D1215191

WITHDRAWN

Contemporary Economic Systems

The Lippincott College Economics Series

330.1
L231c

Contemporary Economic Systems

A COMPARATIVE ANALYSIS

Carl Landauer
University of California, Berkeley

J. B. LIPPINCOTT COMPANY
PHILADELPHIA & NEW YORK

COPYRIGHT © 1964 BY J. B. LIPPINCOTT COMPANY
LIBRARY OF CONGRESS CATALOG CARD NUMBER 64-14849
PRINTED IN THE UNITED STATES OF AMERICA

PREFACE

CA TJan13'65

THE FIELD of comparative economics has no subject matter all its own; most of the problems that it deals with are also the concerns of other fields of instruction and research. The problems of the capitalist market, for instance, are discussed in general economic theory; problems of planning are often considered in the theory of economic growth, in organization theory, or in special courses and research projects on the Soviet economy. A comparative analysis of economic systems, however, is characterized by its special viewpoint, derived from its task to point out the differences of the various systems in structure, operation and achievement and to be applied to much of the total area of economics.

The fact, however, that the subject of comparative economics cuts across a number of other fields raises the question of economy of space. Clearly, no book on comparative economics can repeat the complete analysis of the economic facts and relationships that are central to the nature of economic systems. How much can be left out, however, on the ground that the reader can obtain the relevant information elsewhere? To what extent must such a book restate well-known theorems on the functioning of the capitalist market, rather than refer the reader to works and courses on economic theory? In this book, the decision to include or exclude such material has been made on the principle that the reader should be able to understand every proposition presented here without the use of outside material; for others, whose curiosity may be aroused by such a proposition to the point where they wish to study aspects of a problem that are not necessary for a comprehension of the

11-28-64 Bot 5597

148030

book's content, footnotes and a reading list are provided as guides to further study.

The inclusion in this book of enough economic theory and other subject matter dealt with elsewhere to enable the reasoning of the book to stand on its own does more than spare the reader the inconvenience of investigating other sources. He will find in this book the material he needs to make comparisons between capitalistic, socialistic and communistic institutions. Writings on economic theory, on the other hand, particularly at elementary and intermediate levels, devote more attention to such detail as the conditions of equilibrium than to the ways equilibrium is attained. Consequently, even elementary books on economic theory contain so much detail on economic statics that it is difficult for the student of comparative systems to sort out what he needs for this particular purpose; even fairly sophisticated books on theory fail to include all the material, especially on transitional stages, which is necessary for a valid comparison between the capitalist and other systems. The Sovietologists too—though perhaps to a somewhat less extent than the general theorists—have failed to present their own material in a manner that facilitates comparative studies.

For another reason it seems important to rewrite, for our purposes, many of the propositions and arguments found elsewhere, particularly in books on economic theory. It is the author's hope that the book will supplement readings in Political Science and Sociology, since systems of government, institutions, and practices of different societies cannot be usefully compared without studying similarities and differences in the economic systems. But each of the social sciences tends to develop its own terminology and become unintelligible to the others. The author wishes to make a contribution to the essential unity of the social sciences by dispensing, as far as possible, with the technical language of economics.

The book is designed not merely as a tool of instruction in comparative economic systems but also—if only by implication—as a plea for including this subject in the regular curriculum in economics. There is probably little need to stress the instructional value of looking upon our own economic order from the outside; no device is more helpful to our understanding of the way things are done in our society than to consider alternative ways of doing the same things. Moreover, in judging the performance of an economic system, the comparative approach is vital, since statements can be made only in relative terms. No economic system assures the theoretical maximum of efficiency in production or makes the economy completely sovereign in its relations with the political power or achieves absolute equality or complete protection of human liberty from economic threats. It is equally possible, for instance, to describe present-day American society as equalitarian or as highly stratified by class. It simply depends on whether old world standards or an ideal society of equals is used as a yardstick. Similarly, the contention that we have an "economy of freedom" conveys little meaning since freedom is not absolute in America, but it does make good sense to say that the economic system of the United States is more favorable to personal freedom than that of the Soviet Union.

Although hardly any social scientists would deny these propositions, the comparative analysis of economic systems has so far been treated as a field for specialists rather than as an integral part of economic education, and for good reasons. Whereas the economics of capitalism were susceptible to the simplified presentation suitable for a course of instruction or for a textbook on an elementary or intermediate level, the same could be said only with great reservations about the most important alternative system, that of Soviet Communism. Not long ago, the popularity among economists of research on the Soviet Union was declining rapidly from the high level which it had reached in the 1930's and 1940's because the field proved unrewarding from the point of view of economics. It seemed that the decisive considerations underlying the Soviet plans were in the field of engineering, and that the economic problems, the questions of the relative worthiness of alternative uses of resources, were playing an entirely subordinate role. Recently, however, there has been an important change in this respect. Khrushchev's Russia shows a degree of interest in economic rationality not recognizable in Stalin's Russia; and, as a consequence, efforts to develop a meaningful pricing system are now much stronger. These tendencies play an even greater role in Yugoslavia. Whereas specialists previously had to unearth economic issues involved in Soviet planning and often found the output of that research discouragingly small, these issues have now come to the surface. They are being discussed by Soviet economists as well as by outside observers, and they can be made understandable not only to the Sovietologist but also to those who wish to acquire a general knowledge of economics.

In other words, recent historical developments have brought to light more similarities between the capitalistic and communistic economic systems, and it has therefore become clearer that these systems represent alternative ways to ends which are not so completely different as to preclude any useful comparison. For the first time since the end of the New Economic Policy in the Soviet Union, the economic processes in the two worlds have developed sufficient common traits to make their comparison a proper subject of studies on a non-specialist level.

Strong emotions may color one's approach to the subject of comparative economic systems; and deep-rooted and widespread biases, supported by wishful thinking, make it difficult to reach the minds of an audience with a description of the facts as they are. Yet obviously, such biases cannot go unchallenged. It is bitter but necessary to realize that an economic system that is a product of a hostile ideology may have some points on which its technical performance is superior to that of our system. It is false loyalty to blind ourselves to this possibility. For in a struggle of rival ideologies, victory is not likely to go to those who refuse to see the strong points of the opponent and to learn from him. Of course, we cannot emulate our opponent in those practices that are incompatible with our beliefs even if these practices were found to contribute to success. We must be true to ourselves. But it is simply not true that all the economic techniques which the communists are using are necessarily destructive to freedom or to other values that we cherish. Since the communists have begun to show an inclination to adopt some techniques of capitalist economies, we have every reason to examine the institutions and practices of the other side, to see which of the successful measures could conceivably be fitted into our own system.

But the emphasis on the need for objective scholarship and its value should not make us forget that this objectivity means nothing more than to present the facts as we see them and to make a supreme effort to see them as they are. We are not obliged to suppress or conceal our own value judgments. It is the author's belief that education in the social sciences misses its most important purpose if it does not consist of an effort to teach students two things concurrently: to become more conscious of their basic values and to acquire sufficient knowledge of facts and methods of analysis to apply these values to the world as it is. Teaching, then, becomes not merely the expression of opinions that are the result of logical exercises. On the contrary, the teacher should openly profess that his judgments are ultimately rooted in the belief that some ways of handling human affairs are better than others.

For very effective editorial assistance and collaboration with me in compiling the index, I should like to express my gratitude to Mrs. Thomas Mahan.

Carl Landauer

Berkeley, California
December 17, 1963

CONTENTS

INTRODUCTION

What Is an Economic System?

PRODUCTION OF COMMODITIES is a social activity. Even on the lowest levels of civilization we find a crude division of labor, at least within the family, and at times a combination of effort for some accomplishment which requires the strength of more than one person. The economy of an isolated individual, the Robinson Crusoe economy, has proved useful as a model through which to develop some aspects of economic theory, but it has never been more than an intellectual construct.

The usefulness of the Robinson Crusoe model lies in its simplicity, not in a technological but in a social sense. In this economy all purposes are Robinson Crusoe's and all actions to achieve these purposes are his actions. Although he must make a choice among competing purposes, the choice is his own; should he, for example, use a particular work day to improve his hut or search for food? He must also coordinate his efforts, as in digging the soil and planting but he does not have to weigh his own purposes against those of others before decisions are made.

In a social economy, however, choices must be made between the purposes of different persons, and ways must be found to induce different persons to direct their activities toward a common goal.

Although the determination of production purposes and the coordination of activities are two different problems, the decisions involved jointly determine the allocation of resources: The amount of bread produced in a particular society over a given period reflects both the importance attached to the availability of bread and the success of methods used to induce farmers, millers, transportation workers and others to effect the necessary division of labor and combination of effort. An economic system may be defined as the sum total of the devices by which the preference among alternative purposes of economic activity is determined and by which individual activities are coordinated for the achievement of these purposes. The central problem of any economic system is the allocation of resources.

These economic devices differ according to the customs and institutions of society and need not always be the same even within one country. But except where tradition is especially strong, economic systems must be based on law, and law emanates from government; in modern history, with the prevalence of the nation-state, the larger part of the body of law is national law. For the modern age at least, the devices which constitute an economic system are the same or similar in all parts of a national community; thus we can speak of the economic system of a country. We shall use the term in an even broader sense, however. Although no two countries use exactly the same devices to allocate resources, in most periods of history the traditions and laws of some nations have been sufficiently similar to permit classification of economic systems on a supra-national basis. Without denying the existence of national differences, for instance, we can classify the economic systems of the United States, Japan, and West Germany as capitalistic. Likewise, despite differences between the Russian and Chinese economic systems, they can both be called communist. Although the British Laborites and the Swedish Social Democrats differ somewhat in the kind of society which they would build if elected to power, both parties can be called socialist. Feudalism at its peak developed in so many different ways throughout the world that historians are still debating whether the term should be applied to any phases of Chinese and Islamic development. Yet such decomposed products of feudalism as peonage and sharecropping combined with personal dependency are scattered over a large portion of the globe.

Thus we shall modify the meaning of *economic system* as the anthropologists have done with the concept of race. If race is conceived as a biological group having common hereditary characteristics, then each family forms a race of its own. But for most purposes such a narrow concept of race would not be as useful as one applied to a much wider group. The wider application, however, requires that minor differences among family traits not be regarded as racial characteristics. Similarly, we shall apply the term *economic system* to the typical devices common to a group of countries, not to the peculiar devices used in a particular country. Like every classification by type, the term *economic system,* as used here, is an abstraction, but it is not so far removed from reality as the classical concepts of capitalism, socialism, and communism.

Classical and Contemporary Concepts

Since it is necessary to distinguish the subject of investigation in this book from the "classical" concepts, the latter will have to be briefly described. Capitalism, in the classical sense, is a system of private property in producer and consumer goods, freedom of contract and perfect competition, with government intervention in economic affairs restricted essentially to the protection of property, enforcement of contracts and the prevention of fraud. Classical socialism is a system of complete collectivization of the instruments of production; there are no private profits, but incomes may differ according to individual skills and amount of work done; also, personal property in assets serving consumption directly, such as homes and furniture, is recognized.

In classical communism, as in socialism, all the means of production and distribution are owned and managed by the community. Under this classic system the principle of collective ownership extends to assets serving consumption; thus the very concept of private property disappears under communism. The social product would be distributed "according to need" —an ambiguous phrase intended to mean that shares in the national product should be equal, with only such logical exceptions as medicine available to the sick but not to the healthy. Communist writers assume that in such a society no value calculation is needed either to guide production or to determine income shares, and no coercive machinery is required, since with the disappearance of private property the need for its protection would vanish: Infringement of other personal rights is to be so rare that it is possible to dispense with institutionalized management of justice. Government, therefore, and the use of money and the concept of economic value, are expected to wither away like unused limbs of a body.

Classical feudalism is difficult to describe since inconsistency was one of its characteristics when it was at its peak. For our purposes, it is sufficient to note certain social forms that grew out of the decay of feudal systems. What survives of feudalism today is the authority of the large landowner over the common people in his neighborhood who obtain his protection, the use of some land and other economic assistance in return for labor or rent and the acceptance of dependent status, whether or not this status is fixed by law.

Obviously, we have no classical capitalism today, and the desire for classical socialism has waned. As for classical communism, even the communists now expect to achieve it only in the distant future, and to date, the communist countries have not even moved toward this goal but rather in the opposite direction. Nevertheless, the use of the classical concepts is often defended with the same argument that is applied to highly abstract concepts of economic theory: Models that represent limiting cases can be useful. It is for this purpose that the physicist uses the concept of an absolute vacuum although none exists in reality; it enables him to investigate the properties of an *almost* empty space, which differs from the absolute vacuum only in degree. Such use of a limiting case, indispensable in many parts of economic theory, can also often serve to explain the more complex reality in the analysis of economic systems. But such limiting cases will not be the principal subject of this book. Too many of the important properties of existing systems—existing either as realities or as programs for the immediate future—grow out of the "impurities" and are consequently absent from the "classical" concepts.

Classical concepts cannot help in the exploration of some of the most significant traits of our social life for two reasons: First, each classical model contains inconsistencies which have led to new organizational forms that are not found either in the classical concept itself or in its classical opposite; secondly, some current institutions and practices result from the character of a mixed economy and therefore also are missing in the pure type.

The capitalist system of the present day may serve as an illustration, which is no less useful for the reason that this example also represents the most important case we have to study. Our "mixed" economy, as it is often called, has deviated from laissez-faire capitalism partly under the impact of socialist ideas. Some of these deviations mean simply that our capitalism is more socialistic than classical and our socialism more capitalistic than classical. We have, for instance, more government enterprise than would exist under laissez faire and less than under the kind of socialism described in nineteenth-century socialist programs. To understand these institutions and practices, the classical models would indeed serve us well. But the imperfect character of competition, which is a conspicuous characteristic of contemporary economic life in the United States and other "capitalist" countries, is not due to any socialist ingredients; rather, this feature resulted from inconsistencies in classical capitalism. One of the classical elements was freedom of contract. But contracts that are not made between sellers and buyers, but among sellers to set a minimum price, or among buyers agreeing not to pay more than a maximum price, are destructive of perfect competition; competition is another important element of classical capitalism. Since even the most orthodox defenders of capitalism have admitted some limitations on the freedom of contract—for instance the voiding or outlawing of agreements made for illegal or grossly immoral purposes—attempts have been made to present the prohibition of monopoly and semi-monopoly as equally compatible with the principles of classical capitalism. But while acts such as gambling or extortion can be identified and dealt with by law without interfering with legitimate business, it was soon found that enforcement of perfect competition required far more intense government regulation, so intense as often to be irreconcilable with the laissez-faire philosophy. Thus a two-headed compromise was inevitable: More deviations from perfect competition were tolerated and more government interference was inaugurated than was considered permissible under classical capitalism. Obviously this would have been inevitable even if no socialist had ever written a book or had run for a seat in any legislature. Imperfect competition cannot be explained as a development of our economy that stands between classical socialism and laissez faire.

Second, some of the phenomena resulting from the position of our economies between classical capitalism and socialism arise from problems peculiar to mixed economies and therefore remain outside the scope of any analysis confined to pure types. For instance, public opinion and governments in capitalist countries today have adopted the socialist postulate of a high degree of economic security for the masses. The expense of the policies required to satisfy this demand must be borne by taxation, and the tax burden falls largely upon business. Since business under capitalism is conducted for profit, the question arises of how the impact of taxation, which inevitably deprives those responsible for the management of production of some of the fruits of their endeavors, can be so cushioned as to leave enough incentive for effort and risk-taking. This problem does not exist in laissez-faire capitalism because the basic security postulate is not adopted, and classical socialism knows no such problems because business for profit would not exist there. Similarly, one of the most important difficulties confronting contemporary communist economies arises from the co-existence of planning in physical terms, the sole type of planning under classical communism, with the elements of a price system and a market, which were reinstituted after an approximation of classical communist systems had failed.

From all these considerations, we can now formulate the program of this book. It will compare the economic system of the so-called capitalistic countries, such as the United States and Western European nations, with two other systems:—the one prevailing in Soviet Russia, Eastern Europe and the Chinese mainland, and the one which the democratic socialists of Europe and some Asian countries wish to establish. We shall also compare the capitalist, communist and socialist institutions with some economic institutions which the underdeveloped countries, now apparently on their way to capitalism, socialism or communism, have inherited from their premodern past, some of which we shall call feudalistic because of similarities with the medieval institutions of Europe. Our information on social forms which emerged in Europe when feudalism was disintegrating will help us to understand some of these survivals in Asia, Africa and Latin America.

Common Purposes of Different Economic Systems

A comparison of institutions and practices is not very meaningful unless they have some common purposes. Where purposes are totally different, they can be served only by totally different arrangements. In most cases, only common purposes make it possible to compare performances. If Peter uses his land to raise alfalfa and Paul uses his to raise strawberries, not even the fact that both use land and that all land use requires some similar operations will enable us to say who is working more efficiently, except in extreme instances in which some efforts of Peter or Paul may obviously be waste motions.

In our comparison of economic systems, we are much interested in comparing performances. For example, we want to know whether there are any problems that communism or socialism can solve more efficiently than capitalism. But this question makes sense only if there are problems common to both, and such a community of problems can exist between economic systems only if they share at least some purposes. Here a doubt may arise as to the validity of comparing the performances of capitalism, socialism and communism when the goals and values of the systems are so different.

It is unnecessary and impossible here to spell out all the differences in those values which determine economic activities in the United States and the Soviet Union. But great as these differences are, they still leave room for some likeness of purpose of economic practices and institutions. The communist countries, it is true, are far more prepared to sacrifice the interests of the generation now living to the interests of the future; yet it would be a gross overstatement to say that communist governments are entirely indifferent to the standard of living which they can offer their masses now. On the other hand, capitalist countries are by no means indifferent to the prospects of their own economic development and are willing to make sacrifice for a rate of economic growth which they consider adequate. The Soviet Union, in spite of the communist commitment to achieve economic equality in the future, is prepared to accept greater inequalities now than would be tolerable in the United States and some other capitalistic countries; yet the communists too regard inequality as an evil which they accept only for the sake of a purpose such as greater advances in the armament race.

A meaningful comparison of performance, moreover, is possible even if *ultimate* purposes are completely different, as long as auxiliary goals are alike. Production of steel, for example, is among the auxiliary goals. Steel is required for the construction of hospitals, machinery and tanks. Efficiency in steel production, therefore, is essential whether the economic system emphasizes the welfare of the living generation, rapid economic growth or national power as an end in itself. Although the kind of efficiency directly involved here is engineering efficiency, only an efficient organization of society can produce efficient engineers and research workers. It makes sense to compare economic systems as different as the American and the Russian on the basis of their efficiency in industrial operations. Efficiency in the production of goods, however, is not the only measure of performance. The conditions under which people have to work, the effect of their jobs on their health, their home life and other determinants of their happiness, the distribution of income which results from a particular organization of work must also be considered to obtain a picture of over-all performance. Dependent on our ultimate goals, a system with a higher degree of efficiency in the output of commodities may seem inferior if it fails to satisfy us in one of the other respects.

In comparing economic systems for performance, it is, therefore, impossible to reach an objectively valid conclusion, if by "objective" we mean a judgment that supporters of all economic systems can be logically forced to accept. Our comparison of performance can achieve only two things: It can point out where each system excels the other in meeting certain goals, and it may suggest the extent to which one purpose is sacrificed for another; it may also enable us to decide that we prefer one particular system, because we support the goal which it approaches more closely than do the other systems. It is everybody's right to judge economic systems not only for their efficiency in terms of their own goals but also for the emphasis they place on some goals and not on others. We must not, of course, be surprised to find that those whose goals are different, or who give different weight to the same goals, refuse to accept our judgment.

Economic Systems and the Flow of History

Some authors have treated the concepts of feudalism, capitalism and communism as if they had relatively fixed characteristics throughout history, like definable types of plants and animals. These concepts, however, have been constructed by analysts as convenient categories for classifying observed institutions and practices. Therefore it is unwarranted to assume that elements of one system necessarily operate in a destructive manner in another, as foreign bodies usually do in an organism. Capitalistic institutions and practices, such as large-scale commercial operations, joint-stock companies and free labor contracts, existed in scores of generations, and with growing importance, within feudal society, and these institutions did not detract from the viability of the economy; on the contrary, they greatly enriched the lives of the people in the feudal epoch. It is true that these seeds of capitalism, through their growth, eventually transformed society until all the essential features of feudalism had disappeared; feudalism virtually "died" of the "foreign bodies" growing within its order. But the analogy with organic life is only superficial: The thing that died was no more than an intellectual construct. Real life, the life of the individuals, was not destroyed but benefited. Even for the individuals, to be sure, the transition from feudalism to capitalism was not smooth by any means: Many local distress situations developed, but they were overshadowed by improvements.

We have every reason to believe that contemporary systems are undergoing the same kind of process which can be observed in the transition from feudalism to capitalism. The designations feudalism, capitalism, socialism and communism are nothing but landmarks on the road of social change to enable us better to distinguish sections of the road, not necessarily consecutive sections but often parallel forks.

All Economic Systems Are Built with the Same Bricks

Although there is great diversity among economic systems, they all consist of a very limited number of elements—just as styles of architecture may be exceedingly different when there is much less variety among the bricks used in all the structures.

By what means can men be induced to accept certain goals for their actions and to coordinate their own actions with those of others? First, by command: The goals can be set and everybody told what to do by a superior power which few if any members of society dare resist. This is conceptually the simplest of all devices, although not so simple as it first appears, if the society has an economic horizon encompassing a great variety of goals; the ruler may be equipped with all the power of a Pharaoh, but what he can achieve is still limited by the scarcity of resources, and the determination of priorities for the various goals, if done rationally, will require a complex apparatus. An alternative way of determining goals and coordinating economic activities is that of exchange. Nobody can satisfy his wants exclusively with resources at his immediate, personal disposal, especially with his own labor power, but needs resources at the disposal of others; among these other men there are almost always some over whom he has no power of command. Therefore he induces these fellow members of society to cooperate with him by offering them compensation. This compensation may consist of part of his own resources, e.g. he may try to get his neighbors' help for a particular kind of work by offering them his labor power to combine with theirs on another occasion. This is the method of barter; in the more developed economies, exchange is facilitated by the use of some kind of token, called money, which everybody may earn by putting part of his resources at the disposal of others. In any event, the mutual bidding for resources will establish goals of productive efforts with definite priorities and at the same time will coordinate people's activities for the realization of these goals. Obviously, the greater the role of command in an economic system, the less important will be the role of exchange. An economic system in which the exchange principle predominates is conceivable only where the great majority is free to dispose of its most important resource, its labor power, i.e. where it consists neither of slaves nor of subjects of a despot.

But people are not always guided by self-interest. Sometimes they work in the interest of others, not in the hope of receiving anything in return but because they adopt the purpose of promoting other people's welfare. This motive has often been called altruism; a more fitting term, perhaps, is solidarity. The circle of people to whom we feel tied with sufficiently strong bonds of solidarity, transcending self-interest, may be very wide or very narrow: it may include only the members of our immediate family or it may extend to all mankind. One cannot always draw a hard and fast line between the exchange and solidarity motives. Even loving parents, acting in the interests of their children, may well expect that the children will somehow reciprocate when need arises. On the other hand, a businessman's effort to satisfy an old customer, or to safeguard the welfare of a long-time employee, may not be motivated exclusively by the thought that such action will prove good business, but also by a humane interest in old associates. These difficulties in identifying solidarity as a source of individual action do not affect its importance as a motivation; without it no economic system can be explained.

Command, exchange and solidarity prompt men to act rationally to achieve conscious purposes. But people may also accept goals of economic effort because they are traditional goals and are no longer subject to scrutiny, and they may cooperate for their realization because it has long been customary. The importance of tradition in accepting goals has decreased with the rise of the modern scientific spirit, which weakens the power of tradition, but it would be a mistake to believe that the latter plays no role in the economic life of even the most advanced nations.[1]

This is not a complete list of human motives; the incentives enumerated are those that are important in determining the purposes of management of material goods and services and in coordinating human activities for the sake of such management. None of these incentives is uniquely related to any ultimate impulse: A command may be issued by an infatuated king to serve the whim of a royal mistress, or by a patriotic leader to organize work for a great national purpose, or by a big entrepreneur to improve the coordination of work in his plants in order to increase profits; exchange, obviously, can serve any consumer's purpose, from the purchase of liquor to satisfy a physical craving, to the payment for the education of a child. Although acts of solidarity, by definition, cannot serve an entirely selfish purpose, there is a wide range of possibilities with regard to the kind of people whom we want to serve from motives of solidarity by an appropriate allocation of our labor power or other resources which we control; we may wish to serve our family members or our friends whom we love, or cobelievers in a cause whom we wish to strengthen for our common struggle, or fellow men who have suffered misfortune. Traditions may have originated from almost any motive that can induce men to action.

Command, exchange, solidarity and tradition are the building blocks of every economic system, and it is important that we do not confuse them with the economic systems themselves. There is no economic system which would not make use of all four devices. Even a dictator who decides to regulate all production by command would be foolish not to leave his subjects a wide range of choice in the field of consumption: Why should "Big Brother" tell the individual to eat more apples or more pears? As a consequence, by spending tokens for which he might have obtained pears, the

[1] Some noteworthy thoughts on the role of tradition can be found in a recent book which, unfortunately, is as yet available only in German: Eduard Heimann, *Soziale Theorie der Wirtschaftssysteme,* Tübingen: J. B. C. Mohr, 1963, pp. 36 f.

subject might induce those in charge of production to produce enough apples. Nor is any economy exclusively regulated by exchange: The protection of property, for instance, requires the enforcement power of the state. Moreover, it will be seen later that no large-scale enterprise, even if its relations to customers and suppliers are regulated wholly or mainly by exchange, can be conducted without using the power of command to coordinate efforts. Solidarity and tradition exist in every society and affect economic decisions, but only saints forget their own interests in favor of those of others, and a society that blindly follows tradition in all matters will fail to adjust itself to changing conditions and will soon perish. Thus all the bricks are used in all the structures.[2] But the structures, the economic systems, differ very much in the extent to which they use each type of brick. In some systems the command element prevails, in others exchange, in still others tradition; solidarity may not be the principal element of any system, but it is more important in some than in others.[3]

Economic Systems and Political Systems

Determination of economic goals or coordination of economic activities by command does not always mean the same thing; much depends on the nature of the commanding power. Even the democratic state commands, but in the decision of what the command shall be, the citizen of a democracy is given a voice which the subject of a dictatorship is denied. Because the economy will function very differently, depending on whether the command power of the state is organized democratically or autocratically, economic systems cannot be studied without reference to political systems. Conversely, since economic power can be used for political purposes, any study of a political system which does not consider the economic system

[2] Not only does each economic system consist of all kinds of bricks, but often the same economic decision is determined by a combination of elements: by the command and exchange principles, when the effects of the carrot and the whip are combined; by command and tradition, when people obey not merely from fear of the penalties for disobedience but also from reverence for a custom of subordination; by exchange and tradition in the frequent instances in which a give-and-take was originally found useful and has since been repeated many times with no new examination of its merits.

[3] The idea that all economic systems consist of the same building stones has been expounded by Robert A. Dahl and Charles E. Lindblom in their excellent book *Politics, Economics and Welfare* (New York: Harper and Brothers, 1953), pp. 99 ff. They distinguish four "basic control techniques": spontaneous field control, manipulated field control, command, reciprocity. This arrangement, based on very refined and ingenious definitions of the various control techniques, is useful for some purposes, but for an overall comparison of economic systems the cruder (and, through the inclusion of tradition, more complete) arrangement given above seems preferable.

is at best superficial. Nothing can be gained, however, by blurring the distinction between the methods by which the "will of the state" is formed and those by which economic priorities are determined and economic activities coordinated. Such terms as socialist and capitalist, referring to a form of government, are a source of confusion. Socialism and capitalism are economic systems; democracy and dictatorship are political systems. When we speak of "economic democracy," we refer to the economic and social implications of the philosophy behind democratic systems of government; in this sense the expression is not objectionable, but the temptation to use it loosely, with ensuing confusion, is very great. Even in the case of communism and feudalism, in which political and economic elements are more closely intertwined than in those of socialism and capitalism, the economic and political aspects must be separated in analysis as much as possible.

This distinction would be less important if it were not for the significant role played by the theory that each political system is uniquely related to an economic system. In its most important application, if this theory were true and political democracy and capitalism were interdependent systems, then the attempt to distinguish between political and economic systems might well be wasted effort. This theory is part of the Marxist doctrine, but has gained followers far beyond the circle of Marxists. In fact, it has been upheld with particular insistence by some anti-Marxists, who have argued that the only way to preserve democracy is to retain a capitalist system much like the classical model.

The relationship between democracy and socialism and capitalism will be examined in some detail later; here we are concerned only with the fundamental problem of the relationship between political and economic systems. Not only are they intertwined, as we have indicated, but they form parts of the pattern of social living, which can be fully understood only when visualized as a whole. Before that can be fruitfully done, however, it is necessary to analyze the structure and functioning of the individual parts. As a rule, we understand the purpose of a machine only when observing how it operates as a unit, but we understand this operation only when we understand the shape of the components and know what makes each of them move. Similarly, we can understand society only when we proceed from the separate analysis of its political and economic elements to the consideration of social life as a unit. Neither the initial steps nor the final step must be omitted; to try to undertake them simultaneously is to invite failure.

Certainly not every economic system is compatible with every political system. Just as democratic rights cannot be exercised according to the citizen's own convictions where his livelihood can be arbitrarily controlled by other private interests or by the executive power of the state, so an economic system based on decisions by private enterpreneurs cannot function where the government does not offer sufficient protection of property and enforcement of contracts. It would be easy to find other examples of the incompatibility of some economic and some political arrangements. Although it is true that discrepancies within a social structure can cause intolerable disharmony, it does not follow that there is only one economic system for a given political system. If it is false that a capitalist or a socialist economy can function only if all the parts conform to the classical model, it is equally false that there is only one viable combination of any particular economic system with a political system. If socialist elements within a capitalist economy do not necessarily form a foreign body with lethal effects, then there is even less reason to assume that any economic system different from nineteenth-century capitalism must ruin a liberal or democratic political constitution. Some tension may well exist between economic and political arrangements, just as it may exist between different economic or different political institutions; it is indeed unlikely that the same degree of freedom should exist in all parts of the social structure. Greater freedom in one area will often be used to loosen the bonds in another; but not all tension is harmful; progress toward a better life often depends on the existence of irritants which make for change along with entrenched interests, which limit change.

The compatibility of a wide range of social forms is a great blessing. If the kind of institution in one area were rigidly determined by the kind of institution in another, all parts of the social structure would have to change simultaneously if there were to be any change at all. Thus the evolution of social institutions could never be gradual, since they do not normally change at the same rate and in the same direction. Mankind would therefore be doomed to an infinite series of revolutions: Their destructiveness of material and moral values would be the price we would have to pay for social progress, as radical revolutionaries have indeed maintained for a long time.

Fortunately, we do not have to accept the radical revolutionaries' arguments. All historical experience supports the compatibility of each type of institution in one sector of social life with a wide range of different institutions in other sectors, and therefore we have a right to believe in the possibility of gradualism in social transformation.

I. VALUES AND GOALS

CHAPTER 1

PRODUCTIVITY AND UNDERLYING GOALS

All economic activity is aimed at human goals: the satisfaction of the wants of individual consumers or of a community by material means. The great importance of economic activity to human happiness lies primarily in the dependence of all sorts of material wants on the availability of goods. Man needs material resources not only to feed himself and protect his body through clothing and shelter, but also to build churches and schools, or to procure weapons for the defense of national independence, or to reduce the hazards of illness and death for his loved ones through sanitation and medical service. The second reason why economic activity can do so much to make us happy or unhappy is the large part of our time which it requires. The reader has already been warned against the assumption that in the production and distribution of goods, only the results of our endeavors matter. Not only farming, but all economic activity, is "a way of life." Consequently, people may dislike a particular form of economic activity, or its environment, so much that they do not feel that the good results are worth their efforts. Conversely, they may like the kind or form of activity or the environment so much that they are satisfied with inferior results. In economic life as in other fields of activity, means may assume the role of ends.

Illustrations are easy to find. Some individuals prefer country life to city life, and consequently will remain farmers even if they could earn more in industry; if a whole community shares this preference, industrialization may be rejected. Other individuals may wish to live in a city, with its conveniences, its educational and entertainment facilities and its social graces, although farming may offer more economic security. Among the nations recently liberated from colonial rule, industrialization is often a symbol of the end of "economic imperialism" and, at the expense of primary production, is planned on a larger scale than is justified by the goal of maximum over-all output; strong elements of economic planning are built into the economic system to promote rapid industrialization.

Among the purposes sought in a society through economic activities, many are compatible with one another, although they require different commodities. If you want cake and I want bread, this is no reason for conflict between us: In an economy based mainly on exchange, you will spend the part of your income destined for food from grain on cake and I will do the same with bread; in an economy mainly integrated through command, you will request the commanding power to supply part of your allotment of food in the form of cake and I will request bread, and in such situations no central distributing agency is likely to force either of us to accept what we want less and to forego what we would rather have. Similarly, if I prefer visits to the theater and you would rather eat better and more expensive food, we simply distribute the total amount of consumption allowed to us either by our money income or by other social arrangements according to our respective preferences.

Unfortunately, however, this compatibility of different preferences does not extend to all goals. Suppose I own a house and the city plans to build a freeway which will obstruct my view and cause noise to disturb my sleep, I, therefore, am opposed to the project; whereas you, as a commuter, are interested in the freeway and wish it to be built. The freeway must either be constructed or not constructed; there is no way of satisfying both of us, and if a compromise is at all possible it is likely to involve a different area of want satisfaction: Perhaps I shall receive a financial compensation from the community large enough for me to expand my consumption in other fields and thus find consolation for the reduced pleasure in my home. Or you are a believer in national physical power and I am a pacifist; you want resources to be spent on the construction of tanks and rockets and I am opposed to such use of national wealth; again such tanks and rockets must either be manufactured or not manufactured; only one of us can be satisfied.[1]

[1] Textbooks on economic theory or introductory economics refer to such instances as indivisibilities in want satisfaction. I can limit my consumption of sugar by not eating even half an ounce more than I find pleasurable enough to compensate me for the cost (and perhaps for the pain of becoming overweight), but if I buy or build a house, I cannot draw the limit at the exact point of balance between cost and satisfaction, because I cannot determine the amount of dwelling space as accurately as I can my sugar intake. Availability of lots or structural requirements may make it inevitable that my

Most of the wants for individual consumption are compatible; among the exceptions, probably the larger part involves the use of land, because plots of land are often so located in relation to each other as to make the use of one lot facilitate or impair the use of the neighboring lot. An intermediate case between conflict and compatibility in individual want satisfaction—a case of great practical importance—has been created by standardization in modern production: Suppose 300 individuals are the only customers for an object which can serve its purpose whether it is square, round or triangular, but because the needs or tastes of the customers are slightly different, some prefer the object square, others round, and the last group, triangular. If they all insist on their preferences, the object will be more expensive for each of them, and none will feel that the satisfaction of his own preference is worth the difference in price; yet if the lower price is to be secured for all, only one group will obtain optimal satisfaction—low price plus the shape it prefers—whereas the other two groups will have to sacrifice their particular preference to the advantage of the low price.

The decision whether to introduce standardization at all, and if so by the adoption of what shape, will presumably be made by the manufacturer; he, in turn, will be guided by the preference of the majority, unless the case is complicated by differentials in production costs for the various shapes. Of course, if we are willing to pay for our whims or peculiarities of needs we can generally have our preferences satisfied. In many instances, however, standardization has made this price prohibitive for the average consumer. When Henry Ford, early in his production career, decided that his customers could get "any color they wanted for their car, provided it was black," even a wealthy buyer of his cars would have found it too great a strain on his purse to offer the Ford company a price to induce them to

---

house is either too large or too small for my needs and my spending power. This applies to the sphere of consumption of one particular individual, but an analogous situation is encountered by a government which wants to treat all its citizens equitably, yet in the construction of roads, schools, in defense preparations cannot stop at the exact point at which it feels that any further extension of a particular activity will push the satisfaction of citizen group A beyond the level of satisfactions of citizen group B, which may not be much interested in that particular activity or may even have a contrary interest. (The question of what it means to compare satisfactions of different people, and in what sense this is possible, will be discussed later.) The reason for the impossibility of stopping at that point is that in order to be of any use a school has to have a minimum size, a road has to have a minimum width, quality of surface etc., and armament has to be large enough to deter or defeat an enemy. The government, therefore, cannot help treating some citizens better than others. An extreme case is when all the satisfaction from a particular government activity is with group A, whereas the same activity is a source of unmixed dissatisfaction for group B. Such a situation exists, for example, between believers in national physical power and pacifists in the matter of armament, as mentioned in the text.

paint a few cars white. There are many less extreme examples, however, in which the payment of an extra price is a practicable means for the consumer to free himself from the limitations that standardization puts upon his freedom of choice.

In contradistinction to the area of individual want satisfaction, in which compatibility is the rule, differences in wants usually lead to incompatibility in the field of collective needs, that is needs which must be satisfied by community action. Here the community must either act in one way, or in a different way, or not act at all. The conflict then must be solved by political decision.

The discussion so far has concerned purposes pursued by individuals in their economic activities, including participation in community affairs when decisions of the kind described are at stake. But these are not the only goals which play a role in economic life. In determining our goals, each of us is guided not only by his direct personal needs, but also by our image of a "good society" which expresses itself in desires to influence the character of society—to mold its institutions and the practices of its members to conform with these values. The values may be fraternity, equality, inequality which favors the strong generally or members of a particular race, national power, or any of a large number of others, in part harmonious and in part conflicting. Thus we judge social institutions and practices not only as insiders, as participants, but also as observers or spectators.

In summary: The interests which lead to economic action can be divided into individual interests, as illustrated by the bread-and-cake example; collective interests, as illustrated by the interest of all or most members of a community in good roads or in security from foreign invasion, and spectator interests, for which the desire of pacifists to put a ban on all violence or preparation for violence, or the desire of Christian radicals to eliminate every opportunity for the pursuit of one's own advantage at another person's expense may serve as examples. Individual interests and collective interests may both be called "selfish" interests, in the sense that they both grow out of the individual's desire to have goods and services available for his own purposes. Then the term, however, must be put in quotes, because it includes a number of motivations which ordinarily would be regarded as unselfish, for instance the desire to assist a friend or to fulfill one's religious duty by contributing to the maintenance of a church according to one's means. The values underlying spectator interests may be called "ideals," but again the term, if so used, has a specific meaning; in this application, it is narrower than in ordinary language, in which the motivations of some collective and individual interests are termed idealistic. There is a borderline between collective and spectator interests. For instance, when people support expenditures for national defense, they may do so because they wish to provide collectively for their own protection, or because they cherish the "ideal" of a society which has the will to independence. There are also cases which somewhat blur the dividing line between individual interests and spectator interests, but they are not of major economic importance.[2]

These three categories of interest differ greatly with regard to compatibility. As already explained, individual interests are usually compatible; collective interests are frequently incompatible. The latter, however, are often amenable to compromise. Of course, even the fairest compromise can do no more than limit the consequences of incompatibility. If one group of citizens wants a $100 million road program, and another only a $50 million program, they may settle on $80 million, but such a solution still means that one group has to accept more road building and the other group will obtain less road building than either one prefers. By contrast, in the cake-and-bread example of individual consumption everybody was able to secure optimal use of his share of resources.

What makes a compromise relatively easy in the roadbuilding situation is the absence of strong inhibitions to the striking of a balance of pleasures and pains as long as only "selfish" interests are involved. The advocates of a big road program will feel some frustration when they cope with traffic facilities they consider inadequate, and their opponents will feel regret in having to pay taxes for highways and streets they do not think they need, but the former can enjoy such roads as the compromise grants and the latter can feel gratified over the reduction of the tax load below the requirements of the big program, without the feeling of having betrayed a cause.

"Ideals," on the other hand, are responsible for a large area of irreconcilable conflict in economic and political life, because compromise is impeded by conscientious scruples. We cannot sacrifice part of an "ideal"

[2] A conscientious objector's motivation, for instance, certainly grows out of an "ideal" and not out of a "selfish" orientation, and it has its roots in a particular view of how the community should act, and what would constitute a good society: but in many instances, the conscientious objector's position is too closely related to his own actions to be called entirely a "spectator's" or outsider's position. He not only wants a society without violence, but he also takes the stand that if violence occurs, he will take no part in it: fire no gun, put on no uniform, buy no war bonds or even refuse to pay taxes to finance armament (and in these latter respects his attitude is of direct economic significance) Thus the conscientious objector is motivated not merely by the desire to eliminate violence from the life of society but also, specifically, by the desire to spare himself the burden which he would have on his own conscience if he were to kill enemies or to render support to killing. To the extent that this is his motivation, he also acts as an "insider" rather than as a "spectator" of society, and satisfies an individual need rather than his share in a collective need.

postulate to obtain partial satisfaction of another "ideal" want as easily as we can sacrifice a demand for a "selfish" satisfaction to obtain an alternative satisfaction. We do not feel that "ideals" are commensurate to the point that we could give up one to obtain the other without a sense of disloyalty. This is not to say that we can live without often "betraying" one ideal goal by making a choice in favor of another: Statesmen must do this frequently; as citizens we often cannot avoid supporting them, but the price for the practical solution is usually a bad conscience.

A classical illustration of this difficulty is that crucial sequence of events in American history, the antecedents of the Civil War. The issue of slavery was in part one of immediate personal interests: Northern farmers wanted the Western territories to be reserved for the family farm, in order that they themselves or their sons might acquire cheap land near the frontier, whereas Southern planters wished to expand the plantation system to the West in order to preserve the value of their slave property by having slaves cultivate fresh, fertile soils instead of merely the land of the old South, much of which was exhausted by the continuous growing of cotton. Other "selfish" interests, such as pressure in the North for a protective tariff and the Southern preference for a revenue tariff only, combined with the "free soil" issue to present a more complex picture. Yet, all these conflicts of interest, like all dollars-and -cents issues, might well have been amenable to compromise. If we wish to understand why the many efforts to settle the sectional antagonism by an intermediate solution, from the Missouri Compromise of 1820 to the frantic peace efforts of the spring of 1861, proved futile in the end, we must take into account the troubled consciences in the North which could not consent to the perpetuation of slavery on the national soil, and the belief of Southern leaders that the refined culture which had been built on the foundation of slavery could continue only if the foundation was preserved: This preservation seemed to require not only an enlarged area in which the institution should operate but also repeal of the moral condemnation—expressed for instance in the Northern refusal to enforce the Fugitive Slave Laws—which was slowly undermining its existence. When "selfish" interests are opposed, the cost of the conflict may be greater than any possible gain. This is much less possible, however, when there is a conflict of "ideals."

Conflicts of interests, of course, occur not only in the same category: "ideals" with "ideals," one collective interest with another, one individual interest with another. Equally common are the situations in which a choice must be made between interests of different categories. A particularly important case of conflict between individual and collective interests concerns the alternative of using resources for present consumption or for the provisioning of the future. Normally, individuals wish to provide for satisfaction of their future wants as well as for their present ones, and even beyond their own span of life for the want satisfaction of their progeny; but they have a "time preference," i.e. their interest in acquiring means of want satisfaction for the future is less intense than their interest in acquiring means for present want satisfaction.

The causes and consequences of time preference can best be studied in connection with the phenomenon of interest on capital, and the role of capital, though not confined to capitalism, can be most easily analyzed in its capitalist form. Time preference will therefore first be discussed in the section on capitalism, and its significance in other economic systems will then be explained in the appropriate sections. Here it is only necessary to say that the future appears more important to us when we think of the interests of our national or local community, which we assume to survive far beyond our own limited existence, than when we judge our private affairs in our own life of relatively brief and uncertain duration. This means that our time preference is lower when we act as citizens than when we act as private individuals; as citizens, we may, for instance, approve of expenditures which will yield their fruits in so distant a future as to make a similar investment unattractive for us as private persons. The conflict of social and individual interests which springs from the discrepancy between social and individual time preference has many ramifications which deeply affect the operation of all economic systems.

The Concept of Productivity

We have seen that it is one of the functions of an economic system to determine priorities for economic goals. Economic systems, however, differ not only with regard to the priorities for various goals but also in the efficiency with which the economic effort devoted to these goals is organized. This is not a clear-cut distinction, because often the choice of less efficient methods in working for one goal is prompted by the belief that a more efficient method would create an environment incompatible with the attainment of another goal. In these instances, what appears to be the lower efficiency of one economic system is merely a difference in goal priorities. In the medieval city, for example, the guild system severely limited the opportunities for improving production methods, yet it was maintained largely because it fostered the coherence of the occupational group and the local community spirit, which seemed more important than greater output; even the national rulers, as long as they considered themselves the heads of a feudal society and did not yet aspire to the role of sovereigns of a unified state, favored the restrictive practices of the guilds because unrestrained entrepreneurial initiative was bound to shatter the structure of the feudal caste system. The long survival of feudalism can only be explained by the preference which the leading groups of society gave to values other than maximum production of goods.

But not all instances of deficient performance in an economic system are caused by a conflict of goals; often lack of information, lethargy and other human weaknesses are responsible. In this respect, what occurs in the social machinery which we call an economic system has an analogy in technological experience. When a piece of metal is to be given a particular shape, an ordinary lathe is often an inferior instrument as compared with a specialized stamping or cutting device. Yet there may be good reasons why the lathe is used; not being a specialized instrument, the lathe may serve other purposes as well, or it may fit better into the layout of the plant. Yet again, the lathe may have been chosen merely because the manager has not learned of more efficient devices, or because he is too irresolute or too naturally conservative to introduce an innovation.

The efficiency of an economic system depends on different kinds of achievement. We may achieve a higher or a lower ratio of physical output to physical input; we may be more or less successful in allocating resources to the most important purposes; whereas no economy utilizes all its resources all the time, we may or may not succeed in keeping periods of idleness short and in confining them to a small portion of available resources. The efficiency of an economic system may also be called its productivity if this term is used in its broadest sense; more often, however, the term productivity is used in a narrower sense, the ratio of physical output to physical input.[3] Productivity, so defined, is not quite as difficult to measure as efficiency, and this makes the productivity concept more usable for a comparison of economic systems, since in such a comparison measurement is of great importance; but even efforts to measure productivity in the narrower sense meet with formidable obstacles.

One of the difficulties in measuring physical resource productivity is the necessity of balancing quality against quantity. It would be an invalid judg-

[3] It is sometimes useful to define productivity as the ratio of the value of output to the value of input. Productivity in this sense expresses the success of an economic system (or a nation, or mankind, at a given period of history) in keeping the physical ratio favorable, combined with its success in allocating resources to the most important purposes. In most respects, however, the narrower concept, which involves only the physical ratio, is more useful for our purposes.

ment, for example, to compare the number and size of housing units built in Russia with corresponding figures in the United States, without considering that Soviet home construction is, by all reports, inferior and likely to have a far shorter life than in Western countries. This is not accidental: In an economy that emphasizes central direction, it seems generally easier to hold the production units to a prescribed quantity of output rather than to desirable standards of quality. For purposes of measurement, product quality can sometimes be approximately reduced to quantity: In the case of housing, one may determine the average lifetime of well-built houses the world over, and then convert the output figures of inferior or superior housing into these standard units; to make the calculation more meaningful, one might add some further "premium" to superior housing and subtract a "discount" from the product of inferior construction, to account for the inconvenience of living in a shoddy home. Such procedures, however, can be very arbitrary and should therefore not to be expected to lead to anything like accurate results.

Another difficulty lies in the necessity of taking different kinds of input into account, for little is gained by measuring the productivity of only one type of resource. In a country that is short of capital but has plenty of labor, it is rational to support labor only sparingly with machines; consequently, the physical productivity of labor will be low, whereas the physical productivity of capital goods should be high. Likewise, if labor is scarce and land abundant, agricultural methods should be chosen which make yield per acre low and yield per worker high. Therefore low labor productivity, low capital productivity or low land productivity by no means always indicates inefficiency. We can still recognize the methods of one country as inferior to those of another if we find that in the first country yield per worker, yield per unit of equipment and yield per acre are all lower than in the second. But if we find lower labor productivity combined with higher output per machine unit in one country and the reverse situation in another, we must first answer the question of how much greater the productivity of capital must be to compensate for lower productivity of labor, before we can draw conclusions as to the greater general productivity of one country's methods as compared with those of another; the analagous question arises with regard to the productivity of land in relation to that of other resources. If we were to find a method of answering these questions, and thus to relate output to a magnitude which we might term "combined resources unit," we would still not be able to conclude directly that the economic system of the country showing higher productivity is in this respect superior to the system of the other country, for the result may be due to conditions of climate, topography or soil fertility, racial characteristics of the population or historical background rather than to the economic system. An informed guess may still be made as to which system leads to higher physical productivity of resources: If we consider the reports about the deficiencies in many branches of Soviet industrial production, especially about the shoddy quality of numerous products, together with the low productivity of the Soviet agricultural worker, it seems likely that physical productivity in Soviet Communism is not on the same level with that in U. S. capitalism; this hypothesis will not be refuted by the signs of excellent Soviet performance in limited fields, especially those supporting the country's military effort. But it is impossible to offer any strict proof for this proposition or to measure the overall difference in physical productivity under the two systems with any close approach to accuracy.

All aspects of productivity are significant not only to the present state of the economy, but also to its prospects of growth. It seems expedient to discuss the problem of allocating resources to the most important purposes and the problem of minimizing idleness of resources in the next section, in which we will consider economic growth as a purpose of economic activity and a standard of comparison for economic systems.

Costs and Benefits of Increasing Productivity

In organizing their economic activities into a system, men have never been indifferent to productivity, but they have often permitted other considerations to override this interest. Differences in the attitude toward productivity, the sacrifice in terms of other values that are made to assure or speed up technological progress by which productivity is increased, or the sacrifice in productivity which is accepted to safeguard other values, supply one of the most important criteria by which to distinguish between different types of society in general and between different economic systems in particular.

By technological progress we mean the equipment of human labor with increasingly more effective tools and machines; typically, technological progress requires a) an increased outlay for fixed capital per worker and consequently the establishment within man's living space of increasingly large structures for the performance of mechanical and chemical processes; b) an extensive division of labor which confines the individual worker to one phase of the production process; c) the geographic concentration of workers and factories because of the plant's need for a common supply of labor and materials and the interdependence of specialized plants. These requirements cannot be fulfilled without creating some living conditions which many people find distasteful: Technological progress has a price. If we wish to understand the role which increase of productivity plays among the values in contemporary economic systems, we shall have to examine the achievements and the cost of technological progress in the past and try to gauge its importance and its presumable cost in the future.

It has often been maintained that modern man, in his relentless pursuit of the goal of higher output, has sacrificed the dignity and the pleasure of work and forced himself to accept a disastrous deterioration of his environment—in other words, that he has forgotten that any kind of economic activity must be appraised as a way of life no less than as a means to obtain goods and services. This contention contains some truth and is at least plausible when focused on some periods of recent history or on some segments of the economy in most or all recent periods. The medieval craftsman had more pleasure of work and more pride in his achievement than the textile worker in early capitalism or the man or woman on the assembly line in a twentieth century automobile factory; the monotony of labor which is often as difficult to bear as continuous exertion, and the division of labor which makes it impossible for the individual worker to see the finished product as his own handiwork, have killed much joy. Likewise, when the Industrial Revolution in Britain and other countries turned flourishing villages into ugly factory towns, much that had made life pleasant was destroyed. Yet some further reflections are in order before we condemn those economic systems which are favorable to industrialization—capitalism, modern socialism, communism—and adopt a preference, or develop a nostalgia, for pre-industrial systems.

In the first place, at all times a part of mankind has had to do work which was repugnant. Although the monotony of many factory jobs compares unfavorably with the satisfaction that a craftsman-tailor or a craftsman-turner might have drawn from his work, the typical factory worker's job is hardly more monotonous and is otherwise preferable, when compared with the jobs of many workers in the pre-industrial era who had to pile rock on rock in building strongholds for their masters or to spend day after day at a spinning wheel. Secondly, modern technology has created many jobs which are at least as satisfactory as any type of pre-industrial manual work; this is particularly true of the service industries in which employment is growing faster than in the factories. The truckdriver has a strenuous but interesting job; repair workers of all kinds, from the garage mechanic to the man servicing telephones or household appliances, can take the same pride and the same satisfaction in locating and remedying trouble which the medieval or early modern craftsman took in a job well done. The new army of laboratory technicians, draftsmen, nurses and other professional or semi-professional specialists have obviously an opportunity to show their personality in their work to a higher degree than the great majority of people had in the pre-industrial era.

Finally, for the very reason that work is a way of life and not merely a means to an end, it is necessary to pay attention not only to the working process itself but also to the relationships which it creates among people. Even in the pre-industrial era, fellowship with co-workers was one of the greatest attractions of productive labor. This attraction has been preserved, and may have been increased, if for no other reason than because fellowship now suffers less interference by employers and overseers. It was surely less pleasant for the two or three journeymen in a medieval shop to exchange opinions under the watchful eye of their master, who was always apt to suspect a conspiracy to force a wage raise, than it is for modern workers to chat during intervals of work or at union meetings, or to meet privately after working hours which are much shorter and therefore less exhausting than those of laboring people in earlier centuries.

Confronted with evidence showing that economic conditions of earlier periods were on the whole less conducive to human happiness than those of our own, glorifiers of the past sometimes fall back on a subjective argument: They maintain that our ancestors, with or without sufficient reason, were more content with their lives than we are with ours. Should anything count more than this feeling of contentment? Is it not true, therefore, that a planned return to those conditions would increase rather than decrease our own happiness, and should we not at least warn those nations which now are trying to duplicate our development that they are on the wrong path?

The degree of human happiness in various periods of history obviously cannot be measured and can hardly be the object of even an informed guess. In determining happiness, we must know the characteristics of the mind that is reacting to its environment; the mind's reactions to environmental conditions is as important as the conditions themselves, and we cannot know the minds of past generations with sufficient precision to decide whether their disposition was really happier. But this part of the problem is not relevant to our investigation. As we cannot know all about the mind of a previous generation, neither can we reproduce that sort of mind in ourselves, nor will the intercommunication in the world today permit that disposition to be preserved where it may still exist. Since the low productivity of labor withheld from the masses so many amenities to which even the poor have become accustomed today, the advantages of the economic life of the past are largely illusory, and there is no good reason to doubt that modern man would be unhappy if he had to live under the economic conditions of past centuries, even if the population increase had not made it physically impossible to sustain life under those conditions. This point will be discussed later.

Moreover, even the evidence of subjective happiness under medieval or early modern conditions is to a great extent deceptive. Many analysts of past social conditions have paid more attention to the articulate, educated population groups than the numerical strength of these groups warrants. The educated people, however, were as a rule rich or at least well-to-do, because only people of means could afford an education. Unlike the masses, these people faced no problem in feeding and clothing themselves. Moreover, for the wealthy, the primitiveness of outward conditions was greatly alleviated by the availability of manual labor for personal service. Martha and George Washington would not have been much concerned about the lack of electric washing machines or dishwashers at Mount Vernon, even if they had known that such gadgets could be produced; only a humanitarian desire to lighten their servants' load could have induced them to procure such equipment. This situation prevailed until recently in all countries and still prevails where service labor is available and inexpensive. The point is well illustrated by the story of a European refugee woman, accustomed to household help, who was shown the facilities of a modern American kitchen, but shook her head: "Wonderful," she said, "but my Minna was still better!" For the upper and middle layers of society, many facilities which modern technology has created became important only when the Minnas were diverted from personal service by other employment opportunities. The contentment of the articulate people of past ages proves little about the merits of their type of society.

The assertion that even the people of the lower orders were more content and therefore happier in previous centuries, is refuted by the frequency of revolts whenever the repressive apparatus of the law became ineffective, and especially by the almost ubiquitous banditry in the Middle Ages and the early modern age. A society in which many of the most energetic and self-reliant people preferred to be outlaws rather than peaceful citizens probably contained more frustrations than our own.

Is Technological Progress Still Worthwhile?

"AFFLUENT SOCIETY"?

The philosophy which deprecates technological progress has found many supporters since the middle of the eighteenth century when Jean Jacques Rousseau called for a return to nature. Toward the end of the nineteenth century such influential writers as William Morris and Hilaire Belloc belonged to this school of thought. Elements of the same philosophy are contained in the work of Oswald Spengler, and of many popular writers, especially in the period of the Great Depression.[4] The thinking of the professional economist, however, has rarely been affected by the tendency to regard the simple life of the past as more conducive to happiness than our own civilization of advanced technology. But in regard to the value of technological progress in the future the profession is divided. The book by John K. Galbraith, *The Affluent Society*,[5] which refuses to attribute much importance to such further progress, has found strong support as well as vehement opposition.[6]

Galbraith, to be sure, speaks only for individual consumption when he says that "production for the sake of the goods produced is no longer very urgent."[7] In the whole field of public services he finds an appalling undersupply, and the description of the imbalance between the public and private sectors of the American economy is the most convincing part of his book. It might therefore seem that productivity would still be important if the yield of its progress were used to improve public services. But Galbraith allows this consideration little influence upon his policy conclusions, and this attitude is consistent with his premises. He believes that the private sector is so near the satiation of all important needs as to make it possible, at small cost in human happiness, to reduce the amount of goods for private consumption; the resources thus released could then be used to

[4] Readers conversant with German can find representative passages from the writings of anti-technologists, combined with searching analysis, in the work by Friedrich Dessauer, *Streit um die Technik.* Frankfurt am Main: Josef Knecht, 1952 (abbreviated edition, Freiburg im Breisgau: Verlag Herder KG. 1959).

[5] John Galbraith, *The Affluent Society*, Boston: Houghton Mifflin, 1958.

[6] A voice from the socialist camp—one of the few authors who have dared to trace the course of the socialist movement in the future—has expressed essentially the same idea as Galbraith:

> I no longer regard questions of growth and efficiency as being, on a long view, of primary importance to socialism. We stand, in Britain, on the threshold of mass abundance: and within a decade the average family will enjoy a standard of living, which, whether or not it fully satisfies their aspirations, will certainly convince the reformer that he should turn his attention elsewhere. (C. A. R. Crosland, *The Future of Socialism.* London: Jonathan Cape, 2nd ed. 1957, p. 515.)

[7] Galbraith, *op. cit.*, p. 197.

fill the deficiencies in the public sector without an increase in productivity. But if Galbraith's assumption is invalid, if there are good reasons to believe that further increase in the quantity of goods for private consumption is still important, although a better supply of public services is even more so, then the glaring deficiencies in such areas as education, traffic facilities, city planning, prevention of air pollution will form additional strong arguments for an effort to increase productivity still further.

Are we really in an economy of affluence, of "private opulence," marred merely by "public squalor," and should therefore not be interested in further technological progress? Nobody, of course, can deny that our society is affluent by any standard of the past, but are we really so well provided in the sphere of private consumption as to reduce the usefulness of further increase to near zero?

In 1957, the average personal income per family in the United States was about $6,000 a year. This is a sensational figure when compared with the rest of the world or the American past; yet common experience indicates that the average American family would know how to spend an additional $1,000, $2,000 or $3,000. Subjectively, therefore, we know we are far from the point of want satiation, and since average real income depends most of all on the productivity of labor, it seems that there is still excellent reason to desire a further increase in productivity.

But this argument does not go to the heart of Galbraith's position. He does not doubt that people want more real income with a considerable degree of urgency; he only questions that this urge is spontaneous. He believes that our desire for still greater income to spend on goods is in the main a result of competitive advertising and of our wish to emulate others, "to keep up with the Joneses." It is impossible to measure with any exactness the importance of these two factors; yet some general considerations may help us to form an opinion on the validity of Galbraith's views.

These considerations require a detailed analysis of the different types of advertising—an analysis which has some significance for the task of this book even aside from the Galbraith thesis. Since the right of the consumer to determine what ought to be produced is a characteristic of some economic systems as opposed to others, the question arises of whether this "consumers' sovereignty" is an important principle. It could hardly be judged important if consumers' preferences were manufactured by publicity agents. The distinction between different kinds of advertising will not, it is true, by itself give a conclusive answer to the question of how often the consumer is a dupe of the advertisers—such an answer is impossible within the framework of this book—but it may strengthen the reader's resistance against uncritically accepting the assertion that advertising, where it has been given a free rein, has destroyed the autonomy of consumers' preferences.

ADVERTISING AND HUMAN WANTS

The expansion of sales, which is the purpose of advertising, can be achieved in two ways: Either the advertiser expands the market for his own product at the expense of the sales of his competitors, or the market of the whole industry is expanded by enhancing consumers' interest in its kind of product. The first type, strictly competitive advertising, is an often criticized waste of resources from the social point of view, except for the instances, probably infrequent, in which such advertising conveys to the consumers correct information about the overall superiority of one brand of a commodity over another brand. There is nothing at stake for society in a consumer's decision to prefer one of two types of cars, refrigerators or cigarettes, if the two types are equally well suited to satisfy the need. The second kind of advertising, the promotion of sales for a whole type of product, is useful for society if the characteristics of that product make its increased consumption socially desirable. In the public debate about the merits and demerits of advertising, the defenders have usually emphasized the importance of the second type, arguing that without advertising the consumers would often not become conscious of the possibilities of want satisfaction offered them by modern technology. In appropriate cases, this argument may justify, from a social viewpoint, the expenditure of resources—labor, printing material etc.—on publicity for a product. If, however, increased consumption of the new product is not socially desirable, this kind of advertising is more noxious than the competitive type, because it will lead not only to the expenditure of resources on publicity but also to the usually much greater waste of resources in the production of goods which do not fill any real need. It may well be that originally, before the stage at which it became purely competitive, the advertising of automatic washing machines served an important social function by calling the housewife's attention to the opportunity of lessening her daily labor in the household; but it is difficult to apply the same argument to, say, chewing gum, unless we accept the arguments of some doctors about the benefits of increased exercise of our jaw muscles and regard this advantage as important enough to outweigh the aesthetic demerits of gum chewing.

Galbraith thinks that most advertising is not merely competitive but want-creating,[8] and that most wants so created are not very important. He does not support either of these two assumptions with much evidence;

[8] See especially Galbraith, *op. cit.*, p. 155 footnote.

neither of them appears convincing at first sight, and such examination of individual facts as seems possible also fails to supply anything like a firm foundation for Galbraith's reasoning.

What is the main effect of cigarette advertising, to make us smoke more cigarettes, or to make us increase our consumption of brand A at the expense of brand B? Obviously the latter; presumably, only the small portion of cigarette advertisements that is destined to counteract the impression created by adverse medical findings has any appreciable effect on the total consumption of cigarettes.

What is the main effect of automobile advertising? Probably in the last fifty years nobody who would otherwise have remained a bus commuter has been persuaded by advertisements to buy an automobile; the decision to buy one arises from impulses not created by Madison Avenue. Sometimes the decision to buy a car with automatic instead of conventional gearshift, with hydraulic instead of old-fashioned window lifts, or with some other innovation may be inspired by an advertisement which promotes these improvements as a feature of a particular car model, although they are found in cars of all makes. But even in these cases most of us do not really have to see an advertisement in a newspaper or magazine or on television to learn of the improvements; we could be informed of their availability by the oldest form of sellers' publicity, display in shop windows—a form which even with the most skillful arrangement is less aggressive than advertisements or sales pressure through traveling salesmen and is therefore primarily want-responding rather than want-creating—or we may see the new devices in use by some friends or neighbors who became acquainted with them by accident.[9] From a social point of view, the bulk of advertising represents a waste of printers' labor and of newsprint, but does not cause a misdirection of mechanics' labor, steel, aluminum, and machine capacity.[10]

[9] James S. Duesenberry, in his book *Income, Saving and the Theory of Consumer Behaviour* (Cambridge, Harvard University Press, 1952) calls this the "demonstration effect" of one person's consumption upon another's. For the relationship of Duesenberry's theory to that of Galbraith, see below n. 11.

[10] In discussing the role of advertising, a great deal of attention has been paid to instances in which the consumers have been induced to buy some "new" product which differs from the older ones mainly in appearance but not in technical serviceability, for instance new automobile models with fins. The case of the car fins is of course not essentially different from the general problem of fashion which is most frequently discussed and probably economically most important in the field of clothing. In objects of personal usage the desire for serviceability in an "objective" sense combines, and sometimes competes, with a desire for change in form. This is not a new story; although primitive people cannot change the patterns and the style of their products as frequently as we do, because the lower degree of flexibility of their production methods and sometimes the magic significance of traditional forms impose limitations, the alacrity with which practically all the primitives took to many new articles and patterns when these became available through trade with outsiders, shows their urge for change without regard to

The overestimation of the want-creating effect of present-day advertising, however, is not only due to an underestimation of the merely competitive type of advertising but also to an underrating of the original want-responsive character of many modern innovations and of the producers' publicity—by advertisement or by other means—which was necessary to make these innovations widely known. Of course we cannot want a commodity which has not yet been invented or of which we have no knowledge; in this sense there was no want for washing machines before they were invented. But what was created by technological progress and by the effort to bring it to the consumer's notice was not the want but the possibility of satisfaction: The housewife's back, as she stooped over the tub, ached just as much before she had observed a neighbor using a washing machine as in the time interval during which her decision to buy a machine matured.

TECHNOLOGICAL PROGRESS FOR PRESTIGE-MOTIVATED CONSUMPTION?

Galbraith contends that unsatisfied consumers' wants today are not spontaneous but are created in the process of modern production. The exaggerated belief in the want-creating role of advertising is only one application of that thesis; another is the belief in the dominant role of emulation motivated by prestige in modern consumption.[11] To the extent that

---

serviceability. Fins on automobiles are non-serviceable and—at least in the present writer's opinion—also ugly; but they are no more so than a high hat on the head of an African chief or many of the European-made trinkets on an Indian squaw. The desire for change is not a product of twentieth century technology. We should not silence our adverse judgment when we meet with consumers' desires which, in our opinion, are not worthy of satisfaction; but aside from extreme instances, e.g. the craving of an addict for his drug, every existing want has a claim to satisfaction in a democratic society. In such a society, the way to correct "false" consumers' preferences is consumers' education, not a distinction between valid and invalid preferences, or—what amounts to a variant of such distinction—an advice to policy makers to regard wants beyond an arbitrarily determined level of satisfaction as "not very important."

[11] Emulation of others to gain prestige is only one of many social influences on the demand of individuals for goods. Consequently, Galbraith's theory of want-creation by (advertisement and) prestige-motivated emulation is a much narrower proposition than Duesenberry's thesis, which emphasizes the social determinants of individual wants. Other social determinants are, for instance, the demonstration effect which has been described above, education—the deliberate formation of socially desirable habits such as personal hygiene, interest in books, music etc.—the social conditions which make certain goods suitable for our want satisfaction—suburban living which requires a car—and the multitudinous social factors which determine whether it is desirable to live in a home or in an apartment, in the city or in the country, to take a vacation trip, etc. Still another social determinant of individual wants seems at first sight similar to the prestige-motivated emulation of others but is fundamentally different: In a society, in which economic success is considered a probable result of good character, many an individual

goods are purchased merely for the sake of prestige, the increase and improvement of products has no importance to society, since in the race for prestige, as in every race, only one participant can be the winner. But is consumption exclusively or mainly prestige-motivated even in the area in which this motive is certainly stronger than in any other, that of durable consumer goods, and in the country in which prestige-motivation is believed to be particularly powerful, namely the United States?

Thorstein Veblen's concept of "conspicuous consumption" was one of the great achievements in social science; the desire "to keep up with the Joneses," and if possible to excel the Joneses, is an important motive of consumption in our society. As members of the community most Americans are partisans of social equality; but as individuals we often try to destroy or at least impair that equality by a striving for some extra prestige, and we sometimes attempt to achieve this purpose by having a better car, a finer kitchen, a more impressive house than our neighbors. It is one thing, however, to say that the desire for social prestige is an important motive of buying new and improved commodities, and another to maintain that this is the sole or the most important reason why such purchases are made. We might like to impress our neighbors with our new car, or with our electric kitchen, or with our new washing machine, or with our spacious residence; but the ease and reliability of operation of the improved automobile, the greater cleanliness and time-saving effect of the new household appliances, the privacy which is assured by more rooms would in many cases have been sufficient to induce us to purchase the new product.

A little reflection will substantiate this statement. In the United States, with the world's highest standard of living, it is certainly more common than in other countries for durable consumer goods to be sold by their first owners while they are still serviceable, and sometimes to gain prestige. But there can be no seller without a buyer; and since few of the "prematurely" sold goods are prematurely scrapped,[12] the United States is also the country of the greatest second-hand market for durable goods. In other words, the prestige seekers who wish to exchange their still serviceable com-

---

wants to prove to himself that in a given year he can afford the consumption of some articles which he could not afford the year before, regardless of whether others are aware of the rise in his consumption; whereas in the cases of emulation the individual compares his own consumption level with that of others, in the last mentioned case he compares his present consumption level with that of the past and draws satisfaction from the improvement.

[12] In the year 1957, only 4.3 million passenger cars were scrapped out of 56.8 million registered. *Statistical Abstract of the United States*, 1959, pp. 557 & 558.

modities for new ones always find other Americans who are so little prestige-conscious as to buy second-hand goods.[13]

FURTHER REASONS WHY INCREASE IN PRODUCTIVITY IS IMPORTANT

Even apart from the role of advertising and prestige-seeking, many of our wants today were created by technological progress, and it is likely that this development will continue in the future; the conclusions to be drawn from this fact are different from those drawn by Galbraith. Many of our present-day needs result from urban concentration and vocational specialization, which are themselves a consequence of modern production methods. To a great extent, these needs are social rather than individual; sanitation, urban transportation, prevention of air pollution, water supply, new means of communication and the like, but individual needs are also increased: For instance, many of the hygienic innovations, from sterilized wrapping to modern toilets, have much more significance in modern cities in which each family has to live in close contact with others and the hazards of contamination are therefore much greater, than they were under conditions of sparse settlement. What technological progress yields us is not all net gain; therefore, if we still need technological progress, it is important that we get enough of it to make the net gain, not only the gross yield, adequate to our needs.

The underestimation of the importance of further increases in productivity is also due to the inclination to take too narrow a view of the effects which technological improvements may have on our consumption pattern and thereby on our mode of living. When middle class families, or families below the middle class level, buy a more efficient water heater, a bigger refrigerator, a more adaptable vacuum cleaner, they buy not only some physical amenities or some show pieces which might arouse the envy of neighbors: They buy time for family life, for education, for pleasures which bring color into their lives that would otherwise stay drab. Of course not

[13] The dividing line between buyers who are primarily prestige-motivated and those who are primarily motivated by serviceability is of course not identical with the dividing line between buyers of new and of used cars and gadgets. There are many reasons, other than the desire to outdo the Joneses, why people exchange still serviceable cars, washing machines etc. for new ones, for instance the smaller risk of temporary failure and, in some instances, tax advantages; on the other hand, some second-hand goods may still appear good enough to enhance the owner's prestige in his particular environment. Still, we can draw some conclusions with regard to the importance of the prestige motive in the purchase of durable goods from such information as the following: that 88% of the American car owners were willing to retain or purchase cars older than two years, and that even for cars 8 years and older the figure still amounted to 26% in 1958. *Ibidem,* p. 561.

all the buyers of these objects make good use of the time which they are saving, but in spite of possible misuse the purchase of disposable time through the acquisition of time-saving devices satisfies one of the most important needs of modern man. Increasing demand for time-saving devices is a concomitant of cultural progress, which is served by making these devices more easily available through higher productivity.

If technological progress came to a stop, per capita real income would not only fail to increase but would actually drop for two reasons. In the first place, we are not yet quite safe from the specter which haunted the Malthusians, the effects of the law of diminishing returns in primary production. In recent decades, aside from periods of war and postwar shortages, the products of agriculture and mining have been in abundant supply, and their prices have shown a tendency to fall by comparison with those of manufactured goods; improvement of production and transportation and the development of substitutes have on the whole more than compensated for the higher cost of producing more per acre of soil and for digging deeper mine shafts after the exhaustion of the surface deposits. As to the future, the development of nuclear physics opens a prospect of producing energy in abundance, thereby replacing some mining products and making agricultural operations more productive beyond the dreams of the pre-atomic era; even more important, the knowledge of the nuclear structure of elements opens up the prospect of transforming those in abundant supply into those which are scarce. It is clear, however, that these bright prospects can materialize only through further progress of technology, which alone can utilize the advance of physics; and even if, after some further steps forward, we should see that the bulk of the scarcity problem has been eliminated for all the foreseeable future, some bottlenecks may remain with us, and we may still find ourselves in a race between increasing productivity of labor and increasing difficulties of producing some of the vital primary materials.

Another reason why technological progress will be necessary to maintain per capita national income is the increase in population. If mankind multiplies indefinitely at its present rate, there will eventually be "standing room only." This absolute limit, however, is still far off; at least for the next century, it may be possible to offset the depressive effect of the population increase on the standard of living by technological advance. Only through such advance can we buy temporary freedom in determining the size of our families and for a somewhat later period sufficient time to adjust our habits of life to the necessity of stabilizing the population. This is true for the less crowded countries of the globe; for those already overcrowded, and for some which now have a very high rate of increase, an immediate reduction of that rate plus all the technological progress they can get in the next decades will barely suffice to prevent an aggravation of existing poverty.

The truth and the importance of the latter statement leads obviously to the question: Why adduce any other argument to prove the need for further advances in productivity? If we had One World, or were likely to have it within the foreseeable future, the existing poverty in which the major part of mankind still lives and the danger lest this poverty may be further aggravated by population increase would be sufficient to show that more progress in technology is not only important but desperately needed. But the world is not one; the industrialized countries will hardly strive for higher productivity merely to be able to assist the less fortunate nations more adequately, and they would certainly not make the choice of their own economic system dependent on the criterion of higher productivity if such productivity were merely needed for assistance to others. Reasons of humanity and enlightened self-interest might well recommend that the whole world form a common front against hunger, without any reservations on the part of those who are now well provided, but this will not happen; within this century at least, no nation will devote more than a fraction of its national income to foreign aid. The Galbraith thesis cannot be validly refuted by pointing to an unsatisfied need which we know will remain largely unsatisfied regardless of what happens to productivity. The need for further technological progress will be determined separately by the industrialized and the underdeveloped countries. Whereas the choice of the latter cannot be in doubt, the tempo of further technological advance depends, for obvious reasons, more on the former; it would be unfortunate indeed if the industrialized nations had no reason of their own to seek a higher yield per unit of labor and could afford to choose an economic system without regard to productivity. This is not the case: Material needs, even in the realm of individual consumption, are still important: Further progress in productivity is also needed, even for the industrially advanced nations, to provide us with increased leisure for family life and cultural pursuits, and with some freedom to choose the size of our families without a serious lowering of our standard of living.

CHAPTER 2

ECONOMIC GROWTH

Concept and Presuppositions

ECONOMIC GROWTH can be defined either as growth of production or as growth of the capacity to produce. The difference is easy to recognize from a practical example: Although in the second half of 1960 the national product of the United States fell slightly, the country's capacity to produce undoubtedly increased during this period because new and more effective machinery was introduced and new people entered the labor force. Thus the United States, during that period, had no economic growth in actual production but did have economic growth in productive capacity.

If economic growth is identified with growth of production, should the reference be to gross production or to net production? Obviously, in the process of producing commodities, equipment is worn out; if we wish to know the extent to which our annual labor has contributed to the satisfaction of our wants, we would therefore have to make deductions from our annual gross output. The net output figure at which we would then arrive, would be in principle—that is, disregarding discrepancies that will always arise from different methods of calculation—equal to our national income, meaning the aggregate of all the net incomes of the population: Since these incomes consist of wages, interest payments, rents and profits, and the value of the net product consists of labor costs, payments for other factors of production and net return to enterprises, it is easy to see that the two figures should be equal. The technical terms, national income and gross national product, however, as used by statisticians, differ also in other ways than by the distinction between gross and net output; although these other differences are of no great relevance for the purpose of this book, they must of course be taken into account when actual figures are interpreted.[1]

[1] "Gross National Product at market prices is the market value of the product before deduction of the provisions for the consumption of fixed capital, attributable to the factors of production supplied by normal residents of the given country. It is identically equal to the sum of consumption expenditures and gross domestic capital formation, private and public, and the net exports of goods and services plus the net factor incomes received from abroad.

"Gross Domestic Product at market prices is the market value of the product, before deduction of provisions for the consumption of fixed capital, attributable to factor services rendered to resident producers of the given country. It is identically equal to the sum of consumption expenditures and gross capital formation, private and public, and the net exports of goods and services of the given country. It differs from the Gross National Product at market price by the exclusion of net factor incomes from abroad.

"Gross Domestic Product at factor cost is the value at factor cost of the product before deduction of provisions for the consumption of fixed capital, attributable to factor services rendered to resident producers of the given country. It differs from the Gross Domestic Product at market prices by the exclusion of indirect taxes and subsidies.

"Net National Product at factor cost is the value at factor cost of the product after deduction of provisions for the consumption of fixed capital, attributable to the factors of production supplied by normal residents of the given country. It is identically equal to National Income.

"National Income is the sum of the incomes accruing to factors of production of the given country before deduction of direct taxes." (United Nations Statistical Office, *Yearbook of National Income Accounts,* 1960, p. XI.)

Of these concepts, gross domestic product at factor cost is rarely used; when gross concepts of product are applied, they are usually calculated on the basis of market prices. Capital formation is synonymous with investment. It may be gross investment, including replacements, or net investment, comprising only additions to the capital stock; furthermore, figures may indicate all investment or may exclude additions to inventories, giving only fixed capital formation; finally, investment figures may refer to capital formation anywhere, as long as the assets accrue to residents of the country whose investment is computed, or may be confined to domestic capital formation. These distinctions can of course be combined, as for instance in the expression: gross domestic capital formation, fixed capital only.

The understanding of the concepts used in national income accounting, and therefore in the calculation of economic growth rates, may be facilitated by the following explanation:

"Total output is measured from two principal points of view: as the summation of final products produced by the economy; and as the summation of costs incurred in producing these products. . . .

"The Gross National Product measures the nation's output of goods and services in terms of market value. When expressed in current prices, this series reflects the total dollar value of production; when expressed in constant dollars to eliminate the influence of price changes, it provides an overall index of the volume of goods and services produced by the economy. . . .

"Total output is also measured in terms of the factor costs of producing it, by the National Income—the aggregate earnings of labor and property which arise from current production. This measure differs from Gross National Product chiefly in that it is computed after deduction of indirect business taxes and of depreciation charges and other allowances for business consumption of durable capital goods." (U.S. Department of Commerce, Office of Business Economics, *National Income 1954,* p. 1.)

A number of difficult questions arise in the computation of national income and output figures; whoever wishes to dig more deeply into this part of economic analysis, can find ample guidance in literature. Two well-known books, which can be understood without specialized preparation, are Carl S. Shoup, *Principles of National Income Analysis* Cambridge: Houghton Mifflin Co.—The Riverside Press, 1947, and Richard Ruggles,

Which of the possible definitions of economic growth is most serviceable depends on the particular purpose of the investigation for which it is used. If technical difficulties of calculation could be disregarded, the growth of national income, in global or in per capita figures, would probably be most useful in most cases. Since these difficulties, however, are sometimes important, it is usually advisable to define economic growth as increase in gross national product. In this sense the term will be used here, except where a different meaning is explicitly stated.

Although increase in national product may occur as a consequence of better utilization of capacity without an increase in the latter, this is possible only if there is a slack in the economy—either an actual slack in the form of unemployed resources, or a potential one in the form of resources that can be released from their present employment by more economical procedures without any new installations or other expenditure. If there is no such slack to take up, the economy can grow only if resources are spared from immediate consumption and used for the expansion or improvement of production facilities; in other words: In these cases economic growth presupposes investment.

As used in this context, the term investment refers only to actions which expand the economy's capacity to produce and not, for instance, to every purchase of stock by an "investor." With this reservation, however, the term must in principle be understood in a broad sense, referring not only to the construction of more numerous and efficient machines, transportation facilities and other equipment but also to the use of resources for the better training of workers; whenever a narrower concept of investment is used, attention will be called to this fact. Increase in productivity, both of capital goods and labor, is an important purpose of investment and, unless frustrated by declining utilization of capacity, will result in economic growth. At the same time, increase in productivity will make future growth easier, because it enables an economy to spare resources for further investment without a reduction of consumption, even if all resources are presently utilized.

In later chapters, when economic systems in operation are surveyed, it will be seen that a critical point in economic growth is reached when an economy has exhausted its reservoir of labor readily available for industrial employment—such a reservoir is often found in hidden unemployment on farms, where more hands may be available than are needed to maintain agricultural production—and must rely mainly on improvement of pro-

---

An Introduction to National Income and Income Analysis, New York: McGraw-Hill, 1949.

ductivity for further expansion of production facilities, unless there is a willingness to curtail consumption to such an extent as to make the resource quantities required for the desired rate of growth available.

Aside from the labor reservoir in agriculture, which has played a most important role in the economic growth of the industrialized nations of today and which is now playing an equally crucial role in the developing countries, the most important pool of labor power that can be drained to provide workers for industries is usually represented by married women. From time immemorial, women have participated in productive labor; sometimes they have borne the main burden of that labor. In contrast to many a modern husband in the United States or Europe, an Indian warrior in many tribes would have found it difficult to understand that his pride should prevent him from letting his squaw do some planting or weaving because this would show that "he could not support his family;" rather, he considered it below his dignity to do some kinds of work himself. Female labor became a problem only when women had to go to places of work distant from their homes, so that their jobs seriously interfered with family life, and when, as part of the same development, women had to work under the direction of employers rather than under the control of their husbands and also often became competitors of men for jobs. These circumstances caused many material difficulties and various sorts of emotional resistance against the employment of women. Because an increase in female labor under modern conditions requires adjustments in living arrangements and habits of thinking, it has not always been possible to increase the utilization of this labor reserve as much as called for by the interest in economic growth.

A society has, of course, every right to pay with a sacrifice of economic gain for the protection of a particular form of life; whether increased employment of married women is a curse or a blessing, whether it jeopardizes things more important than economic growth or on the contrary tends to emancipate half the human race from subservience to the other half is not for the economist to decide. He can merely tell the policy makers that here is a pool of potential labor power, that the tapping of this pool may under otherwise favorable circumstances greatly accelerate economic growth, and that if they want such accelerated growth and do not find the social cost too high, they can so shape the economic system—for instance by appropriate measures of tax policy—as to draw more married women into the production process.

The labor force and consequently the national product can, of course, also be increased by population growth. The effects of this increase are different from those of a more thorough utilization of the existing human labor power because a population increase adds to the mouths to be filled and the bodies to be clothed and sheltered as well as to the arms and brains capable of augmenting the flow of goods and services. The rate of increase of the population can be influenced by economic and other policies, notably as in France and in Japan, but its spontaneous determinants, not amenable to social manipulation, still seem to be the most powerful. The greatest significance of population changes for an analysis of economic systems is that of a test of the adaptability of these systems: A slowing down as well as a speeding up of population growth will require a revamping of economic arrangements, and there may be a difference in the promptness and effectiveness of the response to this challenge between systems with more central direction and systems based primarily on the spontaneous activities of economic units. Our present experience, however, does not enable us to make even an informed guess as to which system will stand this test better; in the future, this may well be a vitally important question.

Labor is not the only type of resource that has reserves; often an economy has excess capacity in man-made equipment because in a preceding period more of it was produced than can now be utilized, or because it is being utilized less. Land reserves were at times of enormous importance for economic growth in some countries and many controversies which have played a great role in the history of the United States—for instance the "squatters rights" issue and the Homestead Act—were essentially debates as to the most effective way to make land reserves contribute to national economic growth—to the extent, at least, that these controversies were not merely clashes of selfish interests. At present, land reserves still have some importance for economic growth, as in the Soviet virgin lands program. This importance, however, has been reduced by technological progress in agriculture which has made it relatively easy to raise yields on land already cultivated, whereas rising labor costs often make it more expensive to break in new soil. There are some counteracting tendencies, to be sure, of which probably the improvement of transportation techniques that help open up distant parts for cultivation is the most important; but on balance the advantage for a country in having land reserves and in having an economic system favoring the utilization of these reserves seems to be declining in importance.

In speaking of economies that have a slack in the utilization of resources and those that have no slack, it is necessary to avoid the assumption that a clear-cut line separates these two classes without leaving room for economic systems that are in the middle. Permanent and complete utilization of resources is inconceivable. Workers lose time in moving from one kind of employment to another; some types of labor and some plants can be fully used only in some seasons. Moreover, some of the physically available installations and workers are submarginal in efficiency, although they may be drawn into the production process in periods of heavy demand. Perhaps even more important is the fact that the degree of availability is never the same for all types of resource: Some kinds of equipment and labor may be scarce and may represent bottlenecks of production which prevent the full utilization of other kinds available in abundance. Today the United States has considerable unemployment among unskilled workers and even in some parts of the skilled labor force, while other types, from electricians to physicists, are in short supply. Similar disparities exist in developing countries under a variety of economic systems. Nor is it unusual to find some industries utilizing their equipment fully while others are operating far below plant capacity. This ambiguity of many situations presents grave problems for policy makers: Can the slack in some areas be utilized for growth without intensifying the bottlenecks in others to an unacceptable degree? Not only the wisdom, knowledge and ability of those responsible for economic policy decisions is thereby tested, but also the flexibility of the economic system.

Why Is Economic Growth Desired?

The case for the desirability of economic growth is in part the same as the case for the continued importance of productivity. If our labor and our capital goods are more productive, we are assured of a greater supply of goods now and at the same time can make more investments to increase our future supply of goods. Viewed in reverse, if we were already oversupplied with goods, living in an economy of true and assured abundance, we might not be interested in future production of goods on a larger scale. Therefore the arguments against the Galbraith thesis in the last chapter are also relevant to the question of why economic growth is desired by rationally thinking people.

But these arguments do not make the case for economic growth in industrially advanced nations quite complete; in underdeveloped nations, of course, the case is obvious in any event. Even if people in an advanced nation are not affluent in the strict sense, if they still have some unsatisfied wants which make them wish for an opportunity to buy more goods, this wish might not be urgent enough to make it seem worth the effort to increase the future goods. The strength of the desire for growth, evident even in a nation with so high a standard of living as the United States, calls for an explanation beyond the statement that there are still unsatisfied wants.

A partial explanation lies in the uncertainty of the future. Even if our impulse to increase the flow of goods for consumption—individual and collective—is only moderately strong, we do not know what the future holds; as citizens, we may well be concerned about future contingencies which we can master only if the volume of our economy is greater than today. Many of us think of international contingencies that may arise. War puts a tremendous strain on our resources; even without armed conflict, we may have to use our economic potential to an even higher degree than today to improve our international position by such measures as aid for other nations, and therefore we have a great stake in the future magnitude of that potential. Since international politics is a competitive game, the growth rate of a rival nation is of decisive importance in determining the growth rate which we wish to attain, and the energy with which we pursue this goal.

But we are interested in economic growth not only because we want specific things—two cars for (almost) every family, more schools for our children, travel to the moon and the assurance that the Russians will not be able to beat us. We also desire further increase in production and especially in our capacity to produce because we like the idea of moving ahead—in other words, because we regard economic progress as an end in itself. Whether this desire is a fault or a virtue of modern mankind, whether it contributes to or detracts from human happiness, are questions which the economist must leave to the psychologist and the philosopher, just as he must leave to the historian and the anthropologist the other question of how long this valuation of progress *per se* has existed and whether even today it extends to all human races. In any event, the desire for growth as an end in itself is so important an element, at least in the lives of typically "modern" nations, that it must be recognized in economic analysis. It makes it likely that even a much closer approach to saturation of wants than has been achieved today in the most advanced nations will not bring the drive for further growth to a complete stop.

The Influence of the Economic System upon Economic Growth

RIVAL DETERMINANTS AND COUNTERACTING EFFECTS

It follows from the discussion of the presuppositions of economic growth that any effects which the economic system can have upon the rate of economic growth will compete with the influence of other determinants of that rate. Consequently, the fact that one country has achieved a higher rate of growth than another is no evidence that its economic system is more favorable to growth; rather, the reason may well lie in extraneous circumstances, for instance in the natural endowment of the economy, including the native skills and industry of its population. In empirical observation it is impossible to separate these effects completely from those of the economic system.

To the extent that the economic system acts upon the speed of economic growth, experience makes it unlikely that all these effects will operate in the same direction; it is more probable that some characteristics of the system tend to accelerate and others tend to slow down economic growth. Communism, for instance, generally inculcates a stronger will to economic growth in the minds of the policy makers[2] and at the same time equips them with more effective instruments to break down population resistance against growth-accelerating measures; on the other hand, in many of its operations communism has so far failed to attain as much efficiency as capitalism, and is therefore wasting resources that might be used for economic growth. But there is an ambivalence between the two systems, even in regard to over-all efficiency, because capitalism, having up to now failed to eliminate the business cycle, has not attained the same continuity in the employment of resources that is found in communist countries. The mutually counteracting effects of the different elements in one economic system are not measurable with any close approach to accuracy; even if they could be measured, it would turn out that none of them has equal magnitude in all situations, because in one set of external circumstances the favorable effects of a system upon economic growth and in another set the unfavorable effects may be more important. All this will be discussed more in detail later; here the diversity of effects is mentioned for one reason only: to explain why we must not expect to be able to strike a neat balance, concluding without reservation and qualification that from the point of view of economic growth one system is superior to the other.

To illustrate the ambivalence of the situation, it is useful to compare the growth rates of the Federal Republic of Germany with that of the Soviet Union and the United States. Both West Germany and the United States are capitalist countries, but the West German growth rate has in recent years been more similar to that of the Soviet Union than to the

[2] This is primarily an effect of communist ideology rather than of the communist economic system. However, the two are so much interrelated that any direct effect of one of them is at least an indirect effect of the other.

United States. Production processes are, on the whole, conducted with greater efficiency in West Germany than in the Soviet Union; West Germany has achieved a more continuous utilization, and a closer approach to full utilization, of resources than has the United States; the West German investment rate, although not as high as the Russian, is higher than the American. Yet there is reason to assume that if a world depression occurred, all capitalist countries, including West Germany, would suffer a greater setback in the utilization of resources than the communist countries, especially the Soviet Union. Let us assume for a moment that the West German economy is the type of capitalism most favorable to economic growth; it may still fall greatly behind the Soviet Union if a world-wide depression occurs. On the other hand, it may well be that the resource situation of the Soviet Union will deteriorate in the foreseeable future—especially through the exhaustion of its labor reservoir in agriculture—that therefore its growth will depend more on improvement of productivity of the individual economic process, a task it is less able to cope with than the capitalist countries, and that therefore it will be overtaken in the rate of growth by West Germany and possibly other countries. The case of economies with strong socialist features, such as France or Sweden, has been left out of this discussion, not because their experience is not relevant but because it is too difficult to evaluate before these features have been described in detail.

Particularly important among the factors which must be taken into consideration before valid conclusions can be drawn regarding the effects of the economic system upon economic growth is the stage of development which the country has already reached. As a rule of thumb it can be stated that industrial production grows faster at an early stage of industrialization than at a late one. This is partly a matter of simple arithmetic: Building a second steel works of the same capacity as the first one that is already in operation, means doubling the steel making capacity of the country; adding a third steel works again of the same size adds only 50% to the existing capacity. Assuming that in the early phase most of the equipment has to be bought abroad for each of the three plants, the burden of building the third steel plant is not eased by the existence of the first two and falls with equal weight on the rest of the economy, which in the typical case is agrarian. Thus the same sacrifice of the agrarian sector will add 100% to the country's steel making capacity at stage I and only 50% at stage II; the process continues like this through the early stages of industrialization.

During the later phases, it is true, the industries already existing will contribute to the building of factories and will therefore support the industrialization process. In the meantime, however, other unfavorable factors have usually come into operation, especially the exhaustion of readily available labor reserves from farms, and often also the need for more costly production support services, notably more complex transportation facilities, and for services required for living in metropolitan areas. Growth of industry, of course, is only part of possible economic growth, but it is the most active element, especially because it tends to promote the development of agriculture and commerce. Although after the passing of the earlier phases the process of economic growth becomes too complex to permit the unqualified statement that it will slow down with its own advance, yet more often than not this tendency exists. Detailed analysis of the changes which are occurring in the course of growth under the given circumstances is therefore imperative when rates of growth in two countries at different stages of development are compared with a view to isolating, as far as possible, the effects of their economic systems on their growth rates.

OPERATIONAL CHARACTERISTICS OF ECONOMIC SYSTEMS IN THEIR INFLUENCE ON GROWTH

The Significance of Pricing

More remains to be said on the question of how an economic system may favor or not favor the mobilization of resources which can be used for economic growth. These effects of an economic system are important not only for economic growth but also for consumption; they could have been discussed under the heading of productivity, because their analysis spells out the meaning of efficiency of an economic system. Their particular relationship to economic growth, however, may justify their discussion in this section.

Optimal efficiency of an economic system presupposes maximum capacity to direct resources into the channels in which they can produce the largest quantities of the most useful goods and services. This capacity depends to a great extent on prices which reflect with a high degree of accuracy the existing, and sometimes the prospective, supply and demand conditions. Economic systems differ greatly in their ability to develop such pricing methods. It is therefore essential to see exactly why "correct" prices are so important.

At any level of economic development substantially above the primitive, many types of resource can be used for a variety of purposes, and a given purpose can be satisfied by different production processes; at a high level of technological development, alternatives on both sides are numerous. Facing all these alternatives, the engineer or physical planner is helpless without the assistance of the sales manager and the accountant under capitalism and the persons who fill similar functions in other systems; the individual in charge of sales can give the engineer the relevant demand schedules, but this presupposes a knowledge of prices which consumers are willing to pay for different quantities of different goods; the accountant can help the engineers decide which of alternative production processes are preferable, but only when opportunity costs of different factors, required for alternative production methods, are known, because they are expressed in prices of cost goods.

Any highly centralized system suffers from the temptation to set prices arbitrarily rather than let them express supply and demand conditions. In the presently most important case of such a system, that of Soviet Communism, this tendency is enhanced by the dogmatic commitment of the policy makers to the Marxian labor value theory. That theory maintains that goods are to be[3] exchanged for each other according to labor time socially required for their production, and that prices should reflect labor cost only. But the real cost, to society as well as to an individual operator, of producing a particular quantity of a particular commodity includes not only the expenditure of labor, which involves the sacrifice either of leisure or of alternative uses of labor power, but also the devotion of land and capital equipment which, if not used for the particular purpose, could help produce other goods and services. Any price-cost calculation based on the labor value theory is therefore greatly distorted.

While contemporary communist societies suffer from this distortion of the pricing system to the detriment of efficiency and therefore of economic growth, capitalism suffers from the influence of imperfect competition on prices. Although, in a formal sense, even monopolistic prices reflect supply-demand relations, they do not reflect those conditions of supply which would maximize satisfaction of demand; the more complex aspects of this question will be discussed later. So far, the pricing system of countries of Soviet-type communism is less "correct" than that of capitalist countries; that is to say, the prices under the communist system are more different from those which would have to be established in order to gear production

[3] The original meaning of the Marxian labor value theory is not normative but analytical. In consonance with the teachings of the classical school of economics, specifically with the doctrine of David Ricardo, Marx offered the labor value theory as an explanation of the price forming process under capitalism or in any market economy. In Marx's own writings, however, and in those of his friend and collaborator Friedrich Engels, there are already passages designating value calculation according to socially necessary labor time as the proper method for a post-capitalist—socialist or communist—society as long as the concept of value would be needed at all, and in this prescriptive sense the labor value theory has been in principle adopted by Soviet Communism.

to maximum satisfaction of human wants. In the communist countries, it is true, efforts are being made to rationalize the pricing system; it may be assumed that they will be increasingly successful, because pressure of practical necessity operates in this direction. But whether the decentralization necessary for such a reform will not also produce monopolistic features similar to those observable in capitalist countries remains to be seen.[4]

The imperfections of a pricing system are more important on a high level of economic development than on a low level; notably, their adverse effects on economic growth depend very much on the stage that has already been reached. Where people lack food, clothing and shelter, where capital is relatively scarce and long-range investment therefore confined to programs of obvious necessity, alternatives are relatively few and decisions can be made on the basis of physical considerations alone without much risk of important error. Moreover, if at such an early stage of development a rapid rate of growth is achieved, it does not matter much whether the obvious needs are satisfied in the exact sequence of their importance. If a bridge which is urgently necessary to improve food transport and which should have been built this year with labor that was spent on replacing some huts with brick houses that are also badly needed but not quite as much as the bridge, the consequences are less far-reaching if the turn of the bridge comes next year than if it comes only ten years from now. This is the nucleus of truth in the contention by Abram Bergson that the significance of value calculation in a highly dynamic economy had been overstated.[5] To validate this proposition the low stage of development of the economy is as essential as its dynamic character. When there are many alternatives, both in regard to wants to be satisfied and methods to satisfy them, rapid growth which requires a large volume of investment, much of it long-range, makes the correctness of choice all the more significant. Great waste will result if the wrong choice is made between building more housing, more cars or more refrigerators, or between providing the energy for any of these purposes through hydroelectric projects or atomic power plants, and such mistakes can only be avoided by price calculation and cost accounting.

[4] When the New Economic Policy replaced War Communism, in 1921, and industrial managers were given substantial autonomy, one of the results was widespread collusion to keep prices high. See Maurice Dobb, *Soviet Economic Development since 1917,* New York: International Publishers, 1948, pp. 169 ff; Alexander Baykov, *The Development of the Soviet Economic System,* New York: Macmillan, 1948, p. 57.

[5] See Abram Bergson's comment on "The Soviet Debate on the Law of Value and Price Formation" in Gregory Grossman (ed.), *Value and Plan,* Berkeley and Los Angeles: University of California Press, 1960, pp. 38 f.

THE BUSINESS CYCLE AND ECONOMIC GROWTH

As has been explained, the over-all efficiency of an economic system depends not only on the correct allocation of resources in use but also on the degree of continuity in the utilization of resources. In capitalist countries, this continuity is interrupted by depressions.

At this point it is unnecessary to consider the question of how depressions originate, and it will be seen later that no very precise answers can be given to this question in any event. But it is important to state here that the retardation of economic growth by depressions is not fully measured by the loss of product that could be devoted to investment; the retardation is greater because interruptions in production constitute a major deterrent to the creation of new capacity. The question: "Shall I be able to use the new capacity over at least a large part of its lifetime?" is necessarily raised by the manager of any autonomous production unit when he must make decisions on plant expansion or construction of a new plant. The system of ownership, whether by private shareholders or by the state, makes no difference as long as management can conduct business as it sees fit. To be sure, managerial apprehensions about the possibility of continuous utilization are much stronger under capitalism than under Soviet Communism, but the reason for this is not the different property arrangements; the difference exists, first, because the Soviet manager does not have the experience of temporary underemployment in his plant. But even if he had that experience, he would not have to be much concerned about the hazard of inadequate utilization because of the restricted character of his autonomy and consequently his responsibility. Until recently, if he turned out the quantity of product prescribed by the plan, using up such resources as were allocated to him, his major duties were fulfilled. This situation has not changed much. The planning authorities still determine the capacity that can be used, and provide alternative uses if the original ones do not lead to full utilization. To be largely relieved of this responsibility is of course a boon for the Soviet manager. But responsibility is the reverse side of decision-making power. The same aspects of the Soviet system which, by limiting the responsibility of the managers, have freed them from the fear of excess capacity and thereby have eliminated the resulting inhibition of growth for the whole economy, have also reduced the freedom of action for unit management and thereby have contributed to that overcentralization which has been the great curse of the Soviet system. Gradually, this situation seems to be changing, but it is still too early to see how far the changes will go.

A large part of the problem of autonomy of unit management is the pricing problem viewed from a different angle. Since decisions by unit managers have to be coordinated with each other and adjusted to objective supply conditions and expressions of consumer demand, managers can be granted decision-making power only if prices provide orientation points tending to make the decisions conform to the social optimum, or not to deviate too far from that optimum. Where prices are arbitrarily established, steering the economy by directives issued on the basis of physical considerations alone—such as physical interdependence of industries and physical needs of the population—may be a lesser evil than a self-direction of economic units which will necessarily be misguided by these irrational prices.

The Rate of Time Preference—A Very Preliminary Consideration

Since to a great extent economic growth depends on investment, the will to invest is one of the most important determinants of economic growth. The will to invest is the will to sacrifice present satisfactions for the enlargement of the machinery of production, and this will, in turn, is determined by the importance which we attribute to the future in relation to the present, in other words, by our degree of time preference. This phenomenon will be discussed later in detail, but again—as in the discussion of collective and individual wants—some phases of that explanation must be anticipated. Two interests are at stake here: first, the necessity of time preference in calculating investment projects, and second, the importance of a unified rate of time preference.

In any technologically progressive society there are many opportunities for investment that will promise some return. If all these possible projects were carried out, not enough resources would remain for present consumption, or consumption would drop to an unacceptably low level. Consequently, a selection among investment projects must be made: Those which promise a higher return must, as a general rule, be preferred to those with a lower prospective yield. This rule is not as unambiguous as it may seem at first; for example, how does one compare a project that will bring great benefits for a limited number of years with a project that will bring smaller benefits per year for a longer period? Whatever criteria may be established, however, it is a sound postulate that they be the same regardless which particular project is judged. It may not be possible to express all these criteria in a unified rate of annual return which every project must yield in order to be considered worthwhile, but as a guide for the first steps toward a choice among investment projects such a rate is indispensable—as indispensable as a rational pricing system is for the allocation of resources in general.

In fact, these two requirements are closely related. The purpose of cost-price calculation is to make sure that of resources required for rival purposes of want satisfaction, no unit will be used for a less important purpose while a more important one is left unsatisfied. The unified rate of time preference is to help in making sure that in a choice among rival investment projects, none that is less important will be approved while a more important project fails to be undertaken for lack of resources. The time preference rate expresses the opportunity cost of carrying out a particular project as far as this cost consists in drainage of our general pool of present resources, whereas prices of cost goods express the opportunity cost of undertaking a particular production, whether of an investment or of a current character, with regard to specific kinds of resource.

There is presently no economic system—disregarding primitive societies in remote areas—that would not make use of prices or would not attempt to establish some sort of a unified yardstick for investment decisions. But economic systems differ greatly in the rationality of their pricing system, the role which prices play in the allocation of resources and how close they have come to the establishment of a unified rate of time preference.

THE FACTUAL RECORD OF ECONOMIC GROWTH IN COUNTRIES WITH DIFFERENT ECONOMIC SYSTEMS

Although the growth rates which a country achieves depend on many factors other than its economic system, any analysis that tries to isolate the effects of the economic system must start from a survey of the statistics describing economic growth. Unfortunately, serious obstacles stand in the way of obtaining accurate information on growth rates for purposes of international comparisons.

Even in calculating gross national product (or national income) and its change from year to year for a single country, no high degree of accuracy can be achieved. The reasons are too manifold, and in part too technical, for all to be cited. To mention just one of them: Farmers, more often than not, consume part of their produce in their own households. Even where the other part, the produce that is brought to the market, can be fairly well determined, only the roughest of estimates of farmers' home consumption is usually possible, although this may be an important factor in the gross national product and may change from year to year differently, sometimes even in the inverse direction, from other factors. In international comparisons, this difficulty is extremely significant, because farmers' home consumption plays a different role in different countries; where cash crops prevail, as they do in the United States and also in some tropical monoculture countries, it is much less important than in countries which are closer to subsistence farming, as is the case of Eastern European countries. This is one of the reasons why more reliable information can often be obtained by looking at the growth of industrial production only instead of at the growth of the whole gross national product. In some respects, the growth record of industrial production is also particularly relevant because the increase in industrial production is part of the transformation which many nations are trying to effect through a change or modification of their economic systems. A series of industrial production indices shows probably more clearly than any other set of statistical figures the tempo at which a country approaches its future as a fully developed modern economy.

By the same token, however, the industrial production index gives no full picture of where a country stands at present in its economic development by comparison with others. Even some countries which are already highly developed, for example France, Italy and the Soviet Union, still have a larger agricultural sector than others, such as the United States or West Germany. If this agricultural sector develops more slowly, as it does in most European countries, owing primarily to the traditional conservatism of the rural population, the same rise of the industrial production index means, of course, a slower development of the whole economy.

A particular difficulty in international comparisons of product and income figures is the necessity of using values as common denominators. This requires the analyst to search for proper deflators to take account of inflation and for proper parity ratios to establish the value of one currency in terms of another—questions to which there are no completely satisfactory answers. Everybody knows, for instance, that the 1963 dollar is not the same as the 1939 dollar, but even in a country with statistical methods as highly developed as those of the United States it is not easy to say by what figure to divide a sum of 1963 dollars to reduce ("deflate") it in order to get the same value in 1939 dollars. The use of the cost-of-living index or the wholesale price index can be very misleading, because some prices, for instance those of gasoline, butter and mail service in the United States, have risen much less than the general index, whereas others have risen much more; therefore, the purpose for which the comparison is used, and on which it may depend which commodities should be regarded as the most important, makes a great deal of difference. This is only another way of saying that a general-purpose deflator is necessarily very inaccurate for any particular calculation.[6] Similarly, what a dollar is worth in Greek drachmas, Yugoslav dinars or German marks depends very much on whether the matter is judged from the point of view of an American tourist who has to pay hotel bills, from that of a native who wants to pay for specific American commodities or from that of an American importer who pays for specific products of the foreign country.

From all these facts it follows that no single set of figures of output or income is very reliable for purposes of intertemporal and international comparisons, that the reliability is even less in comparisons which are at the same time international and intertemporal, as that of growth rates of different countries. Therefore, it is useful to look at different sets of figures, for instance industrial production indices and figures of gross national product in constant prices (a concept that is subject only to some of the uncertainties that afflict index figures). Statistical agencies have sometimes been deterred by the difficulties of compiling those tables which would be most useful if they could be constructed in a reliable manner and have been content with more modest endeavors, some of which are of no use to the purposes of this book. This applies especially to output and income figures in current prices, of which quite a few are found in the statistics of United Nations agencies; these figures are too distorted by inflation in a number of important countries. The reader who is tempted to ask why the tables below contain some sets of figures but not others which might have been more informative is therefore requested to withhold criticism until he has investigated whether the more useful figures are available.

In the preceding discussion, the role of investment has been explained. Since the will to invest is the will to sacrifice present satisfaction to the growth of the capacity to produce, the ratio of investment to national income or gross national product—the investment rate—is usually a good indicator of the strength of desire for economic growth.[7]

[6] Moreover, the unequal price movement of different commodities bedevils the establishment of the price indices themselves, because the question arises of how much weight to give to the price changes for an individual commodity. This problem of weighting, which we shall meet again in the discussion of the methods of economic planning, also has no completely satisfactory solution.

[7] Logically, gross investment should be related to gross national product, net investment to national income, but the figures that would permit the most meaningful comparison are not always available.

The distinction between gross and net investment rate is most important when countries at a different stage of industrial development are compared, because the older industrial country, with its larger and older physical plant, must ordinarily use a larger portion of its gross investment for purposes of replacement than the younger country. This difference is important for comparisons between the United States and the Soviet Union. For the same reasons which often make a close approach to correctness harder

A high investment rate—indicating, as it does, a low time preference—means that rapid growth is desired; it does not always mean that rapid growth is achieved. As shown in the table below, in which changes of both output figures and investment rates are found, the countries with the highest investment rates do not always appear to have the highest growth rates. Sometimes this may be a sort of optical illusion: Some investment may be of a long-range character, which will yield much of its return only in a period later than that for which the growth rates are calculated; for instance, if a relatively large part of the investment during the 1950's was in roads, flood protection, power dams, or school buildings, it would obviously be unreasonable to expect the results of such investment to be expressed in the growth rates of the same decade. In other instances part of the investment may have been necessary merely to protect existing production, for instance dike building in countries threatened by floods. The natural environment plays a role also in a more general sense: Where climatic and other aspects of the natural setting are less favorable, investment may be less effective in causing a rise in output. Finally, investment may be partly frustrated by inefficiency of production management; such inefficiency may be a consequence of the economic system, but it may also follow from historical or natural circumstances. It is clear, for instance, that if the industrial labor force consists mostly of former peasants only recently drawn into factories—as in many Eastern European and Asiatic countries—a relatively low productivity of labor must be expected which will inevitably detract from the efficiency of investment until labor has been familiarized with its industrial tasks.

To make a high investment rate possible, it is necessary not only that investment be large in absolute terms, but also that it be large in relation to gross national product (or national income) and therefore to the largest component of the latter, consumer expenditures. However, the desire for economic growth, like any other economic policy, can shape reality only by influencing the actions of individuals in their private spheres: The state may issue exhortations and orders, pay premiums, grant honors or impose penalties, but individuals must work, save and pay taxes. If the material and moral lures and pressures created by the state do not cause the individual to work, save and pay as much as is necessary for the desired amount of investment, that amount will not materialize. The approval of an investment policy by a majority of citizens is no more a guarantee that the citizens as individuals will help carry out that policy by action in their

---

to achieve in calculating national income than gross national product, it is frequently more difficult to find the net than the gross investment rate.

private sphere than the enactment of prohibition in the United States by a democratic procedure assured the obedience to that law by the citizens of the United States. Now it is conceivable that the degree of contentment which is essential for work efficiency, and for an attitude of the individual which causes him generally to act in his private life in consonance with established public policy in regard to economic development, includes a modicum of satisfaction of his present material wants. In this event, it may be impossible to reduce present consumption for the benefit of investment as much as the leaders of the community, or even a majority of citizens acting as members of the community, would desire.

In economies in which free decisions of individuals play a role greater than that irreducible minimum which no centralism can eliminate except at the price of gross inefficiency, another factor, touched upon previously in a different context, establishes a limit to the raising of the investment rate at the expense of consumption. Where managers of enterprises are free to determine investment in pursuit of profit, prospects of ultimate consumption of products must be sufficiently bright to give the production managers reasonable assurance that their products can be sold. In a capitalistic economy, or in a socialist economy (unless the government backs up the investment provisions of the national plan with a sales guarantee for products) or in a communist economy of the Yugoslav type, a curtailment of consumption by taxation, labor arbitration restricting wages or by other means may well result in a reduction rather than an increase of investment and of the investment rate.

All these considerations should be kept in mind when conclusions are drawn from the figures in Table 1. Since in the subsequent sections the capacity of various economic systems to achieve economic growth will have to be investigated, reference to these figures will be made repeatedly. At this point, of course, it has not yet been stated what countries can be regarded as having capitalist, socialist, or communist economies. In some instances the classification is obvious; for the rest, the table should be regarded as raw material for later discussions.

These discussions, however, will not cover all the countries included in the table. The inclusion of the others—especially some of Eastern Europe and Japan—merely serves the purpose of rounding out the picture of the great diversity of growth rates that can exist under like or similar economic systems.

TABLE 1

Production and Capital Formation

Countries	Per Capita product 1960 at constant prices 1953 = 100	Industrial Production 1960 1953 = 100	% ratio of ind. prod. index Jan.-June 1962 Jan.-June 1961	Agricultural production 1959/60 1952/53-1956/57 = 100	Gross Domestic Capital Formation 1960 % of GNP fixed capital only
Bulgaria	155	249	108		
Czechoslovakia	151	193	107		
France	128	161	107	109	18
Germany (Fed. Rep.)	148	179	102	106	24
Italy	144	180	111	119	22
Japan	167	261	116	124	31
United Kingdom	117	126	100		16
United States	105	119	110	110	16
USSR		206	110		
Yugoslavia	163	246	104	166	31

Source: UN Statistical Yearbook 1961, pp. 72 ff, 82, 488 f, 501 ff, ditto 1962 pp. 78 ff.

Gross Industrial Output in Eastern European Countries

% Increase from Previous Year

Countries	1958	1959	1960	1961	1962 Plan
Bulgaria	15	20.5	11.2	9.9	9.9
Czechoslovakia	11.3	10.9	13.4	8.9	9.9
East Germany	11	12.6	8.3	6.2	—
Hungary	12.8	9.4	12.5	11	8
Poland	9.9	9.2	10.9	10.5	8.4
Rumania	9.5	10.2	16.9	15.6	13.5
USSR	10	11.4	10	9.2	8.1

Source: UN Economic Commission for Europe, *European Economic Survey 1960,* Ch. II, p. 2, ditto 1961, Ch. II, p. 2.

CHAPTER 3

EQUALITY AND LIBERTY

Clarification of Concepts

EQUALITY OF LIVING STANDARDS AND EQUALITY OF OPPORTUNITY

Gross inequalities of income are considered undesirable by the great majority. Differences of prestige and power, as well as of income, are integral parts of a structured society, but most of us are prepared to tolerate them only within limits. We have come close to the opinion that all inequalities are a mortgage on the social system in which they exist and, to be accepted, must be justified by some beneficial effects which could not otherwise be achieved, at least not without still more undesirable consequences. There is therefore a near-consensus in most countries, and especially in the most developed ones, that economic affairs should be so ordered as to create or require only a minimum of inequalities. If we had the choice of two or more systems which otherwise perform equally well, most of us would, perhaps with a few reservations, prefer the more equalitarian one.

Sometimes, however, it is maintained that the only equality worth having is equality of opportunity. We want everyone to have an equal chance in life, it is argued, but what everyone makes of his chance is up to him, and the inequalities in the results obtained are not objectionable if there was no privilege at the start. This statement does not correctly describe the majority position in most contemporary societies. It is true that we find it particularly undesirable to have the starting conditions in life unequal, although we must accept the fact that natural endowment varies with individuals; we emphatically do not want our social system to compound the inequalities of heredity by adding inequalities at the start of vocational life. Yet this does not mean that we are indifferent to inequalities resulting from the way people utilize their natural endowment. We are not prepared to leave extreme misery unrelieved, even when it is due to irresponsibility or folly; nor do we like the idea that even the most meritorious conduct should raise a person too high above his fellow humans. We are aware that accidents—illness, victimization by fraud, natural disasters—may lower the economic status of a family beyond the hope of recovery by its own strength, and we want to create protection against these causes of inequality. The desire to limit inequalities even where they are not the result of unequal starting conditions springs from a variety of motives. We want to protect the dignity of even the lowest individual; we fear that misery breeds crime and other socially undesirable actions and attitudes; we also fear that income differentials may be used to make the underprivileged dependent on the well-to-do. Moreover, we realize that qualities most conducive to social and economic advancement are not always the qualities which evoke our highest esteem, and that some great qualities of mind and character are not likely to lead to outstanding positions in economic and social life.

HOW TO COMPARE SATISFACTIONS OF DIFFERENT PERSONS

The problem of equality of income plays a great role in that relatively young branch of economic science, welfare economics, which is concerned with clarifying the concept and the conditions of maximizing the satisfaction of consumers' wants. Seeing the equality problem in the context of welfare economics may lead us to a clearer view of the meaning of economic equality and of the limits within which we may wish to see it realized. Much of the writing on welfare economics, however, has been devoted to the suitability of the price mechanism to fulfill these conditions, and the treatment of this question by the welfare economists will be discussed in the section on capitalism. But there is a fundamental problem involved, significant for all economic systems: Obviously, the concept of maximum satisfaction of consumers' wants requires not only a distinction between higher and lower degrees of want satisfaction of an individual consumer, but also an adding up of the want satisfactions of different consumers and therefore some method by which a minus in the want satisfaction of one consumer can be set off against a plus in the want satisfaction of another. No basis for such an operation can be found in psychology: The proposition that a commodity is desired *n* times as strongly by A as by B has no clearly definable meaning, although it makes good sense to say that the good is high on the scale of preferences of A and low on that of B. Even if the psychologists were to find some basis for comparing the strengths of desires among individuals, such psychological comparison would hardly be significant from the point of view of social analysis. To this point it will be necessary to return when the rationality of price-oriented production will be discussed in the section on capitalism.

A basis for aggregating the importance of want satisfaction of different persons becomes possible only through a value judgment by the analyst, who must weigh the importance of satisfying person A against the importance of satisfying B. He may decide that both are equally important: In this case, and only then, the rule is adopted that desires of different persons should be given equal social weight if they occupy the same positions on the preference scale of each of them. The decision that the want satisfaction of all consumers should be treated as equally important is tantamount to the judgment that all inequality of incomes constitutes a social liability. Like all value judgments, this decision has no objective validity in the sense that anybody could be forced by logical argument to accept it as correct, but since the great majority of living men is inclined toward equalitarianism, the decision to treat the want satisfaction of all members of society as equally important would not deviate very much from the standard which most people would like to see applied. To determine policy, a subjective decision on which almost everyone agrees is as good a basis as objective truth.

If the want satisfaction of all members of society is regarded as equally important, then the concept of maximization of want satisfaction assumes a clearer meaning. It then means that maximum want satisfaction is assured when two conditions are fulfilled: Resources must be used as efficiently as possible, and no want lower on the urgency scale of one individual must be satisfied as long as a want higher on the urgency scale of another individual is left unsatisfied, if both require the same resources.[1]

[1] A condition of maximum welfare is described by the frequently cited formula which Vilfredo Pareto and Enrico Barone have worked out: "it must be impossible by any reallocation of resources to enhance the welfare of one household without reducing that of another." (Reformulation by Abram Bergson, "Socialist Economics," in Howard Ellis, ed., *A Survey of Contemporary Economics*, Philadelphia-Toronto, The Blakiston Company, 1949, p. 414, where also a good evaluation of the Pareto formula can be found.) This condition, however, has little relevance in a comparison of economic systems, in which the question of whether one person should be made better off at the expense of another can usually not be disregarded.

In order to expand the usefulness of the Pareto test of maximum welfare, the following method has been suggested: Whenever a change in the allocation of resources benefits one person while causing injury to another, an increase in total welfare shall be assumed to exist if a tax could be levied on the gain of the benefited person without absorbing that gain, yet sufficient to compensate the loser for his loss. (See Melvin W. Reder, *Studies in the Theory of Welfare Economics*, New York: Columbia University Press, 1951, pp. 14 ff.) Welfare would then be at a maximum when no further change in the allocation of resources were possible that would at the same time result in greater

Equalitarianism and the Requirements of Efficiency

The two requirements of maximizing want satisfaction which have just been stated can hardly ever be fulfilled at the same time: Maximum efficiency in the utilization of resources usually requires premiums upon achievement, and these premiums involve inequalities of income. The basic decision to treat the satisfaction of all members of society as equally important, therefore, does not necessarily or usually imply equality of incomes. We may wish to cut the pie—representing the social product—into equal slices, but we have to realize that an equal distribution of shares would have an adverse effect on the size of the pie, and in order to have a large pie some inequality has to be admitted.

How much inequality is admissible for the sake of enlarging the social product? This again is a matter of subjective value judgment, and opinions probably differ more widely on the question of how large an increase in social product must be to justify a given amount of inequality, than they do on the basic desirability of equality. The only general statement that can be made is that the extremes are rejected by all modern societies: Even the greatest productivity would not reconcile us to a situation in which, say, 1% of the population would receive 90% of the national income; nor would we insist on the elimination of an income differential of 10% between the highest and the lowest quintal of the population if that meant a cut of 50% of the social product. Within so wide a range, the choice between more goods and services and less inequality is one of the basic political issues in all modern countries.

Since a substantial amount of inequality is necessary to prevent too great a shrinkage of the social product, it becomes practically irrelevant that most people would have some reservations on fundamental grounds against a complete equalitarian policy. In any country it is probably no more than a small minority which considers the want satisfaction of a moron as equally important with that of a genius or that of a criminal as equally important with that of a highly moral person. But the income differentials which would be desired on fundamental grounds are generally of the same kind

---

benefits for some persons and in the possibility of sufficient compensation to everybody who suffers a loss. But this device does not touch the core of the difficulty. As Bye has pointed out, the method 'begs the question of unequal incomes.' (Raymond T. Bye, *Social Economy and the Price System*, New York: The Macmillan Company, 1950, p. 5.) If a progressive income tax to finance social benefits deprives high income receivers of $100 million and gives 90 million to the recipients of benefits, while 10 million must be spent on administration, the test would lead to the conclusion that the measure causes a loss in welfare. Obviously, this judgment need not be accepted, because its validity depends on whether the existing distribution of income is regarded as optimal.

and of much less magnitude than the differentials which even those most inclined toward equalitarianism are forced to accept for reasons of expediency. It is therefore still true that in judging economic systems on the basis of an ethical near-consensus we may treat all addition to inequality as a liability.[2]

Equality of incomes would be unimportant in a state of true affluence; if everybody had as much as he wanted, it would obviously make no difference that some could have more. Such a state has nowhere been reached, but even the approach to affluence has the effect of reducing the importance of given income differentials. At a very low standard of living, an income differential of 30 per cent may mean the difference between survival and starvation; at the present American standard of living, it often means no more than driving a Chrysler instead of a Ford, taking a trip to Europe instead of a camping vacation in the nearest national park, and having some more meals in a good restaurant instead of staying at home. Consequently, even if there were no tendency for money incomes to become less unequal—and such a tendency usually arises at the later stages of economic development—there would be a reduction of differences in everyday living as a consequence of the rise in absolute living standards: The upper stratum spends its excess income on some luxuries which have little effect on the general style of living.[3]

Differentials of Power and Prestige

Men want material goods, but they also want power and prestige, of which income is only one of several determinants. It would be conceivable to have small income differentials and still have such differentials of power and prestige as to leave the great majority in a state of unhappiness. The avoidance of such undesirable inequalities is therefore as important as

[2] As explained before, the near-consensus does not extend to the question of how large an increment in social product must be to justify a given amount of inequality, or, in other words, how important it is to reduce inequality. The stand on the latter question has a psychological connection with a person's reservation against complete equality: He who would like to preserve some income differentials will probably also place less importance on the removal of such inequalities which he would prefer to see abolished. This indirect significance of the reservations against complete equality still exists in present-day society.

[3] This might not be the case if one particular kind of luxury which has a greater effect on the style of living than almost any other were not to get out of reach even for the wealthy: the employment of numerous servants. With a rising general standard of living, the class of people who are willing to accept employment in a household where personal independence is inevitably more restricted than in a factory or office becomes all the time less numerous; thus even the upper stratum of society must learn to get along without the personal services of retainers.

avoidance of gross inequalities of income, and since all managerial functions in economic life and some economic functions requiring professional skill are sources of power and prestige, this viewpoint is relevant to a comparative evaluation of economic systems.

Differentials in power and prestige are particularly obnoxious when they are inherited; equality of opportunity is even more important here than in regard to incomes. Most of us are very much opposed to the existing remnants of a caste system, which tend to reverse desirable economic functions for people of "good family"; we want a maximum of social mobility,[4] and not only because of its effect on the material standard of living of the masses. But even if social mobility were perfect, the prestige of those who fill the higher economic functions might be so great and their power so unrestricted as to be oppressive or even unbearable for all the rest of the people. Societies in which equalitarian tendencies are strong will therefore try to develop safeguards against all excessive inequalities of prestige and power.

What does "excessive" mean in this context? Some officials, such as industrial manager, government administrator, teacher, must have authority over those whom they are supposed to organize for work, supervise or teach, and authority means power and prestige. Therefore differentials in regard to these "non-material" privileges are even less avoidable than those in regard to incomes. But modern equalitarian societies do not wish to grant higher differentials of prestige and power to their leading functionaries than is necessary to fill the functions. Such societies may even keep these differentials smaller than would be conducive to the best fulfillment of the functions and deliberately accept a less than perfect performance in industry, administration or education in order to assure a higher degree of equality.

Among the safeguards against undesired differentials of prestige and power, of economic as well as of other origin, the political constitution is of particular importance. Protection of personal liberty against those whose wealth or economic power might marshal the authority of the police or the courts against the lowly is a political matter; so is the prevention of misuse of an employer's power over his employees and the curbing of monopoly power. Less tangible effects of the system of government are sometimes just as important: The ditchdigger whose vote at the polls counts just as much as his employer's thereby gains a consciousness of dignity which will, as a rule, not desert him in talks about wages or about grievances arising

[4] The distinction between this concept and that of the frequency of actual motion across class lines is discussed in the section on capitalism.

from his job. In a modern democracy, nobody is entirely subordinate to any other; everybody remains a little bit of a master of his own superior because as a citizen he participates in the decisions which determine the prestige and power of the superior. Even the soldier, when he goes to the polls, shares in the election of legislators who can make laws curbing the privileges (and determining the pay) of officers. All this adds up to a warning not to overestimate the distinction between political and economic democracy: There is no political democracy without manifold economic effects, and it is difficult to conceive of economic democracy without broad foundations of political democracy.

Once More: The Indispensable Premiums

The rule that differentials in power or prestige should not be greater than required to fulfill the leading functions in society is an equalitarian extension of the principle which distinguishes the modern state from feudalism: that public office must be administered not in the private interest of the officeholder but for the good of the community.[5]

The question arises: Why confine the application of this principle to public office, why not extend it to all social functions, including the management of production and distribution of goods? Classical socialism, at least in its original form, wanted to do just that: The same clear separation between private interest and public interest should be carried out in industry and commerce as exists in the sphere of public administration. The manager of a factory should be a public functionary, bound to his duties by service obligation and not by self-interest; he should act not by his own right but by authority received from the community. Whatever may be the disadvantages of such a system, it would make it possible to keep the differentials in power, prestige and income which the managers enjoy more strictly within the limits of the requirements of the function. But is such a system possible?

[5] Perhaps it may seem that the restriction of prestige and power differentials is an application rather than an extension of that principle. But just as it is possible to pay an officeholder a higher salary than is necessary to attract enough qualified applicants for that office and still prevent him from drawing any further pecuniary gain from his public service, so it is possible to accord him greater prestige than he needs to exercise his functions and still not make him something like a lord of the manor. (Overpayment in prestige may actually be used to compensate for underpayment in salary; for instance, in monarchic Prussia it was often said that the officials were partly "paid in honor.") The absolute size of the emoluments of office, in money or prestige, is one thing; the right of the officeholder to make himself paid through demands upon those over whom he holds authority is another. The opposition to "excessive" size of the emoluments is part of the equalitarian view of society; the rejection of the latter right is a characteristic of the modern state as opposed to feudalism; but the motives of the two are interrelated.

Those who would be inclined to answer this question in the affirmative might point to the change since the time when public administration was based on the economic self-interest of the administrator—was in a sense made an object of private enterprise. The feudal lord was given a territory to administer and defend with the understanding that he should make himself paid by the services and deliveries of the inhabitants and with the right to determine the amount of these emoluments often within wide limits. In a period in which difficulties of transportation and communication made supervision from a distant center difficult—at least without so effective an organization as ancient Rome had known—it proved necessary to bind the self-interest of the administrator and defense commander in this manner to his territory; but the absolute monarchy overcame these difficulties and replaced the feudal barons with paid officials, and the modern state inherited this officialdom. Is it not possible for our organizational technique to be so perfected as to make the separation of self-interest and social function possible in the economic field as it has been made possible in public administration?

Thus far the evidence is against this separation. It is easy enough to separate legal property in factories from management—this is done in business corporations on the one hand and in state enterprises on the other. But the self-interest of the business executives is evoked in many ways to assure good performance: By bonuses, by high power and prestige differentials, by merit promotions. These and similar devices are used not only in capitalist economies; socialist and even communist governments have developed the same or similar incentives for their managers. The tasks of entrepreneurship are sufficiently different from public administration to preclude the development from autonomous enterprise, with its powers of profit-seeking, to officialdom, with its prescribed duties and fixed compensation. The term autonomous enterprise is used in the broad sense in which it may exist even if all its stock is in government hands. It seems that the inequalities arising from this source are irremovable in the sense that their removal would cost too much in terms of the size of the social product.

International Comparisons of Inequality

The task of comparing the degree of inequality in different countries having different economic systems, has proved discouragingly difficult, not only because of the inadequacy of statistical information, but also because of some ambiguity in the concept of equality; this is as true of the distribution of money incomes as of the distribution of prestige and power. Suppose in country A the lowest 10% or 20% of the population have only a very small share in the national income, but the middle group has a relatively large share, thus leaving not very much for the excess incomes of the very rich. In another country B the poor may not be so very poor, but the very rich may be richer. Which country has the more equalitarian income distribution? [6]

With respect to the distribution of power and prestige, ambiguity arises from still other causes. There are different kinds of power: The Roman dictator, for instance, was master over the life and death of the citizens during a brief emergency, after which he had to account for its use; the President of the United States is always bound by the rule of law, and his power is limited by the powers of Congress and the Judiciary, but it lasts longer, and unless he exceeds the constitutional limits of his discretionary powers, he is accountable only to his conscience. Which of the two is more powerful, and consequently which of the two institutions involves greater inequality of power? The prestige of a privileged group may be great in one stratum of the population and negligible in another; or, again, it may be found in all population groups but may be of a lower degree.

The difficulties and ambiguities involved in comparing inequalities frustrate the hope for any clear-cut and accurate results of international comparisons in this field. It will be possible, however, to distinguish extreme cases from one another, and as better statistical information becomes available, we may be able to describe inequalities existing under different economic systems with a fair degree of accuracy, although often the complexities of the phenomena may preclude a summary statement to the effect

[6] Analytical techniques which have been elaborated to measure the degree of inequality and which are not yet very useful for their proper purpose because of the unreliability of the data to which they would have to be applied, can be effective in demonstrating the ambiguity of the equality concept. The simplest device of this kind is the so-called Lorenz curve: On the horizontal axis percentages of population or consumer units are represented, on the vertical axis percentages of national income, both in a cumulative manner. If income distribution were equal, so that 30 per cent of the people had 30 per cent of the national income, the curve would be a straight line rising at an angle of 45 degrees. Since the lowest 30 per cent of the people will have less, and the highest 30 per cent more than 30 per cent of the income, the actual curve will be flatter in the beginning and steeper in the later phases, i.e. it will be concave; the greater the concavity, the more pronounced the inequality of income. It is conceivable that the curve representing the income distribution of a particular country is very flat near the bottom, but at an early point becomes steep, and that the curve for another country would be only moderately flat in the beginning and begin its steep rise only late; these two possibilities correspond to the conditions of countries A and B, respectively, as outlined above. These are only two among many possibilities; a little experimentation with the graph will easily convince the reader that Lorenz curves may vary in very different ways, and that in many instances it will not be possible to summarize their differences in the statement that one curve indicates a more equalitarian distribution than the other.

that one system is more nearly equalitarian than the other. Even now, we can point out the sources of inequality under different systems, even if we cannot compare their quantitative effects.

Attractions and Burdens of Liberty

Man wants to be free. He does not wish to have to do another's man's bidding—to be coerced into action or inaction against his own desires. He wants the right to make his own choices, even if they turn out to be mistakes. If he bows to somebody else's judgment, he wants this to be his own, voluntary decision.

The necessity to make choices, it is true, may sometimes be a burden. People may get "tired of freedom," and may call for a leader to make a wide range of choices, even vital ones, for them. Sometimes bewildered by the intricacy of arguments for and against various propositions that face them, people do not feel that experts can effectively clarify the technicalities that will enable the layman to find alternatives of choice. More often, however, people want to be relieved of choices because they find all the alternatives they can see unacceptable and look for a miracle man to cut the Gordian knot. In any event, however, as soon as things begin to look less confusing or hopeless, people tend to get as tired of their new non-freedom as they did of their previous freedom, and it takes all of the spellbinder's art to keep them in such a state of emotion that they do not think too much of their lost liberty. Basically, man does not want to have a guardian—not even a person of unlimited knowledge, perfect judgment and unimpeachable integrity. Not only does man normally want to make his own decisions, he also wants to prepare for them by free exchange of opinions with others, and to be able to persuade others to join him in his choices to make them effective within society—all this without the risk of being thrown into jail or having to face a firing squad. This is not to say that man, psychically, is all in favor of a free society in normal circumstances. Such a society can exist only if people, in addition to wanting to be free themselves, also are willing to respect the freedom of others, and this is a difficult lesson to learn. It takes a lot of education to hold strong opinions and at the same time to accept the right of others to hold their contradictory views and to argue for them in public. Considering that such acceptance goes against the grain of the average man, it seems more remarkable that freedom of discussion has been so widely upheld than that it is sometimes breached by lapses into intolerance.

Because liberty is a basic human want, a condition of human happiness, it does not have to be justified by its social usefulness to be regarded as a value, but there is no doubt that its long-run effects are highly useful—so much so that even most of the temporary crises which a regime of liberty may produce pale into insignificance by comparison with its blessings. There is no omniscient person of perfect judgment and integrity; all progress, therefore, depends on trial and error. This means that people must have a sphere of freedom in which they can act according to their own judgment; if experimenting were left to a dictator or his puppets, its scope would inevitably be too narrow. This proposition is not refuted by the experience that even under dictatorships technology can flourish; if the dictator leaves his physicists and engineers free to experiment, he can expect good results in these limited fields, but beyond those limits the stifling of the experimenting mind will block progress. Liberty, of course, requires more than merely experimenting with ideas in one's own chamber or laboratory; the trial-and-error process is sterile unless its results can be freely discussed. Consequently, freedom of expression—involving not only the absence of censorship but also the personal security of the dissenter from repressive measures—must be established not only for the sake of the individual, to promote his sense of well-being, but also for the sake of society, because the discovery of truth and the improvment of institutions would either not occur at all or would be infinitely slower without that freedom. All this has been explained with model clarity in John Stuart Mill's classic, *On Liberty.*[7]

Liberty cannot be absolute. One reason, often stated, is the impossibility of protecting liberty except by its opposite, coercion: Without the policeman's gun we would be subject to the bandit's. Another reason is the limited flexibility of social institutions: It is impossible, for example, to organize effective government entirely without patronage, which means a premium on some opinions or party affiliations and therefore a restriction of freedom; it is impossible to assure the individual worker maximum protection from encroachments on his freedom by union leaders and simul-

[7] See the Gateway Edition, Chicago: Henry Regnery Company, 1955. With Introduction by Russell Kirk. The Introduction, however, written from a conservative point of view, is excessively critical of the great liberal essay. There seems to be no good reason, for instance, to agree with the following statement by Kirk: "Mill argues that this peril [of his age] is an unthinking obedience to the dictates of custom; while in actuality, a century later, the real danger is that custom and tradition and prescription will be overthrown utterly by neoterism, the lust after novelty, and that men will be no better than the flies of a summer, oblivious to the wisdom of their ancestors, and forming every opinion solely under the influence of the passion of the hour." (P. 14.) Is this not rather an age, if not of conformity, at least with strong tendencies toward conformity, and are not the views to which people tend to conform mostly those which they have inherited from the past and do not dare to put to the test?

taneously by employers; there may even be instances in which for the sake—but at the same time at the expense—of liberty a political party, aiming at the destruction of liberty, must be suppressed before it can achieve its aim.

Criteria of Liberty: "Absence of Coercion" versus "Range of Choices"

Freedom exists only where man can make choices, but the alternatives among which he can choose are limited not only by coercion on the part of others: They are also limited by objective circumstances which have their origin, for instance, in the limited availability of resources. If we were to define liberty merely as freedom from coercion, we would have to say that a small, independent farmer, working from sunrise to sundown and earning just enough to keep body and soul together, is freer than a factory worker laboring eight hours and then having the pleasant choice of spending a substantial wage income on any of a variety of commodities. But the industrial worker, although he must obey a foreman during working hours, has the chance to determine for himself a large part of his pattern of life, while the poor farmer, since he cannot buy more than the barest necessities in the cheapest way and cannot afford any leisure, has his life prescribed for him by the circumstances under which he exists, as rigidly as they are prescribed for a slave by a harsh master. If we wish to maintain the definition of liberty as absence of coercion by other human beings, we might say that the poor farmer possesses liberty but that it has no value to him; yet this would be a semantic evasion of the problem. Having to work without leisure for a pittance deprives man of freedom in any real sense, whether his predicament is due to oppression by others or to conditions of nonhuman origin. This is true even where such extreme poverty does not lead—as it usually does—to a situation in which the poor sell whatever formal liberties remain to them to people of more fortunate circumstances, with election fraud and prostitution as the consequences.

But if a definition of liberty simply as absence of coercion leads to an unrealistic concept, to define liberty as a maximum of choice would also be unsatisfactory. Our range of choices depends largely on the availability of material wealth; this factor determines not only how numerous the types of commodity are among which we can make our selection for purposes of consumption; material wealth also often determines what we can do to promote causes dear to our heart, how much time we can devote to learning—sometimes even whom we can marry. Other conditions being equal, the richer person is freer than the poorer. But conditions of life are rarely equal for two people, even aside from differences in wealth or income; although the idea that man may be "poor but free" can easily be overstressed, it still contains a core of truth: A legally free person, living in modest circumstances on the yield of a farm, a business or a labor contract, has certainly more liberty in any sense in which it is reasonable to use this term, than a slave whom the whim of a master keeps in luxury; also, around 1938 an American worker, though much poorer, was much freer than many a German businessman whom the Gestapo kept in fear of the concentration camp; an artist or writer, living in Paris or San Francisco on a "beatnik" level, may be freer than his richly rewarded colleague in Moscow, who must toe the party line. In elaborating the implications of the latter example, one would meet another complication: Liberty also has something to do with the pattern of our needs. The man who finds life not worthwhile unless he can have luxuries is likely to be less free than another person who feels happy if more modest wants are satisfied, and it is more than a figure of speech to call a narcotics addict the "slave" of his drug.

To work out a neat definition of liberty, which at the same time is more than an arbitrary construct and really reflects what we mean when we speak of feeling free, is a far more difficult job than appears at first sight. Such a definition, however, is not needed here. For the purpose of this book it is sufficient that the reader should realize that liberty depends both on minimizing coercion and on other measures to widen the range of choices which a person can make in shaping his life; in other words, liberty is reduced if our range of choices is narrowed, and the reduction is particularly detrimental to liberty if it is effected not by objective circumstances but by way of coercion on the part of other human beings. Such a concept of liberty obviously lacks precision. To understand why nevertheless, at least for the purposes of this analysis, it is preferable to an alternative selection of criteria it is useful to consider further the consequences which would follow from a concept of liberty based only on the range of choice or only on the absence of coercion.

As stated before, the first type of definition overemphasizes the significance of material wealth for liberty. The "range of choice" concept of liberty could therefore be easily fitted into the beliefs of many Marxist writers, who consider the rise of productivity *the* motive power of historical development; they tend to identify growth of liberty with economic progress. This tendency is aggravated by Marxist determinism: Since the course of history is essentially predetermined, the individual has no range of sensible choice with regard to super-personal goals; his choices lie in the area of personal activity and consumption, and here the range is of course dependent on the performance of the economy. To be sure, there are other, contradictory lines of thinking in Marxism, but since we are not concerned with an analysis of that complex view of the world for its own sake but wish to give an illustration of the pitfalls in defining liberty merely as a wide range of choices, we may concentrate our attention on that brand of Marxism which displays the defect. This brand finds the basic presupposition of liberty in the recognition of inevitabilities, as shown in the following passage of the most famous book by Friedrich Engels: "Freedom does not consist in the imagined independence from natural laws; it consists in the recognition of these laws and in the possibility, which grows out of this recognition, to make them work for defined purposes according to a plan. This is true with regard to the laws of outer nature as well as with regard to those which regulate the physical and intellectual existence of man himself—two kinds of law which we can separate at the utmost conceptually, but not in reality. . . . The freer man's judgment is with regard to a particular point, the more strict is the necessity with which the content of his judgment is determined; whereas the uncertainty which is based on ignorance and which chooses between different and contradictory alternatives with apparent arbitrariness, thereby proves precisely its unfreedom, its domination by the object which it sought to dominate." [8]

Not all men are equally capable of recognizing historical inevitability; some may be blinded by their class interest, others may be captives of tradition. In the opinion of the Marxist school which builds its philosophy in politics on the ideas indicated in the passage quoted from Engels, those who are aware of the preordained course of history have the duty to widen the range of choice of their fellow humans by promoting economic productivity, and they therefore have a right to determine policy. Since the course of development is essentially predetermined, social experiment is useful only in regard to detail; since no trial and error is necessary in regard to important decisions, error has no usefulness—as it has, by showing some approaches to be blind alleys, if the future is uncertain; consequently, from the point of view of the determinist, those in error have no claim to

[8] Translated from "Herr Eugen Duhrings Ümwälzung der Wissenschaft" in *Marx-Engels Gesamtausgabe*, Sonderausgabe zum vierzigsten Todestag von Friedrich Engels. Moskau-Leningrad: Verlagsgenossenschaft auslaendischer Arbeiter in der USSR, 1935, p. 118. For an English version of the context see Friedrich Engels, *Herr Eugen Dühring's Revolution in Science*, trans. Emile Burns, ed. Palme Dutt. New York: International Publishers, 1939, p. 130. The direct reference of this passage is to the philosophical problem of the freedom of the will from predetermination by natural or quasi-natural laws, but the consequences for the political problem of the freedom of the individual from control are obvious.

participate in decisions. The élite, who know the course of history, will lead mankind to its destiny of abundance of material goods and thereby to the possibility of concentrating on intellectual and cultural enjoyments. Moreover, since economic laws, like natural laws, are to be made to work for human purposes "according to a plan," this means that "men's conditions of living, which so far have dominated men, now come under their domination and control . . . The laws of their own social activities, which so far have confronted man as natural laws, rooted in outside conditions and dominating him, are now applied and thereby controlled by him in full understanding. . . . Only from that moment on, will men make their own history with full consciousness. . . . It is man's leap from the realm of necessity into the realm of liberty." [9] To achieve this great liberating change the élite then seem entitled to use all suitable means, including curbs on liberty for the average citizen.[10] In this way dictatorship is finally made the prelude to freedom—but the prelude is a certainty and the eventual freedom is consigned to an indefinite future.

The identification of liberty with economic progress, given a particularly sinister aspect by the experience with communist totalitarianism, has been a great provocation to many liberals and has induced some of them to maintain all the more firmly the definition of liberty simply as absence of coercion. Friedrich A. Hayek, for instance, considers it the worst of several confusions that have arisen over the concept of liberty to describe it as "the physical 'ability to do what I want,' the power to satisfy our own wishes, or the extent of the choice of alternatives open to us." [11] He would define freedom as "that condition of men in which coercion by others is reduced as much as is possible in society." [12] "In this sense 'freedom' refers solely to men's relation to other men, and the only infringement on it is coercion by

[9] *Sonderausgabe*, pp. 294-295.

[10] Marx and Engels themselves did not clearly draw this conclusion; the term "dictatorship of the proletariat" as used by these two writers has not been given any precise meaning. It was primarily Lenin who worked out the application of Engels' statements on freedom and necessity (which were based on Hegelian ideas and foreshadowed by earlier passages in Marx's writings) to political philosophy. His emphasis on the revolutionary élite is probably in part due to the influence of a non-Marxist kind of socialism, the philosophy of Auguste Blanqui; it is also possible that ideas developed by the pre-Marxist Russian Socialists, the *narodniki,* have contributed to this aspect of Leninism (see on this point, Oliver H. Radkey, *The Agrarian Foes of Bolshevism,* New York: Columbia University Press, p. 22). The basis of the theory of the revolutionary élite and its unrestrained rule, however, is a hardly avoidable conclusion from such statements as the quotation from Engels, however bitterly Marx and Engels personally might have disagreed with it, and however important may have been the contributions to its development from non-Marxist sources.

[11] F. A. Hayek, *The Constitution of Liberty.* Chicago: The University of Chicago Press, 1960, p. 16.

[12] *Ibid.*, p. 11.

men. This means, in particular, that the range of physical possibilities from which a person can choose at a given moment has no direct relevance to freedom." [13] In part, the reasons why this definition is unsatisfactory have already been discussed, but there is still another one of equal importance.

In the most important instances, the question of whether the limitation of choices open to an individual is established by other men and therefore comes under the heading of coercion, or whether it is of "natural" origin is unanswerable because human and "natural" factors are both involved. The occasions in which natural scarcity of resources is so preponderant a reason for poverty that all social factors can be neglected are probably not even frequent in underdeveloped countries; they are almost nonexistent in developed societies. Most frequently there is a complex interaction between social and natural factors in determining the distribution of wealth and income, in causing destitution, comfort, or affluence for particular individuals. Consequently, even if we wanted to understand liberty merely as "relation of men to other men," we could not disregard the economic condition of the masses and their "power to satisfy" their wishes, nor could we, as a rule, draw a line between the narrowing of choices for the multitude by deliberate action of the privileged, a narrowing effect originating from spontaneous social developments and one originating from natural causes. Therefore the definition of liberty based solely on the absence of coercion, aside from being often not meaningful, also would be methodologically impracticable.

Liberty and Equality

THE ALLEGED CONFLICT

Ever since the great French Revolution proclaimed liberty and equality simultaneously as its goals, the opposition has countered with the contention that liberty and equality are incompatible. This contention has been maintained with even greater insistence with regard to economic than to political equality. What is the merit of this argument?

It has already been mentioned that the juxtaposition of poverty and wealth is almost bound to lead to a direct subjection of the underprivileged to the will of the privileged, because the poor are too much tempted to submit to the wishes of the rich in return for some means to satisfy pressing needs. Consequently, extreme inequality of living conditions is highly detrimental to freedom. As inequality is reduced, the hazards to freedom decline rapidly; although complete equality has not even been closely approached in the United States, restrictions on liberty growing out of

[13] *Ibid.*, p. 12.

economic inequality are no longer of general importance in American society. This is a reason not to pay too heavy a price for further approaches to equality, but no good reason to forget that on other levels of development an increase in equality means an increase in liberty, if otherwise the situation remains unchanged; nor is there any justification for overlooking the fact that the approach to equality in the United States is largely the result of policy measures, such as strengthening the labor unions and imposing progressive taxation on incomes, and would be undone if these policies were reversed.

It is important to keep these policy measures in mind because it has been denied that the state can legitimately try to influence the distribution of income to make it more equal. To the extent that this position is based on the explicit or implied assumption that the determination of shares in the national income by marginal productivity can be used for a moral justification of a particular pattern of personal distribution, the basic argument will be discussed in chapter six; other criticisms of equalitarian action by the state are simply a consequence of value judgments too different from those on which our inquiry is based for profitable discussion. One argument, however, brought forth by neoliberal writers must be discussed here: that the state cannot assume the task of influencing the distribution of income because the principle of equality before the law would thereby be violated, and consequently liberty jeopardized. "From the fact that people are very different it follows that, if we treat them equally, the result must be inequality in their actual position, and that the only way to place them in an equal position would be to treat them differently." [14]

Equality before the law is indeed one of the pillars of liberty, but the concept is unambiguous only in its narrow meaning. Liberty cannot exist where the courts mete out one kind of justice to the well-born and another to the lowly, whether they discriminate against the latter because the "rabble" must not do things which are the privilege of its betters, or against the former because they are "capitalists," "*ci-devant* aristocrats," kulaks or other "class enemies." Nor can the principle of equal treatment be confined to the judicial branch of the government. It is now generally recognized in the United States that appointment to public office must not be made dependent on the candidate's race; within a wide range, it can also not be made dependent on the candidate's political affiliation, religion, sex or any other characteristic other than ability tested by performance in examinations or

[14] Hayek, *op. cit.,* 87. In other words, equality before the law requires that the person who, through ability or good luck, is able to earn a higher income, be left in the full enjoyment of that income without impairment, for instance, by progressive taxation.

on the job; other democratic nations have even more stringent provisions assuring equal access to public, appointive office, and the need for such provisions will become greater as the needs of governments for specialists increase. In many fields of legislation, the "due process" clauses of the Fifth and Fourteenth amendments to the Constitution of the United States is a shield against discrimination.

It is an entirely different, in fact untenable, contention, however, that the state should not be entitled to impose obligations on one group of citizens which it does not impose on others. The state requires military service from the young and healthy but not from the aged or infirm; the state forces children of a particular age to attend school and leaves out other age groups. To be sure, this is reasonable. But is it not equally reasonable to have the high-income recipient contribute a larger percentage of his income to public expenses than the low-income earner, since the contribution of the former constitutes no greater and probably still a smaller sacrifice than that of the latter?

THE UNDERLYING ISSUE

To carry the discussion to the core of the problem, it is necessary to trace the arguments against progressive taxation and other measures of economic equalitarianism back to their root. This root is formed by an idea which has rarely if ever been formulated in recent decades; the idea underlies much of the polemics against modern interventionism and especially against equalitarian policies. It is the proposition that the state must take society as it is, that government—and this refers to all its branches—may only, as far as necessary, regulate the functioning of social organs but must not try to influence the structure and the fundamental forces of social living. Viewed from this basic proposition, the anti-interventionist arguments appear stronger than when examined merely by themselves. Many a friend of liberty who does not belong to the Hayek school might well wish that some such firm principle could be established, to make the boundary between freedom and totalitarianism more clearly visible. Yet can we profess that principle without paying too high a price, without finding ourselves forced to violate it until it is more honored in the breach than in compliance and degenerates into a mere pretense?

No modern state has found it possible to refrain from measures intended to shape society. This is not only true of economic measures but also of others, some of which have a particularly strong impact. Compulsory school attendance is in this category, especially since the state determines—with however much restraint—an important part of the content of teaching.

By trying to inculcate the young generation with sympathetic understanding for races not their own or with a concept of patriotism, the state exercises an important influence on the future character of society.

But education, though perhaps the most important tool of the state used in shaping society, is by no means the only one. Some very important ones are in the field of economic policy. One of the most vital decisions, for instance, in determining the economic life of society is the distribution of resources between work for the present and work for the future. The state, even if it follows the advice of those who want to minimize government intervention, cannot avoid influencing that decision by its policy in regard to interest and to public expenditures; it thereby must act either against the preferences of those who want ampler provisions for the future at the expense of the present, or against the wishes of those who have the opposite preference. Furthermore, by either fostering, controlling or combating monopoly, the government deeply influences the structure of the economy and thereby of society; how deeply, will be seen from later discussion where it will be explained that the problem of monopoly in practice is largely coextensive with the problem of the size of enterprises. It is evident that the prevalence of medium business or of giant enterprise in a society greatly influences the non-economic as well as the economic aspects of society; yet who would maintain that the government can be indifferent toward monopoly?

Thus the state cannot in principle be deprived of the right to influence the structure of society and the forces which operate within society. The instrumentality of government must be used to remedy maladjustments in this structure or correct the direction of those forces when they threaten misfortune. The state, indeed, is part and parcel of society; the changes which incessantly transform society cannot be kept from flowing through the channels of political power.

But if no such hard-and-fast line, as some anti-interventionists implicitly assume, can be drawn to limit the state's power over the other elements of society, this does not mean that all limits are unnecessary. What is the difference between a totalitarian state which claims the right to hammer the minds of its citizens into any desired shape and to impose on them any changes in their relationships preferred by the ruling élite, and a democratic state which also claims powers of education and some control over the economic and other relationships among its citizens? The difference obviously lies in the defenses with which the citizens of a democracy are equipped to stave off encroachments by the government upon their interests. These defenses are partly collective and partly applicable by the individual. In the first category is universal suffrage and dependence, full or partial, of the executive upon the legislature; in the second category is the major part of the Bill of Rights in connection with judicial review of executive and legislative acts. The system is based on the expectation that the citizen, if his most elementary rights are protected, can and will use them to defend his other interests against unjustifiable government interference. Naturally, this arrangement involves hazards, but they are smaller than the dangers that would result from so narrowly circumscribing state activity as to freeze too much of the social structure by exempting it from state action. Although in some extreme instances democratic safeguards have broken down, these cases do not indicate that a more far-reaching anti-interventionist rule would have held out better; rather, the lesson seems to be that it is highly dangerous for liberty itself if government tolerates—or has been unable to remedy—faults in the structure of society—faults which, for instance, permit wide swings of the business cycle or excessive differentials in income, prestige or power. A rule obliging the governments to leave those maladjustments untouched would be the most unsuitable means to forestall a repetition of such disasters as Fascism and Nazism or the frustration of the hope for a Russian democracy at the end of the First World War.

It is against the background of these general considerations that the case for equalitarian policies must be examined.

Just as the rejection of too broad a restraint on state activity is not a negation of the need for any restraint, so the realization that a ban on all equalitarian state policy cannot be justified is not meant to suggest that an equalitarian policy can never be dangerous to liberty. If a government were determined to assure complete economic equality among its citizens, it would have to enact such detailed laws and organize so extensive an apparatus of supervision that very little room would be left for the citizen's own decisions. This is true not only with regard to economic equality: Any policy pushed to extremes requires measures to assure a concentration of effort which is detrimental to liberty. This is one of the reasons why liberty inevitably suffers in war; although it is a myth to believe that the most regimented society is the most likely to be superior in armed conflict—since some room for spontaneous action is essential to success even in an emergency—it would be an even greater mistake to assume that a war can be fought without touching freedom. What is true of war against a foreign enemy is true of "war" on vice, of "war" on economic backwardness, of "war" on economic inequality—of any substantive goal that a government regards as supreme and therefore worth every sacrifice. Liberty requires moderation even in the pursuit of highly desirable aims.

DEMOCRACY AND LIBERTY: FURTHER THOUGHTS

Those writers who have tried to show an unbridgeable gap between liberty and equality have often denied that the historical connection between the demand for individual liberty and the demand for an equal voice of all citizens in the government has any inherent justification. The assertion that this connection is arbitrary or completely wrong is heard with particular frequency since it became clear that the masses would use universal suffrage to work for more economic equality.

On the other hand, only the exuberance of some fighters in the early cause of democracy can explain the unwarranted assumption that majority rule combined with universal suffrage is in itself a sufficient guarantee of liberty. Majorities, of course, can be as intolerant as individual despots and have often displayed great cruelty to dissenters. Consequently, a regime based on universal suffrage, just as much as any other system, needs an effective bill of rights to protect the individual's liberties. Protection of these liberties is not only necessary for the individual's own sake but also as a presupposition of free discussion in the interest of society. The peculiar function of a bill of rights in a democratic system is to cause majority rule to make sense. It is a truism to say that the majority is not always right. Democracy is not, as its opponents have often maintained, based on the assumption that the greater number has necessarily the better case. Rather, democracy is based on the assumption that there is an element of rationality in the human mind, that consequently men can learn by experience from the results of intellectual and institutional experiments, provided experiences can be freely discussed; that through such discussion a minority can be turned into a majority; and that therefore in the long run majority rule is more likely to lead to good results than any kind of minority rule. It is the Bill of Rights which assures that free discussion which is so essential a part of the process.

But it is not only that majority rule is incomplete without protection of individual liberties; the reverse is equally true. Universal suffrage is a postulate of liberty. The fundamental reason can be found in the controversies that led to the American Revolution. Why did the colonists object to taxation without representation? Because "taking their money out of their pockets without their consent," to quote the Earl of Chatham, that great sympathizer with the colonial cause, seemed to them an infringement on their liberty.[15] What is true of taxation is true of all matters of policy—economic and others. Since social needs, as felt by the individual citizens, are often incompatible, and the state, wielding its coercive power, must decide

[15] Quoted by Frank Arthur Mumby, *George III and the American Revolution,* Boston and New York: Houghton-Mifflin Company, 1923, Vol. I pp. 126-127.

who should be satisfied and who should not (or how far A should be satisfied at the expense of B, and vice versa), the inevitable encroachment upon the individual's life can only be cushioned by giving him a voice in the formulation of policy. He may still be overruled; but except in the relatively rare instances in which the effects of an action can in no way be undone, he is not finally overruled; he can still work for his cause in the hope of obtaining a majority next time.

Absolute liberty is impossible, let us remember, because—among other reasons—social institutions are not infinitely flexible. We could have more liberty if all our wants were compatible, and therefore we did not need the state as an arbitrator. There is no sense in demanding a degree of liberty which is inconsistent with social living; but there is good sense in demanding that as much liberty as possible be built into the mechanism through which the state exercises its powers. Liberty is not violated if the action of the state meets with the consent of the citizens whose interests are affected; majority rule means that the larger number of citizens is likely[16] to be in that favorable position. Democratic guarantees of individual liberties, on the other hand, mean that the minority in the first place has a voice in the decision before it has been taken, and secondly, that it can work for reconsideration. Who can seriously deny that these elements of democratic government tend to expand the sphere of liberty within the limits compatible with the existence of society?

A bill of rights can exist only where the constitution provides for some separation of powers, at least for a separation of the judicial from the executive and legislative power: Protection of the individual from arbitrary government interference with his life requires an independent judiciary, and no judges can be independent unless their positions are not subject to the whim of the administration or a parliamentary majority. Almost equally important is the principle that those who make the legal rules should not be the same persons or institutions which apply them to the individual case—the principle which the Constitution of the United States is designed to safeguard by its prohibition of bills of attainder in Article I, section 5. But separation of powers is only the most important application of a broader principle, which may be called diffusion of state power.

Writers who wish to minimize the role of the state in economic life have often argued, reasonably, that a citizen's dependence on the government means dependence of one person on others, because the state is an

16 What prevents certainty in this matter are the inevitable deficiencies of representative government, of which so much has been written that an explanation is unnecessary here.

abstraction and state power is exercised by people.[17] But this argument has a reverse side: State power is obviously exercised by a multitude of people; consequently, dependence on the state does not mean dependence on one person. Those who exercise state power will not all be of one mind; unless a rigid, hierarchical pattern is established in the state administration, there will be a competition of ideas and preferences within the governmental apparatus and a chance for the citizen to exercise his own choice among the various tendencies represented among the many agencies which fulfill state functions.

To give a full picture of the importance of the diffusion of state power would require a complete theory of public administration. One example must suffice. It is very important for the job seeker to have a freedom of choice among employers. Now let us consider a society in which all instruments of production are owned by the state. Even in such a society it would not be necessarily true, in a socially relevant sense, that there is only one employer for every job seeker. This would be the effect of wholesale nationalization only if there were one government personnel office to do the hiring for all positions—an arrangement not easy to conceive in a modern state and probably nowhere established. If, on the other hand, every government-owned plant is free to select its personnel and negotiate the terms of employment, the freedom of the job seeker would be the same as if the plants were in private hands, with no understanding among the employers as to the conditions to be offered to their employees; unions, of course, may exist or may not exist or may exist under either government or private ownership. In most instances of state ownership, an intermediate situation prevails: Every office or factory hires its own people, but there are some general rules governing selection of employees and terms of employment. Whether this leaves a greater latitude of choice to the individual applicant than he would have in private industry where some coordination of hiring policies also often takes place among employers, depends on the individual case.

The state confronts its citizen in many other roles than that of an employer, and in any of these functions the diffusion of state power is important. This does not mean that the freedom of the individual is greatest where state power is most diffused. This is not true of hiring: Some general rules of state personnel policy may, for example, prevent racial and political discrimination and thus protect the individual's freedom. Similarly, if I apply for a driver's license or for a building permit, my freedom may be

[17] See for instance the chapter "Who, Whom" in Friedrich Hayek, *The Road to Serfdom*, Chicago: University of Chicago Press, 1944.

severely restricted if too many government offices have a say in the matter; and it certainly will not be conducive to the citizen's freedom if every chief of police can make his own rules for the administration of the law. Thus it is not only the degree of diffusion but also the manner in which state power is diffused that is of significance to the freedom of the individual; but the complexities of the problem should not obscure the fact that a monolithic state is a danger to freedom under all circumstances.

This whole discussion illustrates a statement made in the introduction: The constitution of the state is of the greatest importance for the economic system. No mistake that can be committed in this field is greater than to assume that the liberty of the individual is simply in inverse proportion to the magnitude of the role which the state plays in economic life; the liberty-protecting role of the state as a countervailing power, its welfare-augmenting role which widens the latitude of choices open to the individual in many fields, and the degree and manner in which state power is diffused must be taken into consideration. Large responsibilities of the state, in the economic field as in others, do not by themselves mean state despotism; but state power will indeed degenerate into despotism unless surrounded with those safeguards which mankind has developed for the protection of liberty in the roughly four thousand years in which civilized societies have existed.

II. CAPITALISM

General Characteristics—A capitalist system has the following characteristics: relatively unrestricted rights of private property in both producer and consumer goods, freedom of contract with relatively few exceptions, the right of every individual, except minors subject to compulsory school attendance, conscripted soldiers and incarcerated criminals, to dispose by contract of his labor power, a price system that tends to equilibrate supply and demand, widespread use of money and credit, prevalence of large scale enterprise in at least some important sections of the economy and machinery for the maintenance of public order and the enforcement of contracts to offer a modicum of security for business transactions.

Whoever feels puzzled by the number of qualifications added to each of these criteria ("relatively unrestricted," "relatively few exceptions," etc.) should remember what has been said in the Introduction: First, every economic system, even in its "classical" form, contains all the four "bricks" from which economic systems are built; and since the areas of effectiveness of command, exchange, solidarity and tradition cannot be separated by neatly drawn boundaries, every institution of every system will reflect in its structure and mode of operation the conflicting influences of these principles. Secondly, we are not even describing capitalism as a "classical" system, but capitalism as it exists today, after futher compromises had to be found between mutually antagonistic elements in the classical concept (especially between freedom of contract and free competition) and after "impurities" were introduced into the capitalistic order by socialistic influences. The particular reasons for each qualification will become clearer when the implications of the definition are spelled out—a task which must now be undertaken.

CHAPTER 4

THE PROFIT MOTIVE AND COMPETING INCENTIVES

Importance of the Profit Motive

PRIVATE OWNERSHIP of the larger part of wealth plus freedom of contract with respect to the majority of desired transactions means that the bulk of economic decisions is made within economic units, i.e. economic enterprises and households, and not by a central agency. The economic activities of government are less extensive under capitalism than they would be under most forms of socialism. Only where government leaves the conduct of the larger part of the production and distribution of commodities to private entrepreneurs and where, in general, every individual is permitted to sell to whom he wants and to buy from whom he wants at any price agreeable to buyers and sellers, can a system be reasonably defined as capitalism.

For such a capitalistic system to be established and to operate satisfactorily, the owners of productive wealth must be predominantly motivated, at least in their everyday transactions, by the desire for the greatest surplus of yield over cost, as measured in money terms. This so-called profit motive is a special variety—entrepreneur's incentive—of a more general order, the desire for pecuniary gain, which under capitalism is also a normal guide of an employee in seeking a job or negotiating the terms of employment; all striving for pecuniary gain, in turn, is a subspecies to a still more general motivation, maximization of enjoyments which in a capitalist system requires not only an optimal plan for producing and marketing the goods and services to be sold, but also optimal use of the money income which is received through these sales—consumer rationality along with producer rationality. The large role of the profit motive does not mean that an entrepreneur, to live up to the spirit of capitalism, must be prepared to sell his soul to the devil "if only Mijnheer Satan sends in proper remittances"—as an old Dutch adage said. Every economic system involves some temptation to seek gain (in wealth or prestige or power) by morally objectionable means, and in this respect the worst that can be said about capitalism is that the opportunities it creates for monetary gain offer greater temptations than existed, for instance, under feudalism. On the other hand—as will be explained when we come to the role of tradition—capitalism no less than any other order presupposes that the majority of the citizens, especially those in influential positions, recognize some restraint in the pursuit of personal gain. Moreover, the predominant motive of a leading group is not the only motive of all members of that group at all times; sometimes a capitalist entrepreneur may forego profits in the interests of patriotism, humanitarianism, lust for power or prestige, or friendship or love; in other social groups too the desire for pecuniary gain, even when morally legitimate, is occasionally checked by rival motives. For the functioning of a capitalist system it is only necessary that people are not easily deflected from trying to increase their money income, and especially that entrepreneurs are guided mainly by the profit motive in their everyday decisions on the production and exchange of goods and services.

There are several reasons why the prevalence of the profit motive in economic life is so important a characteristic of the capitalist system. First, the profit motive has enabled capitalism to play its historic role as the great developer of the technique of production and organization, by providing an incentive for effort more powerful than anything known to preceding periods. Whether the prevalence of the profit motive will always secure the best opportunities for technological and organizational progress is a much debated issue, but it is clear that in the late Middle Ages and the Modern Age, at least until recently, no other incentive could have done the work of the profit motive; it has indeed created modern technology. Second, the profit motive makes economic action calculable and thereby creates an indispensable condition for the functioning of a capitalist economy. In an economy directed from above, the coordination of economic activities, beyond the level of an individual plant, is the responsibility of the superior power; therefore, the plant manager need not foresee the actions of other plant managers or of consumers. If Pharaoh or his chief steward ordered the overseer of a kiln to have a certain quantity of bricks manufactured and delivered to a certain place, the overseer had to execute the order regardless of whether he expected the commander of a slave brigade to be present with a sufficient labor force to start the construction. Similarly, a plant manager in a planned economy of the Stalinist type is instructed by the plan to turn out a prescribed quantity of semi-finished goods; it is not his responsibility but that of the planning board to make sure that this is the kind and quantity of material which the processing plant needs, and to see to it that it will actually be taken over by the latter. But when a capitalist entrepreneur decides to produce a commodity and have some quantity of it transported to a place of delivery, he would be foolish to do so unless he expected this other place to be a market on which somebody else—a dealer, a consumer or another producer—is likely to take over the commodity. The functioning of the capitalist system depends on the ability of, say, a steel manufacturer to know what kind and quantity of steel the machine producers will buy; the steel producer must base his guess on the consideration of what machine manufacturers must do in order to maximize their profits, and on the assumption that they will act accordingly. If the supplier miscalculates the interest of his customers, or if the customers, deviating from the norm, do not wish to maximize profits (but for instance prefer to embarrass a hostile government by restricting a profitable production), the web of economic interdependence is broken.

Not only the actions of entrepreneurs but also those of other members of society, especially of employees and of consumers, have to be calculable at least to some extent if the capitalist system is to function well. Although their preferences of a non-pecuniary character, for example, employees' desires for pleasant surroundings during work or consumers' biases in favor of some brand names, can be anticipated by employers or sellers, the labor market would not function if workers were usually unresponsive to changes in wages and there could be no commodity markets if the consumers' purchases could not be influenced by rising or lowering prices. A capitalist order requires that the desire to increase one's money income and the desire to get the greatest possible satisfaction out of one's money income are powerful motives with the majority of people.

This is true for one more reason. The profit motive has helped to shape the cultural and political environment indispensable to the functioning of the capitalist order. The earlier statement that the profit motive has created modern technology does not exhaust the truth; it has been a powerful factor in creating modern civilization, and not only because our civilization would have been impossible without advanced technology. The growth of interest in pecuniary gain under circumstances in which such gain could best be made by individual effort and ingenuity created a widespread belief in the virtue of individual initiative in all human endeavors, and in the freedom which made such initiative possible. Without the will of the individual to greater freedom than he had enjoyed during the Middle Ages, the art, philosophy and theology of the Renaissance period which laid so much of the groundwork for present day culture, would not have come into existence. Nor would the transformation of the feudal state first into the absolute monarchy—which broke the power of the many local rulers and created rational systems of law—and finally into modern democracy been possible if the individual had not learned to use his faculties in the economic field and had not developed a strong desire to be allowed the free use of these gifts.

True as these facts are, we must avoid the temptation to draw unwarranted conclusions. Only in an economy mainly guided by the profit motive could man and society become what they are today, but this does not necessarily mean that democracy, modern law and other institutions we treasure can only be preserved as long as we retain the profit motivation as a principal economic incentive. The requirements of preserving what has once been attained, and even of its further development, may be quite different from those of the original creation. The Middle Ages, for instance, have preserved a considerable part of the heritage of antiquity, although the same ideas and institutions could hardly have developed under feudalism. We shall therefore have to keep our minds open with regard to the possibility that cultural and political achievements of the capitalistic era may survive in a different economic system. Secondly, the truth that capitalism has opened the way to some political and cultural developments must not be interpreted as a one-sided relationship. Without cultural and political preconditions which made possible modern law and modern government administration, capitalism could not have existed any more than modern law and modern government would have been possible without capitalism. Certainly in most, probably in all, periods of history, there has been an intricate interplay between economic and cultural changes. In no single historical case, however, has it been plausibly shown that the first impulse came from the one and not from the other side, and all attempted generalizations, such as the contention that primacy always belongs to the economic factor, remain unconvincing.[1]

[1] A generation ago, Max Weber and R. H. Tawney analyzed the relationship between the emergence of Protestantism, especially in its Calvinistic form, and the spirit of capitalism. Whether or not they were right in all details is controversial, but Protestantism, which emphasizes the direct relationship between the individual and his creator without the need for mediation by Church or saints, certainly has an affinity to an economic system which is based on the right and duty of the individual to strive for economic success without reliance on guilds, manorial communities or protection by feudal lords. This is perhaps a particularly good example to show that one cannot say which came first, the

Agents Not Seeking Their Own Profit

THE PUBLIC SERVANT

Although the dependence of capitalism on particular cultural and political conditions supplies one of the arguments for the historical importance of the profit motive, the same dependence is the most obvious reason why in a capitalist society the desire of pecuniary gain must not be everybody's primary motive in economically important action. The entrepreneur, to be sure, fulfills his function when he strives for the greatest possible income in terms of money, and for employees in private business it is essentially the same, but the situation is quite different for the public servant. He owes his position not to property right but to a mandate from the people. In seeking this mandate, it is proper for him to be guided by the prospects of pecuniary compensation, although actually other interests may be stronger. In any event, once he has accepted the mandate, he is supposed to be guided by the mandate's purpose—which may be anything from the protection of public safety to forest conservation or the maintenance of a postal service—rather than by his own prospects of gain.

The presence of functionaries whose regular actions are not determined by the profit motive is not an anomaly in capitalistic society but a condition of its proper functioning. A number of functions most essential to the operation of capitalist enterprise cannot be properly fulfilled by people whose course of action is motivated by maximum pecuniary gain. If court decisions were to go to the highest bidder for the judge's favor, or if the police were to make leniency or rigorous law enforcement dependent on which pays better, the foundations of capitalism would be undermined. The main actors of the capitalist scene, it is true, are ordinarily supposed to pursue the goal of maximizing their income and to resist this attractive goal only in extraordinary circumstances where otherwise obviously antisocial effects would result. But the capitalist system depends on the availability of a considerable supporting cast of people who may have chosen their careers with an eye to wages and profits—their security as well as their amounts—but who, after having made the choice of their career, will not permit a pecuniary aim to determine their further choices between alternatives of action or inaction. It is no historical coincidence that the rise of capitalist business and of a modern civil service occurred in the same period.

---

economic or the cultural change, since all the evidence points to the conclusion that either of the changes had independent roots: for instance, the economic change in the mentality and the techniques of medieval merchants, and the theological change in the unsatisfactory aspects of medieval scholasticism and in the state of the church. For more on the Webster-Tawney thesis, see pp. 224 ff.

Although the "disinterested" public servant is not an invention of the capitalistic age, he is a more important part of capitalist than of most pre-capitalist societies and was indeed absent in some of the latter. In feudalism public power was normally an appurtenance of private property in land and it was legitimate to use it as a source of private income: The public servant, as the vassal of the king or as the subvassal of a great vassal, was expected to seek compensation from the people whom he had to rule. Much of the "corruption" which existed in the administration of the modern state in the early phases, and which still exists in underdeveloped countries whose political organization only a short time ago resembled feudalism, is probably best understood as a remnant of feudal concepts which were and are slow to die.

THE CORPORATION EXECUTIVE

The entrepreneur-proprietor who runs his own business and strives for maximum profit, and the public servant who must act on the strength and within the limits of his public mandate without regard to personal gain, are two well-defined types within capitalistic society. In twentieth century capitalism, however, a large part of the means of production is managed not by entrepreneur-proprietors but by salaried corporation executives. Their power, like that of individual entrepreneurs, is based on the right of property, although not of their own property: It is power delegated by the shareholders who own the company. But like the public servant, the corporation executive must act within a mandate and is to be guided by the purpose of that mandate—maximization of corporation profits—rather than by his own pecuniary interest.[2] Codes of law have stipulated the obligation of corporation executives and also of the members of the boards of directors, who are charged with supervisory rather than executive duties but whose position involves largely the same problems as that of the ex-

[2] It might be argued that the case of the corporation executive is not essentially different from that of any employee in private business whose work is not narrowly prescribed and who therefore has power of decision. An entrepreneur-proprietor may put the whole conduct of the business into the hands of a trusted employee, whose position will then indeed be similar to that of a corporation executive. Within the realm of non-corporate business, however, such an unlimited power of decision can come to an employee only through accidental circumstances; in a business corporation the executive functions lie by necessity in the hands of people who do not own the business. Moreover, when a private proprietor hands over the management of his business to a salaried employee, there is, as a rule, a relationship of personal trust; the corporation executive is pledged to serve an anonymous organization, and some of the psychological peculiarities of his position result from this fact. The problems of the non-owner charged with entrepreneurial functions can therefore best be studied if the corporation executive is chosen as an object, but it is worth remembering that occasionally the position of higher employees in non-corporate business may show similar traits.

ecutives. The legal rules, however, have not been able to resolve a psychological problem. Unlike the public servant, the corporation officer operates in an atmosphere in which the profit motive is the normal incentive; but if he is to strive for maximum pecuniary gain, why not his own gain? If somebody else's gain, why the gain of the shareholders whose interest the law identifies with that of the corporation but who are usually unknown to the managers? Quite often the managers feel that it would not be good sense to permit their legal commitment to the shareholders' interest to be the exclusive, or even principal, guide of conduct. This does not mean, however, that the managers generally pursue their own gain in conflict with the interest of the corporation, but it often means that they construe the interest of the corporation as different from the interest of the shareholders. The point is well illustrated by the German corporation executive who, when asked why he did not suggest an increased dividend since the company had just had a profitable year, replied: "Why throw good money to strange people?" The expansion of the company, made possible by the retention of profits for self-financing, often becomes a cause which the managers wish to serve, regardless of the preferences of the shareholders, all the more so because such expansion increases the importance and the power of the managerial staff and may increase the security of its position. These goals often appear more desirable to the managers than even an increase in their personal incomes. The attempt to tie the interest of the executives to that of the shareholders through bonuses that fluctuate with the financial success of the company has not completely achieved its purpose. Although the managers' security, prestige and power are enhanced by an increase in company earnings, a security-minded executive may shun risks which in the best interest of the business he should take, and a prestige-minded executive may engage in expansion even where the chances of profit do not justify such a move; preference for spare time to pursue private interests or the desire to be popular with employees or fellow entrepreneurs may also deflect the executive's actions from the course of maximizing the company's net revenue. The corporation president who in his relentless drive for business success develops ulcers, ruins his family life, is known as a ruthless competitor and a hard boss, and finally dies of heart failure is not entirely an invention of fiction writers and sociologists; but it is easy to overestimate the frequency of this type. Although the typical senior executive's life is more fraught with tension and excitement than the medieval guildmaster's, he is not always pursuing the goal of maximum profits with the singlemindedness of a nineteenth century entrepreneur-proprietor, whose very existence could be jeopardized by any deviation from the pursuit of profits. The shareholders, though of course interested in maximum profits, are often unable to enforce the maximization rule against the management for lack of information, or because of their inability to combine for action, or for both these reasons.

Profit Motive and Public Interest

Is the weakening of the profit motive, which resulted from the advance of the corporate form of business, good or bad for society? No clear-cut answer can be given. It cannot be assumed that the man who works twelve or fifteen hours a day will be a better executive than another who takes time off to play golf, have vacations, be sociable with friends and neighbors or read a good book; the case may be even more doubtful if we think of the manager of a firm as a cog in the economic mechanism of society which becomes less effective if frictions are multiplied by the singlemindedness of leading individuals. When the non-economic effects of the business leader's attitude are taken into account, such as mitigation or aggravation of antagonisms among social groups, we may be still less tempted to wish for a restoration of the profit motive in full force. Yet while a frenzied striving for maximum profit is not the most desirable attitude of a business executive in the mid-twentieth century, it is still true that the entrepreneur cannot fulfill his social function unless he is guided largely by the profit motive.

The importance of public relations to business has fostered a tendency among businessmen to represent themselves as engaged in the pursuit of the "public interest" rather than in the pursuit of profits.[3] If they practice this belief to any great extent, the vital distinctions between different functions in society may become seriously blurred. To define the public interest, or the "common good" is not simple in any sense. It requires the weighing of manifold interests against each other—interests of different persons, belonging to different socio-economic groups, age groups, religious groups and others, and the determination of the relative importance of such diverse

[3] Judging from some advertisements and statements of industrial associations, the proverbial man from Mars might assume that entrepreneurs invest not for the purpose of securing additional revenue but to create employment for otherwise jobless citizens, resist wage demands not in order to maintain their rate of profit but to stop inflation, export their products not to sell on a lucrative market but to redress the national balance of payments, and introduce labor saving machinery not to make savings on their payrolls but to win the international race for efficiency for their own nation. This kind of phraseology is fairly innocuous as long as it remains merely a means to create good will and does not influence the attitudes and practices of business itself. But businessmen, like other human beings, are likely to become captives of their own words, and to end up believing that which they have originally said mainly for the benefit of others.

values as material betterment, protection of freedom, satisfactory human relations and so forth. It is not only practically but even conceptually impossible to find an "objective" yardstick for these decisions, and therefore modern man has devised a complex machinery for the play of contradictory interests. This machinery, of which the legislative apparatus with its appurtenances of political parties and political pressure groups forms the core, is operated for the purpose of finding that line of action which is most acceptable, or least unacceptable, to the bulk of the conflicting interests; to use a simile from physics, the purpose is to find the vector of conflicting interests.

To participate in the political conflict from which the line of policy is to evolve in any other capacity than that of a voting citizen, and to read the indicators from which the vector of forces can be recognized, requires special skills; it has consequently become a specialized social function with manifold sub-specializations, including those of the career politician, the political journalist and those government employees who serve as liaison officers between the legislative and administrative branches. The people who are charged with these tasks cannot also be burdened with the responsibilitiies for the technical jobs, from construction of houses and roads to the invention and operation of machines to the administration of hospitals and prisons to the management of business enterprises. Every one of these technical jobs has a defined objective. This is not to say that the specialist must wear blinkers to prevent him from realizing the importance of other tasks: A public health administrator would be foolish not to realize that the reduction of criminality, a joint responsibility of the police, the courts, the juvenile authorities and a number of other agencies, may be as important as the reduction of the incidence of contagious diseases, which is his job. But we would have a poor public health service if its administrators, in framing their policies, were to choose primarily those measures which they think might depress the crime rate, and we would have a very undesirable situation in law enforcement if the police were to think primarily in terms of safeguarding public health. The public health administrator might then refuse to combat the incidence of sickness in families with high criminality in the belief that it is better to have them die out, and the police might arrest any person they vaguely suspect of being a carrier of undesirable hereditary traits on the assumption that he should be prevented from procreation.[4] Nor would the community be well served if all the spe-

[4] Recent history provides an example of such confusion of objectives—with far more serious consequences—in the program of the Nazi government, which was carried out because everybody was supposed to be concerned with the security of the regime and realization of the Nazi ideology and *mystique* of racial purity. Even if these aims had

cialists were to forget their particular tasks over their concern with the national interest, as they understand it—for instance, if they thought more of the impression which their measures would make in the world at large—than of the effect of their actions in their own area of operation. In the fields cited as examples, it is easy to see that the confusion of responsibilities must lead to dilettantism—public functionaries applying criteria from fields in which they are not experts and neglecting those from fields in which their judgment is superior to that of others. Many people, however, fail to realize that the making of profit is just as much the social function of the manager of a productive enterprise as the depression of the crime rate is that of the chief of police or the reduction of the incidence of sickness is the responsibility of the public health administrator. It is a vital interest of society that the difference between cost and return of production be widened; profit is the difference between private costs and private return; to the extent that private costs coincide with social costs and private gain with social gain, the pursuit of private net gain means the same thing as the pursuit of social net gain. It is important to study the instances in which private costs differ from social costs or private gain from social gain; but it is at least of equal importance to understand that more often than not, the two coincide largely or entirely. Because of the frequent coincidence, it makes sense from the point of view of society to have managers of production committed to the pursuit of profit, just as other specialists are committed to the pursuit of other goals.

Division of functions, with its diversity of specific responsibilities, can be found in any kind of modern society, but it is particularly clear and important in capitalism. Because the pursuit of profit by enterpreneurs is within fairly wide limits a way to serve the common good, it is the responsibility of the legislators and other public servants to put up signposts where another course is indicated. It is they who have to define public policy. When a conflict appears between the public interest and the interest of private firms, the former should either be protected by laws which clearly tell the businessman what he must not do in the striving for profits, or profit interest and public interest must be coordinated by such measures as paying bounties for socially desirable conduct and taxing socially undesirable conduct.[5] A businessman who takes it upon himself to act as

---

not required the application of inhumane means, they would have blurred the lines of responsibility, thereby creating a great hazard of arbitrariness in government.

[5] To illustrate: Suppose Congress and the Administration consider it desirable in the public interest that our national oil reserves be husbanded by methods which increase present costs of production more than seems justified, from the point of view of the individual producer, by future advantages. It is then proper to enact a law which makes the

the guardian of the common good in his business policy is bound to substitute his own, subjective interpretation of the public interest for the line which has evolved from the operation of the machinery created for this special purpose, and thus for his part he will invalidate one of the strongest arguments for the capitalist order: that in this system it is easier than under socialism or communism to draw a clear line between political function and the management of enterprises.

To these statements some qualifications must be added. In the first place, some kinds of action which would serve the profit interest of an enterprise may be clearly immoral although not prohibited by law; society functions best if enterpreneurs respect these limits as if they were established by legislation. Secondly, although organizing political forces is a specialized function in our society, these political forces originate in the interests, thoughts and emotions of citizens who are not professional politicians, and entrepreneurs are among these citizens. No hard and fast line can be drawn between the voting citizen, whether an entrepreneur, a worker, a farmer or a housewife, and the political leader or organizer; professionalization of politics is not so complete as to prevent all citizens active in another sphere of life from being elected to Congress or from playing a role in party organization, although fewer and fewer persons find it possible to combine the responsibilities of a political career with anything more than nominal activity in other fields. In many cases, it is true, entrepreneurs have assumed political office after either relinquishing their business interests or taking temporary leave of their enterprises. Their knowledge of business has sometimes helped them, but there is always the danger that former business interests create a bias which makes it impossible for them properly to weigh the interests with which they were identified against those of other groups: This pitfall is well illustrated by the ill-advised statement of a successful business manager turned public servant: "What is good for General Motors is good for the nation." The author of this statement would have done better to say: "What is good for the nation will in the long run also be good for General Motors." By this seemingly slight change in the wording he would not only have evaded political attacks but also made his statement express an essential truth. This is the third reason why it is not easy to draw a hard and fast line between the

---

conservation measures compulsory and their non-application a criminal offense; or it may be decided that the desirable measures may be made profitable by granting subsidies to firms which carry them out; or Congress may put a special tax on all oil produced without conservation measures and thus make it unprofitable to produce oil in this way. Which of the three methods is preferable depends on the circumstances of the case. See footnote on industrial organizations, p. 99.

businessman's function to strive for profit and the consideration of the public interest. Most enterprises can flourish only in a flourishing community. Although a small businessman may still disregard the effects of his own actions on the success of public policy simply because they are negligible, a modern giant corporation is in a different position. When one of the great oil companies exploits Arabian oil resources, when Ford or General Motors make a major contract with an underdeveloped country for the supply of tractors, when the United States Steel Corporation decides to grant or refuse concessions to the steelworkers union, the action influences national welfare as much as many actions of government. Often, especially in cases touching upon foreign policy, the company will act wisely by following the advice of the government even if the preference of its own managers would lie in the opposite direction; but in such matters as price and wage policy, a capitalist enterprise cannot abdicate its responsibilities to the extent of leaving the decision to the government; yet to act rationally, the management of the enterprise cannot ignore the effects of its own decisions on the national economy—effects which in the long run determine the fate of its own company. There is no neat solution for this problem, but in no capitalistic country has it become so acute that it cannot be handled by the tolerable compromises devised by the practical sense of the individuals concerned. If the trend toward concentration in the business world continues, it may well mean the end of the present division of labor between those who mainly pursue profits and those who interpret and safeguard the public interest. This, however, is a bridge which we need not cross yet.

In all capitalist countries there are many exceptions to the rule of private ownership of enterprises. In these instances, obviously, the motive of private profit seeking is not the guide for the conduct of business. An analogous motive, maximization of profit for the government as the owner of the enterprise, is operative in some of these cases, but as the following survey will show, public enterprise is often guided by quite different considerations. The reasons why local, regional or national governments—even those which completely repudiate the philosophy of socialism or communism—have acquired instruments of production, transportation and distribution and are operating them are too numerous for complete enumeration, but some principal categories can be established.

Government Pilot Plants

Whereas in England modern industry was in the main created by private individuals previously active in trade or handicraft, this has been less true on the European continent. Especially in the German states, but to some extent also in France, the spontaneous desire of private entrepreneurs to invest capital in industry originally failed to match the government's desire to have industry develop, and even where the urge on the business side was sufficiently strong, entrepreneurial or private capital resources were often inadequate, or the risks appeared too great for private interests to bear. In the eighteenth century this led to the establishment of government-owned plants, mainly for the purpose of demonstrating to private entrepreneurs the gains that could be won from industrial pursuits, and the best ways to manage industry. Some of these government-owned industries have survived, for example in the continental industries of chinaware. The important role which government pilot plants played in the early industrial development in Europe may well find an analogy in the industrialization of the now underdeveloped countries.

But even in highly developed countries government has had to step in to get some industries started, because the size of required capital outlay, the risks or the prospect of long years of profitless investment before a return could be expected, proved too much of a deterrent for private business. An outstanding example in the United States is the complex of industrial enterprises managed by the Atomic Energy Commission.

Public Ownership for Fiscal Purposes

Governments occasionally find it technically difficult or politically inconvenient to collect enough taxes and therefore seek other ways to secure revenue. One such way is the operation of profitable enterprise. The fiscal purpose will best be served (but other government purposes will conceivably suffer) where the government-owned enterprise possesses a monopoly and the government sets the price as high as the traffic will bear. Monopolies are frequent, especially in the processing and sale of tobacco and alcohol, but the postal service too can be exploited as a financial resource. In some countries government-owned railroads contributed greatly to the public revenue before the widespread use of trucks and automobiles threatened the railroads' profits. In countries where power plants and gas works, or their distribution networks, are government-owned, prices of these necessities have sometimes been kept high enough to make the yield fiscally important.

Public Ownership for Public Service

Governments have often felt that some enterprises cannot be run by private interests in the manner required by the public welfare, and that it is therefore a government duty to operate these enterprises.

In some instances government operation is considered necessary because it is felt that the services involved should be offered free or below cost. Obviously, private enterprise could meet this requirement only if subsidized, and there are many technical and political objections to subsidies paid from the public treasury to private entrepreneurs. But why should the purchaser of goods or services not have to pay for the full cost of production? In some situations gratuitous service is the only way to avoid cumbersome methods of fee collection; this is one of the arguments for toll-free highways. More often, however, the rationale of supplying a service without charge or at relatively low charge and therefore by the government lies in the desire of policy makers to stimulate the particular kind of consumption involved beyond what it would be under "normal" pricing. An outstanding example is education. Our free public school system has been created for two basic reasons: First, in order that a young person's prospects of vocational success should be as independent as possible of his parents' financial situation. Therefore a boy or girl whose family cannot afford to pay enough tuition to cover teachers' salaries and other costs of schooling should still receive at least primary and secondary education. If this were the only consideration, however, many of us might feel that the problem should be solved through scholarships for students from families with inadequate means, while others should be charged the full cost of their education. But even parents whose financial situation would make the payment of full tuition no hardship, or only a bearable one, might refuse to take this burden upon themselves because they do not consider education for their children as important as they should in the opinion of those responsible for public policy. The education of children, however, not only determines their chances of mental and moral development into responsible adulthood, but also the future character of the national community and its standing among other nations. In other words, the social benefits of education, as seen by those who are acting for the community, are often greater than the private benefits which the individuals most directly involved expect to receive.

The possible divergence of social costs and social benefits from private costs and private benefits will be more fully discussed in the section on pricing. Here it will suffice to state that charging for goods or services less than cost is irrational from the point of view of the community and of a private entrepreneur, unless justified by expected social benefits. This may seem a truism, but economic history is full of examples of pressure groups managing to obtain subsidies at the expense of the community where by no stretch of imagination can any social good result in excess of private gain.

Prevention of Competitive Waste or Private Monopoly

Many industries can be rationally operated only if management is highly concentrated. Often an optimal or near-optimal degree of concentration results from competition: Some automobile companies, for instance, may merge, shut down some of their high-cost plants and concentrate operations in the others; their competitors will be forced to initiate a similar process or go out of business. In other fields of production, however, this effect will either not occur at all or will be long delayed. Parallel railroad lines have existed for a long time in the United States; it took decades to bring about a merger of the two nationwide telegraph networks; only nationalization remedied or at least significantly improved the ailing condition of British coal mining which was caused by the uncoordinated efforts of multitudinous producers to exploit the wealth of the subsoil; the similar problem of American oil production was partially alleviated with the aid of state regulations; at least in an area of industrial endeavor which can be roughly described as consisting of public utilities and some types of mining, experience seems to substantiate that competition cannot be relied upon to eliminate the bulk of its own waste, and concentration may have to be produced by a deliberate effort.

This effort can be undertaken by industrial organizations, such as cartels, or government may take over and operate the enterprises. Cartels, however, are outlawed in many countries, at least in principle, and almost no country is prepared to grant private cartels complete freedom of action. Therefore, where cartels attempt to concentrate production in the most efficient plants,[6] they frequently meet with legal obstacles which prevent

[6] Concentration is by no means the purpose of all cartels. On the contrary, many cartels have been formed for the purpose—or have at least the effect—of protecting high-cost producers from extinction by keeping product prices above the cost level of the more efficient firms, which in the event of uninhibited competition would put their less-favored rivals out of business.

To study and classify the politics of industrial organizations in matters of conservation and rationalization—these two purposes are related and often overlap, and concentration of control may be required for either of the two—it is necessary to distinguish between instances in which the association does, and those in which it does not, alter the methods of production. An industrial organization may, by common agreement, introduce measures which would not be profitable for each individual firm unless it were certain that all other firms would adopt the same practices, but which will be profitable for all, or at least for the great majority, provided that condition is fulfilled. The case of the

them from carrying this process to the point of highest productivity. Even where competition itself tends to lead to concentration through one competitor's victory over his rivals, the state sometimes refuses to permit the full exploitation of that victory, lest the result be domination of an industry by a single enterprise, and forces the victorious enterprise to relinquish its acquired holdings.

To escape from the dilemma of permitting either the wastes of competition or the unrestrained use of monopolistic power, the state has often resorted to public regulation, with the dual purpose of assuring efficiency of operation and preventing the misuse of concentrated economic power. But regulation of private industry by the government is often technically difficult; the many litigations resulting from public utility regulations bear witness to this experience.

Public ownership, therefore, is often regarded as the best alternative to either regulated or unregulated monopoly in all industries in which competition fails to work satisfactorily. Preference for government operation of

---

American oil industry may again serve as an example. In this industry, the mutual "raiding" of oil reserves caused great difficulties. When a firm has acquired the right to bring down wells on a certain area of land, this does not mean that it has an underground pool of oil separated from the pools available to other firms; very often several firms are trying to drain the same pool or communicating pools. The location of the wells has therefore often been determined by the interest of the individual firm to get the oil out of the ground before the adjoining concession could pump it out, and there were altogether too many wells for the optimal operation of the industry. The multitude of wells, for instance, reduced the gas pressure which helped to bring up the oil, thereby increasing pumping costs and lowering the percentage of oil in the ground that could be pumped out at all. The industry tried to solve this problem by voluntary agreements, but finally had to call for state regulation—at least large parts of the oil industry raised that demand and were accommodated by most of the oil states.

But many industrial associations exist in fields of industry in which concentration or concerted action is not required to lower production costs or preserve the basis on which the life of the industry rests; and even where prevailing conditions would offer an opportunity for such beneficial action, the association does not always attempt to satisfy the need but simply tries to keep production down by any means that can achieve this purpose, in order to keep prices up. This is the clear case of collusion to limit or eliminate competition—the case which has been the target of many legislative and judicial prohibitions. The task of the analyst and the public policy maker would be simpler if there were never any elements of the first situation in the second and vice versa. Conservation of oil, for instance, means that less oil will reach the market now and that present prices will therefore be higher. To some extent, this undesirable effect will, from the community's point of view, be overcompensated by the benefit to the future consumer; is there any assurance, however, that the oil industry, if organized for the purpose of conservation and rationalization, will not use conservation measures to hold back more oil, and consequently raise prices higher, than those responsible for public policy would wish? Similarly, a cartel or trust in the steel industry may concentrate production in the most efficient plants, lowering costs, but may by monopolistic restrictions keep the price above the lowered cost level, though perhaps below the level prevailing before the concentration. Some of these problems will be discussed below, in the section on monopoly and semi-monopoly.

these industries is logically compatible with the opposite preference in regard to all others, and no serious practical difficulties result from the coexistence of government-owned power dams, telegraph and railroad systems or coal mines with private manufacturing industry. But it would be an error to believe that obstacles to the desirable degree of concentration disappear when an industry comes under government ownership. The administration of the nationalized coal mines in Great Britain has succeeded in shutting down some of the too numerous shafts which private industry had kept in operation, but the unwillingness of the workers to lose their accustomed places of work and to incur the inconveniences and hardships of relocation have prevented such rationalization measures in other instances, and the ultimate dependence of the coal administration on a democratically elected government often made it difficult to resist political pressure by the miners.

The management of publicly owned industries would often have been cumbersome and even unsuccessful if it had been necessary to apply to it the same rules of responsibility which prevail in the civil service, for these rules are too unfavorable to financial risk taking. Public ownership, therefore, gained greatly when it was found that the form of the modern business corporation lends itself as easily to the management of enterprises of which the whole stock belongs to the state as to that of private business.

CHAPTER 5

THE CAPITALISTIC MARKET: BASIC RATIONALITY

The Tendency toward Rationality of Price-Oriented Production

PRICES ARE TERMS OF EXCHANGE; obviously, no exchange is possible without the formation of prices. Without exchange as a regular social institution, i.e. without a market, there could be no social economy in which decisions are made regularly within the individual economy unit. Either all economic units would have to be self-sufficient, each consuming what it produces and producing only what it consumes, with no division of labor among them; consequently there would be no economically integrated society at all, no economic system in the proper sense. Or division of labor and a flow of goods from shops to households would have to take place upon the direction, and therefore at the discretion, of a superior power. Without the market, society would either be an agglomeration of primitive "greater family" households,[1] unrelated to each other, or something like the economy of the Pharaohs,[2] if we disregard the elements of free trading

[1] The reference is to the family household in which several generations are living together, including the spouses of the men (or, in societies in which the man marries into the wife's family, of the women), and are working under the direction of one head, usually the oldest ancestor still alive. Servants, in bondage or free, are also usually found in those households and work within the common scheme. Although most frequent in prehistoric periods and in antiquity, the "greater family" household has survived in Southern Europe until very recently, for instance in the form of the Yugoslav *zadruga,* and may perhaps occasionally be found there even now; it certainly still exists in parts of Asia, Africa and perhaps Latin America.

[2] To choose a modern example instead of the economy of pharaonic despotism, one might refer to the kind of economy which the Russian Bolsheviks tried to establish in the period of War Communism (1918-20); at that time they regarded the collapse of the market—a result of revolution and civil war—not as an evil which made the alloca-

which still existed even in the most despotic periods of ancient Egyptian history. In historic times at least, no society has ever existed without the rudiments of a market: Even among the most self-contained households some exchange has taken place habitually, and economic absolutism has never been carried to the point of excluding all regular exchange. But it is possible to distinguish between societies which show little economic integration, those which are mainly integrated by exchange and those which are mainly integrated by command.

In later chapters it will be explained that even in economic systems in which integration is achieved mainly by command, prices are necessary as guides to rational economic action. In the same function, they are obviously necessary where exchange plays the decisive role as an integrating force, and where therefore most decisions are made within the economic units rather than by a central agency. In such systems, the regularity of exchange leads to the formation of market prices, reflecting not merely the importance which a particular seller and a particular buyer, meeting by accident, attach to the importance of a commodity, but the supply and demand conditions in the whole of society. These prices will be known to the unit managers; they will tell the producers at what sacrifices they can obtain their raw materials and also—before a particular act of production is begun—how much they can expect to receive for the product. Thereby the sellers are enabled to compare input and output—both the input and output of past transactions, from which to draw experience, and the probable input and output of prospective transactions; likewise, the household managers are enabled to compare income and expenditures. Thus prices are the stars from which unit managers can take their bearings. In no historically known economic system has the formation of prices been so

---

tion by command of resources and products necessary as an emergency measure, as did other governments in similar situations, but as an opportunity to substitute the allegedly superior system of moving commodities by directive for the spontaneous movement of commodities under the influence of prices. War Communism was abandoned and replaced by the New Economic Policy, with its restoration of the market, after the famine of 1921-22. For these developments, cf. Landauer, *European Socialism,* I, 763 ff, and the literature cited there. Economic planning as developed in the USSR after 1928 and continued to this day involved a revival of the principles of War Communism, but with strong modifications; this aspect of the matter will be discussed later. War Communism is by no means identical with the "second stage of Communism," or "complete Communism," as distinguished from Socialism in the terminology of Marx and Lenin. As these writers described the two stages of communist development, in complete Communism affluence will prevail and the human character will have reached the level of "socialist ethics," which will have eliminated or restrained greed; for both reasons, society will be able to grant its members perfect freedom to choose, from the common pool of goods, the means to satisfy their needs. Nothing of the kind, of course, was permitted or possible under War Communism, but this decisive difference has apparently not always been present in the minds of the Russian Communists at the time.

regular and widespread as in capitalism, which—in the form of stock and commodity exchanges and similar devices—has even institutionalized the formation of market prices; nowhere, therefore, have prices attained the same importance as guides to economic decisions.

As a general rule, the decisions made by the unit managers under the influence of prices lead to an excess of output over input, of result over sacrifice. Excess of output over input for the individual unit will frequently mean the same for society as a whole; decisions made by the unit managers under the influence of prices will, more often than not, cause more, or more desirable, goods and services to be produced within society than will be consumed in the production process. This may be called the rationality of price-oriented production; it can be described as the tendency of the market to effect the same results which an all-wise and all-powerful manager of the economy, acting in the best interest of the consumers, would achieve by command.[3] The rationality of price-oriented production can exist as a tendency because prices tend to express the economic significance of goods and services—their importance for the satisfaction of consumers' wants. No housewife will knowingly purchase any article which is so highly priced as to deprive her of the means to buy a more desirable article, nor will she leave an article unbought if she knows that the purchase will lead to greater satisfaction for herself and her family than any other use she can make of the same amount of money. Consequently, the prices which producers can get for different commodities depend on the desirability of the latter for consumers. In their own self-interest, producers will not, except by mistake, undertake an act of production which requires an input of goods that could alternatively be used for the creation of products more desired by consumers and therefore able to fetch a higher price; and they will not fail to undertake an act of production if they expect the consumers to be willing to pay a price in excess of the price of the cost goods—

[3] Logical purists may object to the use of the term rationality in this context. To say that a process is rational means primarily that it is suitable to achieve a given purpose; it is doubtful whether the concept of rationality can ever imply a judgment on a purpose. Maximum satisfaction of consumers' wants is not the only conceivable purpose which we may pursue in organizing our economic life; means unsuitable for this purpose may well be suitable for another purpose, and the impediments to maximization of consumers' satisfaction may have their cause not in anyone's failure to realize what such maximization would require, but in the fact that some people pursue different purposes. To avoid involvement in this problem and at the same time the terminological inconvenience of having to dispense with the word "rationality" as applied to the inherent tendency of the price system, let it be understood that the concept as used here, means "rationality in regard to the maximization of consumers' welfare." By the indication of the purpose which the price mechanism tends to serve, it is made clear that the processes which are suitable for this purpose may well be adverse to the achievement of some other goal that members of the society may pursue.

unless there are special reasons, to be discussed below, which make restriction of output preferable from the producers' point of view. When producers are trying to buy raw materials, labor or other cost goods, those who are engaged in the production of articles bringing a higher price will be able to outbid the others; the individual producer therefore will be able to buy cost goods only to the extent that the goods he is planning to produce are more important for the consumers than the goods which any other producer would create from the same resources. Thus, if in each individual economic action output is more important than input, the same, it seems, must be true of the sum total of economic actions. If in an economy guided by prices every consumer and every producer acts rationally, there is a tendency for the whole system to function rationally, i.e. to assure maximum satisfaction of consumers' wants.

The principle that, as far as possible, consumers' preferences should ultimately determine how resources are to be used in the production of goods and services is often called the postulate of consumers' sovereignty. This postulate can only be fulfilled if production is guided by prices, because in no other way can consumers' preferences be effectively transmitted to the production managers. As will be shown later, prices do not always have to be formed by actual competition of buyers and sellers bidding against each other, but may also emerge from the calculations of a central agency, having ascertained basic conditions of supply and demand and working out their consequences on paper. The question of whether prices so calculated can form a basis for consumers' sovereignty should not be prejudged; at this stage it is only important to understand that without prices of some kind consumers' sovereignty could certainly not exist. The principle of consumers' sovereignty has been criticized as meaningless, misleading or inapplicable;[4] from the discussion in this and later chapters it will indeed become clear that this principle is neither unambiguous nor fully realizable. Despite this, if applied with the necessary caution, the concept is sometimes useful to distinguish systems of economic despotism from those in which human liberty is a recognized value.

The rationality of price-oriented production represents merely a tendency which meets with many impeding factors and therefore never asserts itself completely in real life. In anticipating the results of production, the cost of production, or the demand for the product, producers make mistakes, and so do consumers in estimating the usefulness of commodities

[4] See, for example, the debate on "Reappraisal of the Doctrine of Consumers' Sovereignty" at the 1961 convention of the American Economic Association, *American Economic Review*, May 1962, pp. 259 ff.

which they are planning to buy. For these and other more complex reasons, some commodities are produced although they do not serve a sufficiently important purpose, and others are not created although their importance would have justified their production. This is just a preliminary warning not to confuse the tendency toward an optimal pattern of production with the assurance that this pattern will be completely realized, and it may be useful to complement this warning with another against the assumption that the demonstration of limits to the rationality of prices means by itself a condemnation of the market as a guide to economic action. Before the failures of price orientation can be fully explained and weighed against the achievements of the market, a further discussion of its gravitation toward an optimum is necessary; but it is not too early to state the truth that pricing—and the capitalist system in which the guidance of the economy by prices is more prevalent than in other systems—can be properly judged only when the imperfect character of all human institutions and practices is kept in mind.

Basic Rules of Rational Market Behavior

Prices tend to express the significance of commodities for the consumer: This statement is an abbreviated formula for a rather complex truth. When the housewife chooses between buying food or buying pots, this is obviously not a choice between buying only food or only pots; the choice can only exist between buying additional food, or better food, after some has already been obtained, and buying more pots, or more durable ones, when some containers for cooking are already available. Consequently, in the competition of producers for resources, it is never a question of all food processors outbidding all pot manufacturers, or vice-versa; this competition decides merely how much of each type of cost goods is to go into the one or the other production. The consumer tries not to spend any dollar on the purchase of a commodity unit of which he expects less satisfaction—because he is already provided with a number of like units—if he could use it for a unit of another commodity of which he perhaps possesses nothing at all and of which an additional unit would therefore satisfy a more urgent need. Thus the consumer tries to equalize the satisfaction which he expects of the last unit of money in its different uses; in technical language, he tries to equalize the marginal utility of money in all his purchases. So it is the utility of the last unit of a commodity for the consumer—its marginal utility—which must be just covered by the price if the whole production is to be optimally arranged from the consumers' point of view; and this means that the price of any type of resource must just be equaled by the capacity of the last unit of such resource to contribute to consumers' satisfaction—by the marginal productivity of the resource.

The fact that it is marginal utility that determines the price has a number of important consequences; for instance, since marginal utility and not total utility—the utility of the whole available quantity of a commodity—is expressed in the price, no price figure can express the importance to the consumers of all the coal, or all the iron ore, or all the labor in the world; nor is it necessary to have such a figure, since we are never faced with a decision on the amount of sacrifice that would be justified to save all existing iron ore deposits, or our total wealth of coal in the soil, or the totality of any other resource from destruction, or with a choice of either producing a given amount of food or clothing or shelter, for example, or leaving that need entirely unsatisfied. Somewhat less extreme decisions, which still require a judgment on the total utility of the available stock (or procurable quantity) of a commodity, may indeed in rare instances be imposed on individuals or nations, but they are not typical of the kind of decision which the managers of economic units have to make within the framework of the market, and the methods by which such problems can be solved need therefore not be discussed here. The typical decision involves a small addition to—or the prevention of a small reduction of—the stock or flow of a commodity.

Marginal utility is determined by a demand factor and a supply factor—by the urgency of the kind of need which is to be satisfied, for instance whether it is a primary need like hunger, or some want which can be left unsatisfied without bringing much hardship on the individual concerned; and also by the degree to which the need has been satisfied already, which depends on the supply that has already been made available. It is clear that changes in marginal utility, and therefore changes in prices, can be produced by changes in supply as well as by changes in demand—by increased or decreased availability of resources as well as by shifts in consumers' tastes or in their physical needs. The dependence of changes in price on changes in marginal utility makes it easy to study the tendency toward rationality of the price mechanism not only for a given situation but also in changing situations, and this is all the more important because all economic decisions have to be made in response to changes in underlying conditions: If these conditions, availability of resources (including technical knowledge) and consumers' wants, were to remain constant, an optimal situation, once achieved, would automatically continue, and no task would be left for economic management of either households or enterprises. All changes in wants or resource supply produce changes in marginal utility of commodities and therefore in prices. If at the given price more is demanded of a particular commodity because needs or tastes have shifted in that direction, it is in the interest of the consumers that more should be produced, and if such additional production is possible only at higher unit cost, that some restraint be imposed on demand;[5] both these effects are being produced by the rise in price, which puts a premium on additional production, and also tends to limit the quantity demanded. The same effects will be produced when the rise in price occurs as a consequence of an upward change in costs of production. If, on the other hand, prices go down, either because of a lessened need or of a lowering of costs, wise management of resources in the interest of the consumers requires that production be discouraged, or new uses for the commodity be opened up, or both; and, again the price change favors both effects. The market tends to function as the imaginary all-wise manager of the economy would act, regarding himself as the guardian of consumers' interests.

[5] In their restraining effect on consumers' purchases, prices can be compared to point rationing as used by the European nations during World War I and by all belligerents during World War II for daily necessities. The money units in consumers' hands constitute a claim—not in the legal, but in the socio-economic sense—to commodities. But while most ration stamps gave the holder a claim to a definite physical quantity, the quantity to which monetary units represent a claim becomes determined only through the formation of prices. On the other hand, whereas ration stamps can be used only for one or for a very few types of commodity, money entitles the bearer to choose freely among the commodities on the market.

Why do governments feel that in some emergencies they cannot rely on the rationing effect of prices? Probably the most important motives for the introduction of ration stamps results from the inequality of money incomes; the people with higher incomes are to be prevented from purchasing more commodities than those with low income; therefore at each purchase, in addition to the unequally distributed money they have to surrender ration stamps which have been equally distributed among the poor and the rich. Such rationing is a prerequisite of price control; for if the "excess" demand of the high-income groups were permitted to satisfy itself, any price ceiling would make total demand greater than supply, and the consequence would be the formation of lines of people in front of stores, with ruinous effects on morale, health and productivity.

It has been argued, however, that there is no clear line separating emergencies from normal economic situations. Therefore such purposes of economic policy which are important in peace time can hardly be wholly unimportant in war, and vice versa. This is true enough, but when an emergency arises or when normal conditions are restored, different purposes assume a different degree of importance. In war as in peace, it is important to use the self-interest of producers to obtain maximum output, but greater powers of compulsion and moral pressure, such as can be exercised during a national emergency, open alternative ways to this goal. In peace as in war, most of us are interested in preventing extreme inequalities in the standard of living, but in war it becomes more immediately important than in peace to distribute the sources of physical strength equally (or in relation to exertion and usefulness for the war effort) and to forestall that feeling of discontent which extreme inequality would be sure to create. In war, it is the short-run effect that matters; the experience that ration systems and price ceilings eventually are undermined by corruption or circumvented by the production of commodities for which price control is too difficult to administer does not in itself represent a conclusive argument against the introduction of these measures. In peace, however, no government can afford to disregard the long-term effects.

For an understanding of the element of rationality in price-oriented production, one of the most useful concepts in the technical vocabulary of economists is that of opportunity cost. As shown before, the resources needed for a particular act of production can be bought only if the expected price of the product is greater than the price which consumers would pay for another product that could be created from the same resources; otherwise the producers who would create this second product would be able to outbid those of the former in the competition for resources. The importance of the alternative use of coal, or steel, or aluminum, or machinists' labor determines the price of the input in, say, the production of Ford cars on a particular day in a particular factory; that alternative use may be the production of Ford cars in the near future or in another factory, or the production of automobiles of other makes, or the production of any of a large number of commodities for which coal, steel, aluminum and machinists' labor are required. The price which the individual producer must pay for cost goods is ultimately determined by the sacrifice of other opportunities of want satisfaction within society: In this sense, all cost is opportunity cost. Since the price which the producer can pay for resources is determined by the price which the consumer will be willing to pay for the product, consumers are indirectly bidding against each other for the use of the resources: It is through this consumers' competition that the prices of cost goods reflect opportunity cost.

Clarification of the Marginal Utility Concept

The term marginal utility is less frequently used in economic textbooks today than it was by economists a generation ago. The reason why many present-day economists avoid the term is their belief that the concept of utility, and consequently that of marginal utility, cannot be easily freed of the connotation of measurability. Majority opinion among economists today holds that the satisfaction which consumers gain from the consumption of goods and services is not measurable, like weight or length, but merely scaleable, like different degrees of hardness. A consumer can judge that he prefers one commodity to another, and of course every consumer is doing just that all the time; but it is assumed that he cannot, except in self-deception, say by how much, or how many times, he prefers product A to product B. Very ingenious methods have been devised to show that the appraisal of a defined quantity of a commodity A as the equivalent of a definite sum of money, and the appraisal of a defined quantity of a commodity B as the equivalent of twice that sum of money, are possible without the assumption that the satisfactions expected of those quantities of A and B are in proportions that can be expressed in cardinal numbers, i.e. that the difference and the satisfactions themselves can be measured.

The writer is skeptical about the success of these efforts. It seems to him that they do not fully dispose of the apparent contradiction between the assumption of immeasurability and the fact that satisfactions can be increased by measurable additions to an available stock of a commodity or of money, just as the weight of a pile can be increased by adding particles of mass. He finds it difficult to conceive of the possibility that a process of augmenting an existing stock by successive measurable doses should produce results that are merely scaleable; he therefore suspects that in the concepts used by many present-day economists the assumption of measurability of utility is merely hidden but not really eliminated. But the assumption of measurability of utility, based as it has to be on the assumption of the measurability of satisfactions, also meets with difficulties, as long as the psychologists have found no method by which satisfactions can actually be measured, nor assure us that such methods can ever be found.

In these circumstances, the question of whether utility is measurable must be left open here. The reader is asked to think of utility as something merely scaleable, simply because this is the minimum assumption in regard to the problem—everything that is measurable is also scaleable, but not vice versa—and for the purpose of this investigation it is sufficient.

The marginal utility concept, however, must be applied not only to considerations by individuals but also to those by policy makers. As has been explained in the section on Values and Goals, choices between policy alternatives often require an evaluation of the relative importance of the satisfaction of different individuals. The problem of whether, and how, a comparision of the needs of different individuals is possible has often been discussed in the same context as the measurability of utility. It has been argued that even if we could say that product X is twice as useful as product Y for person A, whereas for a person B, X is six times as useful as Y, we could still not compare the satisfactions obtained by A and B from either X or Y. On the other hand, Jan Tinbergen has asserted "that, if utility could be measured, interpersonal comparisons would also be possible." [6]

[6] Jan Tinbergen, "The Theory of the Optimum Regime," Selected Papers, L. H. Klaassen, L. M. Koyck and H. J. Witteveen, ed., Amsterdam: North Holland Publ. Co., 1959, p. 270. The approach to the problem of measurability in the text generally follows Tinbergen. The present writer, however, is not convinced that measurability of individual satisfactions involves interpersonal comparability without an ethical judgment supplying the common denominator; could it not be that the satisfactions of each individual are something *sui generis,* not equal in kind with those of other individuals and therefore with them not quantitatively comparable? This question, interesting as it certainly

However this may be, nothing can free the policy maker from having to form an ethical judgment as a basis for the allotment of claims upon the available flow of commodities and services to different individuals. Even if we could somehow justify the statement that A draws twice the satisfaction from the same amount of commodities as B, it would obviously not follow that A should be allowed a correspondingly higher income than B; although maximization of welfare in the community may well be our goal, it must not be so defined as to force us to draw that conclusion. On the other hand, even if we think of magnitudes of utility as amenable merely to ordering and not to measuring, it still makes sense to say that, as a matter of ethical judgment, the total satisfaction of A should be considered equally important, or twice as important, or only half as important as that of B. With the help of ethical judgments, therefore, individual satisfactions can be put in relation to one another and a concept of social utility, and of social marginal utility, can be formed.[7]

Since measurability of satisfactions is not assumed, it may be asked why the concept of marginal utility has been used at all, although it takes a special mental effort to think of it as a merely scaleable magnitude. The alternative would have been to discuss the problems in terms of the indifference curve approach which contemporary economists have developed for just this purpose, and to replace the concept of marginal utility by that of the "marginal rate of substitution." Suppose an individual is trying to distribute his expenditures rationally between two commodities X and Y, then the "marginal rate of substitution of X for Y is the quantity of Y that would just compensate the consumer for the loss of the marginal unit of X."[8] In terms of this approach, it is possible to analyze the role of consumers' preferences, and of producers' decisions derived from them, in the formation of prices and thus explain the tendency toward rationality of price-oriented production. Such an explanation, however, requires a mathematical apparatus which some readers might find rather formidable. As compared with the necessity of handling the technique of indifference curves, at least the student without much of a mathematical background will find it easier to keep in mind that the concept of marginal utility should, for the purpose

---

is from other points of view, need not be answered here, for the reason indicated in the text: A psychological yardstick for interpersonal comparisons, not based on an ethical judgment, would in no event supply a foundation for policy decisions.

[7] Social utility, as viewed by the policy makers, is of course not necessarily determined by the evaluation of citizens' satisfactions alone, but also may reflect different preferences of the policy makers—their own "spectators' interests."

[8] Bernard Haley, "Value and Distribution," in Howard Ellis (ed.) *A Survey of Contemporary Economics,* Philadelphia and Toronto: Blakiston, 1949, p. 3. Haley's article has a very lucid explanation of the indifference curve approach.

of this discussion, be kept free from the connotation of being necessarily amenable to measurement.

The Meaning of Competition

Competition on the side of consumption is essential to the very existence of a market, in fact to the existence of an economy. Even if there is only one buyer, the situation economists call monopsony, he must have competing wants, otherwise he would have no reason to determine the worthiness of one use of scarce resources as compared with another, which is the essence of economizing. Since consumption is the purpose of economic activity and production the means by which this purpose is achieved, there is not the same conceptual necessity for producers' competition as for that of consumers. An economic system and even a market could exist with only one seller, and with no possibility of substituting one type of resource for another, and consequently no competition among different resources for use in production. Actually, however, instances in which one type of consumers' need can be satisfied only through the use of one particular resource are very rare: Not only can we satisfy our hunger with different kinds of food, use woolens, cotton goods or synthetic silk for clothing, ride on streetcars or in automobiles, but the machines which produce all these goods may be driven either by steam or by electric motors, and if by motors, the electricity may be produced by coal, oil, water power or nuclear fuels; in the manufacturing of either streetcars or automobiles, more steel or more aluminum may be used—the examples could be multiplied a thousandfold. Furthermore, in the market of each of the finished products as well as of the primary commodities necessary for their production, the presence of only one seller is a rare exception; the rule is competition among several sellers. Therefore, although competition on the side of supply is not as indispensable for the existence of an economy as competition on the side of demand, the former is almost as ubiquitous as the latter; the degree of competition, however, differs greatly from industry to industry and from country to country. Sellers' competition is an important factor in contributing to the rationality of price-oriented production. The keener the competition, the harder will every seller attempt to supply as large a quantity as possible at any price above cost plus minimum profit, and in order to do so will try to reduce costs. In this way consumers will receive a maximum of commodities and society will make optimal use of its resource endowment.

In preparation for later analyses in which the limits of competition in contemporary capitalism and its importance in other economic systems will be discussed, it is important to notice that the term competition has been used here in a broad sense, covering not only competition among actual buyers and sellers, but also competition among different wants, even when felt by the same consumer, and competition among different kinds of resource, even when supplied by the same producer. The concept of competition thus includes the case of the housewife who is trying to divide up her husband's income among the competing needs of her family, and that of the chief executive of a giant concern, operating both coal mines and oil wells, who is trying to decide which of the two "competing" fuels he had better use for a particular production job. This broad terminology is expedient, as will become especially clear when we discuss socialism; still, there is a considerable difference between the instances in which alternatives offer themselves merely to the calculating mind in want satisfaction or in the choice of productive resources without any transaction among persons, and other instances in which each rival want or each rival resource is represented by an actual consumer or an actual supplier, who are trying to outbid each other. For lack of better names, the competition of the first type will be called paper competition, and that of the second type personal competition, whenever it is important to distinguish between the two.

CHAPTER 6

THE LIMITS OF RATIONALITY IN PRICE-ORIENTED PRODUCTION

Some General Thoughts

WHEREAS in the ideal market resources and the products created by the use of resources would flow into the same channels into which the all-wise manager of our previous reference would direct them, the situation which the actual market produces falls far short of this ideal—so far short as to have caused serious doubts in many minds about the desirability of an economic system based mainly on the market. It is now necessary to discuss the obstacles which counteract the tendency of the market toward rationality. In the past, economies in which production was determined by decisions within economic units under the influence of prices have found it easier than more centralized economies to direct resources to those uses in which the greatest excess of output over input could be achieved; the institution of a market with personal competition, though it has not always assured the consumer the position of a king, has usually protected him from being treated as a serf. Although this past experience by no means proves that an economy based mainly on exchange will always provide the best protection of consumers' interests, the reasons why such a lesson of history should no longer apply, or should apply only to some areas of economic life and not to others, must be found in specific conditions if the rejection of the lesson is to be justified.

The capitalistic market fails to assure the most perfect satisfaction of consumers' needs partly for reasons that can be found in the functioning of its mechanism and in part because its processes start from presuppositions incompatible with maximum satisfaction of consumers' welfare.

These two causes of partial failure have to be examined separately. Only when all the forces of supply and demand have had time to find a mutual balance is it true that the price just equals the satisfaction which the "last" buyer can draw from a unit of the commodity. Consequently, only in a state of equilibrium is there any likelihood that production will assume that pattern and volume which are optimal for the satisfaction of demand. Since the intermediate stages between two equilibria do not conform to this condition, the degree of rationality of continuous market processes depends on the speed with which the new equilibrium is attained every time in response to a change in conditions determining supply and demand. Since these conditions, however, are changing incessantly under the influence of technological progress, exhaustion of resources and fluctuations in physical and psychic needs, even the speediest adjustment of prices and output cannot catch up with the disequilibrating forces and achieve the new equilibrium before it is again upset by these forces. Consequently, the equilibrium level of prices and output can only be approximated, not reached, and the degree of rationality achieved also depends on the closeness of the approximation.

In some commodity markets the price usually approaches the equilibrium level fast enough and closely enough, and the response of the market parties is prompt and accurate enough to make the pricing process the best device to keep production close to optimum rationality. This is true where the market parties are well informed, possess high business competence where competition is keen, and where changes in underlying conditions are ordinarily not abrupt. Speculation, the attempt of buyers and sellers to anticipate these changes, contributes sometimes, but not always, to the elimination of unnecessary price fluctuations: When a dealer, in a period of ample supply and weak demand anticipates increasing difficulties of production or an increasing demand and accordingly orders more of the commodity at present low prices than he needs to fill his customers' current orders, he contributes to the smoothing of the transition from today's to tomorrow's price level, provided he is right in his estimate of the market tendency; but he may well be wrong, for as an individual businessman he has only limited knowledge of the intentions of other businessmen—competitors and customers—and of the consumers. If he is wrong, his accumulated inventories will aggravate the disparity between demand and supply of the commodity in the coming period. It is also true that speculation offers some opportunities for exploitative practices, but this point has been overstressed in the popular indictment of the speculator. A good case for speculation as a socially useful activity could be made if there were a greater possibility of the speculator's being correct in his estimate or if it were more probable that the mistakes of different speculators would offset each other; but any observer of the commodity or stock exchanges must be aware of the waves of optimism and pessimism which distort the judgment of buyers and sellers, and, of course, always operate in the same direction.

While the effort to anticipate market conditions sometimes lengthens the trial-and-error processes through which the market adjusts to changes in underlying conditions, there are other instances in which the unwarranted assumption that present conditions will prevail in the future contributes to the amplitude and duration of price fluctuations. A case in point is that of the "cobweb theorem," which derives from experience in the hog market. The profitability of hog raising depends on the margin between the prices of mature hogs and feed prices. Suppose a good harvest has depressed the corn price, while the hog supply, and consequently the price of hogs, is still the same as in the preceding period. This situation will induce many hog raisers to increase their output by retaining a larger portion of their litters of pigs. Consequently corn will rise in price, and by the time the pigs that were added to the herds have matured into hogs ready for the market, there will be an oversupply of hogs and therefore a drop in price. The reduced margin then will discourage raisers from maintaining a large volume of operations, and this will tend to reduce the feed prices through declining consumption and to raise the hog prices through a reduction in the supply, and will therefore set the scene for a new increase in production and a repetition of the cycle. Consequently, in some periods there are more hogs on the market than is justified by the importance of pork for the consumers in view of the costs of hog raising, and in other periods the opposite situation prevails; at one time too many resources of the economy are being devoted to this particular branch of production, at other times too few. In the areas of economic activity in which the cobweb phenomenon occurs, it reduces the chances that the equilibrium price, which alone can be presumed to represent the social optimum, will be quickly and closely approached.

Hog production has some special, though by no means unique, features, which are relevant to the example. The demand for corn (or barley in some countries) depends to a particularly great extent on the volume of hog raising—to a greater extent, for instance, than the demand for steel depends on the volume of truck manufacturing or the demand for copper depends on the production of television sets. Whereas an increase in the output of television sets will tend to depress their price but will not appreciably raise the cost of the raw material, an increase in the output of hogs will attack the producer's margin from two sides. Another important factor is the rigidly determined amount of time which must elapse between the start of an increased production program and the time of sale: Hogs require a growing period of many months, which cannot be appreciably shortened to take advantage of favorable market conditions, whereas in a number of other branches of production a speedup or slowdown is possible. But the number of industries in which cobweb conditions prevail is large enough to make this deviation from the optimum practically significant.[1]

The failure of prices to reach the equilibrium level promptly and the frequency of price fluctuations under the influence of temporary changes in supply and demand conditions—or of changes merely in people's estimates of supply and demand—affects the economic fate of different individuals in very different degree; the effect on production also varies greatly from one industry to the other. Generally speaking, price fluctuations are more violent and harmful to a greater number of individuals in primary production than in manufacturing industry. Governments have therefore often attempted to "stabilize" the prices of agricultural products and, not quite so frequently, of mining. Several kinds of tools can be used for this purpose. In a country which imports a large portion of some raw material which it needs, the government can combat price fluctuations by facilitating an increase in imports when the price is high, and making imports more difficult and costly when the price is low: And this can be done either by a sliding scale of the customs tariff, or by manipulation of tariff rates or import quotas at the discretion of the government. Where a given commodity can be produced in excess of domestic needs, a stabilizing effect can sometimes be secured by regulation of exports; or the government may limit production, with or without paying compensation to those producers who cannot completely utilize their resources; or the government may buy up part of the output in years in which foreign and domestic markets together could absorb the whole only at low prices, and sell the acquired quantities in years in which the market is more receptive. The latter plan, plus some limitation of production, underlies the American policy of agricultural price supports; the price which the government is trying to maintain is not defined in absolute terms but by a price ratio between the agricultural product and some industrial products—the so-called parity formula.

[1] For a more detailed discussion of the cobweb theorem, see Archibald M. McIsaac and James G. Smith, *Introduction to Economic Analysis*. Boston: Little, Brown & Co., 1937, pp. 378 ff.

It is at least conceivable that a government agency on the basis of comprehensive statistical information can with some degree of certainty determine the price which would be likely to establish itself through competition in the long run, to be modified only gradually under the influence of structural changes in supply and demand. If the government considers this price the target of its action, it may achieve a beneficial purpose by cutting out price fluctuations. So far, however, the equilibrium price has rarely if ever been the true objective of so-called price stabilization; rather, the political pressure of organized producers has induced the government to manipulate price controls in such a manner as to keep the price above the competitive equilibrium level. The policy pursued can perhaps still be justified as an act of distribution policy: The competitive equilibrium price may under some conditions result in an unfair distribution of the national income, especially when a group has to buy its own articles of consumption or instruments of production at prices enhanced by limitation of competition.[2] In any event, however, a price above the competitive equilibrium means that the consumers cannot buy as much of the product as to make their marginal satisfaction equal to marginal money cost. Even if it is for a good reason that we have deviated from the "optimal" pattern of production and consumption as described before, nevertheless the deviation is no less real: Whatever is gained for distributive justice is at the expense of the volume of consumption, as measured by its satisfying power.

THE COST OF COMPETITION

The argument that the capitalistic market economy reaches the equilibrium level only by delays and harmful price fluctuations is one of several arguments directed against the mode of operation of the capitalistic market mechanism. Even deeper goes the accusation that this mechanism, because of its dependence on personal competition, achieves the optimum only through a process that leaves the road of economic progress strewn with ruins—bankrupt enterprises no longer capable of using their physical plants, workers put out of jobs, human happiness sacrificed on all sides.

The cost of competition has indeed at times been staggering. Every

[2] Although hardly any economist will defend the present system of agricultural price supports in the United States, a system that burdens the government with ever-growing stocks of produce in excess of any useful purpose, the original motive, as distinguished from the level and the technique of support, makes good sense. In earlier periods, American farmers suffered great harm because industrial prices were kept above the equilibrium level by private monopolies which the government never succeeded in controlling to the full extent, whereas agricultural products were sold under conditions approaching perfect competition. This imparity was remedied by the price supports for the agricultural products for which these supports were granted.

student of economic history knows of the painful process by which the small operators in agriculture, handicrafts and retail trade were displaced in various parts of the world through the superior competitive strength of large-scale enterprise, and this process is by no means completed. Even in competition among big business concerns, the human and material losses are often terrifying. Not only the shareholders and managers of the defeated firm have to suffer, but also their employees, creditors and suppliers. Necessary as it is to replace inefficient by efficient methods of operation, could the triumph of efficiency not be secured in a less painful manner? This question has been asked over and over again in the past two centuries.

Concern over the ruthless operation of the competitive process has been increased by the experience that competition, though striking down the inefficient producer more often than the efficient one, offers no guarantee that socially useful behavior will always be rewarded and socially noxious behavior always punished. In some periods of the eighteenth and nineteenth centuries, it is true, people were generally inclined to regard economic success as a reward of ability or even of virtue and economic failure as punishment of those who lacked the qualities needed by society. There was some justification for this attitude in the past, and some justification exists today. Industry, skill, frugality and a reputation for honesty continue to be important assets in all areas of economic activity. But the number of instances in which victory in the competitive struggle is obtained by morally questionable means, or in which people are struck by economic calamity through circumstances beyond their control, are too numerous for us to equate economic success with merit and economic defeat with undesirable qualities. In stable societies of small farmers and craftsmen, personal qualities may in the majority of cases be the main determinants of economic survival, although such factors as crop failure or illness have always been hard to compensate for by competence and industry; even before the machine age, stability was always threatened by a number of forces, such as changes in trade routes, which made the grass grow in the streets of cities prospering a few decades earlier. With the prevalence of large corporate enterprise, however, those whose capabilities can insure the success of a firm represent, as a rule, only a minute fraction of those who suffer if the firm succumbs. The worker on the bench, the stenographer in the office, the salesman, the owner of the small shop to which the big firm had been farming out the manufacturing of special parts, can certainly in no way be blamed for a failure of the corporation on which their existence depends, even if the management of the corporation was at fault. Yet they are all most severely hit. Those among them who possess superior qualifications may have a better chance to be hired by another employer, but even this chance depends on a number of circumstances over which the individual has little or no control: The condition of the industry at large, the degree of difficulty in changing one's residence, the suitability of the worker's own special skills for another and differently organized plant. Moreover, even if employment can be found elsewhere, as a rule the uprooting of a family seriously interferes with the life of its members.

Recognition of these facts has prompted a conglomerate of legislative acts in all capitalistic countries. Reform of the bankruptcy laws has largely lifted the ignominy from the businessman who cannot meet his obligations, and has somewhat improved the chances of avoiding the extreme losses usually resulting from forced liquidation of assets; unemployment insurance has given some protection to the employees of an enterprise that is unable to meet competition; fair trade legislation has reduced the frequency of instances in which victory in competition is won by dishonest means, and has sometimes blunted the edge of competition by "price maintenance" rules—a method of questionable desirability because in some fields of business it may go far beyond a mere alleviation of the economic struggle for survival and permanently protect backward forms of production and distribution. These measures have made the operation of the market less inhumane, but their effect has inevitably been severely limited: If the competitive struggle is to serve as a vehicle of economic progress, the defeated party must be economically displaced, and therefore suffer. Nor can the correlation between desirable social qualities and economic success be radically changed: It is in the nature of the competitive market that the effect of economic action and not its cause determines success or failure. The incompetent man who makes the right guess about market development from sheer good luck will win, and his capable competitor who calculates intelligently may still lose out because of an unforeseeable event; the lazy manager can be saved from disgrace by an energetic and capable subordinate who never receives the credit he deserves. These failings do not vitiate the tendency toward rationality in the price mechanism which operates through competition, because it is still true that good economic performance enhances the probability of economic success, and such a probability suffices to create a tendency toward the survival of the economically most competent of the competitors. But human and moral concern over undeserved calamity cannot be silenced by statistics showing that the incidence of such calamity is not as frequent as either deserved failure or deserved success. The protest against the way competition operates will therefore persist, and it will never obtain complete satisfaction of its grievances. Because the reasons why people succeed or fail can often not be traced to their personal qualities and efforts, society in any economic system will always have to place a premium on success per se and a penalty on failure per se—which is precisely what competition is doing. It will later be seen that competition, even personal competition, is by no means absent from systems other than capitalism. The forms of competition may change and the process of alleviating hardship will very likely continue, but the dream of a society in which nobody looks upon his fellow man as a rival will remain unfulfilled, at least until we have reached a state of true abundance and economizing has ceased.

Competition among the sellers of labor offers special problems and will therefore be discussed separately below.

MONOPOLY AND IMPERFECT COMPETITION

The Determinants of Monopoly Gain

Among the earliest discoveries of writers on economic problems was the realization that, within limits, a seller can gain more by selling a smaller quantity at a higher price rather than a larger quantity at a lower price, and that his exploitation of this possibility is limited to the extent that he must compete with other sellers. While unbridled competition tends to bring down the price to the level of marginal cost, including such profit as to make the seller's exertions worth his while, the absence of competition, monopoly, makes it possible for the seller to increase his total revenue by raising the price above this level.

How much the price which is optimal, from the monopolist's point of view, lies above the competitive price depends on a number of circumstances. In the first place, competition will almost never be absent over the whole range of conceivable prices, and it will be to the interest of the monopolist not to raise the price so high as to attract competitors. He may dominate a local market; but if the price becomes high enough to induce the buyers to make their purchases elsewhere the monopolist loses his market. Or the monopolist may be the only one who sells a particular brand of superior quality (or one which the consumers, influenced perhaps by successful advertising, consider of superior quality); yet if the preferred brand becomes too expensive, substitutes will be bought instead. Even if there is only one seller in the whole industry—as the Aluminum Company of America was the only seller of aluminum during some period preceding the Second World War—the product of that industry will be at least in potential competition with those of others: As long as the price of aluminum was relatively high, steel was used for purposes which might have been better served by aluminum. Ultimately, all consumer goods (and indirectly all producer goods as well) compete for the consumers' dollar: If television sets become more expensive and vacation trips cheaper, many people will refrain from buying television and spend their money on going places.

Even within the limits which potential competition sets to the monopoly power, the exercise of monopoly is restrained by the consideration that only up to a point will the greater revenue per unit compensate the monopolist for the reduction in the number of units sold. Obviously, total revenue will be small if the price is kept so high as to result in the sale of only a negligible quantity; similarly, total revenue will be small if a very large quantity is sold at a price close to zero. Somewhere in between these two extremes lies the price which serves best the interest of the seller who, because of his monopoly position, can freely determine the price. How much the seller loses in quantity sold if he raises the price by a given percentage depends on the degree of elasticity of demand.[3] The demand for bread, for instance, is relatively inelastic in the United States: Given the fact that bread is among the least expensive foodstuffs, also given the public's ideas about a desirable diet, most of us would not consume substantially more bread if the price were drastically lowered, nor substantially less if the price were raised by a considerable amount. Obviously, this is not true of television sets, imported wines or maid's services: Their demand is relatively elastic. As a consequence, a bread monopolist would be tempted to set the price of bread very high, as compared with the amount we have been accustomed to paying per pound, whereas an importer of French wines would have to be more restrained in his price policy to avoid exceeding the optimal point. The determination of the monopoly optimum under a variety of conditions has been a favorite topic of discussion by economic theoreticians, and whoever is interested in the details can easily find information in the ample literature on the subject.

Equally important is the cost structure or—what comes down to the same thing in this context—the elasticity of supply. The monopolist, like every entrepreneur, is interested in maximizing not revenue per se, but the

[3] An economic theoretician may notice that the concept of "elasticity of demand" is used here somewhat loosely and that it would be more appropriate to give the following explanation in terms of a different though related concept, the gradient of the demand curve. The concept of elasticity, however, is easier to understand for the reader who is not accustomed to the use of geometric symbols, especially because the comparison of the gradients of different demand curves involves some problems which in most textbooks on economics are merely mentioned but not sufficiently discussed. The difference between the degree of elasticity and the slope of the demand curve is lucidly defined in Joe S. Bain, *Pricing, Distribution and Employment,* New York: Henry Holt, 1953, p. 45.

difference between total revenue and total cost. The more he raises the price, the less he will sell, and the reduction in sales will reduce his revenue but also his total cost. If he operates under increasing unit cost—which will be true if an increase in production forces him to tap more costly sources of raw material or labor, and if further gains by better utilization of fixed installations and increased specialization of men and machines are not very important—the advantage of cost saving will be considerable; they will be greater if unit costs rise steeply than if they rise slowly. If, on the other hand, unit cost declines with output, which is likely to be true when overhead is important, with capacity not fully utilized or easy to increase, and supplies easily obtainable, in such a situation the entrepreneur has a great interest in keeping sales volume large, and the strength of this interest depends on how quickly unit cost increases as output dwindles. Thus increasing costs tend to push the monopolist's optimal price higher, thereby encouraging a monopolistic price policy which is hard on the consumer; declining costs tend to restrain the monopolist from very drastic price increases above the competitive level. Rapidly decreasing costs may offset the effect of relatively inelastic demand and vice versa.

The monopolist's decision may further be influenced by a conflict between short-range and long-range considerations.[4] When a railroad line is built in a country of still sparse settlement, the railroad company, even if free from public control and safe from competition by other means of transportation, may not set its freight rates as high as to obtain the greatest total net revenue now, because it may wish to attract more settlers into its territory.[5] By the same token, a monopolistic steel manufacturing company may prefer to facilitate the expansion of the steel processing industries rather than maximize present profits, and may therefore set the price below the monopoly optimum. Regard for public opinion may operate in the same direction. After the Second World War, manufacturers of automobiles were faced with an enormous accumulated demand for new cars, and for several years were unable to satisfy that demand. They could have set the price high enough to bring the quantity demanded down to the quantity

[4] For a more detailed discussion of this point, with partly divergent views, see A. D. Kaplan, *Big Enterprise in a Competitive System,* Washington, D. C.: Brookings Institution, 1954, Ch. 9.

[5] The history of American railroads seems to indicate that in many instances long-range considerations were forgotten in the desire to reap maximum short-term profits. (This attitude was in line with the desire of many pioneers and early settlers to exploit resources quickly and to the utmost, with little interest in conservation.) Because other circumstances favored settlement, the increase in population in the western part of the United States was nevertheless rapid by any standard that could be drawn from the history of colonization; but the development of economic activities—industrial activities even more than agricultural—was probably delayed by high freight rates.

they could supply. But each automobile company, and perhaps also the industry as a whole, was afraid to lose good will among the customers, which would be vitally important in the long run; therefore American automobile manufacturers preferred to ration their products by the unprofitable device of waiting lists rather than by the profitable device of the price, at a time when many sellers who were further from a monopolistic position than the automobile manufacturers insisted on fully exploiting the short-term possibilities of gain. The automobile industry is semi-monopolistic because it consists of relatively few large enterprises. Each individual enterprise because of its large size is known all over the nation, thereby making its sales' prospects particularly susceptible to favorable or unfavorable biases aroused in the minds of the consumers. Although the automobile industry is a good example of the importance of good will and its influence on price policy, the case is by no means unique.

The Basic Forms of Monopoly

Monopoly can exist in two basic forms: When a product is sold by a single seller, and when several sellers act in concert to eliminate competition among themselves, thus forming a cartel. A cartel agreement always involves at least one of three stipulations: Not to sell more than a stipulated quantity, not to sell below a given price, or not to invade the sales territory of another firm. The essential effects of every one of these provisions are the same. If the quantity to be sold is limited, the price will go up; if a minimum price is fixed, no more than a limited quantity can be sold, and if every seller is guaranteed his own territory, he is free to set the price as close to the monopoly optimum as he wants, with the effect that a smaller quantity will be sold than would be under competition.

One-firm monopolies are relatively rare. Cartels have never been legal in Anglo-Saxon countries, except to the extent that they were explicitly legalized, as was the case with the Code Authorities of the National Industrial Recovery Act; more recently, even the Continental European countries have tried to restrict, if not to prevent, cartelization of industries. Thus full monopoly is not an important phenomenon in modern capitalism; very important however, are the intermediate stages betwen full monopoly and unrestrained or "perfect" competition.[6] These semi-monopolistic

[6] These two terms are not quite synonymous. By perfect competition, economists mean a situation in which there is such a multitude of independently acting market parties as to make it impossible for any single seller or buyer to influence the price by reducing or increasing his output: There are also other criteria, all involving the absence of any special advantage of one seller over other sellers or one buyer over other buyers, and

conditions result from a great variety of circumstances, which cannot even be enumerated here exhaustively. Instances in which at least one of these circumstances exists and in which competition is therefore not unrestrained are the rule under present-day capitalism: Uninhibited competition is almost as rare as full monopoly.

Techniques to Restrain Competition

Among the practices which enable sellers to maintain a price above the competitive equilibrium without possessing a full monopoly are the following:

1. Product differentiation. A producer gives his product, which otherwise is not essentially different from that of potentially competing producers, some special feature which causes it to be preferred by consumers as long as there is not too great a price differential. The feature may mean a real improvement in quality, or it may be some pleasing subsidiary service connected with the offering of the product, for instance nice packaging or particular courtesy of the sales personnel, or it may be a brand name for which consumers' preference has been established by advertising.

Once the preference for the product of a particular firm is established, the producer can exercise control over the price policy of dealers, by supplying them only on the condition that they will sell at a stipulated price, which indirectly puts a floor and a ceiling on their own margin. The producer is of course interested in preventing an excessive margin which would impair consumers' demand for the product; he is also interested in putting a floor under the dealer's margin because he is protecting his own preferred position by establishing in effect, a retailers' cartel: The retailers do not have to bind themselves by a mutual agreement to maintain a defined margin if each of them is bound by his contract with the producer to sell at a fixed price which will result in the emergence of such a margin. Although individual retailers may rebel against the producer's price rule, the chances are that dealers as a group will be well satisfied with the policy of price maintenance and will reciprocate by trying to confirm their customers in their favorable attitude toward the product.

---

complete rationality of action by all market parties. The classical example of an approximate realization of all these conditions was the wheat market before the establishment of government price supports. Competition, if perfect, is always unrestrained; but even in industries in which the bulk of the output is supplied by a few large firms, each of which could influence the price by varying the volume of its sales, there is sometimes an uninhibited price war which brings the price down to the competitive level or even below the level of long-range costs. Therefore even imperfect competition may be unrestrained.

Producers of preferred brands can practice this policy not only in their relations with retailers but also with wholesalers and processing firms.

2. Acquisition of exclusive control over some resource which can be used to greater advantage than the similar resources available to others. This resource may be location: He who acquires the only vacant lot suitable for an electric repair shop in a small town may set the price for his services anywhere within a substantial range, because it will be troublesome and costly for the townspeople to bring their appliances to shops elsewhere.[7] Or the resource may be the knowledge of a secret process, or the right to use a patented process or instrument. By denying these facilities to potential or actual competitors, or granting them only on the condition of a dampening of competition, the favored entrepreneur can keep his price relatively high.

A market position based on patent rights sometimes amounts to an absolute monopoly, though rarely a stable one, since eventually a rival process is likely to be invented.

A similar case is that of vertical concentration, where it is used to fortify the sales position in the market of a particular product. The term "vertical concentration" signifies a combination of several levels of processing, or of manufacture and distribution, under the same ownership. The classical case is that of steel works, owning on the one hand coal mines and cokeries, on the other hand steel consuming plants, such as pipe factories, shipyards or machine factories.[8] Such a combination may result from any number of motives: The search for profitable investment opportunities for surplus capital, technological considerations[9] or management's desire for "empire building." One possible motive—the one that is important here—is the desire to force some firms, which act as rivals on one level of processing, into a common price policy by the threat of depriving them of the supply of some needed raw material or semi-finished commodity.

A sudden rise in demand for a particular product often creates a monopoly or semi-monopoly for the firms possessing the specialized installations necessary to turn out the product, because a newcomer could not quickly build production facilities and moreover, if the increase in demand

[7] In cases of this kind, it is sometimes difficult to decide whether the extra gain should be regarded as monopoly profit or as ground rent, but this problem need not be discussed here.

[8] By contradistinction, horizontal concentration means either mergers with plants on the same level, e.g. steel plants with steel plants, or establishment of common control for such plants by holding companies, trusts or similar devices.

[9] For instance, steelworks may build a rolling mill to work the steel, when it comes out of the converter "in one heat" into pipes or other shapes, or a plant producing some delicate kind of machinery may acquire a steel plant to make sure that it will always get the quality of steel it needs.

is not likely to be permanent, it would not pay a newcomer to enter into competition with the established firms. The case of the American auto industry after the war, which has been discussed above, is a good example of such a monopoly position based upon possession of production plants which for physical and economic reasons could not be duplicated in time to meet the additional demand.

3. Price leadership. Sometimes an industry consists of one big concern and a number of smaller concerns, and in these instances the small concerns frequently follow the lead of the big firm in setting the price. This may be done from inertia; more often, the motive lies in the consideration that an attempt of the small firms to undersell the large one would lead to a costly price war from which the small firms could hardly emerge as victors.[10]

4. Tacit collusion. In industries in which only a few large firms produce all or nearly all of the output (oligopoly), the advantage to every firm of maintaining a price above the competitive level is often so obvious as to make a formal cartel agreement unnecessary, provided that the firms can trust each other or that any violation of the tacit agreement becomes obvious and exposes the violator to retaliatory underselling by other firms. The latter condition often applies in retail trade, in which every dealer's price policy is bound to become known to the public and therefore also to his competitors; consequently, informal collusion can frequently be maintained in retailing even if a fairly large number of firms is involved. On the other hand, the high markups which the elimination or dampening of competition among small distributors made possible, have offered a powerful temptation to big concerns to cut into these margins by such organizational

[10] A particularly instructive example of this kind of motivation on the part of a small firm can be found in the statements by President Randall of the Riverside Metal Company before the Temporary National Economic Committee in May 1939, on the acquiescence of his firm in the price leadership by the American Brass Company; see TNEC Hearings, Part 5, pp. 2086-2090, reprinted in Corwin D. Edwards, *Big Business and the Policy of Competition* (Cleveland: The Press of Western Reserve University, 1956), pp. 45 ff.

For a small firm, however, the temptation to undersell a big firm holding the price above the competitive level, can be very great, for by keeping the price somewhat below that of the big concern, the small firm may be able to receive still more than it would under unrestrained competition and sell whatever it can produce. Therefore, this is likely to be the policy of the small concern whenever it can expect "big brother" to tolerate the underselling without serious attempt at retaliation. During the early years of the Great Depression in Germany, some Ruhr coal mines with an output representing only a very small fraction of German coal production, remained outside the mining cartel, charged prices only slightly less than the cartel price and sold their whole output, operating at capacity, while the cartel firms could hardly use more than 50 per cent of their capacity. The cartel did not bother to frustrate this policy, although in addition to its economic weapons it probably could have used legal powers because German coal mining at that time was regulated by a law requiring firms to join the cartel.

improvements as department stores, chain stores and supermarkets. This experience, however, has caused legislators to protect the small store by a variety of means, of which the most important ones, aside from tax measures, were promotion instead of suppression of agreements restricting competition. In the United States, the latter type of legislation is represented by many Fair Trade laws and by the Miller-Tydings Act of 1937;[11] although most of these laws refer only to articles protected by trade marks or brand names for which a minimum price is fixed by the manufacturer, this is a wide enough field to reduce competition among retailers substantially. Moreover, the open collusion legalized by these acts with regard to brand-name goods probably facilitates tacit collusion on other articles, because the machinery which retailers will establish through their trade associations to watch over compliance with the Fair Trade laws can easily be used for discouraging efforts at underselling in other fields as well.

In production as in distribution, tacit collusion is probably the most important source of semi-monopoly in countries, which like the United States, in principle permit no open cartels.

Limited Access to Industries

None of the restrictive devices and customs which have been described here, nor any of the others that would have to be included in an exhaustive list, could be applied or practiced if entry into the industry involved were

[11] Similar in purpose is the Robinson-Patman Act of 1936 which prohibits many forms of price discrimination by a seller among different buyers and thereby limits the advantages which large concerns can obtain by buying in quantity, as an antecedent to underselling their smaller competitors. It is significant that both the Miller-Tydings Act and the Robinson-Patman Act originated while the experience of the Great Depression still dominated the minds. At that time the merits of low prices were overshadowed by the conviction that long periods of falling prices must be avoided. A little later, a limited reversal of public policy took place, characterized by the creation of the Temporary National Economic Committee, to investigate the evils of monopolistic price policy, and by a stricter enforcement of the anti-trust laws. It has been suggested that the reason for this change was the slump of 1937-38, which the Administration believed to have been caused by monopolistic exploitation of the improvement of market conditions during the recovery of 1933-37. (See for instance Harold Faulkner, *American Economic History*, New York: Harper and Brothers, 8th ed. p. 672). But the two acts as well as the Fair Trade legislation of the States survived this period, probably in part because they were directed against big business and were thus in consonance with the general tendency of the New Deal, and in part because their provisions could be presented—not without some foundation in fact—as preventives against the establishment of economic power positions which could later be used to exploit the consumer, although the latter had initially been benefited by the practices which the acts prohibited. After World War II, when the danger of inflation was more in the public mind than that of deflation, this kind of legislation was already too well established to be eliminated, but it has come under more criticism; see for instance, John Galbraith, *American Capitalism—The Concept of Countervailing Power*. Boston: Houghton-Mifflin, 1952, pp. 137, 147 ff.

free and easy. Any analysis of the origin of monopolistic and semi-monoplistic devices must, therefore, include an explanation of the restrictive conditions on which the establishment of new enterprises often depends. Part of this explanation has already been given in the discussion of various forms of semi-monopoly, and of the techniques of restraining competition, but some supplementary considerations are needed.

In the industries which account for the bulk of modern manufacturing, access is limited by the requirement of huge capital. This capital, it is true, need not be supplied by a single person or a few partners, but is almost always brought together through the floating of stock among a multitude of shareholders. The organizational ability and the business contacts necessary to organize a modern joint-stock corporation, however, are sufficiently rare to limit access to large-scale industry very effectively. Moreover, since it is hardly ever possible to issue capital stock without the cooperation of credit institutions, the latter are in a position to prevent "overcrowding" of industries, and the financial institutions must use this power, since they want the issues which they underwrite to prove highly profitable.[12]

As an impediment to access, large capital requirements are made even more effective by the condition of declining costs which often prevail in large-scale industry. The importance of overhead as compared with variable cost and the advantages of specialization have created a situation in which it is more important than ever for industries to work at a high utilization of capacity, and to have sales prospects which make it possible so to design capacity as to assure the lowest unit costs; ordinarily,

[12] This is the nucleus of truth in the contention, to be found in the writings of Rudolf Hilferding and other European socialists and finally in those of Lenin, that finance capital organizes the monopolies of industrial capital. See Carl Landauer, *European Socialism* (Berkeley and Los Angeles: University of California Press, 1959), Vol. II, pp. 1576 f, 1596 for relevant literature.

The argument has some relationship to Thorstein Veblen's belief in the domination of the producer by the financier. See his books, *The Engineers and the Price System*, (New York: Huebsch, 1921) and *The Theory of Business Enterprise* (New York: Charles Scribner's Sons, 1912).

Actually, the support which the banks lend to the monopolization of industry is rarely the prime factor in restricting competition. The German D-Banken and the House of Morgan have at times exerted their influence in favor of monopolization in limited fields of industry, but it would be a great error to believe that we would have an economy of essentially free competition if it were not for the influence of banks. The European coal and steel industry, for instance, did not have to rely on banks to limit access, since control of natural resources, including both mining deposits and favorable factory sites, protected the established firms from too many newcomers. The chemical industry in all countries, and large parts of the machine industry, have been sufficiently protected by patents to keep many newcomers out. The general picture of modern capitalism is not one of prevalence of finance capital over industrial capital; often, the power ratio is the inverse.

these optimal conditions exist only in boom periods, and as long as they do not exist, every additional order lowers the cost per unit. Established firms with a substantial stock of orders can therefore easily meet the competition of newcomers. Thus declining costs which are one of the factors limiting the exploitation of a monopolistic position often facilitate its establishment.

In addition to this basic fact of business economics, barriers to entry into a particular industry or profession have been established by a great variety of types of private action and public law, sometimes working in combination. The denial of licenses for patent-protected machines, apparatuses and processes is one of the most effective methods to bar entry to newcomers; how widely it is used, however, is unknown. A variant of this method has attracted special attention: the buying up of patents for new processes by firms which do not intend to use them but merely wish to block others from getting a good start in the industry. Such practices undoubtedly occur, but the number of instances in which an action of this kind has been proven is not great. On the other hand, this is not evidence of infrequency; since the blocking of technological progress would be regarded as obnoxious by public opinion and might lead to corrective judicial or legislative action, it is not likely to be advertised.

Many barriers to entry into an industry and especially into professions and other vocations have been established by public authority, or by industrial or professional organizations, or by both, with the real or alleged motive of safeguarding public interest in the quality of the product or service. Sometimes these barriers take the form of rules for training or examinations; such rules exist almost everywhere for the professions, especially for doctors and other medical personnel and in some countries also for real estate agents, chauffeurs, barbers and other kinds of craftsmen. Some restrictions are motivated by the consideration that too large a number of competitors would either offer too great a temptation to "cut corners," i.e. to neglect safety rules or to resort to deceptive practices in dealing with the consumer, or that unrestrained competition would force all competitors to operate on a highly uneconomical level and would therefore result in much higher prices for consumers; in some instances, in the field of radio and television, the rationale of restriction has been the realization that the physical conditions of producing the service did not permit an unlimited number of producers—there are not enough usable frequencies for an unlimited number of broadcasting stations—and that therefore barriers had to be established if the industry was to exist at all.

Even when restrictive regulations are really indispensable for the public welfare, they often tend to limit access to an occupation for people who might be capable of rendering satisfactory service. All educational restrictions establish effective barriers against the potentially competent as well as the incompetent, if long training periods are demanded without adequate provisions for scholarships. Moreover, any number of accidental conditions, from family obligations to nervousness in tests, may prevent a person from satisfying educational requirements, although he might have performed brilliantly if given a particular job.

Aside from requirements that are truly established for the protection of the public, there have been instances in which this purpose was a mere pretense, where the principal effect of the legislation was to secure an extra profit for the lucky insiders. Still more frequent are the intermediate situations, in which requirements of a needed kind are exaggerated: More comprehensive schooling or more stringent tests may be prescribed than are necessary; the number of licenses granted for taxi cabs and other regulated trades may be fewer than would be conducive to the best kind of service. Sometimes perfectionism—especially in regard to required professional education—combines with selfish interests to raise the barriers unnecessarily high and thus make monopolistic increases in income possible.

Regulatory Agencies

Legislation in the United States and other capitalistic countries has attempted to protect the consumer from monopolistic effects of entrance restrictions into regulated occupations or industries, not only by the general monopoly control laws but also, with regard to public utilities, by imposing special conditions in return for the franchise. Thus rates charged for power, heating gas, transportation service etc., are controlled by public agencies. Sometimes fields of operation are distributed, as in the United States by the Civil Aeronautics Board for the airlines and by the Federal Communications Commission for radio and television broadcasting. Behind such control measures is the intention to put the consumer in at least as favorable a position as he would be if the industry were competitive. But even where the authorities exercise their powers with the greatest sense of responsibility and are well protected from political pressure, the attainment of the goal meets with inherent difficulties. American railroad legislation, for example, requires that the Interstate Commerce Commission, the regulatory agency for the railroads, permit the latter to charge rates which represent a fair return on their capital. But what is that capital? If the nominal value of the original investment is to be taken into account, the amount recognized as investment would be low because of the decline in the value of the dollar; if, however, the cost of reproducing the same physical assets were assumed to be the figure, the valuation and consequently the rates would be impossibly high and would be based on a mere fiction, since in this age of trucks, automobiles and airplanes the present American railroad network would certainly not be constructed if it did not already exist. If an intermediate solution is adopted, as has actually been the case in the more recent decisions of the Interstate Commerce Commission and the courts, the policy of the regulatory agency becomes to a large extent arbitrary, and this absence of strict standards in the treatment of private enterprise is more difficult to reconcile with the rationale of capitalism than government operation of monopolistic industry.

The question of how monopoly control can be maintained in a capitalist system although such control requires a high degree of government interference with business is not peculiar to the regulatory agencies; this problem will be met again in the discussion of general anti-monopoly laws.

The Social Cost of Monopoly

Monopolistic features are not likely to disappear from our economy: This proposition will be more fully substantiated later in the discussion, but probably even at this point few readers will have much doubt about its validity. Since in all probability imperfect competition in its various degrees will stay with us, it is important to make as good an estimate as we can of the harm that monopoly and semi-monopoly inflict on human welfare.

Let us assume a state of the economy in which there is perfect competition in all industries, all resources are employed, and that the economy is in equilibrium. From previous explanations it should be clear that this state of affairs is optimal from the point of view of the consumers. Each industry produces the output which corresponds to the relative strength of consumers' preferences. Consequently, every change must be a deterioration.

In a non-monopolistic situation a deviation from this optimal utilization of resources can occur only if a producer commits a mistake, overestimates or underestimates the quantity demanded at the price just covering marginal costs, and the mistake will soon be corrected since the producers of the industries which are overexpanded in relation to consumers' preferences will not be able to pay for the resources the same prices which had been paid when the resources were optimally distributed among industries, and the resources will therefore tend to flow back to their original uses; other repercussions within production operations will probably also occur to restore the original output situation. Yet if one industry has its output restricted by monopoly or semi-monopoly, the tendencies to restore the original situation will not operate. The consumers will not be able to purchase the commodities which they most want to have in the quantities that the cost situation would permit.

Does monopoly tend to prevent the full employment of resources? Part of the real income which the consumers lose will be gained by the monopolists, and they may spend enough to employ all the resources that have been released by the restriction of output. In fact, if the monopoly is confined to manufacturing enterprise and perfect competition exists among the resource owners—and since labor is the most important of resources, this means complete absence of unions, no effective minimum wage law, etc.—all resources would probably[13] continue to be used, because any unused surplus of any type of resource would lead to a lowering of its price and therefore probably to its re-employment elsewhere. But this is not a frequent case. Labor, even where not unionized, is reluctant to work at less than the prevailing wage for particular skills. Producers of raw materials, even where not cartelized or otherwise working under restricted competition, can often not readily reduce their prices without defaulting on the debts they have contracted to construct their fixed installations, and it requires a time-consuming process of bankruptcies and other adjustments to bring the costs down to a level that restores the full employment of resources. Although monopolization need not impair employment, the possibility that employment will not be affected is quite remote: The probability is that the establishment of a monopoly will restrict the opportunity for resource owners to sell at the prices they are accustomed to receive, and that, as a consequence, a portion of the resources will be temporarily or permanently unemployed.

Thus monopoly is a deviation from optimal market performance: Our resources would be more effectively utilized for the satisfaction of con-

[13] The reason this effect is not certain lies in the significance of lowered resource prices for the distribution of income. The lowering of the price of labor means a decrease of mass purchasing power. It is not certain that the adverse effect of this decline upon employment would be outweighed by the stimulating effect of cost reduction.

sumers if all industries operated under unrestrained competition. How much more effectively? A general answer is impossible. Even for a single industry the difference between price and output under unrestrained competition on the one hand and the same magnitudes under existing monopolistic influences on the other is hard to calculate. To define the price range in which the individual producer or group of producers can set the price without being undersold by potential competitors; to calculate the elasticity of demand which determines how much the industry loses in sales by any given rise of price; to find out in how many plants the cost curve is still declining and in how many it has reached the point from which it starts to rise, these tasks would tax the capabilities of the ablest and best informed econometrician, even for a narrowly limited field, and certainly overtax them when it is a question of generalizing for the economy as a whole. As to the absolute magnitude of the sacrifice which the restraints on competition impose on our economy, we can hardly say more than that this sacrifice was obviously not great enough to outweigh the favorable factors in modern industrial development: Monopoly and semi-monopoly have not prevented the spectacular rise in standards of living in the capitalistic countries during the last half-century—a rise no more than briefly interrupted by such political and economic catastrophes as the two World Wars and the Great Depression.

Whereas the appraisal of the economic cost of monopoly in absolute terms is an insoluble problem, it is possible to form an opinion as to whether this cost is increasing or decreasing. First, the number of instances of high elasticity of demand is increasing at the expense of low demand elasticity. There are two reasons for this: Technology ever more frequently widens the consumer's choice of means to satisfy a given need and thereby makes it possible for him to shift his demand in the direction of the relatively cheaper means; thus automobile transportation has been offered as an alternative to railroad transportation, television entertainment for movie entertainment, aluminum or stainless steel kitchenware for enamelware? Furthermore, as the standard of living rises, an ever larger part of production is devoted to the satisfaction of less urgent needs for which there are alternatives: The choice between the pleasures of travel or those of better home furnishings, between more entertaining at home and more attendance at movies, between one more room in the house or a new car, has either been entirely unknown until recently or plays at least a much greater role in the capitalistic nations today than it did a few decades ago.

It is equally certain that the phenomenon of declining costs is still growing in relative importance. Even where existing plants are operating at optimal utilization of capacity, it would very often be possible to lower costs by building a still larger plant, but this presupposes a sufficiently large market to sell the greater output. Thus the penalty upon restricting the market by monopolistic price increases is growing heavier. (It should be kept in mind, however, that the same phenomenon of declining costs increases the frequency of imperfect competition by favoring industrial giantism.)

Finally, the importance of public relations is probably growing, and the danger for an enterprise of losing good will among its actual or potential customers through ruthless exploitation of a dominant market position is being given more attention. Given the relative decline of the profit motive among the incentives of management in large-scale industry, a more cautious attitude toward exploiting restricted competition is likely.

To be sure, there are some counteracting trends. Some of the new commodities provided by modern technology have a highly inelastic demand, either because they satisfy very urgent needs—as is the case with some drugs—or because they represent small, cheap, but indispensable supplements to facilities we have acquired at high cost: Few people would use the lighting installation in their homes any less if the price of light bulbs were raised by 30 per cent; nobody would fail to replace an outworn screw in the family car even if screws were to double in price. It is probably also true that the technique of monopolization continues to be made more effective: Industries are learning better how to achieve tacit collusion.

To sum up: Although the economic cost of monopoly cannot be calculated, and it is therefore possible that without it we would have proceeded still faster toward the satisfaction of all our needs, the probability is that this cost will decrease. Since in all industrially advanced countries, in which the modern forms of monopoly have become important, mass welfare has grown faster during the development of monopoly than ever before, we may expect that in the future the impediment will not hold us back very much on our march toward affluence.

The Problems of the Anti-Trust Laws

The social cost of monopoly, not merely its economic cost, has alarmed legislators and administrators and has led to the enactment of laws aimed at suppressing or restricting "restraint of trade;" some of the most stringent pieces of such legislation are on the statute books of the United States. But the application and interpretation of these laws have met with considerable difficulties, of which the most important result from the fact that monopoly control requires a degree of government interference with business which cannot be easily reconciled with private enterprise economy. This point has been overlooked by those writers who, *in extenso*, have explained the points of superiority of capitalism over socialism and the dangers of the welfare state, and then briefly added that government action in the field of monopoly control was of course necessary.[14] The elimination or restriction of private monopoly is not a sort of surface correction on the capitalist system; rather, the problem of how to maintain a large amount of competition in a system of privately owned, large-scale industry goes to the very heart of the issue of economic collectivism.

This would be the case even if the government, in its attempt to control monopoly, had to deal only with the monopoly's most vulnerable form, that of open collusion in price fixing among firms otherwise carrying on their activities independently. A prohibition of cartels is an exception to the freedom of contract. Such a prohibition means that contracts can be freely made only between parties on opposite sides of the market: Sellers with buyers, but not sellers with sellers or buyers with buyers. As long as the evils resulting from "restraint of trade" are obvious there is still not much difficulty in justifying the exception to the right of individuals to agree among themselves on any conditions they like: A right can be restricted when it is misused. But where does misuse begin? If ten steel firms, controlling among themselves, say, 90 per cent of the output, decide to raise the price of steel by, say, 25 per cent above the level which existed before and which still enabled them to operate with profit, no court will see any difficulty in condemning such a cartel. But suppose these are corner grocers, who have been engaged in cut-throat competition; some of them have already gone bankrupt, although they and their family members have ruined their health by working long hours trying to save expenses. Now the survivors conclude a price-maintenance agreement to secure a modest retailing margin. A defender of unrestrained competition may still say: They should be compelled by law to continue the ruinous process of competition until they are decimated; then those who remain in business will have a sufficient turnover to exist on a smaller margin. Yet this argument does not do full justice to the basic problem. Whatever the beneficial effects of competition, how far can the state go in denying to the individual the means indispensable for his economic survival, if these means

[14] See Friedrich A. Hayek, *The Road to Serfdom*. Chicago: University of Chicago Press, 1944, *passim*, esp. pp. 198 f.

do not involve crimes like fraud, theft or extortion, but simply an agreement with people in like condition? Historical evidence shows that legislators and judges have often not found it in their hearts and minds to forbid the small man the use of such life savers; this is the most important cause of the emasculation of anti-monopoly policies by fair-trade legislation and by permitting restraint of trade where it seemed "reasonable." In the eighteenth and nineteenth centuries, it is true, the revolt against the guild rules broke down the obstacles to the inexorable operation of the market mechanism, which then crushed innumerable small operators, but the historical presuppositions are different today, especially because now it is not merely a matter of abolishing some laws which stand in the way of competition, but to restore competition by interference of public authority with details of private agreements and business practices. This can be done, to some extent, where the agreements and practices favor the strong as against the weak, but not when the agreements and practices protect the weak from the strong; nor can it always be prevented—in a society based on formal equality before the law—that the strong then use the concessions granted by legislators and courts to the weak. Capitalism is based on the assumption that the individual should be free from detailed prohibitions and prescriptions of what he must do or cannot do in his economic actions, and that such prohibitions and prescriptions are presumed to be wrong, even if in the individual case they serve a good purpose. Detailed regulation to force competition, therefore, operates against the rationale of the existing order; this inconsistency will be tolerated only to the extent that it can be justified as an urgent postulate of social justice.

But explicit collusion among independent producers is still the least difficult form of monopoly to attack, because here the law can strike at defined means of profit making. More difficult are situations in which not the character of the transaction as such but their consequences under particular circumstances must be made the criterion of illegality if monopoly is to be prevented.[15] In a capitalistic economy it cannot be generally forbidden for companies to purchase stock of another company in the same field, because such a purchase may have a number of economically legitimate reasons, such as establishment of production units of optimal size. But the aim may also be the domination of the market. Vertical concentration may be a form of promoting technological progress, and with or without that aim may at the same time lead to monopoly or semi-monopoly. A monopoly

[15] The distinction is completely clear cut only if all collusion is forbidden. If "reasonable" restraint of trade is permitted, the effects of the agreement become to some extent also a criterion of illegality, because the "reasonableness" can in most instances be judged only by the consequences.

may be established by the most legitimate of all business practices: surpassing one's competitors in reducing costs, and thus driving them out of the market—and in industries in which large capital is required, such a monopoly may be, if not permanent, at least of long duration. Tacit collusion, almost by definition, can only be proved by the examination of its consequences.

How is it possible to determine whether a particular transaction creates a monopoly or semi-monopoly? One might first think of the price as a suitable criterion: Since it is the most significant expression of monopoly that the price will be raised above the competitive level, why not make the charging of such an elevated price the mark of illegitimacy? The courts do recognize the price as a criterion, but not as the only one, and to the extent that a high price is an indicator of a monopoly, great difficulties have to be met. In the first place, an adoption of this criterion imposes on the authorities the formidable task of watching the price policies of all industries which are not obviously and highly competitive. Secondly, if a suspicious case is identified, how can it be proved that the price is excessive? Rarely is there a possibility of directly comparing the price which is actually being charged with the competitive price, because the latter does not exist; even where it existed in an earlier phase of development, conditions may have changed fundamentally and the change may make a comparison meaningless. Frequently the competitive price existed only as long as the industry consisted of relatively small enterprises which could not utilize the more efficient technological devices which were introduced later—perhaps they were not even known in the earlier phase. The process of concentration made possible technological innovations which led to a reduction of the price, but at the same time left the market to some giant enterprises not effectively competing with each other and reaping huge profits even at the reduced price, because costs were reduced even more. Where the suspected monopoly price is thus lower than the former competitive price, monopolistic exploitation can be proved on the basis of price policy only if the government agencies go into a detailed cost analysis, to show whether the enterprise is keeping the price too high above cost. Such an investigation involves decisions about the distinction between outlays for capital investments and current costs, and in the case of capital investments about the rate at which the original outlay should be written off. But these are decisions which are part of managerial responsibility; to assume that supervising government officials can competently judge such matters contradicts the rationale of a capitalist economy.[16] The

[16] Government agencies, it is true, must make decisions on the cost structure of enterprises for tax purposes, and this is often difficult enough; yet the responsibility is more

consequences can be made bearable by giving the enterprise the benefit of the doubt in each case; but this means that many instances of "restraint of trade" will escape the control measures. To prevent monopoly control from becoming so spotty as to lose its value, it is necessary to supplement price surveillance with the consideration of other criteria.

Probably the most important criterion of monopolistic power, as applied by the courts, is now the percentage of the market which is under the control of a single enterprise. This involves a compromise between a "means" criterion and an "effect" criterion. An enterprise may reach a given percentage of the total supply of the market by operating efficiently or by consolidation with other companies—in other words: through methods which are not as such frowned upon by the law, and which become illegal only if they bring about the effect of giving the enterprise too large a share of the market. But this effect itself is illegitimate only because it may serve as a means for a monopolistic price policy. Most American court decisions do not even require that the latter purpose be intended, or that the price be actually set at monopolistic levels, but merely that the enterprise has acquired the power to do so.

The drawback in this kind of monopoly control is that it discriminates against bigness, whereas bigness of enterprise is frequently a condition of technological progress. As Corwin D. Edwards wrote: "The anti-trust laws condemn not bigness, but restraint of trade and tendencies toward monopoly. Nevertheless, since the impact of a business practice varies with the size of the concerns that engage in it, types of action that are permissible for business generally may be condemned as monopolistic in tendency when undertaken by big business." [17]

So far, it is true, the administration of American anti-trust laws has not

---

easily bearable than it would be for like decisions in the administration of anti-trust laws, if the price were considered the only criterion for violation. If a tax agency, in judging an entrepreneur's policy in distinguishing between different kinds of cost or his writing-off policy, errs on the side of leniency, nothing worse will happen than that in an individual case the government receives less money than it should, and that the principle of equal treatment of all taxpayers is violated; the latter may appear very bad, but few people would deny that the degree in which the modern state has succeeded in equalizing the impact of taxes is very low in any event. If the government agency errs on the side of severity, the negative effect on the taxpayer's position is, in many instances, still not comparable to that of an analagous misjudgment in the administration of anti-monopoly laws, because in the tax decisions the taxpayer will usually be benefited in later years by the lower permissible rate of write-off or by the charging of a particular expenditure to capital investment rather than to current cost.

[17] See Corwin D. Edwards, *Big Business and the Policy of Competition*. Cleveland: The Press of Western Reserve University, p. 22. Edwards cites a number of instances in which American courts have held the size of an enterprise to be relevant as a criterion of monopoly and briefly characterizes the kind of reasoning the court applied in each case.

visibly impeded technological progress; nor can any such effect be observed in any other country with monopoly control. The reverse effect is more likely to have occurred: The fear of outlawing bigness, which has proved to be a vehicle of economic progress, seems to have induced the courts to exercise additional restraint in applying the anti-trust laws. Whether future technological development will aggravate or alleviate the conflict between the public's interest in controlling monopoly and its interest in promoting technological progress remains to be seen.

The motives behind the condemnation of bigness are not exclusively economic. "Political society in the United States is founded upon distrust of concentrated power. We seek to protect our personal freedom by diffusing governmental authority. . . . Belief in competition is the economic corollary of these political ideas. . . . We are reluctant to see authority over price and production concentrated in one or a few enterprises. We want business rivalries to supply checks and balances that limit the power of each business enterprise." [18] This is the interpretation of the motives of American anti-monopoly policy, as expressed by Corwin D. Edwards, one of the best informed writers on the subject. An eminent American jurist, Supreme Court Justice William O. Douglas, stated his ideas in similar terms: "Power that controls the economy should be in the hands of elected representatives of the people, not in the hands of an industrial oligarchy. Industrial power should be decentralized. It should be scattered into many hands so that the fortunes of the people will not be dependent on the whim or caprice, the political prejudices, the emotional stability of a few self-appointed men. . . . That is the philosophy and the command of the Sherman Act. It is founded on a theory of hostility to the concentration in private hands of power so great that only a government of the people should have it." [19] Another prominent American judge, Learned Hand, said in one of his decisions: "We have been speaking only of the economic reasons which forbid monopoly; but . . . there are others, based upon the belief that great industrial consolidations are inherently undesirable, regardless of their economic results. In the debates in Congress Senator Sherman himself . . . showed that among the purposes of Congress in 1890 was a desire to put an end to great aggregations of capital because of the helplessness of the individual before them. Throughout the history of these statutes it has been constantly assumed that one of their purposes was to perpetuate and

[18] Corwin D. Edwards, *Big Business and the Policy of Competition.* Cleveland: The Press of Western Reserve University, 1956, pp. 1-2.

[19] Justice William O. Douglas in a dissenting opinion in the case *U.S.* v. *Columbia Steel Co.,* 334 U.S. 536.

preserve, for its own sake and in spite of possible cost, an organization of industry in small units which can effectively compete with each other." [20]

Four important thoughts can be found in these statements. The first, of overriding significance, is the conviction that the reasons why political power should be restricted and controlled must by logical necessity be applied also to economic power. The opinion by Justice Douglas even states clearly that if economic power cannot be sufficiently controlled, it should be transferred to the government in order to become subject to those restrictions which have been firmly established for political power. Probably the greatest historical significance of the American anti-trust policy is its expression of faith in the necessity of keeping private power subject to checks and balances for the same reasons that have caused modern man to consider unchecked governmental power intolerable. The Sherman Act has established the principle, more clearly than it has ever been expressed before, that there is nothing in the right of private property that should prevent the state from curbing the exercise of that right if otherwise the freedom of citizens or any of their vital interests, worthy of protection by the community, would be jeopardized. By the anti-trust laws the owner of stock in a corporation was forbidden to dispose of his stock by way of the formation of trusts, or by mergers, in such a fashion as to restrain trade; by the same token, the owner of a factory could be prevented from utilizing his property in such a manner as to restrict unduly the freedom of his workers or jeopardize their health or their family life. The same principle justified the use of the taxing power of the state to adjust power relations among groups of citizens in the sense of greater equity (as for instance in farm support loans to prevent divergent development between fully competitive prices of farm products and less competitive prices of farm supplies).[21] Thus the anti-trust legislation has broken ground in the United States for the social welfare legislation of the subsequent periods, from legal protection of labor's right to organize to social security laws, from the conservation policy to the attempts at adjusting the volume of marketed agricultural products to a magnitude compatible with an equitable price.

Yet from the great historical importance of the anti-trust laws as trail-

[20] Judge Learned Hand in *U.S.* v. *Aluminum Company of America,* 148 Fed. 2nd 416, pp. 428 f.

[21] The justification of the principle, of course, still leaves the question open as to what extent the policy so justified should be pursued. The statement that there is a basic inequity to the disadvantage of the farmer, and the belief that the government is justified in taking remedial action, are not tantamount to maintaining that the "parity prices" established for farm products at any given time are just right, or that the government has chosen the best techniques to achieve its aim.

blazers for a host of social legislation it does not follow that these laws were suitable instruments for the particular purpose for which they were created.

The second thought found in the quoted passages is the belief that bigness in business is undesirable. Indeed, a society in which production is carried out mainly on family farms and in family shops has great advantages. A man's freedom is better protected if he can start his own business and carry it on merely with help from his family. It may be argued that no protective legislation and no union can give a person the same guarantee of his freedom from encroachment by anybody else's economic power as this possibility of producing commodities for an anonymous market. This statement does not contradict the criticism, as given in the chapter on values and goals, of those writings which glorify the past at the expense of the present or deprecate the value of productivity which in small enterprises cannot be improved beyond narrow limits. It is one thing to say that the past with its low productivity offered a better life than the present with its high productivity and another thing to recognize that a price had to be paid for the high productivity of the present by sacrificing the business organization of the past.

But it is not the goal of the anti-trust laws to reduce the size of the economic unit to that of the corner grocery or the craftsman's shop; nor would it be possible to achieve this purpose by anti-monopoly legislation. What anti-trust legislation can do in some instances is to prevent large enterprises from growing into giant enterprises. This does not re-create a situation in which a person of modest means can go into business for himself; it does not relieve the great majority of citizens from the necessity of becoming wage earners. The freedom of the individual is not better protected when he has to work in an enterprise of 1,000 employees than in one with 50,000. For the bulk of the population, the effects of anti-trust legislation upon the structure of industry can make at best only a modest contribution to the protection of individual freedom.

A third thought in the cited court decisions amounts to a questionable historical contention: that the American people have exercised an option against bigness in industry, if not regardless of cost, at least after some sort of an appraisal of what the cost might be, and that public opinion has been in favor of bearing that cost. Actually, the American people have permitted themselves to adopt living habits which would become untenable if bigness were banned from industry; and can there be any doubt how the American people would vote if they had to decide whether to restore the small shop or the medium-sized factory as the prevailing economic unit at the price of renouncing automobiles, refrigerators, gas ranges, improved drugs and many other products of giant industry as articles of mass consumption?

The court decisions and the passage from Edwards contain a fourth thought; it is the belief that competition, per se, among producers, tends to enlarge the freedom of the individual. The buyer's freedom is undoubtedly greater when he can choose among various sellers, the worker's freedom greater when he can choose among various employers, the dealer's freedom greater when he can choose among various brands or other types of product which he will offer to his customers, the farmer's freedom greater when there is not just one dealer or processor to whom he can sell. How important are these contributions which competition makes to the sphere of freedom? This question cannot be separated from the other: For whose freedom is the existence of competition, as far as the anti-trust laws can secure or promote it, of importance? Asking this question is not to imply that society should be less concerned about the freedom of the individual A than about that of individual B. But the freedom of a big corporation to choose among sellers, buyers or intermediaries is not on the same level with the freedom of the worker to choose among employers or the freedom of a small merchant to choose among several manufacturers as suppliers. This is true, first, because the freedom of a corporation to choose among parties on the other side of the market has only an indirect and often tenuous connection with anybody's personal freedom; secondly, because the freedom of anyone in big business is usually greater, regardless of competition, than that of the little man, since the big businessman is likely to have reserves which will sustain him for some time if he does not want to make any deals under the terms offered and from which he can even perhaps draw the capital to shift to another line of business to escape a squeeze. Nevertheless, there is every reason for the legislator to prevent the use of monopoly power even within the sphere of big business as far as this can be done without impairing the attainment of other important goals; but when a choice has to be made between policies, the greater weight has to be given to the protection of the masses with little or no property.

"Countervailing Power"

As a guarantee of the freedom of the worker in capitalistic countries competition is less important than the power of his union; as a guarantee of the freedom of the farmer, competition is today less important in many capitalist countries than the action of government which puts a floor under farm prices and thus reduces his dependence on dealers and processors; as a guarantee of freedom for the small businessman, competition often fails entirely, and it is the formation of monopolistic agreements, with or without the sanction and support of the government, that makes his existence less precarious. In other words, in capitalistic society freedom today depends less on competition than on countervailing power. The book that has introduced the concept of countervailing power into professional and popular discussion—forging a useful tool of economic analysis from vague ideas floating around in the thinking of economists and of jurists concerned with the application of anti-trust laws—is John Kenneth Galbraith's *American Capitalism—The Concept of Countervailing Power.*[22]

Galbraith explained the satisfactory performance of American capitalism, in spite of the weakness of competition in many industries, by checks which buyers' monopoly power is putting on sellers' monopoly power and vice versa, and which government power is putting on both, mostly by bolstering the position of the market party that would otherwise be too weak for effective defense of its interests. He also maintains that the growth of countervailing power was not accidental; that agglomeration on one side of the market, and in one part of society, tended to induce agglomeration on the opposite side.

The existence of countervailing power is hardly contestable; it is also certain, however, that its effects are often unequal. The tendency of monopolistic power of one side to create monopolistic power on the other side has often met with obstacles. In many fields, in spite of chain stores and department stores, production is more concentrated than distribution of goods and "when the big deal with the little, countervailing power is at a minimum." [23] Where only government could supply the countervailing force, it was often hindered by remnants of laissez faire philosophy misapplied. Moreover, the outcome of the struggles of giant buyers and giant sellers may not be what the public interest would require; especially on the labor market, there is considerable danger that the compromises which they might conclude will be at the expense of the consumer. However, these facts, not overlooked by Galbraith, can lead only to qualifications but not to a refutation of the thesis that countervailing power is widespread and on the whole beneficial.

Is Monopoly Control Worth Keeping?

It is hardly a controversial statement to say that the anti-trust laws have been less effective in achieving their purposes—even those purposes on

[22] Boston: Houghton Mifflin Company, 1952.
[23] Edwards, *op. cit.*, p. 100.

which there has been no serious disagreement among courts or legislators—than have been most other acts of penal or civil legislation. The reasons for this relatively low effectiveness are manifold, ranging from such external facts as the ability of big corporations to prepare their defense with the assistance of the most expensive counsel and from the general difficulty of proving the illegal character of intricate business operations "beyond a reasonable doubt," to the conflict between the requirements of monopoly control and some important characteristics of a capitalistic economy. The external difficulties may be alleviated: It is not an immutable law that the techniques of concealment and legal defense of restraint of trade cannot be checkmated by the techniques of detecting these restraints and prosecuting their authors. The internal difficulties of monopoly control, however, will remain, and they alone make it certain that no capitalistic economy will ever be perfectly competitive.

What this means is not that monopoly control is impossible in capitalism, or that it will necessarily destroy the principles on which capitalism is built. The conclusion to be drawn is merely that some of those principles are in conflict with monopoly control, that capitalism cannot be built as an entirely consistent system, that it can exist only by balancing antagonistic tendencies through compromises which prevent any of these tendencies from bringing their advantages to full fruition, because if any of them were given too much rein it would produce intolerable disadvantages.

Neither the limitations to which the anti-monopoly laws—in the United States and in other countries—are obviously subject nor the existence of countervailing power as a partial substitute for competition[24] is likely to lead to the abolition of these laws. There are still strong arguments for maintaining maximum competition provided it is not one-sided. On the other hand, it will prove necessary to apply the rule systematically where it is now applied haphazardly: A monopolistic position countering an opposite monopolistic position which the state has for some reason failed to destroy is worthy of legislative and judicial protection or at least toleration. This amounts to saying that monopoly cannot be treated as a sort of economic vice, or as a crime per se; that, rather, the particular effects of monopoly on the distribution of power and income must be taken into consideration. There is still a tendency to look upon price leadership, labor unions and government bolstering of farm prices in the same way we would look upon gangs of criminals whose actions cannot be validly defended by arguing that they offset or restrict the power of other gangs,

[24] Galbraith himself has argued that the theory of countervailing power does not supply arguments for the removal of the anti-trust laws but merely for modifications in the judicial interpretations of these laws. See Galbraith, op. cit., pp. 141 ff.

equally criminal. The tendency toward monopoly must be understood as an inevitable consequence of the freedom of contract; its often undesirable effects must be forestalled or corrected as the case may be, either by compulsion to compete or by rounding out positions of countervailing power; often the latter alternative will be the only one that promises practical success.

CHAPTER 7

FALSE START: INEQUALITY IN CAPITALISM

What "False Start" Means

In the discussion of the tendency toward rationality of price-oriented production it has been explained that the impediments to this tendency can be divided into those which arise out of the market mechanism itself, as for instance monopolization, and those which result from a "false" starting point —false, that is, if maximum satisfaction of consumers' wants is taken as a goal. The most important factor in the latter category is inequality of incomes. The wants of the recipients of higher incomes exert a stronger pull on the resources of society than the wants of the recipients of a lower income. To use a well-known simile: If price formation is considered as a sort of voting, in which consumers, by handing money units to the sellers, decide what should be produced, then the well-to-do have many times the voting power of the poor. This explains why high-priced luxuries are being produced while some consumers do not receive an adequate supply of necessities.

At this point, however, it is necessary to distinguish between short-term and long-term considerations. From a short-term point of view, all inequalities detract from maximum satisfaction of human wants, if the satisfaction of all consumers is considered equally important. From a long-term (or even a medium-term) point of view, some inequalities are conducive to maximum satisfaction of human wants because of their contribution to the efficiency of production management; this effect has been explained before. Furthermore, whereas inequality of incomes is a determinant of the starting points for the price-forming process, it is also a result of that process. The fact that I have a given income may result from the inheritance of some corporation stock, but it also has to do with the fact that the capital represented by the stock yields a given return, expressed in dividends or appreciation. In technical language, functional distribution—the determination of the shares of different production factors in the social product—is one of the determinants of personal distribution, the determination of the shares of individual persons; and functional distribution is a result of the pricing process, the formation of prices of capital use, land use, of labor and their subdivisions.

The Influence of the Price Mechanism

The basic theorem explaining functional distribution is the rule of marginal productivity: The share of each productive agent is determined by the contribution which the last unit of the agent makes to the product, as measured in value. Obviously, no businessman borrows a single dollar for which he has to pay more interest than it contributes to the product; on the other hand, if there is perfect competition in the capital market, the borrowers will bid up the interest rate until it equals the contribution of the last dollar to the product of the "last" borrower, i.e. the one who makes the least efficient use of loans. If there is no perfect competition, the operation of the law may be modified by monopolistic distortions, but it still would retain at least a limited validity. Bankers may corner the loan market and thus offer less capital than could be supplied, but of the amount supplied it is still true that the contribution of the last dollar to the product of the marginal borrower must equal the rate of interest; and if the borrowers enter into collusion, they may reduce the rate below the marginal productivity of capital, but the reduction cannot go very far without exposing the borrowers' conspiracy to great strain; for as long as each entrepreneur can expand profitable production if only he has more capital, he will be tempted to offer higher interest rates to lenders, and all the more so the greater the difference between his marginal product and the rate of interest. The same considerations apply to land and labor, but the application to these factors is even more complicated.[1] The case of money capital may suffice as an illustration.

The influence of the price mechanism on income distribution is of major

[1] The rule of marginal productivity is directly applicable only insofar as each unit of a factor can be substituted for every other and where the factor can be divided into small units without loss of effectiveness. In the case of money capital, the first condition is completely satisfied, for one dollar is as good as the other; the second condition is satisfied to a sufficiently great extent to permit the application of the marginal productivity principle without essential reservation. But in the case of land, location is so im-

importance in capitalism; in some pre-capitalistic societies, this influence was only a fringe phenomenon. In feudalism, for instance, the income of noblemen had no close relationship to the price of goods or services.[2] The defenders of the capitalist system have laid great weight upon this trait with the correct argument that it distinguishes capitalism from a caste system: Where a person can increase his income by producing something that is urgently wanted, or by reducing production cost of any product or service, there exists a higher degree of social mobility than in a society in which no such opportunity is available. Some of the defenders, however, for instance John Bates Clark,[3] have overshot the goal when they attributed ethical significance to the influence of marginal productivity upon the distribution of incomes. It seemed to these authors that there was basic justice in a rule which made everybody's income dependent on his contribution to the flow of goods and services. But in our society some people are able to make a great contribution to this flow, not because their personal exertion has resulted in supplying something particularly useful, but because they started out with productive wealth which was not available to others. The fact that land yields a rent which is in consonance with its marginal productivity does not by itself morally justify a rent as personal income; it would first have to be shown as a postulate of ethics that land be owned by private persons instead of by the community, and that it be owned by the persons who actually have it in their possession. Moreover, the weight which the pricing process attributes to a person's contribution to the social product is in itself sometimes of questionable moral justification: The person may have a high income merely because he produces a special kind of commodity or service

---

portant that very often one unit of land cannot be substituted for another; nor is it possible to use land in very small units. Let it be emphasized that these qualities of land merely introduce complications in explaining the value of land from marginal productivity; indirectly, the rule applies here too and the way of its application will be found described in any good textbook of economics in the chapter on land rent.

The difficulties of applying the marginal productivity concept to labor follow from the impediments to perfect competition on the labor market. See Chapter 8.

[2] Perhaps it might be thought that there was no relationship at all. Yet aside from instances, frequent especially in the later phases of feudalism, when a nobleman sold some of the products from his estate on the market, the typical relationship between a feudal noble and the king can be interpreted as an exchange of administrative and especially military services for the income—in money or kind—that a fief was able to yield; although it would certainly be stretching the term too far if one were to speak of a "market" for feudal services, noblemen were often competing for fiefs, and the king's decision was not independent of the quality of the services which an aspirant might offer as a "price" for his fief. It might be difficult to find any kind of society in which the elements of the process of price formation are entirely lacking, and wherever they are present they must have had an influence on income distribution.

[3] See Clark's book, *The Distribution of Wealth* (1st ed. 1899, re-ed. New York: Macmillan, 1920); also *Social Justice without Socialism,* New York and Boston: 1914.

that satisfies the whim of some rich people, in which case his own favored position is an effect of the inequality of incomes; or a person may have a relatively low income because the social benefits are not sufficiently expressed by the market price of his services, as is sometimes the case with various groups of intellectual workers; this is why many great scientists earn less than fashion designers or second-rate film stars. It also happens that the social "disutility" may not be reflected in the price: A seller of marijuana earns more than a seller of milk.

With the exception of cases of the latter type, which are hardly common enough to make a proper value judgment of the market mechanism, these arguments do not lead to the conclusion that the determination of incomes as it exists in capitalism is necessarily immoral. They prove only that the existing distribution is not based directly on an ethical principle, and that to hold it justified it is necessary to show that it has some effects which a morally sensitive observer can regard as sufficiently desirable to prefer the existing state of affairs to any other. The most important of these effects is the contribution which some inequalities of income can make to the size of the social product. As has been explained before, there is no objective yardstick by which to judge what amount of inequality could be justified by what increase in the social product, and at this point subjective judgments may differ widely. But this would be a serious difficulty only if we wanted to know whether the system we have—or any other system proposed or in existence elsewhere—is the best we can have; however interesting in itself, to measure the distance of any society from somebody's ideal is not the purpose of this book. For the purpose of comparison between economic systems, it will be sufficient to form a rough idea of how much inequality there is now in fully developed capitalist countries and whether the trend is toward more or toward less inequality; later, similar statements will have to be made with regard to other economic systems. The reasons why it would be hopeless to aim at precision even in this relatively modest enterprise have also been discussed in the section on Values and Goals. The least inaccurate results can obviously be obtained where statistical information is most complete; for this reason, and also because of all the large countries it is most representative of advanced capitalism, the United States offers the most illuminating example.[4]

[4] The United Kingdom would probably be an equally good case—and possibly a better one—with regard to statistical information, but with its comprehensive social welfare system and its important nationalized industries, England is less representative of capitalism.

Income Inequality in the United States

If the total number of families and unattached individuals in the United States is divided into five equal parts, the incomes of each fifth, as received in the years, 1929, 1941, 1946 and 1957, represented the percentages of total personal income shown in Table 2.

TABLE 2

	1929	1941	1946	1957
Lowest Fifth } Second Fifth }	12.5	4.1	5.0	4.8
		9.5	11.1	11.3
Third Fifth	13.8	15.3	16.0	16.3
Fourth Fifth	19.3	22.3	21.8	22.3
Highest Fifth	54.4	48.8	46.1	45.3
Top Five per cent	30.0	24.0	21.3	20.2

Source: U. S. Bureau of the Census, *Historical Statistics of the United States,* Washington, D. C., 1960, p. 166.

A number of conclusions are suggested by this table. The United States is still far from an equalitarian society: Whereas the top 5 per cent receive more than 20 per cent of the total national income, the bottom 20 per cent receive less than 5 per cent. The trend, however, has been continuously one of trimming the top, and almost continuously one of raising the bottom.[5] The table uses income figures before taxes; the impact of the progressive federal income tax naturally further reduced the differences, but not as much as one might expect. The 20.2 per cent of total personal income received by the top 5 per cent of families before taxes in 1957 was reduced to 18.2 per cent after taxes, and the 45.3 per cent which the highest fifth received before taxes was reduced to 43.6 per cent; the lowest fifth received 4.8 per cent before taxes and 5.1 per cent after taxes, and the three intermediate fifths also showed higher after-tax percentages.[6] The equalitarian tendencies are further strengthened by some "fringe benefits" which the lower income groups receive to an increasing extent, for instance relatively inexpensive medical care (in county hospitals and through health plans); low-rent housing operates in the same direction, but it is hard to judge whether this kind of social assistance is increasing.

Since the significance of income differentials depends to some extent on

[5] Only a more detailed analysis than is possible here could reveal why the lowest fifth has not been able to retain completely the percentage gain it had achieved in the first postwar period.

[6] *Survey of Current Business,* April 1959, p. 16.

the absolute level at which the masses live,[7] it is relevant to the problem of inequality that in 1957 the percentages of all American families and unattached individuals indicated in Table 3 received the personal incomes after federal income taxes shown in the table.

TABLE 3

Incomes	Percentages
$3000 and more	74.1%
$4000 and more	60.2
$5000 and more	45.4
$6000 and more	32.8

Source: *Historical Statistics of the United States,* p. 165.

These figures explain why the existing differences in the standard of living of different income groups are not very conspicuous in the United States. A high percentage of families possesses the necessities and the most important amenities of life, and the advantages of the privileged minority are usually not in the important areas of consumption. American living habits are even less different than differences in incomes would cause us to expect.

The prosperous condition of the masses is very largely a product of the last three decades. It is remarkable that this result could be achieved in a period which saw the greatest depression of modern history and a war imposing on the United States tremendous material sacrifices. Table 4 shows the progression.

TABLE 4

Income in Constant (1950) Dollars	Per Cent of all Families and Unattached Individuals		
	1929	1941	1957
$3000 and more	32.8	46.5	69.9
$4000 and more	20.6	30.8	54.6
$5000 and more	13.4	18.5	40.1
$7500 and more	6.0	6.5	17.3

Source: *Historical Statistics of the United States,* p. 165.

The trend indicated by these figures is likely to continue because of the increase in productivity, and consequently in per capita national income,

[7] This thought has been expressed and explained by Robert Solow, *A Survey of Income Inequality Since the War.* Stanford: Center for Advanced Studies in the Behavioral Sciences (mimeographed) pp. 77/78. Quoted by Seymour M. Lipset and Reinhard Bendix, *Social Mobility in Industrial Society,* Berkeley and Los Angeles: Univ. of California Press, 1959, p. 110.

which we have to expect as a consequence of technological innovations. Even if the percentage share of the upper income groups in the total national income remains the same, the advantages which these groups enjoy will be in the satisfaction of less and less important wants.

Will the percentage share of the upper income groups remain the same, or is it likely to grow or to decline? The answer is made difficult because forces operate in opposite directions. On the one hand, it is highly probable that unionization of labor will be extended into industries and sections in which it has not yet taken place on a large scale, and minimum wage laws will probably furnish a less and less inadequate substitute in industries or for types of labor too difficult to organize. Furthermore, technological progress is likely to raise more and more manual workers into the ranks of more highly paid technicians. Against these factors making for more equality, however, others are operating which would tend to increase income differentials. In the first place, the decline of the value of money is likely to continue; although some of its consequences hit the upper income groups more than the lower—the income tax is in effect made more progressive as the same amount of purchasing power is represented by higher nominal incomes to which unchanged rates of progression are applied—yet social security benefits and relief payments are usually adjusted only with great delay, and often incompletely, and therefore a loss is inflicted upon the recipients. This lag in relief payments and social security benefits, especially the former, is in part due to a regrouping of political forces which takes place as a very consequence of raising mass welfare: In the nineteenth century and the early twentieth century, the vast majority of the population consisted of groups whose income was so low as to expose them to a constant danger of being thrown into pauperism by illness, unemployment or incapacitating accidents; consequently, as the masses received the vote, legislative majorities could easily be found for an expansive welfare policy. Today, however, the destitute and those who because of their weak economic position are in danger of becoming destitute are a minority, and it is often difficult to educate the majority to the need for interpreting broadly enough its obligations toward the actual or potential indigents. The regularly employed worker receiving a normal union wage, who owns a comfortable home and is protected by a union welfare fund is not always willing to pay increased taxes to care for those who have fallen victim to the hazards of modern industrial life without being sheltered by powerful organizations.

Non-Economic Group Differentiation

The reduction of inequalities in power and prestige has gone even further in the United States than the reduction of money income differentials. This statement seems to contradict the findings of research that have shown Americans to be status seekers and which have described the hierarchical structure of American society and especially of American business enterprise. Many of the facts reported by these researchers are indisputable, but to judge them in proper perspective it is necessary to keep some other facts in mind. First, in a society with strong equalitarian trends, social distinction is hard to achieve and relatively rare, and just for these reasons, particularly desirable. Although social equality remains part of the American creed, almost every citizen as an individual tries to obtain some prestige and stand out from the crowd. This is often expressed as, "we are all equal, but everybody wants to be a little more equal than the rest." Status seeking, therefore, offers evidence for the strongly equalitarian character of American society rather than against it: Where the gap between social groups is so wide that there is no hope for the individual to rise from bottom to top in one generation, the tendency for the average person is to resign himself to his status.

Second, one might note that in daylight even a strong electric bulb is not very noticeable, while at night, with all other lights extinguished, even a burning match shines brightly. Likewise, in a society in which social differences mean relatively little, remaining differences stand out more clearly than in a strongly stratified society. This is especially true if social equality is a widely accepted ideal and social differences are conspicuous as inconsistencies between ideals and actual conditions.

Third, not much is proved by the belief of the upper groups that a wide social gulf separates them from the lower. Social distinctions are important only when recognized as valid by the lower prestige groups. As long as the "good families" know only themselves that they are "good," the social preference scale is not much more than a toy with which a limited group likes to play. Even if Mr. Smith, who lives in the elegant hills section of his town, is determined to refuse his daughter's hand in marriage to any boy from the wrong side of the tracks, this attitude, though perhaps breaking a few young hearts, has no wider significance as long as the people from the wrong side consider Mr. Smith's refusal unjustified, and not what one might expect. In the United States, the lower economic stratum, though not entirely repudiating the dividing lines within society, regards them as valid only as long as they remain essentially a surface phenomenon; when they threaten to become a vital matter, they are regarded as unacceptable, or "un-American." Class distinctions, therefore, have a tendency to remain a pastime of those who consider themselves privileged.

Many factors have contributed to this effect. The equalitarian tradition with which the United States was born is one of them; the near-universality of American secondary education is another. Since these are special American characteristics, it might seem that they do not permit any conclusions as to the general trends in advanced capitalism. But any examination of European developments shows that, in this respect as in many others, Europe is getting Americanized. Supported by a now firmly entrenched tradition of political equality, the belief in the illegitimacy of social class distinction has been growing fairly rapidly since the end of World War II. Broadening of secondary and higher education is making slow but steady progress; thus the line between the gentleman and the non-gentleman, which so long had been marked in Europe by one's having attended a *Gymnasium* or *lycée*, is gradually being obliterated. The historical causes of the equalitarian trend in Europe and America are in part somewhat different; the effects are becoming more and more similar.

The Chance to Move Upward

What about social mobility? The difficulties of measuring mobility are very great. Some of them result from the inadequacy of data and from the crudeness of the categories with which the statistician has to work. Although it is possible to investigate the correlation between the occupation group of the father and that of the children in a representative population sample, it is difficult to define the occupation on both sides with sufficient accuracy: How great is the variety of social conditions, for example, that is covered by the concept of a farmer. But even if these problems are handled with methods that give meaningful results, what is being measured is not social mobility but social motion, not the chances of the lowly to move upward but the frequency with which they do move upward, which is obviously a joint result of the opportunities offered and the willingness to make use of them. If the chances have improved but the will to use them has weakened, a proper diagnosis would be that social mobility has increased, whereas no proportionate social motion can be observed.

Although there is little that statistics can teach us in this matter, general observation points to the conclusion that this is the actual situation. In all advanced capitalistic countries social handicaps have lost much of their importance. Secondary and higher education have become more accessible;

adult education facilities are offered to those who, because of weak cultural traditions in their families or for accidental reasons, have missed educational opportunities in normal school age. The growing anonymity of business has made personal connections less effective. But the incentives to make the necessary sacrifices in terms of money, time and effort have also become weaker. Since the manual worker can have a nice, well equipped home, an annual vacation and a car, the motivations for improving his standard of living by qualifying for higher jobs seem less urgent than they did before the good things and creature comforts of life were commonly available to workers. In the United States, widespread complaints about low motivation of high school students bear witness to the frequency of this attitude. To be sure, many individuals starting at the bottom of the social ladder still feel strong incentives to rise: Aside from the remaining financial rewards, there is the wish for greater power and prestige and the desire for cultural self-improvement. Although these motives are widespread, in countries with a high and rapidly increasing popular standard of living, their frequency does not seem great enough to justify the expectation that actual social motion will keep pace with social mobility.

It must also be taken into consideration that scholastic requirements, even if established for screening students according to ability without any social bias, do not have the same significance for those from the lower and the upper strata of society. Apart from whether the limitations of natural endowment affect the screening of students from the lower stratum, at least a slower start in intellectual development is usual for a child whose parents have had small exposure to the cultural achievements of the age, as compared with a youngster who grows up in an environment of art, literature and love of learning. Again, the effort which a culturally deprived child is likely to make depends partly on the premiums which society puts on education; and these are smaller when the popular standard of living is high and when the character of society shows already pronounced egalitarian traits, than when the general level of living is low and social differences very pronounced.

The different effects of educational requirements on different social groups have a particularly important bearing on future trends. Social handicaps are almost certain to be reduced, but educational requirements may well become more rigorous, at least for any kind of higher education. On the whole, therefore, the capitalist countries are likely to have great social mobility but perhaps no more actual motion across lines than can be observed now, unless automation reverses the trend by destroying a large part of the employment opportunities for manual labor.[8]

[8] The premiums for moving from the manual workers group to that of white collar

The difference between social mobility and social motion has not received the attention it deserves. Statisticians have often assumed that they were measuring social mobility while actually they were measuring social motion. Colin Clark, for example, after finding that of "the sons of French urban and manual clerical workers a higher proportion succeeded in securing 'social promotion' than in the U.S.A." [9] added the sentence: "This may reflect a better educational system in France." The French *lycée* or *collège* is certainly more effective than the American high school in preparing young people for university studies, but it is far less accessible and therefore not as successful in opening the doors to higher positions to children from the lower social groups. Clark would not have been tempted to make his unconvincing explanation if he had considered the possibility that perhaps the American lower income group may not have the same incentives as their opposite numbers in France to push its young people into higher position at considerable sacrifice. Nor would he probably have drawn the conclusion that "the degree of hereditary stratification in American life is somewhat larger than supposed." [10] "Hereditary stratification" implies that there are rigid boundaries which can be surpassed only with great difficulties, and to say that stratification is greater means that the difficulties are larger than generally assumed; but what Clark's figures measure is not these difficulties but the frequency with which they are overcome, and therefore the combined effect of the degree of difficulty and the force of the push.[11]

---

workers have shown a secular decline, but the penalties of remaining entirely unskilled have increased: The declining numbers of unskilled jobs reduce the employment prospects of those who failed to acquire any qualification for somewhat more demanding jobs. As bulldozers requiring skilled operators take over the ditch-digging, it becomes harder to make a living as a pick-and-shovel man.

[9] Colin Clark, *The Conditions of Economic Progress,* 3rd ed., London and New York: The Macmillan Company, 1957, p. 554.

[10] *Loc. cit.* p. 547. As Clark himself mentions, the samples used are too small for safe conclusions. Moreover, the investigations from which the samples are taken reflect conditions before World War II, and the equalitarian trend has become more pronounced in the post war period. On both grounds, there are doubts whether the data support Clark's tentative conclusions even with regard to social motion, but whether they do or not, they are no adequate basis for judgments on social mobility, in the sense of opportunity to move. Nor is this opportunity clearly distinguished from actual motion across class lines in the otherwise penetrating study by Seymour Lipset and Reinhard Bendix, *Social Mobility in Industrial Society,* Berkeley and Los Angeles. University of California Press, 1959. These authors, however, stress the importance of the widespread belief by Americans that there are great opportunities to rise on the social ladder (although the existence of this belief is treated in the study as a plausible hypothesis rather than a proven truth, see p. 112). It may well be that this "myth" has more reality than would appear from analyses which have merely checked the frequency with which this opportunity is used.

[11] The assumption that weaker impulses to upward motion are responsible for what Clark calls "hereditary stratification" in the United States is supported by Clark's finding that downward mobility in the United States is relatively great—greater at least than in

The actual motion across social group lines has its own importance. In the first place it broadens the basis of selection for the positions of special responsibility. Whether a gifted young person is prevented by insurmountable obstacles of social origin from becoming a leading scholar, a business leader or high government official, or whether he is not enough interested in developing and utilizing his faculties to overcome barriers of only moderate height, in any event society is deprived of the services of a potentially highly competent man or woman. Secondly, motion across group lines is the most striking evidence of social mobility: Where people of humble origin actually get into leading positions in relatively large numbers, nobody can doubt that it can be done. But these merits of actual motion must not obscure the fact that the most important thing is not its occurrence but its possibility, not the rise itself but the chance to rise if there is sufficiently strong interest in making the effort.

Although the acquisition of skills is the most important way to rise on the social ladder, capitalism as well as any other society knows different means—even aside from illegitimate ones—for the same purpose. Without even attending high school, a man may attain well paid positions of great power and prestige in labor unions or other vocational organizations; and a worker, a farmer, a businessman without much formal education may be elected a legislator. Whether these opportunities are increasing, decreasing or showing a pronounced trend in the advanced capitalistic countries is doubtful, because there are two counteracting forces. On the one hand, service in vocational organizations and probably even in political office is getting more professionalized, which involves educational requirements not previously applied; therefore a smaller percentage of such positions is now attainable without advanced schooling. On the other hand, the absolute number of positions in vocational organizations is undoubtedly on the increase, because countervailing power requires that more and more special-interest groups organize. The increase in absolute numbers may well compensate, or more than compensate, for the decline in percentages of those positions which can serve as channels of social advancement for people who have missed their chances of formal education.

Britain, where "sons of proprietors, farmers, managers and professional men show much less probability of becoming manual workers than do their American counterparts" (*op. cit.* p. 553). This would hardly be possible if in the United States fathers were to make as strong an effort to keep their sons from dropping down to a lower group as they do in Britain and probably in all older countries; and where the impulse to prevent a downward movement is weaker, it seems reasonable to expect the same for the achievement of an upward movement.

The Right of Inheritance

For ages equalitarians have complained that there is a way of achieving high income, prestige and power that has nothing to do with skills and service: Inheritance. Although this institution is not peculiar to capitalism, the general rule that everybody is permitted to transmit his possessions to his progeny distinguishes capitalism from communism, under which the same institution exists only in traces, and capitalism from socialism as described by some writers in the past. In the attacks upon the right of inheritance, frequent use has been made of the image of the idle rich, permitted to consume a large part of the social product for no better reason than that their ancestors—often by foul unscrupulous means—were able to accumulate much wealth. The defenders of the right of inheritance countered in the main by two arguments: First, that the desire to provide for one's children was one of the most powerful incentives to productive effort, and therefore socially useful; and that only a class freed through inherited wealth from the necessity of earning a living could devote itself sufficiently to cultural pursuits and thus was a prerequisite of the progress of civilization.

Today, attack and defense strike us as largely irrelevant to the facts of our time. The idle rich are neither numerically important nor an influential group today; they are neither a heavy burden to carry for contemporary society nor does modern civilization depend on their existence. As late as the 1930's, it is true, even so perceptive a writer as John Maynard Keynes could speak of the prospective "euthanasia of the *rentier*," but this just shows how strong is the temptation to argue from the point of view of an age that already belongs to the past: Even in the 1930's the person of working age who, instead of seeking gainful employment, lived on dividends and interest was not an important figure any more. On the other hand, there is little to support the assumption that in a society such as ours, where efficiency in work brings important rewards from higher income to higher prestige, a substantial slackening of effort would follow if people were deprived of the expectation that their labor might benefit their children. General education, shortening of working hours and availability of inexpensive media through which thought and art can be disseminated, have made this age one of mass culture; whatever may be the weaknesses of that culture, they could under no circumstances be remedied by a privileged group out of contact with the basic experiences of contemporary life, of which work is an essential element.

The group that used to live on inheritance is almost extinct for a variety of reasons. Taxation and inflation are reducing inheritable fortunes, but even where these remain large in absolute figures, the social advantages which they can convey have lost in relative significance; for wealth itself is no longer as important a source of income as it was. The rise of labor incomes, absolutely and in comparison with other income categories, has pushed property income, especially income received without expenditure of the owner's labor, into a much less significant position. This change is shown in Table 5. Moreover, the rise of labor incomes has reduced the availability of personal services which is an almost indispensable condition for the enjoyment of high income in idleness. Perhaps the most important causes were cultural: Non-participation in mankind's labors was disapproved; the need to reconcile public opinion with the existence of oversized fortunes made it advisable to use them up in large part in a manner beneficial to the public, instead of transmitting them, unreduced, to the next generation.

Although recent developments have reduced the weight of the arguments on both sides of the controversy, it seems that the position of the critics of inheritance has been weakened more than that of the defenders. Even if the institution is necessary neither to assure sufficient effort nor for the advancement of culture, it is still true that people feel unhappy if they cannot do much for their children beyond their own death; this is an excellent reason to permit them to transmit their wealth if no great social harm is done. To force the surviving playboy-heirs into useful work is desirable, but it cannot justify the frustration of the desires of many working parents

TABLE 5

PER CENT DISTRIBUTION OF NATIONAL INCOME

	Wages & Sal.	Entrepreneurial Income	Dividends	Interest	Rent
1899-1908	59.5	23.8	5.3	5.1	6.4
1939-1948	69.6	18.4	3.5	4.5	4.0

Source: *Historical Statistics of the United States* (1960 ed., p. 141).
For explanations, see *Historical Statistics*, p. 136.

to give their employed children some advantage by leaving them savings, a farm or a business. Moreover, not all the idle rich owe their privileges to inherited wealth; some may find themselves in this favored position by high income earned during a limited period, after which the accumulated money may be lavishly spent. There is certainly a case for progressive inheritance taxes, which limit the possibilities of a luxurious existence without personal effort, but a case can hardly be made for the abolition of the right of inheritance, since it no longer creates major social evils.

CHAPTER 8

WAGE LABOR

The Peculiarities of the Labor Market and the Case for Unionization

THE LABOR MARKET differs in several respects from the market of most other commodities. The over-all supply of labor does not depend on the decisions of any producer, acting under the influence of the market price, but is dependent on the increase of population. Furthermore, in the absence of organization, one side of the labor market, the worker, is normally under much greater pressure to close an employment agreement than the management side: A worker must sell his ability to work to satisfy his vital daily needs and cannot stop selling it for any length of time without sliding into misery, whereas for the employer only a minor advantage is at stake in the hiring of one worker out of dozens, hundreds or thousands. Only in periods of pronounced labor shortage does this inherent disadvantage disappear, as long as the wage bargain is carried on individually: one worker with one employer. Normally the disadvantage can be made to disappear only by collective bargaining, by confronting the employer with a choice of either paying a wage which labor considers equitable, or not obtaining any labor supply. Collective bargaining is the primary purpose of unions.

The imbalance just described is one reason why the presuppositions of perfect competition almost never exist on the labor market. To be sure, there may sometimes be a sector of the labor market in which there is a large number of employers, each of them hiring approximately the same number of workers, and of course there are by necessity even greater numbers on the labor side. Thus one condition of perfect competition, that of a multitude of sellers and buyers with none of them large enough to dominate the market, may be satisfied, although even this is often not the case, because employment may be concentrated in a few enterprises. But perfect competition requires more than the satisfaction of the numbers criterion. Economic theorists usually mention as other criteria, perfect and therefore equal knowledge of the state of the market on the part of all buyers and sellers and no more than a negligible amount of friction—meaning cost, risk and delay—in shifting demand from one seller to the other and supply from one buyer to the other.[1] The absence of unequal pressure to conclude the contract may not be explicitly mentioned, but such inequality is obviously analogous to unequal knowledge of market conditions: Whether a worker is unable to defend his interests as effectively as his employer for lack of knowledge of alternative opportunities to sell his services, or because of an urgent necessity to obtain immediate compensation for these services with no comparable urgency on the employer's side, makes no difference in effect.

There are other reasons which, as a rule, preclude the existence of perfect competition on the labor market. For instance, to change employers, the worker often has to move from one place to the other, or at least to accept higher costs of transportation and greater time loss for the daily trip from residence to working place; this constitutes an important friction. Moreover, the concept of a perfectly competitive market is applicable only where supply can be reduced by a decline in the price; on the labor market, this is often not true: Labor is among the few commodities of which a higher price frequently lowers the supply, and a lower one increases it. If the hourly wage is low, the worker may prefer a long working day; if the wage rate rises, he may insist that the hours be shortened. A working class woman may feel that she can afford to stay home when her husband is making good money; when his wage rate is low, the wife will have to go to work. This means that the employer can get a more ample supply of labor by bringing the wage down, and that a union can shrink the labor supply by forcing the wage up.

Thus there is little chance that under a system of individual labor contracts the wage will be at the level of the perfectly competitive market; usually, unionization of labor will be needed to bring the wage up to the level that corresponds to perfect competition. Although a labor union is formed by collusion of sellers of labor and therefore has the outward marks

[1] See, for example: Frank H. Knight, *Risk, Uncertainty, and Profit,* Boston and New York: Houghton-Mifflin Company, 1921, pp. 76 ff. The absence of emotional or irrational preference of some sellers for a particular buyer or vice versa is also often listed explicitly, but this point is covered by the required absence of friction impeding transfer of supply and demand, if the concept of such friction is broadly interpreted.

of a monopoly, it is not certain that the union will achieve a monopoly price; there may be a case of countervailing power, which just restores the balance of the market. But there is no assurance either that this will be the situation. A union may raise the price to a level which can be maintained only if some workers remain unemployed or if all workers work fewer hours than they would individually be willing to do just at that wage; such a price of labor has to be regarded as a monopoly price by any acceptable definition. This is not to say that such a price is necessarily unjustified; quite often the supply, if unrestricted, would have been so great as to bring the wage down to an amount with which a life of health and decent standards was not possible. Under such circumstances, justice and humanity require that labor be permitted and encouraged to secure a monopoly gain in reducing its own supply by agreement. This effect is accomplished if workers form a union which decides that the wage should have a defined level, even if this means that some workers will not have employment all the time, or that nobody will work longer than forty hours a week, although quite a few workers would be willing to work forty-five or fifty hours if the matter were left to their own discretion.[2] Legislators and courts of law have therefore generally—though not without a long struggle—granted labor the right to organize, even where this required an exemption from anti-monopoly laws.

But until 1918, and in some capitalistic countries even later, the influence of unions on the wage level was substantial only in some industries. The spottiness of union successes was not only due to employers' resistance and an often unsympathetic attitude of courts but also to some inherent handicaps of the union position which could be overcome only after more effective techniques of organization and strategy in labor conflicts had been developed. Since for every employer there are hundreds or thousands of workers, the formation of unions requires the organization of multitudes, which is a task very different from achieving an understanding among a limited number of firms. Whereas the leader or secretary of an employers organization can rely largely on rational arguments, the union leader has to take emotional factors into account to a much greater extent, and since the problems of strategy in collective bargaining call for rational solutions, labor is still under a handicap, unless it can gain a compensating advantage from another source.

When labor unions were first established, a compensating advantage

[2] For the same reason that a monopolistic seller can have a higher total revenue by selling a smaller output at a higher price than a larger output at a lower price, can labor as a whole earn more at a higher wage with some unemployment than at a lower wage with full employment.

was found in the existence of a core of organized workers who regarded their unions not only as a vehicle of personal material advancement, but as a great cause for which they were willing to make sacrifices, not necessarily expecting a proportionate return in dollars and cents. In most countries of Europe this attitude was caused by the influence of the socialist movement, which taught the workers to look upon their organizations as one of the means to achieve an economic system based on human brotherhood. But even in the United States, where socialist influences were less strong, the workers still regarded their unions not as a device which they would use just as long as it yielded to them personally a gain outweighing the cost: One only has to scan the speeches and writings of Samuel Gompers to see that even in business unionism there was more than business, that he regarded the cause of labor as part of a struggle for a better society—better for all men. The presence in a movement of a group which is prepared to support the organization without insisting on a proportionate personal gain is a great source of strength, and the employers had no comparable group in their own organizations.

This advantage of labor, however, has been declining. Even in Europe, labor unionism is now less of a cause and more of a business proposition, and this is even more true of the United States. This development was promoted by the very successes of labor. As unionism expanded it came to include many workers whose natural conservatism or other intellectual or emotional propensities made them less willing to accept the belief in the cause of labor as a supra-personal good. Even more important was the growing belief in the ranks of labor that a basic, deliberate change in the economic system, such as the Socialists and many semi-Socialists had envisaged, could not produce gains proportionate with the risks of such social reconstruction. Through this trend, important causes of internal ideological strife have been eliminated from capitalist society, but the labor unions have lost an element of coherence. Mechanical safeguards were consequently substituted for ideological ties.

The most important of these mechanical safeguards is the closed shop or union shop, which originated much earlier but has acquired new significance in the course of the last decades. The essence of this institution is the obligation of an employer not to hire workers who do not belong to or are not willing to enter the union. The closed shop, which requires the acquisition of union membership before employment, has been outlawed in the United States by the Taft-Hartley Act, but the union shop, which permits the hiring of unorganized workers if they join the union within a specified period, is the rule in large American industries and exists also in other capitalist countries.

The exclusion of workers who refuse to join a labor union has often been attacked as an infringement of personal liberty. Is there any merit in this argument? Obviously a union shop agreement forces the worker to enter into another transaction as a condition to the validity of his own labor contract. In a capitalistic economy, however, it is not unusual that one transaction is made dependent on another. If a real estate developer constructs a dam to secure the water supply for the people who bought homes or lots from him, and refuses to sell water to others, hardly anyone will regard this pressure as an infringement on personal liberty. The more that organization of labor has the aspect of a business matter, the less can there be any objection in principle to the union shop.

Unionization, however, is still somewhat more than a business proposition. It may be a matter of conviction for a worker not to join a union, but he cannot act on this conviction unless he seeks one of the occupations that have no union shop—and at least in the field of manual labor these are usually not the ones in which labor is well compensated. Undeniably, this arrangement involves a restriction of personal freedom; undeniably also, this is only one of many respects in which personal freedom in our society cannot be completely protected because any attempt to do so would be self-defeating. In many communities, a storekeeper will hurt his business if he voices political ideas which are contrary to strongly held preferences of his customers. A junior executive wishing to be promoted or a young lawyer in need of clients would be unwise to oppose the prevailing sentiment of the business community; a doctor will rarely be able to count on the cooperation of his colleagues in professional matters if he advocates compulsory public health insurance. From the democratic point of view, toleration of these conditions can be defended only by the argument that their suppression would create a situation of even greater lack of freedom, because of the controls required. A roughly analogous argument provides a defense of the union shop: Its abolition would endanger the existence of unions, and because unions are indispensable to the freedom of a large number of wage earners, a law prohibiting union shops would be likely to increase rather than reduce the infringement on freedom in society.

The Case for Restraints

SAFEGUARDS FOR INTRA-UNION DEMOCRACY

Union policies are now of great importance for the welfare of the individual worker, especially where his livelihood depends on membership in the union. It is fundamental justice that the internal affairs of the union be settled in a democratic manner, and especially that every member be free to oppose any leader or candidate for leadership without endangering his own standing in the union. In many unions this is assured. There are, however, distressing exceptions. They become possible because the ability to achieve improvement in working conditions through negotiation with employers and sincere devotion to this task is not necessarily incompatible with ruthlessness and even dishonesty in dealing with opponents in the union. Many union members who in their own actions follow high standards of morality are willing to condone despotism or shady dealings on the part of their leaders as long as these leaders "bring home the bacon" of valuable concessions from employers. Internal correctives and checks have therefore not always proved effective against misuses in the operation of unions, and the demand for external correctives, by way of legal restrictions and state supervision, have become widespread. But practically all unions are opposed to such provisions, in the conviction that anything that detracts from the autonomy of the union might be used to frustrate its policies in the struggle with employers. To the degree that these fears can be allayed, progress in eliminating the abuses may become possible.

POLITICAL STRIKES

Aside from anti-democratic practices within unions, external union policies also may lead to conflicts between union goals and the values of a free society. In the past, unions have sometimes tried to coerce governments and legislatures into actions which the majority of voters did not approve. Any extreme case of this sort would be easy to judge: If labor unions, by a general strike, tried to force a democratically elected parliament to enact a law that does not concern labor relations nor endanger the existence of unions or their ability to perform their functions, no defense of such union action could be offered from a democratic point of view. The attempt to impose the will of a minority upon the majority by economic strangulation is no less illegitimate than to do so by force of arms.

But aside from some communist strike calls for purely political purposes, most of them without substantial effect, a clear-cut case of this sort has hardly ever occurred. The few political strikes of the pre-1914 period—for instance the general strikes in Belgium in 1892 and 1913, in Russia in 1905—were not directed against a democratically elected parliament, but were called to wrest from plutocratic or autocratic powers the decision to create democratic institutions; similarly, the German general strike of 1920 was called in defense of a democratic constitution against army leaders who had temporarily usurped power. Some of these actions were necessary for the progress or protection of democracy, in other instances less extreme measures might perhaps have achieved the same purpose at less heavy sacrifice for the community and for the workers themselves; in any event, however, from a democratic point of view it is impossible to deny the workers a fundamental right to use economic weapons in a struggle for democracy.

More difficult to judge is the kind of situation which gave rise to the British general strike of 1926. The cause of this conflict was the unwillingness of the British Government to continue subsidies for the coal mines and the unwillingness of the coal miners to accept a reduction in wages or a lengthening of the hours, which the discontinuation of the subsidies would have necessitated under the then existing system of mine ownership and operation. When the coal miners were locked out, the other unions called a general strike as an act of solidarity. The general strike was a failure, and afterward the Conservatives in control of the British government treated it as an illegitimate attempt to coerce parliament and were—at least at first—supported by public opinion which had been antagonized by the economic losses resulting from union action. But democracy as we understand it is not based on the assumption that a democratically elected legislature has an unlimited right to interfere with economic or other interests of individuals.[3]

A code of democratic ethics defining where legitimate defense of economic interests ends and obstruction of the majority will begins has not yet been written. Only three statements can safely be made about this problem: First, there must be some point beyond which an individual or a group is not obliged to cooperate even with a democratically elected government or

[3] It did not occur to the British government to accuse the mine owners of attempting to put the parliament under undue pressure when they shut down the mines instead of operating them at a loss, and on this account alone the party in power could not be accused of a biased attitude: In a capitalistic economy, the entrepreneur must have a right to discontinue his business if he sees no prospect of profits. It might be argued, however, that the action of the mine owners, unlike that of the workers, was not pointed against the state; they did not demand a continuation of subsidies, probably did not even want it, although they would have had no business reason to discontinue operations if the subsidies had not been stopped; they wanted the conditions of employment to be changed in their favor so as to make unsubsidized mining again profitable. Should it then be regarded as legitimate for employers or workers to bring the economy to a standstill if they do so in the pursuit of the goal of making ends meet without the assistance of the government, but as illegitimate if they demand such assistance? Whether that distinction could be justified in principle, is doubtful; that it would be impracticable, is certain. Any cessation of work in major industries is a concern of the government; it is therefore inevitable that the government negotiate with the parties involved about the conditions for resumption of work; and in the course of such negotiations it is usually inevitable that demands be addressed to the government. Whether a stoppage of work which cannot be profitably continued is a condemnable act of political extortion or a legitimate defense of economic interests can therefore not be made dependent on whether demands are explicitly addressed to the government since such demands, as a rule, are implied in the situation.

legislature in measures which would violate the vital economic interests of this individual or group; second, this right to economic self-defense can apply only to the most fundamental economic conditions of an individual's life and does not justify resistance to majority will merely to avoid inconvenience or obstruct the gradual transformation of society—which by its very gradualness will leave the individual time to adjust to the new framework in which he must live; third, if business has a right to refuse cooperation, labor must enjoy a similar right. If entrepreneurs have a right to go out of business whenever, because of public policy, they see no prospect of continued profits, labor must be permitted to lay down its tools when circumstances justify it, although the grievances have been created by public policy.

It would be futile to argue that nobody denies the right of the individual worker to leave his job, and that only the legitimacy of concerted action by organized labor is at stake. The individual worker is often helpless; since he can effectively negotiate only through his union, it is the union that must decide whether conditions are unfavorable enough to justify cessation of work. American legislation has taken the great step—in 1935, through the National Labor Relations Act—to turn labor's right to organize from a purely negative right—not an illegal kind of action—into a positive right—an action with which nobody can interfere without violating the law. The law implies that the workers have as much right to use their collective decisions for the defense of their interests as property owners have to use property rights for the defense of theirs. The law does not give labor the right to unrestrained concerted action, just as the property owner has no right to use his property for any conceivable purpose; nor does the law draw a clear line between the legitimate and illegitimate use of organization power; rather, much is left to explicatory rules which will have to be established in the light of future experience. But the principle is clear: Just as inalienable rights of the individual may be infringed upon by economic power and may have to be defended by political power, so political power may infringe on inalienable rights which may then be defended by economic action, individually or collectively.

GOVERNMENT ARBITRATION OF LABOR DISPUTES?

Although the question of the legitimate use of union power for resisting political infringements is of great fundamental importance, the issue has become practical only in exceptional situations. Far greater is the immediate practical importance of the question of whether unions—and employers' organizations—may use their power without any limits in the pursuit of their normal functions, influencing the content of labor contracts. There is little reason to raise this question as long as the disputes over conditions of work are too limited in their scope to cause serious distress to the public by the means which parties employ and to influence the general level of prices and employment by their outcome. Today, however, a steel strike, coal strike, a strike in railroad or airplane transportation, may seriously affect the welfare of the community, and the same applies to a lockout. Moreover, the wage levels which may result from the industrial dispute may either be so high as to cause unemployment, because part of the labor force cannot be profitably employed—unless government adds to consumers' purchasing power by creating additional money; or the level may be too low to enable the workers as consumers to spend as much as required by full employment.

For these reasons, several countries have experimented with compulsory arbitration of labor disputes. A government agency, operating as a sort of tribunal, can arbitrate a conflict, preventing the losses which a strike or lockout would impose on the economy; if the agency can obtain enough information, it might conceivably set the wage at a level more likely to serve the common welfare than the level that would result from the fortuitous processes of industrial showdowns. The use which dictatorships have made of this device has caused it to be unpopular in most countries of the West; yet actually, such democratic countries as Australia and New Zealand were the real pioneers in this field, and the labor movement of these countries gave compulsory arbitration strong support. The role of compulsory arbitration in dictatorships, however, is by no means the only reason, and probably not the main one, why interest in compulsory arbitration has declined. To have the position of a court of law, an arbitration board would need a law in which it could find guidance: It is not enough to say that the decision of the board should set conditions consistent with the common welfare and social justice, unless rules are established in which these concepts are so spelled out as to be applicable to an individual case. It may not be impossible to establish such rules, but it is a job that has not yet been seriously undertaken. To calculate the wage optimal from the point of view of the community, it would be necessary to have a full view of the operation of the economy not only at the moment of the award, but also in the period during which the award will be in force. It is doubtful whether this condition can be satisfied in an unplanned economy.

The urge to continue experiments with compulsory arbitration in the period after the Second World War would have been stronger if employers and unions in Western countries had not, on the whole, shown a remarkable ability to avoid industrial warfare through compromise. The few spectacular episodes in which the U.S. economy and those of other countries was temporarily paralyzed by strikes should not blind us to the innumerable settlements that have been reached without work stoppages. The psychological origins of these peaceful tendencies are not entirely clear; it would therefore be rash to prophesy the duration of these trends. It is safe to forecast, however, that as long as unions and employers manage to settle their conflicts of interest with no greater number of major stoppages than the last decade has known, few, if any, pragmatic-minded statesman will assume the task of organizing a compulsory arbitration system.

Labor unions are an indispensable element in the capitalistic system as it exists today. At the same time their presence, like any organized economic power, in a market economy raises problems for which no neat solutions have been found. With some of these problems we may have to live permanently; others may eventually be settled by organizational devices, perhaps by some which are still unknown, perhaps by others which are already being discussed but with which we have so far hoped to dispense. The problems of unionism in the capitalist order provide a particularly impressive object lesson that no economic system operates like a piece of precision machinery, within which all processes are entirely compatible with one another. Unresolved tensions are inevitable in any kind of society; good statesmanship utilizes such tensions to achieve progress without letting them become a source of grave danger.

The Employer as Commander

In the nineteenth century, the employer was supposed to be "master of the house." For a long time, most economists and sociologists failed to realize the contradiction between the demand for political equality and acquiescence in the workers' subjection to the will of the boss. One of the reasons was the veil of voluntarism which was thrown over labor relations. Did the worker not conclude the labor contract out of his free will, and wasn't this contract dissoluble on short notice? Only a few observers realized that for the majority of workers the freedom to leave the job had only limited significance even when jobs were not scarce, because of the frequent difficulty in moving from one plant to another, and because the subjection of the worker to the employer's will was a universal condition of industry. Of course, where conditions were sub-average, the worker could, with some luck, better himself by moving elsewhere, but he could not escape the condition of complete dependence on another man's orders during the working day. If such dependence is wrong in the sphere of government, why should it be right in industry?

Even now, the implications of a democratic philosophy of government for industrial life are not always fully realized. Of course, the employer cannot put an employee in prison; he cannot use physical force to make his will prevail. Also, the aspects of his employee's life which he has any interest in regulating are fewer than those which are regulated by the state. These limitations, however, merely constitute a difference in degree—important, even vital, but not important enough to justify exclusive concentration of safeguarding efforts on the freedom of modern man as a citizen and neglect of the need for safeguarding man's freedom as a worker. Job "law" can be more important to the worker than many state laws. The length of the working day, for instance, originally stipulated by unilateral decision of management, has a much greater influence on the worker's life than many an article in the civil or penal code. The threat of dismissal for disrespect to a foreman can in effect be a more severe sanction than short imprisonment which the state law provides as punishment for, say, small theft. If it is true that the exercise of state power must be limited by the participation of the governed and by rules of due process, then it is certainly desirable to establish similar rules within the area of occupational life.

Even if this truth is well understood, the question remains of whether democratic safeguards can have a place in the organization of a factory. Work discipline is a requirement of industrial efficiency. As long as we want the results of modern production methods, we have to accept their requirements. The worker cannot be his own master as an independent craftsman once was, and therefore an element of command will always be part of life in a factory or an office.

But great progress has been made in developing safeguards against the misuse of the employer's commanding power, without detracting significantly from work efficiency. In most sectors of Western large-scale industry, a framework for these safeguards is established by collective agreement, and these provisions are implemented by elaborate procedures for negotiating grievances. Seniority rules, also protected by collective agreement and supported by habits of thinking which have become widespread in the present generation, limit the employer's right of dismissal and thereby blunt the edge of the sanction with which shop "law" can be enforced. Probably present-day capitalism has gone as far in this direction as is possible without serious impairment of productivity.

Industrial operations are not the only aspect of modern society that makes use of command as an integrating principle. Aside from the obvious example of the army and the equally obvious example of the relationship between the citizen and the organs of justice and public safety, there is the hierarchy of public administration: The subordinate may be protected by civil service rules and by access to courts in the event that he feels seriously wronged by orders of his superiors, but he remains under compulsion to follow orders within wide limits. Absolute freedom is no more compatible with life in society than absolute equality, absolute justice, absolute efficiency or any other absolutes.

CHAPTER 9

CAPITALISM AND ECONOMIC DYNAMICS

The Growth Problem

THE CHOICE BETWEEN CONSUMPTION AND INVESTMENT

A TON OF STEEL used to make kitchenware cannot be used to make machines for the production of more kitchenware next year; an electrician who spends an hour servicing a television set cannot in the same hour repair a motor in a factory producing television sets. At any given moment, in innumerable situations, every economy is faced with the question of how much of its resources should be devoted to present consumption and how much to future consumption, via the production of producer goods.

Wisely chosen investments are productive. This truth means that by using labor and materials for the production of producer goods instead of for the production of consumer goods, we shall have more consumer goods in the end. Much of the essence of technological progress is contained in this statement; when primitive man first spent time on making tools instead of applying his hand directly to wood or skins to make vessels or garments, he produced more and better vessels and garments in the end. When nineteenth-century man learned to use the hammer, the file and the lathe to make machine tools to make needles, spoons and locks, instead of manufacturing these directly with his manual tools, he found that he could get more and (usually) better needles, spoons and locks. Productivity was further greatly increased when machines themselves became products of machines. Thus we have learned that we can improve our standard of living by using "roundabout ways" of production.[1]

[1] This concept was created by Eugen von Böhm-Bawerk, an Austrian economist living around the turn of the century. In his book, *Positive Theory of Capital* (tr. William

Just because this possibility exists in almost innumerable cases, it can be exploited only to a limited extent. If we were to undertake all investment which would yield us more than does direct production, we would deplete the consumers' goods industries of resources. Consequently it is necessary to develop a standard of selection among investment projects: How much more than direct production must an investment project yield to justify the undertaking?

Corresponding to the social need for protection of present consumption against claims of the future, there is an individual time preference in the mind of every person. The roots of this time preference are fairly complex, but its general occurrence can be understood from one simple fact: the uncertainty and limited duration of the human life. Who would not prefer to be able to buy a house now rather than twenty years from now? It is true that most of us have interests extending beyond our own lifetime, because we want our children and our grandchildren to be happy, but even this interest grows weaker with the distance from the present: Few of us permit the fate of our remote progeny to have any great influence on present action. Since we prefer to obtain goods—at least durable goods—now rather than later, we also prefer to obtain sums of money with which we can purchase such goods now rather than later, and usually we will consent to the deferred payment of a sum of money due to us now only if the payment is increased, by means of interest. On the other hand, we do not wish to be without resources in our old age; and since our ability to earn money usually ceases earlier than our life, we wish to make some provisions for the future. Moreover, we also want to provide for a rainy day, for unforeseen contingencies. Therefore, we save and would presumably do so even if we could not receive interest on our savings. But without interest, we would probably not lend money, except in the form of demand deposits, because having money readily available is always preferable to having it invested for a fixed period: We may need funds in an emergency or we may be able to use them for a favorable purchase. Interest is required to compensate us for the chance that either of the two possibilities might materialize. One of its functions is to operate as a premium for not holding cash.

In a capitalist economy, entrepreneurs who wish to take advantage of investment opportunities are bidding for temporary use of the funds which individual savers have accumulated, offering to pay interest from the yield of

---

Smart, New York: Stechert, 1930) he has given a complete and lucid explanation of time preference and its problems. Since valid objections to this theory do not affect the fundamentals, and since few if any contemporary textbooks of economics do full justice to the questions which Böhm-Bawerk posited, the reader may wish to go back to the original.

their investments. (This is the basic form of credit; there are many secondary forms, from consumer credit to mortgages on homes.) In this way a market rate of interest is established. Aside from its significance for individual savers and individual borrowers, it satisfies the social need for a barrier to protect resources for the satisfaction of present consumption from being depleted for the sake of the future.

A NOTE ON TERMINOLOGY AND ARRANGEMENT OF CONCEPTS

The student of economics who has been taught the theory of interest in the language which has become customary since John Maynard Keynes and his disciples rewrote that part of economic analysis, may find it hard to understand how the propositions formulated here are related to those which he has found in his textbook on general economics. The difference, however, is essentially one of terminology, in part merely one of a different emphasis on terms and concepts, and not primarily a difference of substance.[2] Present-day interest theory has not discarded the concept of time preference—although it uses the term less frequently than it was used before—but has merely enriched our knowledge of the reasons for time preference and its determinants. In particular, the preference for keeping funds readily available (liquidity preference), whose significance for the explanation of interest was first fully elucidated by Keynes, is one of the causes of time preference; therefore it would be a mistake to think of a liquidity preference theory of interest as an alternative to a time preference theory. Nor does the recognition that liquidity preference is only one of the reasons why people generally prefer presently available money to money available in the future contradict perhaps the most important policy conclusion from the Keynesian theory: that by satisfying the public's liquidity preference sufficiently through money creation, the government can bring down the rate of interest, and that this is highly desirable in a situation of underemployment. Contemporary theoreticians rarely speak of the

[2] This is not to say that all the details of the Keynesian theory or the most far-reaching Keynesian propositions are compatible with the position taken here; nor have all these theorems been incorporated into the body of doctrine generally accepted by present-day economists. For instance, Keynes' opposition to the "loanable funds theory of interest" —i.e. his aversion to describing the market on which the rate of interest is determined as formed by the supply and demand for loans—is not shared by the majority of contemporary economists. See on this issue, for example, Bernard Haley, "Value and Distribution," in Howard Ellis (ed.), *A Survey of Contemporary Economics,* pp. 40 ff; for a particularly lucid exposition of the Keynesian position see A. P. Lerner, "Interest Theory—Supply and Demand for Loans or Supply and Demand for Cash" in *Review of Economic Statistics,* May 1944, reprinted in Seymour E. Harris (ed.), *The New Economics,* New York: Alfred A. Knopf, 1947, pp. 655 ff.

brevity and insecurity of human life as a cause of time preference, but the existence and importance of this cause has never been disproved—and how could it be disproved? But since the influence of the limitation of the human life on time preference for goods and money is a constant, or very nearly so, and not easy to alter by public policy—in contrast to the effects of liquidity preference[3]—many policy problems in a capitalist system can be analyzed fairly well without reference to the mortality factor.

But a comparative study of economic systems must also deal with communism, a system which bases its policy on an exceedingly low time preference, enforced by a ruling group with a strong sense of historic mission—a sense not shared to the same degree by the citizens. The resulting conflict is one of the central problems of communism. To be sure, the necessity of some time preference can be explained for a communist society, or any other society, by the need for a yardstick of economic selection among the technologically feasible investment projects, which even with the greatest possible restriction of consumption could not all be carried out at the same time. But for the student of communism it is also necessary to understand why this minimum time preference leaves the basic conflict unresolved: that the individual feels aggrieved when he is granted just enough leeway for consumption to keep him effective as a part of the machinery of expansion but not enough to enjoy much of the achievements of technology in his own brief lifespan, and that he is not consoled by thinking of the great benefits which his forced sacrifice will bring to future generations. In other words, the student must be reminded that mortal men can never have the same interest in the future as they have in the present, and that—at least when we judge as individuals—we are unwilling to make any great sacrifices for distant future.

Comparing economic systems requires an investigation of the extent to

[3] Public policy may only indirectly affect the basic determinants of liquidity preference—given the psychic constitution of the individual, these are the probability of emergencies (precautionary motive) and better investment opportunities (speculation motive). But even if these factors are constant, public policy by providing more money, can cause the "liquidity preference schedule"—that is the curve showing how much cash the individual will hold at any particular rate of interest—to shift to the right. In other words, the monetary authorities, although they may not always be able to reduce the risk of emergencies or alter the prospects of more profitable investment possibilities and thus influence the individual's preference for liquid over fixed assets, can bring that preference closer to saturation and thereby cause the individual to be satisfied with a lower rate of interest as a condition for parting with funds in the form of loans.

The assumption that the strength of the speculative and precautionary motives remains constant ignores the probable effect of an increased money supply upon the likelihood of more profitable investment opportunities and emergencies, which would be grossly wrong in a period of unemployment. If these effects are taken into consideration, however, the argument that public policy can influence interest by working on the liquidity preference of the citizens is strengthened.

which phenomena observed in one system also appear in others. The cleavage between the time preference applied in government policy and that of the citizen can never be as drastic in a capitalist society with a democratic constitution as it is under communism. But under capitalism too there is at least a potential conflict of the same kind with regard to public expenditures, taxation and credit policy, since even in a democratic country the policy makers and administrators may have their own sense of mission with a correspondingly lower time preference; the cleavage between the citizen's time preference as an individual and his time preference when judging community matters[4] has even greater significance in a society of the "Western" type because here the citizen has greater influence on the determination of public policy—his time preference as a member of the community has greater relevance than under communism. For the sake of comparison, time preference and its expression in a capitalist and in a socialist society must, as far as possible, be analyzed in the same categories as those applied for the same purpose to communism, and because the terminology and the arrangement of concepts preferred by earlier generations of economists facilitates the application of identical categories, their use in this context seems justified.

THE SOCIALLY OPTIMAL RATE OF INTEREST

Is there any assurance that the market rate of interest will have the magnitude best suited to satisfy the community interest in economic growth?[5] There is a relationship between the determinants of the market

[4] See above p. 23 and below 178 ff.

[5] Many economists—perhaps fewer today than some years ago—discount the importance of the rate of interest on investment decisions. About this tendency in economic thinking, see, for example, James Tobin, "Money Wage Rates and Employment," in Seymour Harris (ed.), *The New Economics*, p. 576; William Fellner, "Employment Theory and Business Cycles," in Howard Ellis (ed.) *A Survey of Contemporary Economics*, pp. 81-82. On public policy, however, this view has had little influence, and in practically all countries the rate of interest is still treated as an effective tool for regulating the allocation of resources as between the present and the future. This writer feels that there is no sufficient evidence to regard this practice as a mistake; he believes that when all forms of credit and indirect as well as direct effects of rate changes are considered, the influence of such changes is indeed important. The text reflects this view.

But if a reader sympathizes with the opinion that sees low efficacy in the rate of interest, he need not on that account disagree with the substance of the propositions; he can satisfy his objections by some minor changes in phrasing. Nobody, however much he emphasizes the role of alterations in the interest rate, will deny that the liberality or illiberality of the banks in granting credit lines or demanding collateral—recommendations of central banks, their reserve requirements and their open market policies, may influence the practices of commercial credit institutions in these matters—will often be more significant to business decisions than the interest rates charged; on the other hand, anyone who questions the importance of the money price of credit will still have to concede that the availability of capital is of major significance for economic expansion.

rate and the socially desirable height of the barrier between production for the present and production for the future. The individual saver's time preference, expressed as the amount of money which he must get in addition to a given sum in order to leave that sum to somebody else for use, indicates also what amount of future commodities, as measured in value, will be regarded by him as equally useful with a given quantity of present commodities, also measured by their value. Assuming given investment opportunities, the average time preference of savers indicates how available resources should be divided between present and future consumption to be in accord with the relative importance that the members of society, when contemplating only individual needs, are attributing to the present and to the future; if the rate of interest equals the prevailing time preference ratio, this division will be achieved. If investment opportunities improve, the same rate of interest would justify too much investment from the point of view of individual consumers, consequently the rate should rise; and it will do just this, because of the higher bids of entrepreneurs who see the prospect of greater profits. The opposite holds true when investment opportunities deteriorate.

Nevertheless, it would be an overstatement to say that the market rate of interest, determined as it is by individual time preferences and investment opportunities, will tend to hold the socially most desirable level. Individual savers, when participating in the formation of the market rate by their demands for interest, weigh the importance which they attribute to the future against the present in their private affairs. When judging as citizens, they attribute a relatively higher importance to the future, because they regard their community and their nation as important beyond the present generation's life expectancy. The collective time preference, therefore, is lower than the individual time preference—meaning the future is discounted less—and the market rate, which is based on individual time preference, tends to cut down investment too much from the point of view of society.

Although only modern economic theory has been able to describe this

---

Therefore, if one does not want to speak of the interest rate as an important regulator of the time pattern of resource allocation, he may simply substitute the expression: terms on which capital is available.

Even the lowest rates will not encourage entrepreneurs to invest capital if they do not expect an adequate net profit in the foreseeable future; similarly, no increase in the rates can in practice be so drastic as to discourage investment substantially if a high wave of optimism affects the expectations of profit. The prospects of profitable product sales, however, are themselves influenced by interest rates and other expressions of credit policy. Cheap mortgages, for instance, will stimulate building, and extensive building activities will create a better market for many goods and services.

difference in precise terms, the phenomenon has always played an important role in public policy. The state has always imposed taxes and other sacrifices upon its citizens for projects which would prove a large part of their usefulness in a future too distant to be of great interest to the citizens as individuals, and the citizens, if called upon to judge the matter as members of the community, have often approved these acts of the government. Even when laissez faire was the most popular creed, governments often financed such long-range improvements as canal or railroad construction, although the return from these projects would not reach the market rate of interest; the usual justification was the argument that the community must provide for its own future.[6]

The magnitude of the margin between the time preference determining public policy and the time preference of the individuals depends to some extent on the political constitution. In an autocracy, the ruler may impose his own time preference as a guide upon state organs. This time preference is often lower than that of the citizens because rulers are often imbued with a stronger sense of historic mission than felt by private individuals, even when acting as citizens. On the other hand, in a democracy the citizens will by their votes prevent a policy which would require excessive present sacrifices for too distant a future: Although their time preference as citizens is lower than that which they apply in their private lives, the two are not without connection. A person who attributes relatively great importance to the future in his private life will usually also attribute to it greater importance in his political decisions than do others, and vice versa. The degree to which a human being discounts the future is an expression of his philosophy, and therefore influenced by acquired beliefs as

[6] The proposition that the state in its projects acts from a lower time preference than indicated by the market rate of interest may, at first glance, seem to contradict the fact that many projects are financed by loans. The borrower finds a particularly great advantage in getting money now, and is willing to pay for this advantage by returning more money later. The borrower, therefore, must have a high time preference—higher at any rate than the lender. How can the fact that the state is a typical borrower and particularly that it borrows funds for great construction projects be reconciled with the contention that it has a low time preference—and particularly that it has a lower time preference than the individual citizens from whom it borrows money for these projects? The answer lies in the significance of the amortization provisions which all these loans contain. The state spreads the cost of construction over a number of years in the relatively near future to secure for the community the advantages of the project for a more distant future without further payment. The low time preference of the state expresses itself in the relatively high valuation of the advantages of the distant future which outweigh the sacrifices of the near future. To be sure, if the state were exclusively guided by its low time preference, it would not borrow at all, but would finance all projects from taxes on a pay-as-you-go basis; but competing interests, especially in avoiding excessive taxation in any given year, call for some spreading of the cost of government expenditures on big projects.

well as by generic personality traits. People holding strong opinions about the future of society will usually have a lower time preference, at least in political decisions, than people whose interests are largely confined to their private affairs. However, a strong sense of family responsibility also tends to lower the time preference, with effects both on private actions and on the attitude toward community problems.

Not only the ordinary citizens, but also the statesmen, administrators and legislators have their own time preferences, determined in each case by character traits and life experience. For basically the same reasons that made the autocrats of former times build for the future in measures excessively onerous for the living generation, the political leaders and the bureaucracy of today sometimes try to put into practice a time preference lower even than the collective time preference of the citizens. It is an important function of democratic government to check this tendency, but how effective is universal suffrage and dependency of the government on the governed in this respect? The factor that most weakens that effectiveness is the highly technical character of many of the decisions through which time preference is applied. It takes an expert to realize the meaning of many measures in taxation, central bank practice, public works programs and other policies. The administrator or legislative specialist may not wish to deceive the public about the ratio of present sacrifice to future social benefit implied in a particular proposal, but it is likely that his own time preference will color the picture which he draws for those whom he has to advise, and, moreover, he may lack the skill to reduce the complicated facts to the relatively simple alternatives which the citizens can understand.

Thus even a democratic society is not completely free of the danger that "planners" preferences may prevail over citizens' preferences in regard to the allocation of resources to production for the present and for the future. Sometimes the fear of this danger, dimly felt, produces a swing of votes to the opposite side, and as a consequence badly needed public investments are rejected. Where public improvement projects have to be submitted to popular vote, the taxpayers' sentiment is often so aroused by previous expenditures that the proposal is defeated, although it would have appeared amply justified by the citizens' collective preference if sober judgment had been applied. This tendency has recently been intensified by an unthinking opposition to public expenditures, as Professor Galbraith has rightly pointed out.

In spite of possible defects in the procedure, a democratic constitution limits the degree to which government can deviate from the prevailing individual time preference of its citizens. Other limits follow from the characteristics of a capitalist organization of the economy. In capitalism, there is a ceiling to the part of the national income which the government can collect by way of taxes at any given time, although the height of the ceiling differs widely from one period to another, influenced by changes in psychological and institutional presuppositions: If income is taxed too severely, it impairs entrepreneurs' and professional workers' incentives; if indirect taxes are too heavy, consumption will be too much restricted. If the government resorts to financing improvements by loans, success depends on the willingness of holders of cash to buy government bonds. Ultimately, limitations of taxation also affect financing by loans, because the latter must be serviced by tax revenue.

The government, it is true, can influence the distribution of resources between production for the present and production for the future not only by projects financed through taxes or by borrowing; it has another powerful instrument in monetary policy. Newly created money usually enters circulation through the channels of credit: It may, for instance, be offered as loans by the Central Bank to other banks which will then lend it to their customers. Thus newly created money tends to lower the market rate of interest. The process may also start at the opposite end: A lowering of the rate of interest, which can be effected by modern government either through its influence on the Central Bank or through other instrumentalities, as for instance the Federal Housing Administration in the United States, will encourage greater use of existing borrowing facilities, and thereby more money will be drawn into circulation. A greater amount of money, borrowed at cheaper rates, for the construction of factories and other capital improvements will obviously result in a greater portion of available production factors devoted to the future. This result will be achieved whether the government spends the newly created money on its own projects or permits private entrepreneurs to utilize it for the expansion or construction of plants.

Even without active government intervention, a similar process may lead to a periodical lowering of the barriers which restrict the flow of resources to production for the future. When a mood of optimism rises in the business community—with or without actual improvement in conditions—banks become less strict in their lending requirements and more willing to reduce their liquidity, and industrialists will become more eager to borrow for expansion projects, while merchants will wish to borrow more in order to finance greater inventories. Thus the volume of credit will grow through a simultaneous increase in supply and demand. Credit is supplied largely in the form of accounts on which borrowers can draw: In this way, private banks too can create money—checking accounts. The government, to be sure, and especially the Central Bank, can limit this money creation by a variety of means, even by the mere refusal to supply a sufficient amount of paper money; although checking accounts serve as money and for many purposes are the most important type, they remain redeemable in legal tender, and for some portion of the amount of checking money circulating, payment in notes or coins will actually be demanded. Up to a point, the private banks can obtain these notes or coins by withdrawing some of their deposits from the Central Bank, but under the American system and that prevailing in many other capitalist countries, the latter can stop the process by increasing the "reserve requirement," i.e. requiring banks to maintain higher deposits with the Central Bank for any given sum which their customers hold on checking account.

Any given act of money creation, whether originating in the government or in the banking system, can no more than temporarily lower the barriers to production for the future. The newly created money cannot be used for investment projects without adding to consumers' incomes, most of all to wages, and will therefore eventually raise consumers' demand, which will result in additional production of consumers' goods; the flow of resources to consumers' goods industries will therefore also be increased, compensating wholly or in part for the original increase of the flow to producer goods industries. As soon as the increase in demand has magnified employment to the point at which some resources are no longer easily procurable, the additional money will create price increases, and finally the funds now available to entrepreneurs for expansion projects will buy no more labor and materials than before the addition to the money supply. A new addition would be needed to maintain a distribution of resources favorable to production for the future, but a sequence of such doses of additional money will bring about a continuous and probably self-accelerating decline in the value of money, involving the economy in the undesirable effects of inflation, which governments, as a rule, cannot afford to accept for any considerable length of time, unless this inflationary phenomenon remains in a low order of magnitude.

This review of the fiscal and monetary means by which a government can give more emphasis to production for the future within a capitalistic society has dealt very summarily with a host of problems on which economic theoreticians have conducted extensive and sophisticated debates. In this context, however, only one result of these discussions is essential: that in a capitalistic economy the government has only a limited possibility to impose its own lower time preference on the decision makers in the economic units. This would be true even if the political constitution were absolutist, oligarchic or plutocratic; democracy adds further restrictions, and therefore a capitalistic system with a democratic constitution will not show as wide a margin as some other systems between the time preference of individuals in their private affairs and the lower time preference which actually determines the distribution of resources between the present and the future in those parts of the economy in which the government has decisive influence.

This feature of capitalism combined with democracy means that the present generation will be protected from the kind of economic despotism which prevailed in Soviet Russia during the First Five Year plan (and with increasing modifications continues to this day) when producer goods industries were built up by reducing consumption to the very minimum required for physical existence and sometimes below that minimum. On the other hand, the limited capacity of government in a capitalist society to lower the barrier between production for the present and production for the future also means that in such a society it will, as a rule, not be possible to achieve the same rates of growth which may be possible where government is less restricted economically and politically. This statement does not mean that in a comparison between two countries, one with a capitalistic and democratic system and the other with a near-omnipotent government, the latter will always show the higher growth rate. The political constitution and the economic system are not the only factors influencing the distribution of resources between the present and the future. Of the other factors, the intensity of the community spirit, determining the interest of the citizens in the future of their local and national community, has already been mentioned. In a capitalistic and democratic society, special conditions might lead to such an intense community spirit as to favor a channeling of a very large part of the available resources to production for the future. If the United States, for example, were to suffer large-scale devastation through a nuclear war, it is conceivable that public opinion would support rapid reconstruction on the basis of a minimum standard of living so strongly as to result in a high rate of re-growth even with the techniques available under capitalism and democracy. Moreover, the achievable rate of growth depends on the standard of living that has already been reached. Although modern totalitarianism has proved unhappily efficient in squeezing resources for growth out of consumers living on a near-starvation level, even the most ruthless dictator must leave his people enough to maintain a modicum of physical strength for work. Inversely, on a level at which life is relatively easy, even the limitations of growth which are inherent in a capitalist economy will not be as stringent as on a lower level—for instance high-income taxation will have less undesirable effects—and popular resistance will be reduced if the sacrifices for the sake of growth involve amenities rather than necessities. On the other hand, there are reasons to assume that the rate of growth will always slow down after the initial phases. The complexities of the problem will be further discussed in the section on Communism; here no more is intended than a warning against the expectation that a capitalist and democratic society will always have a lower rate of growth than, for instance, a communist society.

The Business Cycle: Possible Causes

An economy without growth would not experience any wide fluctuations of economic activity. There might still be changes in consumers' preferences, and consequently some industries might lose their markets and others might expand, but the changes from full employment of nearly all resources to partial unemployment of most resources and back—the phenomenon we call the business cycle—would not be known. Since capitalism was the first economic system in which rapid economic growth occurred, the business cycle is widely regarded as peculiar to a capitalist economy. Aside from this historical experience there are some inherent reasons why a system in which the functions of government are relatively restricted may be more susceptible to the impact of unstabilizing forces than systems which rely more on conscious steering of the economy; at the present stage of analysis, however, these reasons are not cogent enough to justify the contention that the change from prosperity can occur only in capitalism.

Of all the aspects of modern economic life, none has attracted the attention of analysts more than the business cycle, and to no other problem of economics have more persistent efforts been devoted than to the question of what causes the fluctuations of economic activity. Although within the framework of this book there is neither need nor space for a discussion of the refinements of business-cycle theory, a few statements about the nature of the business cycle must be made.

1. The problem of the business cycle is primarily the problem of the origin of depressions. Since even in the most affluent society man's wants are not completely satisfied, why should there be periodically an inadequacy of demand, forcing upon the producers a restriction of supply, thus causing unemployment and "misery in the midst of plenty?" Since no com-

modity can be produced without the creation of incomes fully equal to its value—production costs consist of wages, interest and ground rent, and the difference between cost and product value is profit—how can incomes prove periodically insufficient to buy the whole social product?

2. Obviously, a depression can occur only if some people decide not to spend all the incomes they have received, thus reducing demand and thereby destroying other people's jobs. There are fluctuations in the propensity to consume: At times, people's eagerness to purchase commodities declines; they may decide to save a larger part of their incomes by increasing their bank accounts or by paying debts. Increase in saving, however, does not necessarily lead to a depression. If the savings can be put at the disposal of others via the credit mechanism—if the banks lend the deposits or the creditors re-lend the sums received as repayment to producers or to the government—these borrowers will spend more than their current incomes, and the total amount of spending will be maintained. There is some probability, to be sure, that the reduction of consumers' demand for commodities, which according to the assumption has started the process, will depress producers' profit expectations and will induce them not to borrow or to invest. But this need not be so, since businessmen's expectations of returns from investment are not entirely governed by their experience with present sales; technological innovations—to mention only one possibly relevant factor—may cause heavy business investment in spite of presently declining product sales. On the other hand, businessmen's willingness to borrow and to invest may decline without a reduction of consumers' spending: Entrepreneurs may feel that sales, though satisfactory now, will decline in the future; or, if they are producers of capital goods, they may calculate that they can maintain their present volume of operations only if purchases by ultimate consumers are not only maintained but growing, a point which will be discussed a little later. In any event, a depression will not occur unless the credit mechanism fails to transfer the portions of income not spent by their recipients to others willing to spend them.

3. During rising prosperity, the credit mechanism fulfills this function; there are enough borrowers, and lenders are willing to put out large enough amounts. What can produce a change in this situation? It would be conceivable that such a change might be merely due to a wave of pessimism, causing potential borrowers to doubt that they could profitably use any money and making lenders distrustful of the borrowers' future ability to return the money with reasonable interest. Few present-day business cycle theorists, however, assume such pessimistic expectations to

play a great role in the origin of depressions, unless there are objective developments which give support to pessimism. Such developments would necessarily have to be disproportions developing during prosperity. Some economic magnitudes must have grown too large in relation to other economic magnitudes.

4. In most depressions, producer goods industries have declined before consumer goods industries, and the decline has been more marked in the former than in the latter. This can easily be understood from the fact that no businessman will add to his equipment unless he expects consumption not only to hold its own but to rise. Suppose, for instance, that the amount of clothing bought has been increasing for a while because formerly unemployed workers have found jobs, received normal incomes and therefore have bought more suits and dresses; this will induce the clothing manufacturers to order additional machinery to satisfy the rising demand. Now assume everybody has obtained a job, and that wages, although maintaining their level, are not likely to rise, or at least not rise rapidly; this means that the clothing manufacturers cannot expect further, or at least not rapid, increases, of their sales. They will therefore reduce their orders for machinery to the level required for replacement, or to a level only little higher. Consequently, a critical employment situation will arise in the machine industry, and for similar reasons in other producer goods industries. As the producer goods industries are forced to discharge workers, the latter will lose much of their spending power, and as a consequence consumer goods industries will suffer also: A general depression will be the result. For reasons which can be understood from the history of the business cycle debate, this cause of instability is sometimes called the "acceleration principle operating in reverse." [7]

A similar situation can exist in the durable consumer goods industry. Today even in the United States, the use of dishwashers is far from general. As more and more families acquire a dishwasher, industry will be geared to a demand determined by expansion of the use of the device plus current replacement. Finally, a point will be reached at which every

[7] During the Great Depression of the early 1930's, it was correctly argued that any substantial increase in consumers' incomes through government spending would lead to additional spending by business for equipment, and that business spending, coming on top of increased consumer spending, would accelerate the recovery process. The phenomenon has therefore been called the acceleration principle. It can easily be seen that the process described in the text is the same relationship between the level of consumption and employment in the producer goods industries, only looked upon from a different position in the business cycle. A given increase in consumption requires a given employment in the production of equipment; and the level of employment in equipment industries will be maintained only as long as there is a sufficient increase in consumption and will fall off when consumption merely holds its own.

family that has use for a dishwasher and a sufficient income will possess one; from that time on, the demand will only be equal to replacement.[8]

5. A complex modern economy needs reserve stocks of materials and semi-finished and finished goods, to keep up the supply if for any accidental reasons production is reduced. Under capitalism, however, the size of these inventories is not determined by technical considerations alone, but also by expectations about price movements. When it appears likely to a businessman that prices will go up, he will enlarge his inventories beyond the amount necessary to equalize the flow of goods to the consumer; if the prospect is for low prices, he will reduce the inventories to a point below "normal." If businessmen were always right in their expectations, the changes in inventories would smooth the course of economic processes: The possibility of selling from large inventories at a time when prices soar, owing to an increase in demand relative to supply, will put a rein on this upward movement of prices, and will cushion the strain on resources; when prices are low and are expected to rise, the orders intended to fill up the inventories will reduce unemployment. But businessmen are not always right, and repeatedly in recent years inventories were oversized. The observation that customers' purchases were smaller than expected and therefore could be supplied from stock without new dealers' orders to producers has sometimes led to unemployment in the producing plants and thus may have caused the primary disturbance from which a depression originated. After the depression or recession had lasted for some time, the recovery effect on employment was often delayed because the first increases in demand were met by reduction of inventories, rather than by new orders to producers. On balance, it is at least doubtful whether inventories have been a stabilizing factor in modern capitalism.

6. A substantial part of current unemployment is due to the replacement of men by machines. This process, which of course has been going on at least since the industrial revolution, has not in the past been closely related to the business cycle; at least, nobody has demonstrated that technological unemployment, by depriving workers in some industries of the incomes to which they have been accustomed, has ever caused a sufficient decline in total consumers' spending to create so much idleness in other industries as to make economic paralysis general. Such a development, however, seems conceivable, and its failure to occur in the past is by no means an assurance that it will not occur in the future. Perhaps this is a

[8] This statement must be modified for a situation in which the number of households is increasing, as it will—very rapidly—in the United States during the next few decades, when children of the high birth-rate years (and later their children) reach marriageable age.

question of magnitude: Although the displacement of labor through the technological advances of previous periods did not kindle true depressions, the probably greater displacement through automation in the future may do so. In any event, however, such technological unemployment as we have is an element of economic instability and detracts from the size of the social product.

The classical economists and their disciples tried to allay the concern over technological unemployment with the reasoning that it meant a shift of labor from one industry to the other rather than a reduction in the total demand for labor. Technological improvement, they argued, must increase real incomes, by resulting either in higher profits or in lower product prices, or in a mixture of both. Consequently, entrepreneurs or their customers or both will have free purchasing power which they will spend on commodities and services of some kind, and thus compensatory employment will be created, making up for the loss of jobs in the industry in which the innovation was first introduced. Indeed, there may not be a final loss of jobs even in that industry: Technological improvement may lead to a drastic price reduction and demand may be sufficiently elastic to increase sales to the point where even with the increased labor productivity all workers are needed to turn out enough product.

Obviously, this compensation theory has been correct to the extent that up to now technological innovations have not permanently reduced the number of jobs; otherwise it would be impossible that after two centuries of progressive mechanization the number of employed is many times greater than it was before, and that present-day society, whatever may be the difficulties caused for many categories of workers, finds it less hard to absorb the technologically unemployed than British society at the end of the eighteenth century and in some early decades of the nineteenth century found it to absorb the labor displaced in agriculture through the enclosures. Over this splendid record it is easy to forget not only the suffering of a multitude of workers who had been trained for the old jobs but could not perform the new ones, like the coachmen of the age of horse-drawn stages who could not become railroad engineers or repairmen in railroad shops, but also the loss in potential social product which occurs when in this way manpower remains unused. Only recently has the possibility of retraining and relocating manpower displaced by technological innovations received serious attention, and few countries have so far made a systematic effort in this direction.

7. Common to all these explanations of the actual or possible origins of depressions is the view that an inadequacy of demand is a direct re-

sult of physical or psychological developments. This assumption could not easily be fitted into the picture which the classical economists and their successors had formed of the basic economic processes; therefore some of the latter offered a different explanation; they saw the cause of the collapse of prosperity in a shortage of capital. Great investments have been begun in the boom period; for their completion, they would require new borrowing; but the capital market is not able to provide the required funds at conditions which are consistent with expected profits; therefore, projects are abandoned or completed with losses, and no new projects are begun. This creates unemployment in producer goods industries, and, as a secondary effect, decline in consumption, which then spreads the decrease in employment to consumer goods industries and to the whole economy.

In trying to give the concept of capital shortage a more precise meaning, some of the proponents of this theory have tried to go behind the monetary phenomena and show that under the influence of monetary policies or developments incongruities in the physical structure of the economy have developed when a prosperity collapses. The most convincing of these efforts explain that collapse is caused by an overstrain on the physical resources of society, brought about by too ambitious projects of expansion without a sufficient curtailment of consumption. If the part of society's resources which is devoted to the construction of production facilities is too large to be compatible with the standards of consumption which consumers have the income to maintain, then it will become impossible to complete these projects: The projects will become unprofitable not only because interest rates will become too high, but also because prices of material and labor will be bid up too much through competing producers' and consumers' demand, and unemployment, first in producer goods industries and then in the whole economy, will follow.

At first sight the capital shortage theory seems irreconcilable with the other explanations of the business cycle, which may be broadly described as underconsumption theories. The latter assume that in the boom period consumption fails to grow fast enough to make full employment of all resources possible; the former assumes that there is too much consumption at the height of the boom to permit the continuation of expansion projects which is a presupposition for further full employment. Actually, however, it is conceivable that sometimes the first impulse pushing the economy over the brink comes from a slackening of consumers' demand, and at other times this slackening may be a secondary phenomenon following a collapse of "real" investment as a consequence of an overstrain on resources. Moreover, since resources are not interchangeable without limit, it may be that some types of resource, important for some industries, become scarce while other types are still abundant; such a situation may result in the impossibility for some industries to expand further and in unemployment among the suppliers of their equipment, while in other industries there may still be unused resources which could be put to use if only consumers' demand were greater. Overstrain and insufficiency of demand may then combine their effects to produce general depression.[9]

THE PROBLEM OF PREVENTION

Critics of capitalism have often cited the fluctuations from booms to depressions as evidence of the "anarchic" character of the capitalist order. The rational core in this polemic characterization is the absence in capitalism of a central agency anticipating maladjustments before they occur, and then applying adequate means for their prevention. Although such an arrangement obviously would involve increased responsibilities of government and would therefore seem undesirable to advocates of laissez faire, it is not incompatible with a private enterprise economy; nor is there good reason to assume that the preventives, when discovered, could not be effectively applied. If the government, for instance, could foresee the point from which the demand for a particular commodity would cease to grow, because even in the event of a further rise in incomes consumers' demand were likely to shift to another type of good, the government could warn the suppliers of equipment to adjust in time to the slackening of demand for their output. Such warning would probably be well heeded because no businessman likes to produce merchandise for which there is no sufficient demand; if necessary, however, the government could reinforce the warning by restrictions on credit for the equipment producers, or by appropriate measures of tax or premium policy. The government could also facilitate the transfer of labor from the field affected by the prospective slump to other fields through grants for retraining and relocation. The government might even search for alternative ways of using the same factories and the same type of labor for other production tasks and thus minimize the adverse effects. Analagous measures might be taken if it is foreseen that investment projects are too ambitious to be completed with available resources. If, on the other hand, an overall inadequacy of demand were foreseen, the government could apply a large array of measures, from easing of credit to deficit spending, to forestall a serious maladjust-

[9] The book by Gottfried von Haberler, *Prosperity and Depression* (Geneva: League of Nations, 1939) offers an excellent survey of the main types of theory together with a "synthetic exposition relating to the nature and causes of the business cycle."

ment. Whatever the particular nature of the disproportion, the chance to prevent it from becoming a source of depression could be improved by the foresight of an agency that would anticipate the course of economic events, discover maladjustments which are bound to develop and then apply such preventives as are already in the arsenal of government even in a capitalistic society.

All efforts actually undertaken to free capitalism from the incubus of depressions involve some attempts at perfecting economic foresight. In the United States, the concern over unemployment at the end of World War II led to the establishment of an agency specifically charged with such foresight, the Council of Economic Advisers. In other countries, institutes of business cycle research maintaining contact with the government fulfill the same function. All these efforts, however, have so far failed to produce a sufficiently comprehensive apparatus of economic foresight to guide the economy in a process of economic growth not interrupted by depressions.

One reason for that failure is technical. In order to recognize the present tendencies which will later interrupt the smooth process of growth it is necessary to have a dynamic model of the economy, just as many physical hazards can best be foreseen by building a model of the structures in which they may occur, and then observing how this model is affected by experimentally created strains simulating the forces to which real structures will be exposed. That the economic model will be a "paper" model, consisting of equations, diagrams, matrixes and other symbols or combinations of symbols, rather than of wooden blocks, cement, metal and the like, makes no difference with regard to the function. Only in relatively recent years have economic analysis and the special branch of economics called econometrics reached a stage of development at which the building of models, realistic enough to be useful, became possible. Considerable effort is still necessary to raise the science of model building to the level at which it can form the basis of fully reliable forecasts.[10]

[10] Even with the highest conceivable development of econometrics, forecasts can be fully reliable only with regard to changes from intrinsic causes. Extraneous causes, such as natural disasters or wars, can of course not be anticipated through a technique of economic foresight. Yet an apparatus of economic foresight can still be useful even in the event of such emergencies, because a realistic model of the economy as it would develop if undisturbed may facilitate a forecast of the impact of disturbing forces, provided some plausible hypothesis can be made about the kind and magnitude of the latter. A model of the American economy as it will develop in the absence of extraneous disturbances between now and 1970 will also make it easier to estimate how much that development would be set back if sometime during that period the whole West Coast were to suffer earthquakes of the severity of the 1906 San Francisco disaster, or if consecutive Mississippi floods of the greatest magnitude known were to coincide with an

But the state of economic science is not alone responsible for the failure of the capitalist countries to organize economic foresight. Although economists have been working on the task all the time, though not all of them with a full recognition of the possible practical applications, their efforts have not received the amount of support from public and other institutional funds which the goal of removing the greatest flaw from the capitalist system would have justified. The most intense desire to equip the government with such an apparatus of foresight has been shown by the countries under socialist influence; from another angle, communism approached the problem, but was for a long time—and to some extent still is—handicaped by dogmatism. More about the technique of economic foresight will therefore be found in the sections on socialism and communism.

The failure of capitalist countries to forge adequate tools of economic foresight is to a considerable extent a consequence of the fear that the existence of such machinery may be dangerous to liberty. An apparatus of foresight which tries to determine the conditions of desirable economic development and supplies the basis for a policy that makes action in harmony with such conditions profitable, is something very different from coercive planning which imposes the planners' preferences on the economy; yet the two have very often been confused. Besides, a small core of real hazard is contained in the construction of the machinery of organized foresight: Like every accomplishment of human ingenuity it may fall into the wrong hands and then serve the wrong purposes. If a tyrant is permitted to seize power, he will use any device of economic foresight which already exists, just as he will use the gun factories to equip his bodyguard and the organization of large-scale business to make the workers dependent on his will.

Moreover, to build an apparatus of economic foresight, though requiring only a fraction of the sums that could be gained by avoiding the losses even of minor recessions, is not cheap in itself. Although the task can be greatly facilitated by disregarding variants of consumption and production patterns which are not quantitatively important enough to affect the total level of economic activity, the most refined methods of calculation would

---

unusual accumulation of hurricanes. So far the forecasting of the impact of extraneous forces has been attempted mostly with regard to nuclear war, as for instance in the works of Herman Kahn. Here, however, it is extremely difficult to decide which hypotheses are appropriate. The widespread doubts about the usefulness of these calculations are not directed against the econometrics used but against the basic military and foreign policy assumptions, some of which seem arbitrary and—to this writer at least—unjustifiedly optimistic.

have to be applied and they are equally expensive in terms of equipment and of trained manpower.

The expenses and—fictitious and real—risks of constructing machinery for the elimination of the business cycle would be more willingly borne if public opinion in the capitalist countries were as deeply impressed with the urgency of the problem now as it was in the 1930's. At that time, a great readiness existed in all nations to try almost any approach which appeared at least half-way promising to end the economic paralysis and forestall its return. The prosperity which followed the Second World War, interrupted as it was only by relatively weak and short recessions, has caused the problem to appear less important and its solution not worth a very high price. Moreover, Keynesian theory, the strongest influence in economics since the middle of the 1930's, has created a widespread conviction that in the event of a slackening of economic activity, no more would be necessary than to assure a greater supply of money, to be offered through deficit financing and that thus there was no need for a complex apparatus of economic foresight to guide anticyclical policy.

No such need, it is true, would exist if the only task of business cycle policy were to remedy depressions of the same order of magnitude as that of the early 1930's; by pumping money into circulation when all or most of the industries have succumbed to paralysis, economic life can be revived. Milder depressions, too, can be effectively combatted by an easy money policy, but as a rule not without reducing the value of money: If only some industries show substantial unemployment of men and equipment, the addition of purchasing power to the existing circulation will increase effective demand not only where output of goods can be increased without higher unit costs, but also in markets in which output can either not be raised at all in the short run, or can be raised only at higher unit cost. In either event, a rise of the price level is inevitable. Therefore, the techniques of business cycle control in full use in capitalistic societies—as distinguished from foresight techniques which are still at an embryonic stage—can achieve either an avoidance only of very bad depressions combined with a reasonably stable value of money, or a close approach to permanent full utilization of resources with a constant decline of the value of money in a tempo which makes this decline an element of considerable importance in the life of one generation. If stable money *and* reasonably full employment are desired, new techniques are necessary, which will probably require a selective application of preventive measures, i.e. their concentration upon those industries which are likely to become foci of depressive tendencies, instead of random infusion of new money at the first signs of a slack. Obviously, a selective policy requires anticipation of the points at which such tendencies as the "acceleration principle in reverse," technological unemployment or other causes of job shortage are likely to strike. The beginnings of systematic foresight are therefore likely to be developed with greater energy in the future than they have been in the past.

This expectation seems particularly plausible because of the concern over economic growth in all capitalistic countries. According to many indications, the disappointing tempo of the growth of industrial production in the United States during the last decade has been due less to a lack of willingness and capacity to create more production facilities than to the deficient utilization of such facilities as existed or were built. These two phenomena, to be sure, cannot be cleanly separated, for the creation of new productive capacity is slowed down whenever there is doubt as to the prospects of such capacity being used: Who would want to install new machines when there is a serious chance that much of the time they will stand idle for lack of orders? Yet even this psychological brake seems not to have prevented a rise of industrial capacity faster than that of industrial production.

Some of the reasons why we should be concerned about the growth of industrial production have been explained in the discussion of values and goals. At present, however, the most potent reason why industrial growth appears of vital importance is the competition of the West with the Soviet states. Industrial growth determines the future breadth of the foundation on which military power and such foreign policy actions as foreign aid must be built. Consequently, if our potential enemy overtakes us in industrial development, we may become politically and militarily defenseless. The Sputnik panic in the United States and its various sequels have therefore stimulated efforts to catch up with the Soviet Union in industrial growth. It would not be too difficult to raise, for a time, the portion of the national income invested in plant expansion, but is this a reasonable policy unless we have assurance that there will be sufficient demand for the product of these plants? In other words, does not the solution of the problem of industrial growth presuppose a solution of the business cycle problem?

During the 1950's the rapid growth of industrial production in various European countries, especially West Germany, which knew no more about controlling the business cycle than the United States, has proved that deliberate stabilization of demand is not an absolute prerequisite of a rapid increase in output over a number of years. But at the time of this writing it is doubtful how long the European prosperity will last, and under the perhaps less favorable conditions of the future, American rather than West-European experience may be a more reliable guide. The experience of the United States points to the conclusion that without a more effective assurance against recessions, and therefore without an apparatus of economic foresight reaching farther into the future than the devices we are now using, the tempo will not reach the desired speed.

CHAPTER 10

CAPITALISM AND THE SYSTEM OF GOVERNMENT

Social Integration and Group Autonomy

THE MODERN CONCEPT OF CITIZENSHIP

CAPITALISM HAS OPERATED as a great unifier. Already in that early phase of capitalist production when machines were not yet important and manufacturing—in the literal sense of manual production—was largely carried on in cottage industries under the auspices of a merchant-capitalist who supplied the raw materials and brought the products to distant markets, local self-sufficiency began to be destroyed and the nation became economically integrated. As the factory system developed, standardized products were pushed into all parts of the national territory, and purely local business was further reduced. This process has continued into our own time: It has not only revolutionized business but also changed the lives of individuals. The great business concerns, spreading their supermarkets from coast to coast in the United States and becoming common in other industrialized countries; the mail-order houses; the appliance producers selling the same products in every city and town, all have made consumer habits increasingly similar. Large-scale, nationally unified business has brought the same problems to all parts of the country, and these national issues now largely overshadow the local ones; thereby political subdivisions have lost some of their importance. By reaching beyond the boundaries of nation-states, capitalism has also contributed to international integration. To be sure, there have been countercurrents to the unifying effects of capitalism: Often capitalist business, unwilling to tolerate regulation by national law, has fostered localist or sectionalist sentiment to make its opposition effective; against foreign competition, capitalist entrepreneurs have often allied themselves with the forces of political nationalism. Yet on balance, capitalism has helped greatly to lay an economic foundation for national unity and has stimulated a coalescence of national communities into great continental or even inter-continental blocs, if not yet into one world.

Capitalism has been an agent of social as well as area integration, the two developments being closely related to each other. Capitalism broke down the caste system of the feudal era, by making the old positions of privilege economically untenable, and by increasing the opportunities for individuals to rise above the group into which they were born. In more recent times, capitalism has tended to reduce the income and prestige differentials between the upper and lower groups in society. It has also begun to obliterate the distinctions between agricultural and industrial labor: Farming, where it has reached a high level of technological development, has become a capital-intensive business, and a farmer has to know as much about engines, roller-bearings, and electricity as many a machinist. With this growing similarity of work experience in those two categories of economic life so long divided and separated by habits of thinking and feeling as well as by political preferences, national integration takes a further important step forward.

In breaking down the economic foundations of feudalism, capitalism has helped to create the modern concept of citizenship, which replaced the ideas underlying the medieval "state of estates" (*Ständestaat,* corporate state). In the corporate state, the individual normally participated only through his social group. As a peer of the realm, as a minor vassal or a subvassal, as a merchant-patrician or a guildmaster in a town, as a free yeoman or as a dependent peasant, he had defined rights in the community which he had to exercise, as a rule, jointly with other members of the same group. These rights might be almost nil or they might be very great: In any event, they were determined not by any personal characteristics or achievements of the individual but by his status, which was largely hereditary.[1]

[1] Even in the Middle Ages, ways were open to some individuals to break out of their estate. An unfree peasant, for instance, might qualify for armed service under his lord and thereby gradually rise to knighthood; a large part of the continental European aristocracy consists of descendants of such soldiers of originally unfree status (*ministerales, serjeants*). The medieval Church also served as a social ladder to individuals, in spite of the feudalization of the hierarchy, but in this case the advancement was confined to one person and could not be transmitted to another generation. Later, individuals and their families could rise either through talent and education in the service of a monarch or great lord, or through wealth. Examples of the former can be found among the statesmen serving the Tudors (Thomas Cromwell and Burleigh, both originally commoners) and other dynasties in the transitional period from the Middle Ages to the modern age; an example of the caste-breaking power of wealth in the same period were the Fuggers, originally Augsburg craftsmen, who became true merchant-princes and were finally received into the nobility; even more brilliant was the career of the Medici, of similar ori-

In contrast, the citizen of a modern country goes to the polls as an individual, and he has as much legal power as everybody else to influence the political decisions of the community. Likewise, he enjoys immunity from arbitrary arrest and punishment and many other liberties—among them the right of political organization—as a human being and a member of the nation, and not, as was still true of the guarantees of Magna Charta, merely as a member of a privileged group. Legislative representatives elected by the modern citizen are bound, at least in theory, to represent their constituents as citizens and not as members of a particular class. The most dramatic of the events through which this new concept of citizenship emerged was the decision of the French *états généraux*, the representatives of the estates of the realm, in 1789 to meet and vote no longer separately but jointly; this was the birth of modern parliamentarism on the European continent.

A NEW ERA OF VOCATIONAL REPRESENTATION

The modern concept of citizenship, born in the English, American and French revolutions out of a combination of historical forces of which rising capitalism was perhaps the most powerful, has never been lost in the core countries of Western civilization. The atomization of political society, however, which that concept seemed to many of its originators to imply, has proved to be untenable. Not only did political parties emerge, but beginning with the latter part of the nineteenth century, a new network of organizational ties, based on the individual's economic position, developed in close connection with the changes in the structure of industrial life in the same period—the decline of competition through industrial giantism and producers' combinations. There were not only cartels and similar monopolistic organizations, which now began to hem in the individual; of more direct political significance were those associations which were formed to influence legislation. Almost every branch of industry, commerce and agriculture and most of the professions became organized for this purpose. On the labor side, the rising trade unions also took a stand on many legislative issues. Unlike a political party, to which an individual belongs on the basis of his beliefs and which he can, as a rule, leave without incurring more by way of penalty than frowns of disapproval by his former associates,[2] a voca-

---

gin, who finally were regarded as the equals of royalty. However, to acquire a share of political power, these people had to rise above their original estate and to enter a higher one; from the rank into which they were born, they could not have exercised any substantial political power.

[2] The close association of some vocational interests with political parties has created a few cases of which this is, or was, not quite true. Occasionally, a worker not belonging

tional organization is based on an individual's means of livelihood; if membership in the association is a prerequisite for success in this pursuit, as it often is, then he cannot drop out without changing his mode of economic existence. Thus the individual is often bound to the postulates and the strategy of his vocational organization, not unlike the way in which a guild master was bound to the decisions of his guild.

The political fettering of the individual resulting from the rise of vocational organizations is made less stringent by the fact that most vocational organizations are concerned only with limited sectors of public life: the medical associations primarily with health insurance and related problems, the real estate boards with housing legislation, the labor unions with laws regulating conditions of employment, and so on. But positions taken on a special question often have a bearing on broader issues, and vice versa; professional organizations committed to one side of a struggle over a particular proposal will seek support from ideological groups into whose sets of postulates the vocational aims appear to fit. Thus the medical association which wants to fight "socialized medicine" may merge its effort with other "anti-socialist" groups, and where does this leave the physician who happens to be a socialist? Similarly, in many countries—though not in the United States—the labor unions support the Socialist party to give greater weight to union demands in the legislature, and this puts the anti-socialist worker in a precarious position. A real estate agent who believes in racial equality will suffer a conflict of conscience when the local real estate board cooperates with ideological racialists to oppose anti-discriminatory housing laws.

Obviously, the influence of vocational organizations is stronger on some social groups than on others. In many sectors of economic and social life, however, these organizations stand between the state and the citizen, who has no way to avoid that barrier except at a very high price. Thereby the directness of the relationship between the citizen and his government is reduced, though certainly not abolished as it was by the medieval estates. We cannot alter this situation. Vocational organizations have important functions—some have already been discussed in conjunction with countervailing power; others will be discussed below. This illustrates once again that social forms and relationships are not infinitely pliable and that, because we cannot shape them entirely at will, we often have to accept un-

to a socialist or communist party—or to the wrong party in that sector of the political spectrum—might be boycotted by his fellow workers; an East Elbian large estate owner who refused to join the German Conservative party might perhaps have met not only with social but also economic ostracism by his neighbors. Such instances, however, have always been exceptional.

desirable side effects with developments we approve or find necessary. From another point of view, the modification of the modern concept of citizenship by the rise of vocational organization confirms that the absolute realization of any value, carried to its ultimate consequences, would exact a price that nobody wants to pay. This applies to liberty no less than equality, or any other value.

THE MODERN IDEA OF THE CORPORATE STATE

Not all social analysts had some misgivings about the rise of industrial organization. For a time, this rise captured the imagination of various schools of writers to such a degree as to make them believe that vocational organization should again be made the basis of government. The idea that some constitution modeled after the "state of estates" of the late Middle Ages should be substituted for modern parliamentarism had been held here and there ever since the great French Revolution, but only after the First World War did this idea become the creed of fairly broad movements. The Guild Socialists, mainly a British school of thought, believed that organizations of those working in any particular industry should together manage the affairs of that industry, and own its instruments of production, and an association of these new guilds should take care of the common needs, now fulfilled by the state. In Germany, the revolutionary period of 1918-19 saw various proposals to adapt the Russian system of Workers' and Peasants' Councils to the needs of a society which would not, or not immediately, eliminate all the capitalistic institutions; it was thought that in such a society all the affairs of the various branches of production should be administered by producers' representatives—either the workers alone or the workers and employers, depending on the radicalism or moderation of the particular school of thought. In some of these proposals representation of consumers in the organs administering production was also provided. By a sort of super-council or other devices, the organs of vocational representation should also attend to the tasks of public administration.

After the revolutionary flood had ebbed, several anti-democratic groups in Germany revived nineteenth century ideas of the *Ständestaat;* especially effective as the founder of a school devoted to this concept was the Austrian professor, Othmar Spann. When Italian Fascism needed some camouflage of dictatorship, it chose the outward form of the corporate state, although there was of course no real government by "corporations," which would have meant self-government by groups of vocational representation, under Fascism.[3] In the same period, the corporate state was also recom-

[3] On this point cf. Carl Landauer. *European Socialism,* Vol. II, p. 1263 ff. The cor-

mended in authoritative statements of the Catholic Church: In the *Encyclical Quadragesimo Anno,* Pope Pius XI gave it his endorsement, and many Catholic writers expounded this Papal recommendation and elaborated solutions for the various problems which arose in attempts to put the corporate principle into reality.[4] Nor did Fascist Italy remain alone in the use of a corporate constitution as a means to establish the essence of a dictatorship without letting it become clearly visible: Austria under Chancellor Schuschnigg and Portugal under Premier Salazar followed the Italian example; the constitution of Prime Minister Franco's Spain also shows strong influence of corporate ideology.

But in spite of the remnants on the Iberian peninsula, the role of the idea as a major trend in political thinking ended with the collapse of Fascism. This is a remarkable historical phenomenon: The constitutional concept which seemed to be such a strong rival of parliamentary democracy in the 1930's was all but wiped out in the 1940's. The idea of the corporate state took with it into near-oblivion the belief that Fascism had created a peculiar economic system: It became obvious that it represented just one more instance in which a capitalist economy was subjected to a substantial amount of direction by the state in order to make it serve the power interests of the government, following precedents set under the absolute monarchy.

What were the motivations of the movement in favor of the corporate state, aside from the desire of some dictators to camouflage their regimes?

porate state served the Fascists as a camouflage of their dictatorship in the same way as the Soviet system served the Communists: The regime in Russia was no more a government by soviets, i.e. councils of workers and peasants, than the Italian state of the early 1930's was a government by corporations. Because the Soviet system provided for separate representation of workers and peasants, it even had some outward resemblance to a regime of corporations. But whereas Fascism regarded the fundamental differences between urban and rural life, agricultural and industrial work as lasting phenomena, Communism, in the words of the *Communist Manifesto,* believes in "the gradual abolition of the distinction between town and country"; although this remains a vague idea, the Communists clearly assume a gradual assimilation of urban and rural working conditions and therefore the differentiated representation of peasants and industrial workers has never been regarded as more than a temporary expedient; it had been largely obliterated in the Soviet Union by the Constitution of 1936.

[4] Many Catholic writers, especially French authors, have contributed to the concept of the corporate state. Outstanding among this school of thought in the late nineteenth century was de la Tour du Pin (see his collection of essays: *Vers un ordre social chrétien,* Paris: Gabriel Beauchesne, 1929; see also the analysis of his views and activities—and those of many other Catholic authors—in Parker T. Moon, *The Labor Problem and the Social Catholic Movement in France,* New York: Macmillan, 1921, *passim* and Mathew H. Elbow, *French Corporative Theory,* New York: Columbia Univ. Press, 1953 esp. pp. 53 ff.) However, there is no dogma committing Catholics to the support of the corporate state; Pius XI took pains to point out that in the view of the Church, men could freely choose the constitution under which they wished to live as long as it did not violate any fundamental moral or religious law.

First of all, there was the dissatisfaction of the economically privileged with universal suffrage: To the employer of a thousand workers it seemed unnatural that he, whose actions and omissions in the economic sphere were bound to influence the lives of so many people profoundly, should have only as much political influence as any one of his employees. The employer could easily rationalize this as not only an injustice but an unwholesome arrangement. In trying to keep production costs down and profits high enough to increase capital for new investments, was he not acting for the good of society? Since his success in these actions was largely dependent on public policy, should he not be given political influence commensurate with the importance of the interests he was defending? But simply to give the recipients of higher income, or the owners of property above a defined value, some supplemental votes was against the spirit of the age; moreover, from the point of view of those industrial leaders who adopted this line of thought sincerely, such plural voting would not have been satisfactory because it would have blurred the issue. It was not on account of their greater wealth or income, but because of their function in the economic community that they were claiming additional political influence. They sensed the discrepancy between an essentially aristocratic economic system and a democratic system of government, and believed that the resulting tensions had to be relieved at the expense of political democracy.

A corporate constitution would have satisfied these industrialists (and the large landowners, who were often allied with them) because it would have recognized the importance of the economic function as a determinant of political influence and would automatically have given them a much greater voice in the government than they possessed in a parliamentary system under universal and equal suffrage. In drawing up the constitution of a corporate state, with separate legislative chambers for industry, agriculture, the professions, and perhaps others, with or without subdivisions, it always seemed natural to have each of these chambers composed of an equal number of employers' and employees' representatives, perhaps with the addition of consumers' representatives.[5]

The industrial entrepreneurs, however, never lent more than passive

[5] In Italy, the principle of equal representation of employers and employees has prevailed in all corporations. Often, however, representatives of other groups, such as consumers' societies, independent artisans and technicians, were also added. Invariably, the Fascist party was represented in the corporations. Its representatives could, of course, play the often conflicting interests of the rest of the members against each other and in this way get what they wanted, but they did not even need this strategy. All members of the corporations could hold their office only with the approval of the government, which was identical with the leadership of the Fascist party. Therefore there was no chance of any deviation from the party line being adopted by the corporations; they were just tools of Fascist policy.

support to the idea of a corporate state; even in the heyday of this kind of ideology, there was hardly any industrialist who personally advocated a replacement of parliamentary democracy with a regime of corporations. Probably businessmen generally felt that they could only point out the inadequacy of democracy and must leave it to others to work out the alternative. Thus the spokesmen for the corporate state—and its architects where it was realized—were in the main intellectuals. Nevertheless, the assurance that the power of business would support the movement was indispensable for the degree of success it obtained in the depression years.

A second motive in the drive for a corporate state was the belief that in this way society would be freed from the dangers of the class struggle. The "horizontal" division of society, workers versus employers, seems to lose in importance when the layers are split up by "vertical" organization, uniting the workers of each industry with their employers. But this is merely the outward appearance. Solidarity among workers of different industries rests on the solid foundation of such facts as the interdependence of the wage levels in all or most industries and on the common danger that the commanding power of the employer in the industrial process may interfere too much with the worker's life, if not restricted by labor unions and by protective legislation; these facts cannot be deprived of their effectiveness by any outward form of organization. The antagonism between classes certainly needs to be kept in bounds; but this can be done only by emphasizing the common interests which members of all classes have in the coherence and prosperity of society, not by trying to use an even more narrowly sectional interest, that of a particular industry, as a sort of counter-poison against the class struggle concept.

A third motive of the advocates of the corporate state was contained in the idea of industrial self-government. The corporations were not only supposed to act as cells of a body of general legislation, but they were also intended to regulate the affairs of their particular industries, setting rules for management and adjusting labor relations. Many industrialists were attracted by the idea that to the extent that industry needed regulation, this should be undertaken by industry itself. Sometimes such an arrangement was conceived of as self-government of industrial entrepreneurs only, but in the twentieth century it was not difficult to realize that the concept would not have a chance without labor's participation. In this way, industrial self-government would mean an extension of the principle underlying collective bargaining to affairs other than conditions of employment, such as quality control in production, fairness of competition, and perhaps price policy and determination of volume of production.

Even liberal writers have sometimes ignored or underestimated the grave dangers which would result for society, especially for the consumer, if each industry had the right to regulate itself. Such an arrangement implies that the ways in which each industry is conducting its affairs is essentially a matter of concern only to that industry; actually, this is not at all true. The prices that an industry charges for its products and its decisions on the quality of its products affect all consumers of its goods; so do the standards of truthfulness in advertising. Even in labor relations community interests are often at stake: Unsanitary or dangerous conditions in shops, employment of children at too early an age, an excessively long working day are harmful to society and should not be tolerated even if the workers' representatives, for lack of negotiating strength or for other reasons, fail to insist that these evils disappear. Wage policy, a determinant of the price level on the one hand, and of mass purchasing power on the other, is obviously a matter of public concern. In the Fascist corporations, the dangers of industrial self-government to community interests did not materialize to any great extent because the corporations were not really self-governing, but were tools of a despotic state power—which of course meant that they avoided the evils of industrial self-government only to create evils even more grave. But wherever true industrial self-government has been tried in some sectors of the economy of a democratic state—for example in some German industries after 1919—the result was an alliance between entrepreneurs and workers of an industry against the consumers, and even attempts to protect consumers' interests by special representatives have not been successful. It is safe to assume that the code authorities of the National Recovery Act (NRA) in the early New Deal—perhaps the most comprehensive experiment with industrial self-government, only slightly restricted by the supervisory powers of a democratically elected national administration—would have had the same undesirable consequences if their life had not been cut short by the Supreme Court. As will be explained in the section on socialism, the vestiges of industrial self-government found in British and French nationalized industries have produced few desirable results and were therefore abolished or severely reduced. It will also be shown later why the Yugoslav experiment with workers' self-management has a greater chance of success.

While to most of us today the concept of industrial self-government seems unacceptable because it would deprive the representatives of the whole people of power needed to protect the interests of society at large against special interests, some writers and thinkers of past decades have found special virtue in this weakness of the political government. This may be regarded as a fourth motive of the movement for a corporate state. The medieval "state of estates" on the European Continent had been merely a loose confederation of social classes; the nobility, the clergy, the towns, each had to give its consent to any new taxes and to any other measure under the jurisdiction of the estates. The absolute monarchy, by abolishing the rights of the estates, made a great contribution to national unity. Modern democracy stepped into the shoes of the absolute monarchy and used the power of the unified state for the purposes of which the majority of voters approved. But there were always schools of thought which distrusted all centralized state power. Where regionalism seemed to have a chance, these opponents of central government were in favor of far-reaching provincial autonomy or—in federal unions—of a broad definition of the rights of individual states; where this solution seemed impracticable or inadequate, some of these decentralizers hit upon the idea that "social federalism" could be substituted for regional federalism, and the state again turned into a mere confederation of social groups. Perhaps the most consistent thinker along these lines was the German writer, Konstantin Frantz, who lived around the middle of the nineteenth century; similar ideas can be found with some Catholic writers. Since prevailing church doctrine assigns to the state only a subsidiary function in relation to other forms of social organization, the idea of replacing state power by the power of self-government of organized social groups seemed attractive from a Catholic point of view; secularist "anti-staters" followed the same line of thought.

Widespread enthusiasm for the corporate state during the 1930's would be inexplicable without a fifth reason, which combined with all the others: resentment against political parties. In a true corporate state, parties can hardly exist; the groups which are supposed to act together are not united by a common legislative or administrative program or an ideology underlying such a program, but by identity or similarity of the economic position of all its members. The political party, as an institution, has often aroused an antagonism which is not easy to explain; some writers considered it a particular virtue of the corporate state that it would rid public life of the party system.

But whatever the undesirable features of party politics, the arguments for vocational representation as an alternative are unconvincing. Party lines are fluid; people can cross them if they change their convictions, and experience and arguments can effect such a change. Boundaries among vocational organizations are rigid, because not many people can be expected to change their vocation to belong to another political body; the effects of experience and arguments upon the attitude of vocational bodies is limited for this reason alone. Moreover, vocational bodies, although rarely dominated by ideological fanaticism as it may appear in a political party, are susceptible to a virtually even more dangerous kind of extremism in the defense of economic group interests. To illustrate: A candidate running for a party, even one which finds its voters primarily within a particular class, as the British Labour party does, will usually have to win support from other strata as well; thus a Laborite candidate, even when running for office in an industrial town inhabited mainly by workers, will ordinarily try to attract some votes of lower middle class people and of intellectuals, and will therefore be cautious not to commit himself to demands which would please only workers. Passion may overrule this sort of caution, but this happens only on relatively rare occasions. On the other hand, the leader of a vocational organization, a trade union secretary talking to his membership, a farm bureau official talking to farmers, a leader of a medical association talking to doctors, has only to please his own group, and ordinarily he will succeed best if he makes only a minimum of concessions to the interests of other groups. He will not succeed, it is true, if he refuses to negotiate with others about the practical aims of his group because of an ideological commitment, such as to the idea of an unrestricted class struggle; but in defense of practical group demands the spokesman for vocational interests is usually less amenable to compromise than the party politician. If vocational representation were made the basis of government, as it would be in a corporate state, the most futile of all hopes would probably be the expectation of a more moderate attitude of the representatives.

The character of the corporate state has been discussed here somewhat extensively for two reasons. In the first place, in spite of the demise of the idea as an active political force, it may again play a role in debates of the future; although representative democracy is not seriously challenged at the present time in the advanced countries of the non-communist world, and most of the less advanced countries at least profess faith in democracy as their future system, satisfaction with democratic institutions is not so great as to have completely ended the search for alternatives. Second, the illusory character of most of the virtues attributed to the corporate state should not blind us to the significance of the underlying principle, vocational representation and industrial group autonomy. Group solidarity and the resulting organization of groups is an important fact of life in a capitalistic economy; it may often appear preferable to give these groups a definite place in the process of making decisions for the community rather than to leave them in the position of pressure groups, unrecognized by public law. Moreover, it is one of the great difficulties of modern representative democracy that the elected representatives are often forced to deal with matters requiring more specialized knowledge than they can possibly possess. Although the expert is frequently a person with a special stake in the decision and should therefore not be permitted to wield public power without close supervision whenever there is a conflict between his special interests and those of other members of the community, it might often be best to use him as an adviser or even to give him decision-making powers if there are sufficient safeguards. Such safeguards would be impossible if vocational representation were made the principle for the composition of sovereign legislative bodies; this is the fundamental error committed by the enthusiasts for a true corporate state, and it is important to realize the consequences to which the substitution of vocational for geographic representation would lead by analyzing the corporate state concept. On the other hand, it is equally important to study vocational representation and industrial group autonomy in the subsidiary role they play in many democratic countries; this subsidiary role is designed to assure for legislatures and executive bureaus the expert advice of businessmen, farmers and labor leaders in a formalized manner, or to leave technical matters within their sphere to their decision through processes regulated by the legislature.

VOCATIONAL REPRESENTATION WITHIN PARLIAMENTARY DEMOCRACY

Of the larger countries with capitalist or semi-capitalist economies, the one most amply equipped with institutions of vocational representation and industrial self-government is France. The constitution of the Fifth Republic provides in articles 69 to 71 for an Economic and Social Council, consisting of representatives of all vocational groups both in Metropolitan France and in the overseas dependencies and affiliated independent areas. In their majority these representatives are designated by vocational organizations, with a minority of members appointed by the government. The functions of the Council are advisory; "every plan and every bill containing a program of an economic character is to be submitted to the Council for its advice" (Constitution of the Fifth Republic, Art. 70, last sentence).[6]

For France, the concept of an advisory economic council is by no means new. As far back as 1900, Alexandre Millerand as Minister of Commerce

[6] Translated from Maurice Duverger, *La Cinquième Republic*. Paris: Presses Universitaires de France, 1959, p. 315. On the Economic and Social Council, see also Philip M. Williams and Martin Harrison, *De Gaulle's Republic*. London: Longmans Green & Co., 1960, pp. 254 f.

had created a National Council of Labor, consisting of representatives of unions and employers, with regional subdivisions.[7] An Economic Council, similar in composition to that of the De Gaulle constitution, was created in 1924 and taken over by the Fourth French Republic.

The probability seems to be that the Economic and Social Council of the Fifth Republic will acquire greater significance than its predecessors. Economic pressure groups seem to have become better organized in recent years, and their importance relative to that of political parties has grown. Professor Maurice Duverger, a political sociologist in the Faculty of Law and Political Science at Paris, regards as one of the main reasons the "habit of common action" which the corporate organizations of the semi-fascist Vichy regime has firmly implanted in the minds of French businessmen and agriculturists—the workers have had a strong tradition of organization for a long time—and which persists because it serves the interests of the group concerned.[8] The more the economic groups rely on vocational associations, the more they will need a clearinghouse for their postulates presented by the associations, and this will be found in the Economic and Social Council. In a nation as ideology-minded as the French, however, it is improbable that the Council will ever overshadow parliament.

In parliamentary democracies which are closer than France to a purely capitalistic economic system, general bodies of comprehensive vocational representation are no longer to be found,[9] but public bodies of vocational representation for special purposes are frequent and usually possess a considerable latitude of autonomy in administration and in the issuance of regulations within the limits of their tasks. Such representation is very common, for instance, in the field of social insurance. An American official survey says about old age and survivors insurance programs:

> In the majority of countries . . . responsibility for the actual administration of pension programs is entrusted by law to a variety of types of quasi-autonomous institutions or funds. These agencies are generally subject to at least general supervision by a department or ministry of government, but otherwise are largely self-governing. They commonly are managed by a tripartite board composed of

[7] See Carl Landauer, *European Socialism*. Berkeley and Los Angeles: University of California Press, 1960. Vol. I, pp. 328 f. There was an even earlier body, consisting, however, of government appointees.

[8] Duverger, *op. cit.* p. 292.

[9] The outstanding example of this shrinking of the area in which comprehensive vocational representation was combined with parliamentary democracy is the failure of the Federal Republic of Germany to re-create the *Reichswirtschaftsrat* (Federal Economic Council) which had existed under the Weimar Republic. The reasons why it was decided to dispense with this institution would be worth an investigation.

In the regimes representing remnants of Fascism on the Iberian peninsula, comprehensive vocational representation—or at least its outward forms—of course survives.

representatives of insured persons, employers and the government. In some countries, though, the boards are bipartite, with representatives of insured persons and employers only, or of insured persons and the government.[10]

Among the countries with autonomous or semi-autonomous tripartite boards are Belgium, the Netherlands, Italy, Brazil and Argentina; France has a bipartite arrangement; the United States, the United Kingdom and Germany have government-administered programs without formalized vocational representation. The situation in health insurance is similar, but Germany, for example, administers her health insurance through bipartite boards, whereas Argentina's health insurance is government-administered. Only a detailed comparative study could reveal how much of these differences is accidental and how much results from characteristics of public life and governmental institutions in each country.

Another field in which in many capitalist countries—but not in the United States[11]—group representation plays an important role is industrial conciliation and arbitration. It has often been found useful to put the work for peaceful settlement of labor disputes into the hands not only of one arbitrator or conciliator but of a committee, consisting of an equal number of representatives of labor and management, under a chairman, usually a public official. The labor and management members are usually prominent members of unions and employers organizations, respectively, who do not belong to the industry directly involved in a dispute. The mediation effort is expected to be more effective for the reason that there are members of the committee who are completly familiar with the points of view of either of the contesting parties, and yet have no stake in the dispute itself. Such a system was for instance created for Germany—following some precedents from the period of the Weimar Republic—by the Allied Control Council in August 1946: Every State Labor Department was obliged to form a *Schiedsausschuss* (arbitration board) consisting of a representative of the department as chairman and up to five members each from labor and from management.[12] Although never abrogated, this Control Council

[10] U. S. Department of Health, Education and Welfare (Social Security Administration, Division of Program Research), *Social Security Throughout the World, 1958.* Washington: U. S. Government Printing Office, 1958. p. XII.

[11] On the arbitration boards for the American railroads, however, unions and management are represented. Furthermore, the Federal Mediation and Conciliation Service, which assists management and unions in the amicable settlement of disputes where such assistance is acceptable to the parties, is now supported in this function by a National Labor-Management Board; this board, however, is merely advising the service on policies and does not participate in the settlement of cases.

[12] Control Council Law no. 35 of August 20, 1946, "Conciliation and Arbitration Machinery in Labour Conflicts." Printed in Military Government Gazette, Germany, British Zone of Control, p. 296.

Law has in practice been superseded by an agreement between the National Federation of Employers Associations and the German Federation of Labor of September 17, 1954, which provided for a similar framework for the mediation effort.[13]

Self-governing institutions are one way in which group influence on public affairs may express itself, but not necessarily the only way. Organized labor, for instance, may in some countries possess such great influence on parliament or on the administration that even management of social insurance by government officials alone may still produce results which are similar to those achieved in other countries by labor representation in bipartite or tripartite boards.

Capitalism, Liberty, Democracy

HUMAN LIBERTY HAS GAINED THROUGH CAPITALISM

The development of free political institutions in Western Europe and North America roughly coincided with the rise of capitalism. This was no sheer coincidence. In the first place, the capitalist entrepreneurs needed relief from the fetters of manor and guild, and although the breaking of these bonds did not in itself assure personal and political liberty, the spirit of independence, once released, could not be confined to the economic field: The rise of a class first of merchants and later of manufacturers, both of them inferior in political position to the landed aristocracy, meant that an increasingly influential group strove in its own interest for political guarantees of individual liberty, just as the still older struggle between the feudal nobles and the king had resulted in rudimentary guarantees of the same nature. Furthermore, the capitalists, the landed aristocracy and the monarchy competed for the support of the common people, and this rivalry was conducive to the extension of liberties and political rights. Finally, capitalism tended to make the right of property nearly absolute and inviolable: As long as direct constitutional guarantees of personal freedom were not yet firmly enough established, it was of great importance that wealth could make a man independent of all government favors and immune to a good many governmental threats. Nor was this liberty-protecting function of property invalidated by the fact that only a tiny minority possessed wealth large enough to serve as a shelter from arbitrary government action: It has at times been very important that even a few dissenters could

[13] See Gerhard Erdmann, *Die Entwickelung der deutschen Sozialgesetzgebung.* Göttingen: Musterschmidt-Verlag, 1957, p. 320 f.

speak their minds. This function of property, however, has declined in significance, because the historical situation in which tyrants were more afraid to infringe on a subject's property rights than on his personal liberty was unique and has passed: Under the Nazis, the Jews who owned property rarely fared better than those who did not, unless they saved themselves by early emigration; the property was simply taken from Jewish owners. Nor did the private ownership of factories under dictatorial regimes prevent racial and political discrimination, because the rules of personnel policy were imposed on the private owners by the government.[14]

Among the gains for human freedom which we owe capitalism we must also list the tremendous increase in productivity of human labor which could hardly have been produced by any other system; modern industry could not have been created by the methods which the Pharaohs employed to build their cities. If it is true that the range of choice among material goods has a meaning for freedom, and if that freedom was promoted by social welfare policy which made this range of choice accessible to population groups previously excluded, then the same applies to the institutional presuppositions of the technological improvements which made this range of choice possible in the first place.

Thus, we would have much less liberty in the world if there had never been a capitalistic system: Capitalism has been a liberating force at balance. The latter qualification means that there have been counteracting tendencies. The "wage slavery" in the early factories has often been described. Although many of these "slaves" had been in an even worse kind of thralldom before, working the fields of a lord as serfs, others had been independent craftsmen or had owned a farm before they succumbed to competition or were squeezed out of their holdings by some land-greedy squire. The unrestrained power of the entrepreneur in the period of early industrialism was often as hard to bear as had been the power of a lord over his subjects, but the forces of change which capitalism had unleashed eventually cre-

[14] The respect which in the earlier modern age even arbitrary rulers showed to the rights of property was largely due to the great interest of the absolute monarchy in the rise of capitalism. Although the rise of capitalism would not have been possible without the spontaneous forces of gain-seeking, these forces were not everywhere strong enough to produce a transformation of society. Only in Great Britain and in a few smaller nations, especially the Low Countries and outside of Europe where British civilization was dominant, did modern industrial society grow without strong guidance from the government; in France, in Prussia, in Austria modern industry was far more a child of privilege than of freedom. But the autocratic rulers, once they had committed themselves to the promotion of industry, and having to use entrepreneurship for this purpose in view of the limited success of state enterprises, had to create the legal and political presuppositions under which entrepreneurs could work effectively; and one of the first of these was the protection of private property.

ated an environment in which the power of man over man was put under controls which assured an amount of freedom unheard of in earlier ages.

COUNTERACTING TENDENCIES

Even in capitalism as we know it today, it is true, there are specific tendencies which detract from human freedom—as there are in any conceivable system. Some of these tendencies are still rooted in the power of command which the capitalist, or the hired manager to whom he has delegated power, exercises over his employees, but in the advanced capitalistic countries this power has been put under effective restraints by labor unions and government regulations in the great majority of instances. The Marxist economic morality which prevails in communist states—even in those with a modified communist system such as Poland and Yugoslavia—and which frowns upon or outlaws as exploitation the employment of one person by another for gain regardless of circumstances is an undue generalization from facts which in the highly developed countries have for the most part ceased to exist. Where the starting positions of employer and employee in negotiating the labor contract are largely equalized by union power or government policy, that contract becomes similar to any other bargain, and the dependency which still exists between labor and management becomes truly mutual. The command power of the employer within private enterprise is at least as effectively checked as in public enterprises, where the manager or foreman also must distribute the different tasks within the shop and determine by orders how the work is to be done, thereby necessarily interfering with a part of the worker's life.[15]

More important now is the question of how far the capitalistic system impairs political democracy, which is also basic to human freedom. In capitalistic countries, newspapers, and often also radio stations, are private enterprises and their policies are frequently influenced by what they consider apt to preserve the private enterprise system; this may make these communication media opposed to social reform—or at least far-reaching reform. Moreover, money is important for the success of political parties; private enterprise, by offering profit-making opportunities, enables the entrepreneurial class to influence the outcome of elections, far beyond its voting

[15] It seems now that misuse of management's power over the lives of employees is more frequent with higher echelons of the staff than with manual labor. It has been reported that some American business corporations, in selecting higher personnel, take into account the aptitude of wives to fit into the "community" of employee families, and that a junior executive's career may be impaired if he uses a more expensive type of car than the president of the company. Any discrimination on such a basis, if practiced toward manual workers, would probably end up in the grievance committee and be decided against management.

power, through putting funds at the disposal of the party most favorable to entrepreneurial interests. Although the aggregate of profits represents only a relatively small part of the total national income, the amounts which entrepreneurs can and do spare from their profit income to contribute to campaign funds represents a much larger portion of total campaign expenditure. Contributions by labor unions to the campaign expenses of parties considered favorable to the cause of labor offer a partial compensation but are sometimes restricted by law; the progressive income tax tends to direct entrepreneurs' expenditure for non-personal purposes to charitable and scientific institutions rather than political parties, since contributions to the former are tax-deductible but not those to the latter. In spite of these effects, however, contributions from business interests have usually given the conservative parties financial superiority over their opponents. On the other hand, this superiority has hardly been more than a marginal advantage: In the United States, the party most favored by business has been less successful in recent decades than its rival, and in other countries, for instance West Germany, the most important roots of conservatism seem to lie in psychological propensities of the population rather than in larger financial resources. A well filled party treasury is certainly a convenience for a campaign manager but by itself does not seem to win elections.

Aside from entrepreneurial money, technical advice is a source of extra political power which managers and owners of enterprises can exert in a capitalist system. In economic matters, the average legislator is an educated layman: educated in eliciting and evaluating expert testimony, but not himself an expert on those details which must be settled by legislation. To some extent, he can rely on experts whose biases, from whatever source they come, are usually not determined by their own selfish interests; such experts, for instance, may be professional economists or engineers not in a position to profit or lose through legislative decisions. But often the only people who can give expert advice are those who have a stake in the decision. They may have the will to recommend what is best for the community, but they are rarely aware of conflicts between their own interests and the common good.

This way to influence, however, is open to capitalists not in their capacity as owners but as managers of enterprises. Although in a capitalist economy these roles are intertwined—vested either in the same persons or in persons with largely identical interests, the hired manager being safer in his position if the business is profitable for the owners than if it is not—the managerial function must be filled regardless of the economic system. In other systems, therefore, the managers can also exert influence as expert advisers to the government. Nor would it be correct to assume that only in the capitalist system can managers have interests distinct from and even contradictory to those of other population groups.

CAPITALISM AS A SYSTEM OF DECENTRALIZATION

When we weigh the historical contributions of capitalism to the cause of liberty against the tendencies in capitalism that work against democracy and human freedom, the result will, of course, depend on how much these contributions mean in today's world and how much they will mean in the future. Not what capitalism has done in the past to free mankind from fetters, but what it is doing and will do to keep men free is important for a judgment on which policy decisions are to be based. The past can offer us some hints, but no conclusive evidence, as to the present and future value of capitalism as a protector of liberty.

Most if not all the reasons for the belief that capitalism still has such a protective role to play can be recognized by viewing capitalism as a system of economic decentralization. In capitalism, a large portion of the economic decisions is made in a multitude of business offices, rather than in relatively few government bureaus. The multitude is not as great as it was before important sections of business became highly concentrated; but by comparison with its contemporary rival systems, capitalism is still marked by decentralization. A decentralized economy, it is true, is neither an absolute prerequisite nor an absolute guarantee of personal and political liberty. Fascism has proved that even with a private enterprise system, in which the daily decisions about production were still made in a large number of business offices rather than in a few government bureaus, human liberty could be crushed; on the other hand, there is no valid reason why it should not be possible to surround centralized decisions with sufficient guarantees of due democratic process. Moreover, a large measure of economic decentralization can be achieved in socialist systems, and probably even under communism, if there should be a will to decentralize.

But economic centralization, although not necessarily an instrument of despotism, can be so used. Being a potentially dangerous weapon, it is preferable to have it only where it can serve a good purpose, and then surround it with the necessary safeguards—just as we would want a gun in the house only if we need it for protection, and then storing it where it is as safe as possible from misuse.

In previous parts of the analysis of the capitalist system, it has been shown that there must be centralized economic decisions for the whole nation in some fields, and that the role of centralized decision-making will probably have to be increased, especially for the purpose of eliminating economic fluctuations and regulating the rate of growth. The necessity to centralize some economic decisions, however, is all the more reason to keep others decentralized if this can be done without prohibitive cost.

As an example of a non-capitalistic method of economic decentralization, we may think of workers' self-management as established in Yugoslavia. This system, in which enterprises are run mainly under the direction of workers councils and produce for the market like businesses in capitalism, may prove as effective as capitalist private enterprise in decentralizing economic decisions, although the applicability of the Yugoslav devices to fully developed economies has not yet been conclusively demonstrated. But in any event, economic decentralization is not as safe under the Yugoslav or any similar system as in capitalist countries. A relatively small group of leaders might decide to return to the method of concentrating all decisions in a central agency—as it was once done even in Yugoslavia—which would then order the enterprises what to do. The reason why this hazard exists lies not only in the political constitution, which in all communist and semi-communist countries denies the citizens important rights that can be used in defense against centralizing tendencies, but also in the absence of private property as a basis for management rights. Although property rights do not form an impregnable wall, since they can be breached by despotic governments, they represent an obstacle which anyone—individual despot or central agency—who would arrogate to himself the sole decision-making power in economic affairs must surmount; where the tradition of private property is firmly rooted, the obstacle is important.[16]

[16] The objection might be raised that the right of self-management in Yugoslavia, and even the right of the members of the agricultural collectives in the Soviet Union to run their own production units within the limits of the plan, are established by law, like property rights in a capitalist country. The difference lies—apart from the political constitution—in the firmness of the tradition behind these rights. The protection which statutory or even constitutional provisions can offer to any individual or group is obviously in inverse proportion to the ease with which they can be changed. Where the government or the ruling group has legal power to change them, their effectiveness depends on the extra-legal difficulties with which such a change will meet; an important impediment to the abrogation of rights is the conviction of the great majority that these rights have existed for a long period of time, and that therefore interference with them would cause a widespread feeling of insecurity. When the Yugoslav system of workers' self-management has a tradition of many generations behind it, it may become as difficult to abolish as any capitalistic property rights; but this is not true now.

Obviously, the firmness of the tradition behind property rights is greatly reduced once private property in the instruments of production has been abolished. The decentralization argument, therefore, applies with greater force to the preservation of capitalist institutions where they exist than to their restoration where they have been abolished.

It is a merit of capitalism that it provides the safest and most convenient method of economic decentralization.

HUMAN LIBERTY AND THE EFFICIENCY OF CAPITALISM

The importance of the experience with fascism for the relationship of capitalism and democracy has been mentioned repeatedly, but there is still another aspect of this experience which should not be forgotten. In making the collapse of democracy in the 1930's possible, the weaknesses and the virtues of the capitalist system combined their effects with fatal results. Capitalism had ceased to function effectively, and great mass misery was the consequence. But capitalism had properly been regarded as a system historically associated with the rise of human liberty; therefore when doubts arose as to the viability of the economic institutions of capitalism, the idea grew that liberty had to be sacrificed in order to defeat unemployment and hunger. Dominated by this idea, several nations abandoned the tradition of freedom.

One of the lessons to be drawn from this period is once more the impossibility of completely divorcing the efficiency of an economic system from its significance to human liberty, aside from the narrowing of material choices which lack of efficiency would produce. No fetish should be made of efficiency; even if it were proved that an unfree system supplies us with more goods and services, this would be no cogent reason to prefer it to another in which freedom is protected at the price of a lower output. But a system which causes despair by perpetuating poverty, or, even worse, by plunging people from a relatively high standard of living suddenly into misery, will prepare them to accept the idea that a strong man, free of constitutional restraints, will act as a savior. Perhaps it is not only the creation of acute misery that would have this fatal effect, but also the failure of the economic system to assure progress, especially in a situation in which systems with little or no freedom advance rapidly toward high levels of performance. The feeling of stagnation may suffice to bring about a flight from freedom.

A serious danger is thus revealed in a purist approach to the problem of the economic order. There is much reason to believe that the performance of capitalism can be improved by broadening the economic responsi-

---

In this respect capitalism is much in the same position as the absolute monarchy: The arguments for preservation of absolute monarchies in countries like Great Britain or Sweden are to most of us far more convincing than arguments for its restoration where monarchs have been deposed.

bilities of government in some respects, especially by a better organization of collective economic forethought and by closing the gap between the high satisfaction of many individual wants and the low satisfaction of many public needs. It seems likely that our mixed economic system will have to become even more mixed in order to secure for it a measure of vitality which not only gives people enough material means for consumption but also maintains their confidence that there is no end of progress.

CHAPTER 11

THE FOUR "BRICKS" IN THE CAPITALISTIC SYSTEM

Command and Exchange

In capitalism, exchange is the prevalent method of economic integration and determination of economic priorities. But not only are there areas in which even under capitalism these economic tasks are mainly fulfilled by command; there is also an important interplay between command and exchange. Credit policy by a central bank is an example. Its monopoly of issuing paper money, to determine the reserve requirements of member banks and several other methods by which a central bank controls the supply of credit by the private banks are put at its disposal by the command power of the state. But only to a limited extent is the control of the central bank exercised through direct command addressed to the banks. If the central bank, for instance, raises its rate of rediscount, it virtually notifies the private banks of its intention to demand a higher price for putting its money-creating power at the disposal of the private banks, and that therefore it will become more expensive for the private institutions to improve their liquidity by selling their customer's notes to the central bank. The private banks are not commanded to make credit more expensive for their own customers, but this is the effect which the central bank desires; the private banks usually comply with this desire because the policy of the central bank, based on the state's power of command, has made it profitable for the private banks to seek the necessary amount of liquidity by reducing their loans, through the device of making borrowing less attractive, in order not to be forced to rely on the Central Bank. The Central Bank has signaled to the managers of economic units that in their own best interest they should make dispositions to get along with less credit. Command has not superseded exchange, but has merely set new terms for the exchange relations of which business life exists.

The same indirect kind of steering becomes apparent when we regard the broader aspects of credit policy by governments or central banks. The usual motive for both or either one in desiring a shrinkage of bank loans lies in the field of business cycle policy: fear lest a boom may result in too steep a rise of prices, which is an evil in itself and, according to some business cycle theories, may cause a depression. What is really intended, therefore, is some dampening of business activity, especially reduction in number and scope of projects of industrial expansion. Instead of being ordered to retrench, as would be done in an economy based principally on command, managers of industrial units are discouraged from maintaining or enlarging their projects by an increase in the price and a reduction in the availability of credit. If an industrialist considers his project sufficiently profitable to bear the additional cost—and if he can either finance it from his own resources or convince a bank of the correctness of his estimate—he can still carry it out.

Another example of interaction between command and exchange is the levying of taxes for purposes other than revenue. The best known example is the protective tariff. The collection of tariff duties is an exercise of the government's right to command; its purpose is to reduce imports. Yet the importers are not commanded to restrict their business; the commanding power is merely used to set conditions in which they will find it profitable to do so. In this respect, the tariff is different from import prohibitions or quotas, which have also been used to reduce imports. By the latter method, importers are commanded either to cease importing, or to import no more than a defined quantity of a commodity.

Internal taxes also can be used for regulating economic activities. When Congress created the National Banking System in 1863, it wished all note-issuing banks to comply with its provisions, but it was found that many banks, rather than accept the obligations under the new law, preferred to rely on their state charters and failed to apply for a federal charter. Therefore in 1865 Congress enacted a new law, placing a prohibitive ten per cent annual tax on bank notes not issued under a federal charter. This measure forced the state-chartered banks to choose between giving up their note-issuing privilege or entering the system of national banks and conducting their business in compliance with the federal requirements for note coverage, holding of reserves, liability of stockholders and other conditions.

A more recent example of the use of taxation to eliminate or restrict economic activities which are contrary to public policy is found in the measures for the maintenance of a higher level of farm prices than would exist in a free market. The United States government takes agricultural "surplus" produce out of the market and puts it in storage. If the government's purpose is achieved—whether it has been achieved, at least in most years, is controversial—the price-depressing effect of this surplus is removed, and with it the restraint on production which would have resulted from depressed prices. It therefore becomes necessary for the government to create a new restraint in order to prevent an oversupply, or at least keep it within tolerable limits. In some phases of the agricultural price support program—and here it is neither necessary nor possible to review the many changes that the program has undergone since its initiation in the early 1930's—the government has imposed a penal tax upon some kinds of farm output produced or marketed in excess of established quotas. Here command—the taxing power—supplements the exchange relation between government and farmers.

But in trying to prevent agricultural overproduction, the United States government has relied not only on tax penalties for non-compliance with its policy but has also used premiums for compliance. Farmers receive payments for voluntarily withdrawing acreage from cultivation; this is done, technically, for the sake of soil conservation, especially prevention of erosion, but the reduction of output is at least an important secondary purpose.

The use of premiums instead of taxes to attain an objective of public policy seems superficially to put the measure entirely into the category of exchange, rather than of a combination of exchange and command. In the case of the soil conservation programs, the farmer is free to conclude or not to conclude the agreements,[1] and he has to weigh the advantages and disadvantages as in the case of any private contract. In evaluating an act of fiscal policy, however, spending and the procurement of funds to be spent must be considered together. The funds for paying premiums to farmers have to be raised by taxation, and that means by the commanding power of the state. The premium policy as a whole, therefore, represents another example in which exchange and command are combined.

Just to show the variety of purposes for which the policy of offering tax-financed advantages in return for compliance with policy may be used, let us consider a particular aspect of United States policy with regard to irriga-

[1] The decision which the individual farmer has to make must be distinguished from the choice which the government often requests farmers to make collectively—by taking a vote—between price supports coupled with acreage restrictions, or no supports (or supports at a lower level) and no restrictions. A farmer who belongs to a minority opposing a majority-approved program is just as much commanded to comply under threat of penalty as if the scheme had been directly imposed by public law.

tion. Since the Homestead Act of 1862, it has been the policy of the United States government to favor the family farm, defined (with some exceptions) as property not exceeding 160 acres, over larger holdings. In some section of the United States, especially the Far West, much larger holdings prevail, partly for historical reasons and partly because, without irrigation, the land can be used only in a manner implying a high land-labor ratio. In the last few decades, the federal government has built many multi-purpose dams, which can supply irrigation water and thereby make a more intensive and profitable kind of farming possible. The Federal Reclamation Act, however, stipulates that from federally financed projects water can be supplied only for 160 acres per recipient—a farmer's wife counting as a separate recipient, so that a married couple's holding can comprise 320 acres and still receive water from a federal project. If owners of larger property wish to irrigate their total holdings, they must conclude an agreement with the federal government in which they pledge themselves to sell the excess land within a designated number of years. In this way tax-financed advantages, which the landholder may or may not accept under the terms offered but which under the given physical conditions are conducive to profitable operation, are used to produce a socially more desirable pattern of landholding and thus alter the character of rural society.

What happens in all these instances is a narrowing of the choice open to the individual, and this narrowing is carried out through the commanding power of the state; but since the individual is still able to make a choice, to "buy" or not to "buy" the advantages or the avoidance of the disadvantages by complying with government policy, the element of exchange is still present. In some instances the necessity of avoiding the penalties or obtaining the advantages may be so compelling as to make the choice a mere formality, but this is by no means always true. After 1865, numerous state-chartered banks renounced their note-issuing privileges and did not enter the national banking system; in the San Joaquin Valley of California, where the irrigation problem is acute and the size limitation of recipient farms applies to water from the federally financed Central Valley Project, numerous large landholders have so far retained their big ranches without any sales pledge, continuing their old methods of production if they cannot provide themselves with additional water from other sources. The narrower the choice and the greater the pressure upon the interested party to make the decision desired by the government, the more the element of command overshadows that of exchange, and vice versa.

Whenever it is applicable, the method of using the command power to make desired action attractive, rather than commanding conformity directly, has many advantages. Some of these exist in any economic system; there is usually less need for supervision, and less need to foresee all the effects that the desired action may have, because the greater elasticity of the indirect method will make it possible to avoid or cushion the effects where they might be unexpectedly noxious. An imported commodity, for instance, may be particularly necessary for special purposes. If importation is prohibited, there is danger that the prohibiting authority may not have recognized in advance all these different uses, and the lack of the commodity may do great harm. If the restriction is sought by a tariff, the importance of the need which can only be satisfied by the imported commodity will raise its price and probably the importation will continue although the quantity will be reduced. As will be seen, these advantages have even caused some communist countries to experiment with the indirect method of control. In capitalism, there is the further advantage that the indirect method fits much better into a system which more than others is based on individual initiative.[2]

Solidarity

Solidarity, in the broad sense used here, is important in many various roles in a capitalistic economy. In its beginnings, the capitalistic system would probably have been intolerable if it had not been tempered with human solidarity. There was some truth in the arguments of the early socialists that charity was not only degrading for the recipients but that it was also a pillar of the existing order; they thought mainly of the mentality of the poor, who, by having the extremes of their misery mitigated by charitable gifts, would be prevented from demanding a fundamental change of the social system. On the other hand, there would have been even more defections from the upper classes if their members had been unable to soothe their consciences with the thought that some relief was extended to those who did not find jobs, were incapacitated or became victims of competition.

Although the socialist criticism with respect to short-term effects was well founded, it did not do justice to charity as an expression of general human solidarity and therefore as an effective force to rebuild society. The momentous advance of social legislation, which has fundamentally changed

[2] Dahl and Lindblom, in *Politics, Economics and Welfare* (pp. 104 ff.), use the term "manipulated field control" in a sense for the most part coextensive with the concept of the indirect method of control used here.

the character of the capitalist system, would not have been possible if the workers had not developed their own political and economic power and used it to press for ameliorative laws, but many of the reforms which were enacted would hardly have materialized, or would have come much later, if it had not been for the feelings of shame and anger over the misuses within the industrial system on the part of members of the upper classes. It is impossible to separate the contributions to social change of class "selfishness" among the underprivileged and human solidarity among the privileged; we can only say that both were essential to produce the situation today.

Easier to recognize, though no more important to capitalism today than general human solidarity, is vocational solidarity. Much has been said already about the role of solidarity among members of the same vocational group in the sections on labor and group autonomy. Not all group action, however, is based on solidarity in the sense we use here. This sense implies that the individual participates in the course which the group has chosen, not because he is sure that for himself the gains will outweigh the sacrifices, but because he is willing to count the gains of other members of his group, perhaps even of those who will be members of the group in the future, as important enough to offset some or all of his own sacrifices. Group solidarity in this sense is more important for labor than for most other groups, because—especially in the first stage of labor organization—the individual worker has little assurance that his personal gain in strikes and other campaigns will adequately compensate for his sacrifices. The reason is the greater difficulty in organizing workers, who are much more numerous than employers and often hampered by poor education, a sense of social inferiority, and—far less now than in the past—by their lack of individual financial reserves and dependence on their pay envelopes.

Tradition

Capitalism has been a great innovator; this does not mean that it can function without tradition. No economic system, least of all a system characterized by relative freedom of the individual from close supervision from above, could survive without everybody's being able to rely on the likelihood that others will live up to their obligations even when violations would be more profitable. Since man is not entirely moral, this reliance cannot be absolute; if temptation is too great, many people will weaken; even if under moderate temptation, some will fail to stand the test. For the functioning of the system, however, extremes are not too important; the vital thing is that in the ordinary course of events most participants in the market are reliable.

Man's contemporary moral sense, regardless of its origins, can only have developed in the context of society. Moreover, present-day "do's" and "don't's" are not only prompted by each person's own reflections but are largely the result of social conditioning; that is to say, the individual responds to some situation in the way which is expected of him. The morality that capitalism needs, then, is largely the product of tradition.

What kind of tradition? Clearly, how people manage their economic affairs depends to a considerable extent on their total outlook toward the world. Thus there is good reason to believe that religious attitudes may have an important influence upon economic practices, and if this is true, some religious beliefs may be more conducive than others to the establishment of such a moral tradition as capitalism requires. Max Weber and Richard Tawney, both leaders of sociological thought in their generation, believed that the rise of Protestantism and especially of Calvinism and other forms of Puritanism in the sixteenth century has greatly facilitated the development of capitalism. In proposing this thesis, they have initiated a discussion which has opened up new vistas in viewing the relationship of religious tradition and economic performance.

Both Max Weber and Tawney have pointed out that for its development capitalism required a more specific ethical tradition than that of the Golden Rule, which, of course, all higher religions have taught in one form or another. At least in its earlier phases, capitalism depended on a kind of ethic which emphasized the importance of work and thrift, rather than of the virtues of a contemplative life or of contempt for laying up "treasures upon earth where moth and rust doth corrupt." The Calvinist doctrine of predestination, Tawney and Weber suggested, played a particularly important role in the rise of the capitalistic spirit: Since God had, by a just but incomprehensible judgment, destined some souls to be saved and others to be damned before human beings could acquire merits through good deeds or demerits through evil ones, everybody would naturally search for signs indicating that he was among God's elect. Among these signs of salvation the Calvinists counted a life of honesty, hard labor and self-denial. Therefore, though a man's good works were not a means to secure God's grace, they might indicate that grace had been granted. This explains why Calvinists, and believers in sectarian doctrines influenced by Calvinism, were often even more frantically anxious than Catholics to lead the kind of life which they believed to be pleasing to God: The Catholic might think he could atone for sins by meritorious deeds, but the Calvinist suspected every transgression of being a sign that he was denied divine grace.

If the Weber-Tawney thesis interprets the Reformation as a necessary condition for the rise of capitalism, it is open to serious doubts. Already before the Reformation, practice within the Catholic Church, and theory slowly following practice, had relaxed those precepts which were unfavorable to the new spirit in economic life—especially the prohibition of interest—and the Church had even encouraged in many ways the rise of that spirit, for instance by a favorable attitude toward economic ventures in the latter phases of the crusades. Nor were the regions that turned Protestant the only ones which had an early start in capitalist development: Catholic Northern Italy and the Catholic parts of the Low Countries were just as much in the forefront as Protestant Holland and Britain and the Huguenot regions of France. Also, Calvin as well as Luther condemned covetousness and ruthless pursuit of profit in terms no less strong than any of the medieval Schoolmen; those who heard their preaching could not have felt encouraged to participate in the economic ventures of early capitalism, with its many temptations to deviate from a life of righteousness. Finally, if the proposition is accepted that the doctrine of predestination was a motivation to a life of work and thrift, the question still remains: Why was this kind of work, rather than an attitude of contemplation and withdrawal from the world, considered a sign of divine grace? Weber and Tawney themselves have suggested that this had something to do with the social composition of the Reformed congregations: In spite of the participation of aristocracy in practically all phases of the Reformation, the commercial and industrial groups, for which sobriety and toil were a prerequisite of success and even survival, were more strongly represented among the Protestants than in the European population in general. But this sociological explanation amounts to a reversal of the Tawney-Weber thesis, for it describes the growth of commerce and industry as a cause rather than an effect of the religious change.

Yet there is an important core of truth in the Weber-Tawney thesis. Although the Reformation was not an indispensable condition for the rise of capitalism, it undoubtedly contributed to its progress.[3] In its Lutheran as well as its Calvinist expressions, the Reformation arose in opposition to the sixteenth century Catholic conception of the value of good works. Even as a sign of divine grace, in the Protestant view good works had some value only

[3] Although Tawney and Weber seem to have overstated the magnitude of that contribution, they themselves realized that the new economic order emerged from a number of roots. Tawney was more cautious than Weber in describing the contribution of Protestantism to the rise of capitalism; see his criticism of Weber in *Religion and the Rise of Capitalism,* London: John Murray, 1936, pp 319 ff.

if they were a characteristic of man's whole life; individual acts, perhaps undertaken to obtain remission of past sins, were without religious significance. Thus man must methodically organize his life on the basis of such principles as righteousness, work and thrift; he must systematize his actions, eliminate levities and concentrate upon the tasks before him.[4] This rationalization of human habits and attitudes was of the greatest importance for capitalism. The introduction of modern capitalist enterprise was greatly impeded by the tendency of precapitalistic man to haphazardness and irrational action.[5] By helping to overcome that tendency, the Reformation promoted the development of capitalism.

As Weber himself has pointed out, rationalization of life was already a characteristic of several monastic orders in the Middle Ages, with occasional effects upon the world of laymen. What Protestantism contributed was a more comprehensive adoption of the same principle in daily work. As in many other instances, the change did not remain confined to Protestant believers: The Reformation brought forth the Counter Reformation, and the Jesuit order, the outstanding organizational product and agent of the Counter Reformation, showed at least the same degree of "methodism" as its Calvinist, Puritan or Lutheran antagonists.

At one point the rationalization of life under the influence of Protestant opposition to the old concept of good works was of particular economic importance. Catholic charity had placed primary weight upon the intentions of the giver: He would increase his merits by parting with some of his wealth, whatever use the recipients might make of his beneficence. Protestantism, on the contrary, required the benefactor or those who organized support of the poor on behalf of the community to take responsibility for the effects of charitable action: It was not part of a godly life to encourage sloth or inebriation among the poor. As a consequence, the Protestant countries developed systems of poor relief in which the education to good working habits played a great role. The Elizabethan Poor Law of 1601 already showed the influence of that spirit in its dual-purpose policy: providing work for the able-bodied poor and threatening with severe penalties vagrants who tried to avoid imposed labor by begging. In Holland, the new

[4] Weber calls attention to the significance of the name of Methodism, adopted by the movement of Wesleyan dissenters from the Anglican Church. Although the doctrine and spirit of Methodism differed in many respects from Calvinism and Lutheranism, the Methodists took the postulate of systematization of morality in the practice of daily life from the earlier versions of Protestantism and developed it further.

[5] How much this must have been the case, can be seen today when the same difficulties are encountered in organizing enterprise in underdeveloped countries. Even if the technological and organizational achievements of capitalism are introduced into a new region within the framework of another economic system, socialism or communism, the problem remains the same.

attitude toward poverty contributed in a still more direct way to the development of new forms of production. In that country, as early as the end of the sixteenth century, inmates of poor houses and prisons were organized in "manufactories"—large establishments for the production of various commodities by manual processes but with a high degree of division of labor.[6] The work discipline of the poor house established a model for the work discipline of the factory. It was not merely that the people had to work hard —the medieval master craftsman also had been intolerant of any inclination of his apprentices or journeymen to loaf on the job. The new development was that now workers had to adjust their activities to that of others, with whom they formed a team, rather than to determine their own way of performing the work; also, they could no longer choose to suspend their work and go wandering from town to town: If they did so in search of a job, they now risked being treated as vagrants. Thus work, and rationality of work, became the new categorical imperative, and people had to learn how to get along without many psychological safety valves that had been available in the Middle Ages. This was an important condition for the rapid development of the factory system and thereby for the higher forms of capitalism.

The Weber-Tawney thesis has been treated here at some length because its analysis shows the contribution which religious tradition can make to the development of an economic system. That the contribution was made not so much by the views of Luther and Calvin themselves as by the habits of thinking which grew out of their teaching adds to the significance of the thesis for the role of tradition in the functioning of an economic system. This significance becomes even clearer when it is considered that the attitudes which the Reformation had helped to implant in the human mind survived the belief in predestination, which had played such an important role in the genesis of the tradition. Capitalism today is still drawing much of its strength from the spirit which Calvin helped to create although few contemporaries are Calvinists in the original sense.

The habits of economic thinking which go back to the Reformation, after having survived their religious foundation, may even survive the particular set of circumstances which made them useful. To be sure, work discipline and reliability in business dealings and the whole systematizing of our daily existence are as essential as ever for the economic success of mankind. But can thrift still be regarded unconditionally as a virtue? Over-saving may not so commonly be a cause of calamity as the Keynesian school assumed, and this writer at least would not accept the argument of some apologists for

[6] See Carl Jantke, *Der Vierte Stand,* Freiburg: Herder, 1955, p. 3.

advertising that the latter is necessary as a stimulus to spending to prevent a retrograde development of our economy. But if consumers failed to increase their expenditures approximately in proportion with their incomes, the funds accumulating in the savings institutions would only under exceptional circumstances be taken out by borrowers and spent in the course of investment; and from the accumulation of idle funds, a depression would result. Any drastic rise in the spirit of thrift (decline of the propensity to consume, in the language of present-day economics) would almost certainly lead to such a misfortune.[7]

Aside from the role of moral tradition, there is an enormous variety of technical tradition in the capitalist system. Capitalism could not function if all the useful practices had to be rediscovered by each new generation of businessmen, or even if all of these techniques had to be relearned by fully understanding their foundation in experience. With all its inherent rationality, capitalism must make use of man's inclination to accept some rules without digging for reasons, because if everybody always insisted on a full knowledge why these rules are valid, there would be no time for action. The danger inherent in this need is the same as in all traditions: that rules which have become obsolete may not be questioned before they can do harm. Capitalism, however, has perhaps come closer than any alternative system to a wholesome balance between the necessary force of tradition and the necessary inclination to question traditional practices: On the one hand, the capitalist order is too closely tied to the inquiring spirit of modern

[7] The proposition that unconditional exhortations to thrift may do harm in mature capitalism is explicitly stated, or at least implied, in all writings of the Keynesian school. This proposition is also one of the themes of *The Lonely Crowd* by David Riesman and Associates (New Haven: Yale University Press, 1950; abridged version in Doubleday Anchor Books). Definitions of the maturity of capitalism differ widely; in this context, however, the relevant criterion is that the specter of overproduction begins to overshadow the specter of scarcity even in prosperity—in depressions, despite the misery of the masses, the managers of the economy have always thought in terms of "too many goods." The recognition that capitalism is mature in this sense does not mean to agree with the Galbraith thesis that we are already in a state of true private affluence; it merely means that such a state looms somewhere beyond our present horizon, and that the approach to that state—however long the distance still to be covered—created some specific problems and requires some adjustment in public policy.

In the very distant future, some elements in the economic philosophy of Bernard Mandeville's *The Fable of the Bees* (1714, republished, ed. Douglas Garman, London: Wishart & Co., 1934) may be more appropriate to the situation than the Puritan heritage. Mandeville's satire tells the story of a beehive in which luxury, vice, and tremendous differences in wealth and income existed but trade and production flourished. When under the influence of moralists the bees were converted to thrift and other Puritan virtues, prosperity vanished and returned only when the bees had abandoned moralism. Mandeville's great influence on his contemporaries is one of many indications that the economic teachings of Puritanism evoked strong reaction as early as the first decades of the eighteenth century.

science to acquiesce too long in postulates just because they have been accepted by previous generations; on the other hand, to be an outspoken nonconformist in a business world means a hard life, because one of the basic prerequisites of business success is to be trusted by others, and the typical nonconformist is often mistrusted. Not too many individuals have the strength of character to play this role, and therefore capitalism has, as a rule, had enough conformism to permit the necessary amount of tradition to grow.

III. SOCIALISM

PRESENT MEANING OF THE TERM—Although the meanings of all terms that define economic systems have changed greatly in recent decades and are still in flux, we speak with clearer terms of reference when we speak of capitalism or communism than when we discuss socialism. The traditional meaning of socialism, collective ownership of the instruments of production, is no longer applicable as a basic criterion since practically all socialist parties in the Western world refuse to put primary emphasis on this postulate. In communist parts of the world, where collectivization is still treated as the most important characteristic of a preliminary phase labeled socialism (as distinguished from "full communism," which would be characterized not only by elimination of unearned income through collectivization but also by distribution of the social product according to need instead of according to work performed), the old postulate has lost so much of its humanitarian foundation as to acquire a new meaning, which the old socialists would regard as sinister. In the underdeveloped nations, where many of the governments claim to adhere to socialist principles, the term is understood in a broad sense, certainly not involving nationalization of all instruments of production, except in that minority of cases in which it indicates an emulation of communist practices. Socialism today cannot be considered a clearly definable system either existing or postulated, but only a tendency to look more favorably on some measures and less favorably on others than is done by the supporters of capitalism or communism. Where socialist tendencies are strong, however, they seem to produce policies which complement each other sufficiently to result in arrangements of considerable inner consistency. Perhaps twenty or thirty years from now it may be possible to define socialism as an economic system more clearly than can be done today.

Among the measures that socialists look upon more favorably than supporters of the capitalistic system is still collective ownership of the means of production. The program of the Social Democratic party of West Germany adopted in December 1959, for example, says in its section on "ownership and power," after having approved of protection of "private ownership of the means of production . . . so long as it does not hinder the establishment of social justice:"

> Public ownership is a legitimate form of public control which no modern state can do without. It serves to protect freedom against domination by large economic concerns. In these concerns power is held today by managers who are themselves the servants of anonymous forces . . . Where sound economic power relations cannot be guaranteed by other means, public ownership is appropriate and necessary.[1]

Although this statement shows the great shift away from the old socialist belief in collective ownership as *the* road to the Good Society, it also demonstrates the difference which still exists on this issue between socialist and "bourgeois" parties.

[1] Julius Braunthal (ed.), *Yearbook of the International Socialist Labour Movement.* London: Lincolns-Prager, 1960. Vol. II (1960-61), p. 142. For statements in a similar sense by other socialist parties, see pp. 74 (Austria), 282 (Netherlands) and 323 (Switzerland). The statements by the British Labour Party, still somewhat more positive toward public enterprise (pp. 172, 186 ff) are perhaps less significant because they were adopted in 1956 and 1957 and thus may not reflect the Labour Party's present thoughts very accurately.

CHAPTER 12

COLLECTIVE OWNERSHIP

Nationalization

ENTERPRISE AUTONOMY OR CONTROL FROM THE CENTER

UNDER SOCIALIST INFLUENCE, public ownership has gained much ground in the postwar period. In industrialized parts of the world, the most dramatic advances were not made, however, in the Scandinavian countries, where socialists had stable majorities, but in the United Kingdom and France, where they were only temporarily in power or participated in government coalitions. Coal mines were nationalized in these countries, as were means of transportation, electric power and heating gas, credit institutions, and even parts of the manufacturing industry. The wave of conservatism which followed in the wake of postwar anti-capitalism stopped nationalization but forced only a modicum of retrenchment. Among the motives behind post-war nationalization that were carried out under socialist influence, some have also been important in promoting public ownnership where such influence was weak or absent; these motivating forces have, therefore, been discussed in the section on capitalism—notably the desire to prevent private monopolies as well as wasteful competition, and to render service to the public more effectively or cheaply than private enterprise could do. In addition, nationalization was desired by socialists as an instrument of national planning—it would give the state some "commanding heights" in the economy—and here and there it was viewed as a means to punish private entrepreneurs for undesirable political activities or to prevent political abuse of economic power, especially for the benefit of neo-fascism.

Socialists have done a great deal of thinking about the form of organization under which nationalized industries should be managed and the rules to be laid down for the conduct of their business; socialist influence in the inter-war, especially the post-war, period has made it possible for many of these ideas to be tested in practice. The preferred form of organization is that of a business corporation, the stock of which is held by the government;[1] in many instances even state railways, once administered by the state bureaucracy almost like any branch of public administration, have now been given autonomous status. Only the postal administration is almost everywhere managed in much the same way as other government departments.

For a variety of reasons, socialists, along with many non-socialists, consider bureaucratic organization unsuitable for industrial enterprise. The way that government departments are run, they feel, is not flexible enough for industrial management, because the civil servant is ordinarily too much bound by regulations and directives and conditioned to act in accordance with rules rather than to accept responsibility for a course of action that is not covered by instructions. Furthermore, the business corporation structure seems to make possible the confining of parliamentary control, to which government departments are subject in all details, to broad, general questions of policy. This is regarded as important because otherwise, it is feared, all sorts of political pressures might be exerted on the management of these enterprises.

Another advantage of the business corporation some times cited is that it is not bound by the Civil Service salary scale, and can therefore more easily attract talent in competition with private industry; on the other hand, a corporation executive does not have the secure tenure of a civil

[1] In a number of instances, the legal form chosen is not strictly that of a business corporation, but a special form assimilated to the status of a corporation. In France, for example, only the nationalized banks and insurance companies, which were business corporations (*sociétés anonymes*) before the state took them over, have retained this form, whereas the enterprises for the production and distribution of energy, including coal, have been given the form of "public enterprises of a commercial and industrial character." This distinction may, at least in part, have resulted from the intention that these enterprises should find their purpose not in profit-making but in public service; but this motive cannot be cited as the reason why the Renault automobile factory, when it was nationalized, was also given special status under a still different formula. For the legal forms of French nationalized industries, see M. Boiteux and Assoc. (ed.), *Le Fonctionnement des entreprises nationalisées en France* (Travaux du 3e Colloque des Facultés de Droit) Paris: Librairie Dalloz, 1956 (later referred to as *Le Fonctionnement*), especially the article by Jean Rivero, "L'Evolution du droit des entreprises nationalisées."

From an economic point of view, these legal distinctions are not very important, just as the differences between the special status of the Tennessee Valley Authority and that of other federally owned enterprises having the form of a business corporation do not have much economic significance. As economists, we must make a distinction between such organizations as the post office and those commercial and industrial enterprises of the state which are managed as business firms, regardless of whether the latter have the legal form of a business corporation or some special status.

servant, who is subject to dismissal only for provable cause, and the reduced difficulty of getting rid of managers in the event of unsatisfactory service has also been regarded as desirable.

The corporate form has not fulfilled all the hopes that were held for it before and immediately after the Second World War. H. A. Clegg, for instance, after evaluating briefly but fully Britain's experience with nationalized industries from a socialist point of view, concludes: ". . . the difference between the public corporation and the government department has been exaggerated."[2] His principal reasons for this judgment are the intense supervision exercised by the British cabinet minister in charge of nationalized enterprises over the policies of their management; since the minister himself is subject to political control, Parliament also has concerned itself with issues of prices, working conditions and efficiency in nationalized industries, often going more into detail than had been considered desirable at the time when nationalization was initiated. Clegg sees in this development an inevitable trend and actually recommends that some functions now assigned to the administration boards of individual industries be transferred to the minister. William A. Robson, a distinguished British analyst of problems of nationalized industries, also concludes that "the powers of control which the Government possesses over . . . [the nationalized industries] are right and proper,"[3] although he is skeptical about any plan of bringing the nationalized industries, even in part, under the old pattern of the post office-type of organization.[4] Yet there is no complete unanimity in this respect: A slightly earlier study by the Acton Society Trust, written mainly by P. J. Saynor, suggested reduction of ministerial powers, in part by increased autonomy of the administration boards and in part through "dispersal among other persons or bodies," for instance independent tribunals and commissions.[5]

In Great Britain, increased control of the government, thereby of Parliament, over state-owned corporations was a demand frequently voiced by socialists prior to World War II in criticism of such organizations as the London Passenger Transport Board;[6] therefore, after the Labour victory of

[2] H. A. Clegg, *Industrial Democracy and Nationalization*, A Study Prepared for the Fabian Society. Oxford: Basil Blackwell, 1951, p. 144.

[3] William A. Robson (ed.), *Problems of Nationalized Industry*, London: Allen and Unwin, 1952. Part II (written by the editor), p. 310.

[4] *Ibid.* p. 359 f.

[5] The Acton Society Trust, *The Powers of the Minister* (*Studies in Nationalized Industries*, Gordon Rattray Taylor, ed., no. 2). London: Acton Society, 1951, p. 14.

[6] Clegg, op. cit., p. 42. The study of the Acton Society Trust also makes it clear that the increase in government control over the public corporations was mainly due to criticism of over-extended autonomy by such organizations as the Fabian Society and the Trades Union Congresses. See *The Powers of the Minister*, p. 5. The socialist position in

1945, it was inevitable that the powers of government over public corporations would be increased. Adding to the socialist desire to expand government influence over nationalized industries was the idea that nationalization should be a means to insure the execution of the national economic plan which the Laborites then hoped to establish; to fit coal mining, transportation, power supply and steel production into a national program seemed to require large ministerial powers over the administration of industries. Other factors were operating in the same direction, especially the much larger volume of the industries brought into government ownership after 1945, which caused a strong desire to establish strict accountability for the management of so substantial a portion of the national wealth. To be sure, there was the counteracting trend of guild socialism, a school of thought which sought to dissolve the state into a federation of vocational organizations, with the latter rather than any central agency managing the industries. Guild socialism at times exerted great influence on the British labor movement, but in the 1940's this influence had been reduced to traces. As a result, all the nationalization laws enacted after 1945 gave the minister power to issue "general directives" to the administration boards, which had not been provided for in public ownership laws prior to the war; the tenure of the board members is now normally determined by ministerial regulation, whereas before 1945 it was fixed by law; in their financial operations, especially in borrowing, the corporations are now made far more dependent on the ministry.

In France, the socialists have never exercised governmental power all by themselves, but socialist influence was strong in several phases of the history of the Fourth French Republic, and it has not entirely vanished in the Fifth. This influence, plus a widespread desire not to leave to the Communists a monopoly of restricting the importance of big business, led to a considerable amount of nationalization. A contributing factor was the urge to punish some industrialists for their collaboration with the Nazis and to divest them of their economic power.

In the long run, the tendency to increase ministerial controls over nationalized industries proved to be about as strong in France as in Britain; in France, however, the forces operating in this direction did not gain a clear victory right after the war. The French labor movement, for a long time under the influence of Revolutionary Syndicalism,[7] had more anti-

---

the 1930's and in the post-World War II period signified a change from the earlier guild socialist position. See Clegg, *op. cit.*, p. 10.

[7] On Revolutionary Syndicalism, see Louis Levine (Lewis L. Lorwin), *The Labor Movement in France*, New York: Columbia University Press, 1922; Val R. Lorwin, *The French Labor Movement*, Cambridge: Harvard University Press, 1954; David J. Saposs,

statist tradition than its British counterpart; although this tradition was not as strong in the inter-war period as it had been in 1914, and probably still weaker in 1945 than in 1939, yet "the legislators of 1946 . . . in principle adopted, or believed to adopt, the traditional syndicalist solution of '*nationalisation industrialisée*'." [8] This term means literally "industrialized nationalization;" it signifies an arrangement by which the state, having acquired title to industrial enterprises, hands them over for management to groups of workers, including managers, with participation of consumers, in order that industrial society, rather than the state, takes upon itself the utilization of the plants. This *nationalisation sans étatisation* (nationalization without state management) "would have implied complete administrative and financial autonomy of the enterprise, including complete financial responsibility, but the legislators did not dare to go that far. . . . The laws either are silent on the question of who shall get the profits, as in the case of the banks and insurance companies, or the decision has little homogeneity—in gas and electricity, the profits are to be used for self-financing, in the coal industry, they are to be turned over to the state, after several special charges have been met; the possibility of losses is not even mentioned and therefore these have to be borne by the state." [9] On the other hand, however, the legislation of 1946 gave the workers and the consumers together a majority on the administration boards—a solution which might have looked like dream fulfillment to a British guild socialist of the 1920's, but was unthinkable in Britain after World War II.

It is not easy to decide whether the nationalized enterprises, even before the great reorganization of the spring of 1953, had more real autonomy in France than they had in Britain.[10] The ambivalence and inconsistency of the position of French nationalized industries resulted from a conflict of

---

The Labor Movement in Post-War France, New York: Columbia University Press, 1931; Carl Landauer, *European Socialism,* Berkeley and Los Angeles: University of California Press, 1960, chapts. 11 and *passim.*

[8] Georges Lasserre, "Aspects économiques des nationalisations françaises" in *Le Fonctionnement,* p. 34.

[9] *Ibid.*

[10] Robson, even in that period, was "by no means convinced that Government control is less in France than in Britain. Certainly the minister's power of appointment is much more free under English legislation than under the French system, where interests nominate their representatives. But what about the civil servants who sit on the French boards? What about the power of the French government to fix the prices of coal, gas, electricity etc.? What about the Minister's right to appoint the director-general of each French corporation and to decide the amount of his salary? There are no controls similar to these in Britain." (P. 267.) It is not at all certain, however, that these powers outweigh the greater influence which the British government exercised on the composition of the managing boards.

two trends: On the one hand, there was the syndicalist tradition, which would have demanded far-reaching autonomy; on the other hand, national economic planning was undertaken far more persistently in France than in Britain and most other countries, even in those nations in which the socialists were politically more powerful. In order to fit the nationalized industries into the "plan of modernization and equipment," or rather to make sure that they would set an example for private industry to comply with the plan, it seemed necessary to strengthen government control over state-owned enterprises. Although the early phase of this conflict is of great historical interest, in this context it is unnecessary to discuss in any detail the legal and economic position of the nationalized enterprises prior to the reform of 1953.

The 1953 reform signified the victory of the idea of strong government control over the syndicalist tradition. Representation of consumers on the managing boards was reduced, and it was therefore no longer possible for government representatives to be overruled by a coalition of employees and consumers, which in the previous period had tended to keep wages high and prices low, with the result that for some of its enterprises the state had to cover deficits, and for all of them had to provide more funds for investment than if surpluses had been available for self-financing.[11] The reform has by no means put an end to all deficits, but helped to keep them within limits.

In addition to reducing the application of the tripartite principle, the

[11] Lasserre (*op. cit.* pp. 34-5) thus summarizes the experience of the first period: "In the composition of the managing boards, the legislator seems not to have been able to free himself from the philosophy of parliamentarism (*optique parlementaire*); he based this composition essentially upon the idea of representation; he believed that it was sufficient to distribute equal shares of influence among the various legitimate interests. Therefore the state assumed only part of the entrepreneurial function: it accepted financial responsibility, but held only a minority position on the managing boards, having to face a majority of employees and users who were apt to form a coalition in favor of a policy of low prices and high wages, which meant a deficit. The solution, therefore, was not viable. The state, to be sure, being in control of prices and wages in the directed economy (*économie dirigée*) of the immediate post-war period, has not simply succumbed to that virtual coalition on the managing boards. In the beginning, however, the employees of the nationalized enterprises obtained important advantages, which were subsequently reduced to equalize conditions with the private sector. On the other hand, during the period of inflation the state was challenged every day by private business to 'give a good example' (which business was careful not to emulate) and therefore supplied the products and services of the nationalized enterprises at very low prices, in order to combat the general tendency of rising prices, and thus incurred a deficit which in the last instance meant a massive subsidization of the private sector." According to Warren C. Baum, *The French Economy and the State* (A Rand Corporation Research Study. Princeton: Princeton University Press, 1958, p. 182 f), the inherent weaknesses of the tripartite system were aggravated by Communist representation on the board. Communists as employees' and consumers' representatives had, of course, no interest in proving the French mixed economy workable.

reform subjected the nationalized industries to various control measures. Some of their transactions, involving the disposition of certain kinds of assets and the price policy of the enterprises, had to be approved in advance by a government commissioner, the State Comptroller or government commissions established for this purpose;[12] the control of investments, both administrative and legislative, was reinforced, and the same was true of the control of wages and salaries paid by the nationalized enterprises. The multiplication of controls caused a reaction, which for a moment seemed to result in a restoration of the autonomy of the enterprises as it had existed before, even in its enlargement, but the legislation of 1955 brought little more than a clarification and streamlining of government control;[13] and in 1958, when a new reform—in line with the constitutional changes which marked the assumption of power by De Gaulle—restricted legislative control, "the principal beneficiary . . . was not the nationalized enterprise but the executive power, and it even seems that the autonomy of the former has been further reduced to the advantage of the latter." [14]

It is still very early for any generalization to be drawn from the British and French nationalization experiences, and those of smaller Western countries are even less conclusive. However, it seems safe to assume that the old impulses for guild socialist or syndicalist solutions have exhausted themselves, and that therefore the trend toward *nationalisation industrialisée* will not be revived. Most probably, the development away from this concept was not merely a result of the desire to fit the nationalized industries into the national plan, and of other considerations of expediency, but also of the weakness of workers' desires to participate in management.[15] This con-

[12] Georges Lescuyer, *Le Contrôle de l'état sur les entreprises nationalisées.* Paris: Pichon et Durand-Auzias, 1959, pp. 136 ff. Some of these measures antedate the decrees of 1953.

[13] Lescuyer, *op. cit.,* pp. 160 ff.

[14] *Loc. cit.,* p. 172.

[15] The discussion of labor relations in nationalized industries occupies considerable space in the literature on nationalization. Many socialists hoped that the workers, who as citizens were co-owners of the nationalized plants, would not take as antagonistic a position toward management as they had taken when the plants were owned by private entrepreneurs. These hopes have been largely disappointed, perhaps most severely in France, where labor disputes in nationalized industries were frequent and grave during the first postwar years. "The nationalized sector has been particularly affected by strikes during recent years—in an especially tragic manner in the coal mines (1948); the feeling of being 'at home' (*d'être chez eux*) in the mine has been destroyed with the miners. Although a real *esprit de corps* still exists in the National Railroad Corporation and to a less extent in the Electric Power Authority, in general the integration of the workers into the nationalized enterprises is still inadequate." (George Lasserre, *op. cit.,* p. 36); see also George Levasseur, *"La Situation du personnel dans les enterprises nationalisées";* for the Renault Works, see the somewhat more optimistic picture given by Jean Myon in his article, "La Politique des relations sociales à la Regie Renault," all in M. Boiteux (ed.) *Le Fonctionnement,* p. 394. On British experience, see several Acton Society Trust

clusion is supported by the West-German experience showing that workers' interest in "co-determination" in private industries was not sustained in the degree that the authors of the co-determination schemes had anticipated. In this respect, Western experience is different from that of Yugoslavia, where workers have apparently shown strong interest in managing factories under their own responsibility. But in Yugoslavia the workers' committees have been given a far greater share of entrepreneurial functions than in France or Britain and other Western countries. In engaging the workers' interest in management, half-way measures are apparently not of much use. On the other hand, it is highly improbable that the Western countries will reorganize their nationalized industries according to the principles of the Yugoslav system, and it is by no means certain that these principles would prove fruitful in so different an environment.

In any event, it is interesting to notice that in regard to the powers of state authorities supervising or directing the management of public enterprises, there is a difference in trend between Western and Eastern Europe. In the West, where partial nationalization was imposed on capitalism as a corrective of its maladjustments, it has been found necessary to strengthen the hand of the government vis-à-vis the management of nationalized industries in order to achieve the purpose. In the East, where communism originally made short shrift of capitalist property and the capitalist market system, there is now a tendency either to reintroduce real decentralization, in order that the individual enterprises can act on the market as units with a will of their own, or to bind the central government agencies by rules of economic rationality and thereby curtail their power of forcing the individual enterprises to actions that would adversely affect their financial status, or to introduce both these reforms at the same time. In the most important Eastern country, the USSR, the tendency is still weak; it is nevertheless unmistakable.

INDUSTRIAL GIANTISM VERSUS DECENTRALIZATION

Increasing the power of the state administration over the executives and boards of directors of the nationalized concerns is one kind of centralization, but the problem of how this power should be delimited is not the only form in which the problem of centralization versus decentralization comes up within the nationalized sector; there is also the question of whether it is preferable to establish giant enterprises without autonomous subdivisions,

studies, especially *The Future of the Unions* (1951), *The Framework of Joint Consultation* (1952), and *The Worker's Point of View* (1952); also Robson, *op. cit.*, pp. 338 ff.

or to divide the tasks of production and distribution among smaller enterprises, or to find an intermediate solution by establishing very large enterprises but providing for some subdivisions with a modicum of autonomy. The latter type has become particularly important where regional decentralization is regarded as desirable.

In such fields as electric power and heating gas, the rationale of regional decentralization is the interest of local consumers: In coal mining, the rationale is primarily the dependence of whole communities or even districts on the volume of mine operations. In either respect, the case for regional autonomy is weakened by the frequent necessity to overrule local interests in order to carry out general reforms. Britain, France and other countries with nationalized industries have therefore tried to find a balance between centralization and decentralization.

In the British coal industry, the National Coal Board determines only general policy, while divisional coal boards "appoint the area general managers and hold them to account, coordinate selling policy and activity, provide common services (including engineering advice) and so on. They also negotiate such district wage agreements as still exist. They are authorized to spend up to £100,000 on any one project and, according to the 1948 annual report, out of about £40 million capital expenditures authorized in that year, some £27 million was authorized in the divisions without referring to the National Board."[16] Decentralization in electricity production and distribution is probably somewhat less real than in the coal industry,[17] but the heating gas industry has been effectively decentralized.[18]

The administration of the French nationalized coal mines has from the

[16] Austen Albu, "The Organization of Nationalized Industries and Services," in Robson (ed.), *op. cit.*, p. 82. Robson himself, who in his concluding analysis intended to bring the content of the book up to date (as of 1952), tried to modify the picture given by Albu through the following comment: ". . . a quarter of a century's experience of the BBC has taught shrewd observers the difference between 'managerial decentralization' and true independence. The National Coal Board, like the BBC, is a highly centralized power structure, and any freedom accorded to a division, region, area or colliery is always liable to be overriden by a central organ. No amount of sophisticated talk can set aside this simple fact. Managerial discretion, which depends for its continuance on central aproval and compliance with policies laid down at headquarters, is not to be confused with independence or autonomy" (p. 292). Complete autonomy, of course, would have been assured if each "division" had been organized as a separate corporation, but such a measure would probably have made it impossible to carry out the rationalization process in the British coal industry, which required the partial or complete closing of some mines without too much regard for opposing local interests. Moreover, effective parliamentary control required a substantial degree of centralization of authority: ". . . if the Coal Board (for instance) is to be held responsible for mistakes comitted in the pits, it must have power to rectify those mistakes." (Acton Trust Study #6, *The Extent of Centralization*, Part I, p. 4.)

[17] See Robson (ed.), *op. cit.*, p. 86, 294.

[18] *Loc. cit.*, pp. 294-5.

beginning been more decentralized than its British counterpart, because for each of the coal fields there was a separate body possessing legal personality and exercising the entrepreneurial functions. Above these enterprises, it is true, a coordinating body was established, called *Charbonages de France.* Although the relationship between the *Charbonages* and the individual coal mines still seems in need of further elucidation, the latter undoubtedly possess substantial autonomy.[19]

Originally, considerable regional decentralization was provided for the nationalized French power and heating gas industries, but the degree in which this intention has been realized is difficult to judge because the laws which, according to the original program, were supposed to implement the framework legislation have not been enacted.[20]

The arguments for regional decentralization often overlap with the more general thought that it is unwise to let an enterprise grow too big, because of the various "diseconomies of scale," especially in view of the difficulty for top management to keep all parts of a giant enterprise under close supervision. This problem is, of course, not unknown to private industry, but has particular significance in public ownership because some of the nationalized industries exceed in size all or most of the private business corporations; for instance, the nationalized coal industry in the United Kingdom has more employees than any private enterprise.[21]

A special motive for decentralization of public enterprise is fear of monopoly, although this motive is not important in all nationalized industries; for instance, the nationalized Renault factory in France, exposed as it is to keen national and international competition, can hardly engage in serious monopolistic price policies. Probably the problem is also not too important in the French coal mining industry, because within the European Economic Community, the French coal mines have to meet the competition of Belgian and Dutch coal producers and especially of the German Ruhr,

19 An official French publication describes the situation as follows: "Each of the nationalized coal fields constitutes a legal person and possesses financial and commercial autonomy; it is administered by a managing board consisting of 16 members, appointed by the government for five years: two members representing the supervising ministries (*ministères de tutelle*), two the consumers, six the employees, three chosen 'because of their competence in industrial and financial affairs,' and three delegated by the *Charbonages de France*. A public agency called *Les Charbonages de France* is placed, in effect, above the coal field administration and managed by a board of 15 members, of whom five represent the ministries, two the consumers, five the employees, and three are persons chosen as experts (*intuiti personae*). The board has the task to direct, coordinate and control the technical activities of the coal mines and to play the role of intermediary between them and the public administration." (La Documentation française, *Les Institutions politiques de la France* (Marcel Martin, ed.) Paris: 1959, Vol. I, p. 376.)

20 See *ibid.*, p. 377.

21 See Robson, *op. cit.*, p. 292.

which are all in sufficiently close proximity to sell to French customers.[22] British coal mining , on the other hand, has to meet competition only in export, which would not prevent monopolistic exploitation of the domestic market, and even true competition among the geographic divisions would have such an effect only to a limited extent. Fear of monopolistic exploitation was probably the main reason why it was found necessary to provide for spokesmen for the consumers in the affairs of nationalized industries: In France, the consumers' representatives are members of the managing boards; in Britain, they form separate advisory councils.[23] Consumer representation as a substitute for competition, however, has not proved very effective. Can decentralization restore competition?

Decentralization would have to go very far—as far as it has gone in Yugoslavia, or farther—in order by itself to prevent monopoly pricing, and it is at least doubtful whether such a splitting up into relatively small units is possible in most nationalized industries, which are even less suitable for small-scale operation than many branches of private industry. Wherever the management of individual nationalized enterprises shows a tendency toward monopoly pricing, prevention of such practices often depends on the enforcement of instructions from above to keep the competitive price line. This tendency is more likely to appear, other things being equal, the more intense is the interest of the managers in the financial success of the enterprise. In view of this situation, restricted autonomy of individual enterprises, the opposite of decentralization, will often be a more promising means of protecting the consumer.

These are considerations that can be deduced from economic principles; actual information about the extent of monopolistic price policies by nationalized enterprises is not sufficient to permit a general judgment. The effectiveness of institutional safeguards of consumers' interests, including competition, is only part of the story; such intangibles as the role of the idea of service in the motivation of executives and managing boards of the nationalized industries, or their fear of intensified government control in the event of widespread consumers' dissatisfaction may sometimes give the consumer more protection than any devices deliberately created for this purpose by legislation.

[22] It is a different question, debated publicly among experts, whether the policies of the European Coal and Steel Community are not themselves monopolistic. To the extent that they are, this is a matter beyond the purview of French national policy.

[23] See Robson (ed.), *op. cit.*, pp. 326 ff.

SUCCESS OR FAILURE?

As for the success of nationalization as a venture in economic management, the idea that state ownership necessarily means inefficiency has certainly been disproved, but beyond this point no conclusive statement is possible. The British nationalized coal mines have kept their operational budget in balance but have not earned enough in excess of expenses to pay the full service on the securities issued to the former owners in compensation for their property; considering the state of the industry before nationalization, this appears to be neither a bad nor a splendid record. Railroads, which in all European countries are state-owned, have been under heavy pressure of competition from highway transportation; in view of this handicap, they seem to have done a respectable job, especially in rapid reconstruction after the war, but whether their efficiency compares favorably or unfavorably with the record of privately owned American railroads can only be determined by detailed research, which so far nobody has undertaken. Production and distribution systems for electric power and heating gas, traditional domains of public ownership in Europe, have in all probability expanded their services at least as much as they would have under private management, but then in these fields the advantages of unified planning and administration are particularly great; where the financial results have been disappointing, as in France, this seems due either to unreasonably low rates imposed on the enterprise (in the case of electricity) or to adverse technological developments (in the case of gas).[24] Whether the British experience in the nationalization of highway transport and steel—where partial retrenchment was effected after Labour had gone out of power—proves anything against government ownership is still highly controversial. Perhaps the most interesting cases of public ownership have occurred in the automobile industry: the Renault factory and the Volkswagenwerk. Until the latter became a private enterprise—a recent measure unlikely to have a great effect on efficiency—the two most successful car manufacturing concerns on the European continent were not in private hands.[25]

[24] See André Bisson, *Institutions financières et économiques en France.* Paris: Ed. Berger-Levrault, 1960, pp. 200 ff.

[25] The legal ownership of the Volkswagenwerk was controversial, since capital had originally, in the Nazi period, been provided by private individuals who made deposits for the eventual purchase of a car but never received one in return for their money. Although many of these people claimed to be owners or co-owners of the enterprise, their claims were never recognized and they were not granted any influence upon the administration. In any event, the Volkswagenwerk was actually managed as a government-owned enterprise until 1960-61, when it was reorganized as a private business corporation. This reorganization was by no means the outcome of disappointing financial results, which on the contrary were gratifying, but was a result of the German government's de-

For the French nationalized industries, Lasserre has stated his opinion that their achievements in regard to efficiency have been:

A. Excellent from an engineering point of view, since the nationalized sector has secured immense progress in productivity and in volume of production, such as could not have been expected of the previous private management;

B. Less good from the administrative point of view, since the inherent cumbersomeness (*inconvenients*) of the giant enterprise was difficult to overcome; the facts stated by the control commission, however, do not indicate any faults more serious than those observable in the private sector;

C. Perhaps still less good from the commercial point of view, for just in the area of bargaining relations with private firms, often under bilateral monopoly, the absence of personal interest on the part of negotiators for nationalized enterprise puts the latter in an inferior position with regard to clever maneuvering and hard bargaining.[26]

Lasserre then points out that the nationalized enterprises have not been guilty, to any great extent, of economically favoring vested interests at the expense of their own proper goals—presumably this judgment is not meant to apply to the early period of deficit operations in favor of consumers and employees—and that they have not succumbed to "economic Malthusianism"—meaning acquiescence in stagnation. Lasserre also points out that the nationalized enterprises have faithfully served the modernization plan of the French government.

What Lasserre suggests in regard to the inferior bargaining position of nationalized enterprise in dealings with private firms may have had more validity for France at the time of his writing than it had in countries in which the giant corporation, with its bureaucracy, is more distinctly dominant in the private sector, as it will probably be also in France in the future.[27] Of greater general interest is his suggestion that in nationalized

---

sire to withdraw from competition with private industry. Since part of the stock has remained in government hands and the rest (the majority) has been sold at preferential prices to small stockholders who will be unable to exercise effective influence on management, it seems practically certain that results will not be substantially affected by the change in ownership.

[26] Lasserre, *op. cit.*, p. 36.

[27] Lasserre's reference to "bilateral monopoly" is not necessarily incompatible with this assumption, since even medium-sized enterprises may have a monopolistic or semi-monopolistic position on the basis, for instance, of patent rights. On the other hand, Lasserre offers little if any evidence to substantiate or even illustrate the disadvantageous bargaining position in which he presumes the nationalized enterprise to be, and it seems possible that even so careful an analyst as he has at this point been too much influenced by the widespread belief in a fundamental difference in the motivation of executives ultimately dependent on government and those dependent on private stockholders or banks.

enterprises the engineer's point of view may prevail over commercial management's more often than the interest of profitability—at least short-term profitability—dictates; he speaks, in this context, of "excessive investments" and "technocrat bias." [28] Although the evidence is inadequate to substantiate the general proposition that technological progressiveness is more likely to prevail over other considerations in publicly owned enterprise than in private corporations, some observations do point in this direction; this question provides a fertile field for future research.

Evaluation of the achievements of nationalized industries during the post-World War II period is handicapped by the fact that most of the available studies are based on figures of the early 1950's, when conditions were still far from normal. Although searching French studies have been made more recently than British investigations of the same quality,[29] the effect is even worse in the case of France, which experienced a very rapid rise of industrial output in the second half of the decade—interrupted, it is true, by a setback in 1958, mainly due to a foreign currency crisis. Naturally, the general business situation greatly influences the markets and therefore the financial status of nationalized industries as well as of private industry; actually, in a country such as France, where nationalized plants are largely in industries of high business-cycle sensitivity, the influence of general economic conditions must be felt even more in the public than in the private sector of business. Since France's nationalization experience is at least as important as Britain's for an evaluation of the potentialities of nationalized industries, no definitive results of such an evaluation can be expected until some more up-to-date studies, covering a longer segment of the more dynamic period of the French postwar economy, are available.

Cooperatives

SOME BASIC PROBLEMS

Collective ownership does not necessarily mean state ownership. Since modern socialism exists as a movement, socialists have always seen cooperatives as an alternative, and often it has been the preferred alternative. Although Great Britain is the mother country of modern consumer cooperatives, which still play a great role in the United Kingdom, the cooperative

[28] Lasserre, *op. cit.*, p. 36.

[29] The careful analysis by André Bisson, whose connection with the *Coeur des Comptes*, a judicial body with functions roughly comparable to those of the Comptroller General in the United States, has given him unusual insight into the financial condition of the nationalized industries, was published as recently as 1960 and uses some 1957 figures.

movement has reached an even higher level of development in some smaller countries, notably Belgium, Sweden and Israel.

The cooperative movement, more than the labor unions and more even than political socialism, has proved to be a force shaping habits and philosophy of life in many individuals; the idea of human brotherhood and the belief that the economy should be organized to foster rather than destroy feelings of human brotherhood have found more of a home in the cooperatives than anywhere else in modern times. This is most clear in Belgium, where cooperatives were formed earlier than labor unions of any substantial strength and where the whole longing of a miserably paid working class for a better society crystallized in the cooperative institutions during the last decades of the nineteenth century. The cooperative centers (*maisons du peuple*) became the focus of workers' lives to an extent unheard of elsewhere. For the working class family, they provided not merely purchasing facilities, but also opportunities for education and cultural pursuits, and were headquarters of political, labor union and welfare activities. Thus a cluster of proletarian organizations was formed around the Belgian consumer cooperatives, and the support of these organizations sometimes overshadowed the immediate economic purpose of consumer cooperation. Although much of the force of sentiment which sustained the Belgian cooperative movement before the First World War has been spent, a strong remnant remains.

In Sweden, cooperatives are conducted more like other business enterprises than in Belgium. They are quite active not only in the distribution but also in the production of commodities, and in some industries the output of their enterprises represents a high percentage of national output. In other countries, too, consumers' cooperatives produce a substantial portion of the commodities which they sell in their stores, but in Sweden the cooperative-owned factories sell a great deal on the general market. This means, on the one hand, a greater volume for the cooperative sector, on the other hand, an abandonment, or at least weakening, of the idea that the cooperative sector should be kept clearly separate from capitalist business—that it should form a closed circle in which the profit motive should play no role.

In the older type of literature on the cooperative movement, a very clear line was drawn between consumer cooperatives and producer cooperatives. The latter were defined as groups of workers, possessing their own instruments of production and using them for their own account, sharing profit and loss. In contradistinction, consumer cooperatives were originally associations of consumers formed for the purpose of collectively purchasing and distributing the commodities they needed; gradually, these associations began to produce some commodities in their own factories. These self-producing consumer cooperatives are still distinguished from producer cooperatives by their way of distributing profit—according to purchases instead of in equal shares or by work done—and usually not all members are working in the cooperative factories; but the line has been somewhat blurred.

When cooperative-owned factories supply only cooperative stores, the tasks of management are greatly simplified, because they can count on a steadier market than capitalist enterprises: The cooperative store will always prefer to sell cooperative products; although the customers of the cooperative stores, as those of capitalist business, cannot buy as much during periods of mass unemployment as during prosperity, yet the close familiarity of cooperative management with the situation of consumer members makes it easier to anticipate sales volume and adjust store orders sufficiently in advance to facilitate the dispositions of the production managers. This is an advantage which helps to explain why these cooperatives could successfully compete with profit-motivated enterprises, although the latter often had better-trained managers. Producer cooperatives, however, were not in such a favorable position; they had to sell on the open market.

Another advantage of consumer over producer cooperatives is probably even more important. In producer cooperatives, the whole membership, with rare exceptions, works in the cooperative shop or factory. Managers and foremen are elected by the people whose work they direct. That is to say, the men who are charged with maintaining work discipline are dependent for their positions on those whom they have to discipline; good results, therefore, depend on an unusually high moral standard among the membership. In consumer cooperatives, on the other hand, management is usually supported in its efforts to keep reasonably good work discipline by those members who find their living outside the cooperative sector, and who are typically a majority.

For these reasons most writers have been skeptical about the chances for success of producer cooperatives in modern production; for a long time practical experience generally confirmed this pessimism. Nor has it been disproved by recent developments, but the latter may provide grounds for a more cautious judgment. In very limited areas, especially in the building trades, producer cooperatives seem to have been successful in some Western countries;[1] the crossbreeding of state planning with the principle of

[1] The best known example is the German *Bauhuette,* which flourished especially in the inter-war period.

producer cooperatives, as in Yugoslavia, has great achievements to its credit; most important, in the State of Israel various forms of cooperative production have proved at least moderately successful.

WHAT CAN BE LEARNED FROM THE ISRAELI EXPERIENCE?

In the first place, cooperative landholding and land cultivation have been popular in Israel, and have been one of the pillars of the Israeli economy during the first years of existence of the new state. Although there are some indications that their relative importance may be declining in favor of individual farming—supported, as in other countries, by cooperatives for purchasing supplies, marketing products, and procurement of credit—the *kibbutzim* still represent a substantial section of Israeli agriculture and have retained the loyalty and allegiance of numerous men and women.

This experience is in sharp contrast with that of the Communist countries, in which collectivization of agriculture has been unpopular and its effect on productivity disappointing even where conditions of soil and climate seemed far more favorable to large-scale than to small-scale agriculture, as in Eastern Europe and especially in the Eastern part of Germany.[2] Part of the explanation is undoubtedly that the *kibbutzim* had a very good start, whereas the opposite is true of communist collectivization. From the outset, the *kibbutzim* were true cooperatives, governing themselves completely; the Soviet collective farms, the kolkhozes, were organized by order of the Soviet government against the will of a terrorized peasantry and granted only such limited autonomy as constituted an intermediate form between state farms and cooperatives; a continuous fear on the part of the Soviet authorities lest the kolkhozes develop into centers of resistance operated against abolition of the controls by which the autonomy of the cooperatives was restricted. In those satellite nations where collectivization was carried out, the development was similar, with the aggravating circumstance that the end of individual landholding came as a result of the policies of a foreign power. Furthermore, the Israeli *kibbutzim* were formed by young people whose families had never owned land individually

[2] Much of the area between the Elbe and Oder rivers consists of sandy, not very fertile soils, and the climate is harsh. On the other hand, the country is to a great extent flat and therefore suitable to the application of mechanized equipment. Although in other parts of Eastern Europe, especially in wide areas of the Soviet Union, the soil is fertile, the major part of the land also consists of plains and therefore invites cultivation by the tractor; since mechanized equipment is easier to apply on large contiguous holdings, natural conditions favored the communist collectivizations experiments, and the failure or limited success of these undertakings shows the strength of the adverse psychological factors.

and who often were socialists before they set foot on Palestinian soil. Communist collectivization came to an intensely property-conscious peasantry with a tradition of individual land management—even in European Russia, where property in land (though not the operation of farms) had once been vested in the village community, this institution had been in decay before the revolution. Members of the new Israeli settlements were men and women of good education and of an attitude favorable to scientific innovation;[3] the Russian peasant was just emerging from the level of widespread illiteracy when collectivization began, and, like peasants in most countries, was conservative in methods of work and mistrustful of all manifestations of the scientific mind. It was as easy to teach the Israeli settlers the use of the devices that make large-scale farming superior to small operations as it was difficult to achieve the same purpose in Russia. The Israeli experiment shows that cooperative farming can be popular and successful; the experience of the Soviet Union and its satellites shows that political mistreatment of the peasantry and high-pressure methods in introducing collectivization can frustrate all the advantages of modern agricultural technology.

In the industrial sector of the Israeli economy, many enterprises are owned and managed by a cooperative organization: Some of these factories are run by the *kibbutzim,* mainly as a means to provide supplemental employment for the members.[4] There is also a substantial number of producers' cooperatives founded for the purpose of running an industrial shop, but

[3] Since the initiation of the experiment, new immigrants from Mohammedan countries, many with poor education, may have found their way into the *kibbutzim,* but they have had to fit into the framework of tradition built by the founders.

[4] "When I visited *kibbutz* factories I felt the presence of the shades of Charles Fourier and Robert Owen. *Kibbutz* industry is not only the archaic turned modern but also the utopian turned real. But all the same *kibbutz* industry developed historically out of economic necessities as a response to concrete and pressing situations." Ferdynand Zweig, *The Israeli Worker.* New York: Herzl Press, 1959. The purity of the cooperative principle is marred by the practice of many *kibbutzim* of using hired laborers, rather than exclusively members, in their industrial enterprises during periods of labor shortage (*loc. cit.,* p. 225). This is also becoming more frequent in the agricultural work (*loc. cit.,* p. 91). But it seems that the use of hired labor is due not to the desire of the old members not to let in new ones in order to keep the profits for themselves—the reason which caused some of the successful utopian settlements in early nineteenth century America to turn themselves eventually into business corporations—but to the difference in culture, efficiency and willingness to work between the *kibbutz* members and the laborers. The members are usually immigrants from Europe with a community spirit springing from socialist tradition; the laborers are typically Jews of near Eastern origin who have no such tradition and consider employment by the *kibbutz* in the same category as work for any other employer. The hired man who sees the *kibbutz* member work harder and longer hours for a wage that he cannot even take home has, as a rule, little desire to acquire membership, and the old member often finds these newcomers to Israel culturally and spiritually unsuited to the life of the community and therefore unacceptable as permanent participants.

these groups seem to suffer from the traditional weaknesses of producers' cooperatives and "their death rate exceeds their birth rate." [5] The most important of all the cooperative enterprises, however, are those run by the Histadrut.

The Histadrut is often described as the Israeli labor federation, but it is misleading to regard it as an organization analogous to the American Federation of Labor, the British Trades Union Congress, the *Confédération Générale du Travail* or the *Deutsche Gewerkschaftsbund.* In the first place, affiliated with the Histadrut are not only labor unions but also *kibbutzim,* other cooperatives, housewives and self-employed persons; like the Knights of Labor in the United States during the late nineteenth century, the Histadrut regards itself as an organization of all people "of honorable toil." [6]

In its role as a roof over labor unions, the Histadrut is not a federation: The individual worker must join the Histadrut before he can join a union, and the unions have little autonomy; most of them do not even collect membership fees but are financed from Histadrut funds. The weakness of the position of the individual unions results largely from history: The Histadrut was founded before most of the unions came into existence, and many of the latter were formed through the initiative of the Histadrut. In this respect, the closest analogy to the development of the Israeli labor movement is the labor history of Belgium, where the socialist party existed before there were any strong unions; the socialist party created most of the unions by initiative from above, and for a long time kept them under tutelage, directing labor union activities through a party committee. The analogy with Belgium holds in another respect: The Histadrut maintains an elaborate organization for workers' welfare and cultural advancement.

In addition to all its other functions, however, the Histadrut is the largest employer in Israel. It runs a giant construction firm; through a holding company, it owns and manages all sorts of factories. In some of the Histadrut enterprises private capital has a share; others, especially in the field of transportation, are operated in partnership with the government. For this reason alone the Histadrut sector of the Israeli economy cannot be regarded as having a purely cooperative character, but there is a strong cooperative feature in the Histadrut management of industrial enterprise. The ideas of the Knights of Labor and of British unionists at various

[5] *Ibid.,* p. 233.

[6] The Knights of Labor, however, did not go so far as to organize housewives. As Zweig suggests (p. 249), the purpose of this unique feature of the Histadrut organization is to emphasize the importance of the housewife's role in the new state, to counteract her disabilities under rabbinical law, which in Israel governs family relations among Jews.

times, that labor organizations charged with the functions of unions should also own instruments of production, seem to have come closer to fulfillment in Israel than elsewhere, although in an impure form. But the whole industrial (even the agricultural) organization in Israel appears to be much in flux; critical economic situations will have to be dealt with in the future—especially when the Israeli balance of payments loses the support of the influx of German marks through reparations; the groups which showed the greatest socialist enthusiasm are likely to be gradually overshadowed by recent immigrants who are untouched by that tradition. Thus it would be too early to draw any far-reaching general conclusions from the cooperative experience of Israel; thus far nothing more has been proved than the viability of some forms of producer cooperatives under favorable circumstances.

In spite of the role which cooperative production plays in some smaller countries, for the world as a whole it has remained a fringe phenomenon. In the United States, capitalist production predominates; in the Soviet Union, industry is nationalized, and in agriculture the so-called cooperatives, the kolkhozes, are too restricted in their right of self-government to be regarded as true cooperatives; moreover, it sometimes looks as if the Soviet government might discard or restrict the use of the kolkhoz organization in favor of state-run farms, the Sovkhozes. What form of organization will finally prevail in China after the apparent failure of the agricultural communes is entirely unclear. Although the successes of the cooperative principle in limited areas make it more probable that the role of that principle will be greater than most social scientists assumed a few decades ago, this is entirely a matter of conjecture, and at present the enthusiasts for cooperation hardly have a better case than the skeptics.

One thing, however, is quite certain which was not so clear to the early advocates of cooperative production: Its fate is tied to the fate of the market. Cooperative production, no less than capitalistic production, needs steering by a rational market price. It will be seen later that without rational pricing even a system of completely nationalized industry can have only limited success, but for cooperative production this necessity is still more obvious. Cooperatives are individual enterprises making their own decisions, and there is no way to integrate these self-steering units into economic society except through the market. A centralized industrial administration may, at great sacrifice in efficiency, get along with physical planning alone, at least as long as no high level of development is attained. No such possibility exists where economic units, as cooperatives, are governing themselves.

CHAPTER 13

SOCIALIST PRICING AND PLANNING

The Socialists Accept the Market but Want Planning

SINCE THE TURN OF THE CENTURY socialists have become increasingly converted to the idea that even a wholly nationalized system of production, once it has outgrown the stage at which only primitive needs can be satisfied, cannot function rationally except through a market in which prices are formed. This is one of the most remarkable developments in the history of economic thought.

Previously the socialists tended to regard the competitive market and the prices which emerge from this market as a phenomenon of capitalism which—in so far as they gave any thought to the operational details of the future economy[1]—they wished to replace by a central administration, steering production on the basis of physical considerations alone: So much of each commodity can be produced with resources available and therefore should be produced. In this way the socialists of the nineteenth century be-

[1] From about 1870 to about 1900, the socialist movement on the European Continent and in the United States was under the predominant influence of a Marxist orthodoxy whose outlook was essentially deterministic. The victory of socialism seemed preordained, a historical necessity, because the process of economic concentration would finally leave only a few giant enterprises on the one hand, a huge mass of exploited proletarians on the other, and would thereby destroy the viability of capitalism. Although in the Marxists' own thoughts this deterministic orientation competed with the idea that a revolution would be required to replace capitalism by socialism, the prevailing tendency was to assume that human action could do no more than accelerate the historical process —"shorten the birthpangs"—and that the process could not be planned, either with regard to the destruction of the old order or to the construction of the new one. The elaboration of any detailed proposals for the future society was therefore regarded, by most socialists, as a return to the faulty approach of pre-Marxian writers, the so-called Utopians.

lieved that their system would free mankind not only from the tyranny of the capitalists but also from the tyranny of the profit-and-loss account; that the economic limitations on the use of technological possibilities would be removed, and that for this reason humanity would come to enjoy a state of unheard-of plenty. Now socialists have come to realize that these limitations cannot be removed, because there is never enough labor, equipment and material to produce everything that, from the engineer's point of view, could be produced. Socialists have learned that a comparison of prospective output and required input in terms of their values is necessary to make a choice among the many technologically possible uses of resources. Economic value means importance for the achievement of desired purposes; value calculation is to tell us whether the goods and services we have to sacrifice in a particular production process, performed or contemplated, are more or less important than those we can obtain—whether cost exceeds return or the reverse; since all cost is opportunity cost, this definition is synonymous with the statement that value calculation is to show whether by producing different goods or producing the same goods in a different way, we could gain an opportunity to serve the purposes of production better. For socialists, the purposes of production are determined by the interests of the consumers; to the extent that these interests are mutually compatible, the demand schedule of individual consumers, together with supply conditions, must determine values; for incompatible collective and "spectator" interests, the same task must be solved through the establishment of a priorities schedule by majority decision in the course of a democratic process. (How much should be paid for varying quantities and diverse kinds of defense goods? how much for varying quantities and qualities of teaching service, materials and labor for school buildings? etc.)

On the capitalist market the value of each commodity is found through the bargaining of suppliers and purchasers and expressed in the market price; the government has to participate in this bargaining to satisfy collective needs and utilize collectively owned sources of supply. The market prices supply the orientation points for production. Although price-oriented production, for a variety of reasons, for instance because it does not by itself preclude monopolistic tendencies, does not assure optimal satisfaction of the purposes recognized by society, it comes close enough to convince most of us that this method of steering the economy is preferable to any alternative. This near-unanimity, as far as "Western" countries are concerned, is no longer confined to believers in capitalism. Socialists agree not only that price calculation is necessary, but also that prices should be formed on a "live" market; that is, not to be dictated by a central agency, but to result from bargaining among economic units which must possess the autonomy necessary for such bargaining. Nationalized industries should bid for resources on the market, trying to get supplies as cheaply as possible, and on the other hand should attempt to obtain the best price they can under competition for whatever they have to offer (except that some goods and services should be supplied gratis or below cost at public expense). Consumers should freely bid for all available commodities. If nationalized enterprises compete with private industry, this price is clearly definable, and it will be exceeded only if collusion cannot be prevented. The situation is the same if effective competition among state-owned enterprises in a fully nationalized industry can be enforced. But if the nationalized industry is in a monopoly position, as is usually the case with public utilities and with other industries when administration is highly centralized, then the managers will have to be instructed to set the price which would exist under competition. To find this price may not be an easy task—the problem is well known from monopoly control of private industry in capitalism—and if the managers have a stake in the financial success of the nationalized enterprises, supervision must make sure that the temptation to keep prices above the competitive level will be resisted.

The rationale of instructing managers of nationalized industries not to set the prices above the competitive level is the argument that competitive pricing tends to maximize welfare. Some reservations to the validity of this argument have been discussed before in analyzing capitalism. Another reservation must be added—although it is hardly of practical importance either now or in the foreseeable future—because it has played a considerable role in the discussion on value calculation under socialism. Economic analysis has learned to distinguish between marginal and average cost; the former is the cost of the "last" unit of a given output (defined more precisely: the cost that would be saved if the output were reduced by one unit) and the latter is the total cost divided by the number of units. If unit cost does not vary with output—the case of "constant cost"—average and marginal cost are obviously identical. If more units can only be obtained at higher cost per unit—due for instance to the necessity of using less productive sources of material or less efficient labor when output is to be increased—the marginal cost will be higher than average cost; if greater output can be produced at lower cost per unit, due to the advantages of large-scale production, marginal cost will be below average cost. The price most conducive to maximum welfare—if difficulties in determining and enforcing this price do not absorb too much effort—is the price that equals marginal cost, and thereby causes a volume of demand that makes marginal utility equal to marginal cost; for no unit of a commodity should be produced for which consumers are not willing to refund the cost, and every unit for which consumers are willing to pay the cost of production should be produced.

The rule that the price should be set at marginal cost causes no difficulty in the case of constant cost, or in the case of unit cost rising with output. In the latter case, some units will have additional income which the economic textbook classifies as rent; for instance, if unit costs rise with output because a greater volume of production requires the use of minerals dug from less productive mines, the mining enterprises exploiting the more productive deposits will be paid the relatively high prices covering the costs of the less productive mines. In a socialist economy in which the net revenue of all enterprises goes to the national treasury, the distinction between such rents and the profits dependent on the efficient operation of plants has only theoretical interest, but if the managers or other staff members share in the profits the latter must be distinguished from rent for the very practical purpose of preventing unfair differences of incomes; in either event, the price setting at the point of equality of marginal utility with marginal cost is perfectly feasible. In the event of costs declining with output, however, a policy of setting the price at the point where marginal utility equals marginal cost would force the production units to operate at a loss. Obviously, if marginal cost is lower than average cost, then a price just covering marginal cost will be below average cost. The units then would require a subsidy to stay in operation. In a capitalist economy, nobody will pay such a subsidy, and therefore capitalist enterprises must set the price at average cost in declining cost industries. Consequently, in these industries competitive pricing does not lead to such a delimitation of production as to secure the theoretical maximum of consumers' satisfaction, and therefore the discrepancy between marginal and average cost leads to a reservation with regard to the welfare effect of price-oriented production as it actually operates in a competitive private enterprise economy.

In an economy of old-style socialism, in which all enterprises would be collectivized, the subsidies might be paid from a fund drawing its income from the rents which units exploiting better-than-marginal resources in rising cost industries would have to pay to the community. If necessary, this revenue could be supplemented from the yield of general taxes. But even in a fully nationalized economy, such subsidization would involve formidable organizational and political problems. In a mixed economy of nationalized and private enterprise, the difficulties would be so aggravated as to be hardly capable of solution: Either there would have to be different principles of pricing for private and for nationalized industries, and this would lead to a distorted pattern of resource utilization; or the subsidization scheme would have to include private industry, and such an extension would invite serious misuses. Under these circumstances, pricing on the basis of average cost seems the only practicable solution for declining cost industries in the kind of economy for which contemporary socialists are striving, as well as for capitalist economies.

In no industry can output be increased indefinitely without reaching a point at which unit costs begin to rise and marginal cost therefore approaches and finally exceeds average cost. This is true because as output increases, resource bottlenecks develop; that is, some resources become particularly scarce and can be provided in greater quantities only by a greater production effort; also, to increase output in a particular industry, all sorts of resources must be drawn away from alternative uses of increasing importance; on the other hand, the advantages of large-scale production are bound to exhaust themselves eventually. Therefore, we would have only rising unit cost if for some products the limitation of demand did not forbid the extension of output to the point where units costs begin to rise; in the language of the economic textbook, in these cases the demand curve intersects with the average cost curve while the latter is still in the declining phase. If the rise of the standard of living continues in the industrialized countries and demand for many products therefore increases—meaning a shift of the demand curve to the right—some industries which now operate under declining costs will eventually show increasing costs. The loss of welfare caused by pricing according to average instead of to marginal cost will thereby be reduced but will not disappear, and it will not even become insignificant for a long time.

The problem of average versus marginal cost as a base for pricing may conceivably become practical in the future in the event that communist economies change their methods. With the possible exception of Yugoslavia, these countries are still too far from the application of realistic principles of pricing to make the distinction between average and marginal cost meaningful, and in Yugoslavia which has competition among worker-controlled enterprises, pricing by marginal cost would probably be impossible for the same reasons as in a capitalist economy. Moreover, in all Communist countries concern for consumers' welfare is still overshadowed by interest in rapid growth; since pricing by marginal cost would mean that of some types of consumer goods more would be produced, whereas the government wishes to emphasize producer goods production, application of the marginal cost principle to consumer goods industries would run against the line of policy. If communist price policies are rationalized and if orientation toward the consumer replaces the present emphasis on growth, it may well be that the countries possessing a Soviet type system may try to carry out pricing on the basis of marginal cost; whether they will succeed in solving the problems posited by this method can of course not be foreseen.[2]

Acceptance by the socialists of price formation by actual competition has become all the more inevitable since the socialists have moved away from the idea of total nationalization: If a system comprises both nationalized and private industry, the method of determining prices must be the same for both, if serious maladjustments are to be avoided.

In regard to price formation, it seems, there is no longer any differences between capitalism and socialism. But this appearance is somewhat deceptive. Socialists today are as willing as defenders of capitalism to use the price mechanism and refrain from disturbing it by arbitrary measures, but are not as willing to trust the spontaneous forces of the market to achieve desirable results; it is still a mark of socialist thinking to believe that the market needs a relatively high degree of conscious steering. This means that socialists must try to foresee the development of the market during a period to come, and then decide whether these developments are the most desirable that can be achieved, and if not, how the "signals" should be changed, i.e. how managers and householders can be induced, within the framework of the price mechanism, to take action different from that which they would take if left to their own devices, and thus secure better results for themselves and the economy as a whole. For instance, it may appear that the present pattern of production is bound to lead to an oversupply of some types of durable goods, because private producers fail to take the action of the "acceleration principle in reverse" sufficiently into account. In this event, the government may first call attention to the impending danger, in order to induce the industry to adjust its production schedule to the prospective decline in demand; the warning can then be reinforced by credit policy, both on the producers' and the consumers' side, to prolong the period of equipment demand and smooth the transition to mere replacement demand; finally, the government can take measures to retrain and relocate the part of the labor force which will eventually become superfluous in the afflicted industries. Such economic foresight and the drawing of policy con-

[2] For literature on this problem, see Arthur Pigou, *The Economics of Welfare*, 4th ed. London: The Macmillan Company, 1948; Part II, ch. II and Appendix III; Abba P. Lerner, *The Economics of Control,* New York: Macmillan, 1944, p. 181; Oscar Lange, *op. cit.,* pp. 77-78 (fn. 21); H. D. Dickinson, *Economics of Socialism,* London: Oxford University Press, 1939, pp. 105 ff.

clusions from this foresight is the essence of economic planning; the demand for planning appears in most socialist programs.

The task of improving the spontaneous operation of market forces has been recognized as a government responsibility in present-day capitalism, and the instruments which contemporary socialists would use to influence the market mechanism are also in the arsenal of governments of capitalist countries; even more important, in capitalist countries, too, the apparatus of economic foresight which is the prerequisite of a planned application of these instruments is gradually being improved. In this sense, the significant difference between contemporary capitalism and contemporary socialism is one of degree, and the borderline is flexible and may become increasingly blurred. At the present time, however, the difference is still of great importance. In capitalist countries, great efforts are made to anticipate individual market developments some months before they occur, but attempts to develop devices for comprehensive economic foresight over a period of years are still treated more as interesting intellectual experiments than as a vitally important task of economic reform, whereas the socialists tend to view economic planning as a prerequisite of sound economic policy, and they stress the need for comprehensiveness in foresight. Indeed, since all economic magnitudes and processes are interdependent, any partial effort in this field can achieve only limited success; likewise, since the need for foresight is based on the limitations of present prices as a guide to present economic action, in other words, on the existence of tendencies which may over a number of years frustrate measures to which we are now committing ourselves, short-range foresight has much less chance of showing a high corrective effect in regard to the failings of the market mechanism than long-range foresight. But the development of long-range, comprehensive economic foresight is impeded not only by the prevalence, in capitalistic countries, of the belief that the market mechanism needs only relatively slight correction, but also by great objective difficulties: The technique of such foresight is still at a low stage of evolution. What distinguishes the socialists from those opponents who call themselves conservatives or liberals (sometimes neo-liberals) is a greater willingness to pursue vigorously the goal of elaborating methods of foresight, a greater readiness to experiment with such methods and a greater confidence in the success of such experiments. Although no conclusive answer is yet possible to the question of whether such confidence is justified, partial successes have been obtained—whether they could have been obtained by non-Socialist methods is still controversial.

The Role of Prices in Planning

Comprehensive planning in a market economy is possible only if prospective and desirable developments are foreseen not merely in terms of physical quantities but also in terms of value. Foreseeing future prices, however, means deriving them from their determinants instead of waiting for them to be formed. Therefore the vast amount of literature discussing whether even a completely socialized economy—one in which all means of production would be publicly owned—could have a pricing system is by no means outdated. The arguments found in these writings merely have to be applied to somewhat different assumptions. Those economists who have denied the capacity of socialism to develop a pricing system, especially Ludwig von Mises,[3] argue that prices can be formed only on a "live" market, in which a multitude of buyers and sellers bid against each other. Under socialism, they maintain, there would be only one seller of goods and services, and, at least for labor and producer goods, only one buyer; no rational prices could therefore exist in a socialist system. If this argument were correct, it would not only prove the irrationality of old-style socialism but also the impossibility of devising proper policies for the conscious steering of any economy. Such a policy requires that prices be anticipated; they must, therefore, be calculated by a central agency before they result from the mutual bidding between buyers and sellers. In this case, no less than in that of a centrally administered economy, without a "live" market, it must be possible to determine prices independently of the actual bargaining among the market parties. Whether the "live" market does not exist at all, as in the models of socialism visualized by Mises and other neo-liberals, or whether we do not want to wait for the prices formed on the "live" market but wish to foresee the prices which will result from future supply and demand conditions, makes no difference in this one respect: We need a method of price determination independent of the "live" market. Therefore this need is as great for value planning, which is on the agenda of present-day socialism, as it was for the concepts of a totally nationalized economy without any elements of decentralization.

If the debate[4] had been kept entirely free from the intrusion of policy preferences—if the neo-liberals had had no ideological stake in the outcome—the possibility of determining prices independently of the market would hardly have been denied. Ever since the beginning of modern economics,

[3] See especially Ludwig von Mises, *Socialism* (tr. J. Kahane) New York: The Macmillan Company, 1936.

[4] For the details of the debate, see Carl Landauer, *European Socialism*, Berkeley and Los Angeles: University of California Press, 1960, Vol. II, pp. 1635 ff.

economists have been refining the rules governing equilibrium price. Supply and demand curves were drawn, showing at what prices per unit diverse outputs could be supplied and at what unit prices diverse quantities could be sold, with the point of intersection symbolizing the price at which the quantity that could be produced would equal the quantity that could be sold—the equilibrium price. To draw supply and demand curves is a legitimate method only on the condition that we can calculate prices if we know the supply-demand relationships, which means that we do not have to wait for the market to produce these prices. All modern economic science is based on the assumption that this is indeed possible.

It is true, however, that supply and demand curves are usually not drawn on the basis of ascertained facts, as would have to be done for the purpose of value planning, but under assumed conditions. In principle, to be sure, such assumptions can be verified; for generations, speculators, producers and dealers have been trying to anticipate the effects of changing supply conditions upon prices, and all of them with a modicum of success sufficient to encourage continuation of their efforts. This experience offers a strong argument for the probability that a central agency, equipped with more comprehensive information than any of these groups can possess, will be able to make informed guesses about the relevant data with sufficient accuracy to be practically useful. But on this and the related question of whether data can be evaluated with sufficient speed, a remnant of doubt remains which will be discussed a little later.

The market finds the equilibrium price only after fluctuations, with tentative prices set and then rectified by the forces tending toward an equilibrium; the same process can be undertaken by a central agency, setting prices according to a rough guess, estimating the supply and demand at that price and making the necessary adjustments in order to cause an excess of demand or supply to disappear. Thus a "paper" market can be constructed, on which it may be possible to try out prices in advance of their formation on the "live" market and to determine their effects on production and consumption.[5] In this way indicators may be gained for desirable changes in the "signals." New developments in economic theory and statistics, such as linear programming and the input-output scheme (mathematical techniques to assist the analyst in taking into account the interdependence of industries and in choosing the economically optimal production process), and the growth of that branch of economic science called econometrics (construction of conceptual models combined with an effort to verify the underlying assumptions statistically) may provide shortcuts for

[5] For prices on a paper market, the term "shadow prices" has recently come into use.

the anticipation of prices, but the essential character of that anticipation as a trial-and-error process will not be changed thereby.

It was stated earlier that basically all cost is opportunity cost. If we wish to find out what it will cost society to increase steel production by, say 5 per cent, we would have to calculate the importance of the purposes which will be left unfulfilled if resources are drawn into steel production from other uses. If more coal is used for steel, less can be used for the production of copper, or for the chemical industry, or as fuel in manufacturing, unless coal production can be expanded; and if it can be expanded, more labor and machinery will be needed, which will have to be spared from other uses, unless there is unemployment not only of men but also of equipment for mining and related purposes. On the capitalistic market, the character of the costs incurred by entrepreneurs as opportunity costs becomes obvious when we consider that the businessman who wants to use any resource for his own purpose must outbid other businessmen who wish to use the same resource for theirs; the ability of one entrepreneur to outbid others is ultimately determined by the willingness and ability of consumers to pay for the finished good, and these again are determined by the place of the ultimate want in the social hierarchy of wants. Consequently, the task of a planning agency to calculate opportunity costs for a future period is identical with the task of foreseeing the cost prices which will actually figure in managers' calculations—cost prices which are determined, aside from supply conditions, by rival demands of consumers.

Opportunity costs would be easier to calculate if each producer and consumer good were in itself capable of satisfying a want; but with negligible exceptions all resources have to be used jointly with other resources. Expansion as well as contraction of one industry always affects other industries. To increase any branch of manufacturing industry, we need more coal, but also more steel, perhaps more aluminum or cotton; if demand shifts from aluminum pots to enamelware, aluminum will be released, and its value will drop; since the latter is used in the airplane industry, it may be possible to produce more airplanes provided the complementary resources required for this production are available. Any shift in resources, therefore, has such a multitude of effects that the job of calculating them would indeed be impossible if literally all of them had to be taken into account.

Not only producer goods but also most consumer goods are used in conjunction. It would be of no use to have a refrigerator if food were lacking; even to go hungry to the theater is not an attractive proposition. One needs furniture for a house, and a house for furniture. Moreover, there is interdependence among consumer demands for various commodities through the limited size of incomes: The dollar I spend for a movie ticket I cannot spend on gasoline for a pleasure trip. If demand for a particular commodity declines or grows, which may be due to a change in availability or to a change in needs or tastes, the demand for a large number of other commodities, substitutes or complementary goods, will usually be affected, and thereby the task of the planning agency is further complicated.

Recalling again what has been said in the analysis of the capitalist market, the reader will remember that in a rationally organized economy each resource unit always tends to move to the use in which it can be assigned the highest value. Obviously, movements of resource units will occur until every unit of each resource is in the place in which it can have the same value as any other unit of the same kind—when any resource is so used that all its units have the same marginal utility. This is the state of equilibrium toward which the market is tending at any given moment. Equalization of the marginal utility of all resources is a condition of optimal utilization because as long as a resource unit A is in a place where its utility is lower than that of a unit B of the same kind, it means that unit A is serving a want which is more saturated than the want served by B. By being moved to the point where it will serve the less saturated want, A will acquire a higher utility.[6] As long as the state of equilibrium characterized by equal marginal utilities has not been reached, the utilization of resources, at least for the satisfaction of present wants, can still be improved. A value plan therefore must use the concept of this kind of equilibrium at least as a preliminary target, as a starting point of calculations. The planning agency may deliberately place a resource unit in a use in which it does not presently have the greatest possible utility because such an arrangement seems preferable from a long-term point of view, or for the sake of a purpose which does not figure in the economic calculus, but if so, the agency must calculate the marginal utility of each major resource in its present optimal uses to find the cost of deviating from this pattern.

Too Many Equations to Solve?

The equilibrium situation can be expressed in a system of equations. In each branch of production the value of the various cost goods (resource

[6] This is literally true only of very small units, otherwise the relocation of A will result in another want being oversaturated. Since in fact we often have to deal with indivisible units of substantial size, complete equalization of marginal utilities is impossible. The postulate should be understood as meaning that equalization should be approached as closely as existing indivisibilities permit.

units), including labor and managerial effort, must be equal to the value of the product. If the value of the cost goods were greater, the productive undertaking would not be rational and should be eliminated; if the value of the cost goods were smaller, this would show that their contribution to this particular branch of production has not yet been fully taken into account, and therefore an expansion of production of this branch would be in order. If a change occurs in the availability or in the opportunities of utilizing resources, the new data of course require changes in the system of equations; and because the data change incessantly—through the interdependence of supply and demand for almost all commodities—any change affects the whole system. The determination of the equilibrium, and of the optimal use of resources, is an elusive goal for the "live" market as well as for a planning agency. In order to calculate that optimal use precisely, the central agency would have to solve more equations faster than is humanly possible.

Many opponents of socialism and economic planning have used this argument. The reply of the socialists, most clearly formulated by Oscar Lange in his classic, *On the Theory of Socialism,* was to the effect that the planning agency would have to do nothing that is not being done in the capitalistic system as well. "The only 'equations' that would have to be 'solved' would be those of the consumers and the managers of production plants. These are exactly the same 'equations' which are solved in the present economic system and the persons who do the 'solving' are also the same. Consumers 'solve' them by spending their income so as to get out of it the maximum total utility; and the managers of production plants 'solve' them by finding the combination of factors and the scale of output which minimizes average cost." [7] Indeed, any action by a consumer or production manager is based on a calculation, sometimes rough, sometimes as precise as it can be made, to make sure that the various cost elements do not add up to some magnitude greater than the yield in money or satisfaction of wants; this is a process quite similar to the solving of equations which a central planning board would have to undertake.[8]

[7] Benjamin Lippincott (ed.), *On the Theory of Socialism.* Minneapolis: University of Minnesota Press, 1938, p. 88.

[8] The term "equation solving" is not quite correct when applied to the considerations guiding the economic actions of individuals, because what the individuals are striving for in each case is not equality but an inequality—as great a surplus of yield over costs as possible. However, if an entrepreneur notices that he is making an unusually high profit in one particular line of production, he may decide to expand it although this will bring down the price, at least if his competitors follow suit, and will thus reduce the margin. Therefore, though the effort in each instance is directed toward an inequality, the sum total of all these efforts normally tends to produce a movement toward equality of costs and yield.

Nevertheless, Lange's answer does not settle the problem as it must be put in this context. The equations must be solved on paper before they are solved in reality.[9] The paper process has to be carried out in time to guide economic action; producers and consumers cannot delay actions by which they keep their plants and households going; the question arises of whether the results of the agency's calculations can be transmitted to the economic units early enough to be of any use. This requires a procurement of the necessary data with sufficient speed; it is probably not too optimistic to assume that our statistical services are capable of sufficient improvement to satisfy this requirement. It appears less certain that the utilization of the data can be undertaken quickly enough.

One way to attack this problem is to utilize modern technology to the fullest extent to increase the speed of calculation: The electronic computer will certainly be a great help for planners, and its efficiency is likely to increase in the future. Another means, and perhaps a more important one, is the perfection of the technique of simplification. The speed with which the planning agency can arrive at results is in reverse proportion to the number of equations and to the required accuracy of solution; all methods by which that number can be reduced are helpful, and the wider the tolerance for error the faster can all the procedures be expected to work.

Permissible Inaccuracy

Nobody, of course, has ever proposed that the "paper market" should be drawn up as an advance picture of the real market in all its details. Certainly, no agency can anticipate the decisions of every consumer and

---

Similarly, a central agency planning economic processes will for each such process strive to maximize the surplus of yield over cost, without, of course, providing for monopolistic restriction. If the surplus is great, the planning agency will conclude that this particular production represents a better use of resources than others and therefore should be expanded at the expense of the latter. Whereas an individual manufacturer may prefer, as an alternative to expanding a highly profitable production, to leave well enough alone and enjoy the high profit margin, the planning agency is not interested in superprofits for an individual industry and will, therefore, use whatever means it has available to cause an expansion of the high-margin branch of industry. The activity of the planning agency, therefore, amounts to a search for a new over-all equilibrium, and that means a state in which the former inequalities have become equalities and can be expressed in equations.

[9] It would be a weak argument to say that this means duplication of effort. All price formation and all adjustment of production and consumption to prices is a trial-and-error process. Obviously, it is much cheaper to commit errors on paper than to commit them in actual economic processes; consequently, if paper experiment saves experiment in steel and stone, labor and machinery, there can be great gain.

every producer; estimates of consumption and production can only refer to categories of consumer and producer goods, including labor. But how broad can these categories be without frustrating the purpose? Will it suffice to estimate the production and sales of automobiles, or will it be necessary to make the estimate for each class of cars, and how many classes will have to be distinguished? Is it enough to make a plan for the use of steel, without distinguishing different qualities, and if not, how many kinds of steel must be distinguished? It would certainly not be adequate to lump all machine tools into one category, either as products or as producer goods; but, again, what degree of aggregation is still permissible? Perhaps the most difficult problem arises with regard to labor: What kinds of labor, as distinguished by mental and physical abilities and by acquired skills, must figure in the plan as separate entities?

This problem of the breadth of categories is closely connected with the problem of the required accuracy in planning. Prices on the real market never reflect supply-and-demand conditions with complete accuracy, and a planning board certainly cannot with any chance of success attempt to express the prospective growth or decline of productive capacity and of demand for any particular commodity by the exact percentage, still less calculate the prospective price of a ton of steel or of an automobile to the dollar. But again, what degree of inexactness can be tolerated?

Some very rough idea about the permissible margin of inaccuracy in planning can be derived from a comparison with the margin by which the unplanned market falls short of complete utilization of resources. Not all under-utilization of capacity is irrational: In some industries, for instance power production and most branches of transportation, some reserve capacity is necessary to sustain seasonal and other peak loads and will inevitably be idle in non-peak periods. But much of the idleness of resources is due to a failure of demand to come up to supply either in a particular field or in wide areas of the economy in particular periods; in the latter case, of course, we speak of depressions or recessions. In a market economy, idleness of resources beyond a measure that inevitably follows from the need for reserve capacity indicates a failure of the price mechanism to equilibrate supply and demand; the same is true of the less frequent case that existing demand cannot be satisfied in spite of availability of primary resources, because the latter have not been turned in time into products of such kinds as consumers wish to buy. Both types of failure of the market economy can be classed as inaccuracies of operation, comparable with errors that planners in an economy with more central direction may commit.

In market economies not assisted by comprehensive economic foresight, it is not unusual for the output of several important industries to drop by 20 or even 40 per cent from one year to another or within the span of a few years, to rise again afterwards.[10] As a consequence, a large amount of capacity remains unused and a great many man-hours are lost through forced idleness. If a planning agency anticipated such a drop a year ahead but underestimated its magnitude by 50 per cent, this would still enable the government to take measures which might result in, say, utilizing a quarter of the resources released from their previous use. If, on the other hand, the gap turns out to be only half as large as the agency's advance estimate, some of the measures for stimulating the economy may cause inflationary tendencies, but these can be checked more easily at relatively short notice than it is possible to provide for a stimulative effect (it is always easier to discourage than to encourage borrowing); the measures providing for substitute employment will in part turn out to be wasted motion, but the cost to the economy will be much smaller than that caused by even a mild recession. This extremely crude consideration may show that the range of error in planning which would still not destroy its usefulness is fairly wide, and that the socialists can indeed hope to add to the effectiveness of the economic system by enlarging the scope of economic foresight from its present small magnitude to a measure which would permit a substantial reduction of economic fluctuations.

This is all the more true because planning may not merely reduce or eliminate actual unemployment of men and machines; by providing managers with a more reliable basis for expectations in regard to future utilization of capacity, planning may also remove or diminish hesitancies about enlargement of plants and thus speed up economic growth. From any survey of available statistical data it becomes obvious that some capitalist countries, especially the United States, have for long periods failed by a wide margin to attain the rate of growth which their resources would have permitted, even without any reduction of present consumption, and there is much reason to believe that the main hindrance is the fear of businessmen that demand may not grow sufficiently to utilize increased capacity to produce. If this uncertainty is only in part reduced, economic growth may become much faster.

[10] Two examples among many: Factory sales of passenger cars in the United States dropped from 7.9 million in 1955 to 5.8 million in 1956, to reach, after a further slump in 1958, almost the 1955 level again in 1960; production of radio and television sets dropped from 22 million in 1950 to 18 million in 1951 and continued to fluctuate in approximately the same (and occasionally a wider) range for the rest of the decade. (Historical Statistics of the US, pp. 462, 491; Survey of Current Business, February 1961, p. 40; Statistical Abstract for the US, 1959, p. 780.)

It is, therefore, no valid objection to economic planning to argue that no plan is faultless, that the necessary simplification of devices, the inevitable gaps in basic data and the human limitations of the planners will all result in preventing a perfect plan. Any substantial narrowing of the distance between the economic optimum and the results of the unguided market will, in a country such as the United States, express itself in many billions of dollars of national income. That much can be stated; obviously, it is not enough to prove the case for planning, and thereby for contemporary socialism, but suffices only to repulse some of the attacks by its opponents. With the information now at hand it is neither possible to determine the exact amount of tolerance for mistakes which the planning machinery must not exceed to be of any use, nor to say with certainty that a planning machinery can be constructed which will operate within that margin of error. Those of us who believe that the methods can be sufficiently perfected certainly do not deserve to be treated as visionaries, but those who cannot muster this degree of optimism should not be regarded as defeatists. Planning is certainly possible; whether it will be sufficiently useful to justify itself will for some time to come still remain a matter of faith.

A Lesson from Communism?

Can we not obtain more certainty by analyzing the experience of the communist countries? True, there is no good reason to ignore what this body of experience may teach us about the operation of non-communist systems, but the peculiar circumstances under which the communist planners operate detract from the usefulness of evaluating their methods for the purposes of democratic socialism as well as contemporary capitalism. In the first place, we know too little of the inner machinery of communist planning and the way it works, and many doubts exist even with regard to details of the results: The fear of communist officials to give the outer world an advantage by making known much of the economic conditions and processes in their country compounds the inherent difficulties for Western observers to understand a system which is very different from that to which they are accustomed. But even if this veil of secrecy did not exist, there would be serious obstacles in the way of utilizing communist experiences for planning in the West.

Prior to the Second World War, the only communist planners were those in the Soviet Union, and they were not trying to anticipate developments on a "live" market: They confined themselves mainly to determining what developments were desirable in terms of the goals established by the political authorities, and which of these were feasible in view of the physical limitation of resources; the results of these deliberations, when approved by the party leadership, were then formulated into commands to the administrators. The only sector of the economy in which voluntarism can never be completely excluded, at least as long as money is still used, the purchase of goods by the ultimate consumer, was kept under control by granting the consumer little above the physical minimum of existence and by continuous inflationary pressure, which made it expedient for every household to buy whatever was offered because, restricted as money incomes were, there was always a greater likelihood of having money to spare than of finding goods to buy.

The Soviet economy can no longer be described without qualification in these terms, and other communist economies have grown up in which the role of spontaneity is greater than in the USSR. But the period during which communist planners have been interested in anticipating market reactions is very short, and the change from a command economy, in the strictest sense in which it can exist under modern conditions, to a system in which free exchange plays an important part is still very incomplete. Of the other communist countries, the one whose experiences in planning are of greatest interest to the West is Yugoslavia, because here a "live" market exists, although the plant managers are not under the control of shareholders but of workers' committees. The analysis of the Yugoslav experience, however, has been lagging because of linguistic and other difficulties. More data on the East European planning experience will have to become available before we can find answers to questions that have been raised here, or even to determine the degree in which that experience may be helpful.

The emphasis on prices in the foregoing discussion should not obscure the importance of physical planning. The ultimate reason for many of the shortcomings of an unplanned market economy is the fact that present actions in production and consumption have physical consequences which are inadequately reflected in present-day prices, and that the latter serve as guides for action. In order to remove the shortcomings, it is necessary to calculate the prospective physical developments and to determine which prices are in consonance with their results. Without attempting to anticipate such events as depletion of resources, approaching saturation of some wants, and release of labor through technological improvements, planning would make no sense. All rational planning is necessarily "two column" planning: It must be carried out simultaneously in terms of physical quantities and in terms of values.

In spite of the peculiarities of the communist planning organization, some fundamental problems of planning can be better understood in the context of an analysis of communist systems, where they actually appear as questions for policy makers, and their discussion will therefore be postponed until the next section. The European socialists have so far not used their full influence to attempt comprehensive economic planning; the many verbal commitments to planning in socialist programs do not even always give evidence of a clear concept. At the same time, however, the demand for planning received support from sources outside of the socialist movement. A variety of motives were responsible for this support, ranging from the desire for regional planning for the use of land to the urge to modernize and expand production capacity and to the wish to flatten the business cycle. Attempts at partial planning often revealed wider implications than their authors had anticipated, and the resulting trend toward comprehensiveness led in some instances to the creation of an apparatus for economic foresight that may soon become sufficiently effective to modify the character of the economic system.

CHAPTER 14

SOME RECENT DEVELOPMENTS IN PLANNING

The Beginnings of French Planning[1]

THERE ARE only a few highly developed countries with democratic governments in which planning is undertaken on a sufficiently comprehensive scale to provide an object lesson of the problems encountered in full national planning under democracy. To analyze such experience as is available, it is necessary to keep a distinction in mind which might be considered a truism if it were not so often disregarded: the difference between plan making and plan execution. Drawing up a plan is essentially a statistical job; making economic reality conform to the plan is a job of economic policy. When people talk about planning without making clear whether they have plan making or plan execution in mind, there is danger that they confound thoroughness in plan making with toughness in plan execution. But a plan may be comprehensive, and yet its authors may rely for its execution on persuasion and bounties rather than on compulsion; on the other hand, a plan may be concerned only with one or a few types of economic activity and be carried out with ruthless coercion. France provides an example of the former kind of planning.

Of all the European countries west of the Iron Curtain, apart from Yugoslavia, France has constructed the most comprehensive machinery for national economic planning. Although the French socialists have never

[1] To the extent that it has been thought useful to quote French documents for the purposes of the following discussion, semi-official English translations have been used when they were available, regardless of minor inadequacies in style or vocabulary. Only where no such English versions were known to the author has he himself translated the quoted passages.

been in a position to frame the policy of their country exclusively according to their own ideas, they have at times exerted considerable influence, which was a factor in the adoption of the "Plan for Modernization and Equipment"[2] under which the French economy has operated since 1947. To an even greater extent, however, this plan was a product of the postwar economic emergency as recognized by socialists and non-socialists alike; but the limited extent of socialist influence in its origin does not reduce the significance of the French plan as an example of how socialist ideas about planning may be carried into effect.

After World War II, France was economically prostrate; many buildings and transportation facilities were destroyed and stocks of raw materials and food depleted; most foreign assets had been liquidated or destroyed and foreign currency was extremely scarce. Similar conditions existed in other ex-belligerent countries, but in France the handicaps in overcoming this situation seemed to be particularly serious. Small business, often family-owned and tradition-bound, played a greater role in France than in other Western nations; the stimulus of an increasing population had been absent for a long time prior to World War II; the psychological effects of the Great Depression had been particularly paralyzing in a country of relatively low economic vitality. Yet a high level of productivity was essential if France was to rebuild its homes, factories, roads and railroads rapidly and to restore the equilibrium of its balance of payments through increased exports. "After the short respite which foreign credits and the utilization of our last reserves may give us, the working power of the French will be their only support; to avoid an intolerable lowering of the standard of living, it will be necessary that their working effort be as efficacious as possible, which means that every man-hour of labor must create maximum production, both in agriculture and industry."[3]

The opinion that this effort could not be left to uncoordinated individual initiative prevailed in France. "In order to be successful, the Frenchman must undertake [the work of modernization] from a common point of view, in order that everybody will be assured that the efforts of others will complement his own (*soit assuré d'être épaulé par les autres*) and that there will be no lags, in one activity or another, that would delay the progress of the whole economy. It will, therefore, be necessary to act according to a plan. . . . Such a plan is essentially a method of coordinating activities and a means by which everyone can find the right place for

[2] Later renamed Plan of Equipment and Productivity.

[3] Commissariat Général du Plan de Modernisation et d'Equipment, *Rapport Général,* November 1946-January 1947, p. 9.

his own effort in relation to those of others. In an economy consisting of both a nationalized and a large private sector, the plan must apply equally to the government enterprises and to the businesses of individual citizens, and must therefore be as much a plan of orientation as a plan of direction."[4]

In speaking of their economic system, the French economists usually call it an *économie concertée*—a possible working translation would be "preconcerted economy." At times, attempts were made to distinguish between an *économie concertée* and *économie dirigée*—meaning an economy based on private property but directed by the state through coercive means, such as rationing and allocation, as was done during the war and under fascist regimes. Especially in the early 1950's the *économie concertée* has been distinguished sometimes from an *économie planifiée,* with the meaning of the latter term restricted to a Soviet-type economy; that is, one without private property and with extreme centralization of the decision-making power. Now the term *planification,* which seems to be respectable again in the West, is usually applied without hesitation to the French systems, but to emphasize its difference from communist planning, the French plan is often called *un plan indicatif,* meaning a plan which merely indicates to the producers what it would be best to do and does not order them to do it.

At the outset, the French plan, named the Monnet plan for its principal inaugurator, Jean Monnet, provided specific, physical targets for some basic industries: coal, electric power, cement, steel, agricultural machinery and means of transportation; motor fuels and nitrates were soon added. These areas were singled out because additional supplies of these resources would be necessary "for any expansion of production in whatever direction." For the basic industries, it was possible to guide activities toward the physical targets because these industries represented "in part the nationalized sector (coal mines, electric power, railroads) in which the adoption of the programs by the government and by the organs of administration was equivalent to an order, and in part a sector already strongly organized (steel production, motor fuels, cement) or in the process of organizing (tractors), and here contracts could be made between government agencies and industry."[5]

The rest of the industry, comprising most of the manufacturing branches and agriculture, was in the first phase left without any directives

[4] *Ibid.* p. 21.

[5] Commissariat Général, *Rapport sur les résultats obtenus dans la réalisation du plan de modernisation et d'équipement au cours du premier semester 1947,* p. 57.

as to the level of output, for the two-fold reason that the government did not feel competent to establish specific targets for these industries[6] and that it lacked the means to regulate their activities. In these areas the planning authority "plays a role somewhat like that of an engineering consultant, and the plan is expressed in 'modernization norms,' established by committees including representatives of the plan administration as well as experts from the producing enterprises; these norms are then publicized by government agencies and business organizations, and business is induced to comply with those norms by the use of the various levers which are normally at the disposal of the government (public purchases, fiscal policy, subsidies, changes in the customs tariff, credit policy, and—for the duration of shortages—allocation of materials and foreign currency . . .)"[7]

Owing largely to the investment credits provided by the plan administration through the Modernization Fund,[8] which in turn was in part replenished by Marshall Plan money,[9] the basic industries reached their target figures, although the weaknesses in the nationalized sector during the first years, as discussed above,[10] must have proved a serious obstacle. In 1953, when the period of the first French plan ended, the French economy had overcome its shortages of materials; it had not yet solved the problem of modernization of industry. From now on, the task "was not merely to produce more," but also "to produce better, meaning that quality and price conditions were to be competitive" with those of the technologically advanced countries in the rest of the world.[11]

[6] "One might well debate whether it is preferable to develop or create one branch of manufacturing rather than the other, what volume should be proposed for the output of different branches of agriculture, and what tempo should be chosen for the reconstruction of buildings." (*Rapport Général*, p. 24.)

[7] *Rapport sur les résultats obtenus* . . . p. 57.

[8] In 1955, this fund was merged with two others at the disposal of the plan administration and called Fund for Economic and Social Development.

[9] The necessity of supplying the United States government, through the European Organization of Economic Cooperation (OEEC), with estimates of the prospective development of the French economy in order to obtain Marshall aid, has undoubtedly contributed to the intensity of the French planning effort.

[10] See pp. 237 ff.

[11] Pierre Massé, *French Methods of Planning*. Multigraphed, 1961, p. 10. First the European Coal and Steel Community and later the European Common Market with its reduction of tariffs between France, Germany, the Benelux countries and Italy, intensified the competition which important French industries had to meet. The wars in Indochina and later in Algeria caused additional burdens for the French balance of payments. For these reasons it was all the more important to raise the competitive strength of French industry.

In spite of considerable progress in this respect under the second plan, France suffered a serious crisis in its balance of payments in 1958, at the beginning of the third plan period. The crisis was met by adjustments in the plan, resulting in a temporary slowing down of the rate of growth, and by a currency reform.

How the French Plan Is Working Now

MAKING OF THE PLAN

Once the shortages in basic materials had been relieved, the French economy was no longer automatically responsive to increases in their supply. No policy concentrating on the basic industries could now hope to speed up over-all growth; planning had to be comprehensive to assist in the achievement of this purpose. Consequently, the purview of the second plan was expanded to include all branches of production in its target setting.

Concomitantly, an exclusive engineering approach to planning became less adequate. To be sure, technological improvement was of the utmost importance, but along with the physical efficiency of a contemplated production process and with the availability of the necessary physical resources, the advantages of each act of production and of each change in the production methods had to be judged. Thus it had become imperative to supplement physical planning by more extensive and realistic value considerations. French value-planning was promoted and facilitated by improvements in the compilation of national accounts early in the second plan period.

The task of French planning, as viewed by the legislature, by the cabinet and by the officials in charge—next to the *Commissariat du plan,* the treasury is most directly involved—includes the assurance of rapid and balanced growth, rising living standards and better geographic distribution of French industry, that is, relief of the congested areas, especially the Paris region, and the creation of new employment opportunities in districts with declining industries. These purposes must be achieved without upsetting the equilibrium of outgo and income in international payments. Balanced growth requires physical complementing of the different branches of production—for instance tire production must be expanded in proper proportion with the automobile industry, furniture production at the same pace with home construction, output of energy with manufacturing—and also an equilibrium among aggregates for the whole economy: Enough consumer goods must be available to be purchased with the additional incomes resulting from increased payrolls in producer as well as consumer goods industries, and industries must be sufficient to purchase the consumer goods output; saving must match, but not exceed, investment in production facilities, housing, transportation and community conveniences such as schools and hospitals, plus desired increases in inventories. The adequate solution of these problems requires continuous improvement of statistical techniques and of methods of mathematical calculation. It seems that the *Commissariat du plan* has developed procedures which, though far from perfect, already permit fairly satisfactory results.

The compilation of a new French four-year plan begins with the calculation of an input-output table for the last year of the previous planning period,[12] to apply the experience of the recent past for the anticipation of potential developments in the near future. Preliminary physical calculations about the possibility of expansion then lead to tentative assumptions about the amount of investment required for each of several alternative annual growth rates, and to judgments about the effects of such investment upon the standard of living and upon the balance of payments. For instance, in the deliberation on growth rates during the preliminary work on the current (fourth) plan, scheduled to run from 1962 to 1966, the "6 per cent variant quickly appeared a little too ambitious because it led to a vulnerable balance of foreign payments with practically no safety margin." [13] So high a degree of expansion would have required too much of imported materials and would have diverted too many resources from the exporting industries. Although everything is tentative at this stage, rather detailed "sketches" of the development of individual industries must be worked out as a basis for judging what goals can be achieved at what cost.

Before deciding on the rate of growth and other plan provisions to be proposed to the government, the Planning Commissariat consults with the Investment and Planning Section of the Economic and Social Council. "This . . . reinforces economic democracy and provides those who are often unfairly called technocrats with the possibility of broad contacts." [14] The corrected estimates which result from these consultations are submitted to the government together with reports by the Council. The Commissariat then receives governmental directives, which form the basis for new adjustments in the tentative plan; thereupon the latter are submitted to the

[12] For the sequence of steps in plan compilation, see *Loc. cit.* pp. 16ff. At least for the future, it may be more correct to say that the input-output table for the last year is checked against the actual experience in the execution of the plan, since with the growing application of the input-output technique in French planning such tables will undoubtedly be prepared in advance for each year of every plan; at the start of the new plan, therefore, it will not be necessary to set up the table for the last year of the old one, but merely to discover the deviations of actual performance from the original estimates.

[13] *Loc. cit.*, p. 17. Although French public opinion, including large sections of the business community, seems to support the principle of the *économie concertée* with vigor, the officials in charge of planning are not infrequently suspected of technocrat leanings —meaning a desire to make their own preferences prevail over those of the public. At the conference of the International Economic Association in September 1962 in Vienna, this suspicion was voiced by Professor Robert Mossé of the University of Grenoble.

[14] Massé, *op. cit.*, p. 17.

Modernization Commissions—work teams in which public officials deliberate with those who, as producers, will have to carry out the plan. The Modernization Commissions—25 of them in 1961—"are of two types which can be called vertical and horizontal. The vertical commissions correspond to the various sectors of economic activity: agriculture, energy, chemistry, manufacturing industries, housing, education, social and sanitary equipment etc. . . ." Through the work of these commissions, it becomes possible "to move a step forward from the over-all sketch to more detailed programs for each sector. They set the evolution of technological coefficients and the progress of productivity. They select the production techniques corresponding to the minimum actualized total cost necessary to achieve their objectives. Horizontal commissions work at maintaining basic equilibriums. The Labor Commission deals with employment by qualification and by region. The Comission for General Economic Financing adjusts investments and savings, public receipts and expenditure, currency movements. The Commission for Regional Plans reduces imbalances which the spontaneous economic evolution may have caused between different areas." [15]

From the results of the work of the Modernization Commissions, the Commissariat forms a "provisional synthesis" of the developments in the individual branches of economic activity, particularly for the purpose of a more definite judgment on the obtainable over-all growth rate. But in overhauling the Commissariat's tentative draft, the Commissions, with their more accurate knowledge of the needs and capacities of individual industries, invariably cause discrepancies, since each Commission concentrates on one branch of economic activity. ". . . compared to the stage of preliminary outlines, the Commissions bring more realism and less coherence." [16] To restore the coherence, the Commissariat, in joint deliberations with the Commissions, tries to eliminate contradictions until the final synthesis is achieved. The plan is then submitted to the government and to parliament for approval.

Without the work of the Modernization Commissions, of the Economic and Social Council and of the government departments it would hardly be possible to compile a plan which has a chance of success, but the contributions of all these agencies are based on the original, tentative calculations of the Commissariat, and can be of service only if these original estimates do not overrate or underrate the possibilities too much and also achieve a fairly high degree of consistency. None of the other agencies

[15] *Loc. cit.*, p. 19.
[16] *Loc. cit.*, p. 20.

can do more than correct unsatisfactory details in the draft submitted by the Commissariat, or suggest choices among the alternatives which the Commissariat has pointed out; none of them can work out a whole alternative plan. Therefore the technique by which the Commissariat arrives at its original estimates deserves particular attention.

Like any effort in compiling a comprehensive plan, the original work of the Commissariat consists of two phases: first, the choice of assumptions and setting of targets, both of which are arbitrary in the sense that here the judgment of the planner is decisive; second, the working out of the consequences of assumptions and targets with regard to the output of individual industries and to the technological methods—the state of technology is among the assumptions—which they will have to apply if the targets are to be met with the resources assumed to be available. Since the second phase is merely an exercise of logic in its mathematical and non-mathematical forms, it may be regarded as automatic. When a group of planners assumes that certain quantities of labor, energy and materials are available and that under free choice consumption will follow a certain pattern, they use their judgment with regard to factual probabilities; when they decide that a certain growth rate is desirable as long as the standard of living is not reduced below a defined level, or permitted to grow at the same time to a defined extent,[17] they exercise a value judgment. But when they then calculate how much machinery of every kind, how many millions of pairs of shoes, cars, articles of clothing and food will have to be produced and what labor-saving devices must be applied in each industry in order to reach these goals, this is merely a matter of applying the laws of reasoning and the multiplication table—if the latter term is so understood as to include somewhat refined mathematical techniques. The results obtained in this part of the process are not a matter of

[17] This is a simplified construction which merely illustrates the problem. Planners will not really start by choosing a fixed rate of growth, even on the condition that it must not interfere with a defined level or a defined rise of the standard of living. Rather, they will initially adopt a more open kind of target: a system of priorities between growth and standard of living which are translatable into a map of indifference curves; other goals may also find a place in such a system. Such a procedure means that the task of the mathematicians will be extended into the target-setting phase, to find the optimal combination of goals; mathematical methods for the solution of optimization problems have long been known. Thereby the dividing line between the arbitrary and the automatic parts of the plan-making process may be somewhat blurred, but it is neither removed nor does it lose any of its importance.

From the nature of the task as well as from the statements which M. Pierre Massé, the chief of the planning commissariat, has made at the Vienna congress of the international Economic Association (*Discretionary or Formalized Planning,* multigraphed, 1962, esp. pp. 6 ff.), it is certain that a system of priority rates between growth, living standards and other goals has been established for French planning.

anybody's discretion. They can be proved to be either correct or incorrect —they follow automatically from the presuppositions. The mathematical and therefore automatic phase also includes the determination of the prices which correspond to any given set of assumptions about availability of resources and pattern of targets.

As long as the mathematical operations are carried out with pencil or even with simple calculating machines, the two phases need not be rigidly separated. At many points the calculating process can be interrupted and the intermediate results compared with facts, with the preferences of the planners or with consumers' preferences adopted as planning targets. In this way faults in the assumptions or inconsistencies in the pattern of targets may be discovered. For instance, it may turn out that the satisfaction of consumers' preference for housing would require a cement output that could be obtained only with a large increase in equipment, and that this increase would not leave enough machinery for the reaching of other consumption targets.

However, when the task of calculation is entrusted to the more complicated kind of electronic computer, with the effect that the ultimate consequences of the basic assumptions must be worked out in one continued process, a clear separation of the arbitrary and automatic phases is indispensable. As the French planners express it: "Formalized programming" must be clearly distinguished from "discretionary programming." The French Commissariat is using formalized programming to an increasing degree in the elaboration of the tentative estimates. The reason is not only that formalized programming "enables electronic machines to be used, saves time and makes it possible to investigate a larger number of variants. In addition, by concentrating the assumptions at the beginning of the process, it makes reasonable discussion easier." [18] The latter point is of particular importance in the relations between planning experts and political representatives. Democratic planning requires that government and parliament be confronted with definite alternatives among which they have to choose in full knowledge of the consequences. They should be told: This is what we have; these are the different things we can do with it, and if we want so much of one thing—for instance a particular growth rate, or a particular amount of defense goods, or welfare facilities—then we can have so much less of the other thing, for example private consumption. The clear separation of basic assumptions from the elaboration of the consequences of

[18] Pierre Massé, *Discretionary or Formalized Planning*, p. 1 of the multigraphed English version. The report was delivered in Section 2 of the IEA conference. The conference papers will be published in book form but at the time of writing have not yet been printed.

each choice facilitates this procedure. The role of formalized programming will grow in France with the perfection of statistical and mathematical techniques and the technology of computers; moreover, the greater the importance of the plan for the economy, the more significance will be attributed to the political control of the planning process, and the greater will be the advantage of formalization in making such control more effective.

There will never be a time, however, when all the choices are made at the outset and everything else is treated as an electronic robot's job. To see the reason, it is only necessary to visualize, in concrete terms, the nature of the original decisions. The basic data, from population growth to prospective crop yields and from the emergence of new households to steel-making capacity, must be estimated; patterns of consumption and propensity of the population to save must be anticipated; the optimal allocation of public funds to the various collective wants must be determined; choices must be made with regard to the rate of growth and perhaps with regard to changes in the geographic distribution of industry. Obviously, at each of these steps the planner will encounter a great many uncertainties, some of them concerning physical data, more of them concerning human reactions to economic changes, for instance the effect of a rise in income upon the volume of savings or upon the distribution of expenditures among the various purposes of consumption. The decisions of what growth rate to adopt and how to spend the public revenue are inevitably influenced by optimism or pessimism with regard to assumptions whose validity is always in question. All this means that it is not permissible to build a structure of consequence upon factual and target assumptions as if the latter were an unshakable rock; rather, it will be necessary at every major stage in the elaboration of consequences to re-examine the assumptions. If on the basis of our assumptions about the state of technology, we find that the automobile output we are proposing would involve an amount of steel consumption which is not in accord with the recent sales experience of steel manufacturers, there is reason to ask whether we may have failed to give due consideration to the tendency to replace steel with aluminum. If our calculations show that disposable income would permit the purchase of many more durable goods, the question arises whether consumers will really wish to buy so many television sets, cars and home freezers, or whether they will prefer to increase their savings more than originally assumed. To surrender the elaboration of consequences entirely to electronic robots would be possible only if planners' knowledge were perfect from the beginning, and if the people for whom they are planning were themselves robots whose reactions could be unfailingly precalculated.[19]

THE EXECUTION OF THE PLAN

When a plan is to be carried out in a completely nationalized economy, a failure of the planning authorities to calculate correctly the proportions of expansion in the different industries need not bring the progress of the plan to a standstill, though such mistakes will involve a loss in product and therefore in welfare. The government can write off the loss, issue new orders to the managers of the nationalized industries and insist on their execution.

But if the plan is to guide production where the latter is primarily a task of private enterprise, mistakes of the planning authorities are apt to destroy the first prerequisite of successful plan execution in such an economy: the confidence of the entrepreneurs that planners know what they are doing. If there are major faults in the plan, industrialists in one particular line, when expanding their production in compliance with the plan, might find that consumers' incomes or willingness to spend are inadequate to provide sufficiently receptive markets, or that complementary producer goods needed for expansion have become too highly priced because of inadequate supply. Once a substantial number of entrepreneurs have incurred losses through compliance with planners' intentions, the others are likely to use their freedom of decision to ignore the plan. The fact that this has not happened in France, that on the contrary business has generally supported the planning venture, speaks for the good work that the *Commissariat général du plan* has performed.

Obviously, however, it is not enough that the planners' proposals are objectively feasible and consistent in themselves. Business must be convinced of their feasibility and consistency. In this respect the French Modernization Commissions have undoubtedly done excellent service. Although they have no compulsory power over the individual enterprises, they are not merely instruments of planmaking but also have an important role in plan execution. In the first place, the fact that representatives of industry had a voice in the compilation of the plan tends to strengthen the belief of the business community that the plan is realistic. Furthermore, the contacts created by the Commissions can be used to overcome hesitations and

[19] Since therefore only parts of a plan can be established by formalized procedure, and since a program may be regarded as a part of a plan rather than a whole plan, the term "formalized programming" seems preferable to "formalized planning." Both terms, however, are in use in France.

misgivings on the part of businessmen: The Commissions or their members from the ranks of business can be used as mediators between industry and the planning authorities.[20]

Yet these contacts would hardly have sufficed to maintain the necessary confidence in the plan if the government had not also been able to use other means for its execution. An entrepreneur needs not only assurance that the plan would work well if everybody were to comply; he must also be assured that at least the great majority of producers will act as the plan provides and that the forecast will therefore come true. Hence the government needs powers to bring non-compliant entrepreneurs into line. These powers need not involve compulsion; it will be sufficient if the government has means to make compliance more profitable than non-compliance.

Among the means which the French government applies to this end, those of credit policy are of outstanding importance. The government grants some loans from its own resources, especially from those of the Fund for Economic and Social Development, at an interest rate below that of the market. These direct government loans, however, supply only a relatively minor part of the capital required for industrial and agricultural investments. To be sure, they may have a greater effect upon the allocation of credit to investment projects than their modest amount would seem to warrant: The knowledge that part of the financing of a project is assured by the government on favorable terms enhances the prospect of profitable results and therefore may induce private creditors to lend the balance or investors to subscribe the supplementary stock issues, or may encourage the enterprises themselves to provide additional means from accumulated profits or depreciation funds. In some instances, the government undertakes to guarantee private credits for investment projects which fit into the plan.

In addition to these incentives for approved projects, the government has power to deny access to the most important sectors of the capital market to those would-be borrowers whose projects would conflict with the purposes of the plan. Without the approval of the *Crédit National,* on whose policy the state has decisive influence, no industrial bonds can be issued and not even long or medium-term bank credit be extended to

[20] ". . . agreement achieved while the plan was being drawn up tends spontaneously to extend itself when it comes to implementing the plan. If the real forces of the country have been associated to the scheme, they are more likely to stand together in action. It is the prescience of such a reaction that was one of the motives for adopting the French planning method. Instructions sent to M. Jean Monnet by General de Gaulle, head of the government, on January 10, 1946, said: 'Since the execution of the plan will require everybody's collaboration, it is essential that all vital elements of the nation should collaborate in drawing it up.'" Massé, *French Methods of Planning,* p. 22

industry.[21] Stock issues are technically free now—they were subject to approval by the Treasury prior to 1959—but tax provisions make this method of financing unpopular with business unless there is assurance of special tax benefits which the government can grant.[22] Requests for such benefits and equally requests for permission to borrow by bond issue or from banks are transmitted to the *Commissariat du plan* and are rarely if ever granted without the approval of that agency.

The execution of the plan requires not only that a proper selection be made among investments to be financed, but also that the global amount of credit should neither fall behind nor exceed the limits determined by the requirements of production which the planners have visualized. For this purpose the government can use the traditional techniques of central bank policy, since the Bank of France is a state institution; the borrowing policy of the Treasury can also be used as an instrument of credit regulation.

Taken together, these opportunities for influence provide the government with a fairly tight control over the capital market, but they have little effect on investment which can be financed from a firm's own funds without appeal to the market.[23] The government, however, has supplementary means of control at its disposal. French law permits the government to grant reduction of taxes on the transfer of real estate and preferential fiscal treatment of mergers and of the relations between a mother company and

[21] "It is well known that in France medium-term (2-5 years) or long-term credit (5-20 years) is subject to consent and therefore practically supervised by the *Crédit National*, a private bank whose business policy is controlled by the state. On the basis of an understanding with the planning authority, the latter receives from the Crédit National for comment the files of all cases of credit application if the amount is more than 1 million NF for medium-term or 2.5 million NF for long-term credit. In the same way the Treasury, which has to give its stamp of approval to any bond issue in excess of one million NF, consults the planning authority on the program of the applicant enterprises before approving the dates of issue." (Gilles de La Perrière, Inspecteur des Finances, *Les Moyens d'exécution du plan*, multigraphed, p. 8)

[22] ". . . for a company, the appeal to shareholders is a very onerous means of financing by comparison with an ordinary bond issue. In the first case, what the holders of the securities receive is treated as business expenses and not hit by the corporation tax; in the second case, the same amount is considered earnings and a tax of 50% is due. Therefore the Finance Commission has suggested the adoption of a measure by which the fiscal treatment of the two methods of financing is equalized (Law of June 26, 1957): Up to 5 per cent of the amount paid in as additional capital, a company whose shares are listed at the Stock Exchange can pay dividends to its shareholders free from the corporation tax in each of seven business years, provided that its production program is recognized as consonant with the plan. Practically every corporation which has its securities listed and which increases its capital petitions to have its program examined by a special committee for conformity with the objectives of the plan." (*Loc. cit.*, p. 9)

[23] It may seem that they can have no such effect at all. However, just as cheap government loans which cover part of the cost of a project may induce a firm to supply the rest from its own funds, so the tax provisions which facilitate the appeal to the market for a portion of the cost may cause an enterprise to supply the balance by way of self-financing.

its subsidiaries if transactions are involved which contribute to the success of the plan.[24] Other things being equal, an enterprise will steer its available capital into channels in which it can reap such benefits, in preference to others for which these attractions are not available. Through these advantages a firm may even be induced to use funds productively which it would otherwise keep on bank account. Subsidies granted for special purposes operate in the same direction, because a firm will invest its own capital more readily in projects whose cost is partly borne by the government. Such subsidies are offered mainly for research in connection with expansion projects which fit well into the plan.[25]

In addition, the government has some physical controls which it can use to direct private investment to the points where it serves the approved purposes. The most important is the dependence of all construction on government permits. Since practically all important investment requires new structures, the power to grant or withhold construction permits gives the government a chance to influence the distribution of investments, however financed, among the different branches of economic activity and also among the different regions. The latter point is of particular significance since resistance of private business against the rate of expansion which the plan provides for the various industries is much less widespread than resistance against the programs of geographic redistribution of industrial activity.

In the large area of publicly owned enterprise, the French government can use its influence upon management to promote investment in accordance with the plan. What is done or not done in this area, moreover, also has an influence on the activities of private enterprise. The direction in which the *Electricité de France,* the state-owned power company, extends its network affects the location of new plants, and indirectly the type of industry that can expand; the price policy for power has a similar effect. Publicly financed housing influences the regional as well as the inter-industry distri-

[24] These benefits are sometimes granted through a "quasi-contract:" "A branch of industry or an enterprise establishes an understanding with the government with regard to the goal that it should reach in accordance with the plan; it undertakes to devote its best efforts to the attainment of the goal in return for a promise on the part of the government to grant certain preferential advantages." (*Loc. cit.,* p. 11.) In 1957 such an agreement was concluded between the government and the automobile industry, whereby the latter obligated itself to reserve two-thirds of a contemplated increase in output for export; within three years, the share of exports in French car sales grew from about 10 per cent to about 50 per cent.

[25] They are often refundable in the event that the research proves successful and profitable, but this is no great deterrent, since the major force limiting investment in research is fear of failure. It is usually not too difficult to repay the cost of a successful research venture.

bution of investment since new factories need housing for their workers. The orders which industry receives from nationalized enterprises as well as from such public agencies as the defense ministry, the housing authorities and the school administrations have an obvious influence on the quantity and the kind of increase in productive capacity which firms consider profitable.

Thus the tool shed of the French government is well stocked with instruments for steering business decisions toward plan fulfillment. It is easy to see that the steering devices must be effective; it is somewhat more difficult to recognize the sources from which the motive power has been provided that propelled the French economy on the road of rapid development and thereby fulfilled the hopes of the planners. Many of the measures that keep the French capital market under control are effective only in making business prefer one kind of investment to another, not to strengthen the will to invest. To be sure, cheap capital and tax reductions may contribute to that strength and thereby increase the total volume of investment, but no businessman will touch any expansion project, however low the interest rate and the taxes, unless he believes that demand for the product will be sufficient for satisfactory sales. Tax policy and credit policy can do something to increase consumers' demand, but in the light of American experience, it must be doubted that these means alone could have caused an increase sufficient for such a rapid rate of expansion of productive capacity, following upon a lethargic state of the economy, as has actually occurred in France.

The French government has succeeded in creating a climate of optimism that was essential for the realization of the plan. In explaining this accomplishment one again has to think of the effect of joint consultation of government and business representatives, primarily in the Modernization Commissions. Here the entrepreneurs have become convinced that such fast growth is possible, with great profit for all, if only everybody can be sure "that the efforts of the others will complement his own." The instruments of plan execution in France, credit and tax policy on the one hand, and joint deliberation of government and business on the other, have been effective only because applied in combination.

Has French Planning Been Really Successful?

If the economic development of France in the postwar period is accepted as evidence of the success of the plan, the appraisal must lead to a very favorable opinion.[26] France, it is true, has not matched the economic performance of West Germany, if the whole period since 1948 or 1950 is considered, but in more recent years the industrial production of France, Italy and West Germany rose at approximately the same pace, the lead of the two latter countries being so small that it may even be non-existent, the recorded lead due to inadequacies of statistical technique. But is this splendid achievement the result of the Monnet plan? Nothing like that plan exists in either West Germany or Italy, and the fact that these two countries nevertheless, at least in statistical appearance, did even somewhat better than France seems to suggest that the French planning system had no great influence on the outcome. This conclusion, however, appears implausible when we consider the internal and extraneous circumstances which favored economic development in the two neighboring countries of France and were non-existent or far less important in French economic development.[27]

The difference between the positions of France and West Germany after the war was not merely that the French economy had to overcome a tradition of low economic vitality—economic Malthusianism, as the French themselves call it; there was the additional difference that West Germany started its postwar recovery from a lower level of production, which was due to a still greater disruption of transport and to extensive but largely superficial damage to factories as a result of severe bombing, whereas a strong skeleton of production facilities remained which needed no more than relatively slight repairs to be put into operation. A monetary system disorganized by suppressed inflation and, in conjunction with it, a worn-out machinery of price ceilings, allocation and rationing obstructed the movement of commodities to consumption as much or more than the sad state of the physical traffic facilities. As traffic resumed and the necessary repairs

[26] See table 1, p. 58.

[27] An essentially negative judgment about the results of French planning, even about the reality of an attempt at consistent planning in France, can be found in the book by Warren C. Baum, *The French Economy and the State*, Princeton: Princeton University Press, 1958, pp. 343 ff. It seems, however, that Baum became unduly disturbed by some contradictory tendencies in French economic policy, for instance by simultaneous efforts to modernize industry, which often aim at an increase in plant size, and attempts to maintain small and medium-sized business. Such inconsistencies are partly a result of political pressures, partly a product of the desire to cushion the hardship of necessary reforms. The counteracting tendencies in French policy undoubtedly reduce the modernization effects and the speed of growth resulting from the Monnet plan, but there is much reason to believe that *on balance* the latter greatly contributed to modernization and growth. Without measures for smoothing transition to modern methods, almost nothing could have been achieved because resistance would have been too great. For a more balanced (if critical) and searching analysis, see François Perroux, "Le quatrième plan français 1962-1965" and other articles in *Economie Appliquée*, Janvier-Juin 1962.

were made, the equipment which Germany had inherited from the Nazi period, although somewhat reduced by dismantling, gave the country a high industrial potential. When the currency reform of 1948 swept away the excess money (*Geldüberhang*, as the German economists called it), this potential was rapidly put to full use, and the influx of persons expelled from the East supplemented the labor force of a population decimated by war just at the right time. Thus the German "economic miracle," though not exactly an illusion, was not as miraculous as it appeared, at least not in its early stages: What happened was simply that an existing framework was filled out. France possessed no framework of comparable strength; there had been no industrial armament in France after 1940, whereas Germany continued to create new and very modern plants up to 1944. Nor could France draw upon a source of labor comparable to the German army of expellees, although there was some influx from North Africa. Thus France started its postwar recovery from a higher level than Germany, with fewer resources to support further growth—no wonder that at first the rise of its production was overshadowed by that of its eastern neighbor. French achievement in eventually giving its development a momentum similar to that of Western Germany was great indeed, and it seems plausible that the guidance provided by the Monnet plan was at least jointly responsible for that achievement.

An analogous conclusion suggests itself when French development is compared with Italian. France never achieved such a steep rise of the curve of industrial production during the 1950's as Italy did in the last years of the decade (nor did Germany). Italy has been a much poorer country than France in the nineteenth and twentieth centuries, and also the difference in the level of productivity and welfare between its sections was far more marked, Southern Italy being a region not only underdeveloped, but difficult to develop, whereas Lombardy and parts of Piedmont had gained a good start in industrialization even before World War I. Yet the great poverty of its southern area gave the industrial economy of Northern Italy a labor reservoir which began to be tapped on a large scale as soon as information about the opportunities in the North had spread sufficiently in the southern provinces and some antiquated laws restricting internal migration were invalidated. French internal migration was on a much smaller scale, even if the movement of Algerians into metropolitan France is regarded as "internal." France, to be sure, also has backward agricultural areas, as well as mining regions that have become relatively unproductive and from which some labor has been drawn into areas where it can be used effectively. But the French small farmer, not having fallen so low economically as his

Southern Italian counterpart and possessing different political traditions, showed a stronger inclination to "stay put" and press his legislative representatives into granting him favors at the expense of the government and the consumer; even the relocation of French miners has met with great difficulties.

The high probability that the Monnet plan helped the French economy substantially in achieving its postwar rate of growth is of great interest to other Western countries, because of the community of traditions they share with France. If that country was able to guide its economy effectively by a plan without any harm to its liberties, why should other Western countries not be able to emulate French methods with equal success? It is true that France, more than England, the United States and probably even Germany, had already in the past used government direction to further economic development: Colbert's effort to lay the foundation of modern industrial life by government regulation and stimulation in the seventeenth century were on a larger scale than any similar government activity in other countries; under Napoleon III, ideas of government guidance of economic development, originating in the Utopian Socialist school of Saint-Simon after its ideas had been given a more practical turn by later disciples, largely determined the course of industrial growth. But these differences in tradition cannot overshadow the common heritage of the ideals of freedom and the similarity of economic institutions between France and the other nations of the West. At present, therefore, the French case provides the most relevant test for the proposition that the idea of planning, as held by democratic socialists, can be applied to the economy within a Western framework.

Several other West European countries, especially Norway and the Netherlands, have developed methods of planning along the same general lines as France, although it seems that their planning efforts have not yet reached the same degree of effectiveness in guiding the economy as has been achieved in France. The specific aims, techniques and experiences of these countries—plus those of Italy, which recently has also shown a propensity to plan—would have to be analyzed in a more detailed study of the tendencies of Western nations to remold the private enterprise system by equipping it with an apparatus for economic planning; for the purpose of this book, however, the trend is sufficiently illustrated by the French case.

A new impulse to planning has resulted from the emergence of the Common Market in Western Europe, which is being developed into the European Economic Community. The difficult task of coordinating the economic policies of the six nations now united in this organization is aggravated by uncertainties about the future. The merger of the six economies

—or the four, if the Benelux countries are counted as one[28]—has made necessary the creation of common organs, which will have to make important decisions in the field of social welfare policy, investment policy, regulation of imports, currency and business cycle policy—decisions which will have a profound and prolonged influence upon the economic situation in the participating countries. Any mistake made in these decisions will not only have the same undesirable consequences which blunders in economic policy have on the national scene, but will also compromise the authority of the common organs and thereby jeopardize the coherence of the Community. To reduce the probability of such mistakes, the Commission of the European Economic Community has announced that it will try to organize economic foresight and to draw the policy conclusions from this foresight by short-term and long-term programming.[29] This announcement has provoked Ludwig Erhard, West German Minister of Economics and foe of all government planning, to indignant protests, but it is not likely that he will be able to stop a development which is very logical to the situation.

Swedish Stabilization Policies

Sweden, a country not belonging to the European Economic Community, has been a pioneer in some policies related to planning, though not in planning proper. Having long enjoyed a relatively high standard of living and having suffered no destruction during the war, Sweden did not have to face reconstruction problems of the same urgency as other European countries; since its economy was spontaneously growing at a fairly satisfactory rate, there was all the less reason for Swedish policy makers to concern themselves very much with increase in capacity as an end in itself. Whatever planning Sweden undertook, was, therefore, directed mainly toward the goal of preventing or flattening out business fluctuations. In this endeavor, Sweden has a strong tradition: During the Great Depression, no other Western country achieved so much success in anti-cyclical policy as Sweden.

The principal weapon which Sweden applies in forestalling major de-

[28] Such a procedure, however, would be of doubtful validity in view of the many differences in economic structure and practices between Belgium and the Netherlands in spite of the Benelux agreement.

A number of other countries are associated with the Community,—not being full members—but they have little or no influence on the common policy and therefore on the choice between reliance on spontaneous forces and guidance through economic foresight by the Community organs.

[29] See the memorandum of the Commission on the action program of the Community, issued Oct. 24, 1962.

pression is a tax policy which provides incentives for shifting investments from boom periods to slack periods. Firms are permitted to deduct part of their profits from taxable income, and this portion is put on a blocked account under the control of the National Labor Market Board, a government agency. In periods of recession, this agency permits withdrawals from the account for defined purposes of investment, especially construction work. At the discretion of the government, firms can also receive credit against future tax liabilities for investments made in excess of accumulated reserves during recessions. This regulation of private investment is supplemented by an anticyclical policy of public investment—retrenchment in periods of prosperity, expansion during recessions or depressions—similar to the policy which had been developed during the 1930's.

The laws providing for private investment reserves were inaugurated in the 1940's and strengthened in 1955. So far, the greatest test of the effectiveness of this legislation occurred during the recession of 1957-58. The period during which permissions were granted extended to September 1959, when the Labor Market Board decided that the upswing made further investment stimulation undesirable. It seems that in this period withdrawals to the amount of over 650 million Swedish kronor (about $125 million) were authorized.[30] Sweden has done fairly well during the business fluctuations of the late 1950's; most probably the system of investment reserves had a share in this achievement, but it is difficult to form an opinion on the magnitude of that share. In the first place, not all the investments which were financed by withdrawals from the reserve accounts were additions to the investment programs of the firms; some might have been undertaken in any event. On the other hand, permission to use the reserve funds which otherwise would have remained blocked was apparently a sufficiently strong incentive for some firms to undertake the investment even if the withdrawals from the reserve had to be supplemented from "free" resources; in these instances, the authorizations moved a greater amount than their own into use for investment. In view of these counteracting tendencies, there is no way to determine the exact net effect of the system upon the amount of investment, and consequently the stabilization

[30] See Gideon Nitare, "Investment Reserves." Published by the National Labor Market Board, Stockholm: 1961 (mimeographed.) P. 7. However, Bertil Olsson, director of the Labor Market Board, gives a figure of only 350 million kronor, which, having been supplemented by private funds, he estimates to have caused investment by business firms to the amount of 500 million kronor. The discrepancy is probably due to a difference in the delimitation of the period, since Olsson's figures do not include the 1959 authorizations. Even the smaller amount, however, "equals about one sixth of the annual investment by industry in buildings." "Employment Policy During the Recession," *Skandinaviska Banken Quarterly Review*, April 1959, p. 59.

effect. Moreover, additional public investment provided a stimulus of its own independent of the release of private investment reserves during the 1957-58 recession, and it is impossible to separate the consquences of the two programs for the business situation.

The machinery of withdrawal authorizations is highly flexible; it can be used not only to counteract general recessions or depressions but also islands of unemployment in periods of general prosperity, by permitting firms to withdraw amounts from blocked reserves on the condition that they will be used for the creation of new job opportunities in distressed areas or occupations. To reduce "spot" unemployment, Sweden has also undertaken a substantial program of retraining workers and relocating them when they have to move to places where jobs are available. The government even keeps a reserve stock of prefabricated houses for temporary use in areas with labor shortage in which normal housing is insufficient, in order to make it possible for unemployed workers to move into these areas without delay.[31] No hard and fast line can be drawn between the fight against "spot" unemployment and efforts to combat the business cycle, since in depressions and recessions declining occupations and distressed areas are usually hardest hit.

The Swedish policies to stabilize employment do not themselves constitute planning for they do not directly involve any techniques of economic foresight, but there is a two-fold indirect relationship of these measures to planning. First, both the investment reserve scheme and the retraining and relocation provisions for workers provide incentives to anticipate coming developments, and the same is true to a still higher degree of the anticyclical policies in public works. The efficacy of all these measures depends to a considerable extent on advance preparation. Additional public works require timely fiscal provisions, in addition to backlogs of projects; to determine the amounts which public works will have to provide to supplement private investment, it is necessary to anticipate the response of private industry to the stimulus of the authorization to withdraw blocked funds; and to initiate the retraining and relocation measures in time, it is necessary to foresee an increase in unemployment before it occurs. Even a program like Sweden's, which is mainly intended to respond to the first signs of a slack in business activity by remedial measures rather than to strike at its causes in advance of the start of the downswing, tends to lead to attempts at improved foresight in order to prepare the remedial

[31] Carl G. Uhr, *Sweden's Employment Security Program And its Impact on the Country's Economy*. Pasadena: California Institute of Technology, 1960, p. 12 f.; Gunnar Olsson, *Employment Policy in Sweden*, published by the National Labor Market Board, Stockholm 1961 (mimeographed), *passim*.

measures, just as a physician wants to foresee an epidemic in order to make sure that he has enough drugs and access to hospital beds. If this effect is not yet very noticeable in Sweden—although Swedish economic science has in the past made great contributions to the technique of business cycle forecasting—this may be due to the shortness of time which has so far elapsed since the beginning of serious experimentation with the new measure.

For another reason the Swedish system has significance for planning, though only potential significance. When systematic foresight has been sufficiently developed to represent an economic plan, the investment reserve provisions and the measures to increase local and occupational mobility of labor will be important instruments of plan execution. Although the small size of Sweden as a country and of the Swedish economy may somewhat facilitate the use of the devices, especially their selective application, because it is easier to find the right spots in an area that can be surveyed without difficulty, yet there is no basic reason why other countries should not be able to emulate the Swedish policies with some success. Thus it is possible that the tools developed by an imaginative Swedish policy may be applied as instruments of plan execution in parts of the world which seem to have a greater need for planning because their record of steady employment is not as satisfactory as Sweden's in recent decades.

CHAPTER 15

MORE ASPECTS OF SOCIALIST ECONOMICS

Welfare Policy

HISTORICALLY, the demand for expanded and improved welfare services rendered by government agencies has been one of the most important socialist postulates. It is doubtful, however, whether emphasis on welfare policy can still be regarded as a distinguishing mark of socialism, since the responsibility of the government for the economic protection of those who cannot help themselves is now almost generally acknowledged. Countries still differ widely in the extent and quality of their welfare services, but only with many qualifications can some of the developed countries be said to have more comprehensive or effective welfare systems than others. Often the country which is farther advanced in one field is more backward in others. Sweden, for instance, one of the most socially advanced nations, has no compulsory unemployment insurance; the United States, though without public health insurance, which many other countries have had for a long time, is leading in some phases of municipal welfare work. The Swedish and American examples also show that socialist political influence is only one of many factors determining the extent of a country's welfare services. This can also be verified from British experience. If any country can be regarded as having the most extensive and effective welfare system, it is the United Kingdom. This system, it is true, was created by a Labour administration, but it has been maintained, essentially unchanged, by the conservatives who succeeded the socialists after a brief rule of the latter and have now headed the government for more than a decade.

Although emphasis on welfare services is by no means an exclusive characteristic of socialism, it plays a very important role in socialist ideology. This emphasis is an expression of socialist ethics, which demand a close approach to economic equality and strong human solidarity, animated by the conviction that everybody is his brother's keeper. Socialists want solidarity to extend even to those who are economically unsuccessful through faults of their own—solidarity with "every being having a human countenance," as it has occasionally been expressed in socialist writings; socialist postulates for an extensive welfare policy also often imply a refusal to regard economic success as evidence of human worth. Again, this is not an exclusively socialist opinion, but whereas others may treat failure in economic life as at least presumptive evidence of deficiencies in character or natural endowment, many socialists reject such a presumption.

Critics of extensive welfare policies often argue that when the state assumes responsibility for the support of those who might fall by the wayside, it weakens the individual's sense of responsibility to provide for himself during emergencies; he thus becomes less self-reliant; it has also been contended that since most welfare programs cannot be carried out without a modicum of coercion, they restrict individual liberty, and the socialist emphasis on welfare has been regarded as evidence that the socialists are not as interested as their opponents in preserving a sphere of freedom for the individual. What truth is there in these arguments?

The controversy over welfare policies supplies one of the most instructive object lessons in the difficulties and dangers of generalization. Even if no examples were known, it would be reasonable to assume that individuals will sometimes slacken their efforts at preventing future misery if they know that in an extremity they can rely on welfare benefits. For instance, even if no single case had been verified—and some have been discovered, although the amount of reliable evidence is highly controversial—it would be probable that the provisions for "assistance to needy children" [1] have sometimes blunted the conscience of a father who wanted to desert his family and who might have stayed if support from public funds had not been available to forestall starvation of his children. On the other hand, without welfare benefits many people would be in too desperate a situation to muster the energy to rehabilitate themselves economically; it is a myth that the average person responds to a seemingly hopeless situation with a hard struggle; only people with either extraordinary strength of

[1] This is the term used in the United States. Other countries have programs of similar effect, which therefore raise essentially the same problems, although the legal basis is often quite different. In Great Britain, for instance, aid to children is part of the National Assistance program for all citizens in need; in some other countries care for children's material welfare is embodied in social security legislation.

character or exceptional optimism will do so, whereas as a rule apathy is far more likely to result. In these instances, the measure of help afforded by welfare services is the precondition that induces the individual to help himself further.

Which cases are more frequent, those in which the individual's own efforts are weakened or those in which they are encouraged by public welfare policies? There are, of course, no statistics to provide an answer. If there were, there would still be the question: Which instances are more significant? The father who runs away from a failing marriage, leaving the economic responsibility for his children to the taxpayer, is a liability of the welfare system; does this liability outweigh the asset of having saved the courage of another father to meet economic adversity with the help of some assistance, or the courage of an unwed mother to care for her child, whereas otherwise they might have let themselves sink into delinquency or might have committed suicide? Socialists (and some others) will be inclined to view one rescued human being as more important than two or five or ten cases of failure; critics of socialism and extensive welfare policies will take the opposite position. There is obviously no objective yardstick for a judgment.

It is similar with the coercive aspects of welfare policy. An element of compulsion is part of all public welfare programs because they require financing by compulsory contributions. Even welfare practices which are technically classified as charities based on voluntary contributions are often not financed exclusively by people who would contribute out of their own free will: Often social pressures of all sorts play a great role, including the desire not to endanger one's earning opportunities by not participating in a program that customers or superiors may regard as morally obligatory. It is not necessarily easier, or less hazardous, to refuse contributions when pledges for the community chest are collected in one's office than to dodge a tax which supports the welfare administration of the city or county.

Thus practically all welfare schemes, except those based on genuine charity, which are of declining importance, force an individual to take part in a program of mutual protection although he might have preferred to make his own individual provisions, by saving or by paying as private insurance premiums the funds which he has to contribute to compulsory public insurance campaign. It has sometimes been suggested that individuals who have such a preference be excused from contributions to the general drive, but two factors narrowly limit the feasibility of such concessions to voluntary attitudes. First, any welfare scheme established by the community must afford at least minimum protection to every needy citizen; consequently, a person who has declared his willingness to protect himself by saving or insurance and has then failed to do so, would still have to be provided for at community expense. If, for instance, someone wants to be excused from paying contributions to public old age and disability insurance by stating that he will make his own arrangements with a private company and then fails to pay his premiums regularly and therefore causes his insurance to lapse, he can still not be left to starve in his old age or when disabled by accident: He has to receive minimum support from the welfare agencies. In this way a voluntary scheme will often lead to the exploitation of the conscientious citizen who pays his taxes and contributions by individuals who are either unscrupulous or do not have the energy to carry out their own resolution. Second, some of the most important arrangements for social security in a broad sense are based on a mixture of risks. In any voluntary program, the people representing good risks will feel that they can provide for emergencies at less expense by their own arrangements, and consequently the community scheme is likely to be loaded with an excessive percentage of bad risks making necessary unduly high contributions.

These arguments have been used by socialists, among others, in their advocacy of compulsory provisions for social security and welfare. They are technical arguments of great weight, but they are not convincing to everybody. "Rugged individualists" may still feel that the freedom of the individual to choose his own measure and method of protection should be respected regardless of the harm that is done to those who, for any number of reasons within or beyond their control, have to rely on community provisions. Up to now, "rugged individualists" have been fighting a rear guard action with very limited success. But the ethics of socialism seem to be losing in force even where socialists are still politically influential; whether the ethics of the Judaeo-Christian tradition, which have often operated in the same direction, are gaining in influence is at least doubtful. In affluent societies, the self-interest of those who feel themselves particularly exposed to economic misfortune is declining with their numbers. Thus the further advance of welfare policies, especially in countries which have already built up comprehensive welfare systems, is uncertain, quite in contrast to the situation a few decades ago, when progress in welfare legislation appeared highly probable to its supporters and opponents.[2]

Some other aspects of welfare policy will be discussed in context with human solidarity as a building stone of a socialist system.

[2] This political effect of a generally high standard of living has been explained by John Galbraith, *The Affluent Society,* Cambridge: The Riverside Press, 1958, p. 328 f.

Socialism and the Four "Bricks"

The discussion of socialist pricing has explained the role which the principle of exchange plays in a socialist society as now conceived by the socialists. The role of command in that type of society can be recognized from a brief summation of what has already been said: In socialism, as in capitalism, there is a commanding power of management in the individual enterprise, perhaps more restricted by grievance procedures, perhaps more extensive because unions may feel less free to take steps against management in nationalized industries or against private management complying with a national plan than to challenge private enterprise acting on its own—no general balance of these conflicting tendencies can be struck. Nationalization may be established by the commanding power of the state, although free purchase of private industries by the government has also occurred. If nationalized industries are quantitatively important, the commanding power of the government, based in this case on the right of property, may be used, as it seems to be used in France, to make the management of these industries comply with the plan promptly and thus set a good example for private industry. As supplementary instruments of plan execution, the taxing power, the policing of construction, and other forms of command may also have to be used by the state, as again the French example shows. Some welfare policies, which are likely to be more extensive under socialism than under capitalism, require the use of the state's commanding power because voluntary programs are often impracticable. On the whole, the role of command, relative to that of exchange, is likely to be somewhat greater under socialism than under capitalism, but in either of the two systems the principal means to coordinate the activities of economic units is exchange.

What about the other two bricks of the four which all economic systems contain? Solidarity has always been one of the most important motives of the socialists: They want a society in which the elements of antagonism play a smaller role than in capitalist society, and the elements of conscious human solidarity a greater one. This desire is most obvious in many writings by Utopian socialists, most of whom believed that such a better society could be brought about by an appeal to the natural goodness in man, in other words, that man, if shown the way by rational thinkers of good intentions, would be able and willing to mold institutions according to the principles of human solidarity. Marxist socialism reversed the sequence: When historical forces will have replaced capitalism with an order based on collective ownership of the means of production, man will develop his social instincts to a higher degree, and the combativeness of self-interest will eventually "wither away," just as the compulsory power of the state; human solidarity will remain the dominant incentive.

Socialism has come a long way from its Utopian and Marxist stages. The socialists have tried to meet the criticism of their opponents who argue that socialism can work only if it is true that man is primarily altruistic, whereas obviously his selfish impulses are often far more powerful. No particularly high degree of altruism is assumed in such socialist models as were developed, for instance, by Lange and Dickinson. However, while the socialists now take man as he is, hoping to make him more solidarity-minded in the end but not treating the success of this educational effort as a presupposition of their organizational schemes, they still want so to construct institutions as to make them conform more clearly to the idea that man is man's brother. The practical value of institutionalized welfare can stand on its own merits, independent of its influence on the human character: Even if man's combative proclivities were to remain in full strength in the new welfare society, it would be of great value to reduce the frequency and severity of man's inhumanity to man, and to alleviate the suffering of those who do fall in the struggle. But the hope that institutions which rely for their functioning less on struggle and more on solidarity will have an educational effect has not died out, nor is it likely to. The Marxist idea that man's mind and soul are almost infinitely pliable under the influence of some defined institutional changes—i.e. changes in the property system—[3] must certainly be abandoned, but one does not have to be a Marxist to believe that man's combativeness will decrease, and his brotherly instincts given freer rein, if social institutions are so framed as to teach him by ex-

[3] According to Marxist theory, the property system is itself determined by man's experience in production and thereby by the physical conditions and technological methods of production.

The term "almost infinitely pliable" used in the text above is unavoidably vague, yet this vagueness has its roots in the Marxian system itself. Neither Marx nor his interpreter Engels has ever given a comprehensive statement of what they regard as the stable framework within which the conditions or methods of production can produce changes through alteration of the property system or through other media—if, indeed, they recognized such a stable framework. Most of the time they speak as if they believe that all economic "rules of the game" were subject to change with the system of ownership, although some passages may be interpreted as reflecting the insight that there are some principles of economic rationality which hold true under any system. Similarly, Marx and Engels speak most of the time as if all ethical rules were subject to change with alterations in social relationships, occasionally, however, there appear in Marxist writings traces of the idea that some ethical rules are immutable because they follow from the nature of man as a social being. Similarly, it is impossible to say with certainty whether in the Marxist opinion there is no limit at all to the influence which the property system can exert on the thinking and feeling of man, or whether these limits exist but are extremely wide. If the former interpretation is correct, the word "almost" would have to be deleted from the phrase, "almost infinitely pliable."

perience that his survival depends on cooperation with others rather than on victory over others.

The desire of the socialists to emphasize human solidarity expresses itself most conspicuously in their welfare programs. Of course, welfare institutions do not occur only in socialist societies, or societies dominated by socialists; this, however, merely serves to remind us again that there is no clear-cut dividing line between socialism and capitalism. But does the eagerness of the socialists to provide more comprehensive welfare schemes really widen the influence of human solidarity? Upon the urging of the socialists, public institutions of welfare have to a considerable extent superseded private charity; it might be argued that tax-financed, institutionalized welfare, whatever its practical advantages, provides less opportunity for practicing human solidarity than do voluntary activities based on voluntary contributions. But the recognition by the body social of the duty to provide for its less fortunate members has more far-reaching consequences, psychological as well as material, than the sacrifices of individual benefactors. Although some spontaneity of good will was undoubtedly lost when the professional social worker replaced the volunteer in the service of private charitable organizations, the voluntary decision to care and to give is never a complete substitute for the enactment of the community's obligation to prevent extreme poverty. This is especially true in an age which sees the decline of the influence of religion and its traditional teaching that support of the poor is a duty which no well-to-do person can neglect without committing a sin; for the reverse side of the voluntary character of private charity—if it is voluntary not only in the legal but also in the moral sense—is absence of the right of the poor to be relieved. Yet this right is the first requirement of any welfare policy that aims at rehabilitation rather than humiliation of the recipient, and it is, therefore, necessary to uphold this right in spite of all possible misuses. If all the effects are taken into account, the extension of public welfare as advocated by the socialists has been a true expression of human solidarity.

But it is not in welfare services alone that the socialist emphasis on human solidarity expresses itself. Although the socialists had to abandon their earlier ideas that conscious collective striving for the good of all members of the community should supersede the competitive struggle, in the new concept of a socialist society this struggle tends to be relegated to the status of a tool for executing a plan intended to benefit the whole community. A French entrepreneur who has checked his own production program against the information received from the Monnet plan authorities through the joint committees which help in compiling and executing the plan, acts from the profit motive just as he did before the plan was established. In a way, his selfish interest has been sanctioned as it had not been before, if his program fits into the plan, because it is now recognized as being in harmony with the community interest; yet this arrangement implies that the sanction might be withheld, which, though not making the exercise of entrepreneurial self-interest illegal, would put it in a lower category of legitimacy. Thus the interest of the community, based on solidarity among its citizens, is established as the sovereign principle; action prompted by the profit motive is no longer an absolute right, but is fully legitimate only to the extent that it has the stamp of approval of those who are in charge of the plan and therefore of the community interest. The very existence of a staff of people professionally committed to the protection of that interest in the determination of economic development assigns to the principle of community welfare, and thereby to that of human solidarity, a greater role in the economic system.

Many socialists, especially but not exclusively Marxists, have emphasized class solidarity along with general human solidarity; some schools of socialists, such as the syndicalists, founders of Utopian colonies and cooperators, have tried to build their systems upon the feelings of special solidarity among members of vocational or local groups. There is some indication that in the social structures which socialists may build in the future, solidarity among the workers in individual enterprises may play an important role, as it now does in the Yugoslav system which stands half-way between socialism and communism. No wing of the socialist movement, however, has in principle considered group solidarity or group organization an end in itself, in the way extreme nationalists consider national feelings or the nation-state an end in itself. Rather, for the socialist, the group has always been the representative of mankind. Solidarity among the members of class, labor union or cooperative was cultivated because it was felt that the average human being was not capable of identifying himself with his fellow-humans strongly enough to curb his individual selfishness unless he had more in common with them than mere human existence; also, the group—working class, or labor union—was regarded as the most effective fighting unit to bring about the change that would benefit all humanity. Even extremists of Marxism viewed class organization not as a creation desirable for its own sake but as a vehicle to carry them to the desired goal, a classless society. As in other human pursuits, however, the means sometimes received a degree of glorification which made them appear as ends, but the fatal consequences of this confusion, evident in the extremist interpretation of the class struggle concept and its practical application in communist countries, must not obscure the fact that even in Marxist theory the class is merely regarded as an instrument of the historical process operating for the liberation of mankind. The ultimate reason why socialism and communism parted company was the communist tendency to let class solidarity overshadow human solidarity almost entirely in the present, postponing the realization of human solidarity to an undetermined future.

To assess the role of tradition in socialism is difficult because no completely socialist system exists now, and because the system with strong socialist elements have not existed long enough to develop a tradition of their own. It is clear, however, that the system which socialists want to build would be just as unable to function properly as any other system if every individual had in each case to reason out how he should act instead of often being consciously or unconsciously guided by precedent. Much of this tradition concerns the technique of economic management and the technique of public administration, and in either of these two fields a socialist society will be able to take over a substantial heritage of capitalist tradition. But socialism implies a more involved relationship between these two fields than does capitalism. The technique of the planning board in influencing the decisions of business, and the technique of business in obtaining and utilizing the information which the planning board can give, the technique of the national executive and the national legislature in controlling nationalized enterprises without unduly restricting their freedom of action also will require the forming of a tradition. An important conclusion suggests itself with regard to the degree of patience that should be exercised in judging the effectiveness of such systems as the present French *économie concertée:* They have not existed long enough to establish tradition, and they will probably operate with a closer approach to perfection once time has remedied this weakness.

Aside from these technical traditions, however, there are indispensable traditions embodying moral rules of behavior. In this respect also, socialism must first make use of the heritage from capitalism. The will to perform one's job well, to fulfill contracts faithfully, to resist the temptation to secure one's own profit by means which are contrary to accepted obligations or to public law, are obviously as necessary for socialism as they are for capitalism; neither can socialism, any more than capitalism, rely on an intellectual process by which each individual develops his will through a realization of the social necessity of the attitudes involved; rather, it is necessary that certain loyalties be taken for granted because to deviate from them would place the individual in conflict with his own established habit of thinking and feeling, and he would cease to be a member of the society to which he belongs, a society which has adopted these habits as indispensable to its own coherence.

Does socialism need a specific moral tradition? Since socialists no longer construct their programs on the assumption that individuals will be motivated by a higher degree of altruism than they are now under capitalism, a negative answer suggests itself. Indeed, it would be hard to think of any moral rules, and therefore of any moral tradition, specific to a socialist society; but socialism may well need an even stronger emphasis on some moral rules—and their hardening into an even stronger moral tradition—than does capitalism. Some of these stronger emphases will concern the conduct of public officials, especially their respect for the freedom of the citizen, and the attitude of the citizen, who must regard insistence on the defense of his freedom not only as a right but a duty. A firm tradition of respect for the consumer's sovereignty and for the free choice of employment is highly desirable in capitalism where monopolistic practices and the limitations of social mobility may infringe on these freedoms, but may well be even more necessary under socialism as a safeguard against the misuse of state power.

CHAPTER 16

THE GOVERNMENT AND THE INDIVIDUAL UNDER SOCIALISM: A SUMMING UP

Socialism and Liberty

SOME OF ITS OPPONENTS have decried socialism as the mortal enemy of human freedom; its defenders have often asserted that socialism is the only economic system under which liberty can develop. Socialism, however, is not a prerequisite of a high degree of human freedom, since within the capitalist system of today a greater amount of freedom exists than most, or perhaps all, previous generations knew; similarly, the assertion that socialism cannot be built without destroying the freedom of the citizen is most implausible. Countries in which socialist programs are more advanced than in others have not suffered any impairment of previous guarantees of liberty nor any decline in the vitality of democratic institutions. Representative democracy and the traditional liberties of an Englishman seem to be just as safe in Great Britain today as they were before the Labour Party nationalized some industries and set up welfare services. If the future of democracy is less secure in France, the reason has nothing to do with the nationalization of the coal mines or of the Renault factory, or with the Monnet plan.

Yet the critics of socialism who feared hazards to human freedom were not wholly wrong. These critics were wrong in believing that liberty could exist only under capitalism, but they were right that in no complex economy can liberty be preserved unless at least the bulk of production is regulated by prices which are free to move in order to equilibrate supply and demand. It was through the retention of the price system that socialism made freedom compatible with the extension of government responsibility implied in a socialist order. This connection between human freedom and the existence of a market can be found on several levels of economic reality.

In the first place, the less the necessary coordination of economic activities is achieved by exchange, the more it must be achieved by command. Although command may prevail in limited areas without impairing the free character of society—a democracy, for instance, may show great vitality although it possesses a strictly disciplined army—yet obviously every extension of the areas in which command is the principal coordinating device restricts freedom, and there is much reason to believe that the destructive effect on liberty grows in geometric rather than arithmetic progression with the extension of the field of command. If the producers, however, are not to be told what to produce and how to produce it, it is necessary that they can themselves find the information required to make these decisions with a reasonable approach to correctness; and that information can come to them only through the knowledge of prices for products and cost goods. On the other hand, if everybody is to be told exactly what to do in regard to production, the part of life in which free decisions can be made is seriously restricted.

This argument for the market economy, it is true, has lost some of its force through the prevalence of large concerns. In a factory, internal coordination of individual activities is effected by command. For modern industry only a limited number of managers make independent decisions about the goals and methods of production on the basis of market prices. For this restriction of the area of independent economic choice, modern technology has supplied a twofold compensation. In the first place, its increasing complexity has made it necessary for many individuals in the lower ranks of the industrial hierarchy to make decisions with regard to ways of performing particular jobs, what tool to use for shaping a particular piece of material, what instruments to apply to locate the seat of some trouble, with what speed to run a particular machine for a maximum of efficiency and safety. These are technical decisions, in the narrow sense, but they involve responsibility which often equals in importance that of managerial choices; frequently the avoidance of disaster depends on the nerves, the knowledge and the good sense of subordinate technicians.

Moreover, while a large number of individuals has lost its share in economic decisions within industrial production, that sphere today comprises a much smaller part of the lives of common men and women; modern technology has reduced the hours of work, and this additional leisure time has been a most significant expansion of the sphere in which an individual can live his own life, independent of other people's orders. But these benefits do not depend on the existence of a market per se: Any economic system which is efficient enough to utilize the inventions of physicists, chemists and engineers spreads technological responsibility and leisure.

The steering of production by market forces, however, has preserved substantial areas in which the power of decision-making is far more widely dispersed than in large industry. Agriculture, retail trade and repair services are outstanding examples. Centralizing tendencies, it is true, are infringing also upon these areas: In many parts of the world the family farm is declining, chain stores are often replacing the neighborhood grocer, service departments of large producer or dealer firms are fiercely competing with independent craftsmen. Still, the battle lines are quite fluid; and as long as this is the case, the survival of numerous independent decision makers in production and distribution, who would be eliminated if the economy were entirely steered by directive, must be put on the credit side of the market. All in all, the tendency of the price system to substitute spontaneous decisions for obedience to command in the management of production and distribution of commodities is still of great importance for human freedom, although its significance may, on balance, have declined within the last 100 years.

Even more important, however, is the freedom-protecting effects of the price system on the labor market. In no kind of society is there any assurance that the preferences of individuals for different jobs are distributed in the exact proportions in which these jobs are available Obviously, it would be sheer accident if as many, and no more, teamsters, electricians, stevedores, cabinetmakers and physicists were needed as there are young people who wish to prepare for each of these careers. There are only two ways in which the supply of different types of labor can be adjusted to demand: either by compulsion, young people being drafted into the different vocations in the same manner as recruits in a conscript army may be sent into infantry, artillery or air force according to military requirements, or by making those vocations that are short of candidates more attractive by higher rewards.[1] The free choice of vocation is one of the essential

[1] At first sight it might seem that the latter method should cause wages to reach the highest level in occupations that are most disliked, and the lowest level in occupations that are most satisfactory to most people. This is not the case, of course. Most ditch diggers would prefer to work in an office even if wages were the same, but office workers are usually better paid than ditch diggers. The reason, of course, is that it is easier to qualify as a ditch digger than as an office worker.

Some qualifications are natural: No person without a voice can become a singer, an ugly woman can rarely become a movie actress, no unintelligent man can become a nuclear physicist. Other qualifications can be acquired by training, the cost of which must be reflected in the compensation for the jobs. In addition, even with the modern approach to equality of opportunity, remnants of social qualification are still left: Young

liberties, because it involves the right of an individual to shape a most important part of his own life. It is, therefore, vitally important for a free society to have the vocational distribution of the labor force effected by bargaining for wages and other terms of employment on a labor market rather than by command of superior authority.

But in evaluating the significance of the price system for the promotion of economic freedom, we have to think also of the sphere of consumption. The importance of pricing for the maximization of material welfare has been discussed; here its importance for human freedom is on the agenda. The freedom to determine for ourselves, within the limits of available resources, what goods we shall consume is a large part of the freedom to shape our own lives. Any authority that can tell us arbitrarily what we can and cannot have can set conditions for permitting us to raise our standard of living, and thus has a fair chance to bend our will to its own. This is not to say that any substantial part of our freedom is involved in the question of whether we can buy automatic dishwashers or high fidelity sets; yet it would be equally wrong to think that only the denial of primary necessities can infringe upon our freedom. Although it is possible to get by without electricity or an automobile, in a particular social setting these goods can become so important that it would require a strong will to defy any person

---

people with good connections find it easier to work themselves up to a managerial position than those unconnected; in some communist states, a person of proletarian or peasant origin is given preference in the training for leading positions; in the United States and many other countries, race still plays a role in selection for jobs.

The boundaries between the qualified and the non-qualified are in most instances not rigid but can often be crossed through effort. A person whose brainpower is not much better than average may still become a scientist—though certainly no Einstein—by an unusual willingness for hard work. Even natural obstacles are not always insurmountable: People have become orators in spite of original speech defects, self-development as an actor has sometimes made audiences forget the lack of handsomeness of face or figure. Whenever supply of a particular kind of labor fails to equal demand, in a market economy the compensation will rise until a sufficient number of people have been induced to acquire the qualifications and fill the vacancies.

This effect of a free labor market has little to recommend it from the point of view of justice. We may feel that the worker who has moved into the field by acquiring the qualifications through a special effort, for instance a history teacher who moves into mathematics because mathematics are needed or the auto worker who retrains as a television specialist, or a girl who overcomes a natural aversion to become a laboratory technician, may deserve extra compensation. But the higher wages in the undersupplied vocations benefit not only these marginal workers: The teacher for whom mathematics is easier than history, the man who was trained as a television expert in the first place and liked it, the girl who never thought of becoming anything but a laboratory technician also draw the higher pay. This is the same point that was discussed earlier, when the reader was warned against attributing ethical significance to marginal productivity as a regulator of income distribution. But although without special merit from the point of view of justice, equilibration of supply and demand for different kinds of labor has the enormous advantage of making unnecessary other adjustment methods that would be destructive of liberty.

or agency which has the power to deny us these benefits. In present-day American civilization, it would be intolerable to leave it to the unlimited discretion of a public utility company whether it wants to supply current to a citizen's house, or to the pleasure of the motor vehicles department whether to issue a license plate for a citizen's car.

But the danger lest the power to deny us material satisfactions can be used to make us comply with somebody else's will is not the only infringement of our freedom from which the institution of a market can protect us. Suppose our consumption were determined by a dictator who does not try to extort our compliance with his will by the threat of denying us material comforts, but merely tells us unconditionally what kinds of food, clothing, transportation or recreation we can use. His motives may be benevolent, idealistic or selfish; he may want to force us to eat vitamin-rich food for our own benefit, or to eat less butter in order to release more resources for producing guns. Again, the dictator may deny us the use of automobiles because he owns shares in a local bus company. The mere fact that somebody takes from us the responsibility for the shaping of the material aspects of our lives makes us less free.

This is true not only when the dictate of what to consume or not to consume is conveyed to us by direct command; the infringement of our freedom is essentially the same, though not always felt as distinctly, if the dictator achieves his purpose through a manipulation of prices. To stimulate consumption of some commodities by keeping their prices below cost, at the expense of others which must be higher priced, means imposing a pattern of consumption preferred by the authority which does the imposing and not by the consumer himself. There must, however, be exceptions to the rule that this should not be done. First, again the hazards to freedom grow more than proportionately with the extent of the infringement, and in reverse the hazards are greatly reduced when the area of infringement is kept small. Our liberty is not seriously endangered when the prices of coffee and tobacco are increased by excise taxes. The second and far more important exception to the rule follows from the right and need of society to guide itself, which often requires the encouragement of some types of consumption beyond what they would be when determined by market prices: Free education is the classic example. Overlapping with the idea that comsumption in some areas may have to be enlarged (as it may in less frequent cases, have to be restricted) to make for a better kind of society is the consideration that offering some goods or services free or at low cost may be the best way to combat some particularly undesirable effects of the inequality of incomes. As in all other instances to which consumers' sovereignty is not directly applicable, the power of the community to make decisions affecting the individual's life might lead to a negation of freedom if this power is not subject to democratic safeguards which, one must remember, involve more than a mere majority rule.

To sum up: Steering production by prices is a postulate of the rule of law. According to Hayek's definition, which can be accepted without approving the use to which he puts it, this principle "means that government in all its actions is bound by rules fixed and announced beforehand . . ."[2] Aside from the specific harm which government could inflict on individual liberty by taking away from the individual the right to determine his consumption or to choose a vocation, there is the general need to commit government, in all of its actions, to rules made known in advance in order to preclude favoritism and consequently personal dependence of the citizen upon the executive. One of the purposes of this principle, again in the words of Hayek, is to make it possible for the individual "to foresee with fair certainty how the authority will use its coercive powers in given circumstances and to plan one's individual affairs on the basis of this knowledge."[3] But even if the individual cannot foresee how the rules will work out in his particular case, it is important that he be assured that the government is acting according to rules and not arbitrarily. It is for this reason that in the United States, whenever military necessity required a number of recruits larger than could be provided by voluntary enlistment, but smaller than the total number of those eligible for conscription, the government authorities were still not left free to pick by arbitrary decision those who had to go into the army, but were committed to a random rule through the institution of a kind of lottery, names being drawn out of a wheel or a similar device; this was the original meaning of draft. That such a random rule was found preferable to any arrangement that would have left the selection of recruits more to the discretion of the government is a perfect example of a realization of the dangers inherent in all arbitrary use of power.

Thus it was through the acceptance of the price mechanism that the socialists made their system compatible with liberty. This acceptance was a necessary but also a sufficient condition. With freely moving prices determining production, it is of little significance how production is organized or even how the mechanism is constructed which makes possible the motion of prices to equilibrate supply and demand. The latter point is of particular importance. It has been explained before that prices need not

[2] Friedrich A. Hayek, *The Road to Serfdom*. Chicago: University of Chicago Press, 1944, p. 72

[3] *Ibid.*

result from the actual biddings of individual buyers and sellers, that they can be found through calculation of supply and demand conditions—provided the data are available—and that therefore the market can exist as a "paper market." All the arguments for the freedom value of the price system apply to the paper market as well as to the "live" market, except the argument that has been mentioned first: Only in a "live" market are managers able to steer production by spontaneous response to prices; a system that steers the economy by directives would take this right away from the limited number of individuals who enjoy it now, even if the directives were issued on the basis of "paper" prices. The reasons why this point is probably declining in importance have been explained, but even if there were no such decline, the point could not be held against present-day forms of socialism, since in these forms the "paper market" is not to be substituted for the "live" market but is to serve as its supplement. Socialists of today do not want complete nationalization; they want nationalized enterprises to compete, and their managers to react to prices as private entrepreneurs do. A "paper market" is essential for present-day socialism merely as a planning device, because prices must be anticipated before they appear on the actual market.

The lack of precision in the concept of socialism in contemporary thought has led to a broad interpretation which has brought out more clearly what has always been the core problem in the controversies between socialists and anti-socialists: the delimitation of the economic tasks of the organized community in relation to the economic tasks of the individual. Even if those socialists who lean toward anarchism were right in their belief that the community must not necessarily be organized in the form of the state, that is, be equipped with legitimate means of physical coercion, the problem would be essentially the same, because community pressure can compromise the individual's freedom even without police or prisons. Of fundamental importance to our analysis is the realization that one community is not identical to another, that one government is not identical to another, in economic as in political matters. The amount of government activity in a society is not just the reciprocal of individual freedom existing in that society. The individual can be much freer with extensive government activity, if that government is bound by law and controlled on the one hand by an independent judiciary, on the other hand by the citizens themselves voting in accordance with majority rule after free discussion, than he will be in a society with only limited government activity, where no rule of law exists and the government is independent of the citizens. Nor is it true what many of the neo-liberals have maintained, that in the guidance of economic production the government cannot be bound by a rule of law. In that large part of production which serves individual consumption, government can be committed to consumers' sovereignty, and the latter can be spelled out in a system of prices; for the satisfaction of collective and ideological wants, community action is indispensable in any event, and democracy—it cannot be said too often that this includes an effective bill of rights together with majority rule—is the only conceivable safeguard under modern conditions.

What makes this matter so important is the increasing need to rely on government for vital purposes—not from our wish to avoid individual responsibility but from needs which have arisen through our shift from a rural, agricultural society of poorly educated masses to an urban, industrialized society with a high level of education. An unconditional determination to keep government small would be costly to us, in terms of material well-being and even of liberty itself, because we need government to balance or render innocuous private economic power. The undersupply of public services as compared with the abundance of commodities for private consumption is an economic scandal which John Galbraith has exposed in the chapter, "The Theory of Social Balance" of his book on *The Affluent Society.* The necessity to hold Big Business to obligations of fair and equal treatment of consumers and of employees without union protection is obvious, and unfortunately experience has shown that some labor unions cannot be trusted any more than business to keep their house in order, that is, to protect the freedom of their members from infringement by "bossism;" consequently, some government supervision is also necessary in this field. True, there is no case for big government per se; what can be well done by individuals should be done by individuals. But many vitally important tasks are not in this category, and the bias against government activity is as harmful in some Western countries as the bias against private enterprise has been in communist countries.

Impersonal Forces and Conscious Action

Friedrich Hayek, who is distinguished among neo-liberal writers not only by his extremism but also by his aptitude for developing challenging ideas, has struck a point of fundamental importance in rejecting the notion "that we must learn to master the forces of society in the same manner in which we have learned to master the forces of nature." [4] On the contrary, he reasons, the preservation of our civilization depends "on the coor-

[4] Friedrich A. Hayek, *The Road to Serfdom,* p. 205.

dination of individual efforts by impersonal forces";[5] consequently, he is opposed to the transformation of impersonal forces into deliberate, conscious human action, and economic planning is obviously a prime example of such transformation.

There is certainly no merit in conscious action under all circumstances. The well known story of the centipede whose feet got entangled only after a questioner had made him conscious of their complicated movement applies to some human affairs, in the area of physical, mental and social processes. But this simply means that we should leave well enough alone, or, at the utmost, that we should not extend the area of our conscious action to fields in which we have no reasonable assurance that such action can achieve better results than the "impersonal forces." Conscious action involves responsiblity, and where the author of the action is too often frustrated by the limitations of his technique, useless and socially dangerous recriminations may follow; on the other hand, how could techniques ever be improved if we were always to insist on a high probability of success before attempting conscious action?

No social scientist, however strongly he may support Hayek's fundamental position, can deny that "impersonal forces" do not always produce such good results as to nullify the need for conscious action. Who would say, for instance, that the operation of impersonal forces in the building of our cities has had such good results as to make city planning commissions unnecessary? But if it is true that "coordination of individual efforts by impersonal forces" is not always wholesome, then each case must be examined on its merits; in other words, a bias in favor of the impersonal process is as unfounded as a bias in favor of conscious action. When we apply this rule to the over-all performance of our economy, can we seriously maintain that it works so well as to make an attempt at conscious improvement a frivolous enterprise? To be sure, in the Western countries we have attained a high standard of living; we do not want to lose what we have; it is, therefore, imperative to avoid rash, revolutionary action in substituting new devices for existing social mechanisms. This necessary warning, however, is something entirely different from a ban on the replacement of impersonal processes by conscious action. That such replacement must inevitably result in disaster to our civilization is an assertion which cannot even be made plausible, certainly not proved, and which hardly any social scientist accepts in all its consequences; these consequences would go far beyond a criticism of socialism, planning or extensive social welfare legislation.

[5] *Loc. cit.*, p. 206.

Ever since the emergence of economics as a science, economists have tried to make the operation of impersonal forces in the market mechanism understandable. They did this at first with the primary objective of showing that conscious action often has side effects which are not realized or, in any event, not taken into account when the action is inaugurated, and which may be so harmful as to outweigh any advantageous results. This was the reasoning behind the rejection of mercantilistic commercial policy: Keeping out foreign goods will reduce the country's own exports, because foreigners can buy from us only with money earned in foreign trade, and will deprive us of the advantages of the international division of labor. Equally, it was demonstrated that price ceilings discourage production and do not in the end benefit the consumer. Some of the early economists, especially the physiocrats, tended to generalize these individual criticisms into a broad view of the world based on a natural law concept, and preached that "the world goes by itself" and does not need, in fact cannot tolerate, conscious steering; but with the weakening of natural law philosophy this generalization lost its force, and even in early Victorian England the operation of impersonal forces was corrected by the deliberate creation of such devices as the factory inspector.

Today the belief in the kind of natural law which was the basis of a generalized laissez-faire economics has disappeared, and the disparity between the relatively high degree of control that has been established over the forces of nature and the relatively limited control that has been achieved over the forces of society is keenly felt as a challenge by social scientists. All of them, in whatever special field they are working, attempt to elucidate the social pressures, which means making us conscious of their nature. To maintain that these efforts are undertaken merely to demonstrate that nothing should be done about these processes would be an easily refutable proposition: Not even Professor Hayek himself is really following that rule of abstinence from economic policy. He and some other neo-liberals, however, do not fully realize that the case for reliance on "impersonal forces" as such is destroyed once this reliance is abandoned even in a particular area, for instance, in the sphere of monopoly control. The effort of producers to raise the price of their product by restricting output through collusion is neither more nor less impersonal than the attempt of each of a number of competing sellers to drive the others from the market. In most instances, it is true, the former effort is generally detrimental to consumers' welfare and the latter is beneficial; but this is precisely the point: The operation of impersonal forces can be harmful and call for remedial action; consequently, there is no general case for relying on the operation of impersonal forces. If it is recognized, as the neo-liberals would be the first to maintain, that collusion must be prevented by conscious action, then the idea is refuted that the latter, for some fundamental reason, is always sure to lead to inferior results; and if no presumption exists one way or the other, there is a chance that conscious action will be found necessary in other matters as well—and, of course, the great majority of economists—even many who can in no way be classified as socialists or "planners"—have arrived at the conclusion that other fields also call for community action to control, to limit and supplement the operation of impersonal forces. Part of the task of economists may still consist of teaching respect for the "invisible hand" which, as Adam Smith once explained, causes businessmen to promote the common welfare by actions designed merely to increase their own profits; but such teaching must not imply that this kind of guidance is ubiquitous or, even where it is taking place, is necessarily the most effective kind that can be devised. Just as in medicine respect for the self-healing tendencies of the body would be a bane rather than a boon if it prevented search for cases in which this tendency might usefully be supplemented or superseded by medication and surgery, so economists would fail to exploit the potentialities of their science if their teaching of respect for the "invisible hand" were unconditional.

Political Implications of Big Government

Whether it is good or bad that in modern industrial society we need government as much as we do is a question to which different people will always give different answers. This is only natural, since the benefits and burdens of government action are unequally distributed among individuals; nor can all individuals muster the same degree of patience to meet either the demands of bureaucracy upon the citizen or the natural or social disasters from which government action is to protect them; in fact, each of us may feel differently about that question while making out his income tax return and when receiving a Social Security check. One consideration, however, which should keep us from categorically condemning "big government," has not received the attention it deserves. Nobody, except a small minority of anarchists, maintains that government is superfluous; the issue is whether government can and should be restricted—again, everybody grants a number of exceptions—to such traditional functions as defense, maintenance of public order, and settlement of disputes in civil law. Restriction would mean that in the wide area of our daily activities defining our economic life, government would play only a very minor part. Under these circumstances, would it be possible to maintain the lively popular interest in public affairs which is essential to the functioning of free political institutions? Our democracy is not the Athenian kind which could be supported by the interest in politics of citizens who left many of the economic tasks to slaves; nor do we still have a frontier democracy in which such simple, tangible matters as defense against savages and construction of transportation routes were vital enough to the individual to assure his continuing interest in government. Countries in which a minority of citizens engage in politics as a sport, while the masses remain indifferent, offer a spectacle which certainly does not invite emulation, and the same applies to countries in which the great majority is so preoccupied with money making that they leave public affairs to professional politicians, with little or no control by the citizens. Even the American citizen who regrets the enactment of social security laws or would like to keep the government out of such activities as building power dams may find some consolation in the fact that the controversy over the extent to which social security should be provided and over the merits of individual power projects provides a vital margin of citizens' interests in the affairs of state.

This is obviously not a matter directly related to the advantages or disadvantages of socialism; but the indirect relationship should be clear. The slogan, "creeping socialism," employed by American conservatives to denounce the extension of economic activities of the government contains a core of truth: Since the acceptance of large economic responsibilities by the government is the essence of present-day socialism, an extension of such responsiblities may be seen as a step on the road to socialism. Therefore the arguments, for and against, which apply to the proliferation of governmental economic activities in a capitalist society will apply, with even greater force, to socialism.

The danger inherent in the slogan "creeping socialism" is the implication that the "creeping," once begun, is an irreversible process that cannot be stopped. In most respects, such an inevitability does not exist. If the government establishes one multipurpose dam like the Tennessee Valley Authority, this does not create a compulsion to establish others; if social security is established on a modest scale, it does not follow inevitably that a necessity is created to raise the benefits to ever higher levels; as the example of the United States shows, a country can establish some kinds of social insurance—old age and survivors insurance and unemployment insurance—without establishing another kind that exists elsewhere—in this case, public health insurance. Of course, the experience with one dam project or with one kind of social insurance may be favorable, and therefore the citizens or their representatives may see fit to undertake similar ventures in other areas; but it is one thing to say that we will not be able to stop on a particular road, once we have made a start, and something entirely different to guess, or judge from experience, that we shall not want to stop.

Yet again, there is some truth in the implication that government activity, once started, cannot be stopped at will. The term "cannot" must not be taken literally: No human action is inevitable if we are prepared to pay the cost of omission. Yet sometimes the cost of not rounding out some complex of government policy is rather high. Whereas a country's establishment of unemployment insurance puts no extra penalty on its not having health insurance, the disadvantages of excluding some categories of workers from the operation of any social insurance are often great and sometimes prohibitive. These disadvantages are partly political: The excluded groups may feel a strong grievance and express their resentment in opposition. They may be economic: Giving some industries an advantage over others may distort the pattern of the distribution of capital and entrepreneurship or of the labor market.[5] Such disadvantages have led, for instance, to a gradual rounding out of the old age and survivors insurance program in the United States.

There was a time when many people were resigned to unemployment and other economic misfortunes; these were viewed almost as natural disasters, events beyond human control. This state of mind has never been general and complete, and perhaps in the United States less so than in Europe, as the sequence of movements born of agrarian discontent showed after 1873. But even in the United States, during the nineteenth century, many people were more or less resigned to the assumption that no government could do much about disasters which had their origin in the dynamics of business. This resignation has been destroyed; people today hold the government responsible for preventing economic distress. But how can the government meet this responsibility? To be sure, governments now know more about the working of the economy than they did in the Victorian age, and government tool chests have been better stocked, but they are still far from possessing either the knowledge or the instruments to protect the welfare of the citizens to the degree expected by public opinion. A situation,

[5] The distorting forces are likely to pull in opposite directions: Capital and entrepreneurship will probably be drawn to the industries least affected by social legislation, while labor will tend to move toward the protected occupations, although in both respects there may be important exceptions. There is no probability, of course, that this mutual opposition will result in an equilibrium that leaves the pattern undistorted.

however, in which the government is held responsible for events over which it has little control is a boon to all demagogues. Unless the government acquires new techniques to anticipate and influence the course of economic events, its accountability for economic developments is largely a fiction: The greatest problem of political reconstruction in advanced industrial societies is the task of making that accountability real. Whatever else may be wrong in the concepts of the socialists, they have recognized, though vaguely, this all-important point; outside the socialist camp, too, the task is now more widely understood. The main reason why we are moving along the road to greater government control, which to many people appears an inescapable fate, to be welcomed or cursed, is not that one step requires the next one, although it is true that we cannot stop at just any point of the road without paying very dearly for halting; the principal reason is that the cause of the first steps, the decline of popular acquiescence to economic misfortune, has continued to operate and is not likely to disappear before our economic destinies are brought under the control of responsible government, to the insurmountable limits of human foresight.

At present, it is not only the events that originate in the business world that the government can only inadequately foresee and influence; acts of economic policy even in the traditional sphere, such as the raising or lowering of tariffs, conservation of natural resources or city planning, are necessarily based on assumptions which cannot be tested in advance because economic foresight is not sufficiently developed. Our conjectures about our future balance of payments are quite unreliable; except in the very short range, we know little about the quantities of minerals and other resources which we shall need; no city has a very definite idea of how much industry will be inclined to move into it, or what its traffic density will be twenty years later. Practically none of these developments will ever be foreseeable with complete certainty, because in part they depend on developments in the world at large, on population movements, on beneficial or harmful events in nature, and on future inventions. But a much higher degree of probability could be reached in the estimates if we knew more about the development of our whole economy, by which the development of all its parts is necessarily influenced.

The one point in the socialist program, therefore, which has fundamental significance for the advanced countries, is economic planning. Nationalization is an essentially obsolete demand wherever private enterprise shows vitality; equalization of incomes may or may not be desirable beyond the point which has been reached in the United States and some other countries, but in any event further progress in this direction has become far less important because of the steps toward equality already achieved and because of the absolute rise in the standard of living. But in the field of organized economic foresight, as a basis for coordination of economic policies, much remains to be done, and the same is true of the techniques by which government can induce the spontaneous forces within the economy to respond to the results of such foresight, without depriving them of their spontaneity. The example of France shows that this is no visionary undertaking. We can probably continue to live without these techniques, but at a fairly high price.

IV. COMMUNISM

CHAPTER 17

THE SOVIET ECONOMIC SYSTEM UNDER LENIN AND STALIN

War Communism and the New Economic Policy

TO UNDERSTAND the Soviet economy as it operates today, the student must at least cast a glance at the way it has developed. The Russian Communists, although they finally built up a planned economy, did not, at least in the initial phases, build according to a plan.

The Russian Bolshevik party had in its ranks specialists in the technique of revolution, students of history and philosophy and capable organizers, but it was extremely poor in people who had any understanding of economics. Trying to avoid wholesale nationalization because of preoccupation with political tasks, the Bolsheviks at first experimented with a system called Workers' Control: In the majority of industrial enterprises, the private managers were left in charge, but they were supposed to be controlled by workers' committees. Nobody knew the exact delimitation of the rights of these committees, and the mutual mistrust between the workers and the "capitalists" frustrated any hope for constructive cooperation. The outbreak of a major civil war between Communists and anti-Communists, aggravated by foreign intervention, about half a year after the Communist seizure of power provided the external impetus for the abolition of this untenable system; it was replaced by nationalization of all industries. As in other countries involved in World War I, especially in those suffering invasion, normal economic processes would have been disrupted in Soviet Russia in any event, and many of the measures which the Soviet government took during the civil war, especially the allocation of commodities and materials through rationing and directives rather than through market prices, would have been taken by any government in a similar position; nor was the disastrous inflation, which reduced the purchasing power of the ruble to a negligible amount, without parallel in other countries. What distinguished Soviet policy in this period was that measures which elsewhere were undertaken simply as a necessary part of the war effort were glorified in Russia as the beginning of the Communist age. Naturally enough, this was true of nationalization: Whereas, for instance, the American government took over the railroads because this was the only way to effect an economical use of equipment, and other governments built plants important to the war effort when private industry did not consider them attractive investment propositions, the Soviet government, after overcoming its first hesitation, took pride in fulfilling an old socialist demand: It eliminated private ownership of the means of industrial production; finally, the Russian Communists went to almost ridiculous lengths in this direction, far beyond what the old socialists would have regarded as sensible and proper, by at least theoretically transferring property, even in the smallest one-man shops, to the government.[1]

The glorification of war-generated necessities, however, was not confined to nationalization: The substitution of rationing and directives for the market mechanism in the allocation of resources and consumer goods appeared to the Russian Communists as a victory over capitalism; at times, some of them even believed that inflation was a positive gain, because it destroyed the capitalist institution of money.

This system, which in history books is designated War Communism, collapsed after the end of the civil war, early in 1921; the immediate cause of its collapse was the catastrophic decline of agriculture. In principle, the Russian regulations about food collection from the farms were not very different from those of other European countries during World War I: The needs of the peasant's own household were estimated, and whatever he had produced beyond these needs he was obliged to sell to a state trading agency for the feeding of city populations. In no other country, however, was the system as difficult to administer as in Russia during the civil war. Since the food shortages were very great, only minimum needs of the farming household could be recognized as legitimate, which increased the peas-

[1] The U.S. government returned the railroads to private ownership after the war. Since continued government management would probably have been the only way to secure efficiency in an industry in which competition is naturally imperfect and leads almost inevitably to diseconomies, the undoing of wartime nationalization in the American railroad industry was as much a product of capitalistic ideology as the extent of nationalization in Soviet Russia was one of Communist ideology. In retrospect, to be sure, the American government and the American taxpayer had reason to congratulate themselves on not being saddled with a declining industry, but right after the war the degree to which the competition of the truck would cut into the railroad business could hardly be foreseen.

ant's reluctance to comply with the food regulations except under harsh compulsion. The money which the peasant received for his "excess" food was practically worthless, not only as money value is measured by the price index, but also because the industrial commodities which he would have wished to buy for this money were unavailable. Under these circumstances, the peasants restricted their farming operations as much as they dared, in view of the hazard of government reprisals; when in some parts of Russia natural conditions caused a very poor harvest in 1921, widespread famine was the result, and the Soviet government became deeply alarmed by peasant risings, workers' unrest and a naval mutiny at the Kronstadt base, all resulting from hunger or fear of hunger.

Using his tremendous prestige to overcome resistance, Lenin effected a sudden change of course, and the market was temporarily reinstated as a device of economic coordination. The food-collection scheme was reversed: Instead of being told how much he could retain, the peasant was now told how much produce he had to deliver to the state trading organization as a tax in kind—somewhat later he was permitted to substitute a money tax—and was free to sell the rest at any price he could get. This advantage was made more real by permitting private trading, with the effect that the peasant had a choice among several outlets (government trading organization, cooperatives and private commerce); revocation of the decree nationalizing the small shops—which at that time were still very important in Russia—and a monetary reform rounded out the advantages for the peasant because he could buy something on the market with the money which he received for his produce.

Large industry remained in the property of the state, as did foreign trade; industrial managers, however, were instructed to follow the signals of the market, producing goods they could sell, and to sell them at the prices they could get, and to keep costs down. This whole body of measures was called the New Economic Policy (*Novaia Economicheskaia Politika*, NEP)

It was not easy to rebuild the market mechanism for agricultural products, and apparently even more difficult to do so for industry, but the problem was successfully solved. Not that all hardships disappeared: Agricultural production revived so rapidly that it caused a "scissors" crisis—i.e. farm products dropped so low in price in relation to industrial commodities as to cause a serious parity problem, which tended again to discourage the peasants; the immediate effect was a lag of demand for industrial commodities, because the peasants' incomes were inadequate to purchase the increased output of industry, and industry, whose managers seem to have learned the lesson of collusive techniques of price maintenance rather quickly, was slow in responding to its marketing difficulties by the lowering of prices. Moreover, strong inflationary pressures—a "goods famine"—appeared at times during the NEP period.

The difficulties, however, might well be interpreted as the results of transition. On balance, the New Economic Policy was a great success. Around 1926, Russia reached the prewar level of industrial output. The great majority of the agricultural population was much better off than it had been under the Tsar, and this was probably also true of the workers. Although the middle class and the aristocracy had suffered frightfully, even many of the survivors of these classes in Russia found places as specialists in the Red Army, in government enterprises or in public administration. Why, then, was this period of well-being deliberately brought to an end by the Soviet Government?

The Great Industrialization Debate and the End of NEP

The motives for terminating NEP were a mixture of correct observations on the economic situation, illusions of fear and ideological preferences.

In the latter years of the NEP, deliveries of agricultural produce to the cities proved unsatisfactory; in fact, they never came near the pre-revolutionary figures, and in the case of the most important kind, grains, seem to have reached only one-half of the corresponding figure under Tsarism.[2] The principal reasons for this deficiency were probably inadequate prices for farm products and increased consumption of food by the farm household. To some extent, the latter was the consequence of the former: Because prices offered no great incentive to sell, the peasants consumed more of their own products. Yet consumption of food in the peasant household would in any event have been greater than in the pre-revolutionary period, as an effect of land reform. Under Tsarism, the food consumption of the peasant was kept low by the necessity to sell enough produce to pay taxes and the landlord's rent; even by eating less than they wanted, the poorest peasants and those in the middle stratum of village society—who together accounted for about half the harvest—could supply only little more than one-fourth of the grain placed on the market; the bulk of the supplies came from the big landowners and the rich peasants, the "kulaks." [3] The revolution elimi-

[2] Maurice Dobb, *Soviet Economic Development since 1917,* New York: International Publishers, 1948, p. 214.

[3] The term means literally "fists." This indicates that even in Tsarist times the "rich" peasant, who often had not only more land than the rest but also money to make loans, a windmill or other installations which he might rent to his fellow villagers, or jobs to offer to the poorest peasants at harvest times, was resented by the less fortunate part of village society. On the basis of general experience; it seems indeed likely that many of the kulaks

nated the landlords, and thereby increased the amount of peasant land, at the same time freeing peasants from rent payments; among the peasants, land was redistributed to reduce the kulak holdings. Consequently, the poor and middle peasants now accounted for more than four-fifths of the grain crop and for almost three-fourths of the grain brought to the market.[4] But the poor and middle peasants tended to part only with that portion of their crops which they could spare after having satisfied their own wants for food more amply than they had been able to afford before the war. On the other hand, industrial progress, even if it had not exceeded the speed achieved during the last two pre-revolutionary decades, required an increase of food deliveries to the cities, since increased industrial production was impossible without an additional industrial labor force, and the latter had to be fed. Moreover, increased industrial production required importation of machinery and in some instances of semifinished products, and these had to be paid for by exports. Tsarism had solved this balance of payments problem by exports of grain, made available through the hunger of the peasant population as a consequence of the unequal distribution of land and the pressure of rents and taxes; with the disappearance of these conditions, a large part of the grain once available for export had vanished. Thus there was a vicious circle: The only way to induce the peasantry to bring more grain to the market without compulsion was an increase and rationalization of industrial production that would have provided more industrial commodities on better terms in exchange for food; but that increase in industrial production itself could not be effected without greater grain deliveries to the cities.

The problem was aggravated by the situation in industry. The attainment of the pre-revolutionary level of industrial output around 1926 was a remarkable success, but it also meant that from then on further progress would be more difficult to achieve. Up to that time, it had been sufficient, broadly speaking, to repair existing plants and to restore facilities for traffic, with an economic organization permitting efficient management in order to put the available capacity into operation. Now continued increase depended on new investment in installations, both for the purpose of increasing productivity in existing factories and expanding the industrial base. In this respect, Russian development in the mid-twenties showed some similarity

---

used their advantageous position for exploitative practices, but there is hardly any way of discovering the extent of the abuses. Since with the disappearance of the landlord the kulak became the villain in Communist propaganda—long before the Soviet government turned against him in full force—the Communist assertions must not be taken at face value.

[4] See the table in Dobb, *op. cit.*, p. 217.

to German development in the early 1950's. Germany's economic "miracle" right after World War II was possible because many factories, only slightly damaged, could be put back into operation after quick repairs and after the restoration of traffic facilities and the monetary mechanism; but once existing industrial facilities were fully used, further progress depended on construction of new equipment and could therefore proceed only at a slower pace. Obviously, the Soviet government could not be satisfied with conditions that would have spelled industrial stagnation; it had to break the vicious circle and enter into a period of greater industrial investment. There is every reason to believe that the problem could have been solved without the cruel means that were eventually applied, but the horror of these cruelties must not make us forget that the problem really existed, that the advice to "leave well enough alone" was not applicable here because, despite appearances, conditions were not "well enough."

Whatever might have been the objective advantages of imposing less heavy sacrifices on the peasants and on the consumers for the sake of rapid industrial growth, the idea of assuring the fastest possible growth of Soviet industry by a policy of harshness recommended itself to the impatience prevailing among the more radical faction in the Communist party. One of the motives of this impatience was the belief that the peasantry would always be politically less loyal to the Soviet government than the working class, and that therefore it was imperative to increase as rapidly as possible the number of industrial workers in relation to that of peasants. A second consideration was the fear of war: It seemed essential to many Communists to increase the industrial potential sufficiently and soon enough to make Russia the equal of Western Europe before the latter would renew the effort to destroy the Soviet system by intervention, as France, Britain, Japan and—with some hesitation—the United States had tried to do in 1918-20. It was an irony of fate that the Soviet leaders did not seriously think of the war which eventually—more than a decade after the end of the NEP—was to come, the war with Germany, but were haunted by the specter of a new war with Britain and France, for which not the slightest possibility existed in the late 1920's.

Probably even more important than these considerations was the discontent, for ideological reasons, of many old Communists with conditions as they had developed under the NEP and which were bound to be made even worse by an attempt to carry out industrialization with relatively mild measures. Although the kulaks did not own as large a share of the total agricultural land as they had done in pre-revolutionary days, they had much the better equipped farms.[5] Being the more efficient producers, they had profited more from the opportunities created by the NEP than the rest of the peasantry, and they were sure to profit even more if agricultural prices were raised as an incentive to greater market deliveries. Thus class differentiation in the Soviet villages was on the increase, and would become more pronounced unless the stick rather than the carrot were used to procure more food for the cities.

Another feature of the Soviet economy, which must have been as obnoxious to old-style communists as the class differentiation in agriculture, was the existence of a class of private traders, political outcasts who nevertheless received high profits, at least in the early years of the NEP. Since these "Nepmen," as they were called, had no political rights and were still regarded as a kind of parasite, in spite of the economic function they were filling, they were at the mercy of communist officials; although for understandable reasons there is little tangible evidence, it would be contrary to all experience if the NEPmen had not used part of their high incomes to buy favors from the poorly paid functionaries of state and party. One can easily imagine how the communist ideologists, among whom the tradition of revolutionary puritanism was still strong, must have viewed these signs of corruption in a proletarian state.

Doubts about the effectiveness of the NEP as an instrument of socialist construction of the economy had been expressed as early as 1923 when forty-six leading members of the Communist party in a declaration had warned against the danger that concessions to the peasantry would make it impossible for Soviet industry to earn enough profits for capital accumulation in the interest of industrial expansion; almost at the same time, Trotsky voiced similar ideas in a letter to the Central Committee. In the subsequent years, this program of the Communist left was worked out more clearly, under the intellectual leadership of Eugene Preobrazshensky and with the political support of Leon Trotsky and—at times—Gregory Zinoviev and Lev Kamenev: Industrial prices should be kept relatively high, and available foreign currency should be used for the importation of capital goods, not of consumer goods; Soviet industry should not only be expanded but thoroughly modernized, in order to attain equality and later superiority to that of the capitalist countries; if the higher rate of investment and the refusal to use foreign currency for the importation of consumer goods produced inflation, by keeping the flow of marketable goods so small as to make money chase commodities, this evil would have to be accepted for the time

[5] See Maurice Dobb, *op. cit.*, 1948, pp. 209 ff.

being, because the development of industry must govern currency policies and not vice versa. It is very interesting that in connection with the latter idea the complaint was voiced about "the lack of a plan uniting the work of all the branches of the state economy";[6] it was demanded that the Central Planning Commission (Gosplan), rather than the Commissariat of Finance, and the State Bank be given the preponderant influence in determining the volume of money capital made available to industry.

Although the leftist faction admitted and even emphasized the hazard of a "peasant strike" in retaliation against this policy of "primitive socialist accumulation"[7] at the expense of the peasantry, and ever so often warned of the danger of kulakism and of the rise of the private trader, none of them went so far as to recommend the kind of violent action against the peasants which was applied after 1929. The experience of War Communism was still too close to let such a new aggravation of terror appear acceptable even to most of the extremists. Other Communists were still more strongly influenced by the memory of the events of 1921: Although the "superindustrialists" refrained from demanding a return to outright terrorism, their views found strong opposition. The danger of a complete rupture between workers and peasants, of the destruction of the—always precarious—alliance, the celebrated "smychka," on which Lenin had based his hopes for Communist victory when he admitted individual management of agricultural land instead of insisting on collectivization right after the revolution, appeared to many communists too great; they therefore rejected a policy of "exploiting" the peasants by a continued unfavorable price relationship between agricultural and industrial goods.

[6] This grievance was voiced by Valerien Obolensky-Ossinsky, and quoted in Dobb, *op. cit.*, p. 182.

[7] An expression often used by Preobrazhensky, who took it over from the leftist Soviet economist, V. M. Smirnov; see Alexander Erlich, *The Soviet Industrialization Debate, 1924-1928*, Cambridge: Harvard University Press, 1960, p. 43 fn. The concept of "primitive capitalist accumulation" plays a great role in the writings of Marx, where he describes how the capitalist entrepreneurs obtained the capital for early industrial investment: His answer was that the accumulation had been gained essentially by force, especially through the expropriation of the peasantry by way of enclosures, even though the force was camouflaged by formal legality. "Primitive socialist accumulation" was thought to be an analogy to the Marxist term and to imply that, just as the early capitalists could not have fulfilled their historical role without appropriating by veiled force some income or wealth that belonged to the peasantry, so the socialist state was in essentially the same position, and should not hesitate to use its power to set monopolistic prices for industrial products —and pay relatively low prices for farm produce—for the same purpose.

Like many other Marxian concepts, the accumulation concept as used by Marx can be found in the classical literature of economics. Marx implicitly identified the German term which he used—*urspruengliche Akkumulation*—with the term "previous accumulation" used by Adam Smith. (See Karl Marx, *Das Kapital*, ch. 24.) In English versions of Marxism, the term "primitive accumulation" is more widely used, though "original" would be a more accurate translation.

The intellectual leader of this moderate faction was Nicholas Bukharin, who originally had been on the left wing but had revised his opinions after the crisis of 1921; he was supported by Alexander Rykov, who for a time held a position analogous to that of prime minister, and by Michael Tomsky, leader of the labor unions. This faction proposed increased price incentives for the peasantry, importation of industrial consumer goods to be offered to the peasants in order to stimulate their interest in selling produce, investment primarily in agriculture, and in repairs of even obsolete plants in order to increase as rapidly as possible the output of marketable commodities to counteract inflation, removal of the remnants of the discrimination against kulaks in order to give every peasant an unrestrained interest in improving his operations as much as possible, and for all these reasons a relatively slow pace of industrial expansion.[8]

At first it seemed that the moderates held the stronger position. The most skillful political operator of the period, Joseph Stalin, who already in Lenin's lifetime had become secretary of the Communist Party, sided on the whole with the Bukharin-Rykov-Tomsky faction; the desire of many Communists for a more normal life after the horrors of civil war powerfully supported these tendencies. The surface situation, however, was deceptive: The inherently stronger forces worked for the cause of the extremists.

The generation of Communists governing Russia in the second half of the twenties was still the same one which had split the socialist movement because they were unwilling to accept the restraints which the principles of representative democracy imposed on the labor movement and which made compromise with "capitalist" parties indispensable. The tendency toward extremism was at the heart of the Communist movement. To be sure, the Communists were proud of their mastery of political strategy, which involved deception of the enemy and of temporary retreats to further deceive him and entice him to overreach himself. This pride in shrewdness, reinforced by the belief that history employs "ruses,"[9] facilitated the transition

[8] The domestic issues were intertwined with those of international Communist policy. The leftist faction was inclined to believe—and Trotsky and his personal followers expressed this belief very strongly—that Russia's further development was dependent on world revolution; once the advanced countries of the West had turned Communist, then they would assist Soviet Russia economically so as to raise it to a high level of industrialization; this idea was embodied in Trotsky's theory of "permanent revolution"; he vigorously denied that "socialism in one country" was possible. By a twist of fate, Stalin made the latter idea (if the communist definition of socialism is accepted) come true by adopting, in an exaggerated form, the domestic policies which Trotsky and the other leftists had advocated.

[9] Friedrich Hegel, whose ideas supplied a large part of the philosophical foundations of Marxism, used to speak of the "ruse of history," and Marxist dialectics implies that a move in the opposite direction from one's intended goal can have the effect of making us reach that goal sooner.

to the NEP. But the reverse side of this willingness to compromise was the insistence that the duration of the compromise must be limited: The retreat must prove to be the preparation for a new offensive, the ruse must turn out to be a trap for the enemy. Presumably, no rationalization could extirpate the feeling of humiliation and resentment when the proletarian state was compelled over a considerable sequence of years to conciliate the kulaks in order to obtain enough food supplies for the cities; and when, as happened, the attempts at such conciliation did not produce an effect great enough to sustain hopes that a basis for rapid industrialization could thus be created, when it appeared doubtful whether in this way Soviet Russia could be developed into a first-rate industrial power, it is easy to understand that the idea of following up the weaker doses of concession with stronger ones proved to be too unpopular in the leading Communist circles to be supportable.

There was still another factor operating for a termination of the NEP. Nationalization of industry poses the question of how to prove that a system of nationalized industry is superior in performance to a system of privately owned industry. As has been suggested, an answer to this question had gradually emerged in the minds of socialists and communists: that nationalized industry is superior because it makes it possible, or at least easier, to plan. The idea of planning had grown in Soviet Russia ever since the days of the civil war; while still leading the Red Army against the counter-revolutionists, Trotsky had called for a "single economic plan."[10] A State Planning Commission, Gosplan, had been founded as early as 1920, although at first it had been given only limited functions. In the same year the idea of planning received a further impetus when Lenin worked out a plan for the electrification of Russia ("Goelro" plan). Electrification requires a considerable amount of economic foresight: ideas of where and how industries can develop. All these efforts, however, still fell short of a comprehensive scheme of planned growth for the Soviet economy, although they prepared the soil for such a scheme, and until 1928 the prevailing idea seems to have been that planning could be instituted within the framework of the NEP rather than as an alternative to that policy.

Today, when we have the advantages of hindsight and also of important progress in economic theory, it seems certain that the complete break with the NEP was unnecessary and harmful. To widen the bottleneck in agricultural supplies, the market mechanism could have been used to a much greater extent. Monetary premiums could have been paid for increas-

[10] In a pamphlet, *The Defense of Terrorism,* (London: The Labour Publishing Co. and George Allen & Unwin Ltd., 1921.)

ing market deliveries, perhaps in the form of paying the peasant progressively more for each bushel sold in excess of a defined minimum per acre; such definitions, of course, would vary according to the size and quality of holdings. If such a system, or any kind of strong price incentive, had been followed up by making industrial commodities available in sufficient quantities, without interruptions by "goods famines," to the agricultural population—probably the reliability of the flow of industrial goods was even more important than the price relationship—then there is every reason to believe that agricultural deliveries would have grown considerably; the experience after 1921 had proved that the Russian peasant responded rather quickly to economic incentives. It would have been necessary, however, to supplement these measures by also making capital available for the modernization of agriculture. All this would have added up to a program much like that advocated by the Bukharin-Rykov group: To give the development of agriculture and consumer goods industries, to the extent that the latter was necessary to provide exchange commodities for the agricultural population, priority over the development of capital goods industries in this early phase of industrialization. Since the decisive bottleneck of all industrialization was the food supply problem, it would have been only logical to attack this problem first. In order to hold the burden upon the state budget within manageable limits, it would have been necessary to keep total investment below the amounts spent during the First Five Year Plan. Whether this would have resulted in a slower industrialization during the decade 1928-38 is at least doubtful, since much of the waste of resources would have been avoided.

The market mechanism, however, could not have been used exclusively; it provided proper solutions only for some of the problems, but not for others which had to be met if industrialization was to be carried out with even a modicum of speed. In the first place, food rationing in the cities and other industrial areas was indispensable. Even the wisest agricultural policy could not have succeeded in increasing supplies so much as to make it possible to keep up the level of food consumption which had been attained during the NEP if the urban population was to be rapidly increased; to "ration" food exclusively through its price would have led to intolerable inequalities, especially since differences in money incomes among various categories of workers were bound to become more important as efficiency premiums, indispensable for the success of industrialization, were to be enhanced.

In the organization of industry itself, direction by market incentives was bound to become inadequate during the industrialization period. Physical targets had to be set for the individual industries, even for individual factories. To steer the economy merely by prices if the speed of growth was to come even within a fair distance of the rate achieved under the First Five Year Plan, which more than doubled the output of capital goods in little more than four years, would have required a flexibility of the price system which was inconceivable, even in countries with better trained market operators than existed in the Soviet Union; when similarly rapid changes were required in Western countries, for instance in war emergencies, physical targets and physical allocation of resources also had to be largely substituted for the allocating and rationing functions of prices. Thus during the first phase, Soviet planning had by necessity to be primarily physical planning, whatever the disadvantages of subordinating price considerations to physical calculation.

The drive for rapid industrialization at almost any price found its expression in the First Five Year Plan, inaugurated in 1928, and was officially terminated after only four years in 1932. It was an extremely ambitious plan, and it did not show the people the sacrifices which such a sudden increase of the industrial potential would demand; rather, the plan seemed to promise at the same time an increase in consumption together with the huge expansion of the industrial apparatus. In reality, life became much harder for the Soviet people during this period.[11]

[11] For the results of the First Five Year Plan, see Dobb, *op. cit.*, pp. 254 ff. and—a very pessimistic estimate—Naum Jasny, *Soviet Industrialization 1928-1952*, Chicago: University of Chicago Press, 1961, *passim*, esp. pp. 64 ff. In addition to the inherent difficulties of constructing any production index—a difficulty which is important for global judgments but not necessarily impairing the validity of judgments on individual industries—the reliability of statistics about the results of Soviet industrialization is reduced by inadequate data; for a discussion see Baykov, *op. cit.*, pp. 164 ff.—and by distortion for propaganda purposes. It is therefore not surprising that opinions on the magnitude of Soviet economic achievements have differed widely among experts, especially since even sincere scholars have ideological preferences: These biases may not influence their statements made within the realm of certainty, but often determine to which side they give the benefit of doubt; and the greater the range of doubt, the more important will be the differences of opinion.

By cross-checking various official Soviet data systematically and by applying greatly improved methods of index making, Western experts have been able to narrow their differences of opinion considerably. With improved data, it has been easier than in former years to come to near-agreement on the results of more recent periods and on the results of the whole era of industrialization from 1928 to the present, whereby errors or ambiguities concerning individual phases do not matter too much. For the purposes of this book, controversies about the achievement figures of the First Five Year Plan matter little. By its errors as well as by its positive results, this first phase of industrialization has supplied the experience which formed an indispensable basis for the successes of later years. These successes are as undeniable as the extremely high human cost through which they were achieved.

Jasny has contended that the Five Year Plans in general, and the first one in particular, were primarily instruments of propaganda with little or no influence on reality, that "everything would probably have developed in the same way even if the Five Year Plans had not existed." (*Soviet Industrialization*, p. 27.) Jasny does not maintain that Soviet planning as a whole was ineffective: He believes that the annual plans did provide guid-

SOVIET PLANNING BEFORE WORLD WAR II

The Historic Significance of the First Five Year Plan

The First Five Year Plan was a great historic event not only because it accelerated the process by which one more important country was added to the circle of leading industrial nations; from a secular point of view, the expansion of the industrial plant is not the most significant effect of the change in the organizational principle of the Soviet economy, since the industrialization of Russia would have occurred in any case—under the NEP or even under the Tsar. Rather, it is that change itself which brought something new into the lives of men. For the first time a country made an effort to draw a comprehensive picture of its own economic future in qualitative and quantitative terms and attempted to make it come true by economic policy. To be sure, it was a fumbling effort; what else could it be since it was a first step on a new road?

Although the novelty of the undertaking provides a valid excuse for blunders, the ruthlessness which caused an appalling amount of human

---

ance for the economy, but that they were not in any effective manner integrated into the Five Year Plans.

Whether this extreme view will be accepted by many other Soviet specialists remains to be seen. On general grounds, the present writer remains unconvinced. To be sure, some of the aims of the First Five Year Plan were very unrealistic, and several, especially the simultaneous increase of consumption and investment, were probably not taken seriously by the planners themselves. Deficiencies of achievement occurred also in later plans; and as Jasny pointed out, the plan figures were not always supplied promptly at the beginning of the plan period, which meant that the Soviet economy operated without a Five Year Plan for considerable intervals. But a plan can be very effective in spurring and coordinating economic efforts even though the results remain far behind the proclaimed goals. (Inversely, a plan may be completely fulfilled and yet have been merely a prognosis of the achievements of spontaneous forces, which would have produced the same results if there had not been any plan—an argument implied in some criticisms of French planning.) Nor is the ineffectiveness of the Five Year Plans proved by the fact that some periods were begun without such a plan: In some countries the annual budget has not always been ready at the beginning of the fiscal year, but who would deny that even in these instances budget appropriations ultimately regulated public revenue and expenditure?

With all the window dressing that the Five Year Plans undoubtedly contained, it seems implausible that the plans' only or primary purpose was propaganda. The Soviet Planners could not be content with sketching the development of the economy for one year only, because many investment projects would come to fruition much later; it was necessary to see how the results of several subsequent years would fit together. Therefore plans for a sequence of years had to exist. That the plans for internal use differed in some respects from the published versions is indeed probable, but there is no good reason to assume that they were wholly different plans. Moreover, this is not what Jasny maintains: At least for the Stalin era, he does not believe in the existence of any effective Soviet planning for periods longer than one year. The success of industrialization, even if taken with all the discount that can possibly be justified, would be hard to explain if Jasny's thesis were correct.

suffering as an accompaniment to the introduction of economic planning cannot be defended. Most of this suffering could have been avoided by a modicum of regard for the lot of individuals. Too many observers, looking at these horrible events from their positions of security and comfort in the West, have been inclined to forget the price that had to be paid for the progress that has been achieved. There was often far too much readiness to gloss over the question of why a somewhat slower process, which in all probability would have spared millions of lives, was not chosen. It is true that history is cruel, that no historical achievement would be possible if individual happiness could under no circumstances be sacrificed, but this truth does not grant to the leaders of men license to treat individuals as freely expendable. The efforts of the best minds have long been devoted to the devising of rules and institutions by which historical change should be made possible with less destruction; from a wide area of social relations, we have eliminated violence and arbitrariness, by replacing bullets with ballots as a means of decision-seeking, by substituting orderly legal processes for bloody feuding, by making those who can legally wield armed physical force accountable to those over which such power may be wielded. It is the gravest indictment against Communism that it has caused a retrograde movement in this development, that already under Lenin it had repudiated, for the sake of the class war, the restraints which the evolution of human institutions since the seventeenth century had imposed on state power in its dealings with individuals, and this repudiation has reached its sharpest and most terrifying expression under Stalin in the execution of the First Five Year Plan and in the collectivization of agriculture.

But history must record the credits as well as the debits. Through the organization of economic foresight as a basis for economic policy, an important instrument was added to the tool chest of human endeavors—an instrument which will be applicable in environments and social climates very different from those of its origin. Evidence of this possibility is already forthcoming, France being the most conspicuous example.

Men are often not aware of the most important effects of their innovations. Stalin and his entourage saw themselves as the industrializers of Russia; they put less emphasis on planning as a new technique of controlling the economic fate of mankind. Their ideological bias prevented them from seeing the applicability of this new technique to societies adhering to the democratic traditions of the West, and they would not have been interested if they had recognized this aspect of the matter. One prominent person who seemed to grasp the importance of planning as a new principle was Vladimir G. Groman, a Menshevik by background and the leading light in the Gosplan up to 1928.[12] He was eliminated in the early phase of the new era.

When planning had been discussed in the West prior to the inauguration of Russia's First Five Year Plan—as it was occasionally, for the most part by socialists—the purpose was usually to forestall or abolish "misery in the midst of plenty," that is the destitution of the unemployed in the face of an overabundance of goods, by preventing depressions. The much more extensive discussion of planning contemporaneously with the First Five Year Plan followed the same pattern. This was the period of the great depression all over the non-Soviet world; the great desire was for stability, not for growth. The idea prevailed that the industrialized nations had reached a state of maturity in which further increases in the capacity to produce would only add to the glutting of the markets. The Soviet Union was envied and sometimes admired not so much because it had accelerated its economic development as because the nation had managed to employ all or most of its citizens in useful work while in the rest of the world the governments struggled, often in vain, to reduce involuntary idleness.

On the other hand, the Soviet leaders themselves saw the merits of their plan decidedly in the acceleration of economic development. Since the Second World War, the original Soviet motive has become the dominant motive of planning in the West as well as in the East. In France, in Holland, in India and in many other countries planning is now used or contemplated primarily as a means of promoting economic growth, whereas the concern over unemployment has receded in many parts of the world as the labor market has shown a shortage of supply rather than a deficiency of demand; even in the United States, where unemployment has tended to increase and has been of serious concern for the government, it has appeared as a mass phenomenon only in some sectors of the labor market and is not characteristic of the situation as a whole, as it was in the 1930's. To be sure, the two points of view, desire for growth and desire for full employment, cannot be completely separated: Advanced countries do not seem to be able to sustain full employment over long periods by consumer demand alone, but also need for this purpose a continuous increase in the demand for capital goods, which is possible only if the economy is growing. On the other hand, wherever unemployment exists, the most satisfactory way of

[12] On Groman's role, see Naum Jasny, *Soviet Industrialization,* pp. 435 ff. Groman's great work is *Balance of National Economy of the USSR of 1923-24,* Moscow 1926. This study endeavors to find, through retrospective analysis, suitable forms of expressing the interdependence of industries; these forms could then serve the prospective analysis which is the essence of planning. There is an obvious relationship to input-output analysis.

achieving economic growth is by re-integration of the unemployed into the production process. But the two purposes do not coincide entirely, because at least in the short run full employment can be reached by stimulating consumer demand, and economic growth can be achieved by increase in productivity as well as by increase in employment. It is therefore worth noticing that a circle has been completed in the motivation for planning: Introduced as an instrument of growth, then widely regarded as an instrument to assure full employment, it is now looked upon again as an accelerating device for economic development.

Chaos in Pricing

Although the highly dynamic character of the Soviet economy during the First Five Year Plan made it impossible to rely on the price mechanism for planning, the planning effort and the operation of the economy would have greatly benefited from an early attempt to approach as closely as possible the prices equilibrating supply and demand for all commodities. The importance of the task, however, was not recognized by the Soviet authorities. The pricing system in this period was chaotic. For most consumer goods, both of agricultural and industrial origin, a complicated system of differentiated prices was in force: A basic ration was supplied at a low price and could be supplemented by purchases at higher prices from special state stores or from distributing agencies for the exclusive use of workers in some enterprises. At times, five different price levels existed for the same kind of foodstuff.[13]

The pricing of producer goods was simpler: The basis consisted of labor costs, including both wages in the particular branch of production and the labor value of necessary raw materials and semifinished products; no charge for the consumption of scarce natural resources, beyond the labor costs needed for their production, and no charge for the use of capital, beyond the amortization of equipment valued at labor cost, was permitted. Added to the cost basis, for both producer and consumer goods, was a certain percentage called "planned profit" and a turnover tax which resembled a sales tax and differed greatly for different products;[14] apparently, it was often higher for products of primary necessity than for goods less urgently

[13] See Baykov, Alexander, *The Development of the Soviet Economic System,* New York: Macmillan, 1947, p. 243.

[14] The technical differences between a sales tax and a turnover tax are irrelevant here. The turnover tax is by no means peculiar to communist countries, although nowhere in the West are the rates as high as in the Soviet Union, and in contradistinction to the Russian system there is usually a flat rate for all or most products. The turnover tax has for instance been part of the German fiscal system, both under the Weimar Republic and under the present Federal Republic.

wanted, since with demand generally exceeding supply, it seemed important to restrict the former where the pressure was greatest, and "the ordinary Soviet worker would doubtless be ready to pay much more for a pair of boots than for, say, a dinner service, although the cost price of the two things might be approximately the same." [15] Practically all the prices were fixed by state authorities, except that from 1932 on, the agricultural collectives and their members, after fulfilling their delivery obligations to the state at fixed prices, were permitted to sell produce at the so-called "kolkhoz market" for any price they could get. Thus the managers of industry were not only deprived of the freedom to adjust their output to the demands of the market, since it was prescribed to them by the plan; they could also not vary prices, and in theory at least,[16] their functions were essentially technological: eliminating waste and improving efficiency by good organizational and engineering techniques. Equally important, the maze of differentiated prices made it impossible for the planners to use prices as a measure of the social importance of goods in their own calculations, even when the first great upheaval of price determinants was over and a consistent move toward rational price planning might otherwise have been feasible.

Some attempt at creating the conditions for such a move was actually made in 1935 while the Second Five Year Plan was in operation: In this year food rationing was abolished, and many differentiated prices replaced by unitary ones. However, the differentiation of the turnover tax remained, and therefore there was no question of determining the planned output of each commodity by the equilibrium between marginal utility and marginal or average cost.

The price anarchy under the First Five Year Plan and the inadequacy of the subsequent remedial efforts were in part due to the Marxian theory of value to which the Soviets felt committed. This theory considers the labor spent upon the production of a commodity the sole determinant of its "value." Although Marxists recognize that in a capitalist economy this "value" is not identical with the price—yet supposed to govern it through a complicated mechanism—they insist that in a socialist economy, as long as any price calculation is needed, no other costs but labor costs can form a basis of pricing. Obviously, however, the use of labor for the production of a par-

[15] Hubbard, Leonard, *Soviet Money and Finance*, London: Macmillan, 1936, p. 165. Although the statement refers to the period of the Second Five Year Plan, it certainly applies also to earlier years.

[16] In practice, another function proved to be equally important: To procure, often by illegal means, the materials necessary for the fulfillment of the plan, in supplementation of the usually inadequate official allocations.

ticular commodity does not exhaust the social cost of that production; the consumption of scarce natural resources and the use of capital equipment which is too scarce to permit all technologically possible investment are also sacrifices which society makes to obtain the commodity. If the price is set as low as to cover labor cost alone, demand will exceed supply of most commodities, because the scarcity of non-labor factors limits production.

The differentiated turnover tax was in part an attempt to compensate for the defects of cost calculation. The tax was an instrument by which demand could be more restricted than it would have been through the labor cost price alone; if the instrument had been used exclusively for this purpose, a more rational pricing system might have resulted. It seems, however, that in the determination of the tax scale just as in other forms of price differentiation for consumer goods, ideas about promoting the consumption of some goods rather than others for reasons not connected with price equilibrium played a role. The differentiated prices for basic rations of necessary commodities and for supplementary purchases was fundamentally justified by considerations of social justice, but not the extremely complicated system which was bound to prevent any use of prices as orientation points for planners. De-rationing, however, with the amount of simplification of prices which it did bring, might have started a development toward rational pricing if the new war emergency had not come too early and created conditions under which no orderly pricing was possible.

The Soviet authorities apparently did not expect the great deterioration in the standard of living which occurred during the period of the First Five Year Plan. They may not have really believed that the output of industrial consumer goods would be more than doubled between 1927 and 1928, as the plan provided;[17] they must have had an idea that the concentration of resources in the capital goods industries would put very strict limits to the expansion of consumer goods production. But they probably expected that costs would be far more drastically reduced by the newly applied technology; the fruits of technological progress ripened more slowly than anticipated because too many inexperienced workers were drawn into the production process, and the terroristic measures applied against managers

[17] Baykov, *op. cit.*, p. 154; plan fulfillment in the consumer goods field was 84.9 per cent according to official figures, as compared with 103 per cent for producer goods. (*loc. cit.* pp. 165, 168). Actually, the difference was much greater, because the figures give only the output of large-scale industry. In 1928, when the First Five Year Plan was started, large quantities of consumer goods were still produced in small shops, which during the plan period were closed, to be replaced by factory production (for examples, see *loc. cit.* p. 166). Small shops had played a much less important role—probably a negligible one—in producer goods output, and therefore the 103 per cent represents more nearly net gain.

suspected of incompetence or disloyalty proved a poor substitute for incentive.[18] What the Soviet leaders certainly did not expect, and what would hardly have come about without serious mistakes of policy, was the decline in deliveries and even agricultural production. There seemed to be all the less reason for anticipating such a decline since agriculture was to receive much capital for investment, especially mechanization.[19]

The reasons for the catastrophe in Soviet agriculture will be discussed below. The results consisted not only of extreme deprivations for the population in city and village and of an aggravation in the harshness of the political climate, but also in inflation. The industrial workers did not find enough food to buy with their wages. Since they also did not find enough industrial consumer goods, a great disparity between the amount of money and the amount of goods was the result. Official price ceilings, never completely effective, could do no more than to substitute to some extent suppressed inflation—an excess of money not usable because of lack of merchandise—for open inflation, a situation in which increase in money is used to buy merchandise, thus bidding up the prices of the latter. Inflation would probably have made meaningful price calculation impossible even if arbitrariness in pricing had not created insurmountable obstacles.

Investment Decisions Without a General Rule

Particularly difficult and at the same time particularly important for the Soviet economy was the problem of regulating investment. In a capitalist market economy, the decision of how to select the most worthwhile projects of industrial expansion and improvement among the many which are technologically possible is solved with the help of the market rate of interest: Only those investment projects can be carried out which yield a return exceeding the rate of interest at which capital can be borrowed, unless, of course, the investment is subsidized by the government for reasons of public policy. The Soviet authorities did not have to procure capital from a market in which independent investors can decide how high the interest must be to make them part with their funds;[20] although internal loans

[18] See *loc. cit.* p. 162. An aggravating factor was the decline in the quality of products, caused by emphasis on the quantity of output.

[19] *Loc. cit.*, p. 156.

[20] It is very difficult so to express the differences between capitalist and Soviet methods of making investment decisions without getting involved in the controversies about the nature of interest in a capitalist society. Lord Keynes has taught that in many instances in a capitalistic economy the credit institutions and monetary authorities of a country, between them, can manipulate the rate of interest much as they please. If a Keynesian, therefore, objects to the wording in the text with the argument that the freedom of the Soviet government in setting the interest on its loans makes little or no difference, he should remember that Keynesian economics presupposes that a slack in resources actually

played some part in the financing of planned development, the Soviet government was practically free in setting the rate.[21] But the function which the rate of interest fulfills in a capitalist society as an instrument of selection in investment exists in Soviet society too. Soviet planners have always faced technological opportunities of investment far in excess of what their readily usable resources permitted them to undertake without making the shortages of consumer goods intolerable. If the Soviet government had adopted a policy of steering the economy through the market mechanism, the appropriate solution would have been to charge every enterprise with interest at a sufficiently high rate to discourage investment projects in excess of available resources; but the Soviet government made the opposite decision, to rely primarily on direct controls. The industrial managers were not free to determine the volume of investment, on which the planning authorities had the final word; consequently, they were not free to bid or not to bid for resources, and the rate of interest, whether low or high, could only have caused them to propose more ambitious or less ambitious projects to the planners.

Even without a "live" market for capital, however, a rate of interest would have been important as a calculating device for use by the planners. In each case, they had to make up their minds whether an investment was sufficiently important to justify the capital outlay. Whatever their yardstick

---

exists or is at least a potentiality influencing existing conditions. Under these circumstances, and given other conditions assumed by Keynes, the monetary authorities can satisfy the liquidity preference of the cash holders so as to determine the rate of interest on which they will insist, without causing a general rise in prices and thereby of investment costs. A slack in resources, however, emphatically did not exist in the USSR during the First Five Year Plan or later; if the same conditions are assumed for a capitalistic economy, the possibility of manipulating the rate of interest will be found very limited or nonexistent.

[21] Actually, the formal rates were at times quite high; around 1930, they amounted generally to 8 per cent. (See L. E. Hubbard, *Soviet Money and Finance,* London: Macmillan, 1936, p. 181). However, it must be taken into account that this was a period of inflation, and that even so high a rate was probably inadequate to compensate the bond holder for the loss of purchasing power of his money. It is, therefore, no wonder that Hubbard had to state: "Voluntary saving is so rare that it may be said to be nonexistent" (*Ibid.*). People were induced by all sorts of pressures to buy state loans, and their compulsory or semi-compulsory character was another reason why the government did not have to set the rate so as to equilibrate supply and demand for capital.

In 1936, the interest rate was reduced to 4 per cent; see Arthur Z. Arnold, *Banks, Credit and Money in Soviet Russia,* New York: Columbia University Press, 1937, p. 504.

Aside from interest payments to bond holders and to depositors at savings banks, interest is being paid in the Soviet Union by industrial and agricultural enterprises for short-term loans to the state credit institutions; housing loans also require interest payments. See Arnold, *op. cit.*, p. 385 f.; W. W. Ikonnikow, *Geld und Kreditwesen in der USSR,* Berlin: Verlag Die Wirtschaft, 1954, p. 485. After repeated reductions, the rates are now so low as hardly to cover the cost of administration.

of importance, it was necessary to apply it, as far as possible, equally to all investment decisions. In other words, economic rationality would have required the establishment of a general rate of time preference, to be applied in the screening of investment opportunities.

To be sure, such a general rate of time preference, synonymous with a calculating rate of interest, could not have been applied mechanically, ruling out all investment projects with a lower rate of yield. It is not so applied to government decisions in capitalist countries, first, because it is not always possible to calculate the social benefits ensuing from an investment with enough precision to make them a determinant of a rate of yield, and yet even the most conservative estimate of their magnitude may be important enough to tip the scales in the decision whether or not to undertake that particular project; and second, even a very low time preference—one too low for decisions within the normal range of time—would not sufficiently express the advantage, from the point of view of the community, that a particular investment may yield its benefits for, say, 300 years, whereas competing investments yield a return only for thirty or forty years. These reasons for exception had special weight in a communist economy. But however justifiable the exceptions, to have a standard rate from which the planners would deviate only for special reasons would have been a very great advantage.

To explain why such a rate was not established, requires again an understanding of both objective difficulties and of ideological biases. Very early in the planning period, the difficulties were probably prohibitive. Even in the best organized capital market of a capitalist economy, a rate of interest which truly reflects the relation between the supply of capital and the available investment opportunities and therefore provides a correct yardstick for investment decisions will evolve only if sufficient time is allowed for the market operations to eliminate mistaken or accidental decisions and effect the transfer of capital from those branches of production which are at first oversupplied to those that are undersupplied. Therefore, if a capitalist economy had ever grown as fast as the Soviet economy grew during the First Five Year Plan, such an economy would also not have possessed an equalized rate of interest with any claim to correctness. To be sure, the Soviet planners, unlike capitalist entrepreneurs, did not have to transfer capital from one enterprise to another to balance investment opportunities against capital supply; their trial-and-error process, as a paper process, could have been carried out faster. If a perfect planning mechanism had existed from the outset, a standard rate of time preference could have been developed even during the First Five Year Plan, but such a machinery did not exist. The Soviet ship was sailing uncharted routes; the job of planning had largely to be learned by doing.

Another difficulty lay in the absence of a rational price system. A rate of time preference presupposes that the value of products, which present investment will yield in the future, be related to the value of the capital goods which are now to be invested. Soviet prices were arbitrary during the First Five Year Plan (and later). To go behind the prices and find the real importance of the goods representing the investment and of those representing the yield, would have been most difficult in any event; it was impossible for the Soviet planners, because economic importance of commodities could only be utility, and the acceptance of this concept would have led them straight to a utility concept of value, whereas they were committed to the Marxian idea that value is determined by labor time necessary for production. Without value figures expressing the true importance of commodities, a unified time preference rate would have contributed little, if anything, to rationality.

In other respects also ideological bias stood in the way of the elaboration of a unitary time preference rate. If the institution of a market for goods appeared to Soviet planners as a capitalist heritage which they had to repudiate, this was even more true of a market for capital. Since Marxism had ignored the social sacrifice involved in devoting scarce capital goods to a particular production for a given period of time, a charge for the use of such capital goods seemed without justification, except as a matter of historical inevitability while mankind was going through the capitalist phase. To a Marxist, interest is a share in the gain which the capitalist class secures through the exploitation of workers, a share which the owners of money capital, on the basis of their power position, can force industrial entrepreneurs to pay without receiving anything of substance in return, just as the entrepreneur's gain is won on the basis of a position of power over the worker, only masked by forms of exchange. The distinction between interest as a source of personal income and interest as a calculating device was unacceptable to the Communists because that distinction involves a host of considerations based on marginal utility and therefore a rank heresy from the Marxist point of view.

Still another obstacle to the establishment of a unitary rate of interest as a calculation device was the inclination of the Soviet planners toward the "leading sector" idea. They assumed that within the area of capital goods production, there are some sub-areas which should be particularly emphasized because development in these sub-areas would create an especially effective momentum for the rest of the economy.[22] Originally, electrification had been regarded as the outstanding case of such a leading sector; later, some other industries were included. A unitary rate of interest tends so to spread available capital over all industries as to equalize marginal productivity; the leading sector idea requires that, on the contrary, investment in the "leading" industries be expanded to a point of relatively low marginal productivity.

There would be nothing irrational in this leading sector idea if it were understood as a modifier rather than as a substitute for the marginal productivity rule. Western economists have generally recognized that the expansion of a particular kind of economic activity often has beneficial indirect effects far in excess of those which can be expected of the expansion of another kind of economic activity, and frequently more important than the direct effects. Kenneth Boulding and Pritam Singh, for instance, point out that increase in paper production helps to spread literacy and that bicycle production increases the mobility between urban and rural areas where other forms of transportation are not yet highly developed.[23] Similarly, Harvey Leibenstein stresses that the marginal productivity rule, as usually conceived, "does not allow for. . . . 1) the indirect effect of the investment allocation on the expansion. . . . of entrepreneurship, on the increase of the quality of the labor force, and on the expansion of skills; 2) the effect of the investment allocation on future savings habits and therefore on the future rate of investment. . . ."[24] It is economically legitimate to invest more, at any given time, in industries with such beneficial secondary and tertiary effects, than would be compatible with the equalization of marginal productivities,[25] or, to look at the problem from another angle, with the rule

[22] See John P. Hardt, "Industrial Investment in the USSR," in *Comparisons of United States and Soviet Economies,* pp. 125 ff.

[23] Kenneth Boulding and Pritam Singh, "The Role of the Price Structure in Economic Development," *Papers and Proceedings* of the 74th Annual Meeting of the Am. Econ. Assoc. in New York, 1961. *American Economic Review,* May 1962, p. 35. The argument is used by the authors in a discussion not of investment criteria but of price subsidization, but its bearing on investment policy is obvious.

[24] Harvey Leibenstein, *Economic Backwardness and Economic Growth,* New York: John Wiley & Sons, 1957, pp. 258 f. He enumerates other limitations of the marginal productivity rule, but the quoted examples suffice for an illustration.

See also Alec Nove, *The Soviet Economy,* New York: Frederick A. Praeger, 1961, p. 291 f., and the literature mentioned there. To the present writer, however, it seems that Nove does not fully recognize the difference between the Soviet leading sector idea and the "unbalanced growth" concept in Western literature.

[25] It is possible, of course, to take cognizance of indirect effects in calculating marginal productivity. The term "social marginal productivity," often used in economic discussion, indicates that some of the effects of a production process or of a production increase which do not appear in the bookkeeping system of the entrepreneur or of the

that the return from any investment must cover the unitary rate of interest. As has been mentioned before, deviations from that rule occur in any kind of economic system.

But the Soviet government has so far, and with particular emphasis in the Stalinist period, refused not only to apply that rule rigidly, but to recognize it at all—to have any unitary rate of time preference. The selection among investment opportunities has been made, and is still being made, on the basis of preconceived ideas about which sectors deserve preference, and these sectors have usually been granted all the capital that could be spared from other uses without running into trouble so serious as to be politically unsupportable. This crude method has deprived the Soviet economy of the great advantage of having an adequate prima facie test for the selection of investment opportunities. Not only will the marginal productivity rule lead to conclusive results in a number of instances, but where the results are inconclusive because deviations from the rule seem justified, the compulsion to spell out the specific reasons for the deviation is a most valuable guarantee of rational procedure. There is little doubt that the waste of resources which resulted from the absence of a unitary rate of interest in the Soviet Union has been very great. It may not have been so great in the beginning, because the leading sector originally selected by Lenin, electrification, may in the early phase of economic reconstruction have had such important indirect effects of a beneficial character as to justify all the investment devoted to it, but the preferred list, as it was compiled later, has produced a bad distortion of the investment pattern.[26]

---

investing agency are taken into account. This is of particular importance in the case of investment in the infrastructure of the economy: To measure the productivity of investment in education by the tuition, if any, which students will pay, or the productivity of investment in highways by the toll revenue, if any, or even by the expected increase in tax receipts would mean to underrate that productivity to the point of being unreasonable. On the other hand, if all the indirect effects of investment were included in the concept of marginal productivity, the marginal productivity rule could be pronounced as an unconditional postulate of rational action; but such a broad concept would be inapplicable, because many of these indirect effects cannot be expressed in quantitative terms; yet if we want to compare marginal productivity with a unitary rate of interest, there must be numerical ratios on both sides. It is, therefore, expedient to include in the concept of marginal productivity, even of social marginal productivity, only those effects of investment which can be expressed, at least with some approximation, in figures, and to accept the fact that deviations from that rule will often be necessary "for cause."

26 Not only did projects of direct importance for citizens' welfare suffer, but also a number of possibilities to improve the productive apparatus were neglected. "Structural changes common to other industrializations not stressed in the Soviet approach during the Stalinist period included the shift from solid to liquid fuel; the shift from using ferrous to non-ferrous metals for a number of purposes, especially for construction; and the rise of service industries. This conscious emphasis on structural changes related to electrification and de-emphasis of structural changes common to other industrializations is a cardinal feature of the leading sector approach." (John P. Hardt, *op. cit.*, p. 126).

There is even some reason to believe that the leading sector idea, as practiced in the Soviet Union, has done the Soviet economy more harm than a similar procedure would do in a developing country in commercial intercourse with the Western world. If Ghana or even India, for instance, expands its production unequally, it can still, within fairly wide limits, import those goods of which the production has remained underdeveloped. This possibility is far more limited for the Soviet Union, first, because surpluses may not be available in other countries in sufficient quantity to fill the needs of the Soviet Union with its great economic volume, and second, because for political reasons the exchange of commodities between the Soviet Union and other industrially advanced countries has most of the time been kept to a minimum. Should Ghana need more aluminum, it has a fair chance to buy it in Western Europe or the United States; if the Soviet Union has failed to expand its aluminum industry proportionately to other industries, it will just have to forego a number of technological improvements.

The "Recouping Period"

The advantages of a unitary rate of time preference have not entirely escaped the Soviet policy makers; they developed an instrument which was intended to have the same function, but was supposed to fit better into the framework of Marxist economics. The elaboration of this instrument began with adopting the criterion of "minimization of capital outlays"[27] for investments: Of projects otherwise equally advantageous, the one requiring the least capital expenditure per unit of other factors—mainly labor—should be chosen. Gradually, through the refinement of this rule, the concept of the "recouping period developed;" although its emergence belongs to the post-Stalin phase of Soviet history, it seems expedient to discuss it in this context.

In choosing among investment opportunities, the Soviet planners treated it as a reason for preference if a particular project promised to refund the capital outlay earlier than others. If a standard recouping period had been established within a system knowing rational prices, such a concept would have been synonymous with a standard rate of interest. Obviously, it comes down to the same thing to say that the rate of interest is 10 per cent or that the original outlay will be refunded in ten years (or 7.27 years with compound interest.) In the Soviet Union, however, no single

---

Aside from electrification, the machine-building industries and the chemical industry have been on the preferred list.

[27] See Hardt, *op. cit.*, p. 126.

length of the recouping period is applied; rather, the period is of different length for the different industries, with the preferred branches granted much more time for the refunding of invested capital than the rest. Under these circumstances, the recouping period hardly weakens the leading sector idea, but merely serves as a yardstick to select those technological methods for the achievement of a given investment purpose which will require less capital for a defined period, or a defined amount of capital for a shorter period; the differentiated rates will not affect the place of the investment purpose on the priority list. The concept of the recouping period, as now used in Soviet practice, may for instance lead to the choice of production of electricity more by thermal energy rather than by water power if the former represents a more economical use of capital, or in an analogous case to the choice of one way of producing a certain chemical rather than another way; the preference given to investment in electrification or in the production of the particular chemical will remain unchanged. Even so, the use of the recouping period in investment planning must have led to some improvement.

A development in Soviet economic thought indicates the possibility and perhaps the likelihood of much greater improvement. A general rate of the recouping period is now actually being calculated, although it apparently leads a purely academic existence.[28] If this general rate were applied, as a prima facie test, to the distribution of capital among the sectors, a major step toward economic rationality would be achieved.

But before the general recouping rate can play the role which the rate of interest fills in a capitalistic economy, a reform of the pricing system will be necessary. Calculation of a yield-capital ratio can be rational only to the extent that prices are rational; this statement is not invalidated when the ratio is clothed in the terminology of the recouping period. When arbitrary values are assigned to capital goods or to yield goods or to both, nothing of importance is said by stating that the value of the product will be refunded within ten years or twenty years.[29] Only to the extent that the arbitrary element in Soviet pricing recedes can even a generalized time preference rate operate as a rationalizing element in the Soviet economy.

An attempt has been made by Soviet economists to calculate the yield-capital ratio independently of the rationality of prices, by using cost saving rather than product value in defining the recouping period. In a majority of cases, a particular commodity can be produced either with minimum in-

[28] See Nove, *op. cit.*, p. 212.

[29] The connection between price policy and a yardstick for investment decisions has been pointed out by Maurice Dobb, "Note on Recent Economic Discussion," *Soviet Studies*, April 1961, pp. 343 ff.

vestment of capital and high operating costs, or with maximum investment of capital and low operating costs; usually there also exists a series of intermediate possibilities. It is therefore often correct to say that the purpose of investment is to save operating costs and also that the efficiency of investment of a given magnitude can be measured by the amount of operating costs saved. When all sorts of operating costs are taken into account, as rationality requires, this method is not different in nature from the measurement of efficiency by yield: For instance, electric power can be produced in a hydroelectric or a steampower installation, of which the former usually requires greater capital investment and the latter greater operating costs; to say that every million dollars invested in a hydroelectric plant in excess of the investment necessary for a steam plant, will save *n* thousand dollars annually in fuel, labor, lubricants, etc., which a steam plant would consume in excess of the operating requirements of a hydroelectric plant, is obviously tantamount to saying that the dollar yield of the capital invested in the hydroelectric installation will be $\frac{n \text{ thousand}}{1 \text{ million}}$. But the dependence on meaningful prices also exists for any complete calculation of operating costs: The common denominator, for instance, for aggregating the savings in fuel, labor and lubricants can only be their prices, and if the latter are arbitrarily set, the calculation becomes meaningless.

There are cases, however, in which it seems possible to concentrate exclusively on one kind of cost saved, which is labor, without committing too great an error. If so, the question of pricing becomes less important. It still plays a role, even in evalulating the saving of labor, because labor is not a homogeneous commodity: An ordinary laborer's working hour cannot be treated as equal in importance with that of an engineer and the need for a common denominator is therefore not removed. But if there is a rule of thumb providing coefficients by which different kinds of labor can be expressed in terms of common labor, then it becomes possible to compare the labor-saving effects of different investment by using labor hours rather than price units. This method has been all the more acceptable to the Soviet economists because it seems to fit into the scheme of the Marxian labor value theory. Although a mere comparison of the labor-saving effect gives some indication of the relative efficiency of investments when a more capital-intensive process is to be compared with a more labor-intensive process, yet even there the question arises of how the amount to be invested can be determined. This amount depends on the price of the capital goods, and in the Soviet economy this price has been determined with a great deal of arbitrariness.

For this reason alone the calculation of capital efficiency by labor saving instead of by the use of prices of yield goods did not add very much to the rationality of investment decisions in the Soviet pricing system. But the possible contribution appears even smaller when it is considered that all capital efficiency calculations have the purpose of comparing the worthwhileness of different investment opportunities. Even assuming that capital efficiency were correctly calculated in one instance, the purpose might be missed if the efficiency of investment opportunities which represented the nearest rivals to that project were calculated by false methods. Since efficiency in labor saving at best supplies a yardstick only in projects in which expense for labor is the only important operating cost (or in which other operating costs were equal), the basis of the comparison is so narrow as to make the result not very meaningful except when by accident all competing investment projects are of that type.

"Material Balances"

Even if an economic development plan is not based on an optimal choice of investment opportunities, it must at least be consistent in its physical provisions: The right amount of steel must be provided for the machines which are to be constructed, and the right amount of coke to produce that steel; there must be an increase in transportation facilities sufficient to carry the required materials to the factories and the planned output to the places of consumption; the examples can be easily multiplied. Therefore the Soviet planners drew up schemes showing how different branches of production were to supply each other's needs, and there was a continuous checking of the schemes for consistency. The schemes were called "material balances;" if they all had been fitted together into a general scheme, some matrix essentially identical with Leontieff's input-output scheme would have resulted. But in the period of the First Five Year Plan and later, the planners were content to express only the more obvious interdependencies of different branches of production in schemes drawn up for the purpose and to make those adjustments in the plan which these schemes had shown to be necessary. The neglect of less obvious relations of interdependence was a weakness, but it was of somewhat less practical importance than it would have been in a society based on consumers' sovereignty: Whereas the technological interdependence of industries is of course the same in all economies using the same technology, and some changes in consumption also will ensue from given changes in production whatever the economic system, this is not true of all influences upon consumption patterns following from shifts in production. In a capitalistic economy, for instance, alterations in the structure of production which would require an increase in urbanization would be accompanied by increased demand for some type of recreational facilities—for instance movie theaters—which are less in demand in rural societies; but in a Soviet-type economy, the government may simply refuse to build movie theaters, and then the demand has to turn toward other objects. Whereas a Leontieff matrix, drawn up for the West German[30] economy, would be defective if it did not show an increase in the construction of movie theaters as a consequence of changes in industry which shift people from country to the city, in the Soviet Union the lack of a material balance showing a corresponding relationship will merely be another indication that consumers will often not get what they like best to have.

Western economists have sometimes wondered why the Soviet planners have not developed their material balances into complete input-output matrices.[31] In the beginning, the main reason seems to have been the ideological inhibitions and the reluctance to adopt a method which had its origin in the West. The potential usefulness of the device, however, would probably soon have overcome these hesitations if it had not been for a serious obstacle: the arbitrary elements in the Soviet price system. Although an input-output matrix, like a material balance, is intended to express physical dependencies, it is drawn up in terms of money figures, which serve as indices of physical quantities of commodities.[32] This is necessary because tons of various materials, kilowatt hours of electric energy, hours of labor, units of transportation facilities and so on cannot be compared with each other without a common denominator. In this index function, however, prices are useful only to the extent that they reflect the true supply-demand relationships, and since Soviet prices fulfill this task very inadequately, an effort to expand the system of material balances into complete matrices would hardly have produced satisfactory results. A material bal-

[30] The same could, of course, be said of the economy of the United States, but Germany is probably a better example, because in the United States the living habits of many rural areas have been assimilated to city life.

[31] About more recent tendencies in this direction, see below p. 374.

[32] For reasons which are presumably obvious, "constant" monetary units have to be used if the matrix covers a period in which substantial changes in the purchasing power of money may occur. A matrix, for instance, that would retrospectively describe input and output in the American economy in 1945-50, would best be drawn up in prices of 1949 or 1950. If a matrix is drawn up for planning purposes, that is to picture a prospective rather than a past development, it is generally best to use prices for the most recent year in which the price structure shows relatively few anomalies; since the 1945 American price pattern showed many anomalies due to rationing and ceilings, it would have been difficult to draw up a realistic input-output matrix for 1945-50 at the end of the war. The reason is clearly analogous to the obstacle which the Leontieff method meets in the Soviet Union.

ance, because it is a much narrower concept, can dispense with price figures: One does not need to use values to relate an increase in truck output to the need for more steel or more energy. The hesitations of the Soviet economists to move toward a full utilization of the Leontieff idea is probably one sign among many that the importance of realistic prices is increasingly realized,[33] and this growing insight may well bring about a fundamental price reform in the foreseeable future.

Although the preponderance of physical considerations over the influence of prices in the Soviet economy is one of the profound differences distinguishing contemporary communism from capitalism or from socialism as understood by the socialists of today, it would be an overstatement to say that prices in the Soviet Union have no regulating function. The idea is no less of an exaggeration because it has received some support by slogans which communist authors like to use.[34] Prices exert an influence on production through two interconnected channels: the efforts of the Soviet government to avoid or reduce inflation, and its efforts to increase its profits from industry.

The First Five Year Plan and all subsequent Soviet plans have been drawn up in terms of money as well as in terms of physical quantities; the amounts to be invested in each industry have always been a key element of the plan. Although the Soviet planners disregarded or repudiated important other verities of economic theory, they accepted the proposition that the amount of money in circulation cannot be increased beyond the increase in the quantity of marketable commodities—except in the event of a slowdown in the velocity of circulation—without producing price inflation, which they regarded as an evil. Consequently, the Soviet planners tried to organize production and so set the prices as to recover from the consumers the funds to be invested in expansion, and resorted to money creation only when such recovering seemed to be impossible within the adopted framework of policy.[35] This meant that consumer preferences and demand elasticities had to be taken into account in planning, and this is only another way of saying that the prices were not set in complete disre-

33 This also seems to be Nove's opinion, see *op. cit.* pp. 208 f.

34 "The law of value operates but does not regulate" Quoted by Gregory Grossman, *Value and Plan* (Gregory Grossman, ed. Berkeley and Los Angeles: University of California Press, 1960) p. 9.

35 In addition to the amounts which the Soviet government receives from the consumers by keeping the prices paid above production costs, there is also revenue from direct taxation, but as in other countries with a relatively low living standard, this source yields only a small fraction of the government's needs. See the table in Hubbard, *op. cit.*, p. 113; Dobb, *Soviet Economic Development*, pp. 364, 383 ff.

gard of what the consumers were willing to pay; the revenue which was obtainable through the prices as set was taken into account in determining how much of each commodity was to be produced, although these considerations were often overruled when they came into conflict with the desire to achieve stipulated physical increases of production or other purposes of Soviet policy.

The fiscal interest of the Soviet government has always required that profits be maximized. In the earlier, terroristic phases of Soviet planning, however, the managers of enterprises ran less risk of reprisals if they failed to cover their costs by receipts than if they failed to reach the planned targets of production, defined in terms of physical quantities. Consequently the general tendency was to maximize output rather than profits, and production was expanded even by means which meant uneconomically high costs. The interest in maximization of output, as expressed in tons or units, was also often permitted to overrule the regard for product quality, although the shoddy character naturally made the products less acceptable to the consumers, and "buyers' strikes" might have resulted if inflation had not kept the consumers eager to purchase whatever was on the market.

The difficulties caused by these tendencies were not overlooked by the Soviet leaders, although to this day no more than partially effective remedies have been applied. From the later years of the First Five Year Plan on, the official statements show an increasing emphasis on *khozraschet,* a term indicating responsible management on the basis of correct accounting and efforts to avoid deficits in individual industries. Although the main emphasis remained on the responsibility for reaching physical targets, responsibility for having earnings exceed cost was no longer so completely overshadowed. This modification in the rules of conduct for industrial managers was accompanied by a demand for "synthetic" balances to supplement the material balances in national planning. The term synthetic meant the use of a common denominator for different materials and types of product, in order that all sorts of cost goods and yield goods could be aggregated and thereby an overall balance struck for the individual enterprise and for the whole economy. The only common denominator that could be consistently applied was the monetary unit, although some attempts were made to base synthetic planning on a calculation in labor time units. The Financial Plan, which is intended to show how the money for investments and for other treasury expenditures is to be procured and distributed is the most highly developed form of synthetic planning in the Soviet Union. Synthetic planning thus originated mainly in the macro-economic sphere, that is in the analysis of aggregate magnitudes applying to the whole economy.[36] Obviously, however, neither can the total revenue of the Soviet government be calculated without knowledge of the profits which enterprises will yield, nor the total expenditures without knowledge of the deficits which will have to be covered; moreover, the financial plan, revealing through monetary calculation the difficulty of providing resources for investment, creates a powerful impulse to develop a yardstick of selection among investment project by comparing their prospective monetary yield.[37] In this way, *khozraschet* on the one hand, the evolution of substitutes for a standard rate of interest on the other are extensions of the financial plan, and it was no accident that approximately from the end of the First Five Year Plan on, the emphasis on all these aspects of the planning efforts increased simultaneously. This development meant a gradual evolution of value planning as a complement to physical planning—a recognition, though still a half-hearted one, of the desirability of producing the goods that would yield the greatest surplus of price over cost.

By that time, however, value planning was becoming part of the creed of liberal socialists. Therefore, by the growing emphasis on value planning in the Soviet Union, the distance between the *economic* programs of liberal socialism and Soviet communism was reduced. But this was no period of political liberalization in the Soviet Union: The most outrageous purge trials took place precisely in the second half of the 1930's. There is little point in speculating whether economic liberalization would eventually have gone far enough to modify political terrorism, or whether the despotic forms of government would have strangled the still faint tendencies toward restoring the base for economic rationality and accountability. The threat of war—this time a real and not an illusory threat—and the necessity of

[36] As a consequence of the Keynesian approach and the theories of monopolistic and imperfect competition as developed by E. H. Chamberlin and Joan Robinson, economists are now distinguishing between macro-economics and micro-economics, the latter term signifying the analysis of the decision of the individual enterprise. Everywhere, not only in the Soviet Union, is it a purpose of macro-economic analysis to provide the government with information which will be used to determine how micro-economic decisions should be influenced—by command, premiums, penalties, etc.

[37] Tables showing government revenue and government expenditures can be found in Nove, *op. cit.*, pp. 98 and 104, respectively. The figures given are for 1940, 1950 and 1958.

In the latter year, 47 per cent of the government revenue came from the turnover tax and 20 per cent from profits of state enterprises. Of the expenditures, 45 per cent consisted of "allocations to the national economy," an item that includes investments and subsidies. Of the latter, a substantial portion might perhaps be saved by a more economical operation of enterprises and by more strictly economic criteria for the selection of investment projects.

economic preparations for war soon reversed whatever tendency toward liberalization existed.

How was it possible for the Soviet Union to achieve its unquestionable successes under Stalin's Five Year Plans without a more rational system of pricing and without a standard rate of interest—instruments which Western economists, socialists as well as others, have declared to be indispensable for an efficiently operating economy? The first part of the answer is that the achievements were extremely costly. Efficiency does not merely mean that great results are obtained; it means that whatever results are obtained, they are achieved without unnecessary sacrifice. In these terms, and however narrowly the term "unnecessary" may be interpreted, the Soviet economy was certainly not efficient in the early phase of planning, and even subsequently has failed to achieve a high degree of efficiency.

But the reader who has surveyed the irrationalities in the Soviet system of pricing and investment decisions may ask himself how anything of importance, at whatever cost, could have been obtained under these conditions. Here, it is necessary to remember that statements valid for a relatively slow development of economies that are already far advanced do not necessarily hold true for a rapidly developing economy starting from a primitive level of industrialization and want satisfaction. On that low level of economic development, the danger of satisfying a less urgent purpose before a more urgent one is not very great, because what needs to be done is more obvious than in more developed economies. In addition to commonsense considerations, the Soviet government could use the pattern which the development of capitalist countries had set and which in its most general characteristics would be obligatory for any country. Also, the more rapid the growth of the economy, the greater the chances that tasks neglected today may be fulfilled tomorrow. These relieving factors, however, were bound to lose their force with the very progress of industrialization: Although the levels of want satisfaction and technological complexity which the Soviet Union had reached by the middle of the 1930's were still modest, they must have provided a further incentive to rationalize the price system in all its aspects. Today, the slowing down of the rate of growth is bound to reinforce this incentive.

The Enterprise and the Planning Agencies

An industrial enterprise in the Soviet Union has less freedom of decision than a nationalized enterprise in one of the Western countries. Like many other peculiarities of the Soviet economic system, the dependence of the industrial managers upon the will of central agencies existed to a particularly high degree during the Stalin era.[38]

The Soviet industrial enterprise is primarily an administrative unit, like a local post office in the United States. In principle, it has no rights of its own. The state, being the proprietor of all instruments of production, can take away any capital good from one enterprise and give it to another; in principle also, the profit of an enterprise belongs to the state. Nor does the enterprise have freedom of contract: As a rule, the kind and quantity of supplies which an enterprise can receive, the supplier firms and the prices of the delivered materials are determined from above; so are the kinds and quantities of products which must be turned out and the prices at which the enterprise can sell. The management of the individual enterprise, however, is permitted to produce more than its instructions provide—to overfulfill the plan—if it finds ways to do so with the supplies that are available; such overfulfillment is even treated as highly commendable. Enterprise managers can also, by their own decisions, close loopholes in the directives which they receive from the central offices. These directives can never specify the kind of supplies and products and the terms of delivery in full detail, and therefore the enterprise has some range of choice. Within the limits set by supply allocation and other decisions by central and regional agencies, the managers can, and are expected to, modify technological processes and thereby achieve economies. Finally, there is some range of decision by the enterprise on the use of profits, since the complicated rules governing this matter put part of the earnings in years of success at the disposal of the manager.

No less important, in all probability, than these opportunities for independent decision is the influence which enterprise managers can exert upon the decisions of national and regional agencies concerning the allocation of supplies and the setting of output targets under the plan. In the Soviet system, the manager is half engineer, in his efforts to reduce costs, and half diplomat, in his attempts to obtain from higher authorities the most favorable terms of operation for his firm. The higher authorities cannot determine the potential of the individual enterprise or its supply needs except on the basis of reports made from observations on the spot. Although there are various agencies of inspection and control, of which the local organizations of the Communist Party are the most important, the data which the management of every firm has to communicate to the planning agencies in regard to past

[38] Even under Stalin, in spite of the high degree of centralization, not all the details of the plans were determined in Moscow, but some range of decision was left to regional offices in the capitals of the member republics and in the districts. The much higher degree of regionalization which was introduced in 1957 will be described below.

performance, changes in capacity and needed supplies are still an indispensable basis for the decisions of these agencies. Each manager tries to have the output targets set low so as to be able to fulfill the plan even in the event of minor breakdowns or supply failures, and perhaps to overfulfill it, and to have ample supplies allocated to his firm so as to minimize the hazard of shortages. But these are only the general outlines of the strategy that conditions impose upon him. He must not strive for arrangements that would result in an overfulfillment of the plan by too wide a margin, because this would expose him to the suspicion of having understated the capacity of his plant, and such a suspicion would result, if not in harsher reprisals, at least in the setting of higher plan targets for the next period. In the frequent instances in which an enterprise turns out various kinds of product, it is important for the manager to have the planned output so distributed among these kinds as to emphasize that area of production in which maximization meets with the least obstacles. The manager must not overstate too much his needs for supplies, because hoarding of labor or materials is regarded as a grave offense. For this complicated diplomatic strategy he will need friends and allies. It will therefore often be the part of wisdom for him to help others—superiors, managers of supplier or of customer firms—to conceal their mistakes or have their requests granted, even if this involves some sacrifice for his own firm. Logrolling is an important art in Soviet Russia, and under Stalin, when it was easy for a manager to be accused of sabotage, and particularly dangerous to be friendless, it was sometimes a condition of physical survival.[39]

Whatever decisions are to be made by the firm, they are the manager's decisions; no elements of co-determination by workers exists in the Soviet Union. There are factory committees and cells of the Communist party in every plant, but only in the early revolutionary period have these organs played an independent role. In the NEP period, they had already been put under strict control by the central organs of the party, and this control was further tightened under Stalin. The same is true of the trade unions. All these organizations are instruments of the party, which is essentially identical with the state, and their primary function is to help in reaching the goals of the government, of which the most important is the fulfillment of the plan. A secondary function of trade unions, factory committees and party cells is the disposition of grievances. This function is important, and

[39] On the other hand, one had to be very careful in the selection of one's friends, because it was fatal to have been associated in any way with "enemies of the people," or even with friends of the friends of these enemies, and it took more than ordinary perspicacity to foresee who would be in the ostracized category next year or the year thereafter.

there is no reason to doubt that the worker often has a real chance to have hardships removed or alleviated through grievance procedures, although in the hectic days of the First Five Year Plan—and even more so during the war—when all energies were concentrated on maximizing production, this opportunity must have been considerably smaller than in more quiet years, for instance around 1936. Moreover, even in instances in which it would be in line with government policy to have complaints settled to the satisfaction of the worker, such a settlement could be obstructed by "family circle" relations among the leading figures of business, party and state bureaucracy.[40]

The good will of the employees, however, is important for the Soviet manager. Aside from the reasons that make smooth industrial relations a significant success factor in any enterprise, it generally pays for the manager to be popular because the government, whose functionary he is, wants to be popular, its ample powers of compulsion notwithstanding. But the manager's interest in his own popularity has to be weighed against other interests. He cannot afford to make himself popular by avoiding measures which the workers may not like, if these measures serve the fulfillment, or perhaps the overfulfillment, of the plan. Besides, being too popular with the workers might in the Stalinist period have exposed the manager to the suspicion that he was trying to build for himself a position of power and

[40] "A typical example of the working of such a 'family circle' might be secrecy concerning the progress of worker housing which the factory is expected to build. Where the plant is short of funds and building materials, the director may delay construction of housing in order to speed the erection of an additional production shop. The new shop may seem to him to be far the more urgent of the two projects under conditions where its completion is a precondition of the fulfillment of the factory's production plan. However, the director needs the assistance of the party secretary if the delay in housing construction is to be kept from the ears of higher authorities. The party secretary, who is also judged by his superiors partly according to the plant's production performance, may well go along. The trade union chairman of the factory local may also stick with the director, if only to hide his own feebleness in protecting locally the interests of the factory workers. If the editor of the town newspapers can be brought into the circle, to assure the suppression of indignant letters from the factory's workers, so much the better. If in addition the director's immediate superior, in the administrative organ above the factory, is himself willing to suppress any rumblings he may hear, then the circle is really a tight one." (David Granick, "Soviet-American Management Comparisons" in Joint Economic Committee, U. S. Congress, *Comparisons of the United States and Soviet Economies*, Washington: U. S. Government Printing Office, 1959, Part I. p. 148.)

In this particular case, there would be a fair chance that the director's preference for the production shop turns out to be in line with official policy, although this would not necessarily preclude a decision of the central agencies—if they learned of the matter—to make a scapegoat of the director. In any event, however, the "family circle" relations here described can obviously be used for the frustration of complaints which would be successful if they reached high quarters, for instance protests against errors of judgment or even dishonesty on the part of the director at the expense of the workers. (In Soviet terminology, "director" means "executive.")

thus gain a modicum of independence from the local functionaries of the Communist Party, and such a thought might have induced the latter to take preventive steps against the suspect.

Although the commercial functions of the "red executive" are very modest by comparison with his capitalist counterpart, he does need a great deal of negotiating ability, along with the capacity to recognize the weak and the strong points of the people with whom he has to deal, and he certainly needs as much ruthlessness in exploiting other people's weaknesses as any capitalist entrepreneur anywhere in the world. Although for obvious reasons it is very difficult to draw a rounded picture of the industrial manager in the Soviet Union, we may surmise that the similarities between the president of a Western business corporation and a Soviet industrial manager are probably more important than the differences.

The output targets for the individual enterprises are not contained in the long-term plans (five years under Stalin, recently seven years), but in the one-year plans by which the former are implemented. This means that the instructions to the individual enterprises are formulated after the outlines of the intended development of the economy, especially the amount and the character of the investments, have been determined. Probably the Gosplan, the central planning commission,[41] upon which devolves the technical job of compiling the long-term plan, and the central agencies of the Communist Party, which go over the draft before it is submitted to the Supreme Soviet, the parliament,[42] informally consult the managers of the major enterprises, who in this way have a chance to influence the long-range plan; the bulk of the enterprises, however, can start their attempts to obtain favorable supply and target provisions only when the annual plan is formulated. Since the central agencies are trying to shape the content of the annual plans so as to assure that the goals of the long-range plan will be reached, the elasticity of the framework into which the targets of the individual firms must fit is not very great, and the efforts of the managers amount, for the most part, to a jockeying for favorable positions. The outcome of this jockeying may, of course, be vitally important for the individual firm, but since it decides mainly whose tasks will be the most onerous, and not the magnitude of the tasks, its significance for the national economy is very limited.

Although the fulfillment of the plan is the most important success indicator by which the individual firm and its manager are judged, there are

[41] For the exact position of Gosplan and the changes it has undergone, see Nove, *op. cit.*, pp. 66 f., 75 f.

[42] Before the war, another central agency, the Economic Council, also had important functions in planning.

other indicators too: increase in labor productivity, reduction of costs and the ensuing profitability of the enterprise. Success as evidenced by all the indicators determines the manager's chance to hold his position or be promoted to a more important one, and also his bonus which is a larger part of his income than of that of a typical American executive.[43]

COLLECTIVIZED AGRICULTURE

Terrorism in the Countryside

When the First Five Year Plan was inaugurated in 1928, Stalin apparently did not intend to make any fundamental change in the system of land management before the success of the industrialization program was assured. It was elementary wisdom not to upset conditions in the countryside while the industrial sector was being revolutionized and rather to seek the necessary improvement of agricultural deliveries within the framework of the existing system of landholding. To this day it seems not fully explicable why the Soviet government burdened itself with the immeasurable difficulties of reorganizing agriculture while it had its hands more than full in building up a new industrial system.[44]

Between 1927 and 1929, the inadequacy of grain deliveries reached a critical stage. Some causes of this crisis are fairly obvious. Natural conditions were largely responsible, and a deficit in harvested grain had a tendency to express itself in a more than proportional deficit in marketed grain, because the peasant household would attempt to maintain its own consumption as far as possible and therefore retain a larger share of the smaller crop.[45] Furthermore, difficulties in offering the peasants industrial commodities for purchase appeared at the most unfortunate moment;[46] otherwise their will to sell grain might have been strengthened. Finally, an effort

[43] See Granick, *op. cit.*, 144/5.

[44] Many speeches and articles by Stalin have been printed in the collection, *Leninism.* (New York: International Publishers.) It is interesting to compare the content of the 1928 edition with that of later editions, e.g. that of 1942. In the older edition, Stalin appears as the holder of an intermediate position between the leftists who want an immediate, all-out attack against the kulaks with collectivization as the goal, and the rightists who refuse to believe in a kulak danger and want to leave the agricultural situation undisturbed; the leftist demands are even more vigorously rejected than the rightist policies. In the later editions, the most important passages criticizing the left wing have been eliminated and the desire to acquiesce in the situation which the NEP had created in the villages is pictured as the mortal sin.

[45] It is therefore not surprising that in 1927-28, as Dobb reports, a harvest deficiency of 7 or 8 per cent led to a marketing deficiency of 14 per cent. (Maurice Dobb, *Soviet Economic Development since 1917*, London: Routledge and Kegan Paul, p. 219.) Apparently, however, the Soviet authorities concluded from this difference that some sort of economic sabotage must have aggravated the situation.

[46] *Loc. cit.*, pp. 219-20.

to increase the supply of such technical crops as cotton and flax by raising their prices seems to have led to an extension of the area planted with these products at the expense of the grain area.[47]

Probably, however, the crisis would have been less serious and would have abated in a reasonably short time if the government and the Communist Party had not responded to it with severe reprisals already at an early moment. One has only to read Stalin's speech against the "Right Deviation"—one of his great fanfares after he had turned the edge of his attack from the "leftists" Trotsky, Zinoviev and Kamenev against the "rightists" Rykov, Tomsky and Bucharin—in which he defended the "emergency measures" taken against the kulaks to realize that even before the drive for forced collectivization was started, large-scale terrorism was applied.[48] Not only was the taxation and credit system and the machinery of grain collections so altered as to bring maximum pressure to bear upon all peasants who could produce more than their own needs, but the legal protection of the owners of all but small holdings was apparently suspended in many districts.

Objectively, the situation required a judicious mixture of economic pressure and economic incentive. It was necessary to increase money taxes in order to force the peasant to sell more of his produce; it was also necessary to increase the prices of farm products—as was done in 1929, but apparently not to a sufficient extent—in order to make it profitable for the peasant to bring to the market as much grain as possible. The worst that could be done was to make the kulak a semi-outcast, because that policy was bound to discourage every middle peasant from developing his economy lest he fall into the kulak category. Yet the measures taken in the last two years before the collectivization drive already had this effect: ". . . . the richer a peasant was, the more rapid was his impoverishment." [49]

The greatest objection to the policy of raising agricultural prices as an incentive to increased production was the fear of inflation. The First Five Year Plan, from its financial aspects, was viewed as large-scale investment financed by sacrifices imposed on the peasantry. If farm prices had been raised drastically, this source of financing would have been eliminated or

[47] *Lo. cit.*, p. 220.

[48] The speech was delivered before the Central Committee of the Communist Party of the Soviet Union in April 1929 and is printed in Joseph Stalin, *Leninism*, New York: International Publishers, 1942, pp. 88 ff. The specific reference to "emergency measures" is on p. 129. Although Stalin singled out the kulaks as the object of his attack, he occasionally spoke of "kulaks and the well-to-do elements" (see pp.127-8), thus indicating that the limits of the group treated as a "class enemy" were not rigidly defined.

[49] Leonard E. Hubbard, *The Economics of Soviet Agriculture*, London: Macmillan, 1939, p. 107.

restricted, and only money creation could have taken its place. The Soviet leaders were right in regarding this means as an evil; but few if any processes of rapid industrialization have ever been carried out without some inflation, and it was somewhat ironical to see that the Soviet Communists, so much opposed to economic orthodoxy in other respects, tried to be as conservative in their monetary policies as the majority of pre-Keynesian Western economists and policy makers. By taking this attitude in a situation when they themselves had created conditions under which monetary stability could not be maintained, they were bound to encounter much more serious consequences than limited inflation—among others, inflation running out of control.

When the combination of harsh pressure and modest incentives, as applied in 1929, failed to make a sufficient amount of grain available to the collecting agencies, Stalin decided to go to the limit of harshness in applying pressure by methods with which he apparently expected to solve the agricultural problem once and for all. Individual peasant farming was to be all but abolished within a few years. Although the number of state farms (*Sovkhozy*)[50] was also to be increased, the typical future unit of collectivized farming would be the agricultural *artel* or *kolkhoz,* in which the land of a large number of peasant families would be jointly managed, with only small garden plots reserved for the individual family to produce vegetables and to keep some animals for its own needs. Collectivization would make possible the mechanization, which was too difficult to apply as long as farming units were small. Mechanization would not only save human labor, which could then be drawn into industry, but also land which would no longer be needed to grow feedstuffs for draft animals and could therefore be planted with grain or technical crops. It was not expected that the peasants would respond to collectivization with a great rise of enthusiasm for large-scale market deliveries; therefore an ingenious device to keep the collectives under government control was developed: The machine-tractor stations. The new mechanical equipment was not to become the property of the collective farms, but was to remain in the hands of the government and to be centralized in depots, one such station to serve for a number of collective farms. The equipment had to be hired by the kolkhozes, and the readiness with which the government agencies would respond to requests for tractors would depend on the proven willingness of each collective to comply with government policies. Moreover, the machine-tractor stations were developed as propaganda centers and agencies for political pressure, and became the principal instrument of the Soviet Govern-

[50] See Baykov, *The Development of the Soviet Economic System,* p. 332.

ment to keep the collectives under control and thus to deny them that self-government which is a characteristic of true cooperative organization in agriculture or industry. In order to reduce the presumed focus of anti-collectivization propaganda and possible sabotage, kulaks were not permitted to enter the collective farms; they were despoiled of their land, their houses, their equipment and even of their household effects and sent to labor camps, where many of them perished. The collectivization policy was officially directed against the kulaks, and every effort was made to stimulate the cupidity of the poorer peasants for a share in the accumulated "wealth" of the upper stratum of village society; but since the middle peasants supplied a larger amount, though a smaller one per acre of the grain than the kulaks, it was clear that the main purpose of anti-kulak terrorism was to frighten the middle peasants into complying with the government policies in order to avoid being labeled as kulaks or kulak sympathizers.

Terrorism achieved its immediate purpose: The grain deliveries increased. It seems that in 1932 to 1933, in spite of the partial crop failure in that year, grain deliveries amounted to almost double the quantity of 1926 to 1927.[51] Production, however, fluctuated during the period of the First Five Year Plan, tending to decline rather than increase; the improvement in deliveries, therefore, meant that a greater market supply was squeezed out of the peasantry at the expense of the latter's standard of living. The human cost of this process was tremendous, and the collectivization campaign has rightly been denounced as an outstanding example of state-organized cruelty. But even when measured against the objectives of the ruling Soviet group, especially of Stalin, the debit side of this policy seems so great as to preclude any justification as an act of statesmanship. Collectivization by official terrorism caused an acute shortage of draft animals, which plagued the Soviet economy for a number of years; it replaced the struggle between the collecting agencies of the state and the individual peasant for a maximum of deliveries with a quite similar struggle between

[51] See Alexander Baykov, *The Development of the Soviet Economic System*, Cambridge: University Press, 1950, p. 326. The question of whether statistical information on the Soviet Union is sufficiently reliable to permit firm conclusions has often been debated. For more recent periods, most specialists now agree that it is possible to detect and correct inadequacies to such an extent as to assure an essentially correct picture. Earlier figures can hardly deserve the same amount of credence, even when sifted by such experts as Baykov, because—quite aside from the possibility of deliberate falsification for propaganda purposes—it is a general experience that in times of turbulence and upheaval statistical services suffer with other branches of public administration; yet even the best secondary sources must ultimately rely on the official figures. Considering the violent struggle which was going on in the Soviet agricultural areas between 1929 and 1933, the author cannot entirely free himself from doubts about the validity of figures showing a great increase in grain collections during this period, but there is no way to obtain certainty.

the same agencies and the kolkhozes—hardly less bitter; it saddled Soviet agriculture with an uneconomical distribution of available labor between common land, farmed with relatively extensive methods, and small private plots, on which a disproportionately high amount of labor was, and still is, being used; and it created psychological conditions which seem to be responsible for the otherwise unaccountably slow development of the productivity of agricultural labor in the Soviet Union as compared with other countries. True, the advantages of large-scale over small-scale farming cannot be questioned, at least in regard to grain and most other field crops, whereas there is less certainty in regard to cattle farming. Collectivization opened the way to large-scale cultivation of the soil. But in view of the frightful cost the idea suggests itself that milder methods and less speed would not only have been more humane but also far more economical.

Since not only land but also livestock—with a few exceptions—was to be collectivized, the first response of the peasants to the collectivization program was to slaughter as many of their animals as possible, and feast on the meat. There were not yet enough tractors ready to replace animal power; as a consequence, cultivation suffered, and transporting farm products to the market became far more difficult. Unless the figures indicating an increase in market deliveries are badly misleading, the state and party functionaries in the rural areas who managed to move such large quantities to the urban areas must have shown not only ruthlessness but also high efficiency and great dedication to their task. This is consistent with the signs of high morale and even enthusiasm in a substantial section of the Communist Party during the period of the First Five Year Plan. Many Communists felt that they were privileged to participate in a great venture and that in spite of all severity and sacrifice the result would be a better world. In many hearts, these hopes were crushed after 1937, when in Stalin's purge trials the idealists were liquidated or made to share the fate of the kulaks.

The first shock of terrorism undoubtedly strengthened the position of the government toward the peasantry. It is difficult to say how long this effect lasted, for with the gradual improvement of the conditions of production and the eventual use of the carrot in addition to the whip by the government—especially through the legalization of the free sale of "surplus" product after completion of compulsory deliveries—the market supply was bound to increase spontaneously. Stalin himself has explained that in regard to power relations, not every aspect of collectivization was a permanent net gain for the government. "As long as the peasants were engaged in individual farming," he said, "they were scattered and separated from each other; consequently, the counterrevolutionary designs of anti-Soviet elements within the peasantry could not be very effective. . . . The collective farm gives the peasant a ready-made form of mass organization. Consequently, the penetration of anti-Soviet elements into the collective farms and their anti-Soviet activity may be much more effective."[52] Apart from the assumption that non-compliance with government policies was a sign of counterrevolutionary intentions, whereas in all probability it was merely a response of self-interest to unsatisfactory conditions, the statement is convincing. By forcing the peasants into collectives, the government unwittingly forged for them weapons for resistance which were stronger than any in the possession of individual peasants. Even the machine-tractor stations may not have supplied more than partial compensation for this strengthening of the peasant position, and to break it the government had to fall back on the large-scale use of means which are always at the disposal of a dictatorship: secret police, forced labor, prison and firing squads.

In spite of all the ruthlessness, deliveries did not keep pace with the demand of a rapidly growing urban population for food, and rationing had to be introduced. Needs and supplies remained in precarious balance. In the spring of 1933, when the situation had been aggravated by drought in some important areas, the peasants had hardly enough left to feed themselves; yet the Soviet government demanded the deliveries without regard to peasant needs, and mass starvation stalked the country in the Ukraine and other Southern regions. The number of fatalities has never been ascertained.

Yet the Soviet government survived, and the rations in the cities were kept sufficiently above the starvation level to permit industrialization to proceed. To argue that a given purpose could have been achieved at less cost by alternative methods is always difficult, since this requires the elaboration of consequences of assumed conditions, and the hazard of leaving out side effects is always present in such considerations. But in this case it seems that the long-range goal of consolidated land holding could have been achieved at much less cost through a gradual process, and that the acute deficiency in deliveries was overcome not through collectivization but in spite of collectivization: If the Kremlin found it necessary to impose penalties, resistance would have been both weaker in motive and less effective if individual landholding had continued. Everything the government wanted to avoid by collectivization at the particular moment when it was introduced occurred nevertheless: necessity of severe rationing, inflation, intensified antagonism between country and city.

[52] Joseph Stalin, "Work in the Rural Districts," *op. cit.*, p. 74.

Relaxation

In 1932, as in 1921, a point was reached which even in the opinion of the Soviet leaders called for some concessions to the peasantry, and the reform which ensued from these considerations also had some similarity to measures which had formed part of the NEP, although the general framework was now entirely different. In the first two years of collectivization, the system of food collection had great similarity with the program under War Communism: The agricultural population had to deliver everything produced in excess of its own needs as determined by the government on a basis of a restrictive standard. Now the government re-introduced the NEP principle that after fulfilling the obligatory deliveries at "official" prices all surplus products could either be used for the peasant's own consumption or sold at higher prices on the free market—now called the kolkhoz market. This possibility of free sale applied to both the products of collectivized agriculture and to the products of the "garden" plots of the individual kolkhoz members.[53] The physical facilities—halls, booths, etc.—for marketing the excess products were established by city administrations which were glad to give their citizens a chance of purchasing food beyond their rations. The buyers on the kolkholz market could only be ultimate consumers, because as early as 1929 the legalization of private trading had been repealed and the purchase of any merchandise for resale was now a punishable offense ("speculation") for anyone except the government and cooperative organizations and communal institutions.

In addition to the compulsory deliveries and sales of the open kolkhoz market, a third outlet had already been created in the first phase of collectivization; the roots of this institution go even farther back to the NEP period. This was the selling under contract, either to the state trading organization or to cooperatives, hospitals, restaurants or other institutional consumers. The prices obtained in these contracts were in between those for compulsory deliveries and those on the kolkhoz market. Therefore the peasants would always have preferred to sell their "surplus"—compulsory deliveries had priority over contract sales as well as those on the kolkhoz market—on the latter whenever there was a real choice; but in some instances the kolkhoz markets were too far away, and even more frequently pressure was exerted by government and party agencies to sell a large portion of the surplus product to the state agency under contract.

The 1932 reform had another similarity with the NEP in that it came too late to avert disaster: the man-made famine of the spring of 1933. But after this great calamity, conditions improved, and in 1935 the Soviet gov-

[53] The individual *kolkhozniki* could sell not only the product of their "garden" plots, but also produce that they received as payment in kind for work on collectivized land.

ernment was in a position to abolish rationing. Compulsory deliveries at low prices were continued, and most of the rest of the grain crops went to the state trading organization under sales contract.[54] The kolkhoz markets, however, remained legal and played an important role for livestock and animal products.[55] Government prices to consumers were now intermediate between the former "commercial" prices for "excess" food in state stores and the prices at which rations were supplied. In order to induce the kolkhozes and the kolkhoz members to sell as much as possible, industrial commodities were made available to collectives or individuals with a good record in selling. This system remained in force essentially until the Second World War.

The recovery of agricultural production after 1933 was probably mainly the result of the large investments that had been made in agriculture ever since the beginning of the First Five Year Plan.[56] Motor traction, especially, now became available on a large scale to replace the slaughtered draft animals. The beneficial effect of tractorization was only natural; the extent to which the organizational and marketing arrangements were beneficial to production is more difficult to judge. Undoubtedly, the legalization of the kolkhoz markets and the various premiums for exceeding compulsory deliveries by more or less voluntary sales had a stimulating effect; at the same time, however, they led to a very unequal distribution of labor power over the cultivable land. All reports agree that the kolkhoz members spent as much of their working hours as they could on their "garden" plots, and that most of them tried to reduce the time they had to work on the common land. This meant that in neither of the two kinds of areas was the labor-land ratio optimal: On the kolkhoz area it was too low, on the private plots too high. This problem, has not disappeared even today.

The Economic Position of Kolkhoz Members

The inducement to concentrate labor on the private plots might have been less strong if the remuneration for work on the kolkhoz land had been higher. The kolkhoz paid no fixed money wages, but its unit for labor

[54] See Baykov, *The Soviet Economic System*, p. 311.

[55] *Loc. cit.* p. 312.

[56] A table compiled by Baykov (*op. cit.*, p. 421) from official Soviet figures shows that out of a total investment during the First Five Year Plan period of 50.5 billion rubles, 9.8 billion went into agriculture. The number of tractors grew (in thousands) from 72.1 in 1930 to 422.7 in 1936 (See *loc. cit.* p. 331). Part of this increase, it is true, merely made good the disinvestment through the slaughter of horses and cattle. But the magnitude of total capital at the disposal of agriculture at any given time—even if it could be calculated—is not at issue here; the important point is that the damage done during the collectivization campaign was at least in part remedied by later government investment. Later, increasing urbanization would have required an even heavier investment in agriculture and its auxiliary industries than was forthcoming; hence the continuing difficulties in food procurement.

compensation was—and in the main still is—a "day's work," *trudoden.* But a *trudoden* is by no means a definite number of working hours giving claim to a definite sum of rubles; the system is far more complex.

In the first place, labor compensation in a kolkhoz is on a piece-work basis. The *trudoden* is the amount of work that ought to be performed in a day; if the worker works faster, it is his gain, if he works more slowly, it is his loss. (There are exceptions to this rule, because some work has to be measured by time actually spent: bookkeeping, teaching or care of children, etc.) Second, skilled work is compensated at a higher rate: For work he can perform in a day, a highly skilled mechanic may be credited with several *trudodens.* Third, the value of a *trudoden* in money or kind is determined as a residual after the kolkhoz, at the end of the year, has paid all its taxes and other expenses, and thus represents a share in the earnings of the cooperative unit. The share is usually paid partly in money and partly in produce; of the latter, feedstuffs are particularly important because in the raising of livestock the private activity of the kolkhoz members, on the basis of their individual plots—which, however, would often not provide enough fodder for the animals without the additional supplies from the kolkhoz—plays a much greater role than in grain growing.[57] Against the *trudoden* credits which a worker will earn in the course of a year, advances can be made in order to cover the needs of his household and of the animals he is keeping.

Trudoden credits are not the only source of earnings of a kolkhoz member; in many instances the larger part comes from other sources:[58] from the sale of animals, raised on their plot, or their products, and from outside employment, e.g. in temporary industrial jobs or in other kolkhozes which may need hired help seasonally. The complexity of the system has important effects on the life of the individual member. How well or how badly he fares depends on many conditions beyond his control: Compared with a worker in industry, who receives steady wages, he has less security with respect to the size of his income. Because involved rules regulate the relationship of the private member economy to the kolkhoz economy—the duty to spend a stipulated number of days on kolkhoz work, compulsory delivery

[57] This indicates that the coexistence of small private plots with jointly cultivated land is not always as uneconomical as it may first appear; in some instances a satisfactory division of labor has been achieved, with the private plots sheltering privately owned livestock, fed to a large extent from the produce grown collectively. But the size of the individual plots in relation to the size of the kolkhoz land and the ratio of earning potentials in private work and in work for the kolkhoz are determined by many factors extraneous to economic rationality, and therefore in the majority of cases the distribution of land and labor as between collective and private economies seems to be far from optimal.

[58] See Hubbard, *Economics of Soviet Agriculture,* pp. 176 ff.

of livestock products from the private economy to the kolkhoz and indirectly to the state trading organization, charges by the kolkhoz for marketing products of the private economy—the peasant is to a considerable extent dependent on the interpretation of these rules by the kolkhoz staff, especially the kolkhoz manager and the foreman ("brigadier").[59] According to law, it is true, the meeting of all members is the highest authority, and is supposed to protect the individual from arbitrary decisions by management, but in a dictatorially governed nation local democracy often does not operate effectively even where it is the intent of national law to make it work: A manager who has strong backing by the Communist party cannot be easily challenged by kolkhoz members.

The kolkhoz as a whole is by no means a self-governing cooperative. Its output is planned by state agencies, and it is held by a variety of means to the fulfillment of this plan; although recent reforms, which will be explained later, have loosened these ties somewhat, the vital decision as to what to plant is still very largely not the kolkhoz's own choice. Thus the kolkhoz members "have neither the certainty of income which other Soviet workers possess, nor the control of farm operations exercised by independent farmers (although, like the latter, collective farmers must bear the risks of weather, pests, and plant and animal diseases.)"[60] These factors would have reduced the attractiveness of labor in the kolkhozes even if earnings had been comparable with those in industry; however, they were far below that level in the prewar and immediate postwar periods[61] and have not even reached it today, although there must be very great differences among the individual kolkhozes and even among the individual kolkhoz members.[62] Yet a differential in favor of industrial employment has until recently been an advantage from the point of view of the Soviet government, since it was necessary to have a flow of labor from agriculture to industry; only now is this situation beginning to change.

[59] The labor force of a kolkhoz is divided into "brigades," each of which is assigned a particular area to cultivate or the tending of a particular herd.

[60] Lazar Volin, "Agricultural Policy of the Soviet Union," in *Comparisons of the United States and Soviet Economies,* Part I, p. 291.

[61] "It is true that the money income of the average kolkhoznik represents a ridiculously small purchasing power over manufactured goods consumption compared with the average wages earned by industrial workers, but this is partly compensated by the foodstuffs obtained without payment and by the urban inhabitant's expenditure on such things as transport, house rents and heating, that the peasant avoids." (Hubbard, *Economics of Soviet Agriculture,* p. 217.) The extra expenditures of the city dweller, are, of course, in turn partly or wholly offset by extra conveniences.

[62] *Loc. cit.,* pp. 234 f.

CHAPTER 18

POSTWAR REFORMS

The Organization of Industry

THE END OF THE STALINIST PERIOD

SINCE THIS IS NOT an economic history of the Soviet Union, and references to the past are merely intended to make the most important present problems understandable, it is unnecessary to discuss the Soviet war economy and the phase of postwar reconstruction. In the Soviet Union, as in the West, most of the economic problems caused by warfare had disappeared by the middle of the 1950's; those which had not can be briefly stated.

The war inflicted upon the Soviet Union enormous human losses, and thereby gave a new dimension of significance to the increase in labor productivity. On the other hand, the war has forced the Soviet Union to build many new factories, although this could be done only with superhuman effort. At the price of great additional suffering, postwar reconstruction of the Soviet economy was carried out in a space of time which seems very brief as compared with the magnitude of the task, and the Soviet economy today is undoubtedly much stronger than it was before the war.

At an early stage of the reconstruction period (December 1947), the Soviet government again abolished rationing, effecting the necessary curbing of consumers' demand through prices very high in relation to workers' incomes.[1] In this one respect, therefore, the Soviet government returned to reliance on market controls earlier than some Western countries, but this use of the price mechanism was not characteristic of Soviet economic policy

[1] See Harry Schwartz, *The Red Phoenix*. New York: Frederick A. Praeger, 1961, p. 115.

as a whole during reconstruction. Priority of physical fulfillment of the plan by the individual enterprises was more than ever permitted to overshadow success in terms of the profit-and-loss account. This was certainly not an optimal method for operating the Soviet economy even in the immediate postwar period; yet the specific tasks of reconstruction again made planning in terms of value and control of production by price-cost calculation somewhat less important than they would have been under more normal conditions. The primary task was to restore Soviet industry to its 1940 volume, and this was a job whose requirements could be described in physical terms. To be sure, already in this phase it was important to modify the industrial pattern to allow for the relocation of factories during the war and for the progress of technology—problems which would have required value calculation for their best solution. In all probability, the success of Russian reconstruction—given the same amount of sacrifice imposed on the population—would have been even greater if physical considerations had played a less dominant role. But the tasks of the reconstruction period resembled those of the First Five Year Plan more than those of the late 1930's, and the damage done by the preponderance of physical considerations was, therefore, again less grievous than it would have been in an economy already rebuilt. While value calculation and control of efficiency by prices was less important in the reconstruction period than before the war, it became more important than ever when reconstruction came to an end. It was a significant coincidence that the rebuilding of the Soviet economy was completed only a short time before the death of Stalin in 1953, which opened the way to the rise of new political leaders who could visualize the new economic tasks with less bias in favor of ideas of the preceding phase, although none of them had been free of involvement in Stalinist policies.

SOME RELIEF FOR THE CONSUMER

The reader will have noticed that in the analysis of the industrial system under Stalin, it was impossible consistently to apply the past tense: This would have created the impression that the principal tenets of the Stalinist system had been eliminated by his successors, whereas in fact they have so far been only partially modified.

After the terrible deprivations of the war and immediate postwar periods, the lot of the Soviet consumer had to be substantially improved: On this point, there seems to have been general agreement among Stalin's successors. Great disagreement existed, however, over the time and the measure of consumer relief, and consequently over how early and by what margin the priority of producer goods production should be reduced; this was the essence of the Malenkov-Khrushchev controversy of 1953.[2]

In proposing an early and drastic shift, Malenkov met with resistance not only for practical reasons—especially from the viewpoint of military preparedness—but also on doctrinal grounds. The priority accorded to heavy industry, especially steel and machine production, had become an article of faith. "Unlike the capitalist method," the official newspaper *Izvestia* contended in December 1954, "the Soviet method proceeds from the fact that it is necessary to begin industrialization of the country with heavy, not light industry." [3] There was more behind this belief than a somewhat questionable interpretation of economic history.[4] In developing consumer goods industries, planning authorities play a less active role than in mapping the growth of capital goods industries. In deciding whether to give consumers more trousers or more overcoats, a planning authority would have to be sadistic not to be guided by consumers' preferences; consequently, in the sphere of consumer goods production the planning authorities have to register the desires of the public and use them as guideposts

[2] A brief account of this controversy can be found in Harry Schwartz, *op. cit.*, pp. 176-77.

[3] Quoted by George Daniel Embree, *The Soviet Union between the 19th and 20th Party Congresses, 1952-1956*, s'Gravenhage: Martinus Nijhoff, 1959, p. 163.

[4] It is true that in Britain and some other countries the factory system was introduced on a large scale into the textile industries before it became important in the processing of iron and steel; yet this fact cannot support the generalization, which is obviously the real meaning of the *Izvestia* statement and similar contentions, that capitalist development starts with consumer goods industries as opposed to communist development which starts with producer goods industries. In its very homeland, Britain, the rise of the textile industry would have been impossible without the prior and contemporaneous development of coal mining, which absorbed large investments already in the eighteenth century; in almost all countries heavy investment in transportation facilities—roads and especially canals—preceded large-scale construction of textile factories which would not otherwise have been possible. In capitalist industrialization, the availability of resources and the accidental sequence of inventions determined in the main whether in a particular field of production the process of mechanization started near the base or near the consumption end. The grain of truth in the Communist contention is the fact that production of machinery, in contrast to production of materials on the one side and consumer goods on the other, can be highly mechanized only at a relatively advanced stage of development; in earlier phases, only such relatively simple machines as non-automatic lathes and presses can be used in the machine industry. The ultimate reason why production of machinery by extensive use of machines became possible in a relatively late phase of Western industrialization is the particularly high degree of accuracy required in the machine industry which called for the hand of the skilled workman at critical stages of the process when mechanization could not yet operate with narrow tolerance. Obviously, this historical sequence has nothing to do with economic systems; if twentieth century Russia was freer in selecting the degree of mechanization for its capital goods industries than Britain had been in the early nineteenth century, this was not due to the Communist organization of Russian industry but to the fact that Russia was taking over a technology which had already been developed in the West.

for planning rather than to set these guideposts according to their own judgment. In the capital goods sector, there is more room for judgment by the central agencies: Although ultimately the direction of consumption—public as well as private—determines what capital goods will be needed, the possibility of using capital goods to produce more capital goods makes the producer goods sector for a time independent of consumers' preferences. In these circumstances, the larger the capital goods sector in relation to the consumer goods sector, the more latitude the planners have to shape the economy according to the image they themselves have formed, rather than accept that formed by the consumers.

Although Malenkov was defeated by Khrushchev, this political decision merely limited and delayed but did not prevent the growth of importance of the consumer goods sector. Insistence on rapid growth of heavy industry was maintained, and at first even the percentage of investment in consumer goods production was reduced,[5] but this was a temporary setback: At least since early in 1960 it has been made clear that consumption will not remain the stepchild of Soviet economic policy to anything like the former degree. Thus the branches of production which can fulfill their immediate purpose only if prices are acceptable to consumers are growing and with the increase in the variety of products offered to consumers the exercise of consumers' choices, as influenced by prices, are becoming more important within the consumer goods sector. This latter effect, it is true, has been impaired by the continuation of inflationary pressures within the Soviet economy:[6] Because of the relative abundance of money, the consumer goods sector still tends to remain a seller's market. But again, there is a counteracting tendency: The political relaxation following Stalin's death, and not entirely undone by official reaction to revolts in slave labor camps, to the East German and Hungarian insurrections and to disorders in Poland, gave consumers more freedom in voicing their criticism, and instances in which they could not spend their money on goods of their first choice have become more noticeable and therefore less tolerable.

MORE RECOGNITION FOR MARKET FORCES

The desire to eliminate inflation also became a force operating for increased attention to values. Inflation could have been reduced, of course, by spending less money on armament and on long-range capital investments, but actual cuts in programs—and not only modifications in the use of the annual increment of economic strength—were not acceptable to the

[5] See Embree, *op. cit.*, p. 170.
[6] See Harry Schwartz, *op. cit.*, p. 140 f.

Soviet leaders. Thus the only way to fight inflation was to produce more marketable commodities of greater utility with the resources allocated to the consumer goods sector; this achievement could be made possible only by improvement of the price-cost ratio in the individual enterprise, and by more emphasis on value planning in the central agencies.

Improving the price-cost ratio in the individual enterprise required a reduction of the conflict between the two sets of instructions by which each manager was guided: Avoiding loss, if possible making a profit; and on the other hand, producing the physical quantities for which the plan provided, and if possible exceeding these quantities. As has been explained before, the prevailing emphasis on the second obligation at the expense of the first caused factories to produce large quantities of goods of poor quality, to exceed the optimal utilization of capacity, and as far as management had any influence on the production program, to concentrate on products of which the output could be most easily maximized. The more the emphasis was placed on the profit-and-loss account, the more these evils would be corrected, provided cost prices and product prices, with which price-cost calculation had to be carried out, were not arbitrarily set but rationally determined, either by the enterprises themselves or by the central agencies. Since the central agencies retained for themselves the right to set many prices, it was imperative that they develop the techniques to make these prices express utility in terms of the plan goals; in other words, to combine value planning with physical planning. Even if they had relinquished their price fixing power—and there is very little evidence that Soviet policy makers were so inclined—such a complementing of the planning methods would still have been necessary. If the individual enterprise must make ends meet and is given the necessary freedom of action to achieve this purpose, and if nevertheless the plan is still to be carried out, then it must be so calculated that the actions which are optimal for the fulfillment of the plan will also tend to maximize the gain of the individual enterprise. This can obviously not be assured by a plan calculated primarily in terms of physical quantities. As in the period just before World War II, the government's interest in fiscal and monetary equilibrium operated in favor of rational pricing and value planning, only the pressure of this interest had become greater because of the more advanced stage of economic development which had been reached, with a wider range of choice for the consumers in selecting goods and for the managers in selecting technological methods. So great had the pressure become in the late 1950's that a more determined move was made by many Soviet economists to rehabilitate the price mechanism even in the field in which all such moves met with the greatest resistance, on the capital market. The attempts to introduce a standard rate of interest—as discussed previously—now reached their climax.

Support of these tendencies came from abroad. Since about 1940, Western economists have been developing mathematical techniques that are bound to be even more useful in a planned economy than in unplanned capitalism. These techniques, of which the input-output scheme and linear programming are the most conspicuous examples but which may be more generally described as an extensive use of matrices and indifference curve systems, were to a great extent the outgrowth of the widespread use of mathematics to which economic theory had been inclined ever since the 1920's; it was during that period that the traditions of the Marshall and Pareto schools began to supersede "Austrian" marginalism, which had made use only of the most elementary mathematical concepts. This spontaneous trend in economic science had been strengthened by new requirements of national defense planning: Since the concept of total war, as it had emerged from World War II, made it important to hit the enemy at the most vital spots with the minimum expenditure of resources, it was now imperative for an effective air offense to know as precisely as possible what factories had to be destroyed in the hostile country in order to produce maximum disruption of its economy with minimum commitment of manpower and weapons; it was equally important for defense to know what elements of the economy should receive the highest priority in measures of protection. For this purpose, the theory of interdependence of economic processes, and therefore the input-output matrix, were of obvious importance; likewise, from the point of view of national defense it was vital not only that the optimal combination of resources for the achievment of a particular production purpose should be found but that it be found by a process faster than trial and error on the real market, since in war no type of resource is scarcer than time: For the same reason the defense interest in linear programming was also great.[7]

Although the tension between the West and the Soviet Union and the resulting need for large-scale war planning kept the interest of Western, especially American, defense agencies in these mathematical techniques alive, no field of potential usefulness comparable to that of Soviet economic

[7] More recently, another contribution of mathematical economics has been receiving even greater attention from the defense agencies: the theory of games, which has developed—in spite of a different starting point—largely through its application to economic action. Although the theory of games may eventually gain some importance for the technique of plan execution, this potential development has so far not materialized; therefore, the theory has little present relevance to the problems discussed in this context.

planning existed for them in the West. It was not to be expected that the Communists would let these instruments, almost made to order for their own purposes, lie around unused; but at the same time, the doctrinal obstacles to the use of these techniques in a country of no more than slightly attenuated Marxist orthodoxy were formidable. The input-output matrix, to be sure, can be understood as a rounding out of the system of material balances which the Soviet planners were already employing, and the question of what extension of industry A is necessary to enable industry B to be expanded by a defined percentage is basically a matter of physical calculation to which no Marxist can object on doctrinal grounds. The actual execution of the calculations, however, is not feasible without using values as indices of physical output. For example, if expansion of the automobile industry requires increased production of metal-working machinery, the basic reason is physical: To give pieces of steel and aluminum the shapes which make them parts of an automobile engine or body, all sorts of dies, presses and lathes are needed. But one type of metal-working machinery is obviously not like another; nor do they differ merely by one characteristic, which might make it possible to reduce all of them to one physical standard—just as for many purposes various sizes of railroad cars which differ merely by their carrying capacity can be quantitatively described in terms of one standard size; machine tools, however, differ according to size, shape, purpose, the speed with which they move, and the power they require for operation; they are not mutually substitutable as tools of production. They are, however, to a great extent mutually substitutable as products, because to a great extent the same resources are required for their making. In many phases of the planning process, therefore, a useful purpose is served by aggregating the various types of metal-working machinery—that is, it makes sense to have a category, "metal working machinery," in an input-output program rather than merely individual categories for each type of die, press, lathe and so on. Considering the difficulty of having the results of planning ready in time to guide production, such aggregation is imperative. But what should be the common denominator for aggregating the various machine tools for metal working? The only available one is value, and for the aggregation to make sense, it is necessary that value expresses marginal utility and thereby the opportunity cost of the individual machine. This means that the operation of an input-output scheme requires rational pricing.

The same requirement can be even more easily recognized in the use of linear programming for the establishment of a national plan. Since this device has the purpose of helping to find the most economical process by which a given commodity can be produced, or, alternatively, the most worthwhile product for which given resources can be used, it is clear that these calculations require as some of their data prices which express the true economic importance of product and resource units.

The great potential convenience of the matrix and indifference curve techniques for economic planning caused some Soviet mathematicians to urge their utilization, and since the new techniques could work only in a system of rational pricing, mathematicians became advocates of a reform of pricing that would bring it closer to rationality; to be sure, they attemped to camouflage, or even to conceal from themselves, the deviation from the Marxist labor value theory. The outstanding pioneer of these methods among the Soviet mathematicians seems to have been L. V. Kantorovich, corresponding member of the Academy of Sciences; in any event, we are particularly well informed about his work through an analysis by Benjamin Ward.[8] The details of Kantorovich's work are not important here; the general tendency is clear.

A final impetus for reform came from the realization that overcentralization was a great curse to the industrial system of the Soviet Union. Under Stalin, the more important industries had been under the direction of central agencies, with the rank of Union ministries; industries of only regional importance were directed by central agencies of the member republics. The apparatus of central agencies was subdivided into chief branch administrations, which were often organized on the basis of a combination of geographic and branch principles, such as in the "chief administration of the Donbas and Caucasian coal industry" in the USSR Ministry for the coal industry.[9]

Given the very limited autonomy of the individual enterprise, this organization not only prevented sufficient recognition of regional and local conditions—in spite of the geographical element in delimiting the jurisdiction of some of the chief branch administrations—but also made the job of the central agencies too big. The apparatus was unwieldy, because too much had to be done by the officials in Moscow and in the capitals of the republics—tasks for which these officials first had to obtain information from enterprise managers, make their decisions, transmit them to the managers and then supervise execution of the decisions. This situation was

[8] See Benjamin Ward, "Kantorovich on Economic Calculation," *Journal of Political Economy*, Vol. LXVIII, no. 6 (December 1960), pp. 545 ff. Professor Kantorovich had already published his main work in 1939; he has followed it with several more recent articles; his argument seems to have received more attention in the 1950's than upon the first publication.

[9] See Baykov, *The Development of the Soviet Economic System*, pp. 277 ff., esp. p. 298.

essentially irremediable as long as the enterprises remained subject to double sets of instructions, often conflicting. The manager trying to reconcile compliance with a quantitatively determined plan with the duty—although a duty generally regarded as less important—to make revenue cover expenses, could not be left to his own devices. Often he had to be instructed on the choice he should make; always he had to be supervised to prevent him from using illegitimate means to avoid his dilemma, such means as a deliberate deterioration of product quality. Only by expressing the plan goals in terms of a rational pricing system and leaving the enterprises free to follow the indicators of the price mechanism could the pitfalls of supercentralization and of anarchy in production both be avoided.

In the second half of the 1950's, an apparently strong tendency in Soviet economic thinking was directed toward such a reform. The attention paid to the ideas of Kantorovich, although much of it critical, represented one sympton of this trend. One Soviet economist, for instance, wrote:

> . . . there must be a proper measure of whether a factory is working well or not. This must be stable and constant and not able to be influenced by the administration of the factory itself. The only such indicator is the price, and it must be the profit of the factory which acts as incentive. The price of a product is the economic lever which spurs on or holds back the growth of production. It must encourage the factory not only to engage in simple and easy production but also to produce what the national economy most needs (and what the economy needs must be a source of gain and profit to the factory). Price and the methods of measuring plan fulfillment by value must be retained, and all other obligatory indicators must be reduced to a minimum." [10]

REGIONALIZATION

A major reform was indeed initiated by the Soviet government in 1957, but only one of the weaknesses of the industrial system was made the target: administrative overcentralization, especially where it resulted in a disregard for regional peculiarities. For this purpose, the vertical line of responsibility in the administration of industries was cut near the top. Most of the Union ministries for individual industries were dissolved and their tasks handed over to more than a hundred Regional Economic Councils (*sovnarkhozes*), which are now responsible for more than 70 per cent of Soviet industrial output.[11] As a remedy for the specific disadvantages of ex-

[10] I. Mironov, "Specialization Must Be All Round," Promyshlenno-Ekonomicheskaya Gazeta, July 27, 1956, quoted by R. W. Davies, *Soviet Studies,* 1956-57, p. 435.

[11] See the graph in Gregory Grossman: "Planning: Backbone of a Nation," *Saturday Review,* January 21, 1961, p. 22. In 1962, the number of *sovnarkhozes* was reduced to forty.

cessive bigness, this reform may well achieve its purpose; but it raised problems of its own.

The indubitable evils of overcentralization should not obscure the vitally important functions served by the centralized agencies, with their dominating influence, in an economy such as the Soviet Union's. "We should note," writes Gregory Grossman, "that two of the most powerful forces making for innovation and modernization of products and processes in the market economy are virtually entirely lacking in the Soviet-type system; namely the force of competition and the sales efforts of firms in the capital goods producing industry . . ."[12] Of course, the factory manager is interested in reducing costs, this being the principal field in which he can exercise initiative; but since he is even more interested in bringing the output up to the quantitative norm set in the plan, he will usually not introduce any innovations, even those which promise a substantial reduction of costs, if they would at the same time upset production for any considerable period. This means that the innovating energy of the individual plant manager will operate only within narrow limits, and that more far-reaching innovations must as a rule be imposed from the top, if they are to occur at all. Furthermore, as long as the individual enterprise is largely relieved of the responsibility for marketing what it produces, strict control by central agencies can reduce the danger that plant managers, under pressure to raise quantitative output, resort to undesirable evasion techniques. The sovnarkhozes which are now charged with the supervisory functions do not have the same amount of responsibility for the success of the plan as a whole, as had the ministries and chief administrations; probably their more parochial outlook may make them more willing to acquiesce in the relative technological conservatism of the plant managers, which also helps to prevent temporary disturbances in the regional economy—often an initial result of innovation. To counteract these hazards, additional controls of industrial administration by the party organization have been inaugurated; it remains to be seen whether the remedy is effective and whether undesirable side effects will not detract too much from its benefits.

The transfer of functions from the national to regional agencies creates still another danger: These regional bodies may want to produce as much

[12] Gregory Grossman, "Soviet Growth: Routine, Inertia, and Pressure," *The American Economic Review*, May 1960, p. 65. A somewhat different position is taken by David Granick, who assumes—but as a hypothesis rather than assertion—that because of the engineering background of the typical industrial manager in the USSR, "technical innovations should spread faster through the Russian economy" than through the American economy. (*Comparisons between United States and Soviet Economies.* Part I, p. 144.) To the extent that the two statements contradict each other, Grossman's view seems more convincing to the writer.

as possible for their own consumption, or in any event develop those industries which are most useful for regional needs, although they may be less important from the point of view of the nation. Apparently in order to combat possible autarchic tendencies of the sovnarkhozes, Councils for Coordination and Planning were established recently in 17 "large economic regions," as supervisory bodies for the more than one hundred sovnarkhozes. The addition of these organs has complicated the machinery of economic administration, and it is doubtful whether there will be any gain that will outweigh the disadvantage of a lengthening of the line on which directives and information must move.[13]

In the debate on the organization and methods of planning, which has been carried on in the Soviet Union in a rather lively manner since 1957, the principle of regionalization does not seem to have been seriously criticized. Many Soviet economists, however, realized that this principle, whatever its merits in other respects, did not assure the proper utilization of the potential of individual enterprises, the quality of goods produced, and the use of resources for those kinds of product which were most urgently needed by society. Therefore it was ever more widely understood that mere geographic decentralization was no adequate substitute for that other form of decentralization which would have increased the autonomy of individual plants by giving their managers more responsibility for determining output volume, product mix, purchase of supplies, and for finding outlets for products, while establishing profitability as the decisive success indicator to provide the managers with an incentive to seek optimal solutions for all these tasks; of course, such a reform would also have required a rational pricing system to provide signals for management in the choice of its course. None of the advocates of reform went the whole way toward the postulate of a planned market economy after the Yugoslav model, about which more will be said later. Even the strongest voice among the reformers, Professor J. Liberman, wants to retain the imposition of quantitative output targets with

[13] See Gregory Grossman, "Some Problems of Structure and Organization of the Soviet Economy," *Slavic Review,* XXI:2, June 1962, p. 217. In addition to the "large economic regions," republic Sovnarkhozy have been formed in the Russian Socialist Federative Soviet Republic—Russia proper—, the Ukraine and Kazakhstan with jurisdiction over the local Sovnarkhozy of these member states; USSR State Commissions have been established for several of the major industries, a measure which looks like a partial return to the branch principle of industrial administration. In any event, these additional organs contribute to the complexity of the system.

Two years after the regionalization, the five-year period of planning was replaced by a seven-year period, and the last—the sixth—Five Year Plan was not even allowed to run its full allotted time—up to 1960. The writer would not venture to speculate on the question of whether this lengthening of the period was due to administrative convenience or had more far-reaching significance.

specifications about the product mix upon the individual enterprises. The latter should only be completely free in choosing their sources, quantities and kinds of supply and their technology, and to make their own sales contracts, and their performance should be primarily judged by the yardstick of profitability, which should be made meaningful through a reform of the price system. The emphasis on profitability, to be sure, tended to reduce the importance of quantitative targets, because the more that financial success counts in the event of a conflict with the quantitative success indicator, the less can the managers be held responsible for the reaching of physical plan fulfillment under all circumstances. Moreover, if financial success is given prime importance, the managers will probably find it easier to convince the superior authorities that output and product mix must be so determined as to tend to maximize profits, and since the managers are likely to know the conditions of profit maximization better than anyone else, the reform would probably give them a greater voice in the formation of the plan.

The cause of economic reform was benefited by Khrushchev's report to the Central Committee of the Communist party in November 1962. Khrushchev's move toward reform, however, was still so cautious as to create the impression that he viewed the changes he proposed as an experiment rather than as a matter of settled policy.[14] He pointed out the limitations of gross output as a success indicator and explained that it was necessary to change the system so as to make sure that mere quantitative fulfillment or overfulfillment of the plan would not give one enterprise an advantage over another, which was less successful in regard to quantity but perhaps outstanding in regard to the quality of its products and to the selection of those product varieties which best met consumers' preferences. He emphasized profitability as a success indicator but then weakened this emphasis by stressing the allegedly different significance of profit in micro-economic and

[14] The impression that the course has not yet been definitely determined is also supported by the fact that little of the new orientation has found its way into the new program of the Communist Party of the Soviet Union, adopted in the fall of 1961. (The text of this program can be found in a pamphlet, published by the New Leader, *The New Soviet Society,* New York: 1962. Herbert Ritvo of the Massachusetts Institute of Technology has annotated the program; the section on planning is on pp. 146 ff.) The program contains no more important economic innovations than some fairly noncommittal references to the importance of product quality and of the "operative independence and initiative of enterprises" (pp. 149-50). The lapse of time between the adoption of the program and Khrushchev's speech may have given the new ideas more chance to influence the minds of policy makers. But as compared with a party program, even a pronouncement by the most prominent leader is less of a commitment; thus the greater conservatism of the party program may also be due to its character as a document of intended long-range validity, into which the party leadership did not wish to write any ideas that had not yet been tried out, although the supreme leader was willing to throw them into the debate with a tone of approval.

macro-economic decisions: Maximization of profit was very important as an expression of the efficiency of the individual enterprise, but relatively unimportant for the economy as a whole. This distinction is untenable, and unless excess of output over input, in value terms, is the goal of the whole economy as well as of all its units, it will be impossible to make a reality of the principle which Liberman and others advocated: to assure that for every enterprise that course of action leads to the greatest gain which is the most useful for society.

On the problem of pricing, Khrushchev seems to have been more consistently in line with the reformers' ideas. He emphasized the importance of prices based on "scientifically correct" principles. The resolution of the Central Committee, undoubtedly with his approval, was more specific; it criticized the prevailing practice for "not taking into account the possibility of satisfying the demand for individual commodities, not completely reflecting changes in the quality of products, not stimulating enough the production of needed commodities and not always expressing the conditions of production. . . ."[15]

Thus everything points to the conclusion that the Soviet Union is moving toward a more rational system of planning and industrial organization, but the point of no return seems by no means to have been reached and a reversal appears entirely possible. It also remains to be seen how the changes in the planning machinery, which Khrushchev introduced through his report, will affect the content of the plans and the whole operation of the economic system.[16]

Labor Reform

The changes in the organization and direction of industry, and the forces pressing for these changes, reveal the core problems of the present Soviet economy. For a rounded picture, however, it is necessary to observe how the same forces have worked out in some other areas, particularly labor and agriculture.

15 From an article in the party magazine *Kommunist,* reprinted in German in *Ostprobleme* (Bonn) of January 11, 1963, p. 27.

16 As has been mentioned already, the number of *sovnarkhozy* was reduced from 104 to 40 through consolidation. Possibly of more importance than any of the changes in the organization and jurisdiction of the state agencies will be an alteration in the party apparatus dealing with economic problems. On the central, regional and local levels the economic tasks will be divided between a bureau (or committee) for the guidance of agriculture and one for the guidance of industry. This part of the reform may indicate a design to intensify the surveillance of the party over the economic apparatus of the state, with the absorption of the state apparatus into the party bureaucracy as a possible ultimate aim.

In regard to labor, recent changes can be understood only after a glance at the preceding periods. At the start of the First Five Year Plan, controls over labor had been tightened, first by abolishing the remnants of trade union independence—unions had never had more than very limited autonomy since the establishment of the Soviet regime, because union officers were subject to the discipline of the state party—then by making it difficult for the individual worker to change his job; this latter measure had the twofold purpose of preventing excessive labor turnover because of its adverse effect on productivity and to keep workers in industries where they were needed. Measures were also taken to direct the labor supply into the channels desired by the government. Wage incentives were still used for this purpose, but were considered insufficient: Graduates of vocational schools were often obliged, in return for the education they received, to serve for a limited time where the government wanted to send them; and kulaks and other undesirables were consigned to labor camps to perform compulsory service (and often to perish in the process). All this tightening reached its climax on the eve of the Soviet involvement in World War II, when the government assumed the right to conscript labor and allocate it to jobs. This system, including an extended use of labor in penal camps, remained in force during the reconstruction period;[17] but in the early 1950's shortly after the death of Stalin, compulsory labor allocation was abolished, many inmates of penal camps released, and the proper distribution of labor among industries and enterprises sought through wage differentials. Labor unions have again been given a somewhat greater role.[18] It is easy to imagine the relief which the unfettering of the labor market has brought to the average Soviet citizen.

On the labor market as on the commodity market, however, the abolition of direct controls puts a greater weight of importance on the rationality of the price structure. Even in a capitalist economy, the labor market is still more different from the model of perfect competition than many commodity markets: Union pressure, preponderance of employers' power where no unions exist, lack of mobility of labor and many other influences establish wages which fail to reflect with any accuracy the marginal productivity of labor and are certainly not optimal as far as maximizing the social product is concerned. Yet in a capitalistic economy, wages for different categories of workers will always be influenced by the scarcity or abundance of manpower in each category, although that influence may have to compete with

[17] About the development up to 1940, see Baykov, *The Development of the Soviet Economic System*, pp. 335 ff., esp. 350 ff.

[18] See Gregory Grossman, "Structure and Organization . . .", p. 211.

many others. Consequently, if, say, technicians in biological laboratories are in short supply, there will be a premium on becoming a laboratory technician; and if there is an abundance of truckdrivers, earnings will go down, and the drop will act as a deterrent.[19]

In the Soviet Union, "the freeing of the labor market uncovered many anomalies in wage differentials within local labor markets, among industries, and among regions. Undesirable manpower movements occurred, while desirable ones failed to materialize." [20] Between 1956 and 1960, a great wage reform was carried out in the Soviet Union to remedy these defects.

It is still too early to judge the degree to which the goal has been reached. Some doubts, however, suggest themselves when the principles of the reform are considered. In the first place, competing with the motive of steering the supply of workers to the places where they were most needed was apparently the desire to reduce the inequalities of income which had arisen under the earlier system.[21] Many of these inequalities probably had no sufficient economic justification; in some instances, it seems, favorable wage schedules which had originally been instituted to relieve temporary labor bottlenecks in specific fields—even with direct labor controls, it was easier to move workers from industry to industry with the consent of the individuals concerned than against their resistance—had not been removed when the shortages no longer existed. But how did the Soviet government distinguish between unjustified inequalities and those which were necessary to direct labor into the channels of greatest need? In an economy which, under the most favorable interpretation, is just beginning to develop a rational pricing system for commodities, it is impossible to determine the value of the marginal product of labor even with the modest accuracy in which this can be done under capitalism. Was the desire to eliminate inequalities, and the perhaps equally strong desire to maintain privileges for some groups particularly favored by the government, kept in check by calculation of economic needs and costs? It seems that the elements of such calculation were missing, that therefore the check on motives competing with the drive for rationality cannot have been very effective, and that im-

[19] Wage rates, of course, are only one of the determinants of earnings, which also depend on the weekly or monthly hours of work. Wage rates being fairly "sticky," the drop in earnings caused by an oversupply is likely to come first through more frequent layoffs; but if conditions of oversupply continue over a lengthy period, a drop in real, if not in nominal, wage rates—i.e. a failure of money wages to adjust to rising prices—is highly probable.

[20] Walter Galenson, *The Soviet Wage Reform,* Berkeley: Institute of Industrial Relations, University of California (Reprint #172), 1961, p. 9.

[21] *Loc. cit.*, pp. 3 f.

provement as a consequence of the reform was probably limited to the abolition of obvious abuses.

This tentative conclusion is reinforced by the information that "the basic wage scale is established for each industry primarily on the basis of the industry's importance to the development of the national economy, with arduousness of work and average skill level as additional factors." [22] In judging an industry's importance, the Soviet authorities seem to be largely guided by their bias in favor of heavy industry. Yet for a rational determination of wages, not the global importance of the industry but the marginal importance of its output is decisive. Consequently, even if the place of each industry in the hierarchy of industries is correctly allocated in terms of the purposes pursued, not much is gained for an approach to a rational wage scale.

After the most urgent needs of the most important industries are satisfied, rationality requires that the most urgent needs of the secondary industries be met next, before the less urgent needs of the top-priority industries are satisfied. In the past, Soviet policy has given preference to heavy industry in the procurement of labor as in every other respect; according to an apparent consensus of the top leaders in the Soviet Union, the time has come to modify this policy by allowing the consumer a greater share in the annual increment of the social product. This modification will be hindered by a wage scale which continues to make work in producer goods industries more attractive than jobs in consumer goods industries. The latter will probably be able to get enough workers, but if the best workers flock into such branches of production as the machine industry and power generation, it will be impossible to raise the quality of the goods and services which the consumers purchase directly.[23]

[22] Galenson, *op. cit.*, p. 9.

[23] The whole concept of a hierarchy of industries is questionable for anything but a short-range consideration, because with the exception of the production of luxuries, disregard for the needs of one industry, if continued over a substantial period, will usually hurt the other industries. Soviet Russia had some experience with this kind of interdependence of industries already during the civil war, when some branches of production were singled out as "shock industries" and received high priority with respect to supplies. But since at least small quantities of the products of non-shock industries were vital for the operation of the shock industries—for instance a supply of pencils for the munition industries (and for army and government)—the results were intolerable and the "shock" concept had to be modified. See Maurice Dobb, *Soviet Economic Development,* pp., 114f.

This experience is particularly pertinent to the Soviet scene of today because the Soviet Union is undergoing not only an intensive but also an extensive process of industrialization, related to an analogous process in agriculture: Just as the "virgin lands" reclamation program expanded the cultivated area in Siberia, so new industrial centers are arising there continually. To steer labor into these areas requires increased consumers'

Agricultural Reform

The Soviet Union still employs about 40 per cent of its labor force directly in agriculture and thereby normally feeds the rest of the population but without any great margin for the accumulation of reserves; the United States employs less than 9 per cent of its labor force in the same manner and thereby produces embarrassingly large crops which fill government warehouses to the brim.[24] This statistical fact, together with frequent exhortations by Krushchev and other Soviet leaders to improve agricultural methods, plus the obviously experimental character of many of their present agricultural policies, has tended to obscure the remarkable success which the Soviet Union has obtained in the agricultural field in the 1950's. Between 1953 and 1960, agricultural production was raised by approximately 55 per cent.[25] To be sure, there are several circumstances which detract from the effect of this progress. First, it was achieved only through a great expansion of the cultivated area, Khruschev's virgin lands program. Although this does not make the increase any less real, it means that for its achievement a huge investment was required in what the theoreticians of economic development now call infrastructure: building of roads, communication facilities, homes, government offices and other necessities and conveniences for living in new areas, and this need for investment will continue over a considerable time if the new settlers are to be induced to stay on the former virgin lands. On the other hand, the improvement of the land-labor ratio may work out very well in the long run, and other advantages for the Soviet economy may also flow from the opening up of areas until now relatively unproductive and sparsely settled.

---

facilities on a large scale. See on this point a speech by Premier Khrushchev, reported in an article by Leon Herman, "Inside the Soviet Union; the Labor Force: Who Does What?", *Saturday Review*, January 21, 1961, p. 36.

[24] The figures for the United States are calculated from *Statistical Abstract of the United States*, 1961, p. 207; for the Soviet Union, the *Economic Survey of Europe*, published by the United Nations Economic Commission for Europe, gives a figure of 38.8 per cent of the "total working population"; in the figure for the latter (99 million), however, the members of the armed services (3.6 million) are included, and from the figure for agricultural workers almost 10 million unpaid family members working full time or—undoubtedly more often—part time on individual plots are excluded; therefore for purposes of international comparison a somewhat higher Soviet percentage has to be assumed. All the figures refer to 1959 and are taken from the *Economic Survey* for 1960, Ch. II, p. 35.

[25] Grossman, "The Structure and Organization . . .", p. 221. See also the papers submitted to the Joint Economic Committee of Congress by Gale Johnson, Arcadius Kahan and Nancy Nimitz on Soviet agriculture, and their oral statements before that Committee. *Comparisons of the United States and Soviet Economies*, 80th Congress, 1st Session. Washington: Government Printing Office, 1960, Part I, pp. 201 ff, and Hearings, pp. 103 ff.

Second, per capita availability of foodstuffs has increased much less than total agricultural output since the 1930's[26] One reason is the growth of the population despite war losses; also, there was a far greater output in technical crops than in food. Yet most of the time the consumer's larder seems to be better stocked than it has been at any time since the revolution,[27] and probably since the early phase of World War I. What means, other than the virgin lands program, has the Soviet Union employed in increasing agricultural output?

Since the death of Stalin, prices received by the peasant have been substantially raised, thus providing a stimulus to greater production and deliveries.[28] Moreover, in 1958, multiple pricing in the purchases of the state trading organization was abolished through the elimination of compulsory deliveries in the strict sense of the term. The peasant no longer had to pay a tax in kind by delivering to the state part of his crop at low prices; but since the output of the individual kolkhozes is still planned, and since various pressures are available to make the kolkhozes conform to the expectations expressed in the plan, the peasants are not really free to set the line between their private consumption and that part of their crop which is to be sold. Nor are they at liberty to divide their sales between the state agency and the free kolkhoz market as they see fit, because only if they sell sufficient quantities to the state agency will they be able to buy industrial commodities to anything like the extent of their needs. The importance of the price reform of 1958, therefore, has meant perhaps not so much actual increase in farmers' incomes as the removal of a particularly onerous form of the exploitation of the peasantry by the state.[29] There is no doubt, however, about the very substantial rise in farmer's incomes if the whole period since Stalin's death is taken into account.[30]

The price reform of 1958 coincided with another major change in Soviet

[26] See D. Gale Johnson and Arcadius Kahan, "Soviet Agriculture: Structure and Growth," in *Comparisons of United States and Soviet Economies,* Part I, p. 210.

[27] Also, the larder is stocked with higher quality foods. The table supplied by Johnson and Kahan shows that per capita grain output increased by only 20 per cent, whereas sugar beets show an increase by 80 per cent, milk by 53 per cent, meat by 75 per cent for 1955-58 as compared with 1935-38. On the other hand, the food crisis that the Soviet Union faced in the fall of 1963 as a consequence of deficient deliveries demonstrated that the supply situation was precarious and that any extraordinary event, from a regional crop failure to some hitch in the marketing machinery, can bring about temporary privation for the Soviet consumer.

[28] See the paper by Nancy Nimitz in *Comparison of the United States and Soviet Economies,* Part I, pp. 262 ff.

[29] For the 1958 price reform, see Rudolph Schlesinger, "The New Structure of Soviet Agriculture," *Soviet Studies,* Vol. X (1959), No. 3, pp. 234 ff.

[30] "Between 1952 and 1958 collective farm money income increased threefold. The rise was due entirely to increase in receipts from sales to procurement agencies, and largely to the rise in the level of procurement prices." Nancy Nimitz, *op. cit.,* p. 273.

agricultural policy, the sale of the tractors and tractor-drawn agricultural machinery to the kolkhozes. Since this meant the dissolution of the machine-tractor stations which so long had operated as communist propaganda centers and surveillance agencies, the step represented a move toward autonomy for the kolkhozes, although of course they remained still far from being really autonomous cooperatives. One might well surmise that the step was welcomed by the peasantry, although it was not an unmixed blessing. Payment for the equipment and the obligation to keep it in good repair represented considerable financial burdens, which probably without the price raises most kolkhozes would have been unable to bear.[31] The necessity to meet these obligations provided—and was undoubtedly intended to provide—an element of pressure for increasing the volume of sales of produce.

Soviet agricultural policy during the post-Stalin period has also tried to restrict the labor time which the kolkhoz members can spend on their private plots and their private raising of animals, by increasing the amount of time which each kolkhoz member has to work on the collectively managed land. These measures were certainly unpopular, but probably often economically sound, because they distributed the expenditure of labor more equally upon the available area. Ultimately, it seems, the Soviet leaders intend to liquidate the private plots entirely, at least insofar as they do not merely provide for the household needs of the family. Such a major change, however, would meet with the greatest resistance unless work for the kolkhoz were made more attractive than it is now, especially in the matter of compensation. As a member of the kolkhoz, the peasant bears too much risk to be left without adequate earnings, since the revenue of the kolkhoz is determined as a residual, after all the fixed costs are deducted from the revenue. It might be argued that grievances on this account are unjustified because the kolkhoz peasant cannot have it both ways: If he wishes to be a member of a cooperative with an entrepreneurial role, rather than a worker on the payroll of the state, then he has to accept entrepreneurial risks. The fault in this argument lies in the fact that the kolkhoz members do not have the freedom of decision of a true entrepreneur, and the relationship between costs and chances of profit are not sufficiently favorable in any event to make the bearing of risks worthwhile. True, the situation has improved through removal of the obligation to sell a fixed quantity at decidedly unrewarding prices; before that, a bad crop resulted in a low price per unit sold for the produce of a kolkhoz, because little remained to be sold after the low-priced obligatory deliveries had been effected. Now the unitary price, which will presumably be permitted to fluctuate to some extent with har-

[31] See Rudolph Schlesinger, *op. cit.*, p. 233.

vest results, may cause a tendency of the price "to vary directly with cost, instead of inversely, as under the multiple price system." [32]

The disadvantage from the peasant's point of view in having merely a residual income has not escaped the Soviet authorities, and there are indications that remedial action is considered, or that at least the Soviet government will permit those kolkhozes which by their own efforts have sufficiently strengthened their economic base to give their members greater stability of income. In many kolkhozes, more extensive advance payments or deliveries seem to have been made recently to kolkhoz members against their eventual claims to a share in the kolkhoz income, and some kolkhozes have introduced a system of fixed wages for the *trudoden.*[33] If the latter change becomes more general, the difference between the kolkhoz farm and that of state farms will be reduced, and eventually the state farm may replace the kolkhoz entirely. In recent years the number and area of state farms has already increased considerably.[34] The official tendency to favor "farm giantism," i.e. the merger of kolkhozes of small or middle size, sometimes even of large acreage, will operate in the same direction: The larger a collective farm, the more difficult it becomes to ultilize the potentialities of cooperative organization; the individual will feel unable to exert any appreciable influence on the actions of the collective, and since influence even in smaller units is very much limited by state supervision and regulation, it seems that the stake of the individual member in the preservation of the kolkhoz form is small or non-existent. Especially if the replacement of kolkhozes by state farms is accompanied by an extension of trade union protection to agricultural workers[35]—even in the limited sense in which Soviet

[32] Nancy Nimitz, *op. cit.*, p. 267. The reason why this effect is not certain lies in the question of how far the price will be permitted to fluctuate with crop results. The kolkhoz remains, in fact, obligated to conclude a sales contract with the state trading agency for a fixed quantity. The state agency, a monopolistic buyer, can determine the price and will certainly keep it below prices obtainable on the free kolkhoz market. As before the reform, the kolkhoz can bring less produce to the kolkhoz market, after fulfillment of its contract, in bad years than in good years. The prices on the kolkhoz market will rise if there is a shortage, but often the quantity to be sold there will be too small to have any great effect on the average unit price received by the kolkhoz. That price, in bad years much more than in good years, will be primarily dependent on the contract price; and will the state agency permit this price to go up sufficiently to compensate the kolkhoz for the smallness of the portion of its harvest which in bad years it can spare for sale on the kolkhoz market?

[33] See the paper by Lazar Volin, of the US Department of Agriculture, "Agricultural Policy of the Soviet Union," in *Comparisons of the United States and Soviet Economies,* p. 292.

[34] See Volin, *op. cit.*, p. 293.

[35] There seem to be some tendencies of this kind, induced by the absorption of the personnel of the former machine-tractor stations by the kolkhozes; see Schlesinger, *op. cit.*, p., 239 f.

labor unions can offer such protection—the change may be beneficial to the agricultural population.

The critical importance of agricultural policy for the economic system of the Soviet Union has the same basic cause as it had in earlier periods, but the resulting problems are more difficult to solve. Agriculture has always been the great labor reservoir of Soviet industry; when the First Five Year Plan was initiated, the marginal productivity of labor in agriculture was so low as to make it possible to draw many workers away from the farms without a substantial reduction of agricultural product. Collectivization, intended to strengthen this possibility of maintaining or even increasing agricultural output with a diminished labor force, instead reduced it in the early phase, by creating an extraneous cause of disturbance; only when tractorization became effective did the continued diversion of labor from the farms prove to be compatible with an increased farm production. But tractorization and other forms of mechanization have brought most of the advantages they were able to bring. If further withdrawals of labor from agriculture for the benefit of industrial growth are to be effected without causing a new grave food deficit, increase of agricultural productivity must be sought by other methods, and all of these methods depend on a higher level of education and a greater amount of willing effort in the agricultural population.

There is a qualitative, in addition to the quantitative, problem. "Collective farming cannot fully develop as long as the most capable and ambitious boys and girls are drawn to the towns, nor can their migration be stopped as long as the earnings achievable in agriculture are inferior to industrial ones." [36] Therefore, even if some pockets of agricultural surplus labor can still be found, a continued migration from country to city without assurance that the quality of remaining agricultural labor will not further decline would be unbearable. This makes it urgent to rebuild morale on the farm and offer the agricultural worker attractions which can compete with those of city life. Should the Soviet Union succeed in concluding a disarmament agreement with the West and thus be able to transfer labor from defense industries to consumer goods industries without reducing the output of capital goods, this task will not be too difficult; without disarmament, the problem will be a hard nut to crack for the Soviet leaders.

[36] Schlesinger, *op. cit.*, p. 244.

CHAPTER 19

KHRUSHCHEV'S RUSSIA: THE SOVIET SYSTEM IN TRANSITION

One More Glance at the Soviet Pricing System

LET US CONSIDER the following two statements:

> In the Soviet economy, prices are not an autonomous force determining production, resource allocation, and consumption. Instead, prices are manipulated by the central authorities as one of various instruments intended to accomplish their planned goals.
>
> Morris Bornstein, "The Soviet Price System," *American Economic Review,* March 1962, p. 64.

> Under socialism, goods are produced solely for the satisfaction of specific social needs for them; and it is for this reason that so much attention is paid to the problem of the quality of production, its efficiency and productivity, to the problem of use value, and to the so-called physical indicators as well as value indicators. . . . But what can this have in common with the subjectivist treatment of "marginal utility" in capitalist conditions, where a commodity is produced with an eye to profit and superprofit? In this case not even analogy is possible.
>
> S. Y. Turetski, "Soviet Price Policy: A Rejoinder" [to Maurice Dobb], *Soviet Studies,* Vol. XII (1960-61), pp. 438-9.

The weakness of the Turetski statement is obvious. If it is stripped of elements irrelevant in this context—especially the implication that profit motivation precludes the orientation of production toward consumers' wants—there remains the belief that the marginal utility concept is "subjectivist," i.e. derived from individual psychology, and therefore not applicable to the conscious pursuit of social purposes. Certainly, the theory of marginal utility is related to some elementary facts of individual psychology.

But all human purposes are purposes of individuals, even if they require social activities for their fulfillment and call for a particular organization of society; therefore all needs that play a role in economic calculation are needs felt by individuals, whether they concern a citizen's individual consumption, or a planner's desire to build the foundations of a large industry for the benefit of future generations, or a "spectator's" interest in the prevalence of human solidarity over profit seeking among the driving forces of economic action. All these needs are subject to the rule that their ugency declines with increasing saturation. They are, therefore, subject to the principle that in rational procedure, the least important partial satisfaction must be more important than the addition to total cost required by this partial satisfaction.

Moreover, not only are planners' preferences themselves subject to the principle of marginalism, but planners must also take into account the operation of the same principle in the satisfaction of consumers for which they are planning. Some wants of Soviet planners have little or no reference to consumers' wants; for instance, the desire of Soviet planners to increase the industrial population for the reason that they believe industrial workers to be politically more reliable is probably not shared outside the circle of party leaders who in a broad, non-technical sense can all be regarded as planners. Obviously, however, many incentives for industrialization have sprung from desires for the satisfaction of citizens' wants, either individual or collective, either in the present or in the future. In other words, individual utility, even in the narrower sense of the word in which it does not refer simply to wants felt by individuals—which is true of all wants—but merely to wants for individual consumption, or for collective consumption purposes of the people at large, is an essential element of social utility. What Turetski says about use value implies a recognition of this basic fact, but this recognition is inconsistent with his rejection of "subjectivism."

Nevertheless, because individual satisfaction may compete with other goals in planners' purposes, and especially because the weighing of present against future satisfaction may be carried out with a different scale of priorities by planners than by individual consumers, the prices determined by planners' preferences may differ greatly from the prices determined—in an economy with like resources—by the preferences of individual consumers. But this does not mean that the process of price formation is essentially different; it merely serves other peoples' preferences. Like the forces guiding a ship, the essential difference lies not in the steering mechanism, but in the captain's directives as to where to steer.

Bornstein's statement suffers from the ambiguity of the terms "autonomous" and "manipulated." Since planners' preferences are in part substituted for those of ultimate consumers in the price-determining process, Soviet prices are certainly not autonomous in the sense of being completely determined by some anonymous force. But neither are they set completely arbitrarily, that is in disregard of all determinants outside the will of the price-setting authority. Supply schedules and demand schedules are taken into account, whereby the demand is in part that of ultimate consumers and in part the expression of the planners' own priority schedules. Even in the latter case, however, the Soviet planner of today does not deliberately divorce himself from the limitations which economic rationality imposes on his freedom of action; he still strives to select from purposes competing for a given resource unit the one that is the most important. That he does so with inadequate understanding, because he feels committed to the labor value theory, that therefore the prices are distorted, that they cannot rationally serve as guides for production to the same extent as prices in capitalism or in the Western models of socialism, that they have to be supplemented by a number of "indicators" is all perfectly true. But the element of autonomy which still exists in the Soviet price system should not be obscured, because it alone makes possible the element of rationality in Soviet price calculation without which the Soviet economic successes would become inexplicable.

The term "manipulated" has a similar ambiguity. A car is manipulated by the driver. On a wide and firm salt flat, it may be driven straight, or in zig-zag, or in circles, according to the driver's whim, and with any speed he selects. In dense city traffic, the car has to stay in one lane; its speed is determined by the requirements of safety and law, and the driver, once he has chosen his destination, is, for all further decisions, as much or more the servant of objective necessities as he is master of his automobile. Obviously, there is a great deal of difference between these two kinds of manipulation. In the second alternative, the movements of the car are for the most part determined by forces beyond the will of the driver, though they operate through the driver's mind. In the same sense, Soviet prices, although manipulated, are at the same time largely determined by forces outside of the planners' will, although they operate by being recognized by the planner when he announces the prices and takes measures to assure their observance.

"Manipulated" and "autonomous" are mutually exclusive concepts only if the former is understood in the sense of "manipulated with complete arbitrariness," or if "autonomous" is so defined as to imply not only that a result is determined by forces existing outside the will of any manipulator but also that these forces must assert themselves automatically, that is, not through the will of a manipulator. To return to the automobile driver, the narrower concept of autonomy would require that the necessary adjustment of the movements and the speed of the car to the flow of traffic and to the traffic regulations be controlled automatically, as by an electronic brain, rather than through the mind of the driver. Of course, it is logically possible to define the two terms so as to make them mutually exclusive, but it is not likely that Bornstein or any other contemporary economist—with the possible exception of an extremist of the Mises school[1]—would accept the full consequences of such definitions. Modern economics has generally endorsed the statement by Wicksteed:

> "Price" . . . in the narrower sense of "the money for which a material thing, a service or a privilege can be obtained" is simply a special kind of "price" in the wider sense of "the terms on which alternatives are offered to us"; and to consider whether a thing is worth the price that is asked for it, is to consider whether the possession of it is more to be desired than anything we can have instead of it, and whether it will compensate us for everything we must take along with it.[2]

This statement implies that the important aspect of the price mechanism is not its functioning as an automaton, and that alternatives realized by a "manipulator" who is willing to let himself be guided by this insight—that is, who is not acting arbitrarily—can in principle lead to prices just as rational as those formed on a market of "live" buyers and sellers.

Turetski's and Bornstein's propositions tend to obscure the similarities between the price-forming process and the role of prices in capitalism and in Soviet Communism. At least with Bornstein, whose article is a very informative presentation of several aspects of Soviet pricing, this is not a question of his basic approach but primarily a matter of phrasing a sentence that represents a sort of summary without containing some of the necessary reservations. Yet this choice of misleading terms is characteristic of a fault to which experts on the Soviet economy sometimes succumb: to overemphasize the salient peculiarities of Soviet economic methods in relation to capitalistic methods so that they overshadow the analogous functions which these methods are to serve in both systems, as well as the analogies in the mode of operation of the methods resulting from the analogy of functions. For the purpose of a comparison of systems, it is vitally necessary to recognize the analogy of functions and its consequences, because only by understanding similarities, or even identical elements, in the two systems can we

[1] See above, p. 260.

[2] Philip H. Wicksteed, *The Common Sense of Political Economy* (1910). Re-ed. 1935, Vol. I, p. 28.

hope to understand the differences. The inclination of Soviet economists to deny the analogies to the capitalist system, their claim that Soviet methods of economic operation have much less in common with "bourgeois" economics than in reality they do—the Turetski statement is one example in many—aggravates the task, but it is as necessary to penetrate the fog created by communist illusions and pretenses as to discard other forms of the underestimation of basic similarities among modern economic systems.

When we compare price formation and the role of prices in the Soviet Union and in capitalist countries, therefore, it is necessary to determine in what sense Soviet prices are autonomous and what room the Soviet system leaves for arbitrary influences on prices, and in what ways Soviet prices actually influence production, resources allocation and consumption. Only by this approach is it possible to understand the function of the turnover tax in equilibrating supply and demand, the importance of the new emphasis on profitability of production units for making prices effective orientation points for production, of the fiscal interest of the state as a factor promoting the development of value planning. Against the background of what the two systems have in common in regard to prices, the differences—from the distortions of prices by the labor value theory to the influence of the lower time preference—will appear more clearly.

Even if the economic administration of the Soviet Union were to abandon its commitment to the labor value theory and acknowledge that prices must be determined by the significance of goods for want satisfaction; if, furthermore, the Soviet administrators removed all physical controls, including the imposition of physical production targets on enterprises; if they relied entirely on prices and the profit-and-loss account for making the production units and the consumers comply with the plan, and if they established a unified rate of time preference: Even after such a far-reaching reform the economic processes would still take a different course in the Soviet Union as compared with a capitalist country having the same resources and inhabited by a population with the same individual and collective preferences. This difference would exist because Soviet planners would in part substitute their own preferences for those of the consumers. Although they would not, to repeat an earlier statement, try to make consumers buy unwanted overcoats for wanted trousers, they would produce more military equipment than was desired by consumers, individually or as citizens, and they would also establish a preference for industrial equipment exceeding the wants of the citizens, who would prefer more kitchen utensils, radios, washing machines and motorcycles. In such a reformed Soviet system, the purchasing power of the state, accumulated by collecting—mainly through the turnover tax or a similar device—a large part of the price which the consumer must pay for merchandise, would in turn bid up the price for materials and semifinished products to the point where the competing bids of consumers could obtain only limited satisfaction. Although the Soviet administrators of today are far from confining themselves to the use of the instruments assumed in this example to be the only ones employed, the model is not pure fancy: If present trends within the Soviet economy are not stopped, reality might come close to the model in a decade or two, or even sooner.

Western countries have no planners equipped with powers as great as those in the Soviet Union, but the technical process of transferring purchasing power from individuals to the state and using it for politically determined purposes is of course not unknown in Western-type economies, and here as in the communist orbit this state-appropriated purchasing power is used for bids on the resource markets in competition with the citizens' demand for consumer goods. This is the way that resources are channeled into defense industries, into the building of public schools and hospitals and into road construction in the United States and elsewhere. But there is a most important difference: In the Soviet Union, planners' preferences are uncontrolled, or controlled only indirectly and with low effectiveness, through that modicum of influence which public opinion has even in a dictatorship. In the United States and other countries with Western-type institutions, the public authorities can drain purchasing power into the public funds only to the extent approved by the representatives of the citizens, in theory—and to a considerable extent in practice—expressing the collective judgment of these citizens. Similarly, although the fiscal and monetary authorities in Western countries may take all sorts of measures to promote economic growth, they cannot do so except within the framework of laws which have been approved by popularly elected representatives and which these representatives can change when they deem it desirable. Thus the difference between the Soviet and Western-type economies—capitalist and socialist alike—does not lie exclusively in the techniques used, but even more in the influence of the political constitution upon the economy; even if the difference in techniques were to disappear, the character of the economic systems and the results of their operation would still by no means become alike or even similar—unless the modified techniques were in turn to modify the communist political system. Something like this has happened before: In Western Europe, from the thirteenth century on, the use of monetary techniques by the feudal aristocracy for putting its privileged position to economic advantage has led to progressive disintegration of the political system of feudalism. But it would be hazardous to assume that in this matter history must repeat itself, although it would be equally unwarranted to exclude the possibility.

The Four "Bricks" in Soviet Communism

The large part played by the command principle in the Soviet economy needs merely to be summarized. Industrial enterprises are ordered to comply with specific, quantitive provisions of the plan. It is true that they are given a hearing at the preparatory stage, but once a decision is reached at the government level they must comply. The commanding power of management within the plant seems to be even more pronounced than in the capitalist system; all the regulations emphasize the responsibility and therefore the power of the manager over the personnel. The limitations on the independence of labor unions reduces the protective effect of these organizations for the individual worker, although the restoration of even a limited autonomy has undoubtedly been felt as a benefit by the working population. The extent to which the command principle applies to agriculture has been discussed before; although the abolition of compulsory deliveries at especially low prices has, as a matter of form, substituted exchange for command in the channeling of produce to the consuming centers, this substitution has little if any reality, because the state trading agency still sets the prices for the bulk of agricultural output as it sees fit, through the use of its monopoly power.

The extensive area of command has its concommitant in a relatively small area of exchange. But, though this area is small by comparison with capitalist countries, it has been growing for some time. The abolition of rationing made exchange the instrument for the distribution of consumer goods; the abolition of direct controls over labor did the same for the allocation of human resources to different branches and units of production.

It is difficult to assess the role of solidarity in the Soviet Union. To be sure, the nation has a complete system of social insurance legislation,[3] with fairly satisfactory benefits considering the low general standard of living; the public health service is very good—there is, of course, no organized resistance of the medical profession to "socialized medicine." In offering personal services, such as counseling by welfare workers trained in psychology, the Soviet Union is greatly inferior to the United States, though possibly not to most West European countries. Thus the Soviet Union has faithfully

[3] For details see US Department of Health, Education and Welfare (Social Security Administration), *A Report on Social Security Programs in the Soviet Union,* prepared by a team that visited the USSR under the East-West exchange program in August-September 1958. Washington, D.C.: Government Printing Office, 1960.

carried out the postulates of the older socialist programs in the field of ameliorative legislation, but has not achieved any great progress in those areas where the spirit of human solidarity has carried some Western nations beyond the old concepts. Should this be interpreted as a sign that in the case of the Soviet Union we have to deal with a rather ossified system of welfare policy, which may perhaps be efficient in the operation of its institutions but from which the original impulses have largely vanished? There is little doubt that at times such an interpretation would have been correct: Not only under Stalin, but already under Lenin, Soviet Communism had been struggling against the socialist humanitarian tradition because it tended to impose restraints upon governmental power which the Communists considered unacceptable in the transition from capitalism to communism. The harsh climate which was thus deliberately created must have driven much of the spirit of human solidarity from the administration of public welfare. This spirit cannot be rationed or directed only to some kinds of human misery in disregard of others. It would have been impossible for a welfare administration imbued with the spirit from which all welfare policy ultimately draws its sustenance to disregard the sufferings of despoiled kulak families in the early 1930's or those of the wives and children of the alleged conspirators or dissenters who were exiled, imprisoned or executed between 1936 and 1941, or right after World War II; but any welfare administrators who would have attempted to take up these tasks would have collided head-on with the official policy and would undoubtedly have shared the fate of the victims.

But is the diagnosis of ossification true today, after the various "thaws" which, to be sure, were followed by partial "re-freezing"? There is not sufficient evidence to answer that question. Nor do we have any way of knowing whether in private life the average Soviet citizen, compared with the citizens of capitalist countries, is more inclined, less inclined, or equally inclined to undertake or omit action for reasons other than expectation of personal gain, fear of a commanding power, or staying in the rut of tradition—that is, how often he is motivated by consideration for the good of others. Again, there is much reason to believe that during the previous periods of great stress, when everybody in a wide circle of individuals was afraid lest disaster might strike them and could do little to avert the blow (except perhaps denounce their neighbors), the rule of behavior was on the whole: Every man for himself, and the devil take the hindmost. In those memoirs that have pictured the atmosphere in the years of terror, there is little mention of mutual help among potential or actual victims, or assistance to the latter by people who had no reason to feel threatened—if there were such people. This, of course, does not prove that Russians are less kind or courageous than other nations, but merely that demoralization was general.

It will undoubtedly be years before we can sufficiently probe into the minds of the common man in Russia to arrive at a considered judgment on the role of human solidarity in the contemporary every-day relations among persons in the Soviet Union. When we do find out, we shall have a better clue to some of the characteristics of Soviet society than any analysis of the institutional setup can give us.

As for group solidarity, we have a somewhat stronger basis for an opinion than we had in judging the extent and intensity of general human solidarity. Although the contention that there has been a peasant or a kulak conspiracy has always been a communist political legend, it is likely that some feeling of solidarity united the agricultural population against the authorities, perhaps against the city dwellers in general; almost certainly, members of the same kolkhoz are tied together not only by a partial community of economic interests but also by a willingness to stand together against the outside world, even where such a course does not yield the individual any palpable benefits. The officers of the Red Army undoubtedly have an *esprit de corps,* such as exists in every good army; some features of the Soviet system of government are apt to strengthen this spirit. Compared with the Western democracies, the Soviet system is essentially unstable in the sense that the succession of a ruler, or even continuation of a ruler in power, depends upon the unpredictable decisions of a relatively small circle —the leadership of the Communist Party. Under these conditions, a body which wields superior physical power—even if it never intends to use this power in internal struggles—cannot consistently stay out of politics and it has, therefore, a high stake in its own internal political unity. The army needs political power for self-protection, for without such power it may easily be turned into an instrument of a political faction, the purposes of which it does not approve, and it can have political power only if there is solidarity within its officer corps. Of course, the army may also pursue positive goals, and then has an even greater need for internal solidarity.

After all the ingenious theories that have been developed about the "managerial revolution" of our age,[4] there is great temptation to believe that

[4] The idea that the upper layer of the administrative personnel, both in business and government, was bound to become the dominating class in modern society and would soon shake off control by political leaders and masses was first effectively proposed by James Burnham in his book *The Managerial Revolution* (New York: John Day, 1941). Burnham was an extremist and not too many of his numerous original followers continue to believe in a dictatorship of the managers as the impending fate of mankind, but an

industrial managers in the Soviet Union feel a high degree of "class solidarity," and the narrow and yet fluid limits of their authority would offer good reasons for a development of a feeling that they must either "hang together or hang separately"; but whether such a feeling actually has any strength no outsider can tell. Nor do we know much about the remnants of class solidarity among the workers. The Soviet labor movement has been effectively fragmentized, by sapping the vitality of national labor unions; but this does not mean that workers in an individual enterprise feel nothing any more of the sentiment which makes "an injury to one an injury to all"—a sentiment which was very strong before the revolution.

The role of tradition in Soviet economic policy is strong and largely negative: Marxist value theory is a great impediment to rationalization of the pricing system and to value planning. But when we think of tradition as a coordinating force in the economy, we think primarily of the motivation of the managers of individual economic units—how often they act not under the influence of independent thoughts as to what may be profitable or what may be conducive to the good of others, or what may be necessary to stay out of trouble with the authorities, but simply do what has always—or for a long time—been done by Russians in the same position. Probably management in agriculture is still largely traditional in this sense; otherwise the low productivity of agricultural work in the Soviet Union would hardly be possible. In industry, on the other hand, the changes from NEP to planning, and after the war the changes from the branch administration to territorial administration, with the forms and limitations of the latter still in flux, must have operated against the evolution of a firm tradition; another impediment to this evolution is probably the unsolved problem of how to balance the obligation to achieve physical targets against the obligation to make ends meet in terms of money, because such an open question leads to continuous experimentation with basic rules. If Soviet policy can settle these problems in a manner that will make wholesale reorganization unnecessary for a substantial period, a tradition of business management will undoubtedly grow up and contribute to efficiency; for just as the existence of a tradition too rigid to permit change may lead to stagnation, so the absence or great weakness of technical traditions leads to waste of effort. Optimal solutions cannot be obtained where every manager has to find out for himself how to handle his relations with customers, staff and supervising and directing agencies, without ever being able to rely on precedent.

---

exaggerated idea of the political influence and of the inner coherence of the managerial "class" has remained as a heritage of "Burnhamism."

Soviet Production, Growth and Productivity

PAST RECORD AND PRESENT STATE

The Soviet Union is, and will remain, at least for a long period, inferior to the United States in terms of absolute volume of production. Gerhart Colm of the National Planning Association gives the figures shown in Table 6.

TABLE 6

GROSS NATIONAL PRODUCT OF THE SOVIET UNION IN PER CENT OF GROSS NATIONAL PRODUCT OF THE UNITED STATES ON THE BASIS OF 1958 PRICES [5]

	Actual		Projected	
	1957	1958	1965	1970
Aggregate	40	43	45	48
Per capita	33	36	38	41

[5] See *Comparisons of the US and Soviet Economies,* Part II, p. 534. The table given by Colm is abbreviated here; based on US State Dept. and NPA estimates.

This table, however, has no greater claim to reliability than that it reflects, in Dr. Colm's words, "the general order of magnitude" of the differences as they have existed in the recent past and are likely to exist in some future years. The projected figures may not prove to be very accurate. In the first place, although for the past we know the performance of the United States economy, we do not know what it will be in the future, especially whether any recessions will occur between now and 1970, and how frequent and how serious they will be. On the other hand, although we may assume that at least for the next decade the Soviet economy will not see a business cycle, there are many question marks with respect to future Soviet production, especially the development of productivity which will be discussed a little later. But there are also great uncertainties with regard to the figures of the recent past. The problem of the reliability of Soviet statistical data, it is true, has been greatly reduced not only by a lessening of the influence of propaganda purposes upon Soviet statistics, but also by the progress of methods available to Western analysts in checking Soviet statistics for consistency. Still, not even such seemingly unambiguous terms as output of electric power or of coal mean the same thing in the United States and in the Soviet Union;[6] although many of these discrepancies are known and are taken into account by Western statisticians when comparing production of the Soviet Union with corresponding figures for the United States and other Western countries, the methods by which correction is achieved themselves

[6] See Robert W. Campbell, "Problems of United States-Soviet Economic Comparisons," in *Comparisons of United States and Soviet Economies,* Part I, pp. 15 ff.

involve uncertainties which can often be resolved only by more or less arbitrary judgment. Even more formidable is another problem: ". . . the task of aggregating these separate indicators into total measures"—such as national income or gross national product—"is extremely difficult because of the absence of a meaningful price system for weighting purposes." [7] This, of course, is the same problem of aggregation which has been met before in the discussion of Soviet planning.

The figures in the last table already give some indication of economic growth in the Soviet Union. In the period from 1950 to 1957, the tempo of growth as measured by the increase in gross national product, was 75 per cent faster in the Soviet Union than in the United States (6.3 per cent annually as against 3.6 per cent),[8] and if the comparison were to be carried to 1962, the result would be still more unfavorable for the United States because of the two recessions of 1958 and 1960.

There is a temptation, however, not to regard the United States as representative of countries with a capitalist system in regard to rates of growth, because some European nations have been able to achieve far greater increases in recent years, West Germany being the outstanding example, with some others e.g. Italy, not too far behind;[9] considering the inevitable inaccuracies of statistical methods, which make it advisable to discount small differences, it may be justified to regard the growth of these countries as about as fast as that of the Soviet Union. Is the relatively slow growth of the United States perhaps a characteristic of maturity rather than its ecomonic system, and therefore a phenomenon which must arise in the Soviet Union and other communist countries as well?

[7] See William L. Thorp, "Soviet Economic Growth and US Policy," in *Comparisons of United States and Soviet Economies,* Part III, p. 572.

[8] See Colm, *ibid.*

[9] France could be mentioned too, but it may be regarded as a semi-socialist country and therefore not characteristic of capitalism.

Statistically, Britain offers a far less favorable picture. It is not easy to reconcile this picture with the signs of affluence that meet the eye of the observer of the British scene, and it is hard to avoid the suspicion that fallacies in the statistical procedures are responsible for this discrepancy.

On the other hand Japan, a country with an unquestionably capitalistic system, has the fastest growth of all major nations. However, it seems that the Japanese case has so many peculiar features that it does not easily lend itself to generalizations. Figures of the gross national product of the USSR, West Germany, United Kingdom, France and Italy in percentages of the corresponding figures for the United States in 1960, with projections to 1970, have been given by Stanley Hunter, using estimates by Stanley H. Cohn, in the 1962 hearings before the Joint Economic Committee of Congress. *See Dimensions of Soviet Power,* hearings, together with compilation of studies prepared for the Joint Economic Committee, Congress of the United States, Washington: Government Printing Office, 1962, p. 52. For the decade, the anticipated annual growth rates are: U.S. 4.25, USSR 6.25, West Germany 4.75, U.K. 3.75, France and Italy 5.25 each. The projections, of course, are very rough estimates.

No clear-cut answer to this question is possible. The problem is a special case of a more general ambiguity: Each capitalistic and each communistic country is different not only in its economic system but also in a number of other characteristics, one of which is its stage of maturity. Therefore, empirical evidence, without careful analysis, cannot tell us very much that would be relevant to a comparison of economic systems. But analysis can help us to sort out some differences which are the effect of the economic system from others which are not; there remains, then, an intermediate area in which separation is difficult—sometimes impossible and sometimes feasible merely to the extent of stating the likelihood or improbability of preponderant differences in the system causing certain phenomena. That is true of system comparisons in general, but the intermingling of effects of very different origin is particularly important in regard to the rate of growth.

The example of Western Europe certainly proves that rapid growth is no monopoly of communism. Furthermore, as will be shown later, there is strong reason to assume that Soviet growth will indeed be slowed down as the Soviet economy matures. But it would be rash on this account to dismiss the American experience of slow growth in recent years as irrelevant to the comparative growth potential of differing economic systems and merely characteristic of an advanced stage of development. In the first place, the European experience has simply not lasted long enough to sustain the full weight of serving as evidence for the proposition that capitalism can assure as fast and steady a rate of growth as the Soviet Union has experienced in recent decades. The European economies have been growing rapidly for not much more than one decade—some for a shorter period—and that means approximately 50 per cent longer than the prosperity of the same countries, plus the United States, lasted after the First World War. In contrast, the rapid growth of the Soviet Union, disregarding the years of war and immediate postwar reconstruction, has lasted at least three times as long. It is most unlikely that the European boom will be cut short by a collapse like that of the late 1920's, but neither is it probable that it will continue for decades without interruption, unless new devices of economic foresight and equilibration can be built into the economic system. To show what those devices would have to be, how they might perhaps be developed and made to work, an analysis of the American economy and its growing potential is as important as an analysis of the European economies, especially because the latter, in many respects, are becoming more similar to the economy of the United States.

This leads to the second point. The question cannot be posed simply as a problem of maturity effects or system effects. If we do not merely look at the situation right now but also at the situation of tomorrow, the most important question is how well either system is equipped to handle the problem of further growth from an already mature position, and what changes might be necessary to secure a growth potential that will not become too greatly reduced at a high stage of development. Obviously, for this purpose a comparison between the United States and the Soviet Union is even more relevant than comparing the latter with Western Europe.

In trying to find the reasons why American growth has been slower than the Soviet Union's, one of the steps most obviously called for is a comparison of investment rates. Yet when the rates of gross investment are compared without further analysis, it does not seem that the United States is very far behind its rival. The United States invests 21 per cent of its gross national product, whereas the figure for the Soviet Union is 25 per cent.[10] However, the United States, being the older industrial country, possesses a larger stock of capital equipment. Consequently, a larger portion of gross investment must be used to replace worn-out or obsolete equipment in the United States than in the Soviet Union. It seems that capital consumption allowances in the United States amount to approximately 9 per cent of the gross national product;[11] this would mean that only about 12 per cent of the gross national product of the United States represents net investment. Soviet net investment, while not known with any high degree of accuracy, must represent a much higher percentage of gross investment and therefore of gross national product because of the still smaller size of the physical plant.[12]

Comparing the net investment rates, however, might give too unfavorable a picture of the position of the United States. A substantial part of Soviet investment is devoted to agriculture and is very much needed. A smaller part of American investment is in agriculture, and to raise it would do little good, because the United States does not need a greater output of standard agricultural products than it now has. With respect to none of the targets of competition between the United States and Soviet Union: defense, foreign aid, living standards, would the United States gain any advantage by increasing its production of wheat, corn, butter or cotton. The USSR needs agricultural investment not only because it can very well use greater crops but also because only by applying more labor saving devices on the farms

10 Gerhart Colm, *op. cit.*, p. 535.

11 Calculated from figures in *US Income and Output,* 1959: US Department of Commerce, p. 138, in conjunction with later figures in *Survey of Current Business.*

12 This seems certain although an important part of new Soviet investment—seems to have a much shorter useful life than the same type of investment in the United States, due to the particularly low quality of output in the Soviet construction industry.

can it continue to transfer workers from agriculture to industry. The Soviet Union thus needs substantial agricultural investment to prevent a decline of the industrial rate of growth, or even to keep that decline within tolerable limits; the United States can easily dispense with such investment. This advantage of the United States is important, but not important enough to justify complacence about the present rate of growth, and therefore of net investment, as long as the Soviet Union achieves the increases which it is now obtaining, and as long as the rivalry between the two countries continues.

The different role of agriculture is not the only respect with which the pattern of Soviet investment deviates from the American pattern. The low priority accorded to consumption expresses itself not only in a high share of investment and a correspondingly low share of consumption in gross national product, but also in a high concentration of investment in capital goods industries; obviously, the latter feature is the prerequisite of the former over any period of some length. Among the activities which were more or less starved in the distribution of investment funds were housing and service industries. There is little doubt that the Soviet Union has done less in these fields than would have been optimal even for industrial development—transfer of workers to the places where they were most needed has been impaired by lack of housing; inadequate repair services for productive equipment have probably interfered with output, and in the consumer goods sphere are likely to have forced workers into an excessive "do-it-yourself" activity, at the expense of the energies they could have devoted to their proper work. The United States, on the other hand, has a great deal of investment which serves consumers' convenience without making any appreciable contribution to growth; if economic growth were regarded as the only purpose, both of the patterns would have to be changed—which one the more, cannot now be ascertained.[13]

To what extent is the more rapid rate of growth of the Soviet economy a result of the political and economic system of the Soviet Union? Even before the First Five Year Plan, which brought about so great a reduction of standards of consumption, living standards in the Soviet were too low for a high potential of voluntary saving. Therefore the high rate of investment had to be imposed by the government. But no democratic government could have done this job; any government that would have withheld resources from citizens' consumption to the extent that was done in the early days of Soviet

[13] Since economic growth is a purpose of higher priority in the Soviet Union, the Soviet pattern deviates from the optimum in terms of its own set of purposes, which is not necessarily true of the United States.

planning would have been swept out of office in a country in which the government depended on the consent of the governed. Although today the Soviet citizens have a higher standard of living and therefore can save more without depriving themselves of necessities, there is good reason to believe that even now voluntary savings would not release sufficient funds, and therefore resources, for economic expansion at anything like the pace which Soviet reality shows.

In the United States, per capita income is much greater, and consequently there is much more potential for voluntary saving. Actually, saving in the United States—including accumulation of profits by business corporations—would probably suffice for a much higher rate of investment than the present one, possibly for a rate equal to that of the Soviet Union.[14] In a capitalistic economy, however, there are two decisions to be made in order to effect investment: One is to provide the funds, and the other is to use them for business expansion. These decisions are not entirely independent of one another,[15] but they are not so closely linked as to make sure that all investable funds will really be invested. In the Soviet Union, the government decides what funds to withhold from consumers' incomes and where to invest them. The government has not always succeeded in withholding enough income from consumers to equal the increase in investment, and the consequence has been inflation, but there has never been any doubt that every ruble spared from consumption would find use in investment. The Soviet Union, therefore, has used its productive capacity much more steadily and fully than the United States.[16] This is as important a reason for the difference in growth rates as the ability of the Soviet dictatorship to impose a low time preference on the Soviet economy.

The reason that a businessman in a capitalist system may decide not to invest available funds is usually the uncertainty as to whether the additional

[14] Increased investment—other than the involuntary "investment" of businessmen in inventories which are enlarged merely because merchandise cannot be sold as rapidly as expected—leads to more orders, consequently to more employment, consequently to higher incomes and savings. The funds available at the beginning of a process of increased investment, under conditions of some slack in the economy, are therefore sure to be supplemented by saving brought about through the additional investment. The magnitude of this supplement, however, cannot be foreseen with certainty, and therefore the question of whether in a given economy savings would suffice to sustain greatly increased investment can be answered by nothing better than an informed guess.

[15] Although the followers of John Maynard Keynes are inclined to deny or minimize this interdependence, the author sides with the school of thought which believes that more abundant savings lead to cheapening of credit, and that this cheapening will cause businessmen to engage in expansion projects they otherwise would not undertake.

[16] It is, nevertheless, doubtful whether the Soviet Union has had continuous full employment in the sense in which this term is used in the West, in view of the problem of underemployment of manpower on the farms.

output resulting from increased productive capacity can be sold at rewarding prices. By not using these funds—unless they are borrowed by other entrepreneurs who do use them—the businessman will contribute to a reduction of total expenditures which will further reduce the receptiveness of markets for commodities. If the fear of overcapacity could be taken from the American businessman, this alone might suffice to give the United States the same growth rate which the Soviet Union now has;[17] if this fear is not at least substantially reduced, it is doubtful whether any other measures to raise the American growth rate will be successful because it is hard to think of tax advantages or other government-created incentives that could induce many businessmen to engage in an expansion project unless they believe that there will be a market for additional products. In any event, even if such incentives were to prove temporarily successful, the effect would be bound to die out as overcapacities become evident—as they must unless final consumer demand can be made to grow simultaneously to a sufficient extent.

The fact that in the Soviet Union the decisions to withhold funds from consumption and to use them for economic expansion are both made by the government certainly contributes to the absence of business fluctuations; the question must be raised, however, whether this unity of decision-making is the only reason why the Soviet Union has been able to use its productive capacity without interruption by business cycles. The case is made unclear by the inflationary pressure on the Soviet economy which has existed most, if not all, of the time since the beginning of planning. Where money is chasing goods, there will be no deficiency of demand—provided the pursuit is sufficiently hot, and provided, on the other hand, that the oversupply of money is not so great as to lead to a complete disorganization of the economy. For instance, in the great German inflation of the early 1920's, which has often served as the outstanding example of super-inflation, there was almost continuous full employment except in the very last phase when the dwindling of the value of money had become so rapid as to make business calculation too difficult. To the extent that inflation is responsible for the absence of fluctuations in the Soviet economy, the regularity of the Soviet Union's full use of productive facilities cannot be regarded as an effect of the economic system;[18] and since there has been no opportunity to observe

[17] In West Germany, the experience of an essentially uninterrupted prosperity of more than a decade has brought the fear of overcapacity to a low point. This has enabled the West German gross investment rate to surpass the Soviet rate (about 27 per cent of gross national product); see *Statistisches Jahrbuch fuer die Bundesrepublik Deutschland*, 1963, p. 456.

[18] Another factor which is not an outgrowth of the Communist system and which may

a Soviet system under conditions of prolonged monetary stability, there is no direct evidence from which to judge whether other characteristics of the Soviet system, aside from the close link between saving and investment, have had an important role in keeping the Soviet economy continuously in a state of near-full employment of men and machines, at least in the industrial sector. Some elements of an answer, however, can be found by analysis.

Some of the factors which in capitalist countries are responsible for fluctuations in the utilization of capacity are inherent in modern technology and therefore independent of the economic system. New inventions can make specialized skills of workers and specialized machine capacity obsolete; an industry built up to equip industries or households with some special device will be oversized when equipment demand is superseded by mere replacement demand. In a highly dynamic economy, it is true, even obsolete equipment or skills may be kept in use for a while because installations for the more efficient processes may not be sufficiently available to satisfy the needs, and it will take longer before equipment is completed and demand is cut down to replacement; yet sooner or later these points will be reached in various branches of production in any modern economy. The advantage which the Soviet system possesses in these respects is not the availability of devices for the avoidance of the problem but the existence of a highly developed apparatus of economic foresight which makes it possible to anticipate the task and thus have time to discover new uses for the resources that will be released and to prepare in advance for their utilization. The Soviet system starts from a budgeting of physical resources. While the greatest fault in the present operation of the system is that it does not supplement these physical considerations by adequate value planning, in its physical planning machinery the Soviet Union has an effective device to work for eliminating gaps in the employment of men and machines.

Will the instruments which the Soviet system provides for the elimination of fluctuations in the use of machine capacity and labor power be able to do the full job in the long run? The task is likely to become more difficult. Advanced technology requires greater specialization of machines and skills; this complicates the problem of finding alternative uses for resources released in a particular industry. The problem for which the Soviet system has so far provided only inadequate solutions, meeting consumers' preferences, will become harder to solve as satisfaction of wants reaches down lower in the scale of urgency. It is conceivable that a considerable amount of unem-

---

also help the Soviet Union in avoiding economic fluctuations is its greater chance—as compared with Western countries—of extensive growth. This factor will be considered below.

ployment may arise either from a failure of the planning agencies to anticipate a release of resources in a particular industry through technological change, or from a temporary withholding of purchasing power by consumers when they cannot find on the market the goods which they prefer and do not wish to take those which are offered.

For reasons of technological change and errors in foresight, individual foci of unused capacity emerge incessantly in a communist as in a capitalist system. Although there may be more chance in a capitalist system that errors in foresight will compensate each other, because they are errors of many independent unit managers and not those of a planning agency, and therefore may deviate from the correct results in different directions, this cannot be asserted with certainty, because individual errors often do not conform to a random pattern but are caused rather by widespread moods of optimism or pessimism. In any event, individual foci of idleness of machines or men will not seriously interfere with the operation of the system unless the tendency of such idleness to spread over the body economic remains unchecked. In this respect, the problem is similar for present-day communism as for capitalism. Unemployment in one industry interferes with the opportunities of supplier industries to market their products; incomes in industries which find it impossible to use their full manpower capacity are likely to show a decline of workers' incomes through unemployment or reduction of weekly working hours, and thereby the expenditures of their workers on products of other industries will be limited. The more efficient apparatus of economic foresight which Soviet communism has developed may facilitate the timely application of remedies to prevent the spreading of idleness from its focus, just as under favorable circumstances it may prevent the emergence of the focus; but communism's stock of remedies is not essentially richer than that of capitalism. In both systems the spread of idleness can be prevented by inflation if the consequences are regarded as acceptable. Idleness in the supplier industries of the focus industry can be prevented by opening up alternative uses for the same resources. Failure of consumers' purchasing power can be limited by benefits paid to the unemployed, but unless Soviet Communism decides to return to the method of compulsory allocation of labor, neither system will be able to keep such benefits as high as the level of normal labor income because equality of income of employed and unemployed workers would detract too much from the intensity with which the individual worker will search for the right place to utilize his working power.

It is impossible to say, on the basis of evidence now at hand, whether the Soviet economy will ever experience a degree of unemployment that can fairly be labeled a depression. It is probable, however, that the Soviet Union will find it increasingly harder to maintain as close an approach to the full utilization of capacity as it has been able to achieve in the past, because the increasing complexity of the economy makes it ever harder for the planning agencies to foresee what will happen, and to make such prompt adjustments to shifts in demand and to technological conditions as to keep idleness of men and machines down to an insignificant figure. But for the next decade, at least, the Soviet Union is still more likely to face a labor shortage than a growth of the "industrial reserve army," although particular kinds of labor and machines may be subject to more frequent periods of brief unemployment.

WILL THE SOVIET RATE OF GROWTH DECLINE?

The question of whether the Soviet Union can continue, for the near future, a relatively close approach to full employment has an obvious bearing on the probability that it will be able to maintain the tempo of economic growth which it has attained in the 1950's. Yet most Western economists, though they do not expect major unemployment to appear soon in the Soviet union, consider a slowdown of Soviet growth likely. The Soviet government itself expects only a 62 to 65 per cent increase in national income for the current seven-year period (1958 to 1965) in contrast to a claimed increase of 166 per cent during the nine years 1949 to 1958.[19]

One reason for this expectation is the exhaustion of readily available labor from agriculture. From now on, it seems certain that industry can grow only to the extent that it learns to use its own labor force more effectively, or that more effective use of labor in agriculture will make it possible to spare hands there without reducing output, or rather, without preventing an increase in output, since farm production is still less than optimal and a growing population will need more food. It is very difficult, however, to judge the likelihood of drastic improvement. As will be explained a little later, productivity in the Soviet Union is generally low as measured by Western standards. This fact can be interpreted as meaning either that the Soviet people or the Soviet system is incapable of high efficiency, or that the Soviet Union has a great opportunity to improve the operating efficiency of its economy.

The Soviet Union had to transfer large masses of people from agriculture to industry, and according to all experience such recruits to industrial work

[19] Francis M. Boddy, "National Income and Product of the USSR, Recent Trends and Prospects," *Comparisons of the United States and Soviet Economies,* Part II, pp. 399 f.

need a considerable period of transition to develop the skills for efficient labor; also, the economic system of Soviet Communism has characteristics adverse to efficiency. But these are not insuperable obstacles: As workers learn how to do things better, and as the system modifies itself by softening the dogmatism which stands in the way of rational calculation and optimal provisions for incentives, output per labor hour will increase. The only reservation that must be attached to this forecast arises from the possibility that a new wave of dogmatism may arise and reverse the trend toward rationalization and a greater importance of the price system. Since the political system of the Soviet Union lacks the firm foundation of representative democracy and gives the power of decision to small cliques which can more easily shift from one extreme to another, such a development cannot be precluded; but it is improbable.

In judging the prospects of future increases in Soviet labor productivity, it is important to realize that the relatively low present level is not simply the result of inefficiency. As Professor Warren W. Eason has stated, the cost of using the labor force "more or less 'wastefully' (by Western standards) may have been too small to warrant the effort required to develop a more enlightened manpower policy. From now on, the cost of such waste should be more apparent." [20] This statement does not go far enough. Although some faults of Soviet manpower policy undoubtedly detracted from labor efficiency —for instance, the long retention of direct controls over labor and a sometimes uneconomical structure of wages—and faults of investment policy, such as the unequal distribution of capital increments resulting from the leading sector idea, also detracted from efficiency, it was rational for an economy as relatively poor in capital and rich in labor as that of the Soviet Union to be more reluctant in replacing labor with capital than were Western economies. Many technological innovations, representing transition from labor-intensive to capital-intensive production, will become rational only after some period of time. There is every reason to believe that a number of these innovations will be introduced, thereby counteracting the adverse effect of the exhaustion of the labor reservoir on the speed of growth.

On the other hand, there are a number of reasons, in addition to the problem of labor supply, why a slowing down of Soviet growth appears likely. The growth of the past, which has created large capital equipment, has thereby also caused an increased need for capital replacement; therefore, the same amount of gross investment will in the future mean less net investment. Furthermore, whereas in the past, "the pool of unapplied technological

[20] Warren W. Eason, "Comparison between the United States and Soviet Economies: The Labor Force," in *Comparisons of United States and Soviet Economies*, Part I, p. 91.

possibilities was greater than in the United States," [21] in the future the Soviet Union will not be able to the same extent to exploit improvements already introduced in the West, but will be dependent for further increments in productivity on future technological progress which will in part have to come from the Soviet Union's own research.

The reason that the Soviet Union was so long in a favorable position to exploit technological inventions made elsewhere was her own backwardness. In some measure, this backwardness was the result of the Soviet Union's poverty in capital: It could not afford to introduce improvements that would have required too much equipment. To this extent, the technological backlog available to the Soviet Union was only the other side of the rationality of labor-intensive instead of capital-intensive methods: Because Soviet capital was not sufficient to enable it to introduce all the innovations that the West was using, the Soviet Union had at any given moment a reservoir of known inventions available which it could drain as its capital supply increased. But probably this was not the only reason for the existence of the backlog. In spite of everything we have heard about the large number of engineers being graduated in the Soviet Union every year, and in spite of the magnificent successes of Soviet research and engineering in some fields, there is much reason to believe that personnel of high technical skill has been in short supply at any given time. It is, therefore, likely that not only the shortage of capital, but also the shortage of skills obstructed the introduction of a number of innovations. Clearly, the existence of the backlog is a transitory advantage, but it is very difficult to estimate its size, and therefore the time which will elapse until it is exhausted.

A question also exists with regard to another and potentially vital factor that may make for a slowdown of Soviet growth. In exploiting natural resources, the Soviet Union will in the future have to utilize agricultural soil and mineral resources at a greater distance from the present population centers, and in some cases at least situated in regions with more unfavorable climate. This process has already begun; Khrushchev's new lands program is an example. As the most conveniently located resources are fully used or depleted, this factor is bound to gain in importance. The exploitation of the more distant or otherwise less favorable resources is possible only at a greater cost—in some instances greater initial investment and in others higher operating cost. Therefore, net gain, which can supply the means for consumption and growth, is likely to be smaller. But it is impossible at the present

[21] W. W. Rostow, "Summary and Policy Implications," in *Comparisons of United States and Soviet Economies*, p. 395.

time to make any estimate about the quantitative effect which this phenomenon of diminishing returns will have on Soviet growth.

What makes it particularly difficult to evaluate the effect of diminishing returns is the fact that it is the reverse side of an element favorable to the Soviet economy and its growth. The Soviet Union *has* to extend relatively intense economic activities into areas of scarce population and a hitherto low degree of economic development, but the Soviet Union *can* undertake such an extension to a greater degree than any other large industrial power. The necessity to undertake territorial expansion is a burden; the possibility of undertaking it is an opportunity. One of the positive effects of territorial expansion is its presumably stabilizing influence upon the utilization of capacity. As the Soviet Union as a whole moves into those stages of economic development in which the needs for further investment are less easily discernible, it will be an advantage to have areas still at a lower stage in which problems are simpler because the task of development is, in a large measure, the emulation of the pattern which has already been established in the more advanced areas. To state the same proposition in more technical terms: Although intensive growth is possible for an unforeseeable future not only for the Soviet Union but also for countries already far more advanced, it is also more difficult to achieve in an uninterrupted, smooth fashion than extensive growth; other things being equal, this fact will give a country which has also a possibility of extensive growth a greater assurance of continuous utilization of its manpower and machine capacity than exists in a country which is entirely dependent on intensive growth. With all the difficulty in judging the importance of this advantage, however, it is unlikely to vitiate the previous statement that the Soviet Union must eventually expect increasing difficulty in avoiding some sort of economic fluctuations.

If the Soviet Union's presumable difficulty in maintaining full employment of capacity is viewed together with the other probable impediments to rapid growth, the prediction that the growth of the Soviet economy is more likely to be slowed down than to continue at its previous pace appears well founded. But this is a matter of probabilities; nobody, in or out of the Soviet Union, can forcast the economic future with certainty. Technological improvements might lead to an unexpectedly great increase in productivity of which the Soviet Union is better equipped to take advantage than the West; extensive growth may prove more fruitful than expected; new ideological currents may sweep away the obstacles which dogmatism has put in the way of economic progress more rapidly than seems probable today. The West has no right to take the reduction of speed in Soviet growth for granted.

WHY IS SOVIET GROWTH A DANGER TO THE WEST?

In the section on "Values and Goals," it has been explained that modern nations, to some extent, regard economic growth as a purpose in itself. But for the United States, in its relations with the Soviet Union, this motive is greatly overshadowed by more tangible concerns. The more rapid growth of the Soviet Union is feared by the United States primarily because it means an increased potential for warfare and a greater leeway for using economic resources for purposes of international policy, such as foreign aid or directed foreign trade. Even increases in the standard of living of the Soviet people may have an adverse meaning for the United States because higher living standards add to the prestige which the Soviet Union enjoys among other nations, and prestige is a weapon. All this is important only as long as the present antagonism between the two powers continues. If that antagonism did not exist, the American people might still wish for a rapid growth of its own economy, but it would have no reason to see itself in a race with the Soviet Union.

Is the antagonism a result of the difference of the economic and political systems? Yes and no. Although some people in the United States might feel hostile to the Soviet Union merely because it represents a system of government and economic organization which they abhor, the great majority of the American people considers the form of social living which another nation wishes to choose that nation's own business. Although there is no clear evidence, and much reason to doubt, that the Russian people want to live under the system as it now exists in the Soviet Union, American public opinion is reluctant to support political, not to speak of military, efforts to liberate nations from internal oppression which these nations themselves are unable to remove. There may be exceptional circumstances in which American public opinion might condone, or even demand, the use of economic, political or even military weapons to liberate a foreign country from its own tyrants, but no such exception applies to the Soviet Union. If Russia's economic growth had no military and foreign policy implications, the American people might wonder how long the Russians will tolerate a situation in which so large a portion of the national income is spent on investments and thus withheld from consumption, but Americans would not consider this rapid growth a trend directed against their own well-being, nor would they find it necessary to emulate the Russians.

From the side of the Soviet Union, the situation looks quite different. Communism has a much greater missionary fervor than democracy as represented by the United States in the twentieth century. Whether that fervor is genuine in the minds of the Soviet leaders, or whether they merely believe that it is expedient to show such fervor is irrelevant.[22] Khrushchev's famous challenge: "We will bury you," though not necessarily a profession of belief in war, is at least an expression of the will to convert the world to communism, and whoever would consider such conversion a calamity must view Soviet progress as a threat.

The moment the economic and political system of the Soviet Union is so modified as to make it similar to that of the United States, the rivalry and with it the threat will obviously disappear. To say that it is not really the system but the ideology behind the system that is the source of the communist missionary fervor is correct but immaterial, since with a reduction of the difference in the systems, the missionary zeal would lose its object. Whatever, therefore, is the role of the communist system in making possible the rate of growth which the Soviet Union has achieved, communism is the indispensable condition for Soviet growth to be viewed as a threat by American policy makers.

Since Soviet growth is a danger only because it enables the Soviet Union to achieve some purposes which may improve the political position of the Soviet Union vis-a-vis the United States, it is not growth alone that must be feared but also the ability of the Soviet government to direct that growth to the politically most important objectives. Just as in promoting growth in general in competition with consumption, so also in promoting particular directions of growth in competition with others the Soviet system has some advantages. Of the investible funds in the United States, the major part is used according to the judgment of a large number of business executives, each one acting in the interest of his own business, and only the smaller part is subject to centralized decision. In the Soviet Union, the ratio of magnitudes is just the reverse. Strictly speaking, all investment is subject to government control, but even the limited influence which kolkhozes and industrial managers have upon reinvestment of the profits of their own enterprises extends to a much smaller portion than represented by the part

[22] The expediency in the Communists' showing missionary fervor arises from the identity of expansion of the orbit of Communism with the expansion of Soviet (or Chinese) power. If a Latin American or African country adopts the domestic system of Soviet Communism today, it becomes automatically an ally or satellite of one of the major Communist powers.

Although the case of Yugoslavia may at first sight seem to offer a counter-argument, it actually confirms the interdependence of the domestic system and the foreign policy position of communist countries. Yugoslavia's decision to defy the Soviet Union because the latter attempted to treat Yugoslavia as a satellite led to a revision of the Yugoslav economic system which made its institutions and practices very different from the Russian model.

of investment that is undertaken by private enterprise in the United States. Of course, the United States government has an influence also upon private investment decisions. If the executive and legislative branches agree that orders for a communication satellite should go out, the companies awarded contracts for this purpose will not only order the required equipment but also invest funds in research intended to carry their knowledge about the possibilities in space science to greater perfection. If the Department of Health, Education and Welfare recommends to the cities and counties that a particular vaccine be used in health centers to immunize large sections of the population against a particular disease, chemical firms will spend more on research to improve that vaccine or find cheaper methods of producing it. But the government's influence upon private investment in a capitalistic economy is indirect and works more slowly and less effectively than the Soviet method, which consists of steering the bulk of investment funds into the desired channels by central directives.

This reason for the greater flexibility of Soviet investment decisions is reinforced by effects of the political system of the Soviet Union. In the United States, as in any democratic country, the executive branch of the government needs the consent of the legislature to make expenditures, and it can usually obtain that consent only by convincing public opinion that its general investment policy is sound; details, of course, are usually beyond the understanding of the voters and even of the legislature. The Soviet government is under no such restraint. A relatively small power elite decides what is to be done, and the rise of Khrushchev has shown that the tendency to narrow the circle of decision makers down to one man was not merely a phenomenon of Stalinism but is an inherent trend of the dictatorship.

To be sure, neither the absence of restraints on the executive branch nor the centralization of investment decisions in the hands of the government is an unmixed blessing even from the point of view of promoting purposes of power policy by investment decisions, leaving all other objections aside. Centralization of decisions and absence of restraints increase the danger of mistakes and may thus cause less to be achieved along the desired lines than would have been accomplished under procedures with greater safeguards. This hazard is aggravated by the deficiencies of Soviet cost calculation: Not only may there be mistakes in weighing known cost items against the advantages expected of contemplated investment projects, but the cost which can be known to the decision makers under the Soviet system of calculation will often not be the true costs. However, the Soviet record in those fields which have received priority seems to indicate that for reaching the desired achievements, the advantages inherent in the system have been greater than the disadvantages. A final judgment will be possible only when the secrecy which now veils progress in important areas is lifted. Even if this judgment confirms the preliminary impression that the Soviet Union has effectively directed its investible funds toward the purposes it preferred, the analysts and their audiences will have to remember that these preferences themselves are not completely shared by other nations, and that the other effects of the Soviet system constitute a price which other nations regard as too great for the advantages gained.

Inequality in Communism

If there is any statistical information on income distribution in the Soviet Union, by way of a Lorenz curve or otherwise, it is certainly classified information, not available from open sources. Communism started out as a movement for economic and social equality, for distribution according to needs. Although the Russian Communists have always recognized—and this was good Marxism—that the principle of distribution according to need could not be applied as soon as communist rule was established, but only after a period of transition, they have never hesitated to exploit to the full mankind's deep desire for a society in which everybody is equal to everybody else. But in practice they have never been squeamish about fostering inequality whenever it served their ends; they have been aware, however, that the full revelation of the distance which their own society has to go before it even comes as close to equality as some mature capitalist societies have come would diminish Communism's popularity among those other nations and social groups in which class privileges still prevail.

In the absence of any general survey or analysis, some idea of the degree of inequality in the Soviet Union can still be formed by observing the incomes or standards of living of representative groups. The following statement by David Granick probably reflects the impression which most careful observers have gained about the inequalities within the Soviet industrial sector:

> A director of a successful Soviet factory with 1000 workers would earn some five or six times as much as the average worker; the comparable American executive would be in roughly the same position relative to the American factory worker, although the American's absolute standard of living would, of course, be far superior to the Russian's. In terms of income inequality the relation between worker and manager in Russia and the United States does not differ too greatly. Pretax, the American manager would be a bit ahead; but then, his income tax is higher.[23]

[23] David Granick, "Soviet-American Management Comparisons" in *Comparisons of*

In supplementing the comparisons of individual money incomes, it is necessary to take some other conditions of living into account. There are considerably more wage earners in the average Soviet family than in the average American family. This, of course, makes the gap in average disposable family income between the United States and Russia smaller than it would otherwise be.[24] Whether it also reduces the gaps between the different levels of the economic hierarchy in the Soviet Union, of course depends on whether the greater prevalence of more than one wage earner per family is mainly confined to the lower income groups or extends to the higher ones. On this point, no information seems to be available. Certainly economic necessity would not force a Soviet executive's wife to take a job as frequently as it forces a worker's wife, but economic necessity is not the only conceivable motive. In the Soviet Union, for a married woman to work is a means to obtain social approbation, and an executive's family, being in a more vulnerable position than a worker's family, may be more in need of earning such plaudits or of avoiding criticism for leading an easy life. This is especially important because the executive's wife is likely to have some professional or semi-professional training, and often a high degree of opprobrium is meted out to those who do not recompense the community for the cost of such education by life long work. Moreover, with conveniences such as washing machines, television sets and cars becoming available to the higher income groups, the desire to purchase relatively expensive objects which are not strictly necessary but greatly contribute to the ease of life may supply a motive—the same inducement which so often in the United States causes women to go to work although their bread and butter would be assured by their husbands' incomes. All this, of course, only proves that it would not be surprising to find married women working as frequently in the upper strata as in the lower strata of Soviet life; such work, therefore, may not be a factor reducing income inequality. It has not been proved, however, that such is actually the case. We simply lack the factual information.

Another factor that must be considered in evaluating income differentials is the availability of benefits for which no money, or only a small

---

United States and Soviet Economies, Part I, p. 145. The reader should remember that the term "director" used in the first sentence is synonymous with manager in American usage. For other material on the inequality in the Soviet Union, see the commentary by Herbert Ritvo on the new program of the Communist Party of the Soviet Union, *The New Soviet Society,* pp. 153 ff.

24 Since leisure is also an element in the standard of living, the improvement of the latter would not be as great as the addition to money income, except in those instances in which leisure is in oversupply and therefore the wife wants work for its own sake and not only for the sake of compensation.

money payment, is required. "The Russians provide a considerably larger area of collective or communal consumption, principally the free health and education services, as well as the partially subsidized housing consumption."[25] Free health services and free education[26] benefit the lower income groups relatively more than the higher groups, which would be able to pay from their own funds for medical care and schooling for their children without undue hardship. Probably subsidized housing also tends to reduce inequality of living standards, though this case is more complicated.

"The Soviet government, which is the landlord in most instances, makes no net income or rent on housing; that is, the rent charged is designed only to cover the upkeep of the state property. Judging by the accounts of the upkeep of Soviet housing, rent collections are probably inadequate for even these limited purposes."[27] As a consequence, the average Soviet worker's family spends no more than 4 to 5 per cent of the family budget on housing, including utilities, whereas for the average American family the figure is

[25] Lynn Sturgeon, in testimony before the Joint Economic Committee, Congress of the United States. *Comparisons of the United States and Soviet Economies,* Hearings p. 135.

[26] As compared with the United States, which also provides free elementary and secondary education, the principal advantage of the Soviet worker's family consists of the availability of a more comprehensive system of free pre-school child care. In regard to college education, the comparison is made difficult by the great diversity of conditions in the United States on the one hand—it is a great advantage now, and will be a greater one in the future, for a boy or girl to be a resident of a state with a good state university or state college system—and on the other hand by the fact that in the Soviet Union some types of higher education do not seem to be really free but must be paid for afterwards in the form of an obligation to serve wherever required for a number of years, which may sometimes involve a financial sacrifice. There is little doubt, however, that on the whole higher education is still somewhat more accessible for gifted youth from low income groups in the Soviet Union than is the case in the United States.

Whereas the difference with regard to education is relatively small between the Soviet Union and the United States and somewhat greater between the Soviet Union and Western Europe—although in Western Europe, too, secondary schools and universities are rapidly becoming more accessible—the reverse is true with regard to health service. Here again we meet the difficulty that the effects of economic systems can be recognized only by an analysis of conditions in individual countries, and that in the first place, countries differ with regard to many characteristics other than their economic systems, and that, secondly, no country represents an economic system in anything like its pure type. Any contention that a capitalist system cannot open the way to advanced education for every gifted young person would be refuted by a glance at the situation in the United States and at the obvious prospects of development in Western Europe; likewise, anyone who would argue that capitalism is incompatible with extensive free health services might be asked to look at Great Britain and at other countries of Western Europe. Yet it would be futile to deny that, if not the Soviet system as such, at least the ideology behind the Soviet system has supplied some of the driving force for the establishment of an impressive combination of free facilities.

[27] Lynn Sturgeon, "Levels of Living, Wages and Prices in the Soviet and United States Economies," in *Comparisons of United States and Soviet Economies,* Part I, p. 330. Soviet rents are graduated according to tenants' income, and thereby economic inequality is further reduced.

about 16 per cent, exclusive of utilities other than fuel. Of course, Soviet housing for the typical worker's family is quite inadequate by American standards, much more so than supplies of food and probably also clothing.[28]

But some higher income groups, if perhaps not all of them, seem to be supplied with gratis or low-cost housing of a quality that corresponds to their higher status. We do not know how much better the housing supplied to a successful scientist or artist or to a plant manager is than the housing available to the manual worker or to the kolkhoz member, and it is this difference that alone would enable us to decide whether subsidized housing enhances or reduces inequalities as expressed in money incomes. It is the same with other fringe benefits. The upper level of Soviet society probably has access to a better type of free or low-cost recreation than common man; some of the scientists and artists and most or all of the managers seem to have the use of a car, and some have the opportunity to travel abroad, which is not only greatly desired for its own sake but also offers the chance to buy products not available in the Soviet Union (or available only at excessive prices) and thus to use parts of one's money income more economically. How much of an advantage over the average consumer do these privileges give to the people of higher status in the Soviet Union? The question, unfortunately, is unanswerable.

For the observer who knows the great role played by the progressive income tax in Western countries in reducing the advantages of the highest income groups, it may at first seem surprising that the tax rates in the Soviet Union are relatively low, and that the whole income tax is scheduled to be abolished within the current Seven Year Plan. Yet it can be seen that this is quite logical. In capitalist economies, income differentials arise from market processes. They are not planned, and if they were not modified by taxation, they would often exceed what public opinion and governments regard as necessary incentives. In the Soviet Union, the government controls almost all[29] income differentials at their source, because it regulates all wages and salaries. Having decided that in the interest of production some incomes should be greater than others, the Soviet government considers it basically illogical to reduce these differentials afterwards by taxes.

In both the United States and the Soviet Union the lowest incomes of

[28] Sturgeon assumes that at the subsistence level the difference is less great than at the average workers level, "if one considers the quantity and quality of nonwhite and/or recent immigrant subsistence workers' housing in our large cities" (*ibid.*). Still, it seems that even in the worst American slums the kind of overcrowding that still does not appear unusual in Russia would not be tolerated.

[29] The most important source of income differentials not at their origin under the complete control of the government are incomes obtained through sales on the "free" kolkhoz market.

employed persons are to be found in agriculture rather than in industry. The prosperous farmer is certainly not as rare in the United States as the prosperous kolkhoz member is in the Soviet Union, although great differences of incomes exist even in Soviet agriculture; on the other hand, it is not unlikely that the communal institutions of the kolkhoz and services in health and education provided by the Soviet government[30] prevent such extremes of misery as may be found in the worst sharecropping areas and among some migratory labor groups in the United States.

In any event, the size of the agricultural sector in the Soviet Union makes it inevitable that the low agricultural incomes play a much greater role in the Soviet economy than they do in the economy of the United States. The comparison between the incomes of a typical industrial executive and a typical industrial worker in both countries is misleading unless it takes into account that in the Soviet Union there is a much larger stratum of incomes below that of the industrial worker than in the United States.

In summary, this means that inequalities of money incomes are still more important in the Soviet Union than in the United States, although at the present time at least there is a tendency for these inequalities to be reduced, owing to the agricultural reforms and to some revisions in the scales of wages and salaries. We may guess that fringe benefits somewhat offset the importance of these inequalities, but this cannot be stated categorically. Since the Soviet Union is on a considerably lower absolute level of want satisfaction, any given degree of inequality of money incomes has a greater significance there than in the United States. This truth refutes Communist propaganda which pictures the people in capitalist countries, and especially in the United States, as badly oppressed and exploited by "monopoly capitalism." The combination of a private enterprise economy with strong labor unions and such collective institutions as were created under the pressure of equal suffrage has resulted in an approach to social equality close enough to leave little room for the desire to make it still closer, at the price of a fundamental change in the economic order. The forces which operate in favor of a further transformation of the capitalist system do not arise to any great extent from dissatisfaction with inequalities, but rather from the desire for stable and rapid growth, and other concerns about the efficiency of the organization of production. In the field

[30] Kolkhoz members—except the relatively few who belong to trade unions—are not covered by social insurance. For them, assistance by the mutual aid society, which exists in every kolkhoz, are substituted for social security benefits. However, "the collective farmers and their families have the same provisions for medical care and for family allowances as the remainder of the population." (*A Report on Social Security Programs in the Soviet Union*, p. 68.

from which the strongest impulse of the communist movement originated, communism has not been able to outdo its rival.

The picture looks somewhat better for the Soviet Union if we measure the situation not by the yardstick of Communist claims and aspirations but consider what can be expected of a country at Russia's stage of economic development. Other countries just emerging from a low level of industrial development have often known very great social inequalities. Russia is no longer an underdeveloped nation, although its economy still shows some of the characteristics of the period before it became a great industrial power. Even before the revolution, however, Russia was not an underdeveloped country in the sense which applies to the new nations of Africa and Asia: Its political and economic unity achieved already under the Tsars, the relatively small but efficiently organized industrial core which had emerged in the last two decades before the First World War gave Russia advantages which are lacking in most of the colonial and semi-colonial areas now trying to develop into industrial nations. Since the Soviet Union has only recently entered the circle of highly industrialized nations, it is hardly surprising that she shows greater inequalities than those nations which have earlier reached economic maturity. On the other hand, it is also no reason for astonishment that she does not have the differentials in living standards which can be observed in countries starting from scratch. Perhaps the fairest statement that can be made is that the communist system has tended to make income differentials somewhat narrower than they might be expected in view of the brevity of the period during which Russia has enjoyed the status of an industrially advanced country.

In regard to differentials in the distribution of power and prestige, the picture is very different: The dictatorial system obviously tends to make the shares in these advantages very unequal. They may not be more unequal than in some of the new nations which had not been touched in depth by Western influences before, but the effects of communism on the distance which separates present-day Russia from social equality must be measured against the strong heritage of liberal thought in the broad sense of the term which Russia had acquired already in the nineteenth century. As measured by this yardstick, the Soviet Union has not done very well in the non-economic aspects of social equality.

The foregoing discussion should have established that comparisons of inequalities of income and prestige in the United States and in the Soviet Union are possible only with many reservations and, therefore, can in some respects serve only as a guide to questions which ought to be further investigated, and not yet as answers to questions. It is even more difficult to make comparisons with regard to equality of opportunity. Does a Soviet youngster in a remote kolkhoz have more or less chance to move up the social ladder than the son or daughter of a sharecropper in Alabama? What is the answer if we ask the same question with regard to the children of a Detroit automobile worker and those of a family of similar status in the Soviet Union? Everyone of us may have a guess as to how these comparisons would turn out, but it is not an informed guess and therefore not even worth expressing.

Soviet Communism and Freedom

It is a truism to say that the communist system does not leave as much room for individual freedom as the social system existing in Western countries. It is still necessary, however, to try to find out what specific elements in Soviet communism are responsible for the lack of liberty, and whether it is in any way probable that the changes now occuring in Soviet communism will substantially enlarge the individual's sphere of freedom.

The political system of the Soviet Union is designed to give the executive a maximum of power for the purpose of effecting an economic transformation. This at least was the original rationale of the dictatorship; in the course of years, power greed of the rulers and nationalistic ambitions have provided additional incentives not to reduce the executive power by effective checks and balances, but the economic purpose remains important even today.

It is a fascinating subject—one of the most fascinating in the field of comparative government—how far, and why, some elements of protection of individual freedom are nevertheless operative even in the Soviet system; but this question is too complex to be taken up in full detail here. Fundamentally, two tendencies have been at work in creating such restraints on governmental power. The first can best be recognized by analogy with absolute monarchy in Europe during the early modern age. It has often been stated that for the common man and woman the power of the absolute king was less oppressive than that of the local rulers whom the royal power now held in check. This was true because royal officials, if they were not to become small kings in their own domains as the Carolingian counts had done before—and there was nothing that the national rulers feared more—had to be bound by strict rules. This was also necessary for the sake of efficient government because otherwise uniformity of decisions would not have been assured. These rules, however, even if devised only to reserve the rights of the king, offered some of the benefits of "government of law" to the people. For essentially the same reason, the concept of "Soviet legality" was officially upheld even in the Stalinist period. Its essential meaning was that the right of arbitrary decision was in the main reserved to the dictator and to those to whom he directly delegated that right, whereas the multitude of lesser office holders was bound by rules,—except that for some specified purposes—for instance liquidation of the kulaks—almost any degree of arbitrariness was permitted. Most if not all of these exceptions have been eliminated in the Khrushchev period.

The second fundamental reason why the individual in the Soviet Union is not completely deprived of all freedom is the need for some spontaneity, some personal initiative if the goals of the Soviet leaders are to be reached. This is the reason why autocratic governments, even if they feel safe from the danger of revolution, pay some attention to public opinion: Any government that wants more than just to stay in power, that has to win a war or to reorganize the economy or to accomplish any of a number of conceivable purposes, must have a modicum of voluntary cooperation from its subjects.

Despotic governments, however, have frequently used propaganda as a means to spur the voluntary efforts of the people in the areas in which these efforts were necessary for the purposes of the rulers, without giving free rein to voluntarism over a wider field. The one-party system is a well suited instrument to achieve this end within the limits of possibility. Not only can it prevent crystallization of opposition, but, unhampered by any organized effort working in the opposite direction, it can go a long way to convince large masses of people that the purposes of the government are identical with their own, although there may be a wide gap between what the government wants and what the people would desire spontaneously. The Communist Party of the Soviet Union has proved to be a much more effective propaganda instrument than the Nazi Party during the Hitler period in Germany, in spite of the cleverness of Dr. Joseph Goebbels, Hitler's minister of propaganda.

But there are limits even to the effectiveness of a one-party system. In order to work well, people must have a feeling that they are not just tools, that they have some influence upon their fate and upon the tasks which are assigned to them. Even the members of the party enjoying the monopoly of political organization could not regard themselves as an active part of the regime if they merely had to obey orders, and their enthusiasm is essential if a spirit of cooperation is to be aroused in the population at large.

Not only is it necessary for the achievement of the government's goals that people have the feeling of somehow participating in decisions; they also need, at least in the long run, the feeling of having a reserved private sphere. An abundance of empirical evidence points to the conclusion that man cannot tolerate a life that consists entirely of community affairs—and nothing exhausts the sense of historical mission in the citizen more rapidly than the claim of the rulers that to this sense all private interests must be sacrificed. Totalitarianism, to last more than a limited time, must so limit itself as not to be total in a literal sense.

All this indicates that such changes as have occurred in the Soviet system within approximately the last decade, from the abolition of direct controls over labor to the liberation of the kolkhozes from the surveillance exerted by the machine-tractor stations, were necessary for the purposes of the dictatorial regime. This is no reason to deprecate their importance. Whatever the motives of Khrushchev and other Soviet leaders responsible for the introduction of these alleviating measures, they may initiate a period of progressive relaxation of the dictatorship, although it is just as easily conceivable that the development will be stopped at the present or a slightly later stage.

The dictatorial character of the Soviet regime was the prerequisite of many of the economic changes that have been effected since the Communist seizure of power. Without a dictatorship, only a slower pace of industrialization would have been possible; extensive collectivization of agriculture could not have been accomplished, and a pricing system more responsive to demand would have had to be reestablished. The opposite question is more difficult to answer: Has the economic system helped to maintain the dictatorship? Connected with this question is an even more interesting one: If the economic system is to be progressively rationalized, will this have an influence on the system of government?

In the course of Soviet history, control over the economy has often been used to strengthen the dictatorship. In the crushing of the opposition against Stalin, the power to demote a business manager or high government official to the position of a starving ditchdigger in Siberia for not having supported the dictator with enough show of enthusiasm served the latter as a weapon. The power to withhold the services of the machine-tractor stations from recalcitrant kolkhozes was a means of suppressing peasant opposition. These examples could be multiplied.

But it is one thing to say that elements in the economic system have actually been used to bolster the dictatorship, and something quite different to assert that they were necessary for that purpose. A sword is a formidable weapon and may be used to terrorize an unarmed person but adds little to a man's ability to terrorize others if he already has a machine gun.

The Soviet government's power over the livelihood of its people added little to its ability to control these people because it already wielded the power of life and death.

Again, it is important to look at the past. Such remnants of despotism as had survived in the nineteenth century, for instance the rule of the two Napoleons in France or the Hohenzollern monarchy in Prussia, were limited in their oppressive actions by their inadequate control over the economy. Living in an age in which, on the one hand, an unrestrained use of the firing squad did not seem feasible and on the other hand, the economic development of any country, and thereby the resources of the government, depended on the existence of an entrepreneur class which could function only with substantial freedom of action, the subjects were assured of a modicum of liberty, albeit a modest one, by the availability of jobs outside the government sphere of influence; some measure of liberty was also assured by the adverse reactions of capital markets to government measures so harsh as to invite the suspicion that they were acts of desperation and therefore signs of weakness.

The special circumstances which, in the nineteenth century, made an area of independent economic decisions a refuge of political liberty and individual freedom, or at least an obstacle to arbitrary infringement of personal liberty by the government, are no longer with us. For better or worse, twentieth century governments are far more able to set the determinants of economic decisions than were their predecessors. The best illustration of this truth is the experience of fascism. The fascist governments left many of the essential capitalist institutions untouched. There was only very little nationalization of business; the stock exchange continued to function, and freedom of private investment decisions was not subject to any great restriction. There were some attempts at price and wage controls in Nazi Germany even before the war—in wartime, such controls of course were ubiquitous—but they were neither inescapable nor essential for the functioning of the political system. Those economic measures which the political regime needed for its effectiveness—especially the power to dictate who could hold a job—it could introduce without any substantial reaction in those parts of the economy with which it did not interfere.

As applied to Soviet history, all this means that the Soviet government did not need its own unique economic institutions to maintain itself as a dictatorship. To deny its people the individual freedom which is taken for granted in the West, the Communist regime needed neither a Five Year Plan, carried out in disregard of consumers' wishes, nor collectivization of agriculture, nor even nationalization of industry. The causal relationship runs from political dictatorship to economic despotism, not to any great extent in the opposite direction.

This, at least, is true when we limit our scope to the capacity of government to infringe upon the liberty of its people. But to bring about a dictatorship, not only the capacity but also the will to impose such infringement is required. To be sure, there is great truth in Lord Acton's statement that all power tends to corrupt, and that absolute power corrupts absolutely;[31] as an advice to establish strong institutional guarantees to limit power it is one of the most useful statements that have ever been made. However, it would be misleading if understood as an instruction to historians to take the will to misuse power for granted and to dispense with the investigation of the conditions by which it is created. Whether any institutional guarantees would have proved efficacious if Abraham Lincoln had established a dictatorship is highly doubtful; the important and unquestionable fact is that Lincoln did not want to become a dictator. Nor is this merely a question of a particular personality. If no President of the United States has ever tried to establish himself as a dictator, and if the mere suggestion that some future chief executive in the United States might try to do so strikes most of us as absurd, the reason is not merely that the army might disobey him, or that there might be a general strike or some other repercussion growing out of the revulsion of citizens against unlimited rule; the strongest safeguard is the improbability that anyone raised in the tradition of American political life would seek dictatorial power.

Does the general character of an economic order influence and strengthen the will of its leaders to seek unrestrained power? Specifically, is there something in economic rationality that might restrain that will? Here we are in a field in which certainty of knowledge is impossible and speculation must take its place. But on a subject of such importance even surmises based on nothing better than speculation may be worthwhile.

One does not have to be a Marxist to assume that economic institutions exert an influence upon the mentality of men. Most present-day social scientists believe that economic arrangements represent only one among several determinants of the ideas of an epoch and they would insist that the latter in turn influence economic affairs. The striking historical parallelism between the increased protection of human liberty and the increased role of economic rationality within the last three centuries can be explained by institutional mechanisms and by the influence of changed class relation-

[31] See John Emerich Edward Dahlberg-Acton, Letter to Mandell Creighton, in *Essays on Freedom and Power,* Selected by Gertrude Himmelfarb, Boston: The Beacon Press, and Glencoe: The Free Press of Glencoe, 1948, p. 364.

ships without assuming that economic rationality per se is counteracting power instincts or at least their cruder expressions. Yet the fact that in the analysis of historical experience we can get by without that assumption does not, of course, mean that it must be untrue.

To realize that there are rules of economic rationality means to understand that our freedom of action is limited not only by the will of possible antagonists but also by objective limitations. A good deal of Soviet history has consisted of a process in which the Soviet leaders learned that they had overrated what could be achieved by a struggle against hostile classes and individuals and underrated the dependence of achievement on a kind of economic organization that would in each instance measure the importance of sacrifice against the importance of success.

Education to rationality is education to the necessity of counting costs. This is true not only of economic rationality, but counting economic costs is certainly a way to acquire the sense of the importance of weighing the sacrifice as carefully as possible in any undertaking in any sphere of life. Much of what the communists have done they could do only because they attributed minimum importance to the sacrifices and maximum importance to the goals, which is a way in which their strong sense of historic mission expresses itself. The importance attributed to sacrifices and to goals, if made in full consciousness of all the facts—if the counting of costs has been correctly done—is beyond the judgment of rationality. But there is much reason to believe that very frequently costs are not correctly counted and that, therefore, techniques of rational procedure may lead to a change in the course of action where no readiness exists to bear the full costs; that habitual calculation of costs affects the valuation of sacrifice and success—in other words, the rational procedure may not only lead to the correction of intellectual errors but also may have an effect upon the emotional bases of those value judgments which determine what sacrifices are acceptable for the sake of what successes.

Moreover, as the importance of the incessant striving for rationality is understood it also appears more probable that the significance of voluntary cooperation and spontaneity will be more clearly realized. An individual act of compliance with orders can in most instances be assured by compulsion; the continuity of the effort to lower costs and determine the most favorable product mix requires a greater utilization of self-interest. Of course, even a despot can appeal to self-interest through promising rewards, but he is likely to learn that the individual initiative which is necessary in that particular task can be far more effectively displayed in an atmosphere of at least limited freedom.

If these considerations have any merit—and it cannot be emphasized enough that the empirical evidence is small and the whole prognosis largely a matter of speculation—then we may expect that the trend toward greater economic rationality in the Soviet Union will express itself in a wholesome erosion—wholesome not only for the rest of the world but for the ordinary Soviet citizen as well, an erosion of the will of the rulers to impose by force extreme sacrifices upon the living generation of their people, and in a tendency to give the Soviet citizen more rein for voluntary effort. Although it would be a potentially fatal mistake to rely on a trend whose existence is uncertain and which, even if it exists, may be checked by any of a number of counteracting trends, the fanatical pessimism which is often applied to East-West relations and which considers the motivations of the communist rulers essentially immutable can be just as harmful.

The COMECON

In the East as in the West the postwar period has seen efforts at integrating national economies into larger economic entities. The Eastern effort began as an answer to the Western endeavor growing out of the Marshall Plan: In 1947, when the United States decided to support European recovery through large financial grants, it persuaded the European nations to coordinate their reconstruction efforts in order that a substantial measure of international division of labor might be introduced, instead of every country's trying to build up industries which might uneconomically duplicate production facilities in neighboring nations. It was rightly thought that by such coordination the beneficial effect of American aid could be enhanced. Pursuing the American suggestion, the recipient nations of the Marshall Plan formed the Organization of European Economic Cooperation (OEEC). The Soviet Union, in a move against Polish and Czech tendencies to join this organization in order to qualify for Marshall aid, tried to offer her satellites a substitute by inaugurating the Council for Mutual Economic Assistance—in the West known as COMECON—as an economic alliance of the Soviet-bloc nations.

This sequence of events does not prove that the economic integration movement in the East owes its existence entirely to the desire to emulate the course of the Western countries. The economic advantages of international division of labor are as incontestable from the Marxist point of view as from that of Western economics. The potential benefits of integration must have seemed particularly great in planning countries: Integration of unplanned economies means merely that spontaneous economic forces are given a chance to effect beneficial adjustments; where planning exists, these adjustments can be incorporated into the development programs guiding policy, and thereby made more certain. In the beginning, the reasons why the Eastern countries were unable to exploit this point of potential superiority in their integration efforts were not clear and were therefore not effective as a force operating against the attempt. Thus it is likely that, even without the OEEC, an effort at coordinating the national plans within the Eastern bloc would have been made. But the Western example undoubtedly influenced the intensity of the Eastern effort: As the impetus given by the OEEC led to the establishment of the European Economic Community—a much higher form of integration—the East responded by stronger attempts to facilitate exchange of commodities within the Soviet bloc and to make the national plans complementary to one another.

Although at the present time the groundwork has not yet been laid for a comparative evaluation of the Western and Eastern integration efforts that could produce conclusive results, such evidence as is available suggests that in the East the success was not nearly so great as in the West. The *Economic Bulletin for Europe,* for instance—published by the Secretariat of the United Nations Economic Commission for Europe—speaks of the "growing importance of intra-western European trade in the trade of Europe and in world trade" and continues: "In 1961 this trade rose by 12 per cent so that its share in world trade reached approximately one-fourth compared with only one-fifth in 1957 and 23 per cent in 1960. At the same time the share of intra-eastern European trade also continued to grow, but less fast. For the year as a whole, intra-eastern European trade went up by 9 per cent so that its share in world trade amounted to 6.6 per cent compared with 6.4 per cent in 1960."[32] Figures given in the same Bulletin can be tabulated as shown in Table 7.[33]

TABLE 7

DISTRIBUTION OF EXPORTS
PER MILLE OF WORLD TRADE, IN CURRENT DOLLAR VALUES

	Eastern Europe		Western Europe	
	Internal Trade	World Trade	Internal Trade	World Trade
1953	53	83	180	345
1961	66	104	247	413
Increase (%)	24.5	25.3	37.2	19.7

[32] *Economic Bulletin for Europe,* Sept. 1962 p. 2. Western Europe is, of course, not identical with the EEC. but includes also the member states of the European Free Trade Zone (EFTA) and still others, but the principal increases were within the EEC.

[33] *Loc. cit.,* p. 3.

The second and fourth columns show that the share of Eastern Europe in world trade is, absolutely, much smaller than that of Western Europe, although since 1953, in contradistinction to the most recent phase, the Eastern share has grown faster than that of the West (mainly because of increased eastern exports to Western Europe). As a measure of integration, however, it is important that the share of internal eastern trade in world trade grew much less rapidly than the corresponding share of internal western trade; in fact, as the last line in all four columns shows, Eastern Europe could not quite maintain the role which its internal trade played in its whole trade in 1953, whereas in Western Europe the significance grew very much in relation to its trade with all countries. It should be noticed, however, that the figures in the table indicate shares in world trade, not volume or value of a country's foreign trade. In the latter terms, internal eastern trade grew much more than its share in the world trade, because of the drastic increase of commodity exchange among all countries. The same, of course, is true of internal western trade.

Impressive as these figures are, they do not by themselves permit more than a tentative judgment on how good a use the Eastern European countries have made of their objective opportunities for integration, since these opportunities themselves have not been examined with sufficient thoroughness and compared with those of Western Europe. To grasp the importance of this point, let us assume a bloc of countries with similar natural conditions and with a population showing similar distribution of skills. Obviously, the advantage of each country specializing in particular types of production, and consequently the possible gain from integration, will be smaller in such a bloc than where differences in conditions of production are more important. Where less can be gained, the incentive to achieve a high degree of integration will be weaker. There is no immediately apparent reason to assume that Eastern Europe does not have at least the same opportunities for differentiation—and should, therefore, have at least the same incentive to integrate as Western Europe, but no detailed comparison of these conditions seems yet to have been made, and this would be required for a final judgment.[34]

[34] Exchange among countries is likely to grow with their national incomes. One of the first tasks in refining the comparison between the effectiveness of Eastern and Western efforts at integration would, therefore, be to establish the ratio between growth of internal exchange and growth of national income in both orbits. This task, however, is far more complex than it seems at first sight. Much time has been spent on establishing figures for the national income of the Soviet Union which would be comparable with those of the West. It will be a formidable job to carry out the same modification of official figures for all the other countries of the Soviet bloc.

Even if we could definitely say that Eastern Europe has used its opportunities for integration less well than Western Europe, this would not give us conclusive arguments concerning the relative capacity of the Communist system to carry out integration, since Communist nations, like others, have qualities and aspirations not resulting from their economic system. Some impediments to integration, however, do originate in the characteristics of Communism, either in the sense that they are created by some features of the system or that the effectiveness of tendencies counteracting integration is increased by the centralization of economic power, although these tendencies themselves may have their source in other circumstances.

To think of an example of the latter type, we have only to remember that nationalism is a great force in all the Eastern European countries. Although some of them, for instance Poland and Bulgaria, had once been powerful states, they were for a long time under Turkish, Russian or German domination or tutelage and their experience of independent nationhood—even to the extent that it exists today, under Soviet hegemony—is relatively recent. In contrast, Western Europe, having tasted the fruits—both sweet and bitter—of national sovereignty for a much longer part of the Modern Age, is now beginning to question the value of the nation-state. To be sure, Communist ideology is the official creed in all the nations of the Soviet bloc and establishes a strong bond, at least among the ruling circles. Many observations show, however, that even good Communists have a strong feeling of loyalty to their own nations, all the more so because in the Stalinist period they had to pretend to put the cause of Communism—identified with the national interest of the Soviet Union—above all other considerations. The continued hegemonic position of the Soviet Union, which closes some outlets for satellite nationalism, makes the others more important—among them economic policy. Economic development plans can as well be an instrument to create a great diversity of industries as to concentrate available resources on relatively few, leaving much room for exchange with other nations. The foreign trade monopoly of the state, which exists in all satellite nations as well as in the Soviet Union, makes it possible to prevent any undesired competition from other Soviet-bloc nations as well as from the West. Thus economic nationalism found ready-made tools to obstruct specialization and thereby integration.

Convenience of the planners operates in the same direction. Integration of planned economies may be potentially very fruitful, but it is easier to plan if one has to take only domestic production and consumption into account. Planners may consider it particularly troublesome to participate in a multilateral system of trade: If nation A makes a bilateral agreement with nation B, it is relatively easy to foresee what goods, and approximately how much of each, can be profitably supplied and demanded by either nation, and these quantities—or any portion of them on which both parties can agree—may then be embodied into the national plans. In a multilateral system, when B can transfer to C some export surplus gained in its trade with A, unexpected demands for delivery are more likely; such demands need not be satisfied, but they could only be ignored at the risk of an undesirable accumulation of claims against A in the portfolio of C. This inconvenience of multilateralism is apparently one of the reasons why the efforts to establish a clearing system within COMECON have not led to great practical results, although too short a time has perhaps elapsed since the last such effort—at the fifteenth COMECON conference in Warsaw in December 1961—for a safe judgment of its effectiveness. Free mutual convertibility of currencies within the Soviet bloc is apparently far off, and as long as it is impossible to obtain any desired amount of Soviet rubles for Polish, Czech, Hungarian, Bulgarian or Rumanian money, even the use of Soviet currency for the settling of accounts within the bloc—a generally accepted practice—has only the significance of a minor technical device. In the main, trade within the Soviet bloc consists of exchange of commodities on the basis of bilateral agreements. This is no strong foundation for an integrating process. The European Economic Community, on the other hand, has been led by experience to the introduction of free convertibility of member currencies within fairly wide limits, and the coordination of currency policies which will permit even wider convertibility is making progress.

The manner of pricing commodities for exchange within the Soviet bloc is apt to discourage any reliance on foreign trade. At least between the Soviet Union and the satellites, exchange is usually based on world prices, which, in view of the limited trade relations between the Soviet bloc and the rest of the world, are often pretty meaningless within the Soviet orbit. On this basis, a country may give up a commodity of much greater usefulness than the goods it receives in return.[35] Such cases might not arise so easily if the administration of foreign trade were more closely connected with the management of production than is at present true within the Communist orbit, but a reorganization in this sense, though not incompatible with Communist principles, would require a revamping of important features of the present Communist setup. Until it takes place, tendencies obstructing integration will be strengthened by the thought that the integrating process, based on inadequate pricing, may lead to new irrationalities.

[35] For examples, see Nove, *op. cit.*, p. 191.

On the other hand, integration efforts within the Communist orbit are free from some of the impediments against which their Western counterpart has to struggle. In the East, nothing is comparable to the West European farm lobby which, by opposing concessions to agricultural export interests within the British Commonwealth and in Scandinavia, has powerfully supported De Gaulle's politically motivated veto against British membership in the European Economic Community, and at the time of writing is also an obstacle to expansion of the Community to Northern Europe. In the industrial field, too, protectionist interests have occasionally opposed integration, and in the free political system of the West, they have direct and open access to the places of decision-making, whereas in the East similar tendencies have to be filtered through the apparatus of the Communist Party and will thereby often be weakened. So far, these advantages for the cause of integration in the East seem to have been greatly outweighed by the handicaps. Will the same situation continue in the future?

This is by no means certain. The growth, in absolute terms, of internal eastern trade seems to be due—in addition to growing national incomes—mainly to technical facilitation of exchange among the COMECON countries on the basis of the existing differentiation of production, for instance through the agreement on delivery and transportation of commodities, concluded in 1957. For the reasons explained, the efforts at increasing differentiation by assigning the development of some industries to one country, other industries to another country, have so far existed more in propaganda than in reality. This failure of the COMECON to execute the major portion of a much advertised task on the one hand shows the strength of the obstacles, on the other hand means that an important unexploited opportunity for making the COMECON more useful is still available. Given the great interest of the Communist leadership in all the participating countries in cementing political solidarity by complementary economic action within the bloc, especially if the West can register further progress in this field, one must expect new drives for coordination of plans within COMECON. Whether these impulses can prevail over considerations of national self-sufficiency and planners' convenience remains to be seen.

CHAPTER 20

THE ECONOMIC SYSTEM OF YUGOSLAVIA

The Emergence of Yugoslav "Revisionism"

SINCE THE MIDDLE of the 1950's, a process of differentiation has been under way within the Soviet orbit. The studious emulation of the Soviet pattern during the early postwar years, with only such alterations as were approved or even suggested by Moscow, has given way to an attempt of the satellite states to develop their own methods in the pursuit of the common goal, establishment of a society of full communism. In order to give a completely rounded picture of the economic system as represented by the communist part of the world, it would be necessary to describe the institutions and mode of operation of each of the communist economies. But there is just not enough reliable material accessible to Western analysts for such a comprehensive undertaking. There are, to be sure, monographs on several of the satellite countries and many books and articles on Communist China, but they can only picture the situation as it exists at one given moment; yet the situation is so much in flux as to necessitate observation over a period of several years in order to form an opinion on the trend. For the timebeing, this is a matter for specialists; here it seems best to confine the analysis of communist economies outside the Soviet Union to the country which has deviated earlier and farther than others from the Soviet pattern, and on which we are also provided with relatively ample material: Yugoslavia.

Yugoslavia started the postwar period as a country willingly accepting Stalinist leadership. Under the Serbian Karageorgevich dynasty, which had reigned in Yugoslavia since the latter's creation after the First World War, factions and ethnic groups had always been at loggerheads; there was no united front in the struggle against the German and Italian occupation, but a fierce civil war raged between collaborators and patriots, and also among different groups of the latter. The bitterness of this struggle operated against moderation and thus benefited the communists, who in the person of Josip Broz Tito possessed a more effective leader than any other faction. The role of the Red Army in the liberation of the country further enhanced the prestige of communism and solidified the power of the Communist Party. The general confusion probably made the rigid Soviet pattern appear even to some non-Communists as a desirable kind of order—the only kind attainable under the circumstances.

But the position of Soviet-type communism was not inherently as strong as it appeared to be. Although a well organized hard core of Communists devoted to the Leninist-Stalinist tradition existed in the country, the struggle for liberation had mobilized a multitude of people who, while at the end of the war were thoroughly in sympathy with communism as a political movement, had no full grasp of the Moscow doctrine and would not have accepted it if their understanding had been sufficient for such a decision.

The strong regional differentiation forced from the outset the adoption of a federal constitution. The new communist-led Yugoslavia was divided into five member republics, whose autonomy had more reality than federation in the Soviet Union, where at least under Lenin and Stalin, the Communist Party was so rigidly centralized and so tightly controlled the decisions in the member republics as to leave them no room for a policy of their own.

With ethnic groups and individuals extremely jealous of their right of self-determination, social conditions were even more heterogeneous than they had been in Russia at the time of the revolution. Whereas in some parts of the country landlordism had been important, others were inhabited by independent, property-conscious small farmers. Ethnic antagonisms, largely coinciding with religious divisions, overshadowed class hostility in many areas. Among many participants in the struggle against the occupying powers and collaborators, a strong individualistic spirit prevailed, incompatible with Stalinist dogmatism.

The Soviet pattern of economic life could have been maintained in the long run only if imposed by superior force. This force could have been supplied by Russia, but that would have spelled an end to Yugoslav independence, and most Yugoslavs were not psychologically conditioned to consider such a sacrifice acceptable.

It took time, however, for the tendencies toward deviation from the Soviet model to crystalize in Yugoslavia. Right after the war, the situation was full of contradictory features. Yugoslavia almost skipped the stage of a "people's democracy," which was adopted by the satellites under immediate Soviet control—the phase in which some "bourgeois" parties are permitted to exist and have seats in the legislature on the condition that they accept the leadership of the Communist Party and let the party determine the distribution of seats without an election campaign. After a very brief period of transition, Yugoslavia established a one-party government of Communists. But the Communist Party was less of a closed circle in Yugoslavia than elsewhere, having a larger membership in absolute figures in 1947 than the Communist Party of the Soviet Union had at a comparable stage of historical development in 1921;[1] and the party formed the core of an even wider circle, originally called Popular Front and later renamed Socialist Alliance of the Working People, "which in Yugoslavia is a true mass organization and not—as in some People's Democracies—merely an association of a limited number of representative individuals." Behind the practice of the Communist Party to act through this wider organization is the hope of assuring that "the great majority of the non-party citizens supports (*suive*) the policies of the party instead of simply obeying the party."[2]

In economic matters, similar disparities occurred. As early as the fall of 1946, Yugoslavia introduced complete nationalization of factories, banks, wholesale trade and means of transportation; part of the retail trade was also nationalized. Private enterprise was even abolished in artisans' shops; they were obliged to form cooperatives. Also, a very ambitious Five Year Plan, based on a high degree of centralization with emphasis on the obligation of the managers to turn out prescribed physical quantities rather than to make the enterprises profitable in monetary terms, was introduced in 1947. In contrast to the ardor for change in these fields, the tempo of reform in agriculture was at first slow. Collectives were founded in the main only

[1] For figures, see C. Bobrowski, *La Yougoslavie socialiste* (Cahiers de la Fondation Nationale des Sciences Politiques #77), Paris: Armand Colin, 1956, p. 48. The reason for selecting the year 1921 as comparable with 1947 in Yugoslavia was the end of the Russian civil war in that year. It is debatable, however, whether a somewhat later year should not have been chosen, and if so, the difference would not be quite so striking. Between 1921 and 1924 the membership figures of the Communist Party in Russia almost doubled, because the beginnings of the intra-party struggle for the successorship of Lenin induced some of the aspirants—especially Stalin—to bring in hitherto politically inactive persons to turn them into supporters. But even with that increase, the membership of the Soviet party remained much smaller in proportion to the total population than that of the Yugoslav party.

[2] *Loc. cit.*, p. 50.

for the management of large holdings taken away from their previous owners because the latter had been "ex-enemies"[3] or collaborators; for the rest, the government confined itself to the trimming of "kulak" land holdings for the benefit of the rest of the peasantry.

Strangely enough, Yugoslav agricultural policy experienced its brief period of radicalization only after the break with the Soviet Union in 1948. In 1949, the Communist Party suddenly decided to carry out rapid collectivization on a large scale. This may to some extent have been a result of the desire to disprove the accusations leveled at Belgrade by Moscow, since one of the items of the indictment had been undue moderation in agricultural policy; very likely, however, dissatisfaction with food deliveries by the peasants was an even more important reason: The leaders of Yugoslavia seem to have succumbed to the same error in 1949 as the Russian leaders did 20 years earlier, i.e. they shot at the relatively small target of inadequate deliveries with the big gun of forced collectivization, only to have the latter explode in their faces. Although the Yugoslav collectivization drive did not have the catastrophic effects of its Soviet predecessor because there was no slaughtering of draft animals, the deliveries declined further pretty drastically. The Yugoslav Communists were wise enough to terminate the abortive experiment before the consequences became too serious. Peasants were officially permitted in 1953 to leave the collectives, and very soon the bulk of Yugoslav agriculture was again under private management.

The First Five Year Plan was overambitious from the outset and suffered from all the other faults of Soviet planning,[4] but it would probably not have turned out as badly as it did if the rupture with Moscow had not brought about a cancellation of all Soviet aid and even a blockade by Moscow and its satellites. Subsequently, the industrialization policy was modified, and Western support somewhat relieved the balance of payments. Approximately in 1953, Yugoslavia began her spectacular economic expansion, although it was only in 1958 that per capita personal consumption exceeded the prewar level.[5]

Even before the end of the First Five Year Plan, a basic reform in industrial management had been inaugurated. In 1950, the nationalized en-

[3] This category included all ethnic Germans and Hungarians, regardless of whether of a former foreign or Yugoslav nationality.

[4] For a defense of the methods employed in the First Five Year Plan as the kind of planning necessary in a low-level economy, see Boriboje Jelič, "The Yugoslav Economic Planning System," in *Socialist Thought and Practice*, June 1961, pp. 59-64. The magazine, appearing in Belgrade, has at least a semi-official character.

[5] See George W. Hoffman and Fred W. Neal, *Yugoslavia and the New Communism*, New York: Twentieth Century Fund, 1962, p. 365.

terprises were handed over to workers' councils to be run, within the framework of general regulations, for the benefit of the workers in the enterprise. During the subsequent years, Yugoslavia has moved ever closer to a "socialist market economy," if this term means a condition in which workers have the determining voice in the management of industries and are free to act essentially as entrepreneurs do in a capitalist system. The characteristic of the Yugoslav system, however, is the coexistence of this market economy with a plan, which the Yugoslav government is trying to carry out in the main by setting the signals for the market orientation of the enterprises. In this respect—and in spite of great differences in many details of importance—the Yugoslav system has some similarity with the French *économie concertée.*

There is a temptation to view the rupture between Moscow and Belgrade as a consequence of the latter's economic heresies, because today the differences of the economic methods play a considerable role in the violent denunciations of Yugoslav "revisionism" by the Chinese Communists and in the echo which these denunications find elsewhere within the Communist world. Moreover, it is quite possible that the peculiarities of the Yugoslav economic and psychological situation would in any event have produced deviations of economic policy which the Soviet Union might have been unwilling to tolerate in a member country of the Soviet bloc. In the actual development of events, however, the causal relationship was the reverse. The reasons for the break were essentially political, with economic grievances of Moscow against Belgrade providing only some camouflage; for the most part, Moscow was antagonized by the Yugoslav independence of spirit, the unwillingness of the Yugoslavs—in spite of great gratitude for Soviet military help—to regard their liberation as the exclusive accomplishment of the Red Army and thus minimize the role of the partisans, and to accept for their country the function of a mere executor of Moscow politics. Yugoslav plans for a federation or confederation with Bulgaria and possibly other Balkan states probably played a role too, although Moscow's attitude toward special ties among the Balkan states has been contradictory and enigmatic. The political rupture destroyed some of the prestige of the Soviet Union in Yugoslavia and gave the country the inner as well as the outer freedom to go its own way in reshaping its economy.

The Present Organization of the Yugoslav Economy

WORKERS' SELF-MANAGEMENT

The Internal Organization of the Firm

The decision of the Yugoslav state to surrender the right to operate production facilities—though not the property—to the workers of each enterprise grew out of a combination of practical and fundamental considerations. On the practical side, it was thought that in this way the incentive to work efficiently could be strengthened and the dangers of overcentralization avoided. On the side of principle, Yugoslav leadership liked to think that self-management of workers in industry, just as self-government in communes and other institutions, was the prerequisite for the eventual "withering away of the state" which Marx had foreseen for the condition of full communism. By laying the foundations of a society which might later exist without the machinery of the state, the Yugoslavs believed that they were proving themselves better Marxists than the Soviet Communists, who merely paid lip service to that Marxian tenet while establishing a most rigid system of centralization.

To almost any Western observer, the belief in the "withering away of the state" appears visionary. There is no reason, however, to doubt that most Titoists held—and are still holding—this belief in all sincerity, and that for this reason as well as for the sake of practical advantages they have tried to make a reality of the principle of workers' self-management. They encountered the difficulty that the economic system they were creating required spontaneity on the part of individuals, whereas the political forms which they were trying to maintain were far more suited for a direction of all efforts from above. Although the political structure has gradually been loosened up, the conflict is by no means over.

Workers' self-management is intended to put into practice, within the framework of the firm, a democratic principle of organization. It could not function, however, as direct democracy; essentially, it has to be representative democracy. Although the workers of an enterprise convene from time to time to lay down some basic rules for the policy of the firm, for the most part the task to define business policy belongs to an elected body, the workers' council, which thus acquires a position between that of a shareholders' meeting and a board of directors in a capitalist enterprise. The workers' council elects a management board, to explain the defined policies in detail, especially in regard to personnel. The final decision on the distribution of profits is reserved for the workers' council. For the executive tasks in the narrower sense of the word, a chief manager ("director") is appointed who has approximately the function of an American corporation president.

The appointment of the chief manager is not in the hands of the workers' representatives of the individual enterprise, although they have a voice in this appointment. The appointment is made under the authority of the commune, but the selection is up to a joint committee of the workers' council of the enterprise concerned and the special committee of the commune.[6] As far as judgment is possible on the basis of still limited experience, this seems to be a good compromise; it avoids the danger to work discipline which would arise if the executives were dependent for their positions exclusively on the workers' representatives in the enterprise—this point is well known from the controversies over consumers' versus producers' cooperatives in the West—yet it does not deny the workers all influence on the selection of those under whom they have to work. The commune is closer to the interests of the workers than would be a state organ, and the special committee consists mainly of members of workers' councils within the commune; they are as a rule responsive enough to the workers' desires not to elect a manager who could not get along with the workers of his enterprise. On the other hand, the fiscal interest of the commune in the profitable operation of the enterprises is sufficient guarantee that competence will not be overshadowed by popularity as a determinant in the choice of leading personnel. To minimize favoritism, the chief manager is usually chosen after a competitive examination, following upon public advertisement of the position with an indication of the required qualifications.

Although the procedure in electing the chief manager tends to reduce the danger of conflict between him and the workers' council, this danger cannot be entirely eliminated. Actually, the chief manager bears a double responsibility, toward the workers' council and toward the commune, and indirectly toward the state.[7] He may find himself caught between the two

[6] For the constitution and the functions of the commune, see below. Before the constitutional reform of 1963, the managers ("directors") were "selected by the people's committees from among candidates who apply in response to public advertisement of the vacancy, under the guidance of a special subcommission of the people's committee appointed for the purpose, and in which one-third of the members are representatives of the workers' council of the enterprise concerned." (*1000 Facts about Yugoslavia*, Belgrade: Publishing House Jugoslavia, 1961, p. 35.) The constitution of 1963 has given the people's committee the new name of communal assembly, but does not seem to have changed the procedure of appointing directors in any important respect. Undoubtedly, the "subcommission" which "guides" the communal assembly in these matters was, and is, the de facto appointing agency.

[7] It seems that the chief manager's responsibility toward the commune and the state is expressed in the stipulation that he is "directly responsible for the execution of the laws." (Art. 36 of the law of 1953, regulating workers' self-management, as printed in

horns of a dilemma if the wishes of the workers conflict too much with the interests of the community at large. The principle of workers' self-management would require that the manager could be recalled by the workers' council just as the members of the management board, but obviously this would frustrate his responsibility toward the commune. Therefore a set of complicated rules for the dismissal of managers was adopted, which in effect mean that the workers' council can take the initiative for the removal of an unpopular manager and can ultimately obtain it if the council persists in this demand and is backed by the workers, but that the commune and state authorities also can remove a manager on their own initiative.[8]

The Firm and the Government

Within the rules of policy laid down by the workers' council and the management council, the executive decides on output, product mix, methods of production and—with the exception of a number of products on which price ceilings or limitations of profit margins still exist—on prices. Although the national planning authorities estimate in advance the output of the various industries—otherwise there would be no plan—the managers of the enterprises are under no obligation to turn out the goods which the planners expect to be forthcoming; rather, it is the planners' obligation to propose policies which will make it profitable for the individual enterprises to make their proper contributions to the fulfillment of the plan. This is one of the decisive differences between the Yugoslav and Soviet systems.

In disposing of gross profits, the workers' council is obliged to make proper allowances for depreciation and depletion of capital and for reserves, and for meeting tax obligations. The rules which require the maintenance of capital are intended to safeguard the interest of the nation as the owner of the instruments of production, and are probably stricter than the rules

---

Bobrowski, *op. cit.*, p. 170.) This, of course, means a responsibility merely for the legality but not for the expediency of the activities which the firm undertakes under his direction. Whether this distinction is practically as significant in Yugoslavia as it would be in a country with a clear separation of powers cannot be ascertained at the present time.

[8] See Hoffman and Neal, *op. cit.*, p. 241. The position of the "director" is well analyzed in Harry Schleicher, *Das System der betrieblichen Selbstverwaltung in Jugoslawien*, Berlin: Duncker & Humblot, 1961, pp. 244 ff. Schleicher points out that a director whose dismissal has not been demanded by the workers' council can only be removed for violation of a law but not because he has failed to raise the profit of the enterprise to its maximum level (p. 248). Clearly, this sets limits to the discretion of the public authorities with regard to a director's dismissal, but whether this means that except upon demand of the workers' council a director cannot be dismissed for such unwise actions as to show incompetence is doubtful, since the conduct of business according to the rules of prudence is undoubtedly among his legal duties.

in capitalist countries in which they are intended to protect the investing public. After these obligations are met, the workers' council is free to decide on the use of profits. These may be used for investment, for social purposes —for instance the construction of workers' homes, recreational facilities and so on—or may be distributed among the workers as their individual shares in the earnings. As a consequence of the great difficulties which the Yugoslav economy experienced in 1961, the government took some measures to induce the enterprises to increase their allocations to the investment fund at the expense of the individual shares in profit, but it seems that the power of the workers' councils to decide on these allocations was maintained at least in principle.

In regard to price policy, the autonomy of the enterprise is not complete. Yugoslav prices are not all freely formed on the market. There are some price ceilings and more instances in which the margin of wholesalers and processors is limited by authoritative decision. Since 1959, the number of these instances has even increased. In addition to federal regulations limiting prices or margins for various commodities a temporary law has been enacted to give the communes general power to regulate the margins for retailers of commodities for daily use, such as food, fuel and other necessities. But the Yugoslav authorities are generally aware that price regulating powers must not be used to impose prices lower than those that would just clear the market; what they want to prevent is prices which are kept above this level by monopolistic power.[9]

The monopoly problem is serious in Yugoslavia because the limited size of the country makes it inevitable that there can be no more than a small number of modern factories in any line of production. Consequently, one big enterprise may sometimes dominate a regional or perhaps even the national market, and more often enterprises of any importance will be few and tacit collusion between them will be easy. Tito himself considered the matter important enough to address this warning to managers and workers on the occasion of the fifth congress of the Socialist Alliance:

[9] This is not always indicated as the purpose of the limitations; perhaps more frequently, their avowed purpose is to combat inflation. In a perfectly competitive market, however, inflation cannot begin with price rises; only an increase in money (or in the circulation of money) can start the inflationary process; barring such an increase, competition will put any seller who attempts to raise the price above cost plus normal profit out of the market. In an economy with monopolistic features, however, the reverse sequence is possible; here it can happen that prices rise first and that then the monetary authorities feel compelled to issue the amounts of money necessary for the purchase of the higher-priced goods and services because otherwise a slump would ensue. Therefore, to say that price rises must be prevented because they might cause inflation is only another way of saying that monopoly must be controlled because, aside from other undesirable effects, it might reduce the purchasing power of money.

Workers' management includes the right of economic organizations to form business associations for the purpose of cooperating and specializing in different branches of production and ensuring a better division of labor. . . . Certainly, association at the top designed to secure monopoly on the market, to liquidate or merge small enterprises with big economic units would be harmful as would also be the establishment of one or another type of unproductive workers' supercouncil. This would be a gross infringement of socialist relations of production, because the working collectives in the small enterprises would be deprived of the right of self-management. Associations of the nature of monopolies, cartels or similar organizations tending to replace workers' management by bodies which would be above the workers' councils, are incompatible with our system— We have often said that enterprises should cooperate because it is essential to achieve the specialization of production as it is also necessary for the small enterprises, as independent production units, to supplement the larger enterprises and to cooperate with them. As a result, costs of production would be lowered to a considerable extent. But fusion for the purpose of achieving a monopoly position on the market and raising prices must on no account be the purpose of the cooperation I have just mentioned. Instead of liquidating small enterprises by merging them with bigger ones, we must on the contrary endeavor to stimulate the construction of many more suitable enterprises, especially in the underdeveloped areas, where suitable conditions for such type of enterprise exist.[10]

This statement shows that the fear of monopoly combines with other considerations to cause some skepticism about the blessings of very large enterprises, especially when they are formed by swallowing up or merging a number of smaller ones. The greatest virtue of the Yugoslav system, the active participation of manual workers in the management of industries, has the greatest practical significance in small and middle-sized enterprises, whereas giantism necessarily leads to a preponderance of managerial bureaucracy. At least some of the Yugoslav leaders understand this well, and also seem to recognize that it is irrational to replace small production units by large ones where inadequacy of transportation facilities and market organization favor local production on a limited scale, and where an ample supply of cheap labor detracts from the usefulness of labor-saving devices, as is generally the case in the underdeveloped parts of the country. On the other hand, fanaticism for modernity, and therefore preference for plants of very large size, is also to be found among Yugoslav policy makers. But even if all irrational preferences for large-sized plants were eliminated, the average size would have to grow as the country progresses, exhausts its

[10] Josip Broz Tito, "The Building of Socialism and the Role and Tasks of the Socialist Alliance of the Working People of Yugoslavia." *Report to the Fifth Congress of the Socialist Alliance of the Working People of Yugoslavia in Belgrade, April 18, 1960,* pp. 23 f.

easily available labor reserves and undertakes kinds of production which are just not feasible in other than huge installations; a country so short of capital and therefore not able to afford too much obsolescence, will also often have to build on a scale too large for today but just right for tomorrow. As it will continue to be necessary, in many instances, to replace the small shop with the big factory, and the big factory with a bigger one, the hazard of monopoly will remain and may become more acute. Yet administrative limitations of prices and margins not only bring back a feature which the Titoists wanted to eliminate from their economy, but they are also clumsy instruments of monopoly control. They may work a little better in an economy with a plan, which makes it easier to recognize the determinants of the price that would establish itself under perfect competition, than they would under unplanned capitalism, but they can hardly work well enough to suppress monopoly pricing. The most effective way of solving this problem—to the extent that it can be solved at all, for Yugoslavia can hardly be expected to develop a one hundred per cent effective anti-trust policy when no other country has succeeded in so doing—will be a still greater participation of Yugoslavia in foreign trade, which will expose Yugoslav enterprises to greater competition at home and abroad and at the same time give them a chance to sell the output of modern-sized plants in the market of a greater area if calculation is close enough. But this solution has a number of economic and political pre-conditions, which cannot be created overnight. In the meantime, it is of particular importance that, wherever market conditions warrant it, the formation of new enterprises be assured to prevent monopoly positions of existing ones.[11]

As a matter of form, any group of Yugoslav citizens has the right to organize a new firm, after having complied with defined legal requirements.[12] But these requirements include the founders' obligation to provide the necessary capital either from their own resources or through credit obtained from a bank of the state or a commune. Obviously, a group of "technicians interested in a particular project or . . . a group of workers who want to secure employment for themselves"[13] will hardly be able to supply the

[11] See on the related problems of expansion and of the creation of new enterprises Bobrowski, *op. cit.*, pp. 173 ff.

[12] Of course, no hired help can be used. Therefore, if the labor of the founders is not sufficient for the operation of the enterprise, they must admit outsiders as associates with full rights. This requirement is onerous in many instances and probably one of the reasons why the founding of new enterprises by private citizens is no longer of great importance —if indeed it ever was.

[13] These are some of the examples mentioned by Bobrowski, *op. cit.*, p. 174, to illustrate the possibilities of how new firms may emerge. Djordje Mijič, in a statement made three years after the publication of Bobrowski's book, mentions only the public bodies and other enterprises as possible founders of firms, probably because in the realm of large-

necessary funds for a large productive undertaking without outside help, though they may be able to finance a laboratory, a repair shop or a small hotel. New industrial firms are sometimes founded by existing enterprises—either by a single enterprise or by a group of enterprises, which may wish thus to create new outlets for their products or new suppliers for raw materials or equipment. There is no assurance, however, that in this way effective competition can be introduced where monopoly or semi-monopoly exists because the circumstances which create an inducement for existing firms to organize new ones are not always present; moreover, the new firm, especially a dealer firm created by producers, may become an instrument rather than an antidote of monopoly. An agency is needed whose task it is to take the initiative for the creation of new firms if this seems economically feasible and desirable, and if no initiative is forthcoming from any other quarter. In the Yugoslav system, this task is within the responsibility of the communes.

The Communes

THE STRUCTURE OF THE COMMUNES

The Yugoslav concept of the commune (*obština*) has little in common with the Chinese concept,[14] nor is it strictly synonymous with the concept of a local community in Western countries. Like the latter, it is also an administrative unit, but it has much wider socio-economic functions; furthermore, the Yugoslav commune is a relatively large body for a local unit in a country with so low a degree of urbanization.[15]

The most important organ of the commune is the communal assembly.

---

scale production citizens' groups are in practice unimportant. See Djordje Mijić, "La Gestion d'entreprise, partie integrante de la gestion sociale" in Institut de Sociologie Solvay (Université Libre de Bruxelles), *Le Régime et les institutions de la république populaire fédérative de Yougoslavia,* Bruxelles: Centre national pour l'étude des pays à régime communiste, 1959, pp. 70 f.

14 The Chinese concept originated in Russia. Soon after the Russian revolution, various forms of collective management of agriculture were developed, and the most extreme one, involving community of all property and strictly communal ways of living, was called commune. When collectivization on a large scale was introduced, however, the form normally chosen was not the commune but the artel, also called kolkhoz, in which only the major part of the land, of livestock and of implements was collectivized, but some property remains to the individuals who also have some privacy in their lives.

15 In 1960, there were 782 communes, comprising on the average 34 settlements with 23,000 inhabitants. Whereas 28 communes had less than 5000 inhabitants, about one-eighth of the total number had more than 40,000 and about one half between 5000 and 20,000. The 782 communes were grouped into 75 districts (Sreten Bjeličić, *Communal System in Yugoslavia,* Belgrade: Publicističko Izdavački Zavod "Jugogoslavija," 1961 pp. 14 f.) The role of the district (*srez*) as a unit of self-government is declining.

It combines legislative with some executive functions and is divided into two chambers: The political chamber and the chamber of working committees. The former is elected through direct and equal suffrage; the members of the latter are also chosen in direct elections, but the votes of the individual citizens do not have equal weight. For the purpose of electing the latter chamber, all the voters are divided into two groups: The workers in industry, in commerce and in the handicrafts on the one hand, individuals engaged in agriculture on the other. Between these two groups the number of seats in the council are distributed "according to the percentage share of either group in the social product of the commune, as determined in the economic plan." [16] Since the per capita social product is smaller in agriculture than in industry, the industrial worker has more voting power than the farmer; thus the system results in a reduction of the political influence of the agricultural population below its numerical importance, except in purely agricultural communes. The chamber is part of the communal assembly which decides many issues as vital for the farmers as for the workers in industry and commerce, and the former are handicapped in the defense of their interests by the political discrimination. The inequality in the distribution of votes is not found only on the commune level, but also on the national level, as will be seen later. Although nothing remotely comparable to the anti-peasant policy in the Soviet Union can be found in Yugoslavia, the Titoist political system is also committed to the idea that the struggle for the good society is the historical task of the industrial worker rather than that of the peasant, and as a consequence gives the industrial workers greater political weight.

For some time considerations have been under way, however, to modify if not to abolish the discrimination against the peasantry in matters of political rights. This may indicate that the Titoist leadership believes that the regime is becoming increasingly popular with the agricultural population; in any event, with the constant migration from the country to the city, the

[16] Jovan Djordjević, "Le Self-gouvernment local ou le systeme communal de la Yougoslavie" Institut de Sociologie Solvay, *Le Regime et les institutions de la republique populaire federative de Yougoslavie,* p. 113. The official *Statistical Pocket Book of Yugoslavia,* 1963, states that for the chamber of working communities the number of delegates for each economic activity "corresponds to the economic significance and strength of each individual branch" (p. 17). This statement seems to be identical in meaning with Djordjević's explanation; apparently, therefore, there was no change in the composition of this communal chamber as a consequence of the constitutional reform of 1963. The latter, while splitting up vocational representation on the federal level into four chambers (see below), has retained the bicameral system as the regular arrangement for the commune, "although the constitutions of the republics may provide for the formation of several chambers of working communities." *The Constitution of the Socialist Federal Republic of Yugoslavia,* trans. Petar Mijušković, Belgrade: Secretariat for Information of the Federal Executive Council, 1963, Art. 76 (p. 33).

political influence of the peasants is decreasing automatically on the national level and on that of the member republics, and to a less extent in many communes; thus it may appear to the regime that it can dispense with discrimination. The new constitution of 1963 has in principle retained the discrimination, but apparently reduced it in degree; since the new system is very complicated, the effect of the provisions cannot be determined with certainty before practical experience is available.[17]

GENERAL FUNCTIONS OF THE COMMUNES

"After having defined the new situation of the commune, the law of 1955 on the organization of the commune and the district stipulated a presumption of competence in favor of the commune; therefore only those functions which are reserved for the federation, the member republic or the district are exempt from the communal competence." [18] Thus the commune, according to the letter of the law, has the same kind of residual power which the individual states have in the American union. At present, the practical significance of this power of the commune is limited by the great importance of the tasks which can only be fulfilled on a national scale and which therefore devolve upon the federal government; it may well be the same in the future. The commune now has no functions which the federal government has not willingly granted and which it could not take back at any time, even if this required a change of the constitution. The principal importance of the residual power in theory granted to the communes lies in what it tells about the intention of the Yugoslav leadership. Some of them at least regard the commune as the cell of the decentralized socialist society of the future, and envisage the replacement of the present national government by a loose federation of communes, much as Marx at times visualized the replacement of the state by a federation of local communities modeled after the Paris commune of 1871. Here again, official Titoist theory claims that the Yugoslav development will lead to the fulfillment of Marx' prophesy that the state will "wither away." [19]

On the practical side, the commune is at the same time the handmaiden of the federal and the republic governments for all purposes for which

[17] For elements of discrimination against the peasantry which would remain even after such a constitutional change, see Hoffman and Neal, *op. cit.*, p. 218.

[18] Djordjevic, *op. cit.*, p. 114.

[19] See Tito, *op. cit.*, p. 17. The withering-away process is supposed to apply not only to national but also to local government. "As it develops further, the commune—which anyway was never envisaged to be a miniature form of the state, but a basic form of socialist social relations—should gradually lose the feature of a body of government and increasingly acquire the character of a social and economic organization of persons working with socially owned means of production and participating in management in line with their individual and collective interests" (*loc. cit.*, p. 34).

these have not created special organs, and an organizational device by which the local population can pursue any common purpose within the limits of national law. The commune is in charge of welfare and health services, of education, of the maintenance of public order; it supervises the enterprises within its jurisdiction with a view to the legality of their activities, and often it supplies them with credit or with guarantees which make it possible for them to obtain capital from the state. There is no doubt that the role of the communes in loosening up the dictatorship and building elements of spontaneity into the system has been important. Although the promotion of the communes in Yugoslavia has some superficial resemblance to the regionalization introduced in the Soviet Union through the Sovnarkhozy the two situations are in fact very different. The Yugolsav commune is a much smaller body, in absolute terms and even in relation to the size of the country, and this difference not only makes another delimitation of functions inevitable—a much larger part of the activities of the Yugoslav commune is devoted to local public services—but also precludes any serious attempt to strive for autarchy, although the danger of excessive "localism" is not entirely absent.

The role of the communes is enhanced by the absence of smaller bodies with more than a trace of self-government. There are local bureaus or councils established by large communes for villages and small towns, and "neighborhood councils" for parts of large cities, but their authority derives from the commune, which remains the center of self-government.[20] Between the commune and the republic stands the district (*srez*), legally an association of communes and possessing similarly constituted organs; but the role of the districts has been dwindling as that of the communes was rising.

THE COMMUNES AND MONOPOLY CONTROL

"The commune is interested . . . in changing the social structure by creating collectives (*Communautés*) of active producers working with the socially owned means of production. This interest is of a material nature. The magnitude of the financial means and the other resources of the commune depend essentially on the volume of economic activity, or rather on the economic strength of the citizens and primarily on the revenues which result from the individual and collective labor of the producers and other workers." [21]

[20] See Bjeličić, *op. cit.*, pp. 87 ff.; Hoffman and Neal, *op. cit.*, pp. 215, 233 f.

[21] Djordjević, *op. cit.*, p. 126. The phrase "producers and other workers" may be puzzling, because what workers would there be except producers? But in the particular interpretation of Marxist theory which modern communism has adopted and which is upheld even in Yugoslavia, services are no part of the national income, although they may be useful or even indispensable for production or for the life of the community. A person render-

Since the commune is interested in the full utilization of all the economic resources within its jurisdiction, it has an incentive to encourage the creation of new production units in any field in which it seems that the volume of production, and consequently of employment, is restricted by imperfect competition. The commune can provide the capital for these units either from its own resources or by guaranteeing loans which the new enterprises may obtain from the state bank. Whether the incentive is strong enough, and the knowledge and ability of the commune leaders sufficient to check monopolistic tendencies remains to be seen. The mere fact that the national leaders still worry about monopoly[22] does not provide definitive evidence that the communes have failed in this task, because it is only in recent years that they have been equipped with sufficient financial resources to play a very active role in economic life, and they have hardly had time to acquire the necessary experience and develop the techniques to counteract monopolistic trends. On the other hand, the communes are interested in the level of earnings of existing local enterprises. There is no a priori assurance that their interest in maximum employment will always outweigh their incentive to help existing firms to obtain maximum profits; economic history knows many instances in which localism and monopoly have entered into an alliance. Yugoslavia may still be forced to create instruments of anti-monopoly policy less open to hazards of economic irrationality than the price ceilings imposed by national agencies and more

---

ing services, for instance a teacher or a policeman, is, therefore, not regarded as a producer, although he earns an income.

[22] In addition to the speech by Tito quoted above, the official pamphlet explaining the current Five Year Plan gives evidence of this concern. Speaking of the necessity "to eliminate large price disparities as much as possible so as to mitigate and remove high and economically unwarranted unevenesses in the economy of individual branches and types of production," the pamphlet first speaks of instances in which "regulated or ceiling prices" are in need of revision, and then continues: "In the case of disparities which had sprung up freely on the market it should be sought, through a correct investment and production policy, to eliminate intensive disharmonies between supply and demand, thereby mitigating sharp price differences and eliminating the unwarranted earnings of individual working collectives which do not originate from their own labour and efforts." (*The Five Year Plan of Economic Development of Yugoslavia 1961-1965*, Belgrad: Secretariat for Information of the Federal Executive Council, 1961, p. 119.) The source of earnings which collectives enjoy without having earned them through their own efforts and which should be corrected through price adjustments can only have resulted from monopolistic or semi-monopolistic positions. Unearned extra-incomes, it is true, may also exist in cases of differential rent, for instance when a mining enterprise exploits a particularly favorable mineral deposit while the price for the mineral is kept relatively high by the necessity to cover the costs of mines less favored by natural conditions; in these instances, however, the remedy would be a higher charge imposed on the favored enterprise by the national community for the use of resources. Since the report speaks of cases which call for price adjustments, the reference is obviously to instances where monopolistic pricing has resulted either from a one-firm monopoly or from collusion.

protected from counteracting incentives than the watchdog functions of the communes.

The National Plan

PLANNING GOALS

The plan as worked out by the federal planning office and eventually enacted as a federal law has for its main purpose the establishment of the rate of economic growth for the whole of Yugoslavia and also for the individual sections of the country, thus providing for a subsidization of the development of the less developed sections at the expense of those already more developed. The tasks involve a planned division of national income into funds for investment and funds for consumption. In planning consumption as well as in distributing the investment funds among consumer goods industries, the Yugoslav planning authorities are in principle guided by consumer preferences, but the time preference adopted by the planners is certainly lower than that which the individuals apply in their private lives and in all probability also lower than that which the individuals, as citizens, would wish to see applied in community decisions.

In order to see this cleavage in the right perspective, however, some other facts must be taken into account. There is a particularly strong case in Yugoslavia for making sure that the economy will grow rapidly. People from the country are pushing into the cities in large numbers, lured by the higher earnings of industrial workers, but they cannot immediately be provided with jobs; meanwhile, they have to subsist on a minimum standard of living. Thus there is a great human need—aside from all prestige considerations and also from the consumers' interest in an increased supply of industrial commodities—for the creation of new production facilities in which people can be employed. The country-city migration could only be reduced by measures that would infringe even more drastically on people's liberty than the imposition of a relatively low time preference. The measures by which the latter effect is achieved are, therefore, significant not only from the aspect of production policy but also from that of social equalization: The industrial workers, though still living on a very low standard as compared with American workers, are better off than the peasants and much better off than the applicants for industrial jobs newly arrived in the cities, and if they are limited in the free use of their incomes in order to relieve the economic pressure on those poorer members of the nation, this is in essence an equalitarian policy.

It must not be assumed that these considerations of equity operate only in the minds of the planners. To be sure, there is no reason to believe that Yugoslavs, just because they live in a state which calls itself socialist and is under the leadership of an elite group which calls itself communist, are more altruistic than people of other lands. There is also no reason, however, why motives of solidarity should be less effective there than elsewhere: The Yugoslav worker, seeing the urgent need for new factory jobs, can hardly be unresponsive to the demand of maintaining a high rate of investment when called upon to judge matters as a citizen, however anxious he may be as a private person for a rapid increase in his presently spendable income in view of the many conveniences which this would enable him to acquire. Willing acquiescence on the part of the average Yugoslav worker in this aspect of state policy is all the more probable for the reason that he has already experienced a great improvement of his living standards and that, barring some disaster, this improvement will continue even with a high investment rate; it is only the tempo of the improvement that is at stake.[23] The understanding which the common man develops for the importance of investment brings his time preference in his capacity as citizen closer to that of the planners. In view of the strength of the factors which make for such understanding, it seems fair to assume that the gap between the planners' time preference and that of the individuals as citizens—the private time preference of the individuals is a different matter[24]—is not as wide in Yugoslavia as it is in the Soviet Union.

If it were otherwise, the Yugoslav system would in all probability have gone to pieces years ago, because the political instruments at the gov-

[23] Since shocks suffered in the past often have an influence on individuals' present attitudes, it may also be of importance that there are no memories in Yugoslavia of such bitter suffering of consumers through public policy like the experience of the Soviet consumer between 1929 and 1933, although the Yugoslav First Five Year Plan was also very hard on the average person. First, as far as can be judged, the actual deprivations were less grave because the agricultural crisis did not reach the same degree of severity. Second, the Yugoslav First Five Year Plan was not a setback in the standard of living as was the Russian, which followed upon the period of relative well-being under the New Economic Policy. The antecedents of the first Yugoslav plan were the even greater deprivations of wartime. Although the Yugoslav plan of 1947 was technically less successful than the Russian Five Year Plan of 1928, its sacrifices and failures were likely to cause less bitterness because it did not appear as a cause of retrogression in consumers' standards deliberately brought about by the government for the sake of a historic mission in which the interest of the population was so much less intense than that of the planners. This might have been different if the hardships and disappoinments of the Yugoslav First Five Year Plan had not been largely attributed to the hostile acts of the Soviet Union.

[24] The gap between planners' and citizens' time preference on the one hand and individuals' private time preference on the other may be greater in Yugoslavia than in the USSR because motorcycles, sewing machines, and even refrigerators may have come within the realm of imagination of more Yugoslavs than Russians. On the other hand, because the Yugoslav system gives the individual more chance and reason to identify himself with public policy, a wider gap between public and private time preference is probably tolerable.

ernment's disposal would hardly enable the latter to carry out low-time-preference plans strongly disapproved by the great majority of citizens. It is true that Yugoslavia has a one-party system, party discipline, a secret police and other trappings of modern dictatorship, but all this is less stringent than in the Soviet Union, and is in part compensated for by a deliberate encouragement of spontaneity. Even the Yugoslav "League of Communists"—as the Communist Party has been renamed—is a body very different from the Communist parties in the Soviet bloc countries; party discipline does not go so far, for instance, as to stifle the vigorous defense of regional interests. An anti-consumer policy as has been carried out in the Soviet Union would require a rebuilding of the political institutions of Yugoslavia. The improbability of such an undertaking makes it unlikely that the restriction of consumption in favor of investment will go very much further than the larger part of public opinion will approve.

The Yugoslav system permits the consumer to use his own money according to his preferences, and the profit interest of the enterprises assures that they will try to satisfy these preferences. Prices are intended to be so formed as to assure that the market will be cleared and that the consumer who wants to buy a commodity does not have to go home unsatisfied because the stock was exhausted before it was his turn in the line of purchasers. It is also the government policy to prevent sellers' monopolies from so raising the price as to restrict the quantity demanded below what it would be if the price were set at marginal (or, in the case of a declining cost curve, at average) cost plus normal profit. All this is obviously in the interest of the consumer. But since planners have a lower time preference than individual consumers, and they wish to develop some areas faster than others, whose inhabitants may not approve of that policy, it would be an overstatement to say that consumers' preferences are the lodestar that exclusively guides economic planning in Yugoslavia. The pursuit of these purposes in planning is made compatible with the functioning of the price mechanism by the use of fiscal means: Individuals and enterprises are taxed to fill the investment funds and thereby left with less purchasing power, the amount of taxes being greater than what individuals, if they decided freely, would put up for investments through voluntary saving; individuals and enterprises in Slovenia and Croatia are taxed more heavily to provide increased investment funds for Montenegro and Macedonia, which means that some consumers are left with less purchasing power and others—through the income-raising effect of investments—are given more, which means a steering of demand by the planners. There are, of course, reasons for these measures which may completely justify them even in the eyes of a strong supporter of consumers' sovereignty, and there are analogies in Western economies, but the fact remains that in these instances demand is being manipulated.

In another respect, too, there arises at least a question whether such manipulation is not taking place—manipulation in the sense that demand is not permitted to extend to the point of equality between unit utility and unit cost.

Yugoslavia, like the Soviet Union, has a turnover tax, meaning a levy collected as a percentage of aggregate sales from the producer, and differentiated with respect to different kinds of product. The producer, of course, has to count the turnover tax as part of his cost; therefore the price which the consumer has to pay and which limits his demand includes the turnover tax. If the same percentage tax were laid upon all products, the turnover tax would raise no problems other than any kind of indirect taxation. The problematic feature of a differentiated turnover tax lies in the fact that it causes the consumer to distribute his purchasing power among various commodities in a manner different from the distribution which he would choose if the goods were available to him at prices merely covering costs. The turnover tax can, therefore, be used as an instrument of planners to establish an outward balance of supply and demand for each commodity while denying the consumer true influence on the use of resources. There is no doubt that the turnover tax is largely used in this manner in the Soviet Union.

But this is not to say that a differentiated turnover tax always amounts to such a distortion of the pattern of resource distribution. Even a purist believer in consumers' sovereignty cannot object to such a differentiated levy where the price demanded by the producer does not express all the social cost of production, and the tax is only high enough to restrict the quantity demanded to the point of equilibrium between price and marginal social cost. Assume, for instance, that a commodity requires a substantial amount of raw material from abroad, of which the balance of payments can sustain only a relatively small importation. In a country like Yugoslavia, where this is common, the social sacrifice of burdening the balance of payments is not fully expressed in the cost of the material to the producer. (It might be argued that, therefore, the currency rate should be changed so as to lower the value of the national currency in terms of other moneys and thus make the foreign material more expensive for the producer, but changes in currency rates often cause repercussions which limit the applicability of this means.)[25] The supply, therefore, cannot be extended to the point of

[25] A currency reform, intended to eliminate the gap between the external and the internal value of the dinar through devaluation of the latter and thus to make dinar prices

equality between price and marginal private cost, including normal profit. If the government merely used foreign exchange control to limit the importation of material to the point which the balance of payments can stand, the enhancement of the product price by the restriction of supply would accrue to the producers as a monopoly gain. The imposition of a heavier turnover tax on this product than on others means that the government drains this extra gain off into the public treasury.

Does the differentiated turnover tax play only this role in Yugoslavia, or does it mean a distortion of the pattern of resource use as it does in the Soviet Union? The available material does not permit a conclusive answer, but on general experience it seems likely that neither of the two possibilities materializes to the exclusion of the other. In all probability, there is some distortion of demand in Yugoslavia through the turnover tax; but since the tax rates are lower, the distorting effect is less important than in the Soviet Union. Moreover, while with Soviet leaders the principle that guidance of production by prices, as determined by consumer demand and objective supply conditions, meets with antagonistic attitudes ranging from grudging acceptance to outright rejection, this principle is affirmed in Yugoslavia. At the worst, therefore, the Yugoslav turnover tax serves as a means to cover up planners' mistakes in giving the consumers what they most want; in the Soviet Union it serves largely as an instrument of a deliberate policy to make the consumers buy what, in the planners' opinion, they ought to want.

The turnover tax is not the only fiscal instrument which can be used to influence the distribution of resources among the various purposes; the following discussion will show other examples. Most of these other devices, however, bear a closer resemblance to instruments of policy used in the Western World, and hardly any of them is capable of being used to the same degree to replace citizens' by planners' preferences.

MEANS OF PLAN EXECUTION

Among the means by which the national authorities induce the firms and communes to take such action as will make the national plan a reality, credit policy plays a prominent role. The plan determines the amounts which will be put at the disposal of enterprises for purposes of expansion by the national investment fund—as it also determines the direct investments by national agencies in highways, defense and many other fields—and the normal way in which the additional capital is made available to the enter-

---

of imported goods more nearly expressive of the social cost of importation, has actually been introduced in January 1961. Since the balance of payments difficulties continued, the purpose, as here described, has not been fully achieved.

prises is through loans. The investible funds have to be collected mainly by taxation; thereby a link between fiscal policy and the steering of the economy by credit policy is created, but the structure as well as the yield of taxes are important in making individuals and firms comply with the plan. Taxation of profits of firms for investment is so devised as to put a premium on distributing the earnings between payments available to members, enlargement of social welfare funds and investment in the way provided by the national plan.

Determination of the percentage of the national income to be invested is a political decision. The same applies to the distribution of the funds available for investment among regions and industries. These decisions provide the basis for the credit and tax measures which are to be taken, and to which the individuals and their organizations are supposed to respond in such a manner as to make the plan come true. The planning authorities make global estimates of these responses and incorporate them into the plan. Of course, the plan neither determines nor estimates the response of each individual household; that would be impossible and has not even been attempted in the Soviet Union. It is more remarkable that the Yugoslav plan neither determines nor estimates the output which the individual firm will create in response to the tax and credit measures, and only in exceptional cases allocates investment funds directly to enterprises. The response is to be essentially free; the realm of political decisions or even of collective foresight is essentially confined to the macro-economic sphere.

Different enterprises or communes compete with each other for the capital which the Federal Investment Fund and the investment funds of the member republics have available for lending in a given area and for a given kind of industrial expansion or social improvement. There was a time when the competition consisted of the borrowing agencies outbidding each other by offers of interest rates,[26] with only minor importance attributed to other considerations, such as the security of repayment, the length of the period within which repayment will take place, or advantages accruing to the whole economy from the way in which the firm will carry out its investment project, for instance by using domestic rather than foreign materials and thus relieving the balance of payments, or by establishing a plant in a locality with surplus labor. In the present opinion of Yugoslav policy makers, the emphasis on interest rates was a mistake; many managers offered more than they could fulfill. It is probably also true that under the special con-

[26] Between 1954 and 1956, it was even customary to arrange "credit auctions," by which the available funds were allocated to the highest bidders. See Eugene Neuberger, "The Yugoslav Investment Auctions," *Quarterly Journal of Economics,* Feb. 1956; Hoffman and Neal, *op. cit.,* p. 251.

ditions in which Yugoslavia finds itself, the indirect effects of a particular investment, for instance the absorbing of a local labor surplus, will frequently be more important than the degree of profitability on which the offer of a higher interest rate has to be based. The system, therefore, has been changed, and the rate of interest is now fixed in advance, differently for broad categories of investment. The criteria of selection which previously played a secondary role are now governing the decision. It is practically impossible for any enterprise to obtain a state loan without a guarantee by the commune in whose territory the enterprise is located, and the financial strength of the commune in relation to the sum total of its guarantees and other obligations is a major factor in deciding the competition.

The reasons for eliminating differences in the rate of interest offered from the means of competition seem plausible, but the decision meant that an easily measurable criterion of the efficiency of investment was replaced by criteria which are far less measurable and must be interpreted by the lending authority with more room for ambiguity and arbitrariness. There is no point, of course, in applying criteria which express only too small a part of the social benefits to be expected of an investment, or which represent visionary promises rather than realistic expectations. Yet there is a danger that the greater latitude which the new method gives to the interpretation of criteria by the government lending agency will lead to a blunting of the method of selection by prospective productivity and to an infiltration of criteria extraneous to proper economic considerations. This danger is already inherent in the advance decisions concerning the distribution by area and industry of the funds available for lending—in fact, there is no economic criterion in the strict sense by which it could be decided how much of its standard of living Slovenia should have to give up for the sake of speeding the economic development of Montenegro; it would be exceptional if the political considerations by which these issues must be decided were kept free from personal favoritism as well as from illusions about the economically achievable. The original attempt of the Yugoslav leadership to apply a yardstick of sharp economic selection at least within the individual area and industry bears testimony to its will to achieve economic rationality; this policy's failure to work out as intended is another illustration of the difficulty of introducing into an underdeveloped country the safeguards of economic rationality which have originated in developed market economies.

The importance of credit policy as a means of plan execution constitutes a similarity between the Yugoslav and French systems; the same is true of the supplementation of credit policy by fiscal measures. The analogy can be carried further: The use of the layout of power networks, railroads and highways, which are all under direct government control, for regulating the relative growth of industries and the relative development of areas is very important in both countries, although probably more so in Yugoslavia, where facilities are still farther from being ubiquitous than in France. The similarity in the means of plan execution between two countries so different in their political and economic structure follows from the limited number of instruments available to a government which has decided to guide the economy of the country on the basis of collective foresight but to do so by changing the market signals, not to replace the market by government directives; and these basic traits are common to Yugoslavia and to France.

WHY DID PLAN EXECUTION SUCCEED?

Up to 1961, the plan was essentially carried out as drawn up, except for agriculture, where in some years crop failures resulted in deficiencies. On the whole, the industries turned out the goods which the government wanted to see produced. The government was also able to reduce the differences among the several regions in regard to their levels of production and living by an appropriate distribution of investments. The causes of the recent crisis constitute a separate problem; to gauge the future prospects of the methods applied, it is necessary first to analyze the presuppositions of their success over more than half a decade.

The main reason why the planning authorities were able to steer the Yugoslav market economy largely with the aid of credit policy was the scarcity of capital. Although it seems likely that in some branches of production the firms, coveting monopoly gains, wanted to produce less than the government wished them to do, and less than capital supply would have permitted them to produce, such instances seem to have been relatively rare. This, of course, does not mean that monopoly was, or is, rare, but merely that the causal relationship is the other way: The limited availability of capital reduces the prospects that a sufficient number of enterprises will be created to provide effective competition. In any event, for every firm which may have held back with demand for capital because of monopolistic temptations, there were apparently many other firms and Communes to take up the offer of capital.

The absence of sluggishness in the response of economic units to the intentions and the capital offers of the government indicates that the managers had confidence in the plan, to the extent that they assumed the volume of output which the plan provided for each industry would be purchased by the consumers. It is an open question whether the managers would have had that confidence to the same degree if the Yugoslav economy had not been continually under inflationary pressure. Yugoslav policy makers regard inflation as an evil to be eliminated, and at times it has reached proportions which were indeed highly undesirable.[27] But on the other hand, by creating a sellers' market, inflation greatly reduced the hazard for firm managers of not being able to sell what they had produced, provided reasonable attention was paid to quality and consumers' tastes.

Some Yugoslav economists have misgivings about the durability of this condition, Mijić reports that one day, a few years before the time of writing (1959) an economist from Western Europe told him:

> You Yugoslavs have the good fortune of encountering only one problem, that of production. You are pushing ahead with production in your factories, and you do not know the problem of product marketing (*placement*), the problem of the outlets (*débouchés*).

Mijić commented:

> This was true at that time; it is still true for some enterprises today, but it is becoming less true every day. The market asserts itself and the equilibrium between supply and demand is being established. . . ."[28]

Before the crisis of 1961, the change which Mijić expected had materialized only to a small extent, and even during that crisis the difficulties in selling output were by no means general. Undoubtedly, in the last five years Yugoslav industrial producers have had to make increasingly greater efforts to satisfy their customers' tastes and to maintain an efficient sales organization, since with the greater diversity of products offered the consumer has become more careful about how to spend his money. For some highly priced goods, the domestic market has at times not proved receptive enough to provide a substitute for exports which failed to rise sufficiently because of the inadequate competitive strength of Yugoslav industry, but for articles of daily usage, and probably also for some in the near-luxury class, there is no deficiency of demand: On the whole, money is still chasing goods rather than vice versa.

The successful execution of the future economic plans of Yugoslavia will depend on the continuation of keen competition for capital on the part of the producers and collective consumers. As long as the state can make a selection among applicants for capital, it has the power to steer the economy. Should this condition vanish, the government could only carry out the plan

[27] From 1958 to 1961, the index of retail prices rose from 92 to 108. As a consequence of this upward movement of prices, the index of workers' real wages fell from 110 in 1958-1959 to 108 in 1959-60 and to 99 in 1961-62. During 1962, however, there was a drastic rise (a change in the basis of the index makes the 1962 figures not precisely comparable with those of previous years). See Federal Institute of Statistics, *Statistical Pocket Book of Yugoslavia*, Belgrade: May 1962, pp. 88, 89. May 1963, p. 90.

[28] Mijić, *op. cit.*, p. 73.

by again setting production targets for the individual enterprises, with all the consequences harmful to freedom as well as to efficiency.

This thought leads to an important generalization. If planning is to guide rather than to supplant the market, the plan offers no substitute for the will of the producers to avail themselves of opportunities for expansion. The plan can only help to preserve that will by forestalling disappointments through economic foresight, which may detect inconsistencies or other drifts into distress situations—overbuilding in some sectors, development of a general discrepancy between consumer demand and construction of production facilities, beginning saturation of demand for new durable goods, growing capital shortage or developing production bottlenecks—before a critical point is reached and it is too late to apply preventives. The future of the Yugoslav system will depend on the realization by the policy makers that the spontaneous will to progress in the "cells" of the economy is just as essential for this system as for capitalism, that just as in capitalism defects in that will can bring about economic paralysis in spite of the plan, and that the conceivable superiority which planning creates can be found merely in its use as a basis for prevention and exists only to the extent that the plan is so employed.

Agriculture

In spite of remarkable progress, agriculture still represents the most important bottleneck of Yugoslav economic development. One illustration is that in 1959 almost the same percentage of the wheat supply had to be imported as in 1952, and in the years between (probably also in 1961) the percentage was even higher.[29] Since foreign currency is also badly needed for the importation of machinery, the importation of wheat represents a heavy sacrifice.

Why could this sacrifice not be eliminated or at least greatly reduced? Part of the answer lies in the population figures, showing a rapid increase, and in the weather record, showing a number of unfavorable years.[30] It is worth asking, however, whether faults of economic organization or policy have not also detracted from the productivity of Yugoslav agriculture.

There is no reason to believe that peasant dissatisfaction with government policies has an adverse influence on agricultural production as it undoubtedly had in the period of forced collectivization and immediately afterwards when the memory of that struggle was still fresh and the state

[29] See Hoffman and Neal, *op. cit.*, p. 274.
[30] See *loc. cit.*, p. 293.

authorities continued to view private agriculture with misgivings. Since the middle of the 1950's, however, the farming population has on the whole been well treated. The peasants are selling their produce in part directly to consumers on local markets, in part through cooperatives to processors and distant consumers. For the latter sales, government guarantees put a floor under prices. On the other hand, the government can use various methods to limit price rises—perhaps the most effective is manipulation of agricultural imports. The federal tax is a flat rate, determined by size and quality of the holding, and therefore puts a premium on the best use of the land; Commune taxes, however, are progressive.[31] Availability of credits, originally scanty, is now ample. Peasant incomes, though still far below those of the industrial population, have in recent years grown somewhat faster than workers' incomes.[32] The peasants, supported by cooperative organizations—"general cooperatives" as distinguished from the relatively few "work cooperatives" modeled after the Soviet kolkhozes—for all sorts of services, including tractor plowing and technical advice, have improved their methods of cultivation. But there is an important obstacle to the application of the most efficient methods: the small size of the average holding.

Under the circumstances, this obstacle can only be overcome by an expansion of the "socialized sector" of agriculture, either in the form of state farms or of land-managing cooperatives. The Yugoslav leaders recognize this problem. They reject forced collectivization but they hope that the peasant population will open the way to an expansion of the socialized sector by voluntary decisions. What are the chances that this hope will come true?

About 88 per cent of the agricultural area and 90 per cent of the arable area of the country is still under private farming.[33] These figures are probably not as significant as they appear at first sight, because a substantial part of the soil lies in mountainous regions in which large contiguous holdings are made impossible by the terrain, and therefore the advantages of collective management could not materialize in any event; but even of the land in valleys and plains, where consolidation would be highly beneficial, only a small part is now held by collectives or by the state. Socially owned farms were responsible for only 11.6 per cent of total agricultural production in

[31] See *loc. cit.*, p. 289. The reverse side of the premium effect of the flat federal tax rate is that, in the words of a United Nations report: "The present system of taxation implies a smaller proportionate deduction from peasant incomes in years of good harvests than in years of bad ones." (*UN Economic Survey of Europe 1960*, Ch. I, p. 55.) In this respect the situation is similar in kind, but not in degree, to the system of compulsory deliveries from the Soviet kolkhozes before the Khrushchev reforms, and would hardly be acceptable to the peasants if the Yugoslav tax rates were not fairly moderate.

[32] See Hoffman and Neal, *op. cit.*, p. 281.

[33] See *Statistical Pocket Book of Yugoslavia*, 1963, p. 39.

1959; their share of market supplies, however, was undoubtedly greater, although it is difficult to give credence to the high estimates in some sources.[34]

Two developments favor an increase of the socialized sector. The lure of the higher earnings in industry is so strong that in some areas peasants are willing to sell their land to cooperatives or to the state in order to migrate to the cities. The speed of this process naturally depends on the tempo by which new industrial jobs are created. If rapid progress of industrialization can be maintained, it is conceivable that in this way the share of the socialized sector, especially in the areas suited for large-scale production, can be substantially increased.

The second method of socializing agriculture is to permeate private farm management with cooperative features. The general cooperatives sometimes conclude an agreement with a private owner by which they take over the land management entirely, paying the owner a sort of rent—mostly on a sharecrop basis—and leaving him free to seek other employment, or they may farm the land together with the owner, in conjunction with neighboring farms which may be managed under a like agreement, or with cooperatively owned land, because the general cooperatives have acquired some land for the establishment of model farms and other purposes.[35]

At this juncture it seems that the hopes of the Yugoslav policy makers for an expansion of the socialized sector have some chance of fulfillment.

Achievements of the Titoist system

GROWTH AND PRODUCTIVITY

UP TO 1961

Whoever looks at the table on page 58 must realize that the economic performance of Yugoslavia compares very favorably with that of other countries, on the Soviet side as well as on the Western side of the Iron Curtain.

Yugoslavia has achieved its impressive performance in production growth

[34] For the share of the socialized sector in total production and its development from 1956 to 1959, see Hoffman and Neal, *op. cit.*, p. 291. The authors refer to an official statement which maintains that the socialized sector supplied 76 per cent of the marketable surplus of wheat in the unfavorable crop year of 1958, which dropped to 53 per cent in 1959 when the weather was far more favorable. It is certainly possible that in poor crop years the peasants, with more people per unit of land to feed than the collective and state farms, can spare only a lower percentage of produce from household consumption, and that therefore the share of the socialized sector in produce sold must be higher; but the percentages seem very high for both years. Perhaps the official statement used an unduly broad definition of "socialized sector;" as is explained in the text, there are instances of such close collaboration between "general cooperatives" and private farmers in land management as to blur the dividing line of private and cooperative enterprises.

[35] See Hoffman and Neal, *op. cit.*, pp. 280, 284.

in spite of the fact that agriculture, which almost everywhere grows more slowly than industry, has a greater share in the national output of Yugoslavia than in that of many other countries listed in the table. There are also other factors which make the Yugoslav achievement in economic growth even more remarkable than the mere figures indicate. She has a very heterogeneous population: There are Serbs, Croats, Slovenes, Montenegrins, Magyars, Albanians, Turks, "Macedonians" (who themselves are of various ethnic origin but are often lumped together) and various splinter groups. These groups are divided by language, religion and living habits, and these differences must be a great obstacle to labor mobility, on which the increase of industrial production and general economic growth largely depends.

Among several of the population groups there exists a tradition of bitter hostility. In the Kingdom of Yugoslavia as established after the First World War, the antagonism of Serbs and Croats threatened to tear the state apart, and most minorities were perpetually discontented. Massacres during World War II have greatly added to the bitterness, and anyone who reads the record must marvel how it was at all possible for the Yugoslav state to reemerge from the ordeal. The communist ideology of the ruling elite has proved to be a tie which has reduced the antagonism of ethnic groups within that elite, and however much diluted that ideology may be among the masses, there too it has had a unifying effect. But the old rivalries and jealousies have merely been attenuated; they still exist and are a factor in politics—in the decision of economic policy issues as well as of others. The more advanced areas, especially Slovenia and Croatia, are being taxed for financing a rapid development of such backward regions as Macedonia and Montenegro. This causes resentment and some degree of political resistance in the parts from which a "surplus" is taken; it is reasonable to assume that the amount of subsidies for the underdeveloped territories cannot be determined by economic criteria alone, but that various political considerations must enter into the picture, and that the effort necessary to prevent or dampen mutual recriminations detracts from the energies that can be spent on the economic tasks.

In addition to these structural difficulties, Yugoslavia has had to cope with the economic consequences of the abrupt break with the Soviet Union in 1948, when Russian assistance suddenly ceased and a blockade cut off all trade with the Eastern bloc. Western assistance has, it is true, alleviated the consequences of this loss.[36] On the other hand, Yugoslavia itself aggravated

[36] One might wish for a clear statement in figures as to whether Western economic aid has been a complete substitute for Yugoslavia's loss through the hostile acts of the

the effects by its ill-considered venture into forced collectivization of agriculture, in an apparent attempt to defend its reputation as a communist power against Stalinist criticism. The final success was on that account harder to achieve and speaks even more strongly for the combination of prudence and audacity with which Yugoslav economic policies were pursued in the second half of the 1950's. It is true that the Yugoslav policy makers have not succeeded in achieving a smooth development of their economy: Inflation, monopolistic pricing, food shortages appeared at times even before the crisis of 1961-62. But erroneous actions in handling individual problems have to be expected when policies without precedent are being tried out, and stresses and strains cannot be avoided when economic development is as rapid as it has been in Yugoslavia during the last decade. To have overtaken almost the whole Soviet bloc and all capitalist countries, except Japan, in the increase of industrial output, and still to have afforded the population a continuous and rapid improvement of its standard of living at least between 1955 and 1961[37] remains a great achievement, although

---

Soviet Union and its satellites, but such a statement cannot be made categorically. United States and West European assistance between 1950 and 1959 alone reached the figure of $219 million (Hoffman and Neal, *op. cit.*, p. 354); the Soviet Union, in 1947, had promised credits for capital goods in the amount of $135 million but by the time of the rupture in 1948 had delivered only capital goods of a value of $800,000 (*loc. cit.*, p. 118). As to trade, more than half of the exports went to the Soviet bloc countries prior to the break and approximately the same portion of imports came from there (*loc. cit.*, p. 332). Then trade with the Soviet bloc dwindled to almost nothing, but revived in the middle of the 1950's and from there on fluctuated with the changing political atmosphere and also, to some extent, economic circumstances. In 1961, exports to the United States, the United Kingdom, Italy and Western Germany were about twice as large as exports to the USSR, Poland, Czechoslovakia, Hungary and Eastern Germany, and imports from the same Western countries were more than three times as large as those from the Eastern countries listed. (See *Statistical Pocket Book of Yugoslavia,* 1962, pp. 68, 69).

These figures leave no doubt that relations with the West are of vastly greater economic importance to Yugoslavia than ties with the Soviet bloc. It is also likely that the aid which Yugoslavia received from the West, and of which it would have received nothing or only a small fraction if the break with the USSR had not occurred, was greater than anything she would have received from the East. But it is not entirely impossible that the USSR might have followed up the $135 million credit with other loans or grants in the event of friendly relations (on the other hand, of course, she might also have defaulted on the promise of the 135 million.) A further point of uncertainty is the damage that was done to the Yugoslav economy by the abruptness of the break with the Soviet Union in view of the inevitable delay in the granting of Western aid. If trade is considered, it cannot be taken for granted that Yugoslavia would have had no commercial intercourse with the West without the rupture with the East, although this intercourse would certainly have been reduced by discrimination to an undefinable extent.

To sum up: It is likely, but not certain, that Yugoslavia gained more than it lost for the external conditions of its economic well-being through its rupture with the Soviet Union. To measure the probable gain even approximately is not feasible.

[37] The decline in workers' real wages in some of the years—see footnote 27, p. 457—does not vitiate this statement. Against the reduction in the purchasing power of wages must be set the increase in income of the newcomers to industry who were able to earn

some items have to be put on the debit side of the ledger. The fact that this achievement was possible in a system which allotted a much greater role to spontaneous effort and tried to assure a much closer approach to economic rationality than the Soviet system is a gain for human freedom which is not extinguished by the considerable remnants in Yugoslavia from its recent past as a totalitarian country.

Increase of productivity is a strong concern of the Yugoslav leaders. One of the methods employed was the insistence on piece work as a wage system. For a considerable time, the government tried to impose this system if not by outright compulsion, at least by moral pressure exerted through the trade union organization. The self-interest of the workers in maximum profit of their enterprises might have been thought to make them more ready to accept and support this policy, but the old antagonism of workers in almost all countries against piece work proved stronger: Only a minority of enterprises introduced the system, and in 1961 the government removed the pressure and instead strengthened the incentive to productivity by a tax reform.[38]

It seems that in industry, labor productivity grew by about 4 per cent per year between 1952 and 1960,[39] which appears very high in view of the continuous augmentation of the labor force by raw recruits from agriculture who had to be trained and whose low productivity during the initial period must have depressed the average. Of course, the increase in productivity was not merely a result of better performance by the individual worker but also, and perhaps even more, an effect of technological improvement.

Yugoslavia has still considerably greater possibilities than the Soviet Union to increase national product by transferring labor from agriculture to

---

much more than they had done in agriculture, although over the whole period of the 1950's agricultural incomes rose too, probably in excess of price increases for the goods bought by the rural population. That the net effect of these various factors upon the average standard of living was favorable is shown by increased figures of personal consumption (See Hoffman and Neal, *op. cit.*, p. 370 f.) Moreover, it is likely that improvements in housing—although they required higher rents—and in various kinds of collective consumption also contributed to a rise in the standard of living.

[38] See Hoffman and Neal, *op. cit.*, p. 257.

[39] "In the past eight years productivity as a whole grew at an average yearly rate of 8.8 per cent. According to a global estimate, a part of this increase, about 4.8 per cent, is the result of structural changes in the economy, and transfers of the population from agricultural to non-agricultural activities while about 4 per cent on an average is the result of increased productivity on individual operations" (Tito, *op. cit.*, p. 64). Although Tito did not explicitly say so, it seems that "individual operations" were understood to be operations in individual industries, to the exclusion of agriculture. Increase in the productivity of agricultural labor is difficult to ascertain in a meaningful manner, because outside factors, especially weather conditions, have so great an influence on the output of every worker. For the increase of industrial productivity in individual years, see *Statistical Pocket Book of Yugoslavia*, 1963, p. 55.

industry. No estimates are available of the period during which it will be able to make such transfers without seriously reducing agricultural output; naturally, this period will be lengthened if technological improvements can be introduced on farms more rapidly than has been possible up to now. It is at least conceivable that the draining off of agricultural labor into industry will speed up this process not only because such migration will facilitate consolidation of holdings, but also because it brings home to the individual farmer the importance of labor-saving devices. The Yugoslav farmer of today has an obvious interest in increasing his yield by better seed selection, better feeding methods for cattle and poultry, and similar devices not involving mechanization; but as long as labor—mostly labor of members of his family whom he has to support in any event—is abundantly available, he is not particularly interested in tractorization that would enable him to dispense with workers for the care of draft animals, or in the use of reapers and similar machinery which would cut down labor requirements for harvesting. As his sons and daughters, attracted by industrial wages, leave the farm, the farmer will learn to appreciate the advantage of letting machines do the work of man. If he does not sell out to a collective farm or the state and follows the younger generation to the city, he will—in many instances at least—try to combine with his neighbors to organize the cooperative purchase and use of machinery.

The Crisis of 1961-62

From 1960 to 1961, the index of industrial production showed an increase of only 17 points as against 32 points from 1959 to 1960; for manufacturing alone—leaving out production of electric power with its (probably) rising secular trend—the slowdown was even somewhat greater (18 points as against 36).[40] The loss of momentum in production increases, however, was a general European rather than a Yugoslav phenomenon; only Italy, which had begun its great postwar rise belatedly, remained almost unaffected. Thus it may at first sight seem rather inexplicable why the Yugoslav leaders, as well as outside observers, regarded the signs as sufficient reason to suspect major faults in the machinery of the Titoist system or in its mode of operation. But closer inspection of the facts reveals that this suspicion could be supported by good arguments.

In the first place, the figures probably understate the setback to Yugoslav industrial growth. It stands to reason that Yugoslav managers, who cannot reduce the number of workers as easily as capitalist employers, will try to absorb sales resistance for a considerable period by increasing inventories

[40] United Nations Monthly *Statistical Bulletin,* July 1962, p. 22.

rather than by reducing output. This cannot have applied to all industries, because in some of them growth was impeded not by marketing difficulties but by shortages of important raw materials and equipment: They could have sold more than they were able to produce. But where sales resistance was experienced, part of the output was most probably put on stock, and the realizable value of this part may well have been much smaller than the statistical figure.

Second, when the figures for Yugoslavia are compared with those of France or West Germany, it is necessary to consider that one production bottleneck which is important in the case of the two large West European countries, and most of the smaller ones, does not exist to nearly the same extent in Yugoslavia: labor shortage. Many types of skilled labor are scarce in Yugoslavia, but the still unexhausted reservoir of unskilled labor has no counterpart in Western Europe, except perhaps Italy. If a country's economic growth is slowed down because it is scraping the bottom of its labor reservoir, the deceleration may still present some problems of how to bear an increased load of social overhead, for instance defense; but such a slowing down does not normally indicate a fault in the economic system or in its management, since under any system the availability of labor limits output. But if a country's production grows more slowly than before, although the labor reserves are still ample, this means that the country's ability to make use of its manpower has declined, and there is reason to investigate whether the economic system has structural defects, or perhaps has not been properly operated.

Another aggravating aspect of the Yugoslav situation was the coincidence of inflationary and recession symptoms. This is not an entirely unique experience; whereas in earlier decades price declines almost invariably accompanied a decline in economic activity, just as rising prices, growing use of credit and an increase in the circulation of money were characteristic of a general upswing, recently there seems to be a growing number of instances in which the border line between upswing and downswing is obscured, and a decline or stagnation of output and sales occurs in large sectors of the market simultaneous with an upward movement of prices and corresponding changes in the monetary field. In Yugoslavia the index of retail prices rose by 8 per cent from 1960 to 1961,[41] and the currency circulation on December 31, 1961, stood at 246.6 as compared with 193.1 a year

[41] *Statistical Pocket Book for Yugoslavia,* 1962, p. 88. The cost-of-living index, however, receded slightly, owing to a reduction of rents, presumably at government expense. The effect of this boon to the consumer began to fade out already during 1961: In December of that year the cost of living index was already 10 per cent higher than it had been in March (*loc. cit.,* p. 89).

earlier.[42] Such a strong inflationary trend at a moment when many enterprises were experiencing sales resistance suggests that the discrepancy between price trends and business activity was unusually great in Yugoslavia even for the present period and that serious faults existed in the use of economic resources: Although consumers had a relatively large amount of money at their disposal and must have been impressed with the experience of continually rising prices, which makes it advisable to turn money into goods as soon as possible, they were apparently unwilling to buy all the products of industry; they must have felt that even under these circumstances a number of commodities were not worth the money for which they could have been purchased. On the other hand, the price rise was bound to aggravate the balance-of-payments situation.[43]

The Yugoslav difficulties of 1961 to 1962 consisted to a great extent of a balance-of-payments crisis. This was the most conspicuous symptom and in turn made it more difficult to overcome the industrial stagnation, because increases in production required foreign materials and equipment which had to be bought with foreign currency. Although the rapid progress of inflation in 1960 and 1961 may have been the factor that brought matters to a climax, the rapid industrial growth in the preceding years had already put a heavy strain on the foreign currency resources. In the 1950's, the large imports of materials and machinery could not be fully offset by commodity exports and tourist trade, and the remaining deficits were precariously covered by foreign aid. Occasionally, the situation was aggravated by poor crops, requiring food imports. Thus Yugoslavia had been teetering on the verge of a balance-of-payments crisis before the breaking point was reached in the second half of 1961, and shortage of foreign currency forced a curtailment of economic growth. A new partial crop failure had contributed to the result. Finally, a measure which at another time would have represented a move in the right direction was taken at the wrong moment: Early in 1961, many import controls had been lifted, leaving it to the industrial and commercial enterprises to determine the quantities of producer and con-

[42] *Loc. cit.*, p. 85. The figure was probably somewhat higher as a result of the currency reform of January 1, 1961, which reduced the value of the dinar in terms of foreign currencies to less than one-half the previous official rate. This change, however, was generally regarded as an adaptation of the external value to the internal value of the Yugoslav currency, the former rate having been out of line with the purchasing power of the dinar for many commodities important in international exchange; moreover, even before January 1961, dinars had been sold for specified purposes for a much lower price in foreign currency (or the latter bought by monetary authorities at a higher dinar price from specified sources.) The effect of the devaluation upon the amount of circulating money can, therefore, hardly have been very great; most of the increase must have been due to internal causes.

[43] It also tended to frustrate, at least in part, the relief which might have been expected from the currency reform of 1961.

sumer goods to be imported according to their production plans or to their estimates of market receptiveness. This liberalization was part of the currency reform of January 1961, which involved a devaluation of the dinar. The government apparently expected that the higher dinar prices of foreign currency, and consequently of foreign products, would sufficiently restrict their use without special controls. This deterrent, however, was not sufficiently strong to keep imports within manageable limits.

The majority of Yugoslav experts have not been content with regarding the difficulties of their country as just one more balance-of-payments crisis, caused by too rapid expansion in coincidence with some unlucky circumstances, such as had occurred repeatedly, since the end of World War II, in Britain and France. Rather, they have been asking themselves what had caused the failure of Yugoslav exports to rise to a level at which the balance of payments would have attained equilibrium. Obviously, this question leads to an investigation of all the possible defects of the country's economy.

The most important of these defects is the relatively low productivity of labor.[44] If Yugoslavia were as large a country as the Soviet Union or the United States, and foreign trade therefore unimportant by comparison with the domestic market, or if she possessed natural resources for the supply of a readily exportable commodity such as oil, like Venezuela, relatively low productivity could hardly have become a cause of crisis, though of course it

[44] According to official statistics, labor productivity in Yugoslav industries grew by something over 5 per cent annually between 1956 and 1961, whereas the increase of 1960 to 1961 was only 3.4 per cent. (See *Statistical Pocket Book for Yugoslavia,* p. 54.) It seems, however, that this index is calculated by dividing the statistical value of the output by the number of employed persons, and therefore does not provide a reliable measure of the rationality of operations. In the first place, statistical output value may have been overstated, as it was probably in 1961 and 1962, because commodities which were unsalable were presumably put on stock. Second, when workers are retained who cannot be fully employed within the plant—and this very likely was the situation in some Yugoslav factories during 1961 to 1962—the divisor is kept high "artificially;" under these circumstances the statistical decline of the growth rate of productivity is a crisis symptom, but does not measure that which a productivity index is supposed to measure, and rather indicates the existence of hidden unemployment.

A valid comparison between the productivity of Yugoslav and Western labor would require the study of individual operations; as far as the writer knows, no such studies are available, and the difficulty which would be encountered in undertaking them are obvious. However, many observers from other countries have had experience, as tourists, with Yugoslav hotels and passenger boats. Here the quality of service has been much improved in recent years and now compares favorably with conditions in other countries. The running of a hotel or a steamer requires as much diligence and good teamwork as managing a factory, and success in this field may prove that the Yugoslav worker has the basic capacity to reach the Western level of efficiency in industry also. But conditions of work in the tourist trade and work in factories are still too different to permit the conclusion that the high level of efficiency in the former gives assurance that the efficiency in the latter has also reached the Western level; there is general agreement that such is not the case.

would in any event have detracted from the standard of living. But Yugoslavia is a small country, dependent on import to a degree which requires more export than it can sustain with crude materials alone. Consequently, Yugoslavia is compelled to export industrial goods to markets on which it must compete with more advanced countries. Obviously, Yugoslav industries can hope to succeed there only if the productivity of their labor is not inferior to that of their foreign competitors by a greater margin than can be compensated for by the lower Yugoslav wage level.

Since the wage level is of decisive importance, Yugoslavia's competitive strength depends on the productivity of its labor not only in the export industries but in the whole economy. Rising productivity of labor in those industries which produce important consumer goods—for instance clothing, furniture, dwellings, bicycles, processed foods—is the most effective force to counteract inflationary trends, which are inevitable in a country that has been growing as rapidly as has Yugoslavia between 1955 and 1961. The faster the tempo of inflation and consequently the rise in the cost of living, the greater the pressure to increase nominal labor incomes, a pressure which under Yugoslav conditions the government finds it more difficult to resist than is the case in the Soviet bloc. The problem is aggravated by a number of circumstances growing out of the particular situation of Yugoslavia.

In the first place, the progress of rapid industrialization and urbanization means that large parts of the agricultural population are annually drawn into the cities and factory towns and thereby lose the high degree of self-sufficiency which they possessed as relatively primitive farmers. Their incomes are much higher in industrial jobs, but they are more dependent on purchased goods, and unless these goods are offered them at prices which do not rise faster than their industrial wages, the adjustment problems of these newcomers to industry are made more difficult. As soon as they feel such a squeeze and have learned to defend their interests in their new surroundings, they will make great efforts to obtain compensatory wage increases.

Second, the government cannot even wish that compensatory wage increases should be prevented, except perhaps for brief periods of transition, because—aside from all considerations of social equity—in order to develop competitive strength internationally, Yugoslav industries need a broad inner market, which cannot exist with shrinking real incomes of the masses. A number of Yugoslav factories are designed for mass production, and if they are to utilize their capacity must have an output for which present markets are not sufficiently receptive. To sell more of their potential surplus abroad, it is necessary that production for the internal market bear a proper share in the overhead.

Third, countries such as Yugoslavia find themselves in a dilemma created by modern technology.[45] Their relatively low wage level seems to make it advisable for them to go slowly in replacing human labor with machines, but in following such a moderate course these countries might build factories which, in many instances, would soon be obsolete because the progress of automation will probably enable the advanced countries in the relatively near future to undersell even many cheap labor products. Moreover, continuity of technological progress is a presupposition of the full adjustment of the Yugoslav working population to the requirements of the modern age. This means that Yugoslavia has to make a number of industrial investments which correspond to the situation of tomorrow rather than to that of today, and therefore increase her short-run difficulties. To be sure, by concentrating technological progress in fields in which it makes labor more productive without reducing employment so much that the low price of labor ceases to be an important advantage, the framers of industrial policy can alleviate the problem, but it cannot be removed. To make the short-run difficulties bearable, it is all the more essential to preserve a substantial wage differential in favor of Yugoslav industry for a considerable time to come. Although the goal must be to remove the need for a wage differential in the end—since Yugoslav policy makers can hardly be content to defend the international position of their country permanently through a low wage level—it would be fatal to let that differential disappear too quickly.

To reconcile the preservation of a wage differential with a growing inner market and to prevent inflation from impairing the competitive strength of Yugoslav industries to an intolerable degree, continual improvement of labor productivity is essential. This can be secured in part by investment which enhances plant efficiency, but much depends also on the adaptation of the individual worker to his task. Yugoslavia cannot live without speeding up the transformation of yesterday's peasants into efficient industrial workers.

As has been explained, there are important circumstances, independent of the economic system, that make it inevitable that labor productivity, specifically the efficiency with which the individual worker performs his task, is below that of the Western countries. We do not know how large

[45] This problem has been much discussed in the context of development theory. See, for instance, Albert O. Hirschman, *The Strategy of Economic Development*, New Haven: Yale University Press, 1961, pp. 145 ff.

the margin is, but it is easy to see that the over-all efficiency of industrial labor in Yugoslavia is subject to two counteracting forces: On the one hand the workers who are already in industry are acquiring skills for better performance, and newcomers are entering industry and are inevitably depressing the average with their lower skills. Therefore, even if we had studies about average labor performance in Yugoslavia and its changes as compared with other countries, we would not know the most important figure—most important for a judgment on the economic system from the viewpoint of labor efficiency: the effectiveness of the system in inducing the worker who is already in the factory to improve his performance. But even in the absence of data necessary for a judgment, it is important to consider the points at which the economic system, or those who handled its controls, may conceivably have incurred a responsibility for the difficulties. Has the appeal to the worker's self-interest in good performance, on which the institution of workers' self-management is based, proved effective enough? Has the monopolistic or semi-monopolistic position of many enterprises perhaps caused too much slackness in efforts to rationalize production, and have these tendencies been combated with enough vigor? Has capital that ought to have gone into improving plant productivity been diverted into other channels by non-optimal decisions of planning authorities? Have the Yugoslav policy makers exploited to the full the peculiar advantages offered by their system—such as the opportunities to educate the workers to the realization of their self-interest in the success of their enterprises, the powers of the top agencies to scrutinize investment projects for their promise on the basis of more comprehensive knowledge than is available in an unplanned economy, the possibility to apply strong monopoly controls? If these questions will ever be answered, it can only be after many years, when economic analysts, with the advantage of hindsight, have scrutinized the events and their causes. In the meantime, the success of the remedial measures taken by the Yugoslav government has proved that the principal causes of the crisis were really to be found within the wide areas indicated by the list of possible weaknesses of the system and of faults in its operation. It was just against defects of this kind, and their consequences for the balance of payments, that those measures were aimed.

"Wage controls were tightened in such a way as to gear changes in income to changes in productivity since 1960." [46] Because in 1961 real wages

[46] United Nations Economic Commission for Europe, Economic Bulletin for Europe, Vol. XIV: 2, p. 54. Presently available information does not permit a view of the legal technique by which this linkage between productivity increases and wage increases was established, but the measure must have dealt not only with the payment of wages in the narrow sense of the word, but also with the division of profits into workers' individual

had increased faster than productivity, they were scaled down—in the first seven months of 1962 they fell 6 per cent below the corresponding 1961 level.[47] Some special measures were taken against high salaries of managers—perhaps as much from considerations of social equity as from the thought that some kinds of luxury consumption put a particularly great stress on the balance of payments, cars of foreign make being an outstanding example. In the same period, building activity was curtailed, which resulted not only in relaxing the strain on physical resources but also in a budget surplus which permitted some sterilization of funds as an anti-inflationary action. Interest rates were raised and credit to enterprises was also restricted in other ways;[48] taken together with the wage controls, this policy

---

shares and accretions to the investment fund or the reserves of the enterprise; otherwise, the limitation of wages would have missed its purpose, since lower wages mean higher profits (other things being equal), and if the right of the workers to dispose of profits had remained unrestricted, they could have taken in the form of additional profit shares that which was denied them in the form of wages proper.

It can well be argued that surpluses of an individual enterprise which are not due to increase in productivity are no true profits, because they result from price raises which will add to inflation and therefore in the end will harm the enterprise in which the profits were made, together with the whole of society. Making these "profits" unavailable for distribution, would not, in principle, infringe upon workers' self-management any more than obligating the plant community to make adequate depreciation allowances or build up proper reserves. But increases in productivity are difficult to measure, and probably even more so for an individual enterprise than for the economy as a whole. The interpretation of the criteria may give the state authorities more power over the enterprises, but whether this is really the case can only be judged when more experience is available. At present, it is not even clear whether the attempt to establish a linkage between productivity and wage increases in the individual enterprise will turn out to be part of a permanent policy or merely an emergency measure. Nor is it quite certain that regulation of the use of enterprise profits will always be confined to making increases in workers' disposable incomes dependent on growth of productivity; they could perhaps also be used to reserve part of productivity increases for investment. The measures to combat the crisis of 1961 had to be taken under the old constitution, but the relevant provisions of the constitution of 1963 are indicative of the belief of Yugoslav policy makers that federal regulation of the use which enterprises make of their profits may be necessary. The constitution stipulates:

"The Federation may 1) prescribe as obligatory that the working organizations shall utilize part of their freely disposable income to develop the material bases of their work, or their economic and social development, if this is necessary for economic stability or for the attainment of the basic material relations established by the social plan for Yugoslavia; 2) temporarily prohibit the use of certain social resources by the working organizations and social-political communities, when this is indispensable in order to prevent or eliminate major disturbances in the economy and major disproportions in the fulfillment of the social plan of Yugoslavia, or when the needs of national defense or other special needs of the country so enjoin. . . .

"These measures may be prescribed by law."

The *Constitution of the Socialist Federal Republic of Yugoslavia,* tr. Petar Mijušković, Belgrade: Secretariat for Information, 1963, Art. 124 (p. 33).

[47] U. N. Economic Bulletin for Europe, Vol. XIV: 2 p. 54.

[48] Credit restriction was applied on a selective basis, "favoring export industries and certain industries which lack the means of expansion even though demand for their prod-

meant that enterprises were induced to finance a larger portion of their investments at the expense of consumption of their members rather than through credits from the state bank or the communes. The tightening up of credit supply and the higher interest rates must have resulted in higher standards of profitability in the selection of investment projects; the knowledge of the workers that wage increases depended on increases of productivity within the enterprise tended to induce acquiescence in, or even insistence upon, a high degree of work discipline. Very probably these effects were reinforced by moral pressure on the part of the Communist League and the labor unions upon the workers' councils. There is reason to believe that anti-monopoly policies were also sharpened. As a result of all these measures, the worst was over by the fall of 1962.

In the first nine months of 1962, Yugoslav exports rose by 15 per cent, whereas imports increased only by 4.8 per cent. It was particularly important that the increase in exports occurred in relations with the non-communist world, with a corresponding yield in currency usable for imports which Yugoslavia needed, whereas there was an actual decline in exports to communist countries[49] which usually pay in blocked accounts, difficult to liquidate because Yugoslavia cannot use many of the products which the Soviet bloc has to offer. With this improvement in the balance of trade the first prerequisite of industrial progress, the possibility of importing enough materials and machinery, was restored. In the third quarter of 1962, the index of industrial production (1958 = 100) stood at 152 as compared with 140 in the same period of 1961 and 132 in the same period of 1960.[50] The cost of living index still stood at 130 in the third quarter of 1962 as compared with 120 in the third quarter of 1961 (1958 = 100), but it had dropped considerably from its peak of 139 in the second quarter of 1962,[51] and thus the progress of inflation seems to have been halted. ". . . real wages had almost regained their mid-1961 level by the end of the summer [of 1962]." [52]

At the time of writing, it is still too early for a reliable judgment on future prospects. Perhaps even more than in the past, the economic development of Yugoslavia will in the years to come depend on factors beyond Yugoslav control. Considering the large role of Western Europe among the recipients of Yugoslav exports, the policy of the European Economic Com-

---

ucts is keen." (*loc. cit.*, p. 55). For methods of credit restriction, see *Economic Survey of Europe in 1961*, Part I, Ch. I, p. 46 fn.

[49] *Economic Bulletin for Europe*, XIV: 2, p. 37.

[50] *Loc. cit.*, p. 40.

[51] *Loc. cit.*, p. 46.

[52] *Loc. cit.*, p. 54.

munity and the question of whether this Community will be preserved, expanded or dissolved, must greatly affect Yugoslavia. Of similar importance for the country will be the policy of the United States in regard to foreign aid and especially to the sale of surplus agricultural products, of which Yugoslavia has in the past been able to obtain a share in times of need on very favorable terms.

But however uncertain many determinants of Yugoslavia's economic future may be, the way in which the crisis of 1961 to 1962 was handled has proved a good deal about the flexibility of the system, about its capacity to provide remedies for maladjustments, and also about the ability of the leaders to learn from experience. Obviously, the leaders had failed to foresee the impasse, and this was a major deficiency in the management of an economic system which includes an apparatus of economic foresight as one of its essential elements. But just as obviously, planning is an art that must be learned. For the long-run prospects, the fact that the crisis could occur seems less important than that it could be overcome. Its origin has proved that the system has built-in hazards; the success of the remedial measures suggests that with proper management of the system, the hazards either need not materialize or that the consequences can be strictly limited. The experience seems to indicate that the Yugoslav government has more effective means available to combat economic maladjustments than have governments in capitalistic countries, and that it can judge more reliably—because of the indicators provided by the market—what remedies to apply in what doses than is possible for the Soviet-bloc countries. This statement still represents a hypothesis rather than a hard-and-fast conclusion, because of the difficulty in comparing the conditions of success in a relatively small country such as Yugoslavia with those in the countries of the West and in the Soviet Union with their large and highly diversified economies. The hypothesis, however, appears more plausible than any alternative evaluation of the events that have occurred in Yugoslavia since 1961.

Liberty and Equality under Titoism

FREEDOM IN THE APPARATUS OF PRODUCTION

Obviously, command in relation to exchange plays a smaller role in the economic system of Yugoslavia than in the Soviet Union or its satellites, but a larger role—on balance—than in the Western economies. In Yugoslavia, plans for physical output are not translated into orders to individual enterprises as they are under Soviet Communism; rather, these enterprises are free to respond or not to respond to the stimuli provided by government action. Within the enterprises also, there is not the same prevalence of the command principle as there is in the USSR, because to a considerable extent the workers in their plants govern themselves, and society tries to buy good performance from the workers by granting them shares in the profits instead of simply ordering them to work efficiently, under the threat of penalties. (The difference is not absolute, since the Soviet system also has premiums for efficient work.) An especially important part of the self-government of the workers in the plants is their right to determine the ratio between the portions of profit to be used for investment and for consumption, individual and collective; in this way the workers themselves have some influence, though a modest one, upon the rate of time preference applied in society. Therefore, if this right were seriously restricted as a consequence of the 1961 crisis—there are some indications to this effect—part of the line of distinction between Titoism and Soviet Communism would be blurred. Another vitally important mark of distinction between these two systems—important for the respective roles of command and exchange—is the freedom of Yugoslav peasants to join or not join collective farms, and the steering of agricultural production in the main by market stimuli, whereas in the Soviet Union collective land management is obligatory, and orders issued to kolkhozes are more important than responses to price policy in determining what farms produce and how they divide their output between selling and self-consumption.

The greater role of the command principle in Yugoslavia as compared with Western economies is evident in the existence of price ceilings, in the stricter and more detailed regulations about the use of gross profits and in some features of the Yugoslav taxing system, especially the turnover tax, which interferes with consumers' sovereignty. Against these features must be held the smaller role of the command principle within the plants—smaller for the same reasons which in this respect distinguish the Yugoslav from the Soviet system.

Since workers' self-management has a great bearing upon the respective roles of command and exchange, and therefore of coercion and liberty within the Yugoslav economy, it is very important to form an opinion on the effectiveness of the legal provisions which give the workers councils the right to determine the business policy of the enterprises.

There is no good reason to doubt that the Yugoslav leaders, at least in the great majority, desire to make a reality of workers' self-management. They are very proud of this innovation, and they believe that the combination of this principle with economic planning will lead to an order of humanistic socialism, avoiding the most important social evils that have emerged in either capitalism or Soviet communism. But genuine desire to see a principle realized does not necessarily imply readiness to pay any price for its complete realization; nor would such willingness always make good sense. To choose a familiar example from American public life: Certainly Americans wish to uphold freedom of speech, but even those who jealously guard that principle recognize the necessity of limitations where the exercise of that right would create a "clear and present danger" to individuals or to the community. By the same token, however sincerely the Yugoslav leaders may wish to establish workers' self-management, they cannot be expected to sacrifice everything to its realization. In the conflict which recently seems to have arisen between workers' self-management and the requirements of economic growth, the Yugoslav government has apparently thought it necessary to impose some restriction upon the freedom of the factory community to dispose of the fruits of their earnings. Even before these measures were taken, this freedom was of course restricted by the use of the government's taxing power, and by the regulation protecting the state property in the plants. But whatever interpretation may be put on these measures, the recent ones and the older ones, in matters of business management there can be no doubt that regulations still leave a greater sphere of decision to the workers of the individual enterprise than exists in any other country.

But are the decisions of the workers' assemblies and the workers' councils really free? They are guided to a considerable extent by labor unions; the labor unions are under the strong influence of the League of Communists,[53] and the League, the re-named Communist Party, is the ruling power in the state in which it holds a monopoly of political organization. It would be easy to draw up a scheme implying that the state dominates the workers' councils, if only indirectly, and that implication could be supported by analogies with the Soviet Union, in which formally granted rights of self-government—especially territorial self-government—have been frustrated through the domination of the allegedly self-governing bodies by a centrally controlled Communist Party. Yet the scheme would be misleading. The danger to workers' self-management does exist, but it has not materialized to nearly the extent which the analogy with the Soviet Union would suggest. If any doubt in this respect existed prior to 1961, it should have been removed by the experience that the workers' councils made decisions with regard to the relative size of investment and wage funds in contradiction to the policy which the government wanted to pursue. To be sure, measures have been taken to correct this situation, but they were taken after the de-

[53] See Hoffman and Neal, *op. cit.*, pp. 244-45.

cisions were made and put into practice. Nevertheless, the corrective measures prove that the workers' right to self-management is not unconditional, but the fact that on a cardinal point a cleavage between the policies of the workers' councils and those of the government could arise at all shows that the workers and their representatives in the councils vote mainly according to their own interests and beliefs.

Yet there is some guidance by the trade unions, and there must be, because many workers are inexperienced by comparison with Western workers, and even in the West the workers have often had difficulties in understanding the problems which must be faced in managing industries. It would be contrary to all experience to assume that labor unions, in providing this guidance, offer merely technical advice, without attempting to influence the course of action of the workers' councils in the sense of their own policies—and in Yugoslavia this means, in the main, the policies of the government. But these attempts do not seem to have been carried to the point at which the councils would have become government instruments and workers' self-management a mere sham.

The analogy to the fate of self-government in the Soviet Union would presumably be correct if the Yugoslav League of Communists had the same monolithic character and the same degree of party discipline as the Communist Party in all countries of the Soviet bloc, and the Communist Parties in the West as well. The line of command which, in the Bolshevik parties, leads down from the party directorate to the smallest communist cell in any enterprise is less tight in Yugoslavia.[54] We shall have to know more about internal relations within the League of the Communists, its relations to the National Syndicate of Labor Unions and the unions' structure and mode of operation before we can determine exactly to what extent and in what forms the policy aims of the government are transmitted to the workers'

[54] This is true in spite of the tightening-up of the party organization in 1956 (following upon an ideological tightening-up in 1953, which seems to have caused Milovan Djilas to start his opposition to the party leadership). See Hoffman and Neal, pp. 187 ff. The reforms of 1956 probably were designed to counteract at the same time the impact of Djilas' criticism and some of the abuses which he had criticized. When it turned out that some of these abuses were intensified rather than remedied by the reforms, the latter were modified by a circular letter of the Central Committee of the League of Communists in February 1958.

The difference from the Bolshevik system, at least as the latter had developed under Stalin, was well illustrated during the ideological tightening which followed the party congress of 1953. To be sure, there was a purge, and 72,000 members—about 10 per cent of the membership—were expelled from the party. But almost half that number—32,000 left the party of their own accord (*loc. cit.*, p. 196), which seems to indicate that voluntary resignation was not regarded as a demonstration of dissent that would invite sanctions, and that the personal advantages of belonging to the party were not great enough —at least in the case of ordinary citizens—to check such a wave of resignations.

councils (and other self-government organizations, especially the communes) through the party and the unions, but we know enough to support the belief that there is no more than a moderate influence of the government upon the decisions of the workers' councils.

Although workers' self-management means, in sum, a gain for liberty, it is not an unmixed gain. Its advantages must be weighed against the fact that the Yugoslav system leaves little room for the normal functions of labor unions. The influence of the party upon the unions adds another item to the debit side, but even if the unions were independent, the narrow limits in which they can become active would still be a liability. Although theoretically the right to strike is recognized, and at least one major strike did occur in 1958 when the workers' council of a coal mine acted against the wishes of the miners in regard to wages,[55] obviously such an occurrence can only be caused by a malfunctioning of workers' self-management. Nor does there seem to be much room for collective bargaining. Thus the functions of the labor unions are mainly educational, constituting a link between the Communist Party and the workers. They are not so important an arena of workers' free activities as are unions in the United States, in spite of bossism and other scourges of the American labor movement.

Now it may be argued that workers cannot expect to be their own employers, as they are in principle in Yugoslavia, and at the same time be free to bargain about wages as if they were hired hands. The answer is that workers' self-management may be worth all that it costs, but that it has its costs, and that among them is the limitation which the system places on union activities. It takes some weighing of advantages and disadvantages to decide whether it really is desirably for workers to own their enterprises, or whether it is preferable, from their point of view, to leave the responsibility of management to the appointees of capitalistic owners and reserve their own freedom of pressing for greater rewards of labor.

THE DETERMINATION OF PUBLIC POLICIES

The Representation of the People

The one-party system is a threat to the genuine character of workers' self-management; this and other survivals from the Bolshevik past of Yugoslav communism have equally far-reaching economic effects in other areas. The exclusive privilege of organizing political power confines to a small circle of men the major part of the influence on the allocation of resources—how much of them are to be used for collective and how much for individual

[55] See Hoffman and Neal, *op. cit.*, p. 398.

consumption, how much on benefits for the present generation and how much for provisioning the future. It would, of course, be erroneous to assume that such an exclusive power of the elite cannot exist because the constitution makes these decisions dependent on the vote of elected representatives of the people. Without freedom of political organization, there is always a strong possibility that the vote of the representatives can be managed by the elite and any assembly turned into a gathering of yes-men.

But the degree in which this possibility will materialize can be very different, depending on the ideology and the character traits of the elite, on its coherence and on the rigidity or flexibility with which the inner circle itself is organized. These questions are at least as important as the formal provisions for the organization of state power. Nevertheless, before the character and the organization of the governing elite can be discussed, it is necessary to survey the constitutional provisions.

As has been explained, the organs which, theoretically, at least, have a general presumption of legislative and administrative competence are the communes. This constitutional provision expresses the idea that sovereignty rests with the people as a whole; the people surrender only specific rights of decision by empowering their representatives to act for them in defined matters, but retain all other powers. The analogy to the concepts underlying the American constitution and the origin of this principle in natural law are obvious. The members of the bicameral communal assembly, being the representatives closest to the sovereign people, are, therefore, considered to have the most valid title to all rights which cannot be exercised by the people directly and are not expressly attributed to another state organ. For the time being all this is of little if any practical consequence, because necessity requires much concentration of powers, but especially in a society which takes its ideology as seriously as is done in Yugoslavia it would be rash to assume that ideas professed but now frustrated by practical requirements can play no role in the future.

The national legislative body, the Federal Assembly, used to consist of two chambers, one composed of deputies elected by direct universal and equal suffrage, plus a minority of representatives of member republics and autonomous areas, and the other formed by delegations from vocational organizations.

In the new constitution of 1963, this bicameral system has been superseded by a complex multicameral arrangement. The greatest political power rests with the Federal Chamber, which consists mainly of delegates from the communes; these delegates are nominated by groups of citizens, elected by the Communal Assembly, and then confirmed by the citizens through a direct and equal vote. The Federal Chamber also has members representing the member republics and autonomous areas, and these members, on some occasions, act as a chamber of nationalities, for the purpose of "safeguarding the equality of the peoples of Yugoslavia and the rights of the republics, as determined by the Constitution." [56] There is also an Economic Chamber, a Chamber of Education and Culture, a Chamber of Social Welfare and Health, and an Organizational-Political Chamber; these chambers are composed of representatives of "working communities," from industrial enterprises to universities, health centers and many others. Thus the Economic Chamber consists of representatives of the workers' councils or the workers' assemblies in individual enterprises, of agricultural cooperatives and perhaps also of such organizations as industrial associations and labor unions. Although many details of this arrangement will become clear only when the laws implementing the constitution can be studied and experience with their application is available, it is certain that the four special chambers are intended to be bodies of vocational representation. But their members, though supposed to represent the "working communities," are only nominated but not delegated by these communities: Like the members of the Federal Chamber, they are appointed by the communes. The constitution stipulates: "The deputies to the chambers of the Federal Assembly which represent working communities shall be elected by the Communal Assemblies." [57] The election of these delegates, unlike that of the deputies to the Federal Chamber, does not even have to be ratified by those whom they are to represent. The vocational chambers may, therefore, become a particularly effective instrument of the communes to influence federal policy.

But are the Communal Assemblies completely free in the decision on whom to elect? Specifically, are they not bound by any rules about the relative strength of the representation of subgroups? The most important case of this kind concerns the representation of peasants as compared with that of industrial workers in the Economic Chamber. As has been stated before, in the Chamber of Working Communities of the Communal Assemblies the subgroups are represented according to the "economic significance and strength of every branch," which presumably means its contribution to the social product—a principle that involves discrimination against the agricultural population because of the lower per capita output, in value terms, in agriculture as compared with industry. Presumably, the Communal Assemblies use the same principle for the appointment of delegates to the federal Chamber

[56] *The Constitution of the Federal Republic of Yugoslavia,* Art. 165 (p. 61).
[57] *Loc. cit.* Art. 167 (p. 62).

of Working Communities, or at least for the appointment of delegates to the Economic Chamber,[58] but whether this is just the presumable practice or a legal prescription is still unclear.

The Federal Chamber has a position of preeminence, since it deals with the most important affairs of state—international relations, defense and internal security—and also decisively influences the composition of the federal executive. Furthermore, the Federal Chamber participates in all decisions, on equal terms with the chamber having special competence for the subject matter, if the issue is one "of concern to the working communities." [59] This rules out binding decisions by the vocational chambers alone and restricts their independent activities to debates, reports and recommendations. In contrast, the single vocational chamber of the old bicameral system, the Council of Producers, possessed exclusive authority on a number of economic matters.[60] Moreover, the splitting up of vocational representation into four bodies has probably reduced its significance: Each of them now seems to be more of an appendage to the Federal Chamber than an autonomous body. On the other hand, the basis of vocational representation has been broadened: Whereas before it was confined to the population active in industry, agriculture, commerce and the handicrafts, now professional workers of all kinds, from university professors to doctors to welfare workers, are also represented.

The preeminence of the Federal Chamber may have reduced the importance of the discrimination against the peasantry. To be sure, the delegates to all chambers are elected by the Communal Assemblies, and these Assemblies, in which agriculture often has a smaller representation than the size of the agricultural population would warrant, might wish to discriminate against the peasantry as much in the delegation to the Federal Chamber as in the Economic Chamber and other vocational bodies. But whereas in the choice of delegates to the latter the Communal Assembly has a free hand, the delegates to the Federal Chamber must be ratified in a general vote in which all citizens have equal suffrage.[61] Again, however, the question arises: How much real choice does the voter have? To what extent is the outcome of these elections predetermined by decisions of the leadership of the League of Communists? These questions can be answered only in the years to come; probably not even the authors of the new constitution are able to foresee how all the provisions which they have created will work out in practice.

[58] It seems somewhat difficult to assume that the contribution to the social product should determine appointments, for instance, to the Chamber of Education and Culture.

[59] *Loc. cit.*, Articles 173, 174, 175, 176, 177 (p. 64).

[60] See Hoffman and Neal, *op. cit.*, p. 216.

[61] *The Constitution of the Socialist Federal Republic of Yugoslavia,* Art. 35 (p. 23).

The One-Party System and Civil Liberties

The problem that arises with regard to the ratifying vote on the delegation to the Federal Chamber has a broader application: Do the masses have a share in the formulation of politics, and therefore of economic policies, or does Tito himself or the governing elite use its power and prestige to arrogate to themselves all the decisions? If the masses do have a share, can an opinion be formed as to its magnitude?

The postwar history of Yugoslavia indicates that the Titoist government is much more responsive to public opinion than the Soviet government. The abandonment of collectivization in agriculture and the mild response to industrial unrest would alone be evidence of this responsiveness; the whole atmosphere of the nation confirms the proposition that there is a modicum of identification of the people with the government, inconceivable unless the people believe that the government is not excluding them from a voice in their fate.

Such responsiveness, however, is only a partial substitute for legal influence of the citizen upon the conduct of affairs. The Yugoslav constitution provides for such influence by establishing popular representation, if not on a basis of political equality, at least without any degree of discrimination that would diminish the individual citizen's opportunity to elect representatives of his own choice. But as long as only Communists have a right to political organization, even if a wide variety of beliefs and loose groupings are permitted within the Communist Party, any opposition on fundamental grounds to the policies pursued will remain fragmented and therefore ineffective. It must not be assumed that the particular forms of democracy which have developed in the West are the only conceivable ones; the great diversity of forms which are found in the West—from the differences between a presidential system and pure parliamentarism to the varying nature of the party system in individual countries—shows that there is no one particular form in which people can govern themselves, and should we expect that all imaginable forms have already found their counterpart in reality? But the denial of the right to organized political activity to all opinion groups except one is not a matter of form merely; it denies the essence of political freedom.

To be sure, vocational representation, as realized by the Yugoslav vocational chambers, is a sort of partial substitute for a multi-party system. The representatives of the various branches of production and commodity distribution are supposed to represent their divergent interests. Although interests are by no means the only, or even the most important, source of beliefs, there is an interrelationship between the two. Moreover, where the law, as it does in Yugoslavia, recognizes the legitimacy of organized representation of divergent interests, the organizations which are supposed to represent interest may also accommodate some beliefs that would otherwise find no organized representation. Peasant representatives, for instance, may well defend not only the economic interests of their constituents but also their ideological demands, for instance in state-church relations; no empirical evidence is available, however, that would show the extent to which this possibility has materialized.

There can be no doubt that even with the mitigations inherent in vocational representation and in a party discipline which is loose by comparison with other Communist parties, the one-party system of Yugoslavia stifles the expression of the political will of the citizens to a high degree. Thereby the average person in Yugoslavia is deprived of the measure of influence which he can exert on collective decisions, in the economic as in other fields, in countries with free political organization. This is only another way of saying that he is not to the same extent as Westerners master of his own fate—that his liberty is seriously restricted.

What about other kinds of freedom—those which are usually called civil liberties, in the narrower sense, meaning habeas corpus, the right of free expression in speech and in writing, the right of assembly. The Yugoslav constitution has an extensive catalogue of citizens' rights, but there is no constitutional guarantee of the independence of judges. Although the constitution stipulates that "the courts shall be autonomous in the performance of their judicial functions"[62] and that "a judge . . . shall not be called to account for an opinion given in the performance of judicial functions,"[63] the judges are elected by "the assembly of the corresponding social-political community"—the judges of the Communal Court, for instance, by the Communal Assembly—and the same body that has elected them can also remove the judges from office.[64] Even in democratic countries there is some question whether judges who hold their office by election can be fully independent; under the Yugoslav one-party system it seems unlikely that a judge could retain his position if his interpretation of the law were in serious conflict with the wishes of the League of Communists, which can exercise decisive influence in all the "social-political communities." There is good reason to believe that this influence is used with more restraint than that of the Communist Party in the Soviet Union, but no judge whose professional fate depends on the approval of the ruling party can be a strong guardian of civil

[62] *Loc. cit.* Art. 136 (p. 52).
[63] *Loc. cit.* Art. 138 (p. 52).
[64] *Loc. cit.* Art. 137 (p. 52).

liberties, and without such guardianship by the judiciary no bill of rights can be very effective. Civil rights have a dual relationship to the economic system: The economic power of the state may be used to infringe upon them, and their guarantee is a condition for the free exercise of such influence upon policy as other constitutional provisions grant the citizens. Moreover, the assurance of civil liberties facilitates the formation of an independent public opinion, which the government may to some extent respect even aside from legal provisions, and which thus may become a determinant of economic policies.

Although there is too little evidence to form a very reliable judgment, it does not seem that in Yugoslavia economic pressure is used to any great extent to penalize opponents of the government. For occupations which involve the making of decisions of political importance, membership in the party, or at the very least a conforming attitude, is of course prerequisite, but as far as can be judged from individual instances, the government seems anxious to utilize the services of experts—in a broad sense—without too much scrutiny of their political record. Certainly ordinary workers, whether blue collar or white collar, are not subject to economic sanctions for known or suspected heresies. Nor do there seem to be other forms of persecution for privately held opinions. The police apparently do not pry into the opinions of individuals—except where eligibility for "sensitive" positions is involved—as long as they are not publicly expressed.

Public expressions of convictions is a different matter. In this respect the case of Milovan Djilas is widely supposed—in the West—to have proved that Titoist Yugoslavia is still an unfree country, and an analysis of the case confirms the conclusion to the extent that the amount of freedom in Yugoslavia is more restricted than in countries possessing an effective bill of rights. Because of the symptomatic significance of the case, it is necessary to summarize its essentials.

Djilas was one of the co-leaders of the Communist partisan movement, one of Tito's closest friends, and in the first period after the war an advocate of communist extremism. He had a change of mind, for reasons which are not entirely clear but among which the impression—gained at first hand—of Stalin's ruthlessness was certainly a major factor. The rejection of Soviet-type communism by Yugoslavia did not go far enough for him, and in 1953 he started a campaign of journalistic criticism of the party and tried to continue it even after Tito had expressed disapproval. Developing ever more extreme opposition to the party and all its works, he was censured—only his friend Vladimir Dedidjer supported him (and eventually went to London as an exile.) Still refusing to be silenced, Djilas now published his criticism abroad, first through an interview with the foreign press and then through the publication of his book *The New Class*, the manuscript of which was smuggled out of Yugoslavia in 1956. Even before the book appeared, he was sentenced to prison for "hostile propaganda"—according to the official interpretation, not for holding his views but for disseminating them abroad—and after the publication of *The New Class* he was actually imprisoned, later released but made to serve another sentence after having inaugurated the publication of a new book about conversations which he had with Stalin early in the postwar period.

The statutory provisions against "hostile propaganda" under which Djilas was sentenced are typical legalistic rubber, capable of being stretched according to the preference of a court which is not even in any true sense independent, because the judges can be removed by the government. This aspect of the matter is no less objectionable from a democratic point of view for the reason that the opinions held and propagandized by Djilas were indeed extreme, as shown especially by the following passage:

> Viewed from the standpoint of freedom, a military dictatorship in a Communist system would denote great progress. It would signify the termination of totalitarian party control, or party oligarchy. Theoretically speaking, however, a military dictatorship would be possible only in the case of a military defeat or an exceptional political crisis.[65]

Even in a democratic country, such as Western Germany, publication of such views might have been prohibited as propaganda directed against the principles of the constitution, though criminal prosecution would hardly have been instituted. To be sure, a democratic country which leaves a safety valve in the form of a machinery for peaceful change has a greater moral right to protect itself against propaganda that advocates violent change than a government which closes (or half-closes) that safety valve. But a government which is not committed to democracy in the Western sense can hardly be expected to see matters in this light.

The Djilas affair was only the most spectacular among a number of political prosecutions under the elastic provisions of Yugoslav law. Although it is impossible to make a firm judgment on the basis of the information available, at first sight some of them seem even more objectionable than the conviction of Djilas. An opinion as to the amount of political freedom in Yugoslavia naturally depends on what yardstick is used. As compared with the Soviet Union, punishment for political opposition is neither frequent nor harsh; a comparison with Western countries shows that Yugo-

[65] Milovan Djilas, *The New Class*, an analysis of the Communist System. New York, Frederick A. Praeger, 1957, p. 78.

slavia is not a free country. Worse than the degree of restriction that is now being applied is the wide latitude which the government possesses in the event that it wants to inaugurate a more severe policy.[66]

In its economic effects, this policy of leniency with reservations means essentially that nobody is seriously hindered in defending his economic interests in the public arena as long as his arguments do not strike at the fundamentals of the system, but that no propaganda against the established economic order is tolerated.

INEQUALITY

As in the Soviet Union, the possibility of measuring economic and social inequality is even more limited in Yugoslavia than in Western countries. From all descriptions, it is obvious that peasant income is generally lower than the income of industrial workers, with great differences among the several agricultural regions, and that the higher administrative and business personnel have a standard of living far above the ordinary worker.

This latter point has been the special target of Milovan Djilas.[67] The title of his most important book, *The New Class*, is in itself an attack upon the individuals who are in charge of the conduct of economic and political affairs under Tito.

Djilas maintains that under any kind of communist regime, including Titoism, the upper crust of society "owns" the instruments of production in essentially the same sense as the capitalists do under capitalism. There is no doubt that the people who hold political power ultimately control the use of all economic resources in Yugoslavia as well as in the Soviet Union. To describe this control as a matter of ownership may be satisfactory to a Marxist—and Djilas has retained a good deal of the Marxist approach—who tends to think of social differentiation as caused exclusively by ownership or non-ownership of the means of production, although Marx himself would not have followed this tendency to extreme conclusions. But ideological preconceptions aside, the concept of ownership of material means implies the right to use them for one's own advantage, except to the extent that ethics and law forbid a particular use because it would cause too much harm to others. What Djilas means, of course, is not that the "new class" has any such formal right, or even openly claims it, but that the "class" acts as if it were in the possession of such a right. What element of truth is in that contention, so far as Yugoslavia is concerned?

66 This is also the opinion of Hoffman and Neal. See *op. cit.*, 393 ff. The authors give some examples of prosecutions and sentences imposed.

67 On the effect of Djilas' heresy upon Yugoslav communism, see Hoffman and Neal, *op. cit.*, pp. 196 ff.

Yugoslavia has accepted the principle that pay should largely depend on the contribution that a person makes to the social product. Consequently, not only must measurable effort be compensated, but also greater intelligence, higher education and greater responsibility. Since the people who are in power have created these rules, from which they and their immediate subordinates profit, it is true that they have not acted like ascetics. They have been guided by the belief that all members of society, including themselves, work better if given a material stake in the results. But this is not to say that they are guided primarily by their own interests even if these conflict with those of the rest of the community. Whoever has had contact with Yugoslav leaders must have got the impression that this group contains a substantial number of individuals dedicated to their tasks, and if results are the proper basis for judgment, few power elites have a better claim to recognition by the masses than that of Titoist Yugoslavia.

To raise Yugoslavia from the state in which it found herself after the war to its present level of relative economic well-being and give it the prospects for the future which Yugoslavia's current growth rate indicates, required enormous effort, wisdom and initiative on the part of leaders and subleaders. To find a sufficient number of people who would strain their capacities to the necessary degree in order to develop their own faculties as much as the task required, would have been impossible in a strictly equalitarian society. Material gain is certainly not the only incentive that spurs individuals to effort, but those who make a supreme effort without prospect of material premiums are few. Yet supposing that, by some miracle, revolutionary purists had been sufficiently numerous, the chances are that most of them would have been zealots whose power would have taken a greater toll, though not in material goods, among the citizenry than the power of leaders who expected some material reward for their special qualifications. It is not enough to say that in the regular case premiums of a material nature are needed to get important work done; it is also true that with rare exceptions those who would entirely forget about themselves and work merely for the sake of the cause will be as hard on others as they are on themselves, and are therefore undesirable holders of power.

At various stages of the development of the last ten years there was a feeling in the Yugoslav legislative bodies that living standards of many business and political leaders were too high and efforts were made to reduce income differentials regarded as excessive. It may well be that the advantages were substantially larger than necessary or desirable. The Yugoslav system gives well-managed firms great opportunities for profit, and it is logical that workers who have greatly profited from the work of a successful manager will not grudge him a particularly high compensation. In the political sphere, it would have been an extraordinary event if the tradition that public office can be exploited for private gain—a tradition which had grown very strong under Turkish rule and had been continued to a great extent when the Balkan nations became independent—had been entirely uprooted by the Yugoslav revolution. It is very important for Titoism to fight these tendencies, but mostly for the reason that any toleration of excessive or illegal incomes would compromise the regime morally and diminish its authority; since the material effects are not preventing a steep rise of the standard of living of the masses, they do not seem to be a great economic liability in themselves.

The Yugoslav system must deal with the vital question of how income differentials, inevitable as they are, can be prevented from leading to class stratification by becoming hereditary so often as to obstruct inter-class mobility. A business manager, a high government official, a university professor, a high-level engineer will naturally use part of his higher income to give his children a better education, and especially to give them the cultural background which makes schooling more effective. Thereby they will be prepared again to occupy higher positions in the future than the great majority of workers' and peasants' children. This effect cannot be eliminated without imposing intolerable restrictions on the individual and largely frustrating the purposes for which income differentials exist. On the other hand, in a society as dynamic as that of present-day Yugoslavia, new top and near-top positions are created every day; even if it is harder for a boy or girl from the bottom layers of society to rise than for those whose parents already occupy higher positions to remain above the average level, this phenomenon will not lead to dangerous stratification as long as every gifted young person has the opportunity for substantial advancement. One of the historical tests that Titoism faces is whether by scholarships and by raising the cultural level of the masses, mobility will be maintained, even when the dynamism of the Yugoslav economy has diminished—a development which eventually is bound to occur.

V. OTHER SYSTEMS IN TRANSITION

CHAPTER 21

PRIMITIVE AND UNDERDEVELOPED ECONOMIES

Purpose and Limitations of This Survey

IN DEALING with underdeveloped areas, social scientists have generally proceeded along two different lines. Some of them have investigated the mores and institutions of primitive ethnic groups as they existed before effective contact with industrial nations, or at least before recent efforts at systematic economic development: These investigations have been inclined to focus upon individual areas. Following another line, other investigators have worked out theories about the political, social and economic presuppositions of economic development: These efforts have tended toward generalization. The two different approaches have left a gap in the literature: No general survey of the various types of primitive society seems to be available or easily accessible. The empirical studies of the first kind of investigation contain a wealth of material for a general typology, but the very abundance of data makes it difficult to search the works of these writers for information on those institutions that may be characteristic not just of the particular society under investigation, but of other primitive societies as well. In some instances, however, the authors of the empirical studies have engaged in a comparative analysis of different societies found within the same general area, and these efforts facilitate further work directed toward a typology. On the other hand, the theorists of economic development have supported their generalizations with illustrations taken from the studies of the empiricists, and thereby fitted some individual facts into a general framework. Thus the gap between description of individual primitive societies and a survey of their types has been narrowed from both sides, but it has not disappeared.[1]

[1] The book which perhaps comes closer than any other to giving such a survey is

Although this book cannot close the gap, a survey of contemporary economic systems would be incomplete without an attempt at classification of those economies which have not yet fully met the impact of modern industrial life. Difficulties arising from the inadequacy of previous studies for our purpose preclude the possibility of completing the task now; more spadework needs to be done for future authors.

Thus there are two unavoidable shortcomings: First, the typology of primitive economies to be drawn up here is a rough sketch—a framework without much detail, apart from some cases that will serve only as illustrations. Second, although our objective is to make present-day conditions understandable, it will be necessary to some extent to describe not only what exists today, but what existed until recently. Economic primitivism is disintegrating rapidly, even though it will be many decades before its institutions vanish completely. Thus it is difficult to determine in every case how far the process has gone and to describe the institutions in all their fading-out phases. It is easier to describe them as they were before they disintegrated; the student must then keep in mind that institutions so described have undergone some weakening and that each stage of the weakening cannot be precisely defined.

The principal interest in comparing economic systems grows out of the fact that they exist in the same world, that they influence each other, that their differences lead to conflicts or aggravate those which arise from other causes, and that they require mutual accommodation. In other words, we wish to compare economic systems primarily because of the possibility of their interaction. In the case of primitive economies, one particularly interesting aspect of that interaction lies in the certainty that these economies, as they outgrow the primitive stage, must either follow the path of capitalism, socialism, or communism, or adopt some synthesis of the elements contained in these systems; and the system to which the majority of the now underdeveloped nations will turn, or to which the system eventually adopted by that majority will show the greatest similarity, will thereby gain in competitive strength over the rival systems. All this means that there is little interest in dealing with systems that are not in interaction with others; and by this same token there is no need to deal with people in the least accessible regions of the Amazon basin or in the innermost recesses of the Congo area,

---

Melville J. Herskovits' *Economic Anthropology,* New York: Alfred A. Knopf, 1952. It supplies much valuable information on a variety of types of social organization of primitive peoples, but it concerns itself very little with situations in which the subordination of the cultivators of the soil to large estate owners is an important feature, except where such cultivators were slaves. This omission seems to have been caused by confinement of the scope of the book to non-literate societies.

people who may not have passed the stage of mere foodgathering. The primitive economies to be described here are predominantly agricultural or pastoral, with well and often highly developed handicrafts. Although households are to a much higher degree self-sufficient than they are in industrial nations, there is more than occasional trading, and in many of these economies traders exist as a separate vocational group. Money is in use; credit may or may not play a role, and where it does, the source is the village money lender rather than a bank or a cooperative society. The countries in this group, and frequently even various regions within the same country, differ widely in regard to the influence which advanced economic techniques have gained in their economies. Some areas are still truly primitive, with a prevalence of subsistence farming; others already show a considerable degree of economic differentiation, with a fair amount of production for the market, often for the world market; they deserve to be called underdeveloped rather than primitive. No clear line of distinction, however, can be drawn between these two sub-categories.

Since land use is central to economic activities, the system of landholding provides the most important mark of distinction among the various types of primitive societies. To bring any sort of order into the bewildering multitude of these landholding systems, it is well to distinguish between three archetypes. There is, first, collective ownership or control of land by the tribe, the clan or the "great" family; second, there is private ownership by the individual or the "small" family with no sufficient differences in the size of property to lead to a division between a landowner and a tenant class or otherwise to political and social preponderance of big landowners; third, there are systems in which such a preponderance exists, often in the form in which the rights in the same plot of land are divided between an overlord and a dependent peasant, as they were during the Middle Ages in Europe.

Common Ownership or Control of Land

Common control of land has a variety of meanings, depending on the nature of the group which holds the rights over land and also on the delimitation of group rights as against those of the individual. Rarely, if ever, is land in joint ownership and management; often some lands are held and managed in common, while other tracts are left to individual property or at least to individual cultivation; again no land may be managed collectively, but all land may be subject to social control, perhaps only in the sense that the community reserves the right to redistribute the land when changes in family size make it desirable, or perhaps in the sense that the community also determines the crops that should be planted by individual "small" families and the proper time for planting and harvesting. As for the nature of the controlling group, it is not only important whether the group represents a more extended or a narrower circle—tribe, village, clan or "great" family—but the political arrangement is also significant: In the frequent instances in which a chieftain acts as trustee of his village or tribe in exercising social control, much depends on how his power is limited—how effective, for instance, is the control exercised over him by the elders or by all members of the community.

The extent or intensity of group control is influenced by those factors, physical or cultural, which favor one kind of land use over others. Where hunting is an important means of sustenance, uncleared land must be held in common as hunting grounds; in a merely pastoral economy, too, joint holding by tribe, village, clan or other kinship groups avoids problems that would be caused by recognition of individual rights.[2] On the other hand, where crops are raised for which the land must first be cleared, this clearing is often an individual effort, and it seems reasonable and just to reserve some or all benefits over the cleared land to the individual and his wife and children. But even in these cases, the community may not surrender all rights to the land: To reserve the right of redistribution of the arable land may be the only way to prevent distress in families that have grown too large for their holdings and thus to preserve social and political stability; to restrict the right of the individual to sell land may be necessary to prevent the intrusion of outsiders or the acquisition of control over the community by foreign capitalists.

The great variety of arrangements shows that many primitive population groups do not have—at least not in regard to land—the same absolute concept of property which modern law has inherited from Roman law; rather, very often we find a bundle of overlapping rights, some complementary, some conflicting, in the same plot of land, and sometimes it is even difficult to determine whether we are dealing with mere custom or with law.[3] Not

[2] One does not have to go to primitive economies to find instances of the kind. In European countries there are to this day villages which, as a collective entity, own forests and meadows for essentially the same purposes as in the Middle Ages and in antiquity: to have cattle and sheep of the villagers pastured in one herd, and to provide lumber and fuel for the villagers.

In addition to these instances, modern living conditions have led to collective landowning for different reasons. The national forests and national parks of the United States, for instance, owe their existence to the need for conservation of natural resources.

[3] Melville J. Herskovits questions whether it is a "helpful usage" to make a hard and fast distinction between custom and law in primitive societies. See his article, "Some Problems of Land Tenure in Contemporary Africa" in Kenneth H. Parsons and Associates, ed. *Land Tenure* (Proceedings of the International Conference on Land Tenure and Re-

only are overlapping rights regarded as compatible, but often property titles, especially those of tribal property, are not thought of as totally exclusive toward outsiders. C. Daryll Forde, for instance, reports that in some sections of Oceania a tribe or village community may consider part of the wild country nearby its own in the sense of a land reserve but, as long as no actual cultivation is undertaken, regards it as proper for people from other villages to hunt or collect fruit on that land.[4]

The vagueness of the property concept facilitates the balancing of communal controls and private rights of usage which we find in many primitive societies, with the balance shifting in either direction as practical necessities change under the impact of physical or social factors (population increase, soil exhaustion, loss of territory through war or natural disaster). Although illustrations could be found in many parts of the world, sub-Saharan Africa contains especially interesting examples of communal control over land and its relationship to private rights and individual efforts. ". . . in all Africa, so far as it is possible to determine, one finds group control and discipline at a very high level.[5] One root of this power of the community lies in religious concepts which attribute to past and future generations claims on the land. As one Nigerian chief put it: "I conceive that land belongs to a vast family of whom many are dead, few are living, and countless members are still unborn." [6]

---

lated Problems in World Agriculture, Held at Madison, Wisconsin, 1951), Madison: University of Wisconsin Press, 1956, p. 235.

[4] See C. Daryll Forde, *Habitat, Economy and Society,* London: Methuen & Co., 1961, p. 192.

[5] Melville J. Herskovits, "Some Problems of Land Tenure in Contemporary Africa," p. 235. See also his article "Economic Change and Cultural Dynamics" in Ralph Braibanti and Joseph J. Spengler, *Tradition, Values and Socio-Economic Development,* Durham: Duke University Press, 1961, p. 132. Although he speaks of "all Africa" in an effort to point out what African societies have in common, he seems not to include—or to include only as marginal cases—the North African areas. Also, his statement would have a different meaning—though it may be literally valid—for those African areas, like Ethiopia, in which strong feudalistic traits appear in the social structure. In this part of our discussion we are, of course, concerned only with social control in non-feudalistic societies.

[6] Reported by Charles K. Meek, *Land Law and Custom in the Colonies,* London: Oxford University Press, 1949, p. 178. Land tenure systems often have some roots in cultural factors other than religion. In an article on land tenure, Robert Lowie stated:

"Property rights are correlated with other social phenomena, so that a complete functional study of land tenure among primitive peoples requires a consideration of their clan and family organization, economic technology and religion." (*Encyclopaedia of the Social Sciences,* New York: Macmillan, 1933, Vol. IX, p. 76.) Even this enumeration, however, is illustrative rather than exhaustive. The amount of social coherence, of desire for "togetherness," even to the extent that it has not crystallized into a particularly close clan or family organization, may have an influence on land tenure arrangements. Jan K. Boeke, for instance, reports that in those parts of Indonesia in which European influence has not penetrated too deeply, social control over land—especially the community's power to take excess land from one family and give it to another—is still generally accepted, but

The variety of landholding arrangements in tropical Africa is so great and each case is so complex as to make it impossible in this context to go into details of description in more than one example. For this purpose Bechuanaland, a British protectorate bordering South Africa and Southern Rhodesia, appears particularly suitable, because social controls there are very far-reaching but, on the other hand, educational facilities and other factors tend to stimulate individual initiative.[7] Some land in the Bechuanaland protectorate is reserved for communal cultivation; for this area the chief of the tribe provides seed, but the members of the tribe have to do the work with their own draft animals and utensils. "The corn that is harvested is stored in the Chief's granaries. He is supposed to use it on behalf of the tribe, e.g. by helping indigent people, providing for his subjects in times of starvation, feeding the regiments that he summons to work for him, and entertaining visitors." [8]

Aside from these "tribal lands," and apparently covering much the larger area, there are lands which are cultivated by individuals under control by the tribe and its subdivisions. ". . . as head of the tribe, the Chief controls the tenure of all the land in his Reserve. Acting through subordinate authorities, he distributes holdings among the people for various purposes." [9] The position of the chief is hereditary, but he has to act as a trustee for his tribe, and in important matters he can decide only with the approval of the tribal assembly. Furthermore, custom requires him to consult about tribal affairs informally with the notables of the tribe, among whom his own relatives are usually prominent, and more formally with a council formed by the headmen

---

he regards it as ancillary to other functions of the village community. "The village is not primarily a center of work, of production, but of repose, and only when reposing does a human being truly live." (Jan K. Boeke, *Economic Policy and Dual Societies as Exemplified by Indonesia,* New York: Inst. of Pacific Relations, 1953, p. 26. See also pp. 31 ff.)

[7] Among these other factors is employment outside the tribe, especially as migratory labor in the gold mining industry of the Union of South Africa.

[8] Isaac Schapera, *Native Land Tenure in the Bechuanaland Protectorate,* Lovedale: The Lovedale Press, 1943, p. 156. The "regiments" mentioned in the quotation are age classes of men and women which can be called up by the chief for work of usefulness for the tribe and at least to a limited extent work of benefit to himself. "Regiments may be called for services necessary in times of national emergency in order to avert a calamity or threatened calamity or to deal with any circumstance that would endanger the existence or well-being of the whole or part of the population. A single regiment or more regiments may be demanded to: look for strayed cattle, make dams, build schools or churches, hunt dangerous animals of prey like lions, clear trees from the chief's crop fields, clear show grounds, etc." S. M. Gabatshawane, *Introduction to the Bechuanaland Protectorate, History and Administration,* Kanye: S. M. Gabatshawane, 1957, p. 77. Only men who are properly enrolled in their age class can participate in the tribal assembly. See Schapera, *op. cit.,* p. 28. Service in the regiments is nevertheless not very popular because it must in principle be rendered without compensation and often extends over as much as 3 months. See Gabatshawane, *op. cit., p.* 77.

[9] Schapera, *op. cit.,* p. 42.

of "wards"—settlements which may represent a village or part of a village, each of these, as a rule, representing a kinship group of which the headman is a prominent member.[10]

The tribal authorities determine what land shall be used for dwellings, for grazing, for cultivation, and what land shall be temporarily or permanently withdrawn from usage; also, what land shall be used in common by the tribe and what should be parceled out for use to families. The land to be distributed is allocated to the wards, and the headmen of the wards then assign the plots to individuals. From the headman every married man in the ward can claim enough land for residence and cultivation to accommodate his family.[11] Once land has been taken for cultivation, the family to which it has been assigned remains in possession as long as it continues the use; redistribution of land under cultivation or in use as pasture has not yet become a practical necessity because of the relative abundance of land reserves in most parts of Bechuanaland. Since it is possible to assign land to a family in a ward other than the one in which it lives, reserves in one location can be used to relieve population pressure in a neighboring area,[12] and individual hardship cases have been alleviated by such measures as "borrowing" land from temporarily absent neighbors or plowing up grazing lands if existing cattle herds can be sustained on a smaller area by sinking new wells.[13] No one, however, can possess more land than he is able to use with the labor of his family, except that as far as land reserves permit, he may keep some land for his sons if they are old enough to establish themselves as heads of their own families within the next few years. If he abandons his fields permanently, the land reverts to the ward or the tribe; complicated rules, differing from tribe to tribe, determine when land will be regarded as abandoned.[14]

[10] See A. Sillery, *The Bechuanaland Protectorate,* Capetown and London: Oxford University Press, 1952, p. 200.

[11] For details see Schapera, *op. cit.,* pp. 44 ff.

[12] Such assignments, of course, have the disadvantage of lengthening the distance between the cultivator's home and his plot of land. But the inhabitants of the protectorate are accustomed to such distances because custom forces them to live in large villages or towns, rather than in farmsteads near their fields. See Schapera, *op. cit.,* pp. 269 ff.; Sillery, *op. cit.,* 199 ff.

[13] See Schapera, *op. cit.,* pp. 136 ff., 215 ff. The latter remedy, however, becomes increasingly inapplicable because overgrazing is already a great problem, and all the improvements in the water supply may be needed to make the grazing area in use sustain the amount of cattle the people need. The plowing area has been increased also by land purchases from European settlers and by grants of crown land. But unless outside employment increases rapidly enough to relieve population pressure more drastically, the tribes of Bechuanaland may have to limit the land which an individual family can cultivate and introduce periodic redistribution.

[14] *Loc. cit.,* pp. 176 ff.

Among all Bechuanaland tribes sale of land is forbidden.[15] Sometimes, to be sure, a man may be compensated for his labor in clearing the land when he is moving away, or for other reasons is unable to cultivate it any longer, and a new user has to take over. The right to the land itself is inheritable within the family according to fixed rules, which cannot be changed by testamentary disposition.[16] Prohibition of sale applies not only to agricultural but also to residential land, but under certain conditions and with the permission of the chief, a user who is moving out may demolish his dwelling and sell the materials.[17] Nor can wells be sold, even if they have been dug by private effort, but a price can be charged for water when used by somebody other than the possessor; frequently, however, it is freely shared.[18]

In addition to control over the possession of land, tribal authorities have retained some power to determine the seasonal beginning and end of the various agricultural activities.[19] The rules in this matter, to the extent that they do not have their origin in magic beliefs, probably had the same basis as similar rules in the European manorial communities of the Middle Ages: to prevent cultivators from getting into each other's way when planting or harvesting. Since some of these rules now seem to hinder individual effort to improve agricultural methods, chiefs have become more liberal in their enforcement of the rules.

A great variety of orders and regulations is issued by the tribal chiefs for the purpose of conserving the natural resources of the territory, especially the fertility of the soil, water and timber.[20] As in many other parts of Africa, primitive methods of agriculture sometimes make it necessary to shift cultivation to new areas, because the old fields are exhausted or—more often—eroded or overrun with weeds.[21] As a consequence, homes and towns must also be relocated; the chief can order such moves and they cannot be made without his permission.[22] Relocation to better soils and population increases require the parceling out of new portions of the land reserve with relative frequency and thereby make the authority of the chief and the ward headman, and ultimately of the tribal assembly, over these matters more important.

Social control by the tribal authorities over individual economic activities

[15] See Schapera, p. 152.

[16] *Loc. cit.*, pp. 152 ff.

[17] *Loc. cit.*, p. 101.

[18] *Loc. cit.*, p. 246.

[19] *Loc. cit.*, pp. 188 ff.

[20] *Loc. cit.*, p. 42 f.

[21] Exhaustion of the soil is fairly infrequent because many drought periods force the cultivator to let part of his land lie fallow about four or five seasons out of ten. See *loc. cit.*, p. 177.

[22] *Loc. cit.*, p. 42 f., 144 f.

goes beyond the powers directly related to land tenure. The individual may be called up for "regimental labor," as has already been explained. Moreover, the ability of a man and his family to earn a living depends to a great extent on where he lives, and this can be determined by the chief. Not only can he order the relocation of villages, but he can also banish individuals from their home community and force them to live elsewhere. This kind of measure is either punishment for asocial behavior or a preventive against further trouble. The records show that typical reasons for banishment are insubordination or intrigues against the chief, quarreling with or inflicting violence upon other members of the community, and suspected sorcery.[23]

The High Commissioner for Bechuanaland, Basutaland and Swaziland, representing the government of the United Kingdom, exercises legislative authority in addition to his duty of supervising the tribal administration. He acts through resident commissioners, one for each of the three territories, and through district commissioners. The resident commissioner is supported by an African Advisory Council, a European Advisory Council[24] and a joint Advisory Council; as the names imply, the votes of these bodies do not bind the government, but they are frequently followed.[25] The African Council consists mainly of the tribal chiefs.

Against decisions by the tribal authorities, appeals to the resident commissioner and ultimately to the High Commissioner are possible; courts of the colonial administration handle appeals from the tribal courts, and generally the more serious cases. The tendency of the British authorities has been to strengthen the powers of the chiefs in the conservation of resources, but at the same time to emphasize the character of the chieftainship as a trusteeship. Since the chief normally holds his position by inheritance, that is as a matter of his own right, there is danger that the chief might become a sort of feudal ruler if there were no check on this tendency provided by the policy of the colonial administration. Specifically, without that counteracting force, such chiefly privileges as the right to use labor "regiments" for personal advantage as well as for public works might become a lever for changing the whole character of native society.

In Africa today there are few if any places where such far-reaching powers of colonial administration as the High Commissioner exercises in Bechuanaland are accepted by the native population with so little opposition; the only reform that is strongly desired by the residents of the Protectorate—or at least the chiefs—is the endowment of the African Council with

[23] See Schapera, *op. cit.*, p. 104.
[24] European settlements exist in the border districts of Bechuanaland.
[25] See S. M. Gabatshawane, *op. cit.*, p. 82.

legislative rights[26] and there is little doubt that this demand will eventually be met. The reason for native acquiescence in the rule by the United Kingdom lies in geography, combined with the political situation in the neighboring countries. Like the residents of the two other territories under the High Commissioner, which are completely surrounded by the Union of South Africa, the people of Bechuanaland fear that in the event of a withdrawal of the United Kingdom's claim to sovereignty, they would come under the much harsher rule of the Boers; nor are these fears allayed by the fact that Bechuanaland, unlike Basutoland and Swaziland, has a common border with Southern Rhodesia.

Although the power of the High Commissioner is now an anomaly in Africa outside the Portuguese and Spanish colonies, it does not make the situation of Bechuanaland atypical in the sense that it offers no lessons applicable to other areas. On the contrary: The national governments which in the new African states have taken over from the colonial administrations are encountering many of the problems with which those administrations had to cope, and which the High Commissioner has to handle in Bechuanaland and the two other protectorates. Outstanding among these problems is the relationship of the central government to the tribes: It is vitally important not only because on its solution depends the inner coherence of the new states, but also because of its bearing upon the exercise of social controls over individual economic activities, since these controls require direction and regulation from the center. These controls, however, can only be administered by regional and local authorities, such as the tribal chieftains, tribal assemblies and village headmen.

At present, most of the new governments have great difficulty in coping with the problem of their own relations with the tribes. Often the national rulers have to play one tribe against the other, or have to rely mainly on the power of their own tribe, much as in the European Middle Ages the kings of France or the German emperors could maintain the authority of the national government only by exploiting the rivalries between regional rulers, or by utilizing the military resources of their own family possessions. The British High Commissioners in the South African protectorates are in a more fortunate position. Backed by an outside power whose role is regarded as protective rather than oppressive, they are able to exercise their authority over the chieftains and their tribes in an impartial manner. The new independent states of Africa must reach the same stage to secure their existence as nations. In this sense Bechuanaland, otherwise not one of the more important areas of the continent, holds before the new nations a picture of their

[26] See Gabatshawane, *op. cit.*, p. 83.

own future. Not the least among the problems which they will have to solve by balancing tribal against national authority is that of social controls. Should they be strengthened, maintained, reduced, allowed to disintegrate or deliberately abolished? This problem is not peculiar to Africa. The old issue of state interventionism versus laissez faire presents itself in a new form in many of the countries which have recently achieved independence, because their communal traditions and institutions might perhaps be modernized in order to serve purposes which have become important through changes in technology and related developments.

Will such modernization be possible? Will not tribes, village communities and kinship groups disintegrate under the impact of the economic changes that are unavoidable? Some experts regard this as an inevitable conclusion. "Gradually, the original tenures are giving way to individual holdings of a peasant type or to the plantation type of operations for the production of cash crops." [27] Tendencies of this nature obviously exist, and they may well prevail ultimately; it is still an open question whether they will not have to prevail in order to make possible a modern economy. Small farmers, not hampered in their decisions by chieftains, headmen of villages or the ruling elders of "great" families, may be easier to fit into an economy with substantial industrial and commercial sectors such as the African and Asian states are trying to build. The same may be true of a system of plantations provided it does not develop into a sort of feudalism.

But there is another side to the question, which warrants the warning not to take for granted the disappearance of extensive social controls in underdeveloped countries or to consider it optimal for economic development. The rise of industries is possible only with simultaneous improvement of agricultural yields, because otherwise the food for a growing urban population could not be provided; in many instances it will also be necessary to pay for importation of machinery with increased agricultural exports. It is by no means certain that the small farmer, if all decisions are left to him, will learn quickly enough to take advantage of modern scientific methods. On the other hand, to let the whole agricultural sector develop into a private plantation economy is contrary to the ideological preferences in practically all underdeveloped countries and would probably prove a cause of political instability, even if the workers were assured of more satisfactory conditions of employment and living than prevail now on many plantations. Great advantages would therefore be gained if the social controls, under which the small native farmer in many of the underdeveloped countries, and especially

[27] Melville Herskovits, "Some Problems of Land Tenure in Contemporary Africa," *Land Tenure,* p. 7.

in African countries, now works, were so altered as to make them effective instruments of technological and economic progress and social justice.

Without considerable reconstruction, existing social controls can hardly survive and certainly not fulfill any useful function once the development toward an industrial economy is further advanced. One point is that the rise of non-agricultural opportunities will lead to the accumulation of private fortunes, and it is hardly conceivable that the authority of a tribal chief or a village headman, as now constituted, could be maintained against the opposition of someone who has acquired much greater wealth. In this event, social controls can be effective only if exercised clearly on behalf of the community, not merely as a matter of hereditary or kinship rights, and if their application is approved by elected representatives of the members of the community. Even with such democratic sanction it will not be easy for the tribal and local authorities to exercise control over the rich as well as over the poor—it has not always been easy even in developed democratic countries for the public power to hold its own against the power of wealth. But without popular support more systematically institutionalized than is presently the case in many tribal communities of Africa and other continents, there is not much hope for social controls to be maintained.

In another respect, too, the foundation of social controls has to be revamped if they are to be maintained and made to serve the purposes of a developing economy. In many underdeveloped areas, social control rests mostly with kinship groups; even where tribal authority is of great importance it is largely exercised through kinship groups, as it is in Bechuanaland where the wards are based mainly on family relations. But the requirements of a modern economy are incompatible with the concept of the overriding importance of kinship ties. The comprehensive concept of kinship solidarity which exists in most underdeveloped countries implies that all members of the group have a claim to sharing the benefits of success which any one of them achieves. The existence of such claims might be reconciled with the requirement of an efficient economy if a tradition of economic self-reliance were to restrict the demands to cases of true indigence; but such a tradition does not yet exist, or at least is not yet strong. Under these circumstances, the obligation to share the fruits of one's labor with others constitutes a deterrent to efforts at economic advancement: It is expecting too much of an individual that he should work hard for economic success if he is then obliged to let others, who have taken no such pains, obtain a great share in the benefits.

Moreover, the obligations of kinship solidarity often extend to non-agricultural activities, and here they are even less compatible with economic efficiency. An African who has become a shopkeeper may have to let his relatives take freely what they want from his stocks; if he has entered one of the professions, his earnings are often at the disposal of the poorer members of his kinship group; if he is a civil servant who has to appoint subordinates, he is supposed to exercise patronage in favor of his kin.[28]

The kinship ties cannot be loosened unless a sufficiently effective machinery of public support for the needy is established; the democratization of tribal controls cannot be successfully carried out except if accompanied by a growth of the awareness of individual civic responsibility and of at least rudimentary mass education. But difficult as such reform is, there is still no evidence that it is impossible. Belatedly, it is being recognized that effective popular government with effective guarantees of individual rights cannot be expected to emerge on short notice in the underdeveloped countries. Although these countries have been informed about the philosophy and the techniques of democracy through the example of the West, it is only by their own experience that they can learn to build and manage political controls. Similarly, to assume that a textbook knowledge of modern technology and methods of business administration will by itself create a modern economy is an error: The habits of thinking which entrepreneurs must possess are not acquired overnight; neither is the different but equally essential set of attitudes which must prevail within the public administration.

On the other hand, it is an equally great error to regard present-day societies in underdeveloped countries as static. Most tribes and nations living in primitive conditions have had to make numerous changes in habits of living and of production merely to survive—changes which affected all phases of their existence. Numerous primitive communities, for instance, made the transition from nomadic to settled life; and if it took many decades to see even the beginnings of a rise of a native class of businessmen in many parts of Western Africa, this tempo does not compare unfavorably with Western experience at comparable stages of economic development. Basically, the mistake of expecting too much of relatively primitive societies, and the other mistake of underestimating the capacity of adaptation in these societies has the same root: failure to realize that modern forms of living require a great many prior changes in practices and attitudes which are less spectacular than the eventual break-through of modern types of organization. Because the preliminary changes are less spectacular, it is easy to forget their indispensability, and it is also easy to overlook their actual occurrence.

[28] See Melville J. Herskovits, "Economic Change and Cultural Dynamics," in Ralph Braibanti and Joseph J. Spengler (eds.), *Tradition, Values and Socio-Economic Development,* Durham: Duke University Press, 1961, p. 132.

Realistically appraised, the prevailing evidence speaks for the capacity of present-day tribal economies to develop either along individualistic lines, which in agriculture would mean an independent peasantry, or to modernize their system of social controls.

As for the latter possibility, the question arises whether these controls, after undergoing the necessary modification of their mechanism, could not even be intensified. In most of the areas with highly developed social controls the actual cultivation of the fields remains an individual responsibility, although private ownership of the land either does not exist or is highly restricted. Even in the Bechuanaland example, only a part of the arable lands, the tribal fields, are plowed, planted and harvested by common labor, whereas work on all other lands is done by individual "small" families. Throughout the world, in areas still in the pre-industrial phase, there are many other instances in which the community possesses paramount rights over land, especially in regard to supervision, regulation of crops and periodic redistribution, while cultivation remains a private matter. Yet in this way social control does not yield all its potential advantages. Many achievements of modern agricultural technology, particularly farm machinery, can be much more effectively used in larger than in smaller areas and therefore on collectively rather than individually cultivated fields. This is true not only of tractor-operated machines, which in most underdeveloped countries will probably not come into large-scale use for quite some time, but also of much simpler equipment, even of animal-drawn plows. Would it not be the best course to develop community rights of control over land into a system of collective land management?

In this question, the emphasis is not only on collective management, but also on the possibility that it might be made to grow out of the existing institutions of communal control. In Israel and—with very different sociopolitical implications—in the Soviet Union and some other communist countries, collective agriculture has been created without regard to historical antecedents;[29] the communist experience is not encouraging, and the success

[29] Russian peasantry did have a communal tradition: In many parts of Russia before the revolution, title to the land was vested in the village community, the *obshchina;* the more familiar term is perhaps *mir*. Cultivation was done by individuals, but the community redistributed the land when the size of the holdings no longer roughly conformed to the size of the families. Although in the nineteenth century one wing of the Russian socialist movement—the so-called Populists—was in favor of using the *obshchina* as a cell of collective production, the Marxists were never sympathetic with this idea, and by the time of the revolution the *obshchina* was in such a state of disintegration that in all probability any attempt to so use it would have been hopeless. The Russian peasant had become an economic individualist and showed it by his resistance to collectivization.

An even stricter kind of collectivisim was represented by the *zadruga* of the Southern

of the *kibbutzim* in Israel is the result of conditions which do not exist elsewhere. Thus it would seem a particular advantage of those countries which still have a strong communal tradition that they might be able to develop collective land management from native roots and thereby find a solution to their agricultural problem which would have the advantages of large-scale management without the evils of a system of private latifundia or of forced collectivization.

During World War II, an experiment of this kind was conducted on a limited scale by the British administration in Bechuanaland. In order to increase the food supply for native troops, the tribal authorities were requested to have additional lands taken under cultivation and the work done by a joint effort of all the families in the neighborhood. The outcome does not seem to have been quite conclusive, but the thinking behind the scheme might perhaps lead to an attempt at vitalizing the management of tribal lands.[30]

A much more important attempt of this kind has been undertaken in Mexico, initiated under President Lazaro Cardenas, who in the framework of his land reform program tried to modernize the ancient Indian form of the *ejido*. This is the name for a village community that maintains supercontrol over allotments which were, in the past, individually cultivated. After the revolution of 1911 and prior to the Cardenas administration (1934-1940), various Mexican administrations acquired the land from large estates and handed it over to the village communities for distribution to formerly landless peasants, who eventually were to receive full title. Within the schemes of the pre-Cardenas land reform, the *ejido* therefore represented only a transitional form. In regions in which large estates had not been important enough to require or justify land distribution, such *ejidos* as still existed seem to have been in a state of decay. Cardenas viewed the *ejido* as a permanent institution; he tried to revitalize it by supplying technical and financial assistance, and he took the decisive step of inducing *ejidos*—

Slavs. This was an extended kinship group which held and cultivated the land jointly. It also was in decay when modern collectivism had its triumph: It seems that Titoism has not attempted to use the *zadruga* tradition.

[30] See Schapera, *op. cit.*, pp. 157 ff. A passage he quotes from a 1935-36 report of the Director of Native Agriculture in the Union (p. 159) makes it clear that the experiment, though initiated as a wartime measure, was based on considerations which had been on the minds of British officials for some time. These officials observed that many of the native farmers did not have enough draft animals for the proper cultivation of their fields, and that too often the work on individual holdings was interrupted at a critical moment because the farmer or members of his family sought temporary jobs in industry outside the protectorate. These officials believed that collective farming, under responsible leadership, would make possible a more adequate use of manpower and animals.

where conditions favored such a course—to introduce collective instead of individual cultivation.[31]

Subsequent administrations abandoned some of Cardenas' ideas and favored the establishment of individual holdings. At the time of writing, the future of the *ejido* seems uncertain. In any event, however, the Cardenas policy has historical significance as a systematic attempt to develop a modern form of land cultivation out of an ancient form of collectivism. Other Latin American governments seem to have toyed with similar ideas, but no systematic effort has apparently come out of their vague plans.

In view of the preference shown by many governments in underdeveloped countries for socialist forms of organization, and their frequent desire to picture their own policies as an expression of national traditions, it may seem strange that the strengthening of communal controls over land does not figure greatly among the measures undertaken by the leaders of new nations. Part of the explanation may be the widespread belief, held by economic individualists and Marxists alike, that the old communal forms represent just so much rubble which must be cleared away to make effective reconstruction possible. It may be also, however, that the peasants themselves no longer feel satisfied with the old ties, that the new economic opportunities which have appeared on the horizon have created a groundswell of individualistic sentiment which, though not yet apparent on the surface, is perhaps dimly felt by the leaders who are therefore hesitant to apply their socialist formulas to land problems. That there are such feelings among the peasant masses of Asia and Africa can hardly be doubted, but it is too early to assess their strength or that of opposite tendencies on which a policy of revitalizing the communal institutions might rely.

The underdeveloped countries will have to develop their industries either along capitalist or communist lines—whereby mixtures remain possible—and they will either have to strengthen or abolish social controls in agriculture. The two sets of decisions are no more than loosely interconnected. One might suppose that a government insisting on nationalization of industries will give some preference to communal forms of land cultivation, but most governments of underdeveloped countries which have professed a commitment to socialism have not applied this concept to agriculture, or have interpreted it as meaning support of a peasant economy. Governments that prefer private enterprise without planning in industry may be inclined to rely on the initiative of the individual cultivator in farming, but it would be conceivable for voluntarily formed agricultural collec-

[31] See Sanford A. Mosk, *Industrial Revolution in Mexico,* Berkeley: University of California Press, 1954, pp. 53 ff. and *passim.*

tives to operate within a free market for which, on the industrial side, production is carried on by private business. Thus a commitment to communal or to private forms in agriculture does not carry with it a like commitment for industry, or vice versa.

Remnants of Feudalism

THE CONCEPT

Western historiography has formed its ideas about the characteristics of feudalism through an analysis of the social order that existed in Europe during the Middle Ages and reached its most elaborate stage in France during the crusades. The most important institutions of that order were the *feudum,* the fief, and a web of personal relationships called vassalage in its upper part and the manorial system or villeinage in its lower part. These two institutions were closely interrelated. The fief was a piece of territory which a nobleman, a vassal, held under the supercontrol of a greater lord, who might be the king or a chief vassal of the king. The vassal owed to his superior allegiance, counsel and military support, and he was obligated to maintain law and order in the fief, to defend it, and to mobilize its resources for the support of the king's wars. The vassal was entitled to some deliveries in kind and especially to labor services from the population of his fief, and in turn owed the people protection and emergency support. The population consisted of peasants, sometimes with a sprinkling of craftsmen who usually were part-time agriculturists. Each peasant family held a plot in which its right was contingent upon fulfillment of its obligations to the lord, just as the vassal's rights in his fief were contingent upon the fulfillment of his obligations toward the chief vassal or the king. The peasants also had obligations to each other: The village was a sort of cooperative organization, which arranged for the settlement of many locally important matters, for instance the choice and succession of crops, in order that cultivation and harvesting work on one plot might not hinder operations on the neighboring plot, and everybody had to abide by the decision of the community.

Among the many points in which this system differed from capitalism, two are of outstanding importance for this survey. In the first place, there was no absolute unitary property right in any piece of land: The king, the lord (possibly both a higher and a lower lord) and the peasant all had rights in the same area. Second, there was no clear distinction between public and private law—rights and duties under the one and the other. The fief was handed to the vassal for the purpose not only of administration and defense, but also as a compensation for his services. The peasant's obligations were based at the same time on his position as a subject of the king, who was represented by the lord, as a member of the local community over which the lord had special rights under public law, and as a cultivator of a plot of land in which the lord had a sort of super property.

There were great differences in the positions of vassals and peasants from locality to locality, and even within the same area. Some of these differences were caused by the way in which feudal relationships had originated: Sometimes the lord had originally held the land as his private property under Roman law, which once had been the law of the land in most of Western Europe, and had accepted the super-control of the king or a greater lord for the sake of protection; in that case, he usually had stronger rights than if he had received the land originally from the sovereign, or if he had been defeated by the latter in a feud. The peasant, too, may have been originally a free proprietor who had thought it wise to accept the protection of a lord, or he might have been a man without property, even a slave, and might have received the land from the lord's domain; in the latter event, his position would probably be weak, he might be a serf tied to the soil.

Some of the differences, however, would be based less on the origin of the relationship than on the economic situation. Where land was abundant, the fief itself might be less important than the personal obligations: for the king to have the allegiance of the lord, for the lord to have the protection of the king and the services of the peasants, for the peasants to have the lord maintain law and order, to arrange for local defense and to afford relief in an emergency. In settled areas where land had considerable value the significance of the fief itself was likely to be greater.

The controversies among historians over the definition of feudalism arise largely from those cases in which importance either of the rights in the land or of the personal relationship is so preponderant that only one of the two principal criteria of the feudal order seems to be fully satisfied. For our purpose here, controversies of this kind can be disregarded. We have to deal not with full-fledged feudalism, but with remnants of a feudal order, and it stands to reason that some features of feudalism will disappear or become unimportant earlier than others. Therefore, it is of no interest in this context whether or not, at an earlier stage, all the main characteristics of a feudal order were fully developed, or some, such as the personal relationships or, on the contrary, the rights in the fief, were overshadowed by others. Here we shall speak of survivals of feudalism whenever a large landowner has *de facto* economic power and exercises some sort of socio-political control over the cultivators of the soil. Within these limits of the concept, the arrangements which we shall survey will differ greatly. There are plantation owners who work with hired laborers receiving money wages; there are landowners who give their land out to sharecroppers whose position will vary with the provisions of their contract, although it will almost always be one of great social inferiority; the cultivators may be tenants paying money rents, and their position in relation to the landowner may range from dependency as strict as that of a typical sharecropper to near-equality. The landowner may be an overlord in the legal sense, exercising police power over the peasants in addition to keeping them in economic dependence; he may, on the other hand, have no formal legal power over the cultivators but may supply them with protection and leadership too useful to be dispensed with, and may thereby alone obtain a large measure of control over their economic activities as well as over their attitudes in political and other affairs.

REASONS FOR FEUDAL SURVIVALS

Underlying all these possibilities are some facts basic to an agricultural society in which there are large differences in the size of holdings. In farming, one man often depends on the help of his neighbor, and if the neighbor is rich in land, equipment and perhaps even cash, he will invariably be the supplier rather than the receiver of aid and can therefore impose conditions. This situation is aggravated if the rich neighbor is able to offer job opportunities during seasons in which the cultivator cannot use his labor power sufficiently on his own plot of land, or under circumstances in which the plot of land is too small for full sustenance, or when the marketing of products is too difficult and some cash is needed to supplement subsistence agriculture.

Furthermore, where produce must be shipped over considerable distances and therefore, as a rule, through trade channels, the large estate owner has the advantage that traders usually prefer to deal with him rather than with a multitude of small farmers. This may be due to the savings in cost and effort if large quantities can be bought from one supplier, or to the likelihood that the product of large estates will be superior in quality, because more specialized use of land and labor is possible there and often the level of technical competence is also higher. Under these circumstances, the small cultivators can either leave to their big neighbor the raising of crops for the market and confine themselves to subsistence farming, a choice which would almost certainly increase the economic superiority of the large landowner over the villagers; or they may put themselves under the guidance of the large landowner, using his good offices in dealing with the traders and perhaps also rely on him for advice and technical assistance in the raising of crops, and perhaps financial assistance in the purchase of equipment; obviously they will thereby come under the landowner's sway.

Finally, not only the traders but also the public authorities will often find it convenient to rely on the landowner. His economic power can be used to support or to obstruct public policy; it is therefore easier for the policy makers to work with him than against him. In return for his support, and to make this support more effective, they frequently entrust him with the exercise of public powers, or protect this position with special legal sanctions, for instance by making breach of contract on the part of his laborers or sharecroppers a penal offense, whereas other contractual relationships are protected only by civil law. All these measures in turn tend to increase the economic power of the landowner and his control over the activities of the cultivators.

In an agrarian society, even more than in an industrial society, economic power tends to breed political power, because of the need of the farmer for such support as only a rich neighbor can give, and because of the need of public authorities for such services as only a rich man can render. Although the power of a landlord class may be broken by a peasant revolution or by a democratic reform, the achievements are not likely to be permanent unless political and economic arrangements can be made to assure that the functions filled by the big landowners will be taken care of in other ways—by cooperatives, agricultural counseling, peasant education in self government and public welfare services. Where a policy directed against landlordism fails to provide these necessary complements, the chances are that either the landlords will regain their former position of power in different legal forms, or if the change was so radical as to drive the landlords from the countryside, the economy is likely to decay and the peasants will suffer so much as to look longingly back to the old system and become hostile to the government that has inaugurated the change.

PEONAGE

It is now time to survey some of the forms in which large landowners are exercising—or have exercised until recently—control over peasants in underdeveloped countries. In the Western Hemisphere, the most common of these forms is peonage. A tenant—usually a sharecropper—or laborer, who has been supplied by the landlord with food, seeds and other necessities, sometimes also with the use of draft animals, thereby accumulates a debt and is prevented by the police power of the state from leaving the land until he has either repaid or worked off the full amount. Since his chances to do so are often small and sometimes nonexistent, he is in most instances bound to the soil as long as the landlord wishes to continue the relationship. In the Spanish-speaking countries, a person in this state of dependency is called a peon, which originally meant a foot soldier in contradistinction to the *caballero,* the knight, and then in a broader sense a lowly person. Deprived of the chance to seek other employment—for which the prospects would usually be small in any event—the peon must accept the terms offered by the landlord, even if they interfere with his private life or with his rights as a citizen. Largely the same effect as by penal sanctions against not working off a debt can be caused by vagrancy laws which make it a crime to be "without visible means of support," if acceptance of employment under conditions impairing personal liberty is the only way to escape the law's penalties.[32]

Peonage is an institution which assures landlords of great power over those who cultivate the soil; it is not always a system of ruthless exploitation. Landlord and peon may look upon their relationship as upon a web of mutual rights and duties, with the sanctions of tradition keeping demands on the tenant within customary and tolerable limits. Steady employment may compensate the peon for the restriction of his freedom, and he may prefer his own position to that of a free laborer whose sustenance is not assured. To understand what a system of dependency—even serfdom or slavery—means in human terms, we must always know much more than the details of the formal relationship: the character of the people on both sides, the mores of the society, the forces forming public opinion and its power. Only one thing is always certain: Every such system means a lack of freedom for the individuals in the lower group. People who are tradition-bound and live on a level of bare subsistence often value security more highly than personal freedom, but this is likely to change as traditions disintegrate under the impact of outside forces and the prospects, if not yet the reality, of improvement in living standards appear.

Peonage has been called a capitalistic institution.[33] It would be better to say that this relationship is most frequently found in areas in which capitalistic forms of commerce have already intruded through contacts with more developed countries, and in which the political development has already advanced far enough toward the realization of modern constitutional

[32] Such vagrancy laws played a great role in the United States during the first two years after the Civil War, when they were used by several of the former Confederate states to force negroes back into a condition of dependency. These laws ("black codes") aroused indignation in the North and thus helped to strengthen the position of extremists to the point where they could win majorities in both houses of Congress and thus impose reconstruction on the South.

[33] "Peonage is to be found exclusively in capitalistic societies." George McCutchen McBride, "Peonage," *Encyclopaedia of the Social Sciences,* Vol. XII, p. 70.

concepts to give even the lowly a vague desire for some modicum of independence. Where these preconditions are lacking, the predominance of the landlord over those who actually do the work on the soil is likely to assume still cruder forms, such as slavery or serfdom.[34]

Peonage has been officially abolished in Latin America, but many sources indicate that for all practical purposes it continues to exist in some areas, especially on the eastern slope of the Andes and in some parts of Central America. This is not surprising because a firmly entrenched system of labor relations, responding, however inadequately, to some practical needs, cannot be uprooted overnight in parts of the world in which the low efficiency of public administration and the traditionalism of the people make it hard to replace the old system with a better one. It is very difficult to ascertain how much of peonage is left in spite of official abolition, and what subterfuges are used. Any description, therefore, must refer to a situation as it existed some time ago and of which we can only be sure that some considerable remnants have been left.

One of the Latin American republics in which the formal abolition of peonage came late is Guatemala. Because this fact makes Guatemalan experience more relevant to the present, and because it shows also the substitutes invented when the debt became inapplicable as an instrument to impose forced labor, that country is well suited as the object of a little case study to illustrate the operation of a peonage system. It seems that in Guatemala coffee played a similar role for peonage to that which cotton played in the southern United States for slavery. The great expansion of coffee production in the last two decades of the nineteenth century—according to available statistics, probably incomplete, production rose about 60

[34] Slavery can also occur in areas in which business in capitalistic forms is already important, as the *ante-bellum* situation in the southern United States demonstrates. Serfdom is more vulnerable under the disintegrating effects of capitalism because the serf has some personal rights, and a capitalistic environment frequently offers him an opportunity to use these rights, especially the right to own property, for his social advancement.

In the context of this discussion, one particular form of serfdom, the *encomienda* is of special interest, because it was the parent system of peonage. In the Spanish colonies, following some precedents of Spain itself, the king used to commit the inhabitants of an Indian village or town to a Spanish official or a favorite of the Crown, with the right of the beneficiary to exact labor service and deliveries in kind. Although the natives so committed, like the serfs in Europe, were considered persons and not chattel before the law, this kind of bondage was worse for those subjected to it than European serfdom. The serf peasant in most European countries was to some extent protected by traditional restraints upon the lord's rule—the "custom of the manor" in English feudal law—and often by the interest of the king who tried to maintain some direct bonds of allegiance between the peasantry and the Crown, whereas in the Spanish colonies protective traditions had not had time to grow and the king was far away. From 1512 and especially from 1543 on, the Spanish kings issued laws restricting the abuses of the *ecomienda* system and looking toward its eventual abolition, but the reform laws were largely evaded with the connivance of the royal officials.

per cent between the early 1880's and the end of the century[35]—favored a plantation system when otherwise there might have been an advance of production by individual peasants. The coffee planters believed that the Indians, who represented the bulk of the labor supply available for coffee growing, would work only under compulsion. Already during the colonial period, however, the old system of Indian serfdom (*encomienda*) had fallen into disuse because the landlord's rights interfered too much with the fiscal interest of the king who wanted to tax the Indians, and the assignment of natives to varying masters for a tour of service (*repartimiento*, later *mandamiento*) had been at least nominally abolished in 1878,[36] when a liberal movement swept the country. As as substitute, a system of peonage was developed which consisted of criminal prosecution for evasion of workers' debt obligations or nonfulfillment of labor contracts, combined with official pressure on all Indians not fully occupied on their own land to enter into such contracts. In 1909, a Presidential decree ordered the appointment of "agricultural judges" in each district. "These were to keep a list of workmen on each plantation and of their debts and a list of those not under contract who were fit to work. The judges were to 'aid instantly, with energy and without any excuse, in the apprehension and capture of workmen who are fugitives or remiss in the fulfillment of their obligations and contracts to work.' Captured 'fraudulent workmen' were thrown into jail and, barring settlement of their accounts, delivered over to the employer to work off their debts. If workers on plantations refused to do the tasks assigned they were fined or put on labor gangs for public works. If in spite of such measures, the labor supply was still short, the lists of those not under labor contracts were available for the recruiting agents." [37] The labor recruiting agents of the plantations had the assistance of the authorities who did not fail to use extra-legal pressure to induce the Indians listed as available to accept employment.[38]

In 1923, all Central American republics concluded a treaty by which they obligated themselves to abolish all legal devices for compulsory labor; Guatemala had not thought it politically possible to abstain from signing this treaty. But in the opinion of the Guatemalan authorities and the coffee planters, who believed in the incurable laziness of the Indian, compliance

[35] See Chester Lloyd Jones, *Guatemala, Past and Present*, Minneapolis: University of Minnesota Press, 1940 (Copyright by the University of Minnesota), p. 209. Recently bananas have become an important export crop, but their production still has not reached the value of coffee.

[36] On *encomienda, repartimiento* and *mandamiento* see Chester Lloyd Jones, *op. cit., Guatemala, Past and Present*, pp. 13, 113 ff., 141 ff.

[37] *Loc. cit.*, p. 157.

[38] *Loc. cit.*, p. 158.

with the spirit as well as the letter of the treaty would have meant the decline of the country's economy. Gradually, the idea of an evasive device was worked out, and in 1934 it crystallized into a law which, on the one hand, prohibited advances to laborers in order that they might not be encumbered by debts, and on the other established stringent provisions for the punishment of "vagrants," defined either as persons who had broken a labor contract or had failed to conclude one without cultivating land of their own above a minimum yield. The punishment was imprisonment, but the "criminal" could be released if an employer took him off the hands of the authorities; if the laborer refused to accept employment, this was a new crime.[39]

The vagrancy law remained in effect until 1944. The new constitution adopted in 1945 upheld the principle that labor was a "social obligation" as well as an "individual right," and that vagrancy was a crime. But with the old law abolished and no new laws enacted for the prosecution of "vagrants," it seems likely that direct compulsion to work is no longer a fact in Guatemala.

Has this made the agricultural worker truly a free citizen? To answer this requires a distinction between the two main categories of workers on coffee plantations.[40] The migratory workers, who live in their native villages and come to the plantations only for seasonal work, are now in all probability freer than before. Their wages and other conditions of employment on the plantations are poor, and they may feel an increased economic necessity to go to work, because the slow intrusion of industrial products

[39] *Loc. cit.,* pp. 160 ff., esp. 162. The prohibition of advances to workers probably meant no more than that such debts were not legally enforceable; considering the whole structure of the employer-worker relationship under the new law, the former had enough means of indirect enforcement to dispense with the means formerly at his disposal. Nevertheless, the indebtedness of the workers was presumably reduced by more reluctance on the part of planters to make advances, which were no longer the chief means to keep the workers in a state of dependency.

[40] Work on banana plantations, all of them in the coastal area and most of them under foreign ownership, is in a different category. The employers, as foreigners, have to watch their steps because of their politically vulnerable position, and must in these times be careful to abstain from any undue pressure on their workers. Moreover, work on banana plantations is done mainly by *ladinos,* not by people classified as Indians. In Guatemala, this seemingly ethnic distinction has become a dividing line not between two races but between two modes of life. The number of those of pure European descent is too small to count. The *ladino* category comprises all persons who live in a (modified) European way—a little more than half the population (See Nathan L. Whetten, *Guatemala, The Land and the People,* New Haven: Yale University Press, pp. 53 ff.). Most of these are *mestizos,* but pure Indian blood does not exclude a person from being counted in this category if he has living habits regarded as European.

Ladino workers are less pliable because they do not feel the helplessness of the Indian in the face of authority. The vagrancy law of the period 1934 to 1945 was enforced only against Indians.

into the communities of even the "traditional Indians"[41] must increase the need for money incomes. But once the seasonal worker has returned to his village to till his own little field, he is a free man; since apparently he no longer has to fear arrest if he spurns the offers of the recruiting agent from a particular plantation, he is at least free to choose his employer for seasonal work or even to stay at home for a season if he so prefers.

But a large portion of Guatemalan Indians are not migratory workers: They are *colonos,* that is agricultural workers settled on a plantation, having been given the use of a little land and a cabin by the management in return for the obligation to work a specified amount of their time.[42] The *colono* can send his children to the plantation school, and he receives other benefits as needs arise and the conditions on the plantation permit, for instance the right to cut fuel wood for his household, and in some cases medical care or emergency support.[43] Just because the *colono* has these advantages, however, he will be most reluctant to leave the plantation or to assert his independence in a manner which may spoil his relationship to the plantation owner. As a rule, he is probably better off in regard to his material welfare than he was under the old laws which forced him to remain on the plantation, because now the plantation management, no longer equipped with legal instruments of compulsion—at least if the authorities keep within the law—, has to attract its permanent labor force by economic advantages. But whether he has more freedom than a peon is doubtful.

Under the pro-Communist Arbenz government (1951-1954), an agrarian law was enacted in 1952 which was intended to put an end to the *colono* system, by giving the *colonos* title to the plots which they cultivated for their own use; expropriation of plantation lands (with modest compensation) not actually cultivated was also provided in the law.[44] The provisions of the law were more moderate than similar measures taken in comparable situations elsewhere, but apparently failed to offer an adequate substitute for the labor system established on the plantations; whether Arbenz and his advisers could have worked out a practicable solution if they had had more time cannot be answered. Arbenz was overthrown by Castillo Armas with an invasion force of exiles and with assistance from army elements within the country. The unsympathetic attitude of the United States toward Arbenz because of his foreign policy was a factor, although its importance is controversial. Armas suspended the Arbenz agrarian law but tried to carry

[41] See Whetten, *op. cit.,* p. 69 ff. and *passim* for the distinction between "traditional" and the "transitional" Indian.

[42] *Loc. cit.,* pp. 98 f.

[43] Whetten, *op. cit.,* pp. 98, 158.

[44] *Loc. cit.,* pp. 153 ff.

out a reform program of his own; his successors also continued attempts at agrarian reform. The impediments are obviously great. Within the system of private plantations, the independence of the permanent workers can hardly be assured; to nationalize plantations—some of them have actually been expropriated during the war as property of enemy aliens—would not be a solution as long as the politics of the country are not thoroughly reformed, because otherwise the dependence of the *colono* on the plantation owner would be replaced by his dependence on government officials, which might be worse. To turn the plantations into workers' cooperatives would ruin them unless the measure were preceded by a successful educational campaign; breaking up the large holdings would have similar effects. The country, depending on coffee exports for its balance of payments, cannot stand any serious loss of productivity; diversification of Guatemalan agriculture, with new products becoming available for export (in addition to bananas) may not be impossible but will take a long time.

These economic difficulties are compounded by political ones: The division of the population into *ladinos* and Indians, with the former not having a great stake in the removal of leftovers from peonage and the latter largely lethargic and divided among themselves by tribal antagonisms, makes it difficult to organize sustained political support for long-range reform measures. The lack of an efficient and incorruptible administration is a further obstacle.

In all these respects Guatemala represents a case in which conditions existing in various parts of Latin America appear perhaps somewhat magnified but not distorted; nor is it certain that Asia and Africa are entirely free of conditions similar to Latin American peonage.

THE LANDLORD AS WIELDER OF PUBLIC POWER

Whereas in a system of peonage the state puts its police power at the disposal of landlords to keep their tenants or laborers in a state of dependency, there are other systems in which such dependency is maintained by making the landlord part of the state mechanism. Thus he does not have to apply to a judge or a police chief for keeping those who work for him in subjection, because he himself wields the judiciary and enforcement powers. Such a system is even more similar to medieval European feudalism than is peonage, and in nineteenth century Europe there were still considerable remnants of the endowment of large estate owners with public powers. In Britain, the justice of the peace was, as a rule, the local squire, and in the first decades of the nineteenth century, when the agricultural laborers were unruly, the ample powers of his office could be used to keep them in their place. Even more to the point, because in this case the connection between the big landholders' position and public office existed not only *de facto* but *de jure,* was the situation in the Eastern provinces of the Prussian monarchy where the large estate, as a rule, was a police district (*Gutsbezirk*) with the owner entitled to function as the head officer or to appoint one of his employees to this position.

Here we are interested in analogous cases existing in primitive or underdeveloped countries. The Empire of Ethiopia may serve as an example.

The very difficulties of describing the Ethiopian situation are characteristic of a country with important remnants of feudalism. Although there is a dependence of the small cultivator upon the big landowner in most, if not all, regions of Ethiopia, the terms on which land is held and cultivated differ tremendously from one area to the other. Ethiopia has not had a continuous period of centralization by a strong national government to overcome these regional differences. At this point the analogy with Europe is striking: Despite all that the great French statesmen Richelieu and Mazarin did for the establishment of a centralized regime of royal absolutism, important differences in the laws, customs and economic institutions of the French provinces continued up to the revolution; even more to the point is the example of Prussia, where the absolutism of the Hohenzollern rulers from the Great Elector in the middle of the seventeenth century to Frederic the Great in the latter part of the eighteenth had not been able to eradicate the differences in the land tenure systems which prior to the Napoleonic wars still varied from almost unmitigated serfdom in Pomerania to mild dependency of the peasants on the landowner in the western parts of the realm. In the light of European history, it takes a long time to unify the agrarian system after the heyday of feudal rule, and the Ethiopian case confirms this experience. Apparently, the complexity of the land tenure problem in that country has up to now deterred writers from working out a comprehensive analytical description of the Ethiopian system, or rather systems; the only two attempts known to this author's knowledge and which are cited below, those by Worq and by Hufnagel, are too brief to supply an analysis in depth.[45]

Under these circumstances, it is impossible to discuss here the terms of land tenure in all of Ethiopia; nor is such a complete survey necessary for

[45] A serious attempt at such an analysis has been made by Richard K. Pankhurst for the earlier periods of Ethiopian history. His book, *An Introduction to the Economic History of Ethiopia,* London: Lalibela House, 1961, deals with developments only up to 1800. If he were to continue this analysis up to the present, not only the specialists on Ethiopia but also the students of economic systems would have reason to regard this as an important gain.

the purpose of this book. Some illustrations will suffice, and as one of them the conditions in Shoa, the region which includes the capital city, Addis Ababa, may serve.

In that area landowners hold land partly as full property (*rist*) [46] and partly as state land given them as a sort of fief (in regard to the latter the landowner is called a *geter melkegna*).[47] The land was in part given out by the landlord (*balabat, melkegna*) to tenants, who status varied; the rest was retained as the lord's land, to be worked by teams of peasants (*gebbars*).[48] The crown retained some land for its own use and for the compensation of people who had rendered special services to the emperor.[49] The peasants work the land of the lord or of the crown under the supervision of a bailiff (*mislenne*). In addition to work for the landowner, all peasants, except perhaps those with very small holdings, have a number of public obligations. They have to pay a land tax either in money or in kind; the place of this obligation is often taken by labor service on the land given the governor or other officials as compensation for the exercise of their functions.[50] Some further obligations devolving upon the peasants are now probably obsolete, such as the transporting of "a mule load of honey, flour or similar footstuffs" in wartime or escorting prisoners to the nearest imperial court.[51]

The land tax—as a rule—is paid directly to the government or its agent but it is the duty of the landlord to see to it that the payment is on time.[52]

[46] The terms in Amharic (the official Ethiopian language) are given to make it easier for the reader interested in details to trace the explanations to the sources. The sources are very vague on the question of how much of all these institutions still exists; probably conditions are fluid in which the exact situation cannot be ascertained even by specialists. The reader should therefore not assume from the present tense used in the text that all the practices described are still found in the same form. More will be developed on this point later.

[47] See Gebre—Wold—Ingida Worq, "Ethiopia's Traditional System of Land Tenure and Taxation," *Ethiopian Observer*, Vol. V (1962), p. 304. In Worq's description, the title to the land appears as reward for first cultivation. This may well have been the regular origin of land titles, but it must not be assumed that the clearing of land was usually an effort of an individual small cultivator working for himself; rather, since shortly afterwards Worq says that the recipient of the title gave out land to tenants "or any other persons of his preference," the clearing of the land from wild growth or from pests which had prevented cultivation must have been organized by persons with means at their disposal sufficient for a fairly large operation, in the typical case probably a nobleman.

[48] H. P. Hufnagel *Agriculture in Ethiopia*, Rome: F.A.O., 1961, uses the term *geber* (e.g. p. 105), whereas according to Worq this term means the tax, and the peasant is called a *gebbar*, a word of apparently different origin.

[49] The term for land retained by either the landlord or the crown is *hudad*, but Worq is not entirely clear on the question of whether this means all such land or only that which is to be cultivated by peasants in teamwork.

[50] See Worq, *op. cit.*, p. 306.

[51] *Ibidem.*

[52] Worq, *op. cit.*, p. 305.

The exercise of a direct taxing power over the population, including the peasants dependent on a landlord, obviously is an attempt by the government to prevent each landlord from becoming a small king in his own domain; the history of medieval Europe abounds with illustrations of both this danger and similar efforts by national rulers to establish direct ties with the population under their vassals' suzerainty. One of the presuppositions of a system of national land taxation, and generally a means to assert the authority of the national government, is a survey of the land. William the Conqueror had undertaken something quite similar, and for essentially the same reasons, when he ordered the inquiry which resulted in the Domesday Book. The Imperial Government of Ethiopia also understood the economic and political value of such a measure, but the survey it initiated has not yet been extended to all parts of the country.

In the regions "where the land has not yet been measured," there existed, according to Hufnagel, a hierarchy of chieftains and sub-chieftains. "These chieftains were not nominated by the central government but by the ancient landholders." Obviously, the feudal structure in these areas antedates any effective effort to establish the authority of the central government. The peasants "were obliged to build the houses of the province chief, and to erect fences for him, and to care for one or two of his mules. In wartime, some of the 'gebers' [53] followed the chief and carried camping equipment; those who remained acted as territorial guards. In peacetime, the 'gebers' helped in building and repairing churches and gave five liters of grain for the clergy. They were in charge of maintenance of the telephone posts." [54] From this description it seems that in these regions which have not been reached by the government survey the labor services are probably more varied and important than deliveries in kind and money payments. This is quite plausible, because these areas were not surveyed because of distance and obstacles to traffic, and for the same reason it must be difficult for the landlord to market any surplus of produce over his own needs; it must be even more difficult for the peasants to pay money rent since they cannot transport much of their produce to a place where it can be sold for money. Thus labor service is the mutually most convenient manner in which peasants can fulfill obligations to the landlord. At the same time, however, labor service establishes the authority of the landlord over the peasant's person more firmly than would delivery and payment obligations.

The sources used here give their description of the Ethiopian forms of land tenure in the past tense, thus perhaps suggesting to the reader that the

[53] See footnote 48.
[54] Hufnagel, *op. cit.*, p. 104 f.

remnants of feudalism have already been swept away. Indeed, a law of the early 1930's decreed: "All obligations of personal service are herewith entirely abolished, and no governor or chief of any sort shall exact such services from the cultivators." Such a reform, if carried out to the letter, would have gone a long way toward the elimination of feudal institutions and practices. Apparently, however, the law does not mean what it seems to say, because another provision says: "When the landed proprietors have made an agreement with their 'tissainya' [55] in which it is stipulated that the latter shall work a certain number of days for the owners, this work cannot be exacted during the agricultural period, but only in other months." [56] Perhaps the general rule should be interpreted to mean that labor service should be abolished as far as it was a public obligation, which would imply that it was to be maintained as far as the obligation followed from private contracts. This line of distinction, however, cannot be clearly drawn because of the very nature of feudalism: In feudal societies the roles of the landed aristocrat as a public administrator and as a private landowner, and consequently his claims for benefits in lieu of an administrator's salary and his claims for benefits in lieu of rent, are merged. No land reform which attempts this distinction instead of abolishing all permanent obligations to render labor service can successfully emancipate the peasant; European experience, especially the Prussian reform legislation of the early nineteenth century, is rather conclusive in this respect. On the other hand, in an economy in which the use of money is limited it is very difficult to replace such a permanent obligation, as a burden resting on the user of a particular plot of land, with any other form of obligation, or to abolish it without replacement. This, of course, is only another way of saying that in such countries as Ethiopia feudal institutions have not yet ceased to represent the most practical answer to some real problems.[57]

That the landlord plays a role in the collection of the land tax, even if merely as a supervisor where the tax is paid directly to the government, illustrates the difficulty for the national ruler in a primitive country of dispensing with the services of local landowners in any exercise of authority,

[55] Cultivators with precarious titles. See *Ethiopian Observer*, Vol. V, no. 4, p. 313.

[56] Hufnagel, *op. cit.*, p. 120.

[57] The intention to reduce the feudal character of Ethiopian institutions can also be seen from the difference between the two constitutions of 1931 and 1955. The former provides that "temporarily, and until the people are in a position to elect them themselves, the members of the Chamber of Deputies shall be chosen by the nobility . . . and the local chiefs." The Constitution of 1955, however, gives the vote to "all Ethiopian subjects by birth, 21 years of age or more, who are regularly domiciled and habitually present in any election district . . ." *Ethiopian Observer*, Vol. V (1962), no. 4, pp. 364, 375.

including taxation, however hazardous it may be for the central government to use and thereby strengthen the position of the landowning class.

The logical consequence of entrusting landlords with the collection of taxes for the government would have been to hold them financially responsible for the peasants' tax payments. Whether this consequence has ever materialized in Ethiopia is doubtful. The clearest case of the landlord's position as a responsible fiscal intermediary between the government and the peasants—and a case in which this position became a cornerstone of the social system—has occurred in British India.

In some parts of India, such as Bengal, a class of landlords, called *zamindari,* collected payments from the peasantry called *ryots* and paid a share to the government. Whether the *zamindari* were originally owners of the land and the *ryots* their tenants, or whether the *zamindari* were collectors or tax farmers for the Mogul and other pre-British governments seems to be doubtful, but in any event the East India Company recognized them as owners of the soil.[58] The *zamindari* had to pay a fixed tax; what they collected from their tenants was originally left to their discretion, although this indifference of the British administration to the condition of the *ryots* gave way to attempts at protection during the nineteenth century. Aside from legal rights, the economic superiority of the *zamindari* was so great as to make the *ryots* helpless and frequently unable to resist any demands—economic, political or other—which these local lords cared to make.[59]

The situation became more complicated during the nineteenth century when individual *ryots* withdrew from the personal cultivation of the land and leased that land to others who actually did the work.[60] Although this new class of landlords did not have the traditional position of the *zamindari,* they probably acquired considerable power over the peasants because by their decisions to renew or not to renew the lease contracts they often held

[58] See Vera Anstey, *The Economic Development of India,* London: Longmans-Green, 1957, p. 98.

[59] Aside from the *zamindari* system, two other systems of land tenure and taxation existed in India under company rule. The one was the assessment of individual *ryots* by company agents, which presupposed the recognition that the *ryots* were the owners of the soil; where this system was used, either no *zamindari* had existed or they were eliminated through the direct relationship between government and peasantry. (It is doubtful whether this system was generally preferable from the point of view of the peasantry, since the integrity of the agents whom the company employed for the assessment and collection of the tax often left much to be desired. See Romesh Dutt, *The Economic History of India,* first publ. 1882, reprint Delhi: The Ministry of Information, 1960, Vol. II, p. 42 and *passim.*) The other alternative to the *zamindari* system was an assessment of the whole village community, which remained jointly responsible for the payment of the tax. This system was made possible by the tradition of communal land control in some parts of India and at the same time tended to continue the system.

[60] See Anstey, *op. cit.,* pp. 99, 377.

the fate of peasant families in their hands: Where abject poverty exists on the one hand and economic well-being, if only in a very relative sense, on the other, the formal equality which modern law provides for partners in business transactions still tends to result in relations of dependency not unlike those under feudalism. Moreover, the fact that the new landlords remained responsible for the payment of the land tax made them a type of money collector for the government and thereby strengthened their control over the peasants.

After independence, the Indian government abolished the *zamindari* system by legislation which tried to give the actual cultivators title to the soil. Whether this goal has been reached and more equality has actually been established in the Indian village cannot yet be judged. Success of this kind is possible only if the land taken from the traditional landlord class does not get into the possession of a new kind of relatively large owner who again leases the land to tenants in a position of dependency. Some observations make it appear doubtful whether this danger actually has been prevented.[61] The student of history who goes over the preliminary records of these Indian experiences is reminded of the effect of the French Revolution upon the landholding system: The confiscated lands of the aristocracy at first passed mainly into the hands of a new landlord class.[62] To be sure, the development during the later nineteenth century in France would teach an encouraging lesson: The French peasant, freed from the cruder forms of dependency and equipped, most of the time, with the right to vote, gradually turned legal emancipation into economic reality. But will the same thing happen in today's caste-ridden India, where the impediments to social mobility and even to the full realization of citizenship are probably greater than they ever were in post-Renaissance Europe? [63]

The use of the *zamindari* system by the East India Company is an illuminating example of how early capitalist enterprise took advantage of feudal

[61] See the following contributions to Richard L. Park and Irene Tinker, *Leadership and Political Institutions in India,* Princeton: Princeton University Press, 1959: Morris E. Opler, "Factors of Tradition and Change in a Local Election in Rural India," p. 143 which shows how not only wealth in land but also the higher education that goes with it can operate as a factor to make the peasants politically dependent on their relatively rich neighbors, and how the reform laws themselves can be used for this purpose; and John T. Hitchcock, "Leadership in a North Indian Village: Two Case Studies," p. 407, which shows the inequitable distribution of former *zamindari* land as a consequence of the power structure in the village under investigation. The role of the caste system in aggravating or recreating dependency relations is also made clear.

[62] See Herbert Heaton, *Economic History of Europe,* New York: Harper and Brothers, 1948, pp. 434 ff., and the literature indicated there.

[63] India, however, has a government determined to eliminate gross inequalities, and this could not be said of any French government in the nineteenth century, except possibly during the short-lived Second Republic, 1848-52.

traditions to serve profit interests. Although money had been in use in India for a long time, the *zamindari* system of pre-British days was based largely on deliveries in kind, which the landlord with his family and servants consumed. The East India Company was interested in monetary gain; it had not necessarily any objection to payments in kind, as long as the *zamindari* or the company itself could sell the produce. This meant as long as the produce consisted of cash crops, and the market was well enough organized to permit regular sales. These conditions, to the extent that they had not existed before, were established under company rule, and thus a hybrid system of feudal and capitalist practices proved satisfactory from the point of view of the European corporation, which at least in the *zamindari* areas held the position of the sovereign in a feudal state, and of the *zamindaris* themselves,[64] though decidely not of the cultivators of the soil.

The rise of some *ryots* to the position of large landowners during the nineteenth century shows that even the social structure of India, in spite of the impediments to social mobility created by the caste system, was not completely rigid. However strongly the stratification of a society may be fortified by tradition and taboos, it is never completely protected from the endeavors of intelligent and shrewd individuals of low birth who possess the will power and the drive to make their way to the top. It is an advantage for such an individual to be able to accumulate the fruits of his industry or drive in the form of money, which is the most versatile form of wealth. lending itself to a great variety of uses. Therefore, and because the opportunities to use individual gifts for personal advancement are greater in the kind of underdeveloped society which is already in extensive contact with the industrialized world, the instances of a successful attack of men from the lower ranks upon traditional privileges are more frequent there than in a society in which those contacts are still scarce. It is particularly important that monetary wealth can be acquired abroad, outside the established hierarchical controls, and then transferred to the home area to serve as a source of power.

"BIG MAN"

Individual initiative in primitive societies can threaten not only privilege but also equality. In areas in which approximate equality of rank exists, if

[64] Except in periods and localities in which the rule of the company was so arbitrary as to make the position of the *zamindari* precarious. The outstanding example of such arbitrariness occurred under the governorship of Warren Hastings at the end of the eighteenth century; see Dutt, *op. cit.*, Vol. I, pp. 42 ff. It should not be assumed, however, that in later periods established rights were always respected when they came into conflict with the profit interest of the company.

not among individuals at least among households, the appearance of the so-called Big Man has been noted by anthropologists as a fairly frequent phenomenon. An individual, without any kind of institutional sanction of his leadership, attains that leadership position through personal power. Marshall D. Sahlins has described this process as it operates within Melanesian societies, and he has clarified the economic side of this process.[65] To rise above the others, a man must first establish a faction. He can do this by impressing others with heroic or otherwise outstanding qualities, in combination with that power of inspiring admiration and loyalty which the great German sociologist Max Weber has called *charisma;* but sooner or later there will come the moment when he will have to produce tangible advantages for his followers, and in many instances these advantages will have to be economic. In a primitive economy, however, the chances of an individual leader's introducing such innovations as will result in substantial economic gain are limited, especially since the followers are not likely to be patient enough to wait for the results of long-range plans. Even if opportunities of this sort exist, the typical Big Man is probably not, as a rule, the kind of person to utilize them effectively. He is more likely to wage feuds or wars and reward his followers with the spoils, but even this opportunity may be absent. Moreover, to wage wars or feuds, it is necessary to make the faction as large as possible, and this often requires the distribution of largesse among those members of the community who do not yet belong to the faction. For these purposes economic resources are required. The Big Man may have private wealth, or he may be able to tap the wealth of relatives who are interested in promoting his success for the sake of family prestige; where women are an economic asset because of their productive work, multiple marriages may equip him with means to invest in his career. In most instances, however, the Big Man will sometimes have to ask his followers for contributions to the pool of resources to promote the interest of the faction; he therefore cannot afford to be a mere dispenser of wealth; he must also, at times, be a recipient, and one of his most important qualities is the gift of striking a tolerable balance between what he exacts from his followers and what they receive from him. The Big Man may impress his faction with the necessity of creating a surplus over daily needs by a special effort at work, and may then divert this surplus into a common treasure from which an enterprise, peaceful or bellicose, may be financed. At times he may be

[65] Marshall D. Sahlins, "Poor Man, Rich Man, Big Man, Chief: Political Types in Melanesia and Polynesia." *Comparative Studies in Society and History,* Vol. V, no. 3 (April 1963), pp. 285 ff.

able to make his followers pay much more than he gives them, covering the balance with hope for the future; he may even for a long time persuade them to "eat the leaders' renown," [66] which means to accept deprivations for the sake of the glory which he brings to the faction. But discontent is eventually bound to arise if the followers have nothing tangible to show for their sacrifices. Therefore the position of the Big Man is inevitably insecure—much less stable than that of a leader who owes his position not merely to personal qualities but to the prestige and power inherent in an institution. A feudal or a hereditary chieftain is not under the same pressure to secure benefits for his immediate followers and enhance his popularity by distributing gifts within the community. Operating from a more stable position, the leader whose authority is derived from his office rather than from his personal superiority is able to make more long-range plans—organize the storage of food reserves, or drainage and irrigation projects, development of handicrafts and commerce—and use the economic surplus thus created for strengthening of his power as well as for the enhancement of the people's living standards.[67]

It would therefore be natural for the Big Man to try to establish himself in a position which is surrounded by institutional sanctions—traditional chieftain, high priest, king. In differentiated societies possessing a trained armed force of which a popular leader can seize control, many such instances have occurred. In a truly primitive society, where no such organized apparatus of power exists, the feat of a newcomer's surrounding his position with sanctions that elsewhere protect chiefs and aristocrats would be more formidable. It can probably be solved only as society becomes more differentiated, especially with regard to the control of land, and where the Big Man therefore not only may have a chance to create a firm economic basis for his own rule, but also can play antagonistic interests of social groups against one another.

This is the reason for mentioning the Big Man phenomenon in this context. It is not a remnant of feudalism, but it is a possible source of a tendency toward the creation of institutions resembling those remnants. How often,

66 Sahlins, *op. cit.*, p. 293, quoting a saying common in the Solomon Islands.

67 Sahlins contrasts the Melanesian Big Man situation with the Polynesian situation characterized by a complicated structure of paramount chiefs and lesser chiefs, each owing his authority to his office rather than to his personal charisma. Sahlins emphasizes the advantages which this system has not only for the men in power but also for society, because the works necessary for progress can be undertaken on a larger scale. The advantages are real; the reverse side is the possibility that the chieftain, secure behind the wall of religious and other traditional sanctions, may let the people slave for his greater glory without allowing them any substantial share in the results.

and under what conditions, a charismatic leader has succeeded in building up a position of feudal or semi-feudal power is an open question, which only future research by cultural anthropologists can answer.

Peasant Societies with Individual Property

On all continents, there are underdeveloped areas in which the small family cultivates the land with a minimum of social control, and often with full property title. There is no survey to tell us whether these instances are more frequent than those in which tribal authorities, village communities or extended kinship groups exercise far-reaching controls over the land and the cultivator, but individual peasant property, or a degree of peasant independence approximating property rights, seems to be more frequent the less primitive are the methods of cultivation and the more the economy has been integrated into the world market. An exception is where technological progress and connection with the world market has led to the growth of plantations.

Individual ownership of land is possible only where the state of agricultural technology and the physical conditions of farming permit the necessary operations to be conducted by the small family in a sufficiently economical manner. Where, for instance, a great effort at irrigation or drainage or protection from floods is required, a basic likelihood exists for either the community to overshadow the individual, who by his own resources cannot manage such undertakings, or for a great lord to be accepted as master of land and people in return for his leadership and supply of material and labor from the outside in order that the necessary work be accomplished. Thus individual land ownership will, as a rule, exist only in areas in which no great obstacles to farming operations must be overcome, and in which the inhabitants know enough of farming to support themselves under these conditions, although their techniques may be quite primitive as compared with those of highly developed countries.

In addition to these physical and technological presuppositions, sociopolitical factors may also favor or prevent independent land-holding by the small family. Such a system can hardly exist under a powerful aristocracy, because even if the latter does not have control over the land in the first place, it will almost certainly acquire it through its political strength and reduce the small cultivator to a dependent status. On the other hand, independence of spirit and a tradition of self-reliance among a peasant population makes it likely that, given the external conditions, every family wants to possess and cultivate its own piece of ground, and if this striving meets with obstacles of social origin, will use whatever economic and political power it possesses to overcome these obstacles. Where the mode of making a living and the structure of society leaves the peasants a choice to have the title rest with tribal or extended kinship groups or with individual small families, the choice apparently depends much on historical "accident" —i.e. on events and traditions unrelated in origin to present circumstances. It seems futile to explain the choice by arguing that some ethnic groups are inherently more community-minded than others. The Russian peasants, who for some time were regarded—inside and outside of Russia—as having a collectivist type of mind, maintained their resistance to collectivization for decades; Jews, in other environments almost proverbial individualists, have established collective settlements in Israel.

Although unrestricted political power of an aristocracy is incompatible with the existence of an economically independent peasantry, the latter can exist even in a highly structured society, provided there is enough dispersion of power within the upper stratum not to leave a free rein to the aspirations of any one privileged group. A case in point is Thailand, the former Siam, the only country of Southeast Asia which has never been a colony and whose economic and social development was therefore less influenced from the outside than, for instance, that of India and Indonesia.

Thailand is emphatically not a country in which all citizens are social equals. There is a gradation of social rank with the king at the top, the members of the royal family next, and then a hierarchy of nobles, the commercial classes below them and the peasantry at the bottom. Until the end of the nineteenth century there was even slavery, which could have formed the basis of a plantation economy in the hands of the upper-crust members of society, and here and there such a development actually took place. But the bulk of the land is—and has been in the past—in the hands of peasant proprietors, who on the average own about ten acres.[68] By far the most important crop is rice, but a little more than one-half of the farms can only supply enough of it for the needs of the owner's family; fruit and—in some regions—rubber are important as cash crops, although the share of all non-rice crops in the cultivated area amounts to less than one-fourth.[69] A considerable number of proprietors are mere subsistence farmers.

Thailand's agriculture shows the typical strong points as well as the typi-

[68] See *A Public Development Program for Thailand,* report of a mission organized by the International Bank for Reconstruction and Development at the request of the government of Thailand, Baltimore: The Johns Hopkins Press, 1959, p. 33; Robert L. Pendleton, *Thailand,* New York: Duell, Sloan and Pearce, 1962, p. 154.

[69] Pendleton, *op. cit.,* p. 149, 154. In value of output, however, rice accounts for no more than 40 per cent; see *A Public Development Program for Thailand,* p. 34.

cal weaknesses of small-scale, individual landholding in an underdeveloped country. The mere fact that this system could survive in a social environment that contained at least some of the seeds of feudalism and against the—at least potential—competition of large-scale commercial farming with its many technical advantages, testifies to the tenacity with which the peasants held on to their soil, and their vital interest in proprietorship must have expressed itself in an effort to cultivate the land well within the limits of their knowledge, and to maintain the fertility of the soil. On the other hand, in their techniques the peasants are tradition-bound, which is especially shown by their failure to use the natural opportunities for crop diversification,[70] in spite of the economic advantages that could have been expected of such a change. Thai agriculture also shows great fragmentation of land: The individual peasant's holding is generally not a continuous area but divided into several lots—between two and three on the average—which often lie at a considerable distance;[71] the effect is loss of time for the cultivator and his draft animals, and the near-impossibility of using any mechanical contrivances, because the individual lots are too small. This fragmentation is typical of peasant economies, in which inheritance and forced sales to pay off pressing debts will often split the holdings and make one part the property of another family.

In the course of Thailand history, occasional infringement on the peasant's economic liberty have occurred; for instance, persons whom the king had granted titles of nobility had the right to claim some labor service from the population until the system was abolished around the turn of the century.[72] But only in very limited areas, if at all, did the aristocracy ever obtain control of the land. Aside from political presuppositions, the preservation of peasant independence was due to the conservatism of the Thai peasant in the management of the land: He did not undertake any improvements—irrigation or drainage of soil—which were beyond his resources and which, until recently, he could not have carried out without committing himself to a master in return for assistance. "In large measure the past development of Thailand's agricultural resources has been the result of the unguided and unassisted efforts of the individual Thai farmer . . . Government aid has been confined until quite recently to minor irrigation works and the con-

[70] See for these opportunities *A Public Development Program for Thailand,* p. 33 ff. The results of this later and apparently more comprehensive investigation seem to have refuted the opinion still expressed by Pendleton that "only rice can be grown on most Thai agricultural land" (*op. cit.,* p. 149).

[71] See Pendleton, *op. cit.,* p. 155.

[72] See J. G. D. Campbell, *Siam in the XXth Century,* London: Edward Arnold, 1902, p. 76. For details see also James C. Ingram, *Economic Change in Thailand since 1850,* Stanford: Stanford University Press, 1955, pp. 14 ff.

struction of the railway system."[73] Traditionalism, which now tends to become a curse, has in the past tended to preserve relatively sound social conditions: Great works of improvement were postponed until a machinery of modern government was created which now can undertake these tasks without destroying peasant independence.[74]

Even restraint in initiating improvements, however, could not have preserved the independence of the Thai peasant if the aristocracy had been politically strong. In Thailand, the kings never, for any extended period, lost control of the nobility. Noble rank was, in the main, an appurtenance of office by royal appointment rather than of landed wealth.[75] At least as a matter of form, noble titles are non-hereditary, although it was, and may still be, customary that the son of a nobleman receives a rank which enhances his status over that of a commoner.[76]

But high office has never been monopolized by the prominent families: At least from the fifteenth century on, "most of the working officials were commoners who had been elevated to high ranks. . . ."[77] Today, "the leaders of Thai society . . . in government, in education, in the professions, in business—come increasingly from humble peasant background, from Sino-Thai merchant families. . . ."[78] This feature is in contrast with the conditions in many other underdeveloped countries, where the positions created by the expansion of government services and by the growth of business tend to be in the hands of the traditional upper classes and to develop into self-perpetuating sources of private power. As the role of government in the economic development of the country increases, it becomes increasingly significant that government influence is not likely to become a

[73] *A Public Development Program for Thailand,* p. 33.

[74] The absence of strong population pressure made it easier to abstain from major improvement schemes.

[75] Campbell, a British school administrator who for a time served as educational adviser to the Thai Government, contrasts the "personal feudalism" of Thailand with the "territorial feudalism" of medieval Europe (pp. 76 f.). Perhaps some qualification should be attached to this distinction when it is drawn in such sharp terms, and not only because European feudalism also involved personal relationships. Campbell himself reports that "the dignity of various grades of nobility is measured in terms of land" (p. 77): When the king enobles a man, he fictitiously endows him with an estate of a magnitude corresponding to his new rank. However fictitious this conveying of a fief may have been already in the nineteenth century, it points to a past in which control of the land was not so entirely dissociated from noble rank as it is today. This is confirmed by Pendleton's presentation (*op. cit.,* p. 13) and the same conclusion is suggested by the report that tenants—in those relatively small areas in which tenancy prevails—often prostrate themselves before their landlord (See Noel F. Bush, *Thailand,* Princeton: D. Van Nostrand Co., 1959, p. 70). Nevertheless, there is no doubt that in Thailand feudalistic tendencies have never had more than very shallow roots.

[76] Campbell, *op. cit.,* p. 76 f.; Pendleton, *op. cit.,* p. 14.

[77] Pendleton, *op. cit.,* p. 13.

[78] *Loc. cit.,* p. 32.

weapon in the hands of traditionally privileged groups to protect their vested interests.

There may be a number of reasons for the limited influence of the aristocracy in Thailand. If Campbell is right in assuming that such feudalism as existed in the country was not indigenous but was due to influences from Cambodia, and that nobility was not firmly instituted before the fifteenth century,[79] this may be a partial explanation. In any event, however, the weakness of the aristocracy has been the concomitant of the strength of the monarchy. Whatever old customs and laws may have limited the power of the king,[80] such limitations could become effective only through moral force; nobody had any legal remedy against royal decisions; there was nothing like a Magna Charta in Thailand.

The great power of the king made it possible for Thailand to take the first energetic steps toward modernization with relative smoothness. In the second half of the nineteenth century, King Mongkut and his son and successor Chulalongkorn Westernized many of the institutions of the country without meeting either serious resistance on the part of conservatives or arousing the zeal of revolutionaries who would force a tempo faster than the king found it wise to adopt. Subsequently, however, both resistance to change and impatience increased, and the royal power which might have held these antagonistic forces in check, turned out to be weaker than before. This weakness was probably in part a matter of personality: Neither of the two sons of Chulalongkorn who followed him seem to have had the strength of their father and grandfather. But they also faced a harder task because Westernization of government and economic practices, even though still limited, had already affected "the magical-religious rationale of the traditional monarchy. Abandonment of royal ceremonies to dispel flood waters in favor of building dams and dykes to control floods, left the government vulnerable to evaluation in terms of its technical and administrative efficiency." [81] Naturally, in spite of the reforms, this efficiency did not yet appear very high in the eyes of the considerable number of Thai intellectuals who had studied abroad, compared conditions of their own country with the Western models and rarely understood that societies cannot be reconstructed as fast as one type of machine can be put in the place of another. Thus the king's power to promote and control the modernization of

[79] Campbell, *op. cit.*, pp. 75, 77.

[80] See about this point, Pendleton, *op. cit.*, p. 12. The statement refers to the period from the fifteenth to the eighteenth century, the so-called Ayutthaya period—named for the city which was then the capital—but it may be assumed that the same situation prevailed until the contemporary era, since changes of dynasties, even if effected by a *coup d'état,* did not break the continuity of basic laws in Thailand.

[81] Pendleton, *op. cit.*, p. 26.

the country declined, and in 1932, when existing maladjustments had been aggravated by economic crisis, the machinery of government broke down. A coup forced King Prajadhipok to grant a constitution with a parliament. The king resigned; his young nephew, Ananda Mahidol, succeeded, and political stability was lost; it does not seem to have been regained. Although there is apparently no revolutionary sentiment among the general population, the rivalry of cliques in the army, the administration and the palace are no longer restrained by any institution of such unquestioned authority, as the king still retained in nineteenth century Thailand and as the institutions of representative democracy can possess where they are firmly established.[82] At this writing there is a sort of military dictatorship. Although this is not a satisfactory state of affairs, the danger of a feudalistic development at the expense of the peasantry has passed. In this respect, royal absolutism has fulfilled its historic mission.

Political instability would be less of a danger if the economic development of the country were not at a point at which it depends very largely on government guidance. In spite of fragmentation and other technical drawbacks, a peasant economy offers a healthier basis for further progress than a semi-feudal large estate economy. Even when the latter shows more rapid technical progress—though in many countries great landlords have failed to take much advantage of technological innovations—a semi-feudal system is so vulnerable to social upheavals and so little conducive to the development of mass purchasing power which is a presupposition of the rise of industry as to make the impediments to progress in a peasant economy definitely appear as the lower hurdle. With government promotion of cooperatives and education in modern methods of agriculture, there is a chance to overcome these impediments—if there is a stable government, devoted to the task of enhancing the well-being of the masses. In spite of coups and intrigues among the various factions, the Thai government has worked on this task with some degree of effectiveness—with more, in any event, than some other governments in Asia and Africa. Yet even the World Bank mission, though obliged to exercise diplomatic caution, has expressed the opinion that in assisting individual economic effort, the government's contribution, "although substantial, has been less than might reasonably have been expected in view of the large financial resources that have been devoted to public investment." [83] The mission tries to explain these deficiencies

[82] A good sketch of these developments can be found in Pendleton, *op. cit.*, pp. 27 ff. See also Busch, *op. cit.*, pp. 71 ff. The latter states that between 1932 and 1959, Thailand has six times received a new constitution (see p. 97).

[83] *A Public Development Program for Thailand*, p. 3. Ingram, on the other hand, believes that the government did not spend enough to give the country a good start

by faults in administrative techniques, such as the refusal of government officials and even cabinet ministers to make decisions within their competence and the resulting paralysis of the cabinet which is overloaded with trivial matters that should have been settled on a lower level.[84] But such technical faults can be remedied only if the administration has a firm political basis. Where every government functionary must expect to become involved in a life and death struggle with a rival clique, he will naturally be wary not to make himself vulnerable by accepting responsibilities he can avoid.

The case of Thailand permits some degree of generalization. In Europe, the basis and the instruments of popular sovereignty were created largely during a struggle between feudal aristocracy and absolute monarchy. The conflict of these two forces gave the social groups which eventually built democracy—middle class and workers—a chance to grow in power and experience; modern parliaments grew out of the feudal assemblies of estates, guarantees of individual liberty originated from the restrictions by which the nobles tried to limit the arbitrariness of the king. This process can hardly be repeated in any of the now underdeveloped countries. In the first place, there is no time for such a protracted process; in the second place, there are few kings left, and those who still reign in countries in need of development are often Ibn Sauds and not Mongkuts or Chulalongkorns. A feudal aristocracy, firmly entrenched and not checked by royal power, is unlikely to lead the country on the path to progress: Such countries as Thailand, where the land system is unfavorable to a strong aristocracy, are surely in a happier position, but that does not prevent their lower degree of socio-economic stratification from creating its own problems. With the masses illiterate, largely indifferent toward political issues and without organization or experience, an absence or decline of royal power without a strong aristocracy leaves a vacuum which invites the attempts of either rabble rousers or a man on horseback to seize power.

---

on the road of modernization, and that this failure was due to "conservative monetary and fiscal policies," adopted largely for reasons of foreign policy (*op. cit.*, pp. 170, 212). Ingram mentions, however, that government expenditures for investment have sharply increased between 1951 and 1954—the terminal date of his study, four years earlier than that of the World Bank investigation—partly as a result of U.S. foreign aid.

In addition to governmental caution in fiscal matters, Ingram holds the sluggishness of the people's response to monetary stimuli accountable for the relative slowness of Thailand's economic development. Although Ingram carefully weighs the economic cost of an accelerated development against its advantages, he does not examine the question of whether the reluctance to take advantage of economic opportunities is not characteristic of a peasant economy at an early stage of development, and if so, whether the social and political advantages of preserving that system were not perhaps a sufficient compensation for the loss of speed in economic growth.

[84] *Loc. cit.*, pp. 225 f.

Whoever has given serious thought to the political problems of underdeveloped countries will acquire a substantial tolerance for forms of rule which deviate from the Western democratic pattern, not because these peoples are "lesser breeds" incapable of enjoying the blessings of democracy, but because the sociological foundations which made democracy possible in Europe cannot be created overnight. Even the distinction, often ridiculed, between "good" dictators and "bad" dictators is easier to deprecate than to reject in practice. The trouble is only that so many "good" dictators turn into decidedly bad ones: This has been an ever-repeated story in Latin America; some of the worst oppressors, like Batista of Cuba and Trujillo of the Dominican Republic, began as representatives of popular movements with a program of social reform.

The ultimate solution can lie only in the education of the masses to the acceptance of political responsibility and their equipment with the knowledge necessary for the exercise of this responsibility; it is just because the chances for this solution are better in a society of the Thailand type than in one in which peonage or other remnants of feudalism prevail, that the specific weaknesses of a peasant economy represent the lesser evil. An important intermediate stage will be reached when commercial and industrial development has created an urban society numerous and educated enough to give vitality to the institutions of popular government; if we again draw the analogy with Europe, this was largely the situation of Italy between the achievement of national unity in 1870 and the First World War, when a reasonable approach to democracy existed in that country on an essentially urban basis, while the rural population, especially in central and southern Italy, took little interest in political life. Before even this stage is reached, any underdeveloped country is fortunate if it can live under a government, however constituted, that provides the necessary guidance in economic development, prevents internal disorder without resorting to firing squads, does not overheat the passions of nationalism so as to make them explode in aggression or in frustration of outside economic assistance, and does not stifle the development which is to create the foundations of government by the people.

What Future Systems in Underdeveloped Countries?

Today the underdeveloped countries form an arena of the Cold War. When one of the conflicting ideologies gains ascendancy over the other in a particular country, this outcome will necessarily affect the country's economic system. But unless the victory of an ideology is as complete as it was in China, it will be only one of several factors, and not necessarily the most powerful, in determining the economic system of the future. Other forces, arising from practical needs, from aspirations of groups and individuals and from limitations caused by the country's past may be more important than ideological preferences in shaping the institutions and practices of the nations now at a pre-industrial stage. Socialist slogans are widely used in all these countries; sometimes they express real beliefs of the masses or at least of a ruling group and may lead to a deliberate nationalization policy; in parts of North Africa and Latin America, such a policy is already under way. Often, however, the decision of whether the economy will conform to a private enterprise pattern or show a prevalence of public ownership may depend primarily on practical possibilities and necessities. In most of these countries the number of individuals capable and willing to play the role of industrial entrepreneurs is limited, and so is the number of people who are fit to act as public functionaries in economic management. Sometimes the one, sometimes the other of these shortages may be easier to overcome; in some countries the group of businessmen, though small, may be eager for a chance to build up industries; in other countries traditional lethargy or the preference of businessmen for commerce, with its more rapid turnover of capital, as against industry which requires long-term investment, may be insuperable. These factors can have a greater effect in determining the future role of the state in production than any political program. Nor is the choice between democratic government with a capitalistic or socialistic economic organization on the one hand and communism on the other exclusively a matter of propaganda, infiltration or foreign policy ties with the East or the West. In pre-industrial nations the funds necessary for the development of industries cannot come out of voluntary mass savings because the common people are too poor. Where proceeds from the sales of cash crops on the world markets, oil or mining royalties or foreign aid supply funds for industrialization, the temptation to adopt communist methods for squeezing the necessary funds out of a prevailingly agrarian society can as a rule be resisted; where such other sources are not available, the temptation will be much stronger, and the procurement of development funds by compulsion is likely to lead to a dictatorship, which may or may not bear the communist label.

In none of the now underdeveloped countries, however, is there any chance for a laissez-faire policy, or for any policy even resembling laissez faire. The need for an apparatus of collective foresight and for machinery to make the economy conform to the pattern which appears most desirable on the basis of that foresight plays a role even in already industrialized countries but is still greater in underdeveloped nations which now wish to cover within a few years the distance which it took the West almost two centuries to travel. Consequently, almost all the governments of the new nations have worked out, or are working out, schemes for economic planning, and some of them, primarily India, have reached a stage at which they are encountering many of the problems with which so advanced a country as France has to cope in its efforts to guide its economic development.

It will be a fascinating but formidable task to compare the methods which the various underdeveloped countries apply in their planning; today, the material is not yet available, or at least is so difficult to obtain that the comparison would be out of date before it could be completed, since the situation in all these countries is very much in flux. When such a study becomes feasible, it will not only be of great scholarly interest but may also assist the various parts of the pre-industrial world in learning from each other's successes and mistakes. Although the underdeveloped countries themselves have the greatest immediate interest in the elaboration of sound planning methods adapted to their specific needs, the rest of the world also has a vitally important stake in helping to bring these efforts to a good end, in order that the present imbalance in economic well-being among the underdeveloped and the industrial nations may be ended before it becomes more dangerous to world peace.

CHAPTER 22

CONCLUDING THOUGHTS: CONVERGING DEVELOPMENT PATTERN OF ECONOMIC SYSTEMS

COMMUNISM seems to be moving toward recognition of the importance of prices equilibrating supply and demand, and is likely, in the foreseeable future, to introduce into its system the necessary machinery for forming such prices. Essentially, this would mean adoption by communist countries of the institution of the market—even if only in the broad sense which conceives of prices as the expression of "the terms on which alternatives are open to us." The market, however, has historically reached its more efficient forms only under capitalism; therefore the evolution of a rational pricing system under communism would mean that the latter is adopting one of the characteristic features of capitalism. On the other hand, in capitalist countries collective action has become increasingly important; many of them are now trying to achieve comprehensive economic foresight by collective endeavor, and to build machinery to direct the economy so as to avoid undesirable developments and assure desirable ones.

The plans emerging in capitalist countries differ from communist planning by structure and by the choice of means of execution. In spite of these differences, however, the efforts to coordinate and direct economic developments on the basis of collective, systematic foresight mean that the capitalist countries are trying to do in their own way what communism began to do, in its ruthless manner and by techniques distorted through dogmatism, more than thirty years ago.

These facts justify the statement, made by contemporary observers, that in some very important respects the lines of development of capitalism and communism tend to converge. Can the economic order toward which their development seems to gravitate be described as socialism? That depends on what is meant by socialism. If complete nationalization, or even nationalization of major industries, were considered a characteristic of a socialist order, then no tendency could be detected in the capitalist countries of today to assimilate to socialism; but if enlargement of other collective responsibilities, especially the elaboration of machinery for collective economic planning, is viewed as socialistic, then one could indeed foresee that capitalism and communism will eventually meet under the sign of socialism—*provided the present tendencies are not stopped or reversed before the meeting takes place.*

On the capitalist side, such a stoppage or reversal is unlikely. The idea that the instrumentality of government should be used to correct defects of the market mechanism has been growing within the Western countries for more than a century. This trend has proved strong enough to overcome all sorts of hindrances: laissez-faire dogmatism, selfish interests, anti-statism as a reaction to ill-considered and arbitrary government policies. Organized collective foresight as a guide to economic policy is a postulate of rationality, a step toward the elimination of waste motion, in an age in which the endeavor to increase the efficiency of human action in all fields has become the order of the day. Moreover, the arguments with which the trend toward planning is opposed derive their force mainly from antipathies caused by state action under circumstances which no longer exist in the Western countries. It is not very likely that democratically controlled governments, committed to the principle of giving consumers what they want within the limits of available resources and in accordance with rules approved by the representatives of the governed, will use any enlarged economic responsibilities granted to them as an opportunity to cripple the liberties of the citizens. As the experience of fascism fades into the background, as the old laissez-faire slogans sound increasingly time-worn, the usefulness of rational planning will probably prevail over the obstacles erected by the past in the minds of men.

In the communist sphere, the development is more doubtful. To be sure, the introduction of a rational pricing system with more freedom of decision for enterprise management would be at least as useful to the Soviet Union as a mechanism of comprehensive economic foresight would be for the capitalist countries. Therefore Soviet pragmatists can make as good a case, even a stronger one, for that kind of reform as Western pragmatists can for planning. But the resistance to pragmatism is greater on the Soviet side: Communist dogmatism is more firmly entrenched than are the neo-liberal biases in the Western countries. This alone makes the outcome more uncertain in the East.

But even assuming that Soviet pricing will be rationalized and that management will in the foreseeable future be instructed to regard maximization of profits as its principal responsibility, and will be freed from restrictions to pursue this goal, the political basis of this new situation will be precarious as long as the political organization of the Soviet system remains as it is. In Western societies abrupt changes of trends are rare; reforms once achieved are not often abolished; when they are, it is usually on the basis of prolonged adverse experience. The reason for this relative conservatism is the necessity to convince masses of voters of the desirability of a change. In the Soviet Union decisions are made within the small ruling group of the Communist Party; a few individuals may turn a minority into a majority, and their attitude may not be determined so much by the merits of the case as by considerations of personal or factional power, as happened during the struggle among Stalin, Trotsky, Zinoviev and Bukharin.

This is but one of the points at which the problem of possible converging patterns of the economic systems is connected with the future of the corresponding governmental systems. Among the modifications in the political system of the Soviet Union and its satellites since Stalin's death have been the replacement of outright terror by milder forms of control, and some easing of the concept of heresy. But the one-party system has remained intact and does not seem to have been mitigated—as it has in Yugoslavia—by at least a limited recognition and toleration of conflicting group interests. The principle that no thoughts can be publicly expressed which contradict the basic tenets of Soviet Communism or criticize its practical application in anything but superficial terms has been maintained. Also, in spite of the posthumous downgrading of Stalin, the infallibility of the party—meaning the national leadership—is one of the dogmas which cannot be opposed without inviting severe penalties on the deviationist. Any change in these fundamentals of the Soviet political system would surely meet with great resistance, because it would impair or abolish the monopoly of political power in the possession of the inner circle of the party. This inner circle would lose nothing, in fact would gain, by a rationalization of the economic system unless it had political consequences; nor has it lost anything by the post-Stalin relaxing of control methods. But it is hard to imagine that this group would consent to any reform that would deprive it of its privilege to hold the helm of state without interference by any group of citizens.

The question may be raised: Will economic reform not lead to a political change, even against the wishes of the ruling group? At first sight it may seem beyond doubt that historical experience supports this view. Is it not true that the introduction of capitalist practices, involving a rationalization of economic life, has proved to be the most powerful force in the destruction of feudalism? Has the same rationalization at a later stage not had a decisive share in the breakdown of absolute monarchy? Can we not assume that the advance of economic rationality in the Soviet Union and other communist countries will have the same effect?

The rise of capitalism, however, meant the rise of a new class which had previously been excluded from political power—to the extent that it existed at all. This class, the commercial and industrial entrepreneurs, wanted political influence; moreover, their position outside the social hierarchy, or on a low level of that hierarchy, had opened their eyes to the wrongness of privilege. Finally, the rise of modern industry activated still another class, the workers. Their numbers were tremendously increased, and their striking power slowly grew as modern technology gathered thousands of them in one plant, whereas their predecessors, the journeymen of the handicrafts, had been isolated from one another during the working day in their small shops; also, modern industry required a higher amount of general education, at least in the upper echelons of skilled labor, than workers had previously possessed, and more knowledge meant more weapons in the struggle for political emancipation. To sum up, the rise of capitalism influenced the political system largely through its effects upon class structure and class relationships.

No similar development, providing greater economic independence for the managers of Soviet enterprises, seems likely in the case of those economic reforms now on the agenda in the Soviet Union. But these managers are already integrated into the Soviet hierarchy; there is nothing to indicate that they want any political change. From a reform of the political system that would give the masses a decisive voice in public affairs they could not expect any improvement of their position. Even under the present circumstances, in which the manager is forced to questionable maneuvers in order to show success by the official indicators and often finds himself in a vulnerable position, little if anything points to acute dissatisfaction within this group; if the managers are freed from at least an important portion of their present fetters, as they would be through economic reform, why should they try to force a change in the political system by the use of their economic influence—even if that could be done with any prospect of success?

This means merely that the economic reform which seems to be probable in the near future will not influence the political organization of the communist countries through that channel which was the most important in the age of rising capitalism: changed class relationships. The larger question of whether economic reform may not perhaps affect the system of government in other ways cannot be answered. Certainly, the manner in which economic problems are handled affects prevailing habits of thinking; the way we think in one field of endeavor influences our thinking in other areas, and finally has an impact on the structure and operation of institutions. But the ways in which this interdependence of thought, activities and organizational arrangements operates are subtle; no sociologist or historian has yet succeeded in elucidating them entirely. It is impossible to deny categorically that economic rationalization may in the long run have a corroding influence upon the totalitarian character of communism; it is equally impossible to affirm such an influence.

For the foreseeable future, fundamental differences in the social systems of the communist countries and of the West will remain, and the practical task is to prevent the antagonism between the two blocs from causing a nuclear holocaust. It is reasonable to expect that with decreasing differences between the economic systems, ideological antagonism, along with international tension, will also decrease. We would not be justified, however, in predicting this in the near future. The communists will not love us any more than they do now if we develop a system of economic planning; on the contrary, they have always been particularly hostile to any attempt to show that one can go beyond capitalism without embracing the whole communist system. Nor will their acceptance of the capitalist market mechanism immediately lessen their contempt and hatred for other features of the Western system. It will take some time before the psychological consequences of changes in the economic system can reinforce the deterrent effect of the fear of nuclear warfare.

It would be unwise now—except as a matter of speculation without commitment—to look beyond that stage into a future in which the balance of terror may become unnecessary because the differences in the way of living have declined to such a degree that no nation can believe any more in its historic mission to impose its own system upon others. Such a day may come; but here and now, our task is primarily to eliminate the danger to man's survival without sacrificing those guarantees of human freedom and justice which are the fruits of a long and painful development.

SELECTED READING LIST

The purpose of this list is to indicate where the reader can find more extensive discussions or factual information on the subjects dealt with in the text. Since these problems have occupied the minds of many thinkers and cover a broad field, it is impossible to list every work that could add substantially to the reader's comprehension of the problems. An effort has been made to include the books most useful for this purpose—which are not always the books that have contributed most to the advancement of scholarly knowledge. In most of the works mentioned, however, the reader will find further references to pertinent literature, and in using them he will receive additional stimulation and assistance in pursuing the lines of thought in which he is particularly interested.

In order not to enlarge the list unduly, no general reference works such as textbooks on economics or encyclopaedias have been listed, except where a passage or article in such a reference work contains a piece of analysis or information of specific relevance to a problem dealt with in the book.

The list contains books which have been cited or quoted in the text, but only if they are related to some point of more than marginal significance to the subject of contemporary economic systems. On the other hand, books not quoted or cited have been included in the list if they contain analysis or information sufficiently useful for its purpose.

No book has been listed more than once; if a book is relevant to more than one part of the text, it has been listed under the part for which it appears most important. Books in foreign language have been included only when they contained information or analysis of great relevance to the subject matter, such as could not be found in English-language literature. Some informative publications were excluded from the list because, as multigraphed papers destined for limited circulation only, they are not easily available to the reader.

Introduction and Part I, Values and Goals

American Economic Association, "Reappraisal of the Doctrine of Consumers' Sovereignty," *Papers and Proceedings,* 74th Annual Convention, Dec. 1961, in *American Economic Review,* May 1962

Baumol, William J., *Welfare Economics and the Theory of the State,* Cambridge (Mass.): Harvard University Press, 1952

Clark, John M., *Economic Institutions and Human Welfare,* New York: Knopf, 1957

Dahl, Robert A, and Charles E. Lindblom, *Politics, Economics and Welfare,* New York: Harper and Brothers, 1953

Dessauer, Friedrich, *Streit um die Technik,* Frankfurt: Joseph Knecht, 1952

Engels, Friedrich, *Herr Eugen Dühring's Revolution in Science,* tr. Emile Burns, ed. R. Palme Dutt, New York: International Publishers, 1939

Galbraith, J. Kenneth, *The Affluent Society,* Boston: Houghton-Mifflin, 1958

Golob, Eugene, *The "Isms,"* New York: Harper and Brothers, 1954

Hayek, Friedrich A., *The Road to Serfdom,* Chicago: University of Chicago Press, 1944

———, *The Constitution of Liberty,* Chicago: University of Chicago Press, 1960

Heimann, Eduard, "The Affluent Society," *Kyklos,* Vol. XII (1959) no. 2

———, *Soziale Theorie der Wirtschaftssysteme,* Tübingen: J. C. B. Mohr, 1963

Hoover, Calvin, *The Economy, Liberty and the State,* New York: Twentieth Century Fund, 1959

Rostow, Walt, *The Stages of Economic Growth,* Cambridge (England): University Press, 1960

Scitovsky, Tibor, *Welfare and Competition,* Chicago: Richard D. Irwin, 1951

Simon, Yves, *Philosophy of Democratic Government,* Chicago: University of Chicago Press, 1951

Tinbergen, Jan, "The Theory of the Optimum Regime," *Selected Papers,* L. H. Klaassen, L. Koyck and H. J. Witteven, ed.; Amsterdam: North Holland Publ. Co., 1959

Ward, Dudley, *Goals of Economic Life,* New York: Harpers, 1953

Part II, Capitalism

Anderson, Thomas J., *Our Competitive System and Public Policy,* Cincinnati: South Western Publ. Co., 1958

Bain, Joe S., *Pricing, Distribution and Employment,* New York: Henry Holt, 1953
Bendix, Reinhard, *Work and Authority in Industry,* New York: Wiley, 1956
Böhm-Bawerk, Eugen von, *Positive Theory of Capital,* tr. William Smart, New York: Stechert, 1930
Berle, Adolf, and Gardiner Means, *The Modern Corporation and Private Property,* New York: Macmillan, 1932; reprint 1962
Brady, Robert A., *Business as a System of Power,* New York: Columbia University Press, 1943
Burns, Arthur, *The Decline of Competition,* New York: McGraw-Hill, 1936
Chamberlin, Edward H., *The Theory of Monopolistic Competition,* Cambridge (Mass.): Harvard University Press, 1946
Clark, Colin, *The Conditions of Economic Progress,* London and New York: Macmillan, 1957
Clark, John B., *The Distribution of Wealth,* New York: Macmillan, 1920
Colm, Gerhart, and Theodore Geiger, *The Economy of the American People,* Washington, D.C.: National Planning Association, 1961
Edwards, Corwin D., *Big Business and the Policy of Competition,* Cleveland: The Press of Western Reserve University, 1956
Elbow, Mathew, *French Corporative Theory,* New York: Columbia University Press, 1953
Finer, Herman, *Mussolini's Italy,* London: Golancz, 1935
Galbraith, J. Kenneth, *American Capitalism: The Concept of Countervailing Power,* Boston: Houghton-Mifflin, 1952
Gordon, Robert A., *Business Leadership in the Large Corporation,* Washington, D. C.: The Brookings Institution, 1945
———, *Business Fluctuations,* New York: Harpers, 1952
Haberler, Gottfried von, *Prosperity and Depression,* Geneva, League of Nations, 1939
Haley, Bernard, "Value and Distribution," in Howard Ellis (ed.), *A Survey of Contemporary Economics,* Philadelphia: Blakiston, 1949
Hansen, Alvin, *The American Economy,* New York: McGraw-Hill, 1957
Harris, Seymour (ed. and author of section), *The New Economics,* New York: Knopf, 1947
Kaplan, A. D., *Big Enterprise in a Competitive System,* Washington, D. C.: The Brookings Institution, 1954
Katona, George, *Psychological Analysis and Economic Behavior,* New York: McGraw-Hill, 1951
Keynes, John Maynard, *The General Theory of Employment, Interest and Money,* New York: Macmillan, 1936
Knight, Frank H., *Risk, Uncertainty and Profit,* Boston and New York: Houghton-Mifflin, 1921
Lipset, Seymour, and Reinhard Bendix, *Social Mobility in Industrial Society,* Berkeley: University of Calif. Press, 1959

Lorwin, Lewis, *Advisory Economic Councils,* Washington, D.C.: The Brookings Institution, 1931

Lorwin, Val, *The Labor Movement in France,* New York: Columbia University Press, 1954

Moon, Parker T., *The Labor Problem and the Social Catholic Movement in France,* New York: Macmillan, 1921

Pigou, A. C., *The Economics of Welfare,* London: Macmillan, 1932

Reynolds, Lloyd, *Labor Economics and Labor Relations,* Englewood Cliffs: Prentice-Hall, 1960

Tawney, Richard, *The Acquisitive Society,* New York: Harcourt, 1920

———, *Religion and the Rise of Capitalism,* London: John Murray, 1936

Ulman, Lloyd, *American Trade Unionism—Past and Present,* Berkeley: Institute of Industrial Relations, 1962 (reprint)

U.S. Department of Health, Education and Welfare, *Social Security Programs Throughout the World,* Washington, D.C.: Gov't Printing Office, 1961

Veblen, Thorstein, *The Engineers and the Price System,* New York: Huebsch, 1921

———, *The Theory of Business Enterprise,* New York: Scribner's, 1912

Wright, David McCord, *Capitalism,* New York: McGraw-Hill, 1951

Williams, Philip M., and Martin Harrison, *De Gaulle's Republic,* London: Longmans Green, 1960

Part III, Socialism

The Acton Society Trust, *The Extent of Centralization,* London, Acton Society, 1951

———, *The Framework of Joint Consultation,* London: Acton Society, 1952

———, *The Future of Unions,* London: Acton Society, 1951

———, *The Powers of the Minister,* London: Acton Society, 1951

———, *The Worker's Point of View,* London: Acton Society, 1952

Baum, Warren, *The French Economy and the State,* Princeton: Princeton University Press, 1958

Bedi, Raghubans Dev, *Theory, History and Practice of Cooperation,* Meerut: Int. Publ. House, 1961

Bergson, Abram, "Socialist Economics," in Howard Ellis (ed), *A Survey of Contemporary Economics,* Philadelphia: Blakiston, 1949

Brisson, André, *Institutions financières et économiques en France,* Paris: Ed. Berger-Leorault, 1960

Boiteux, M., and Associates, *Le Fonctionnement des entreprises nationalisées en France* Paris: Library Dalloz, 1956

Braunthal, Julius, *Yearbook of the International Socialist Labour Movement,* Lincoln-Prager, 1960

Clegg, H. A., *Industrial Democracy and Nationalization,* Oxford: Basil Blackwell, 1951

Cole, G. D. H., *A History of Socialist Thought,* London: Macmillan, 1953-60

———, *A Century of Cooperation,* Manchester: The Cooperative Union, 1945

Commissariat Général du Plan de Modernisation et d'Equipment, *Rapport Général,* Nov. 1946-January 1947

———, *Rapport sur les résultats obtenus dans la réalisation du plan de modernisations et d' équipment au cours du Premier semester* 1947

Crosland, C. A. R., *The Future of Socialism,* London: Jonathan Cape, 1957

Dickinson, H. D., *Economics of Socialism,* London: Oxford University Press, 1939

Dorfman, Robert, Paul A. Samuelson and Robert M. Solow, *Linear Programming and Economic Analysis,* New York: McGraw-Hill, 1958

Dorfman, Robert, "The Nature and Significance of Input-Output," *Review of Economic Statistics,* May 1954

French Information Service, *France and Economic Planning,* New York: 1963

Hackett, John, and Ann-marie Hackett, *Economic Planning in France,* London: Allen and Unwin, 1963

International Economic Association, *Proceedings of the Vienna Convention, 1963* (Sect. 2, Development Planning) when available.

Landauer, Carl, *European Socialism,* Berkeley: University of Calif. Press, 1960

Lerner, Abba P., *The Economics of Control,* New York: Macmillan, 1944

Lescuyer, Georges, *Le Contrôle de l'état sur les entreprises nationalisées,* Paris: Pichon et Durand Anzias, 1959

Meade, James E., *Planning and the Price Mechanism,* London: Allen and Unwin, 1948

Mises, Ludwig von, *Socialism,* tr. J. Kahane, New York: Macmillan, 1936

Perroux, François, "Le Quatrième plan français, 1962-1965," *Economie Appliquée,* January-June 1962

Pigou, A. C., *Socialism versus Capitalism,* London: Macmillan, 1937

P. E. P., *Economic Planning in France,* London: PEP Broadsheet #454, 1961

Robson, William A., (ed.) *Problems of Nationalized Industries,* London: Allen and Unwin, 1952

Schumpeter, Joseph, *Capitalism, Socialism and Democracy,* New York: Harpers, 1942

Spaull, Hebe, and D. H. Kay, *The Cooperative Movement at Home and Abroad,* London: Macmillan, 1947

Uhr, Carl, *Sweden's Employment Security Program and Its Impact on the Country's Economy,* Pasadena: California Inst. of Technology, 1960

Wicksteed, Philip, *The Common Sense of Political Economy,* London: Routledge, 1933 (reprint)

Zweig, Ferdynand, *The Israeli Worker,* New York: Herzl Press, 1959

Part IV, Communism

Arnold, Arthur, *Banks, Credit and Money in Soviet Russia,* New York: Columbia University Press, 1937

Baykov, Alexander, *The Development of the Soviet Economic System,* New York: Macmillan, 1947

Bjeliči, Sreten, *Communal System in Yugoslavia,* Belgrade: Publicističko Izdavački Zavod "Jugoslavija," 1961

Bobrowski, C., *La Yougoslavie socialiste,* Paris: Armand Colin, 1956

Bornstein, Morris, "The Soviet Price System," *Am. Economic Review,* March 1962

Boulding, Kenneth, and Pritam Singh, "The Role of the Price Structure in Economic Development," Papers and Proceedings of the 74th Annual Meeting of the Am. Econ. Ass. 1961, *Am. Economic Review,* May 1962

The Constitution of the Socialist Federal Republic of Yugoslavia, tr. Petar Mijušković, Belgrade: Secretariat for Information of the Federal Executive Council, 1963

Djilas, Milovan, *The New Class,* New York: Frederick A. Praeger, 1957

Dobb, Maurice, *Soviet Economic Development since 1917,* New York: Int. Publishers, 1948

———, "Note on Recent Economic Discussion," Soviet Studies, April 1961

Embree, George D., *The Soviet Union between the 19th and 20th Party Congresses, 1952-1956,* s'Gravenhage: Martinus Nijhoff, 1959

Erlich, Alexander, *The Soviet Industrialization Debate, 1924-1928,* Cambridge: Harvard University Press, 1960

Federal Institute of Statistics, *Statistical Pocket Book of Yugoslavia,* Belgrade, May 1963

The Five Year Plan of Economic Development of Yugoslavia, 1961-1965, Belgrade: Secretariat for Information of the Fed. Ex. Council, 1961

Galenson, Walter, *The Soviet Wage Reform,* Berkeley: Institute of Industrial Rel., Univ. of Calif., 1961

Granick, David, *The Red Executive,* Garden City: Doubleday, 1960

Grossman, Gregory (ed.), *Value and Plan,* Berkeley: Univ. of Calif. Press, 1960

———, "Soviet Growth, Routine, Inertia and Pressure" *Am. Economic Review,* May 1960

———, "Planning: Backbone of a Nation," *Saturday Review,* January 21, 1963

———, "Some Problems of Structure and Organization of the Soviet Economy," *Slavic Review,* Vol.: XXI: 2, June 1962

Germann, Leon, "Inside the Soviet Union; the Labor Force: Who Does What?" *Saturday Review,* January 21, 1961

Hoffman, George, and Fred Neal, *Yugoslavia and the New Communism*, New York: Twentieth Century Fund, 1962
Hubbard, Leonard, *Soviet Money and Finance*, London: Macmillan, 1936
———, *The Economics of Soviet Agriculture*, London: Macmillan, 1939
Information Service Yugoslavia, *Social Management in Yugoslavia*, Belgrade: Edition Yugoslavija, 1961
Institut de Sociologie Solvay (Université Libre de Bruxelles), *Le Regime et les institutions de la république populaire fédérative de Yougoslavie*, Centre National pour l'Etude des Pays à Régime Communiste, 1959
Jasny, Naum, *The Socialized Agriculture of the USSR: Plans and Performance*, Stanford: Stanford University Press, 1949
———, *Soviet Industrialization, 1928-1952*, Chicago: Univ. of Chicago Press, 1961
Montias, John Michael, *Planning in Poland*, New Haven: Yale Univ. Press, 1961
Nove, Alec, *The Soviet Economy*, New York: Frederick A. Praeger, 1961
Ritvo, Herbert (ed.), *The New Soviet Society* [The 1961 Program of the Communist Party of the Soviet Union], New York: The New Leader, 1962
Schlesinger, Rudolph, *The New Structure of Soviet Agriculture*, Soviet Studies, Vol. X, 1959
Schwartz, Harry, *The Red Phoenix*, New York: Frederick A. Praeger, 1961
Spulber, Nicholas, *The Soviet Economy: Structure, Principles, Problems*, New York: Norton, 1962
Stalin, Joseph, *Leninism*, New York: Int. Publishers, 1942, and earlier editions
Schleicher, Harry, *Das System der betrieblichen Selbstverwaltung in Jugoslawien*, Berlin: Duncker und Humblot, 1961
Tito, Josip Broz, "The Building of Socialism and the Role and Tasks of the Socialist Alliance of the Working People of Yugoslavia," *Report to the Fifth Congress of the Soc. Alliance of the Working People of Yugoslavia*, Belgrade, April 18, 1960
Tinbergen, Jan, "Do Communist and Free Economies Show a Converging Pattern?" *Soviet Studies* XII: 4 (1961), pp. 333ff
Trotsky, Leon, *The Defense of Terrorism*, London: Allen and Unwin, 1921
Turetsky, S. Y., "Soviet Price Policy: A Rejoinder" [to Maurice Dobb] *Soviet Studies*, Vol. XIII (1960-61)
U.S. Congress, Joint Economic Committee, *Comparisons of the United States and Soviet Economies*, Washington, D.C.: Gov't Printing Office, 1959
———, *Dimensions of Soviet Economic Power*, Washington, D.C.: Government Printing Office, 1962
U.S. Department of Health, Education and Welfare, *A Report on Social Security Programs in the Soviet Union*, Washington, D.C., Gov't Printing Office, 1960

Ward, Benjamin, "Workers' Management in Yugoslavia," *Journal of Political Economy*, October 1957

———, "Kantorovich on Economic Calculation," *Journal of Political Economy*, December 1960

PART V. OTHER SYSTEMS IN TRANSITION

For writings on particular areas, see citations in the text and general reference sources

Braibanti, Ralph, and Joseph Spengler, *Tradition, Values and Socio-Economic Development*, Durham: Duke Univ. Press, 1961

Coulborn, Rushton, *Feudalism in History*, Princeton: Princeton University Press, 1956

Encyclopaedia of the Social Sciences, articles "Land Tenure," Vol. IX, and "Peonage," Vol. XII

Forde, C. Daryll, *Habitat, Economy and Society*, London: Methuen, 1961

Herskovits, Melville J., *Economic Anthropology*, New York: Knopf, 1952

Meek, Charles, *Land Law and Customs in the Colonies*, London: Oxford University Press, 1949

Parsons, Kenneth *et al*, *Land Tenure* (Proceedings of the International Conference on Land Tenure and Related Problems in World Agriculture, Held at Madison, Wisc., 1951) Madison: Univ. of Wisconsin Press, 1956

INDEX